THE OFFICE BUILDING

THE OFFICE BUILDING

From Concept to Investment Reality

Editor in Chief
John Robert White, CRE, MAI

Executive Editor
Ellen L. Romano

A Joint Publication of the
Counselors of Real Estate
(American Society of Real Estate Counselors)
Appraisal Institute
Society of Industrial and Office REALTORS®
Educational Fund

The Office Building is endorsed
by the Building Owners and Managers
Association International and the
Institute of Real Estate Management

Credits

Managing Editor,
The Office Building
From Concept to Investment Reality
Staff Vice President,
Counselors of Real Estate:
Linda Magad

Vice President, Publications,
Appraisal Institute:
Christopher Bettin

Programs Director,
Society of Industrial and
Office REALTORS®:
Mark Crowley

Design:
Stuart Paterson

Cover Photo:
Charles Thatcher/Tony Stone
Worldwide

Counselors of Real Estate
430 North Michigan Avenue
Chicago, Illinois 60611-4089
312.329.8427

Appraisal Institute
875 North Michigan Avenue
Chicago, Illinois 60611-1980
312.335.4100

Society of Industrial and Office
REALTORS® Educational Fund
777 14th Street, N.W.
Washington, D.C. 20005-3271
202.737.1150

The Office Building From Concept to Investment Reality is recommended by the Homer Hoyt Institute of Maryland and the National Society For Real Estate Finance of Washington, D.C.

Library of Congress Catalog Card Number:
92-76112

Printed in the United States of America
10 9 8 7 6 5 4 3 2 1

ISBN 0-939653-01-X

ABOUT THE EDITOR IN CHIEF

John Robert White is a renaissance man: appraiser, dealmaker, author, board member, broker, counselor, economic forecaster, friend, mentor, president, professor.

As the head of Landauer Associates, Inc., of New York, he held many titles and originated or participated in many of the headline-making transactions of the country's largest city and leading financial market.

He has served his professional organizations well, most recently as the editor in chief and a contributor to this book. He is a widely published author and has served on the editorial board of *Real Estate Issues*, published by the Counselors of Real Estate; and on the editorial board and as editor in chief of the *Appraisal Journal*, published by the Appraisal Institute.

John is an outstanding economic forecaster. During his years with Landauer, he was regularly quoted for his accurate predictions about the direction of the real estate industry. The Annual Economic Forecast of the Counselors of Real Estate, which he moderated for many years, attracted standing room only audiences as people came to hear John Robert White's words of wisdom.

John Robert White has served as adjunct professor of real estate at the School of Commerce of New York University and was executive-in-residence at Columbia University Graduate School of Business.

John's current assignment as editor in chief of *The Office Building: From Concept to Investment Reality* is the latest challenge and success in an outstanding career. His organizational skills and dedication to the timeline as well as the bottom line have enabled this publication to stay generally on time and on budget. The section captains and authors, volunteers all, are busy professionals, yet John Robert White motivated this geographically scattered and intellectually diverse group to produce their portion of the book as promised. The effectiveness of his leadership is evident in both the quality of this publication and its timely production.

To our own renaissance man, past president and good friend, many thanks. The members of the Counselors of Real Estate, Appraisal Institute and Society of Industrial and Office REALTORS® Educational Fund, as well as readers of this book, will learn much from your insight and guidance.

Jean C. Felts, CRE
1993 President
Counselors of Real Estate

ACKNOWLEDGMENTS

Task Force On Education/Text Development

Jonathan H. Avery, CRE, MAI, Chairman
Peter D. Bowes, CRE, MAI
Robert K. Brown, CRE
Eugene P. Carver, CRE
James E. Gibbons, CRE, MAI
James J. Hawk, CRE
Maury Seldin, CRE
Jared Shlaes, CRE, MAI
Richard D. Simmons, Sr., CRE
John R. White, CRE, MAI

Consulting Editor

Maury Seldin, CRE, President, Homer Hoyt Institute

Section Captains

Part I: Jared Shlaes, CRE, MAI
Part II: Judith Reynolds, CRE, MAI
Part III: Roland J. Rives, CRE, MAI
Part IV: Rocky Tarantello, CRE
Part V: Donald J. Hartman, CRE, MAI, SIOR
             David T. Houston, CRE, SIOR
Part VI: John J. Grinch, CRE
Part VII: Rocky Tarantello, CRE
Part VIII: James E. Gibbons, CRE, MAI
             Richard Marchitelli, CRE, MAI

1992 Presidents

Lawrence A. Kell, CRE, Counselors of Real Estate
Patricia J. Marshall, MAI, CRE, Appraisal Institute
James J. Casey, SIOR, Society of Industrial and Office REALTORS®
Educational Fund

ABOUT THE PUBLISHERS

Counselors of Real Estate

The Counselors of Real Estate are recognized authorities who provide counseling services mainly for agreed fees in such areas as lease and sale transactions, financing, asset management, land utilization, market studies, debt restructuring and investment analysis. The organization's CRE designation (Counselor of Real Estate) is awarded to all members and attests to the practitioner's expertise, reputation and adherence to a stringent Code of Ethics. CREs include practicing counselors of prominent real estate, financial, legal and accounting firms and leaders in government and academia. Membership is selective, extended by invitation on either a self-initiated or sponsored basis. The Counselors offer quality publications, networking opportunities and educational programs.

Appraisal Institute

The Appraisal Institute is the world's leading organization of professional real estate appraisers, with general appraisal members who hold the MAI, SRPA or SREA designation and residential appraisal members who hold the SRA or RM designation. These members are identified by their experience and knowledge of real estate valuation and adhere to a strictly enforced Code of Professional Ethics and Standards of Professional Appraisal Practice. Currently, the Appraisal Institute confers one general designation, the MAI, and one residential designation, the SRA. To increase appraisal knowledge and foster professional excellence, the Appraisal Institute publishes more than 60 books and sponsors a full curriculum of courses and seminars on the valuation of residential and commercial properties.

Society of Industrial and Office REALTORS®
Educational Fund

The Society of Industrial and Office REALTORS® Educational Fund (SIOREF), through its involvement in research, publications and educational programs, provides forums for experienced practitioners to share ideas and expand their knowledge and also provides basic education for individuals who are new to the field of commercial real estate. Among the goals of SIOREF are promoting effective information and knowledge of industrial and office real estate in the United States, Canada and overseas; and improving the flow of information and knowledge between industrial and office real estate brokers, their clients, developers, lenders, governmental bodies and the public. SIOREF challenges commercial real estate professionals to achieve excellence.

FOREWORD

As the title suggests, *The Office Building: From Concept to Investment Reality* is not just another book about office buildings. It looks at office buildings both as an enterprise and as a real estate asset. Ownership of an office building involves more than simply valuation, leasing or sales. This book views every aspect of a property and its operations and presents this comprehensive analysis within the covers of a single volume. It is intended to be a valuable reference for professional practitioners, developers, appraisers, counselors, loan officers, property managers, leasing agents, architects, engineers and students.

Synergism is the action of two or more components to achieve an effect of which each is individually incapable, and this volume is a synergistic work. *The Office Building* represents the work of 43 volunteer authors, all practicing professionals specializing in various phases of the office building enterprise. Their individual chapters bring to the reader direct personal, professional and practical experience. In its entirety, the book provides a useful reference as well as an insightful and fresh look at office buildings.

This book was originally conceived by a task force of the Counselors of Real Estate. This task force foresaw the need for a work on office buildings that would appeal to those in the industry as well as to a broad spectrum in finance and market economics. It envisioned a book that would serve its readers well over time, a reference that would be useful in both up and down markets. When this project was first discussed, office construction was active and well-located office buildings were sought by most institutional onshore and offshore investors and lenders. While the current market is very different, this book is a valuable addition to your library because it will serve you well in volatile as well as stable markets.

The book is a joint publication of three professional organizations: The Counselors of Real Estate, the Appraisal Institute, and the Society of Industrial and Office REALTORS® Educational Fund.

John Robert White, CRE, MAI, 1969 president of the Counselors and retired chairman of Landauer Associates, Inc., with the assistance of association staff, has guided the volunteer efforts of the nine section captains and 44 authors in the creation of this work. The guidance and dedication of the Task Force on Education/Text Development under the chairmanship of Jonathan Avery, CRE, MAI, has moved this project forward during four presidential terms. Jeff Fisher and Sherrie Henry at

Indiana University's Center for Real Estate Studies assisted with the bibliography. As 1992 president of the Counselors, it is my privilege to thank those who have devoted so much to making this book a reality. As you read this book, perhaps more than once, you will come to appreciate how much knowledge there is within its covers and the efforts of those who made it a reality.

Lawrence A. Kell, CRE
1992 President
Counselors of Real Estate

PREFACE

In 1988, a group of real estate counselors (CREs), led by Jared Shlaes, CRE, MAI, and advised by Maury Seldin, CRE, met to discuss the prospect of creating a series of books on the various types of investment real estate. It was decided that the first book would be about the office building as emblematic of commercial real estate.

Many of the original participants were also members of the Appraisal Institute and the Society of Industrial and Office REALTORS®. The committee's principal task was to decide whether it was possible to produce a book with individual chapters contributed by specialists in every functional area relating to office buildings without the finished product resembling a manual. The group felt strongly that it was indeed feasible to create a book with each chapter reflecting the voice of its individual author(s), yet which would flow sequentially in a logical progression and which would avoid the duplication and lack of coherence frequently characteristic of a manual.

It was also decided that the book would be designed to appeal to the highest level of practitioner. Because it would be unusually comprehensive, it would not be possible to include every fact, circumstance, technique or financial model. However, the footnotes, citations and suggested readings would offer an intellectual blueprint for those who wished to pursue any specialized subject. Above all, the book would be structured to present an executive perspective of how the office building industry operates. This overview is critical to success in the office field.

Another feature of the book is its recognition of the importance of relationships. Of course factual knowledge, supported by a mastery of analytical techniques and mathematically based models, is indispensable in a technologically oriented business environment. However, our authors stressed that readers must understand the manner in which relationships with clients, customers, consultants and suppliers are created and administered. It is fair to say that successful relationships are equally as important as market knowledge. Relationships start with a written contract so that principal and contractor have a clear understanding of what is required but that is only the beginning of the process of gaining trust and confidence.

The authors also stress the critical importance of continued, timely and relevant communication. Nothing dissipates a relationship faster than lengthy periods of silence by the contractor. Keeping the client informed is the most effective way to maintain sound relations.

This book represents an artful blend of historical perspective; regulatory functions; requirements of market and investment analysis; development concerns; financing considerations; operating and managerial factors; and the various ways in which performance may be measured. I'm confident you will be excited by the quality of the book and challenged by its contribution to your knowledge.

John R. White, CRE, MAI
Editor in Chief

CONTENTS

CHARACTERISTICS OF OFFICE BUILDINGS AND OFFICE MARKETS

1

EVOLUTION OF THE OFFICE BUILDING

by Jared Shlaes with Marc A. Weiss

INTRODUCTION

The roots of the office building reach deep into ancient times. Its ancestors, almost as old as the written word, appear for the first time in the form of chambers set aside for record-keeping in the palaces of the earliest kings. Much later, during the Italian Renaissance, the freestanding dedicated office building would begin to take shape in the *palazzi* of the great Italian banking houses. But it was not until a burst of technological innovation in the late 19th century allowed it to reach new heights of efficiency and structure that the office building would assume its modern form.

ORIGINS

"The king was in his countinghouse, counting out his money..."

Precursors of the modern office building first appeared about 6,000 years ago, in the palaces and temples of the earliest civilizations to leave written records. There, in the treasuries and warehouses of ancient kingdoms, much of the business essential to organized agriculture and trade was carried on.

Five-and-a-half millennia later, the spread of capitalism would lead to a wider distribution of office functions, their gradual separation from domestic functions and their consolidation into special buildings. For almost all of human history, though, beginning with the great river civilizations of the

3

Middle East—Egypt, India and China—dedicated office spaces of any size could have been found only in the palaces and outposts of kings and ecclesiastics who kept their books in the buildings where they lived.

THE INDUSTRIAL REVOLUTION

Through the Middle Ages, little happened to advance office development until the Renaissance brought the invention of double-entry bookkeeping, discount banking and modern capitalism. These inventions stimulated business capitals such as Venice, Florence, London and Amsterdam to impose a new order on the world. As early as 1480, powerful banking and trading houses headquartered in these new financial centers were building large, solid houses, some of which are still in use as banks and corporate headquarters.[1]

The late 18th and early 19th centuries brought with them a broad range of technological innovations and a radical rearrangement of the landscape. They also brought vast economic and social changes. Water-powered and later coal-powered manufacturing slashed costs and allowed the distribution of low-priced manufactured goods to an eager world marketplace. Standards of living rose and urban populations soared as immigrants poured in from the farm to share in the new prosperity, often by way of the new railroad and steamship lines. While many suffered from the associated dislocations, the general effect was to increase the wealth of the industrializing countries.

Among the consequences was a regrouping of business along new lines of travel and communication. River and canal crossings, road junctions and ports had always attracted trade and manufacturing. Now, as manufacturing was enabled by the coming of the steam engine to move down from the hills where water power was most readily harnessed, rail lines and especially the rail transfer points located in the cities began to compete with them for growth. In James Heilbrun's phrase, railroads "proved to be the most powerful agglomerative invention of all time," an observation confirmed by the vast influx of jobs, people and capital along the paths carved by the new trackage.

As the Industrial Revolution spread and prospered, cities in Great Britain and America launched upon a period of expansion that would be interrupted only by periodic financial panics. Growing inter-city and interregional trade, made easier by the new rail lines and communications, stimulated business and manufacturing activity of every kind. Centers like London, Manchester, Liverpool, Boston, Philadelphia and New York

---

[1] Nikolaus Pevsner, *A History of Building Types* (Princeton: Princeton University Press, 1976); Spiro Kostoff, *A History of Architecture* (New York: Oxford University Press, 1985).

became magnets for capital investment as well as for people in search of jobs and business opportunities, quickly absorbing the surplus population of nearby rural areas.[2]

To meet the growing need for business space in these cities, office buildings began to appear in some numbers as early as the 1830s. These four- and five-story structures, almost insignificant by modern standards, were imposing in their day and would spawn many imitators.[3]

The form of the city was changing in response to its new dynamism. For one thing, rapid horizontal expansion had been made possible by the horsecars and steam trains common in the 1850s and the electric tramways which appeared later in the century. Many people and businesses took advantage of this opportunity to move outward toward the suburbs, where the air was cleaner, the streets safer and the housing costs less, commuting downtown for work, shopping, and recreation.[4]

Another effect of rapid growth was that traffic congestion and rising land prices in the downtown districts soon began to force out those who could not afford downtown space costs. This freed up the city center, where the docks, railheads, banks, wholesalers and government agencies were already located, for functions that wanted to be close to them and could afford to pay the high rents and taxes.

Available sites were soon taken up by newspaper and book publishers, real estate and insurance firms, professional offices of every kind, light manufacturers, wholesalers, department stores, hotels and service enterprises, all of them able to use multi-story structures that could support downtown land values. The influx left city cores no choice but to grow denser and more vertical.

Office buildings began to rise in large numbers as the growth continued. At first, they generally took the form of multi-story, masonry-walled, store-and-office buildings, often 50 feet wide or less, with modest entrances between the storefronts. Visitors climbed upstairs by way of narrow stairhalls to the high-ceilinged offices above, which were lit by gas or whale oil and heated by stoves and fireplaces. Sanitary facilities were of the simplest and fire protection was primitive.

Technical Innovation

Office work was changing in response to new inventions and technical improvements such as the typewriter. Just as important to the comfort and

---

[2] James Heilbrun, *Urban Economics and Public Policy*, 3rd ed. (New York: St. Martin's Press, 1987); Adna F. Weber, *The Growth of Cities in the Nineteenth Century* (Ithaca, New York: Cornell University Press, 1963).

[3] Richard MacCormac, "The Dignity of Office," *The Architectural Review*, (May 1992): 76-82; Fletcher, *A History of Architecture*.

[4] Mark Girouard, *Cities and People* (New Haven: Yale University Press, 1985).

productivity of office workers was gas light, invented by Lavoisier shortly before he was guillotined in the French Revolution. It became practical with the founding of the first gas company in London (1813) and was common by 1860, reaching a peak of perfection with the 1885 invention of the gas mantle, which multiplied the lumens it produced. Meanwhile, Thomas Edison had registered his patent on the incandescent electric bulb in 1879 and would open the Pearl Street Power Station in 1885, making electric light a commercial reality.[5]

White-collar work was growing more efficient in other ways thanks to the development of modern communications. By 1868 most American cities were connected by Samuel F. B. Morse's telegraph, which had seen its first public use as early as 1844. The telephone, independently invented by Elisha Gray and Alexander Graham Bell in the 1870s (Bell's patent dates to 1876), was in commercial use by 1878, and in 1887 the list of subscribers had more than 150,000 names. Soon the telephone and telegraph would be supplemented by Guglielmo Marconi's wireless telegraphy, which had reached across the English Channel in 1889 and would cross the Atlantic in 1901.

Toilets, Lifts and Skeletons

Three other key inventions were essential before the modern office building could take shape: the flush toilet, the passenger elevator and skeleton construction. The first of these had appeared at the Minoan court four millennia ago and reappeared in various forms over the years. It would come to near-perfection only with Alexander Cumming's 1875 patent for a toilet with a "stink trap" that prevented sewer gases from backing up through the drains. Cumming's invention allowed office tenants previously dependent on chamber pots to enjoy upstairs accommodations without paying servants to dump their deposits. The growth in the size, number and comfort of office buildings would not have been possible without corresponding improvements in sanitary and storm sewer installations.[6]

The second key to the future of the office building was the new safety-equipped, steam-driven passenger elevator exhibited by Elisha Graves Otis at the Crystal Palace Exposition of 1853 in New York City. Otis's elevator, which first appeared in practical form about 1858 in the Haughwout Building (designed by J. P. Gaynor and Daniel Badger) at Broadway and Broome Street in New York City, was far from the first mechanical

---

[5] Charles Panati, *Panati's Extraordinary Origins of Everyday Things* (New York: Harper & Row, 1987); Charles Panati, *Panati's Browser's Book of Beginnings* (Boston: Houghton Mifflin Company, 1984); Arnold Lehman, "The New York Skyscraper—A History of its Development 1870-1939," (Ph.D. diss., Yale University, May 1974).

[6] See Panati, *Origins of Everyday Things* and *Browser's Book of Beginnings*.

means of vertical transportation. Hand-operated hoists without rails had been used in the third century B.C., and Queen Anne had installed a lift at Windsor Castle in 1700. But Otis's inventions—a speed governor, the "automatic gravity-wedge safety" and the "automatic safety stop"—made them safe for human passengers even when operated at the high speeds made possible by steam power and electricity.[7]

However, it was only with the application of steam power to the improved hydraulic elevators in use by 1890 that buildings could comfortably reach to a height of 10 or 12 stories. There was much more to come. In 1898 a new high-speed direct plunger design allowed them to attain a dramatic 30 stories, tall enough to be taken seriously as skyscrapers. By the turn of the century, electric drive, push-button controls and speeds of 700 feet per minute were available.

The Skeleton Frame

These devices improved the practicality of the cast-iron and glass buildings pioneered by Daniel Badger and James Bogardus in the 1840s. Theirs was not the first use of these materials. Iron had been around since roughly 1200 B.C., though it was then too costly for use in construction. New 19th century technology made it much cheaper, and by 1830 cast iron columns, beams and store fronts were going up all over Europe and the United States. In New York, the Lorillard Building (1837) had a cast iron front, with cast iron beams and columns in its two lower stories. Of special architectural interest toward the end of this period was the elegant iron, stone and glass facade of Peter Ellis's Oriel Chambers in Liverpool (1864-65), which had cantilevered bay-window oriels in a repetitive pattern that anticipated the designs of the Chicago School later in the century.

Cast iron, which had been preferred to wrought iron and steel in structural columns because of its greater compressive strength, was discredited by the Chicago Fire of 1871 and the Boston fire of 1872, though "it was not until the Worth Street fire of January 1870 in New York that the history of cast iron in that city was severely curtailed."[8] Hidden defects in iron columns also caused problems; these were solved with the development of the box column, a riveted assemblage of plates and angles made at first of wrought iron and later of steel.

The Chicago, Boston and New York fires had other consequences. Among them were increasing use of terra cotta fireproofing wrapped around the iron and steel structural members and the development of the

---

[7] See Lehman, *The New York Skyscraper*; Thomas E. Tallmadge, ed., "The Origin of the Skyscraper, Report of the Committee appointed by the Trustees of the Estate of Marshall Field for the Examination of the Structure of the Home Insurance Building," (Chicago: The Alderbrink Press, 1939).

[8] Lehman, 14.

tile arch floor, a method of bridging the distance between cross-beams with flat arches of hollow terra cotta tiles, the flanges of which covered the I-beams to protect them. Steel lathing was used with "adamant" plaster for greater fire resistance; so was terra cotta partitioning covered with plaster, a technique still common in the 1950s.

Toward the end of the century, new foundation techniques employing grillages of steel embedded in concrete made it safe for architects such as Burnham & Root to push structures 300 feet into the air, as they did at the Masonic Temple Building at State and Randolph Streets in Chicago (1890). This impressive mixed-use development had 14 hydraulic passenger elevators and retail stores on its lower floors. It would set a standard for many subsequent buildings aimed at the prestige market.[9]

START OF THE MODERN ERA: LATE 19th AND EARLY 20th CENTURY

Through most of the 19th century serious commercial building had been characterized by masonry construction. It was limited to about six stories in height by its own weight and by the inability or unwillingness of most people to climb any higher in dim stairwells.

L. S. Buffington of Minneapolis had worked out the principles of steel framing in 1871 and patented a 28-story design in 1878. There followed a variety of skeleton-framed buildings in Europe and America. The technique reached a climax in 1884-85 with the competition entries of Frederick Baumann and William LeBaron Jenney for what would turn out to be Jenney's fire-resistant Home Insurance Company Building in Chicago, a ten-story marvel of skeleton framing and the first exemplar of the new Chicago school of architecture. The structure, completely self-supporting, incorporated the first steel I-beams rolled by the Carnegie Phipps Company of Pittsburgh, which sold them to Jenney for use in conjunction with the wrought iron beams and cast iron columns called for in the design.[10]

Soon after came the fully skeleton-framed Tacoma Building by Holabird and Roche (1887-89), which had riveted junctions for added structural rigidity. Home Insurance and Tacoma were bellwethers for the school of architecture that almost immediately formed itself on the principles of skeleton-frame construction: lightweight curtain walls of brick, stone and terra cotta; generous wooden "Chicago" windows grouped in threes; simple ornamentation and rational floor plans. This "Chicago School" would set the style for office buildings around the world.[11]

---

[9] *Masonic Temple* (New York: Exhibit Publishing Company, no date).

[10] See Lehman and Tallmadge.

[11] John Zukowsky, editor, *Chicago Architecture 1872-1922* (Munich: Prestel-Verlag, 1987).

The Home Insurance Company Building (1884-85), Chicago, by architect William LeBaron Jenney, incorporated skeleton framing and was one of the first examples of the new Chicago School of Architecture. *(Chicago Historical Society/ Photo by J. W. Taylor ICHi-00989)*

The First Big Boom

Office buildings were rising at a great rate in downtowns all over America. In the central business district of Pittsburgh, for example, over 400 buildings were completed within five years beginning in the late 1880s. New York, Boston, Buffalo, Cleveland and many other cities saw their skylines rise and their business lives transformed as these new developments multiplied.[12]

The burgeoning downtowns attracted all kinds of facilities to feed, clothe, water, house and entertain their numerous employees and visitors:

---

[12] Earle Schultz and Walter Simmons, *Offices in the Sky* (Indianapolis: Bobbs-Merrill, 1959).

retail stores, restaurants, hotels, taverns, theaters, churches, schools and bawdy houses. More than ever, downtown was now the vibrant heart of the American city. It would continue to capture the bulk of new office construction for almost a hundred years, until suburban development began to take hold on a large scale in the late 1960s.

Steel-framed structures predominated but reinforced concrete was on the march. It had already been used for floor slabs in Great Britain since 1854, and Portland cement had been used in the United States since 1872.[13] French technology featured at the Paris Exposition of 1867 encouraged its wider use in the United States and elsewhere. Thirty years later, in 1902-03, the 16-story Ingalls Building in Cincinnati became "the first reinforced concrete skyscraper",[14] and by 1908 C.A.P. Turner published his system for manufacturing beamless floor slabs of this material.

Employers found that the advantages of the office space offered by these centrally located buildings more than offset its relatively high cost and

New York's Flatiron Building, constructed in 1902-03, was part of a wave of multi-tenant speculative structures built in response to businesses' demand for a downtown location. *(Library of Congress)*

occasional discomforts. It was strategically positioned on or near main transit lines, close to clients, and convenient to more visitors and employees than any outlying office was likely to be. It was also, as space went in those days, attractive, light and airy, easily cleanable and often with impressive upper-floor views.

The design of the buildings where this space was accommodated gave employers a chance to demonstrate their wealth and power, especially in New York, where rents were higher and tastes less Spartan. Many of the earliest and most prominent office structures were erected by large life insurance companies to house their headquarters and impress their current and future policyholders, using for this purpose the investment funds set aside to cover policy obligations. By the late 19th century, Equitable, Prudential, Manhattan Life, Metropolitan and others were battling to build the most impressive structure in Manhattan.

Driving a large share of the growth was the sheer convenience of doing business from a downtown location. All the facilities needed by busy entrepreneurs—post offices, banks, law firms, commodities and securities markets, repair services, equipment suppliers, advertising and employment agencies, clubs, restaurants, taverns and everything else one might want—were within easy walking distance. It would have been near-idiocy to choose a location anywhere else. The powerful socio-economic forces of agglomeration impelled both commercial and residential clustering.

Downtown: A New Kind of Information Processor

For many tenants, these assets were more than sufficient; for others, there was an even more powerful inducement to overcome any lingering distaste for the dirt and hurly-burly of the business district. This was the free flow of information available in downtown settings where businessmen could talk informally to customers and competitors on a daily basis.

In the larger buildings being built, with their many small tenants, new ideas could be floated and tested with great efficiency. The relevant experts and decision makers could often be found under the same roof, or at least within a few blocks' distance. Everywhere there was the cross-fertilization of different disciplines working together in an open environment. With faster access to the latest ideas, businesses located downtown could gain a leg up on the competition. Those that knew how to capitalize upon these opportunities found themselves blooming amid the smoke and noise, increasing the demand for yet more office building construction.

The result was a wave of multi-tenant speculative structures of which a notable example was New York's Flatiron Building (originally the Fuller

---

13 Lehman, 24.

14 Carl W. Condit, *American Building* (Chicago: University of Chicago Press, 1968) 291.

Building), a triangular structure built to the designs of Daniel H. Burnham and Company in 1902-03 at Fifth Avenue and Broadway. Many of these buildings were aimed at particular trades and industries: railroad companies, stockbrokers, insurance agents, lawyers, doctors, real estate men.[15]

Mechanical Systems

Long before the start of the Great War all new buildings were equipped with central heating. In various forms, it dated back to Roman times. Hot water systems fired by coal which distributed heat to cast iron radiators below the windows had been used through much of the 19th century. Steam heat, quieter than the burbling hot water systems common at the time, appeared toward 1890, the year the Masonic Temple Building was built in Chicago.

Coupled with electric lighting, steam heat made office buildings habitable, though uncomfortably dry, even on dark, cold winter days. Soon they would be tolerable even on hot summer days. Air cooling with ice and blowers was an old idea which had been revived by Adler and Sullivan at the Auditorium Theater Building (1887-89) in Chicago. It would be reinvented by Willis Carrier in 1902 with a system that controlled humidity and air movement as well as temperature, and used by Frank Lloyd Wright in the Larkin Building (Buffalo, New York, 1904). Later, in the 1920s, the first fully air-conditioned office building would be erected by architect George Willis: the Milam Building in San Antonio, Texas (1928).[16]

During the long years before air conditioning became common, office buildings generally lacked all but the most primitive artificial ventilation (vertical air shafts in the toilet rooms and sometimes fresh air inlets behind the radiators). Tenants were obliged to leave their windows open through the summer, despite air that was full of soot and would remain so until strict clean-air ordinances began to be enacted at mid-20th century.

In due course, technological progress and economic change would multiply the size of the new buildings and their efficiency as places of business. Steam-powered rapid transit lines to bring in the workers would make them more accessible to outlying residents. So would the improved roads and widespread automobile ownership that followed Henry Ford's application of mass production techniques and mass-market pricing to the private car. Commuters, customers and clients who had migrated outward toward the suburbs could now find their way downtown to the new office buildings with relative ease, and once there could enjoy the views from their upper-floor offices, however those views might be obscured by coal smoke and neighboring buildings.

---

[15] See Lehman.

[16] *Encyclopedia of Architectural Design, Engineering and Construction*, vol.3 (New York: John Wiley & Sons, 1989).

While this was happening, land values in Lower Manhattan were reaching $200-$600 per square foot and office rents as much as $40 per square foot in 1912.[17] New York's 1916 zoning ordinance would alter the skyline with the wedding-cake designs encouraged by its setback requirements, which would soon be echoed in Chicago and other cities. There would be more to come; office tenants everywhere were growing larger and demanding more space. Yet over the 20th century, growth has been like a roller coaster, with severe cyclical swings in rents and land values.

THE PROHIBITION ERA

When center-city development reached a new peak in the 1920s, the downtowns of the larger American cities had become striking if confused agglomerations of tall office buildings, fancy department stores, palace hotels, shops, restaurants, saloons, betting parlors, factories and wholesale establishments of various kinds. These buildings, often heavily ornamented in a variety of quasi-historical styles, were built to the sidewalk lines under zoning ordinances that offered no rewards for open space at ground level, though by 1925 they generally required setbacks higher up to allow the passage of light and air. Soaring above the stores at ground floor level, they ranged in height up to the 1,250 feet reached by the 85-story Empire State Building (Shreve, Lamb & Harmon, 1931; a tower carries it upward to 102 stories) and in rentable area up to more than a million square feet. More typically they were 20 to 30 stories high with areas of less than 400,000 square feet. The very density of the new downtowns provided customers for a broad range of retail and service outlets which in turn made life easier and more agreeable for employees and their bosses.[18]

Fire safety, always a sensitive issue even though the structures were inherently fire-resistant, was greatly improved, though there were no sprinklers and floors were of hardwood or tile. Office buildings still had large openable windows to provide natural light and ventilation, and ceiling heights still ran 10 to 12 feet for greater tenant comfort in an era when cigar smoking was the rule among male employees who could afford it. The typewriter, the telephone and the teletype made it possible to do business more easily, cheaply and effectively than ever before.

Tenants during this period were still relatively small for the most part; it was a rare building that had more than one multi-floor tenant, so that the social and business interchange among renters and between buildings remained far greater than in today's large corporation-tenanted structures. Along with this advantage came other, sometimes less desirable

[17] Lehman, 9; Moses King, *King's Views of New York, 1911-12* (New York: Moses King, 1912).
[18] See Lehman.

consequences of the new situation. Tenants in the new offices, separated from the manufacturing and agricultural operations that fed them, grew more specialized, their workers forming a new white-collar class that seldom had to dirty its hands with physical work. As it multiplied, this class would make new demands and force massive social changes.

While New York had almost 2,500 of the 4,800 buildings in 1929 that were 10 stories or higher, many other cities had significant numbers. Chicago, Los Angeles, Philadelphia, Detroit and Boston as well as New York each had more than 100 such buildings, while St. Louis, Pittsburgh, Kansas City, San Francisco, Cleveland, Seattle, Baltimore, Minneapolis, Tulsa, Dallas and Houston each had more than 30.[19]

Chicago's stainless-steel-clad Inland Steel Building (1955-57), by international style architects Skidmore, Owings and Merrill, paved the way for new cladding materials. *(Photo by Jon Miller/Hedrich-Blessing. Courtesy of Skidmore, Owings and Merrill)*

In a world where paper and information were fast replacing gold and commodities as the basic currencies, boom-bust cycles had become familiar. The office building boom of the 1920s came to a resounding halt with the depression of the 1930s, which bankrupted tenants, pushed most properties into receivership and wiped out many owners. A few major office structures, notably New York's Rockefeller Center (1931-40), a model grouping of quality buildings, and Chicago's Field Building (1934), were started during the Depression years, but World War II put a stop to all non-defense construction until late 1945.

THE POSTWAR YEARS

At the war's end, a generation of white collar workers reared in suburbia would in due course find its way back to the heart of the city. Employers there awaited them with open arms. Those cities fortunate enough to enjoy good commuter rail networks, modern expressway systems and attractive downtowns were special beneficiaries. Available space was in short supply, driving office rents to new highs.

Most cities, though, experienced no real resurgence of office development until at least the 1950s, when Lever House in New York (1952) and the stainless-steel-clad Inland Steel Building in Chicago (1955-57), both by international style architects Skidmore, Owings and Merrill (SOM), gave proof that the office building was still a viable art form, if not yet a guarantee of financial success for investors. The metal-and-glass skins of these two buildings would pave the way for other cladding materials. These included glass, stamped aluminum (Harrison & Abramovitz's 1953 Alcoa Building in Pittsburgh), precast concrete (most notably at the 1960 Pan Am Building in New York, by Walter Gropius with The Architects' Collaborative and Belluschi & Roth), composite insulating panels, and the oxidizing steel (actually a steel-copper alloy) used at Chicago's Civic Center (now the Richard J. Daley Civic Center, by Jacques Brownson with C. F. Murphy and Son, 1963-65) and the U.S. Steel Building in Pittsburgh (Harrison & Abramowitz, 1969). Stainless steel, discovered by accident in 1912 but little used for building before the Inland Steel Building because of its cost, would be used again at the Harris Bank Building in Chicago, also an SOM design, and at the Mobil Oil Building in New York.[20]

---

[19] See Lehman.

[20] See, for example, William Brubaker, "The Evolution of Chicago's Tall Office Buildings," *Chicago Office* (Chicago: Building Owners and Managers Association, 1991); Robert Bruegmann et al., *A Guide to 150 Years of Chicago Architecture* (Chicago: Chicago Review Press, 1985); Paul Goldberger, *The Skyscraper* (New York: Alfred A. Knopf, 1982); Henry-Russell Hitchcock, *Architecture: Nineteenth and Twentieth Centuries, 3rd. ed.* (Baltimore: Penguin Books, 1971); Pauline A. Saliga, ed. *The Sky's the Limit: A Century of Chicago Skyscrapers* (New York: Rizzoli International Publications, Inc., 1990).

The design of these buildings, which rose straight up from the ground without setbacks and left much of the lot open, would also encourage major revisions to the zoning ordinances of New York, Chicago and other cities. Inside, the space was laid out to the new standards made possible by central air conditioning. The Inland Steel Building, for example, had all its mechanical services in a separate core, allowing its office tower to be designed without interior columns.

Central air conditioning, now refined to provide for supply and return zones, and a rising demand for the larger spaces it made possible, encouraged the new buildings to increase their floor sizes, though floor plates of 15,000 square feet or less remained common. At the same time, new building forms were made possible by zoning reforms such as those of the Chicago Zoning Ordinance of 1957 and the New York Ordinance of 1961, which set limits on floor area ratios instead of imposing height limits or requiring upper-floor setbacks. These reforms, reflective of international style architectural canons, allowed greater design flexibility and encouraged setbacks at grade rather than at the upper floors, often granting bonuses for arcades, plazas and other amenities.[21]

Technology had been evolving behind the scenes during the quiet years, and elevator manufacturers like Otis and Westinghouse were ready with new high-speed operatorless systems that could move people to the top of a 40-story building in less than a minute, popping eyes as well as ears. A shift from direct to alternating electric current and improvements in fluorescent lighting (invented 1938) reduced power consumption while encouraging light levels to rise. Oil and sometimes gas-fired boilers had begun to replace the stoker-fired coal boilers of an earlier era. Later, electric heating, cheaper to install and maintain, would have its turn.

Central air conditioning, still fairly rare in the 1950s because of its cost, became common and in fact almost mandatory during the 1960s. It reduced ceiling heights to as little as eight feet, though ceilings of nine feet or more remained the standard in Class A buildings. Also possible with air conditioning were floor plans far larger and more flexible than in the past, with greater core-to-perimeter distances and greater amounts of window-less space lighted by fluorescent fixtures. Older buildings through the period were often retrofitted with window air conditioners or package units serving selected tenants.

Meanwhile asphalt, rubber tile and carpet floor coverings were becoming common, and fire-resistant gypsum-based plasterboard, generally mounted on structural tile block or metal studs for reduced flammability, had appeared as a lower-cost partitioning material which allowed faster

[21] Seymour Toll, *Zoned America* (New York: Grossman, 1969).

and cleaner revision of tenant layouts. During the same period, mass-produced curtain wall elements were reducing costs and construction time for many buildings.

Decentralization Creates Major Locational Shifts

A system of interstate highways launched during the Eisenhower Administration—and the suburbanization that accompanied it—would at first contribute to the vitality of the downtown marketplace, now more accessible than ever to outlying users. Later, the rapid expansion of urban blight and the ensuing flight to the suburbs of office businesses and employees, facilitated by new expressways and transit lines, would begin to undermine the attractiveness and viability of many central cities. Suburban communities eager for new revenues fought to attract office development with liberal zoning and other incentives.

As a result, office buildings began to dot the suburban landscape, at first in isolation but soon, especially after about 1965, in growing clusters served by the new expressways. Industrial parks with carefully planned streets and facilities had been commonplace since the 1920s. Now office parks with landscaping and off-street parking were beginning to appear in many markets.

Tenants would also increasingly influence the location of office building sites. Wanting to work closer to home, and when possible to commute by private car rather than public transportation, the executives of the 1970s and 1980s would induce the development of exurban office concentrations in the "urban villages" or "edge cities" and along the growth corridors of sprawling American metropolises. Tyson's Corner near Washington, D. C., the Woodfield area near Chicago, and Route 1 near Princeton, New Jersey, are among the most striking examples. Perhaps the most notable individual buildings reflecting this phenomenon are a tower by architect Helmut Jahn some 17 miles west of Chicago in Oakbrook Terrace and the 1.6 million-square-foot 64-story Transco Tower, by Philip Johnson and John Burgee, in the Post Oak area of Houston, the tallest building ever built in an essentially suburban setting.

Through this period floor plates and building sizes continued to grow larger. Column spacing began to standardize on the five-foot module increasingly preferred for facilities planning, producing bays 30' x 30', 30' x 50' and 40' x 40'. These cost more to build than less costly 20' x 20' bays but allowed more flexibility in tenant layouts. Specially designed computer rooms were installed to accommodate the growing computer needs of tenants; movable partitioning had made its appearance, while wall-to-wall carpet and vinyl tile floor coverings largely replaced the rugs and the asbestos-laden asphalt tile that had covered most floors until the 1960s. By 1965, asbestos, an ancient building material commonly used for fireproofing, was beginning to be rejected in favor of safer materials. Later, it would

become a serious problem for many building owners and manufacturers of building materials because of the health hazard it posed.

Electric heating systems and floor-to-ceiling windows had become common by the 1960s, but the energy crisis of 1973-74, when oil prices soared and people lined up for gasoline on the streets, yielded a new generation of buildings designed to conserve energy. These tight new structures were heated mainly by gas, often with provision for the use of oil as an alternate fuel. They came with low rooflines, reduced heat-wasting perimeter wall areas, insulating skins sealed to minimize heat loss, and smaller double-glazed non-openable metal sash equipped with thermal barriers.

In the 1980s a new problem was becoming apparent. The artificially-supplied air which replaced air that had formerly come in through the windows allowed toxic substances and germs released in the course of ordinary operations to accumulate inside, making breathing a riskier proposition. Also of growing concern was the danger of terrorist attack, which led many owners to rearrange their building entrances and install alarm systems for greater security.

In Chicago, major structures such as the John Hancock Center (Skidmore, Owings and Merrill, 1970), Sears Tower (SOM, 1974), the Amoco Building (Edward Durrell Stone with Perkins and Will, 1974) and Water Tower Place, an instant mixed-use landmark (Loebl, Schlossman, Bennett and Dart, 1975-76), dominated their market for several years. Far from the Chicago scene in the roughneck city of Houston, a new architectural standard would be set by Johnson and Burgee's Pennzoil Place (1972-76), which demonstrated to the world that good architecture could be worth its cost. Meanwhile, in New York, Donald Trump was proving at Trump Tower (Swanke, Hayden, Connell and Partners, 1976) that mixed-use design could be sybaritic as well as more or less functional.

THE EASY EIGHTIES

By 1982, when the country experienced a serious manufacturing recession and blue-collar jobs were lost by the million, people began to believe that the future of the United States lay with the service industries. Large amounts of space would be necessary to accommodate their growth, much of it in the suburbs where suburban baby boomers could get white-collar jobs close to home. The impact of IBM's first personal computer was multiplied by the proliferation of the photocopier, the telefax and the modem, novelties which greatly increased the flow of information and stimulated the creation of new businesses. Communication via satellite, fiber optic cable and laser printing increased unbelievably the speed of the information flow and enabled companies to move anywhere.

In the suburbs, office building development in many markets was proceeding even faster than in traditional downtowns, where construction continued apace. Some of this construction took the form of "smart buildings" prewired for computer networks and fiber optic communications, often with central computer and fax services available to tenants. Vertical chases were made larger to accommodate tenants' telephone lines and special wiring. Heating and air conditioning were by now integrated in new computer-controlled energy-conserving forms, often based on electricity rather than gas or oil, that allowed tenants to exert a high degree of control over temperature and airflow and shielded them from outside atmospheric conditions to such an extent that "sick buildings," with air contaminated by internal effluvia, would become a problem. Improvements in the art of slicing and fastening marble and granite veneers allowed them to be used as facing materials for tall buildings, but as the failure of numerous building skins would show, this flexibility was not without its perils.

Coming into fashion as the decade progressed was an almost frivolous post-modernism exemplified by Johnson and Burgee's Chippendale-style AT&T Building in New York (1984) and by two Michael Graves designs: the Portland Municipal Services Building (1980) and the Humana Building in Louisville (1982). New York's towering World Trade Center (Minoru Yamasaki and Associates, 1972-74) had been built in the international style, as would be Cesar Pelli's World Financial Center (1985-88) in New York, but European and Japanese architects as well as American post-modernists were beginning to come on the scene with buildings such as Kenzo Tange's AMA Center (1991) and Ricardo Bofill's R. R. Donnelley Building (1992) in Chicago. Daring, sometimes dazzling, office buildings by architects such as Jahn, Bofill, Richard Rogers, Michael Hopkins and many others meanwhile were rising in Europe and the Far East.

The great strides made in office technology had improved worker productivity throughout this period, allowing many office tenants to think about space and staff cuts as they modernized. They could also think about the kinds of new activities made possible by greatly improved information-handling and communications facilities. World capital markets were now increasingly integrated and able to operate with lightning speed, which facilitated the movement of funds across regional and national lines.

In response, decentralization became the order of the day. One result was the emergence of fast-growing global service businesses that could place their operations wherever labor costs might dictate, almost without regard to location. Another was the spreading institutionalization of real estate ownership and management as the insurance companies and pension funds, hoping for investment returns higher than they could earn as mere mortgage lenders, involved themselves more deeply in the property markets.

NOT THE END OF THE STORY

As the new century approaches, it is evident that the shape and function of the office building will continue to evolve, though the directions they will take are not yet clearly discernible. So will the office building's investment dynamics and its relationship to its community. Like a living creature, the office building must adapt to the vagaries of chance and change, as it always has done in the past, forever ready to make new—and possibly quite different—economic and social contributions to the constantly unfolding capitalist society which gave it birth.

ABOUT THE AUTHORS

Jared Shlaes, CRE, MAI, is the author of *Real Estate Counseling in a Plain Brown Wrapper*, published by the Counselors of Real Estate in 1992. Recently retired as director for special real estate services for Arthur Andersen & Co., Shlaes had also been founder-president of Shlaes & Co., a real estate counseling and appraisal firm, and senior vice president of Arthur Rubloff & Co. in charge of counseling and appraisal services. Shlaes is a national authority on the economics of landmark properties and the use of preservation easements, and was co-originator of the internationally acclaimed Chicago Plan for landmark preservation, a transferable development rights scheme.

Marc A. Weiss, Ph.D., is director of the Real Estate Development Research Center and associate professor in the Graduate School of Architecture, Planning and Preservation at Columbia University. He previously taught at MIT. He is author of *The Rise of the Community Builders* and co-author of *Real Estate Development Principles and Process*. Weiss has written many articles on urban development and is now writing and producing *Prime Property*, a public television series on the history of American real estate. He holds an undergraduate degree from Stanford University and a Ph.D. from the University of California, Berkeley.

2

THE CHARACTERISTICS OF TODAY'S OFFICE BUILDINGS

by James Goettsch

INTRODUCTION

Chapter 1 described how societal and economic forces generate changing requirements for buildings to house office activities. This chapter presents the office building as it is found today in most of North America. The latest buildings in Europe, Africa and Asia are adopting similar forms as technology overwhelms regional differences.

Office buildings vary greatly in location, size, height, class, configuration, building services and equipment, cost, age, origin, use and markets served. Although the accepted categories are not clear-cut, it is possible to classify office buildings in terms of these characteristics, which are discussed later in the chapter.

MODERN OFFICE BUILDINGS

The office building types commonly seen today began to emerge in quantity during the 1950s. At first relatively modest in size, they grew through the 1960s and 1970s until, by the 1980s, a downtown building of 1,000,000 square feet or more was not unusual in the larger cities.

The author wishes to thank John F. Hartray, Jr., FAIA and Jared Shlaes for their comments and assistance.

In most of these new buildings, tenant spaces were left in a raw state, to be completed by or for unknown future users. To be considered desirable, this "shell space" had to be relatively open, encumbered as little as possible by fixed structural or mechanical elements that might impose limitations on tenant layouts. Equally important, it had to be fitted with the latest heating and air-conditioning systems and be able to accommodate increasing numbers of office machines. Older buildings, with their small floor plates, irregular column spacing, low floor-to-floor heights, inadequate wiring and lack of air conditioning, could seldom be adequately modified to satisfy these new requirements.

Since its appearance in the 1950s, the postwar office building has been in a continual state of evolution. Significant changes affecting its design have occurred in:

- The economics of construction technology and of real estate investment
- Standards of space utilization by larger tenants
- Standards of environmental acceptability
- User and developer preferences

The international style, with its ornament-free, clearly expressed structures, was prominent through most of this period, but it has been largely succeeded by post-modernism and other architectural styles. Simple, box-like slabs with regularly spaced columns, sometimes elaborately and expensively detailed, are giving way to more complicated shapes, partly to provide more corner offices per floor and partly to provide a more distinctive architectural form. Meanwhile a constant struggle for efficiency in construction, operation and maintenance has been coupled with a growing preference for large tenants with needs often different from those of smaller ones. The result has generally been more efficient floor plates with large bays and very efficient utility cores. However, during the boom years of the 1980s, owners, lenders and tenants showed an increasing preference for dramatic lobbies and for facilities such as health clubs, day-care centers, employee cafeterias and auditoriums.

THE U.S. OFFICE BUILDING STOCK

This influx of funds, coupled with the tremendous growth in the service industries which followed World War II and accelerated during the 1980s, led to a corresponding surge in office employment and office building development.

White collar employment, according to data from the Bureau of Labor Statistics and Cognetics, Inc.,[1] swelled by 38.6% in the 1960s, 36.5% in the 1970s and 29.8% in the 1980s. This growth encouraged office development on a large scale. Since 1960 the U.S. has added over 9.22 billion square feet of rentable space to its office space stock; 5.38 billion of this was added in the period between 1980 and 1989. By 1990, the total inventory of office space had reached about 11 billion square feet—some 44 square feet per capita—with a value of over $1 trillion.[2] Allowing 200 square feet per employee, a commonly used yardstick, this inventory would accommodate 44 million workers and executives. The social and economic consequences of this major business use of office space are discussed in Chapter 3.

Data from Salomon Brothers cited by Mike E. Miles[3] give an indication of how office space is distributed regionally.

Regional Concentrations of Office Properties

January 1988	
Region	Share of Inventory
New England	3.9%
Mid-Atlantic	28.6
Industrial Midwest	19.4
Farm Belt	1.1
Mineral Regions	18.8
So. California	10.3
No. California	8.8

Sources: U.S. Bureau of Labor Statistics, The WEFA Group, and Salomon Brothers, Inc.

Statistics for Chicago, where good office building data are available through The Chicago REsource, provide an idea of the distribution of commercially available office space across a metropolitan market. Only a quarter century ago, almost all the space would have been concentrated in the downtown area. The following table reflects 1991 inventories.

---

[1] *Fortune*, January 28, 1991, page 44.

[2] Data from *Managing the Future: Real Estate in the 1990s*, a 1991 study by Arthur Andersen & Co. for the Institute of Real Estate Management Foundation. Other estimates, such as those by F. W. Dodge, Salomon Brothers and Stephen Roulac/Equitable Real Estate Investment Management, were taken into account by the Andersen study. Another contributor to the study, Mike E. Miles, conveniently summarized these in "What Is the Value of All U.S. Real Estate?" (*Real Estate Review*, Volume 2, Number 2, Summer 1990, pp. 69-77). Miles is executive vice president, Prudential Realty Group, Newark, N.J.

[3] Adapted from Miles, *op. cit.*, p. 76.

1991 Chicago Office Space Inventory

Zone		Net Rentable Area
Chicago (Central)		122,684,828 sq. ft.
Suburban		
North	19,479,942	
Northwest	24,960,172	
O'Hare	16,057,009	
West	32,443,544	
West and South Cook	5,268,933	
Total Suburban		98,209,600 sq. ft.
Grand Total		220,894,428 sq. ft.

This total, which does not include space not available for commercial use, amounts to roughly 35 square feet per capita for the Chicago metropolitan area. Most markets have less space per capita, but a few, notably New York, which has by far the largest stock in the world, have much more.

DESIGN AND VALUATION FACTORS

To understand office buildings, it is necessary to recognize the fundamental aspects of this varied building type. They include:

1. Location
2. Size and height
3. Class
4. Configuration
5. Building services and equipment
6. Building costs
7. Age
8. Origin
9. Use and ownership
10. Markets

Location

Some office buildings are found in the central city ("downtown office buildings"), others in the suburbs and exurbs ("suburban office buildings"). Where they are located makes a difference in their design, utility and value. Buildings in traditional downtown areas are generally taller than buildings in suburban and outlying areas because of higher downtown land costs and usually more permissive zoning. Rents, operating costs, development cost and value all tend to be higher on a square foot basis than in outlying areas.

Centrally located office buildings generally have fewer parking requirements than suburban buildings because public transportation and commercial parking facilities can meet most or all of their needs. Often downtown buildings can also depend on the services provided by outside restaurants, health clubs, day-care centers and other facilities. Suburban buildings, on the other hand, must provide their own parking lots or decks, and often must include restaurants and other amenities in their planning.

Size and Height

Some buildings are large (1,000,000 square feet and more), some middle-sized, some as small as 5,000 square feet or even less. Some are high-rise (16 stories and up), some mid-rise (4-15 stories), some low-rise (1-3 stories). Size and height also affect use and value.

Most office builders, public or private, try to build as much square footage as the law allows, although the economics of construction and local laws may hold them in check. The objective is to minimize land cost as a percentage of total development cost so that rents in the finished building will be competitive. As land costs go up, the pressure to build a larger building increases.

Limits can be imposed by soil conditions. Taller buildings require foundations that can be costly if the soil lacks adequate bearing capacity. Depending on where they are located, very tall buildings (35 stories and up) can only be built on caissons that reach down to bedrock or on special foundations such as a large concrete mat (sometimes 15 feet thick) covering the entire site. A smaller building that can be built on less expensive spread foundations might save money in such cases and be preferred.

Local building codes often set a break point between mid- and high-rise buildings based on the height that can be reached by fire department equipment. Chicago's break point is 80 feet; in Whitewater, Wisconsin, it is 3 stories. Above the break point, building code requirements are stiffer and costs go up, sometimes prohibitively. Special exit, ventilation and fire safety requirements imposed on buildings with heights or floor sizes exceeding certain threshholds can be so costly that they constitute effective limits to size and height.

Most commonly the size of the office building is imposed by the local market, which can only absorb a certain amount of space at a time, or by local zoning, which may set a maximum building area or height. Since the 1950s, building size is usually capped in terms of floor area ratio (FAR). This is the maximum ratio allowed between the gross area of the building (GBA) and the gross or net area of the site (SA): FAR = GBA/SA.

Zoning may set the maximum height of a building, but more often it is determined by a reconciliation between the maximum building area and the optimal floor plate size. The area of the ideal floor plate divided into the total building area determines the number of floors to be built.

Height is also affected by the preferences of developers and other building sponsors who, for various personal, business and political reasons, may prefer a building that is taller or shorter than the competition. Since upper-floor offices are generally considered more desirable than those on lower floors and command higher rents, adding height frequently adds to building value. Absolute limits on building height may be imposed by the Federal Aviation Administration (FAA), which caps the height of buildings that might otherwise interfere with the safe use of nearby airports.

In build-to-suit projects, public and private, there is seemingly no need to consider market preferences regarding floor size or building height. However, in an era of rapid change when companies are growing and shrinking unpredictably, prudent sponsors will take into account the possibility of an eventual conversion to multi-tenant use and the likely market appeal of the space.

Several other factors may influence the size and height of an office building:

- **Market demands:** The needs of tenants often dictate not only total rentable area but also column spacing and floor plate sizes. Tenant preferences may also suggest that buildings be taller to provide more upper-floor space or irregularly shaped to allow more corner offices.
- **Economies of scale:** In general, larger floors and buildings cost less per square foot to build and operate. Beyond a certain scale, though, buildings can be difficult to build, fill and manage.
- **Field conditions and construction technology:** The presence or absence of on-site room for the contractor's equipment may dictate the maximum size of the typical floor. Though conditions vary from market to market, some slab sizes are cheaper to form and pour than others, which also affects the choice.
- **Elevatoring:** An individual elevator that serves too many floors causes undue delays because it must make too many stops. Tall buildings thus may require zoned and even stacked elevators that can take up floor space and add to costs. Often the solution is to limit the size of the building rather than install a more expensive or more complicated elevator system.
- **Aesthetic objectives:** Many developers care about appearance as well as economics, and will scale their buildings accordingly.

Class

Class A buildings, the best in their markets, are generally the most attractive, rentable and efficient. While some are relatively old, they must have modern mechanical systems, allow good tenant layouts and have prestige tenants to qualify. Class B and C buildings, by definition less appealing to tenants, may be deficient in a number of respects including floor plans, condition, facilities and quality of management. They lack prestige and must depend chiefly on lower price to attract tenants and investors. Trophy buildings, the ones most eagerly sought by investors willing to pay a premium for quality, are the cream of Class A, and often are designed by architects whose names are immediately recognizable.

Typical features of the different classes of office buildings are as follows (these may vary from one market to another):

- **Trophy building:** Extremely desirable as an investment, suitable for the most selective portfolios. Generally one-of-a-kind, with unique shape and floor plans, notable architectural design, excellent and possibly outstanding location. Best quality materials and workmanship; expensive trim and interior fittings. First-rate maintenance and management. Prestige tenants.
- **Class A:** Investment-grade property, well located and offering high-quality space. Good design, above-average workmanship and materials. Well maintained and managed, exceptionally so if an older building. Quality tenants.

Trophy buildings such as the Bank of America building in San Francisco are extremely desirable as an investment. *(Photo by Ezra Stoller/ESTO. Courtesy of Skidmore, Owings and Merrill)*

- **Class B:** Generally a more speculative investment. Offers utilitarian space without special attractions. Ordinary design, if new or fairly new; good to excellent space and design if an older non-landmark building. Average to good maintenance and management. Average tenants.
- **Class C:** Basic space in a no-frills older building. Below-average maintenance and management. Mixed or low tenant prestige. Inferior elevators and mechanical/electrical systems.

Configuration

Some office buildings (mostly downtown) cover the lot, with parking inside or below or in adjacent public parking lots, while others (mostly suburban) are landscaped and provide outside parking; shapes range from cubic to free-form.

A Class A building such as the PPG Headquarters in Pittsburgh, with its outstanding design and above-average workmanship and materials, is considered an investment-grade property. *(Photo by Ted Trimbur. Courtesy of PPG Industries, Inc. and John Burgee Architects)*

The shape and arrangement of a building as well as its height and mass can affect its first cost, maintenance costs, market appeal and value. Among other things, they influence the choice of structural system and building skin. In turn, they are influenced by a host of factors including zoning, building codes, development costs, and market factors such as natural light. Even downtown there are often setbacks, particularly at common lot lines, to provide daylight on all sides.

A number of different structural systems are used for office buildings.

Steel Frame

Steel frame offers the advantage of large scale application with less load on the foundations than a concrete structure, good speed of erection, large spans, flexibility of modification and the ability to accommodate changing loading conditions. These advantages can be offset by the limited number of structural steel suppliers, which can result in large fluctuations in prices, and by the long lead time sometimes required between date of order and delivery to the job site. In addition, except in special circumstances, steel requires 6 to 12 inch higher floor heights, resulting in a dramatic increase in the cubic content of the building and thus in the costs of skin and mechanical systems. For tall buildings, wind bracing is also an important design and cost consideration.

Reinforced Concrete

Concrete is in many ways the counterpart to steel. Traditionally the number of suppliers is greater than with steel frame construction (though they may be individually smaller), speed of erection is slower, foundations must be stronger to carry the greater weight, floor-to-floor height is lower, and wind bracing has less impact on the cost of the structure. Compared to steel, floor-to-floor height can be reduced by 6 to 12 inches with resulting cost savings. Disadvantages include shorter spans, the difficulty of making major modifications to the structure after completion and the fact that the concrete structure takes up floor space and reduces rentable area.

Composite Construction

In high-rise buildings, the concrete core with steel framing beyond has resulted in an almost perfect union of the advantages of steel and concrete construction for:

- Speed of construction
- Flexibility of design, even during construction
- Minimum wind bracing
- Reduced structural spans in occupied areas

- Maximum competition among contractors

Alignment and differential settlement have in the past created problems, but experience has taught builders how to prevent them.

Other Types of Construction

The use of unprotected steel is usually limited to industrial and small suburban office buildings, though there are conspicuous exceptions such as the State of Illinois Center in Chicago and the Knights of Columbus Building in New Haven, Connecticut. Other types of building construction—mill, ordinary construction and light frame—are not typically used except in small, low-cost office buildings.

Building Services and Equipment

Configuration, class and other aspects of the office building are also influenced by the facilities to be provided, the market to be served and the aesthetic impression to be made. Significant changes have occurred within the last 30 to 35 years.

Environmental

There have been three or four generations of changes in heating, ventilation and air conditioning systems. In addition to meeting basic environmental provisions (e.g., reducing noxious emissions from motors or old, recirculated air), mechanical systems can respond to specific considerations such as operating costs, energy conservation and first cost. Rising concerns about the supply and cost of energy make the efficiency of these systems a primary concern of owners and tenants alike.

Life Safety

Life safety in high-rise buildings has been highly refined through extensive cost studies and experimentation. State-of-the-art systems are provided in almost all new office buildings, high-rise or low-rise, and include sprinklers, heat/smoke detectors, alarm reporting systems, smoke evacuation systems, and so on. These affect insurance rates and can be important to tenants as well as owners.

Building Codes

Codes are continually changing, and while existing buildings legally may be able to avoid compliance with new code provisions, their value tends to decline if they are not readily upgradable. Some provisions, such as the accessibility codes under the Americans with Disabilities Act of 1991, may require uniform compliance and provoke exceptional costs just in widened exit stairs. Among the issues are:

- Life safety/high-rise codes
- Accessibility codes
- Hazardous materials (chiefly asbestos)
- Window-washing equipment (tall buildings)

Communications

Buildings that provide computer-based information processing and communication services to tenants have yet to live up to expectations. Still, the importance of telephone, telefax, teleconferencing, duplicating and computer technology has continued to grow. Architects and developers must struggle to keep up with changing tenant demands as these technologies evolve, seemingly at an ever-increasing pace.

Control Systems

"Smart buildings" that are programmed to make efficient use of energy and to monitor air quality and temperature have become the rule. Another round of innovation will likely result in still more operational, security and user improvements.

Building Cost

Original cost is recognized in the class of the building and also affects market appeal, operating efficiency and value within classes. An expensive building may not only be more attractive and rentable than an economy model of similar size but may also be cheaper to maintain and operate.

The cost of construction varies dramatically depending on location, size, height, design concept, interior finishes and mechanical systems. To establish the extremes, one might compare the detailed component costs as well as the shell-and-core costs of a downtown high-rise with those of a suburban mid-rise building.

Component	Urban High-Rise	Suburban Mid-Rise
Structure	$22.12/sq. ft.	$11.09/sq. ft.
Exterior Enclosure	22.69/sq. ft.	11.10/sq. ft.
Elevators	5.53/sq. ft.	3.26/sq. ft.
Lobby Finishes	4.26/sq. ft.	.75/sq. ft.
Mechanical, Electrical	14.10/sq. ft.	14.00/sq. ft.
Misc. Arch. Items	13.77/sq. ft.	6.95/sq. ft.
Total	$82.47/sq. ft.	$47.15/sq. ft.

These costs, accurate for Chicago in 1990, will differ from year to year and from one part of the country to another, according to the size and quality of the building and the health of the economy. However, the proportional costs of the components and the relationship between urban high-rise and suburban mid-rise will hold roughly constant throughout the country. To the above figures must be added the cost of tenant improvements (interior space installation and outfitting), which can range from $20 to $50 per square foot and more. Developers will also add land cost, capital costs during development and rent-up, and the costs of carrying the project through to completion, which may include maintenance, housekeeping, taxes, administration, marketing, legal and management fees, leasing commissions, rent concessions and similar items.

The following factors influence building costs.

Location

Urban sites with restrictions on deliveries and limited staging areas assure major complications in the construction process. During the 1980s in New York, for example, from Thanksgiving to Christmas deliveries to construction sites were not allowed between 8 a.m. and 6 p.m.

Ownership

Developers who focus on short-term gains will often plan and build their buildings very differently than owner-builders more interested in the long term. Prestige-conscious tenant-owners, whether corporate or institutional, may be willing to pay a premium for superior designs that is not justified by ordinary real estate economic analysis.

Size and Height

As buildings increase in height, the foundations, the elevatoring, the structures required and the logistics of the construction process can all result in additional costs per square foot. On the other hand, savings can result from quantity purchasing and from the repetition and special construction techniques possible with tall buildings. Concrete forms, for example, can often be lifted from floor to floor at a considerable savings from the cost of one-time use. The size of the floor plate is also a factor in most markets.

Design Intent

The shape of a building and the selection of exterior materials have a major impact on cost. The cheapest rectangular enclosure of precast concrete with strips of skin and windows may cost $20 per square foot. Better curtain walling for a high-rise structure of good quality may cost $38-$42 per square foot, while the enclosure of a "trophy building" can reach $50-$60 per square foot. Unusual design concepts intended to stand out from the crowd can prove costly to build.

Also important is the choice of interior finishes. Extensive use of costly materials in public areas, such as marble and rare woods, can have a significant effect on project cost.

Building Services

There is a generally understood level of base building standards for mechanical, electrical and plumbing (MEP) systems. Depending on the desires of the owner or user there may be a need for additional MEP/building costs to cover additional capacity, energy-conservation measures, high-density occupancy or greater than normal structural capacity. Anything out of the ordinary can increase costs.

Any improvement in the overall quality of the building or the scope of services to be provided is likely to increase the cost of its amenities, which generally must be gauged in proportion to the project's intended market. Typical amenities that must be considered in the modern office building include:

- Parking
- Recreational facilities
- Day care
- Subsidized retail and/or food service

Age

Buildings range in age along a continuum from new to very old indeed. Old buildings may be landmarks, gaining value with the years; others are just candidates for the wrecking ball. The age of a building affects its utility, its marketability, and its value. However, age alone does not dictate an office building's value. Many are capable of total modernization.

The period from 1932 to 1946, when few office buildings were developed because of the Depression and World War II, constitutes a gulf between those buildings built before it and those that came after. "Older buildings" is now coming to mean buildings built more than a generation ago, but to many it still means those built before the Great Depression. The differences among buildings built at different times can be numerous (see Chapter 1); each era has its characteristic building sizes, configurations, bay sizes, mechanical systems and architecture.

Use and Ownership

Different kinds of users—government, corporations, mixed use—generally need different kinds of buildings. The nature of the user, whether owner or tenant, influences the design and operation of the office building. Perhaps the most important distinction is that between single-tenant buildings, usually designed for a specific user, and multi-tenant buildings, which must appeal to a broad market.

Single-tenant buildings, mostly found in the suburbs, often have larger floor plates and higher efficiency ratios than multi-tenant buildings. Bay depth (distance from core to windows) can often be greater, partitions can be fewer, and the core, elevatoring and facilities can be designed to the specific requirements of the intended user instead of for a generalized office space market.

Multi-tenant buildings must be designed to accommodate a wide variety of potential users. Typical floors must be standardized to allow efficient space planning for likely tenant classes such as law and accounting firms. Because the marketability of the space is so important, such buildings often provide varied tenant facilities and as many corner offices as possible.

These factors make a difference in operating as well as initial capital costs. They also influence value. So does the nature of the building's occupancy and ownership.

Government

Buildings intended for government use in our tax-conscious times are usually designed to appeal to the most conservative design instincts with the implicit goal of offending as few people as possible. In spite of this, they are seldom low in cost, primarily because design details usually reflect government's desire to:

- Minimize operating costs even at the expense of higher capital cost
- Avoid criticism in its contractual procedures which, because government must usually accept the lowest bid, tend to result in large change orders and construction delays
- Maintain the highest level of local building code compliance

Single Tenant

Corporate institutional office buildings, whether leased or owned, are unlike government buildings in that they must meet the aesthetic and business objectives of a particular organization. These objectives may be ceremonial as well as functional. Structures are often designed for prestige, ease of maintenance and the specific layout requirements of the user rather than to minimize capital cost.

Multi-tenant

Buildings intended for unknown tenants must be designed and built to appeal to a broad spectrum of the office market. Primary factors for consideration include initial cost per square foot, operating costs, floor size, lease span, efficiency, flexibility, location, building services, amenities and aesthetics.

Mixed Use

These are buildings that incorporate multiple uses within a single structure. The range of uses may include two or more of the following:

- Office
- Parking
- Hotel
- Recreational
- Retail
- Cultural
- Residential

The design and operation of a mixed-use building are difficult because each use may have a different set of structural and operating requirements, such as bay size or floor loads. Satisfying all these requirements at the same time can be awkward and costly. Frequently the uses must be kept functionally separate, with individual entrances, elevator banks and mechanical systems. Under the best circumstances, the synergism of mixed use may result in significantly higher values for all the uses to offset the higher cost of the project.

Markets Served

Different buildings appeal to different kinds of tenants and are marketed accordingly. How well its space marketing program is geared to the potential tenant market has a major influence on the success of a building. Also relevant is the investment market in which the property will be traded, the behavior of which determines the value of the property.

With everything else changing it is natural that marketing strategies must change as well. In general, these strategies reflect the following concerns.

Economics

The cost per square foot of leasing space becomes a matter of interpretation when one starts to include:

- Credits toward costs of tenant improvements
- Deferred rent payments
- Assumptions of other leases
- Rights to equity ownership

Still, first cost is at or near the top of the space marketer's concerns. In good times or bad, tenants prefer not to waste money, and a building that is too costly will be handicapped in the marketplace. However, a well-designed and aesthetically appealing building need not necessarily be significantly more expensive; this is the constant architectural challenge.

Changing economic conditions affect building design as tenants and owners seek to:

- Reduce maintenance and operating costs, for example in response to an energy crisis
- Accommodate aggressive real estate brokers or depressed space markets
- Capitalize on improvements in construction technology, for example by using prefabricated instead of on-site assembly

Mixed use buildings such as New York's City Spire incorporate multiple uses within a single structure. Each use may have a different set of structural and operating requirements, resulting in higher costs for the project. *(Courtesy of Murphy/ Jahn Architects)*

Efficiency

Layout becomes important as one building is compared to another. The issues include the loss factor (the percentage of gross building area lost to unrentable space) and the efficiency of the layouts possible within the leasing envelope. A properly located building core, minimal intrusions into the space by mechanical equipment or columns, and correct sizing of bays and modules can make an obvious difference in the utility of the space.

Aesthetics

The overheated market of the 1980s put a renewed emphasis on aesthetics. More than ever, architecture became a marketable commodity, something that was perceived to have value because it affected the project's ability to attract and sell future tenants. From their own viewpoint, marketing-conscious tenants, anxious to project the right image, often appreciated superior design.

Fresh ideas as well as fashion and practical considerations drive the movement in architectural styles. Architecture is a reflection of the world that surrounds it. Styles such as modernism, post-modernism, historicism, deconstructionism and late modernism are merely visual expressions of what is happening in society at large. Social evolution and especially technological developments—new materials, new structural techniques, new environmental capabilities—force change in building design. The introduction of the structural steel frame, modern elevatoring and central air conditioning launched revolutions in their day. More recently, the developing glass industry has brought about significant changes with each new product. The complex nature of modern communications equipment has brought about changes in electrical installations.

CONCLUSION

Following the overproduction of the 1980s, the office building has temporarily fallen out of favor as an investment. White-collar employment growth that for years absorbed vast quantities of space in the U.S. has slowed dramatically from its peak, and relatively little new development is anticipated for the balance of the 1990s. What the office building of the future will look like is uncertain, but it undoubtedly will be different, at least in subtle ways, from the office buildings of today. New philosophies of office space design and use are taking shape as this is being written, tending away from the longstanding pattern of individual private offices and a shared secretarial pool.

This shift in the thinking of office planners is triggered by a proliferation of small, portable computers and versatile telephones which allow their users to get the job done at home, in the car or hotel room, at the client's, or in a satellite office. Increasingly, mind-workers are being freed from their traditional bondage to the office desk and will need less personal space in the company headquarters. The next buildings may well feature general work and meeting spaces furnished more like hotel lobbies and living rooms than like traditional offices, with generous common facilities and meeting rooms plus small workstations where workers returning from the field can plug in.

The structural design and general configuration of office buildings have changed little since the invention of the skeleton frame and are likely to remain very much like the ones today into the indefinite future. Still, the imagination and creative energy of architects and developers can be counted on for at least a few surprises as they approach the 21st century. How people work, and how well they enjoy their work, will be strongly influenced by what these architects and developers do.

ABOUT THE AUTHOR

James Goettsch, FAIA, is a principal with Lohan Associates, Chicago. He was with the firm of Murphy/Jahn for 19 years, where he was executive vice president and associate director of planning and design. He was the principal in charge of the firm's New York office from 1983-1988. He has been involved in all phases of the design and construction of more than 80 major buildings, including high-rise and low-rise office buildings, throughout the United States and overseas. He holds a Bachelor of Architecture degree from Iowa State University, and has served as an adjunct professor in the Department of Architecture at the University of Illinois.

3

THE OFFICE BUILDING AS AN ECONOMIC GENERATOR AND CONTRIBUTOR

by Richard J. Roddewig

INTRODUCTION

What is the image invoked by the words "office building"? To a farmer, it may be the bank building in the regional center where he banks, shops or dines. To a suburban housewife, it may be the glass box surrounded by a sea of parked cars across from the regional mall. To a young urban professional, it may be the post-modern skyscraper in which he or she works. To a retired pensioner, it may be the landmark building downtown where a lifetime was spent toiling for a corporation. The image called up will differ depending upon the age, place of residence and occupation of the person asked the question.

Each person has a corresponding image of the office building's function as well. The suburban housewife may view the office building only as a source of the gridlock that plagues the arterial streets around the suburban shopping mall during morning and evening drive times. The mayor of a major city may view the office building as a generater of additional jobs and tax revenues, and the announcement of a new office building as a prime photo opportunity. The CEO of a major corporation may see the company's home office building as a symbol of the company's importance, as a metaphor for the company's image, or even as a marketing opportunity, e.g., Sears derives immeasurable free publicity from having its name attached to the world's tallest building.

Most people, most of the time, think about the office building in terms of its most basic function: providing space in which individuals and organizations conduct business. Looking more deeply, however, the office building has a variety of functions, business as well as civic, public as well as private, social as well as personal, aesthetic as well as functional, symbolic as well as actual. People use office buildings in a variety of ways that, when combined, define its function in today's world.

In this chapter, those various perceptions and functions are investigated, along with the creative tension derived from the fact that the office building must serve a diversity of oftentimes conflicting purposes. Understanding the basis of that dynamic tension can provide insight concerning why office buildings are planned and built in the way they are, and the continually evolving manner in which office buildings are related to each other, to other portions of the built and natural environment, and ultimately to society's business, social, cultural and political needs.

THE OFFICE BUILDING AS A GENERATOR AND CONTRIBUTOR

The Office Building as an Economic Generator

On the most basic level, the office building generates business activity. It is built and developed to serve the need of contemporary businesses, institutions, governments and individuals for an enclosed space in which to conduct their activities. The economic activity the office building generates is both direct and indirect. It also induces, or creates, some forms of economic activity. These concepts of direct, indirect, and induced economic impacts are commonly used in economic impact analysis and have equal applicability to an analysis of the office building as a generator of and as a contributor to economic activity.[1]

Because the office building is essential to the operation of modern business, it is partly responsible for the generation of the wages and salaries of the workers who work in it. This is the most obvious of the office building's directly generated economic products. In addition, the office building houses companies that create profits and losses, to which the building contributes in two ways. First, as the locus of the business activity, it directly participates in, and contributes to, the profit or loss generated by the business. Second, its actual design or operation may increase or decrease profit or loss.

---

[1] See, for example, Robert Burchel and David Listokin, *The Fiscal Impact Handbook* (New Brunswick, New Jersey: Center for Urban Policy Research) p. 323.

Social reformers of the late 19th and early 20th centuries began to recognize the significant connection between the workplace environment and the emotional and even physical health of the workers who occupy it.[2] One result was the invention of the "Chicago window"[3] and the interior light court that allowed more light and air into even the remotest corner of a high-rise office building. Healthy office workers are more productive workers.[4]

Even the color of the walls, the type of carpet and the style of furniture may have an impact on worker morale and productivity. There is increasing concern about the health implications of working in potentially toxic buildings, or under fluorescent lights or in front of video screens.[5]

The office building is both a consumer of products and services and a producer of products and services. Its construction requires steel, wood, stone, glass, metal and concrete, the raw materials of the shell. Electrical, HVAC, plumbing and vertical transportation systems are purchased and installed in the shell. The interiors are finished with insulation, stud walls, plaster and gypsum board, wall coverings, acoustical ceiling tile, wood, stone, glass, paint and carpeting to the specifications and needs of the occupants and tenants.

Direct and indirect services too are consumed during construction. The developer who has the concept, the attorney who closes the acquisition of the land, the planner who lays out the site, the architect who designs the building, the contractor who supervises the construction, the banker who provides the financing, even the public officials who review the plans and issue the permits and approvals, are among the countless providers of services related to the construction of the building. Indirect services may be provided by the equipment dealer who maintains the construction equipment, the accountant who prepares the contractor's annual tax return, and even the owner of the fast food restaurant where the construction workers eat lunch.

The building also generates taxes and fees for federal, state and local governments. These too are indirect and induced, as well as direct. The occupants of the building pay federal (and often state) income taxes on corporate and individual income; the contractors pay sales tax on the

---

[2] For a more contemporary discussion of this relationship, see William H. Whyte, *City: Rediscovering the Center*, (New York: Doubleday, 1988) p. 230.

[3] "A window occupying the full width of a bay and divided into a large fixed sash flanked by a narrow movable sash on each side, as in the Marquette Building by Holabird and Roche (1894) and Sullivan's Carson Pirie & Scott Store (1899-1904) in Chicago." John Fleming et al., *Penguin Dictionary of Architecture*, (New York: Penguin Books, 1972 ed.) p. 60.

[4] See Beverly Russell, *Architecture & Design 1970-1980: New Ideas in America*, (New York: Harry Abrams, Inc., 1989) p. 51.

[5] See generally, D. Geoffrey Hayward, "Psychological Factors in the Use of Light and Lighting in Buildings," in *Designing for Human Behavior: Architecture and the Behavioral Sciences, Community Development Series*, Vol. 6, p. 121.

materials used in construction; and the building pays property taxes to the various local government units that levy a millage rate against the value of the property. Increasingly, office buildings must pay more than simply real estate taxes. Many states require developers to pay "impact fees" before development approval is granted. Finally, connection fees for water or sewer hook-up, permit fees for reviewing architectural or site plans, and occupancy permit fees are other common government charges imposed during the construction process.

Office buildings directly consume far fewer public services than most other types of real estate development. Office precincts are usually among the safest, and therefore consume fewer police services (except for traffic control). Retail shopping districts, even suburban regional malls, make heavier demands on local police departments to respond to calls concerning theft, shoplifting and disorderly conduct incidents. Residential neighborhoods not only consume more police and fire services, but also create demand for schools, parks and libraries.

While office complexes indirectly generate demand for some types of public services, most notably road and highway construction, so too do shopping complexes and residential subdivisions. Most communities that have carefully compared office building development to residential projects quickly conclude that office construction generates more public income than it demands in services.

For many communities, then, it is the office building—not the single-family home—that is the most important development in the community. The location and amount of office construction defines the community's economic character. During the 1980s, the United States lost over 850,000 manufacturing jobs but gained over 2 million white-collar, service sector jobs. Most of those new jobs were located in office buildings. Although the explosion of the service sector job base more than offset the devastating erosion of the manufacturing job base, not every community benefitted equally. Many cities and suburbs were not able to replace lost manufacturing (industrial building) jobs with an equal number of service sector (office building) jobs. Many cities that had no manufacturing base became centers for office building development and employment.

The office building has replaced the manufacturing plant as the most important symbol of political and economic stability in America. Construction of an office building brings jobs, the top objective of every community's economic development program. And because the office building typically consumes fewer public services than residential or retail development, and generates far more in tax revenues than it costs the public for services, it is a potent force in the community for political and economic stability. A community's success in attracting office development allows it to keep taxes on single-family homes lower than would otherwise be possible, however inequitable this practice may be. That in turn increases the likelihood that local officials will be re-elected, because high property taxes are the most significant political issue in most communities. It is no wonder that for many local elected officials, the amount of new office development during their term is a surrogate measure of the success of their economic development policies and programs, and is often the best measure of their chances for re-election.

The Office Building as a Social Center

Americans spend more of their waking hours[6] at their place of employment than they do in their homes. And with the typical work week now longer than it was in the 1960s,[7] Americans are spending more time at the office than ever before. As a result, work increasingly defines who people are, and in large measure how they socialize and how they play. With more than 20 million Americans employed in managerial and professional occupations,[8] the office setting has become the center of many people's social lives.

Consider how high a percentage of social and recreational time is business or company related. The company golf outing, picnic, holiday party, management retreat and sports team have become permanent fixtures in the social calendar. Sales personnel, managers and professionals market through social activities, and senior management is involved in charitable or civic affairs to assure the company's image as a good corporate citizen.

These trends have increased the importance of the workplace as a social center. First, more Americans, both in numbers and in percentage of total household units, work in office buildings. Second, in two-income families, a higher percentage of family social time is devoted to work-related activities, as both wife and husband must meet social obligations generated by their employment. The office building has become the dominant organizing force in Americans' social life.

Office buildings can also play a role in public events. The lavish public lobbies of many buildings have become attractive settings for civic functions. Large expanses of space, use of exquisite materials, fountains, atria and other attractive design features make lobbies attractive spaces for banquets, concerts, fundraisers, political rallies and other events. The

---

[6] See, for example, Walter Kiechel II, "Overscheduled and Not Loving It," *Fortune* (April 8, 1991) p.105.

[7] There is considerable controversy about whether the typical American work week has increased or decreased over the past two decades. The consensus seems to be that in white-collar business and professional occupations, the work week has indeed increased. See, for example, "Time Vise Tiff: Do People Really Work More Now?", *The Wall Street Journal* (March 24, 1992) p. A17 (N), p.A21 (L); *Los Angeles Times* (February 23, 1992) p.D2, Col. 1; "Time for Overworked Americans to Lobby for More Precious Time Off," *The Washington Post* (January 22, 1992) p. F3, Col. 1.

[8] *Statistical Abstract of the United States*, p. 395.

lobbies of some office buildings, such as the IDS Centre in Minneapolis or the Citicorp Building and Philip Morris Building in New York, have become part of the fabric of downtown life. Their many events and activities make them an enclosed equivalent to the town square.

Other office projects have created exterior spaces that serve these public functions. Such exciting "people places" as First National Bank Plaza in Chicago, and Seagram Plaza and Chase Manhattan Plaza in New York City, attract large lunchtime crowds. Often the buildings plan special events in these spaces, with the cost of the events seen as good marketing and image enhancement by the company or institution whose name is on the building.

The Office Building as an Activity Generator

Every office building is like a stone cast into a pond—it creates ripples of activity that emanate from it as energy emanates from the star at the center

The lobbies of some office buildings, such as the Crystal Court of the IDS Centre in Minneapolis, have become part of the fabric of downtown life, an enclosed equivalent to the town square. *(Photo © Richard Payne, FAIA 1989. Courtesy of John Burgee Architects)*

of a solar system. Perhaps a better analogy is that of nuclear fission. Splitting an atom creates a chain reaction of dissembled nuclear particles ricocheting and further splitting other atoms. Successful construction and leasing of an office building generates activity that has impacts in the business world, in the surrounding neighborhoods, in the political and social culture of the community, in the nearby streets and expressways, in public transit usage, in residential construction and sales, and even in the halls of government and financial institutions.

Office buildings also beget other office buildings. Despite the innovations of modern communication technology, many types of businesses still have a strong need to relate to each other face to face. The complex relationships between law firms, accountants, banks, title companies, real estate brokers, and county courthouses necessary to complete even a simple real estate transaction such as the sale of a single-family home is an example of office space users who need to be near each other for the sake of convenience and efficiency. The same kind of specialized locational agglomeration is even more pronounced in office neighborhoods such as Wall Street in New York or LaSalle Street in Chicago (stock and commodity market centers).

Development of an office building also has a profound impact on the character of the surrounding neighborhood. This is because of the business impacts, the aesthetic and traffic impacts, and the way local government thinks about an area where office buildings have been developed. In the early stages of a neighborhood's transition from another use to office use, there may be an abrupt spatial transition between the previous land uses (for example, low-density, low-height and low-coverage buildings with open landscaped space in a campus atmosphere) and the new office use. That dichotomy changes quickly once a neighborhood is clearly perceived as an office and commercial district. Property is purchased with the expectation of future office development. Land speculation begins and the previous residential or industrial structures are demolished. If the market is strong, construction may proceed rapidly on the vacant sites, and there may be little elapsed time between purchase, demolition and new construction. In "greenfield" office development, especially where agricultural use continues to receive deferential property tax treatment, there may be no noticeable change in the pattern of use in the surrounding neighborhood — farm fields will remain so until financing and an anchor tenant are secured for the next office building project.

Typically, however, the marketplace overestimates the demand for office development. More sites are bought for office development than current demand can support.[9] Land values are bid up, and the prices paid for sites

---

[9] To some extent, this is necessary to make a market truly cost efficient. There must be a greater supply of sites than current demand requires if the market is to work effectively, providing choices and allowing competition that avoids payment of monopoly prices for land.

cannot be supported by the income that can be generated by the existing structures on the sites. In downtown markets, interim uses may appear. For example, existing structures may be demolished and replaced by surface parking lots (or even structured parking) catering to surrounding office uses; some sites may sit vacant for years. Local governments bent on encouraging more office construction frequently zone or rezone areas for office development far in excess of any reasonable near-term projections of office demand.

The political tenor of a community, especially smaller suburban communities, can be completely transformed by office building development. Entire political campaigns have been based, and careers made, on issues surrounding the need for, or problems created by, office building development. Suburban residential neighborhoods may actively oppose, and support candidates who oppose, more office development. Even inner city neighborhoods have been known to rally around a campaign to limit downtown office building construction as a way of encouraging

Exterior spaces of office buildings also serve public functions. The First National Bank Plaza in Chicago attracts large lunchtime crowds. *(Courtesy of The First National Bank of Chicago)*

more neighborhood development. But the number of new office buildings is more likely to be used as a politician's measure of a city's economic health.

Perhaps the most generally acknowledged activity generated by an office building is the trip to and from work. These trips create traffic in the immediate vicinity of the structure, as well as on the arterials, highways, expressways and interstates serving the community. The gridlock that plagues expressways in most major metropolitan areas during morning and evening rush hours is a direct result of office building development. That traffic in turn creates a demand for parking, unless the applicable zoning code requires ample on-site parking for all workers and likely daily visitors.[10] Public transit use may also be enhanced, especially if the office building is conveniently located near a mass transit stop or on a major bus line.

Construction of an office building can have a major impact on nearby cultural facilities. Museums located near new office buildings often notice a marked increase in new members and lunchtime traffic. Theaters and concert halls can garner increased attendance and even new board members or corporate sponsors. Parks and open space may experience more lunchtime strollers and morning and evening joggers when a new office building opens nearby. Other types of investment may also be stimulated by the construction of an office building. Other businesses may desire to be located nearby, causing funds to be channeled to the neighborhood of the new building.

Finally, construction of an office building can also generate regulatory activities. Office building development is not without its critics. The traffic, aesthetic, environmental and streetscape impacts of particular buildings or groups of buildings can cause public officials to rethink zoning and building codes. In one celebrated case, the New York City planning commission turned down a major new office development adjacent to the southwest corner of Central Park because of the shadow it would cast on the park (blocking of sunlight). New planning techniques, such as computer imaging or wind analysis, have been developed to pre-test the impact of particular office building designs or shapes on sunlight and shadow and wind patterns in the area around the development site.

When new modern office buildings replace historic landmarks, the result often is enactment of historic preservation ordinances to protect the best of the past from demolition. And many cities are starting to dictate the construction materials of office buildings, for example by banning

---

[10] Not all zoning codes require on-site parking. While this is the standard model in the suburbs, most big city downtown office districts do not require parking on-site in a deliberate attempt to encourage more use of public transportation or a more "pedestrian-friendly" and aesthetically pleasing streetscape.

reflective glass or by requiring materials that are compatible with those of nearby buildings, in order to eliminate adverse impacts perceived to have occurred from previous office development in the same locale.

The Office Building as a Community Contributor

The office building contributes to the community precisely because it is an economic generator, a social activity generator, and a business, political, and investment generator. But the sheer presence of an office building on the skyline can contribute to the community in another way. The office building creates an image of a community. In many major cities, the relationship between buildings actually defines that city's image to the world.

The architecture of the office building is a form of public art, and Americans probably engage in more public discussion about whether they

One office building, such as the IDS Tower in Minneapolis, can become the symbol for a city. *(Photo by Thorney Lieberman. Courtesy of John Burgee Architects)*

like or dislike the design of a new building than they do about any other form of artistic expression. It is appropriate that they do so. Unlike works by a painter or sculptor[11] that get hidden away in galleries or private collections, the office building is there as a work of art for everyone in the community to view every day. And because of its scale and quantity, it has much more of an impact than residential construction or even public sculpture.

One office building can become the symbol for a city. The Empire State Building (or more recently the World Trade Center) in New York, the Sears Tower in Chicago, The TransAmerica Building in San Francisco, the IDS Tower in Minneapolis, the PPG Building in Pittsburgh, Humana Tower in Louisville, all have become part of the image and attraction of the city where they were built. And before each of these buildings was built, another office building evoked the image of that city in a previous era.[12]

An irony of office building development is that a building attacked as an architectural abomination when first proposed can become an icon for the next generation. Alien buildings, in their location and design, can later become heroes. Well-designed office buildings, or even prominent badly-designed office buildings, become "landmarks" in the broadest sense of the word. They become familiar parts of the built environment and as important psychologically and emotionally as the tattered armchair passed down from Aunt Martha or the high school graduation picture buried in a box in the attic. As John Costonis, dean of Vanderbilt University Law School put it:

> We bond to our (architectural) icons for reassurance; and they, in turn, reinforce our sense of order in the world no less than religion or popular culture.[13]

Real estate developers and interior designers have long known that light, color, sound, smell, shape and pattern can be manipulated in retail and residential environments to stimulate moods conducive to one type of activity but adverse to another. They routinely design interior spaces in shopping centers or restaurants to stimulate a mood conducive to shopping or dining.

Architects, urban planners, sociologists and psychologists have found that the same principles apply to the entire built environment. The style, shape, massing and materials of an office building can dramatically affect

---

[11] Even public sculpture has a much more modest impact on the perceived character of a community than office building design and development.

[12] Consider the Flatiron Building, Equitable Building or the Metropolitan Life Insurance Building in New York, or the Prudential Building, Tribune Tower or Wrigley Building in Chicago.

[13] John J. Costonis, *Icons and Aliens: Law, Aesthetics, and Environmental Change* (Urbana: University of Illinois, 1989) p. 46.

its appeal in the marketplace and stimulate a positive reaction. The debate continues as to whether there is some archetypal "aesthetic sense" hot-wired into man's genetic code, or whether people are simply tired of plain glass boxes and will eventually become equally bored with post-modernist historical allusions and deconstructivist assemblages. However, for the first time fundamental questions are being asked about the relationship between the design of office buildings and the fundamental emotional, psychological and social health of a city or nation.

How to handle parking generated by office development became the character-defining question for most developers and planning officials. While suburban developers and planners unanimously answered this question through mandatory on-site parking and stipulated ratios between total office area in a building and required parking spaces,[14] downtown the answer has taken on a variety of forms. In some cities, like Houston, downtown developers created a series of free-standing, self-contained buildings containing plenty of structured parking (often on the first few floors or in an attached parking structure) and supporting retail/service uses. When the pervasive curb cuts to the parking structures were combined with underground pedestrian connectors between buildings, the result was a streetscape devoid of pedestrian activity, a diversity of uses, or any continuity of design character from one block to another. In other cities, like Chicago, developers and public officials sought to continue a predominantly pedestrian orientation by prohibiting curb cuts and on-site parking in order to encourage greater use of public transportation and by constructing centralized parking on the edge of downtown.

Many downtown office developers also appreciate how the relationship between their building and neighboring buildings can have a profound effect on the appeal of their building and its long-term financial success. Many projects are designed with attractive public plazas or pedestrian arcades designed to provide an amenity for workers in the building and to lure nearby office workers to the shops, restaurants or services offered on their property. Well-placed (and designed) public plazas and pocket parks have often given one downtown office precinct a competitive edge over another. On the other hand, poorly located, policed, designed or

---

[14] In the late 1980s and early 1990s, this uniformity began to dissolve. There were increasing cries that the solution to the traffic gridlock plaguing suburban office centers was higher density and mixed uses in a concept called "urban villages." Later neo-traditional planning called for the extension of the traditional downtown pre-automobile, or at least early automobile, pattern of development, i.e., continuous streetscapes of mixed office, retail and residential uses with the automobile relegated to underground or peripheral car parks, and strenuous attempts to make the pedestrian superior to the car. See, for example, Joel Garreau, "Cities on the Edge," in *Architecture*, Volume 80, No. 12, (December 1991) pp. 45-47; and Suzanne Crowhurst Lennard and Henry L. Lennard, *Livable Cities*, (Southampton, New York: Gondolier Press, 1987) pp. 98-102.

maintained public spaces, or too many public spaces in one office precinct, can deaden a formerly lively office environment.[15]

The Office Building as Part of an Ecosystem

There is an intimate relationship between the office building and the society in which it is built. As society has gradually recognized the environmental problems facing mankind, it has begun to ask what role the office building plays in contributing to, or solving, environmental problems. Four of the major environmental issues affecting office buildings are air pollution, waste disposal, energy and environmental health.

Office buildings both directly and indirectly contribute to (or solve) environmental problems. For example, it is well documented that low-density, dispersed suburban office building development is one of the principal generators of automobile use and therefore a prime contributor to the serious air pollution problems in such cities as Los Angeles, Phoenix and Denver. At the same time, the pattern of downtown office building development in places like New York, Philadelphia, Chicago and San Francisco actually lessens auto emissions by stimulating public transit ridership.

Office building development also contributes to the waste and landfill crisis.[16] Demand for new office buildings results in the demolition and destruction of older buildings. The demolished buildings are hauled off and dumped in landfills. It is estimated that construction-related demand accounts for about 6% of landfill space demand.

Office building users consume and throw away huge amounts of paper, contributing to demand for more timber cutting as well as landfill space. Yet large office buildings present intriguing possibilities for cost-effective collection and recycling of paper products, and in fact innovative programs to design and operate office buildings with paper recycling as one objective have been developed.[17]

In the 1970s the energy crisis came to the fore on the environmental agenda. While the decline of oil prices in the mid to late 1980s relegated the energy crisis to a less prominent position, it continues to be one of the most significant problems. By generating automobile trips, office buildings

---

[15] See Whyte, *supra*, p. 312.

[16] One South Carolina government agency did an internal study of its paper waste generation and discovered that an office of 100 employees discarded an average of 75 pounds of high-grade paper every day. Richard M. Payne, "Business Papers: The Time to Recycle is Now," in *The Office: Magazine of Information Systems and Management* Vol. 115 (April 1992) p. 30.

[17] See, for example, Payne, *supra*; Patrick J. O'Connor, "Face It: Recycling is a Job That Must Be Done," in *The Office* Vol. 113, No. 6 (June 1991) pp. 35-37; and William C. Johnson, "Office Recycling: One of the 50 Ways to Save the Planet," in *Facility Management Journal* (November/December 1991) pp. 32-34.

cause the consumption of oil reserves. By requiring light and power, office buildings generate demand for electricity. If that electricity is generated by nuclear or coal power plants, it in turn can contribute to hazardous waste disposal or air pollution problems.

Nowhere is the difficulty of finding true solutions to environmental problems more evident than in office building development. In an effort to make buildings safer and more energy efficient, developers in the 1960s and early 1970s used asbestos as a fire retardant and an insulator. When the environmental dangers of asbestos became known, developers switched to fiberglass and other substitutes. Then fiberglass began to be questioned as environmentally unsafe.[18] And the efforts to tighten up office buildings in the 1970s to make them more energy efficient have resulted in another environmental problem, the sick building syndrome.

The safety of the office environment itself has come under increasing scrutiny. Concerns about the health dangers of recirculated office air, prolonged exposure to ultraviolet light, the dangers of computer screens and chemicals in office carpeting and furniture are just some of the office environmental issues that have emerged.

THE OFFICE BUILDING AS A SYSTEM AND SUBSYSTEM

The office building can also be considered as part of a system. Because it generates activity and contributes to the community, it is part of the system in which those activities and contributions occur. The five principal components of the system in which the office building operates are money flow, people flow, information flow, energy flow, and materials flow.

Money Flow

Major office buildings are not only physical icons in the neighborhood where they are built, but are financial icons as well. They attract and concentrate economic power and money in a way that few other investments can match, and the skyline of a city is a living testament to the ebb and flow of money and wealth from one era to another. During the "go-go" years of the 1980s, the office building development deal was to real estate finance what the leveraged buyout was to corporate finance—the ultimate expression of the era's search for ways to create large amounts of new wealth from comparatively small equity investments.

---

[18] See, for example, "OSHA Reaffirms Hazard Warnings for Fibrous Glass," in *Textile World* Vol. 141, No. 9 (September 1991) p. 20.

Capital investment flows into office building projects. This occurs over and over again during the life of an office building as the property is developed, financed, sold, refinanced, refurbished and modernized, and sold again. Fortune 500 corporations, limited partnerships consisting of individual sophisticated investors, financial institutions, insurance companies and wealthy families were traditionally the principal sources of capital investment for office building projects in the 1920s and again in the 1950s. In the 1960s, 1970s and 1980s, new legal concepts such as the real estate investment trust, combined with changes in the tax laws and the emergence of new concentrations of financial power in pension funds and offshore investors, accelerated the flow of money into and through office building projects.

The money that flows into an office building project for development or renovation then circulates out into the hands of the architects, contractors, tradesmen and developers involved. When an office building is sold, money flows to the mortgage lender to pay off the existing loan, allowing that lender to invest it elsewhere, perhaps in a loan on another office building project. Even the profits for the owner or developer who sells the building may stimulate development of a new project elsewhere.

Rent and other charges to tenants are another piece of the money flow. Tenants operate their businesses according to a plan and budget that will generate income sufficient to pay their rent, utility charges and other expenses associated with occupancy. When those rent and occupancy charges exceed what they consider to be an acceptable percentage of revenues, they may go elsewhere, thereby changing the course of money through the system.

From the rent generated, the owner or developer pays the costs of operating the building. Maintenance and repairs, utilities, cleaning and janitorial services, property taxes, legal and accounting fees, and management fees consume from 35% to 60% of total rental income in newer office buildings and represent outflows from the rent collected.

One of the largest single outflows from rent collected typically goes to the mortgage lender to pay debt service. On a 20-year self-amortizing loan carrying a 10% interest rate, at a debt coverage ratio of 1.25, and a net operating income that represents 60% of effective gross revenues, outflows for debt service payments will be about 48% of effective gross revenues.

Some of the rent that the property generates, combined with some of the proceeds of sale when the office building is eventually sold, however, stays in the hands of the developer and his equity investors. But because of the nature of money flows in the economic system, that too is dispersed into consumption of goods as well as investments in stocks, bonds and other types of real estate investments.

People Flow

An office building is simply, therefore, a money-processing facility when the capital flows are considered. It is also a people-processing facility. The hustle and bustle of the streets of major American downtowns is generated mainly by traffic into and out of its office buildings. As downtowns have lost their prominence as retailing centers, their importance as office centers has increased. Office building tenants and their employees account for most of the people on the streets in major downtown office centers during the morning and evening rush hours. During the business day, the interplay between businesses accounts for the flow of people between major downtown office buildings and the visitors to a particular building.

In the suburbs, where office densities are lower and automobile use replaces pedestrian activity, the people flow component of the system may be less visible. But it is still there.

The operating staff of an office building, its managers, administrative support and operating engineers, are another component of the people flow system. So too are the repairmen, leasing agents and salesmen who visit the building in the course of dealing with its management.

Information Flow

Office buildings are also cogs in an extended information flow system that connects them to every point on the globe. By telephone, by modem, by mail, by fax, by delivery service, and by word of mouth, information enters the office building, is reviewed, stored, digested, analyzed and reconfigured, and then sent out in a new form. The office building also works internally as an information network. The day-to-day operation of any of the businesses conducted by any of its tenants is most likely based on the sharing and analysis of information compiled in the brains of its employees.

Materials Flow

Paper, pens, pencils, typewriters, computers, furniture, food, water, metals, plastics, and chemicals flow into an office building on a constant basis. Waste products associated with those materials then flow out daily. Some of the materials that enter the building, such as the original construction materials, or the interior finishings, may not generate any waste products for months or even years. But other types of materials are tossed into the wastebasket within minutes or hours of entering the building. All of that waste eventually exits through sewage lines, incinerators or trucks that take it to recycling centers or disposal sites.

Energy Flow

The office building is also part of an energy flow system. It is connected to the sources of electricity and gas that provide the light, heat and energy to operate the office equipment that receives, processes and stores the information generated by the tenants. The activities carried on in the office building also create a demand for more energy and stimulate the production of energy in other offices tied to it in the network of capital flows, people flows, information flows and material flows.

THE OFFICE BUILDING AS A PRODUCT OF EXTERNALITIES

Office buildings are the product of external forces. They would not exist except for the fact that there is a demand for them, there is usually an available source of funds to build them, there are entrepreneurs skilled in developing them, and there is a public that tolerates and even actively encourages their construction.

Real Estate Entrepreneurship

Office buildings don't get built without a developer. In the United States, the developer has historically been an entrepreneur. To be successful, he or she must have a unique set of talents. First and foremost is an ability to work with people because the developer's essential role is that of a coordinator. The developer coordinates the activities of architects, engineers, contractors, lawyers, accountants, lenders, investors, regulators and brokers. Each has a different personality and mindset and the developer must be able to understand and work with each type. The developer must know enough about the technical aspects of those professions and disciplines to be able to communicate effectively and efficiently.

Next, the developer is a problem solver. A person who cannot find a creative solution or compromise for a tough problem will never be a successful developer. The developer must be able to juggle a variety of tasks and activities at once, enjoy being on the telephone constantly and be available at any time of the day or night to solve problems.

The developer is also a salesman. The office building is a product to be sold to lenders and equity investors, to public officials and to prospective tenants. The developer must know where to find sources of equity and debt and be able to convince lenders and investors to invest their money. The developer must understand the motivations and needs of elected officials and be willing to make the compromises in a project necessary to win public approval. And the developer must intimately understand what the users of office buildings need in the way of a product and what price they are willing to pay to acquire it.

The Educational System

Office buildings will not get built without an experienced cadre of developers ready and available to undertake the project. And despite the recent rise of education programs designed to teach real estate development, the skills needed must be learned on the job, not in the classroom. But the educational background of the developer does affect the development process. Developers who lack any grounding in political science, urban planning, architecture and aesthetics are likely to produce a different type of office building than those with this background. Many developers today emerge from the world of corporate or real estate finance. Too often, developers with a background in only the numbers side of real estate lack the education necessary to appreciate the function of the office building as a community contributor and as a generator of activities far more comprehensive than simply the businesses conducted by its tenants.

Capital Availability and Cost

Skilled developers without adequate capital cannot develop office buildings. But as was made clear in the 1980s, too much readily available capital creates too many developers, many of whom lack the skill or judgment necessary to successfully complete an office building. The office building development process, and its boom or bust cycles, is the product of the capital markets. When capital is in short supply, office buildings simply do not get built. This is sometimes true even when there is strong demand for office space. When capital is in oversupply, too many office buildings get built, even in the face of obviously limited demand for office space.

Interest rate fluctuations, not only in mortgages but in corporate and government notes and bonds and even in foreign currencies, also affect the office building development process. Usually, equity positions in real estate demand a slightly higher rate of return than debt positions in real estate, which in turn demand a higher rate of return than less risky, more liquid investments such as stocks and bonds. When yields for those alternative investments drop, yields on real estate also typically drop, but the margin of the difference can have a significant impact on how much money seeks real estate as an investment.

The investment policies of large institutional investors such as insurance companies and pension funds are another external factor that dramatically affects the development of real estate including office buildings. While insurance companies have long been involved in real estate as a way of diversifying their investment portfolio,[19] pension funds only began expanding into real estate investments in the late 1970s. The dramatic commercial real estate downturn of the early 1990s caused many institutional investors (and off-shore investors) to slow and even curtail their real estate investing.

Market Demand

Office buildings should not be built if there is no demand. Unfortunately, if there is a plentiful supply of money available for real estate, projects often are built even in the absence of demand. Eventually, however, lack of demand will dry up the money for commercial real estate. Fundamentally, it is the demand for space that drives the commercial office market.

What drives the demand for office space is the basic health of the American and international economies combined with the impact of demographic, sociological and technological change, and the current availability of space to meet that demand. The 1970s and 1980s saw an unprecedented expansion of demand for office space in the United States. This was fueled by two basic demographic facts. First, the baby boom generation was coming of age and entering the work force. More than 80 million Americans were born between 1946 and 1964. More highly educated than any previous generation in American history,[20] they entered the white-collar work force and office space had to be developed to accommodate them.

Second, women entered the workforce in unprecedented numbers. In 1960, only about 35% of American women were employed. That percentage had increased to 40% by 1970, and close to 50% in 1980. By 1990, it was estimated that 55% of all American women were employed, and by the year 2000, the percentage is expected to increase to 60%. Once again, office space had to be created for these new additions to the white-collar work force.

CONCLUSION

The office building has a dynamic role in American life and society. Each office building is a unique product forged out of the many social and governmental influences that have created society as a whole.

But the office building also helps to shape society and contributes to its definition. It is not only an economic generator, but a social generator as well. So many of Americans' daily activities flow in, through, or by the

---

[19] For a discussion of insurance company investment in real estate, see "ULI Development Trends 1991," Vol. 50, No. 3 (Washington, D.C.: Urban Land Institute, March 1991) p. 12.

[20] Nearly half of those born during the period have been to college for at least one year, with about 25% having graduated from college. See Cheryl Russell, "On the Baby Boom Bandwagon," *American Demographics* Vol. 13, No. 5 (May 1991) p. 27.

modern office building that most people probably give little thought to its contribution to their culture. But when one stands back and gives the office building careful consideration, it becomes apparent that the quality office building has become a cultural icon. It has a presence not only in the physical landscape of America's cities and suburbs, but in the landscape of Americans' minds as well.

ABOUT THE AUTHOR

Richard J. Roddewig, CRE, MAI, is president of Clarion Associates, a real estate consulting firm with offices in Chicago and Denver. He has extensive experience in land use and zoning, real estate economics, and historic preservation. Roddewig is past chair of the Midwest Chapter of the Counselors of Real Estate, and is active in the Land Use, Planning and Zoning Committee of the American Bar Association Section on Urban State and Local Government Law. Roddewig has a BA in history and government from the University of Notre Dame and an MA and JD from the University of Chicago. He has taught land use law, real estate feasibility analysis and appraisal at several universities and has authored or co-authored numerous books and articles on real estate and land use issues.

4

THE STRUCTURE OF
THE OFFICE INDUSTRY

by Beth S. Krugman and
Brian A. Furlong

INTRODUCTION

This chapter introduces the major equity and debt players involved with office buildings. It describes the role of each player, the tasks they perform, the parties they represent, how they get paid and how they are regulated.

To understand the roles assumed and the tasks performed in the office building industry, it is important to understand not only how buildings are built and operated, but also how and why people and institutions develop and operate the buildings. Equity and debt sources invest in office buildings in the expectation of earning a reasonable return. Professional service providers build, manage, lease, renovate, finance, sell and otherwise operate the structure throughout its life cycle for their clients. These services are provided to earn fee income rather than a return on invested capital.

Part One of the chapter analyzes the participants who provide the equity and debt capital to build, own and operate the building. Part Two discusses the life cycle of an office building and the roles of the others: their tasks, motivations and regulatory constraints.

PART ONE: THE FINANCIAL PARTICIPANTS

Providers of Equity Capital

The developer can seek equity funding from many sources. He may develop the project solely from his own funds and hold it for his own account or, at the other extreme, he may develop the project for a fee and have no equity position. The developer may also build as a principal with temporary financing and then sell the equity portion for a profit, retaining little or no financial interest in the building. Depending on the number of tasks done "in-house," fees may be sufficient reward for the task of development in cases where the developer is not a principal.

Probable equity investors in office buildings include pension funds, real estate investment trusts (REITs) and life insurance companies. These institutional equity sources represent and have a fiduciary responsibility to their investors. Other sources of financing include private investors, corporations and the government. In dealing with investors, the developer may retain a full or a partial interest in the project. When he shares equity, the developer may act for his own account, as general partner in a limited partnership or as the managing partner in a joint venture with an institutional or corporate source of equity funds. Each of these equity investors will be examined here. For a more detailed discussion of equity investors in office buildings, see Chapter 22.

The Individual Investor

The fulcrum of the office equity market has always been the individual private investor. Historically, he has been the backbone of the industry. In many small communities, the individual owner/investor/developer still dominates ownership of office buildings, sometimes joining with small groups of family and friends but often acting alone.

An individual investor's ownership objectives include income, potential asset appreciation, a hedge against inflation, tax shelter, managerial control and pride of ownership. Under the sole proprietorship or general partnership forms of ownership, however, the individual suffers the major disadvantage of unlimited liability for all losses. To protect his private assets, he may adopt other legal forms of business organization. Limited partnerships, corporations and closely held corporations ("S" corporations) all trade limitations on liability for limitations on control. However, the individual investor's objectives remain the same.

As office structures have increased in size, complexity and cost, the visibility of the individual has faded. Public limited partnerships and real estate investment trusts (REITs) arose as ownership forms to allow the individual to share in larger and more remote investments, to diversify investments and to benefit from centralized, professional management, although at the expense of ceding control. Indeed, depositors in a bank or savings and loan association or purchasers of a life insurance policy or pension may be unaware of the secondary institution's specific real estate investments.

Recently, the ownership of office equity has become increasingly institutional. This is a function both of the increasing cost and complexity of the office investments themselves and of the softness in the national office market. In many cases during the early 1990s, falling rents and property values resulted in the reversion of these buildings to their institutional lenders. Some of this increase in institutional ownership may be temporary. With the recovery of the economy and the office market, the individual owner should become evident once again.

Pension Funds

Motivated by labor's demand for increased benefits and security, the first pension fund was set up in 1875, and the first pension fund to accumulate funds was set up in 1924. The tremendous growth of pension funds is a phenomenon of this century. Pension fund earnings are free of income and capital gains taxes until they are distributed, and their time frame is long.

With about $3 trillion in their coffers, pension funds are the second largest financial intermediary, after commercial banks. Pension funds invest in real estate equity, debt and hybrids of debt and equity. It is difficult to tabulate the amount they have invested in real estate, but it is far less than they invest in stocks, bonds and cash equivalents. As of year-end 1991, the 50 largest real estate advisors had a total of $123.94 billion of tax-exempt assets; about 82% of that was invested in equity real estate and some 37% of the total invested in real estate was in office properties.[1]

Pension fund managers invest in real estate equity for a variety of reasons. They seek long-term capital appreciation, conservation of capital and diversification of their investment portfolios. Over the long term, they expect internal rates of return to compare favorably with equity stock positions.

Pension fund advisors historically have charged fees to acquire, manage and dispose of real estate assets. But with the downturn in real estate transactions in the early 1990s, they began turning to more performance-based methods of compensation tying compensation to the performance level of the fund.

---

[1] *Pension and Investment Age*, September 16, 1991.

State laws regulate the actions of pension funds, but in nearly all states and on the national level, the prudent man rule is the standard by which their fiduciary responsibility is judged. This rule has been stated as follows:

> In investing, reinvesting, purchasing, acquiring, exchanging, selling and managing property for the benefit of another, a trustee shall exercise the judgment and care, under the circumstances then prevailing, which men of prudence, discretion and intelligence exercise in the management of their own affairs, not in regard to speculation, but in regard to the permanent disposition of their funds, considering the probable income, as well as the probable safety of their capital.[2]

At the federal level, the Employment Retirement Income Security Act of 1974 (ERISA) lays out standards for participation, vesting, survivor benefits, minimum funding, fiduciary responsibilities, reporting, disclosure, auditing and the like. The National Council of Real Estate Investment Fiduciaries (NCREIF) and the Pension Real Estate Association (PREA) are the main professional associations of pension fund advisory firms.

Real Estate Investment Trusts

Created by legislation in 1960, REITs are a securitization vehicle that allows investors to pool money for shares in the returns generated by large real estate projects and portfolios. The REIT format provides the limited liability of a corporate structure while avoiding double taxation. A REIT must have at least 100 investors; in this sense, a REIT is a syndication. As long as the investors receive dividends equal to at least 95% of the REIT's profits, the REIT corporation or trust pays no income tax. REITs also provide centralized management, risk diversification and liquidity to the investor. Most REIT shares trade publicly.

As with other securitized financial instruments, the gauge of REIT performance is return on investment. Shareholders receive regular dividends, the prospect of capital appreciation, tax benefits, risk diversification and investment liquidity. The primary source of equity returns is rents, but shareholders may also realize capital gains from property sales. Profits on the disposition of properties may be paid out to shareholders or reinvested.

REITs are highly regulated. State laws govern the offering and sale of securities and may impose other organizational and operational requirements. The Securities and Exchange Commission (SEC) regulates public REIT offerings, reporting and disclosure, while the Internal Revenue Service (IRS) specifies rules for qualifying and filing. The National Association of Real Investment Trusts (NAREIT) is this industry's leading trade organization.

---

[2] William Atteberry, *Modern Real Estate Finance* (Columbus, Ohio: Grid Publishing, Inc., 1980)

Real Estate Limited Partnerships

Until the tax reforms of 1986, real estate limited partnerships were a preferred way of raising money for real estate ventures. They offered limited liability to their limited partners, a direct pass-through of profits and losses to the partners without taxation at the entity level, and a convenient vehicle for small investors to share in the ownership of large properties or groups of properties.

Prior to 1987, when the 1986 reforms went into effect, tax losses from real estate could be used to shelter investors' ordinary income from any source. The tax code allowed limited partners to generate substantial tax losses even when they earned a positive return. Investors seeking tax shelter responded enthusiastically to this favorable tax treatment, and an enormous quantity of money flowed into limited partnership shares.

A general partner organizes and manages the affairs of the partnership and receives a return on its invested capital. In addition, a general partner may obtain income from fees charged for such services as organizing the partnership, selling the limited partnership shares, property acquisition, disposition, management, leasing, renovation and even such operational services as cleaning. These fees often have been substantial compared to the earnings of the real estate.

The limited partners typically provide most of the equity, but by law they play a passive role in management. Limited partners are compensated by cash earnings on their investment plus a participation in the taxable profit and loss from the partnership.

On January 1, 1987, the new 1986 tax law greatly limited deductible losses. Since then, most limited partnerships have earned low after-tax returns, performing so poorly in recent years that they have attracted little new money. Chapter 31 addresses the income tax consequences of the 1986 tax act.

Business Corporations

The business corporate owner, incident to its main business, may develop a building itself, contract with a developer (build-to-suit) or purchase a new or existing building. Corporate equity ownership is typically of a whole office building but is sometimes of a condominium share. The benefits of corporate ownership (often in a subsidiary corporation) include limited liability, long-term capital appreciation, a hedge against inflation in ownership costs and pride of ownership.

Most corporations view their ownership as a cost of doing business. Sometimes, however, firms manage their real estate separately as a profit center. Profit center managers take an active role in managing the corporate real estate; this may include debt financing, transactions, leasing, design and property management.

The corporation represents only itself and its shareholders. Typically, the firm takes a long-term perspective. If the real estate is actively managed as a profit center, this time frame may be shortened.

Government

Some factors that motivate corporate ownership also motivate government ownership: the desire to control occupancy and operating costs and pride of ownership. In addition, government office buildings frequently have special features that differentiate them from speculative rental office buildings and encourage direct ownership. Government office buildings may include extra large elevators and lobbies and elaborate finishes in keeping with their ceremonial purpose. The locations of buildings often lie outside established office markets, limiting their potential for reuse by private sector office occupants.

Foreign Investors

Foreigners have invested in the United States from the country's earliest history. The British and French funded the country's westward expansion, and foreigners financed part of the Gold Rush. Baring Brothers of London financed the Louisiana Purchase when Thomas Jefferson was president. European investors today include British, Dutch and German nationals. Foreign investors have also expanded to include Canadians, Arabs, South and Central Americans, Australians, and Asians from Japan, China, Hong Kong and Korea. Quantitatively, Canadians have the largest total investment in the U.S., followed by British and Dutch investors, but the Japanese are close behind.

Foreign investors use several different kinds of investing entities. European pension funds are very old compared to their U.S. counterparts and have a much higher percentage of investments in real estate. Property companies are publicly traded development companies that raise money to fund new construction through stock issues. Unitrusts are real estate mutual funds similar to REITs. Commercial foreign banks with lending capacities increasingly are opening offices in the United States. Finally, wealthy individuals and families represent a prominent segment of the foreign investor market.

Each of these groups has its own investment criteria. Factors that have made foreign investment in commercial real estate desirable include a hedge against inflation, greater cash flows than in the home country, a cheap dollar relative to the Deutschmark and other currencies, a perception that U.S. real estate is undervalued compared to other countries, diversification of investment portfolios, U.S. political and monetary stability, the lack of official controls, and tax considerations. In addition, the U.S. trade deficit and the worldwide integration of economies and capital have played major roles in attracting foreign capital to U.S. property markets. Different foreign investor groups have bought different real estate products, but office buildings have been foreign investors' preferred investment property type.

Recent large-scale foreign investment in U.S. real estate has raised vague fears that the country is selling its birthright, as well as more concrete fears about dependence on foreign capital and the effects of foreign purchases on escalating prices and tax assessments. As values have tumbled, these fears have subsided, while leaving some foreign investors with doubts about the wisdom of their purchases.

Joint Ventures

Equity joint ventures can be of two types. In one type, an entrepreneur provides expertise and staffing for a development while a money partner provides the capital. In the other type, an office tenant receives an equity interest as part of the leasing commitment. In either instance, a joint venture is a contractual arrangement and not necessarily a legal entity.

Typically, the developer provides expertise while a "deep pockets" investor provides patient money in the form of equity capital and sometimes also as debt capital. Patient money may be defined as mainly long-term institutional capital invested in the belief that the IRR over an extended time period will be superior; it tends not to be unduly influenced by short-term conditions. The equity investor seeks a share of cash flow (rents), a share in the building's capital appreciation, the tax benefits of ownership and sometimes a degree of managerial control. The developer may have to relinquish a portion of these privileges to realize the development. The equity partner may earn a preferred return, and the debt portion may include an equity kicker for the lender, which is senior to any equity return to the co-venturers but may be junior to the preferred return and to the equity return as well.

In an overbuilt market, the lead tenant in a new office building may receive equity participation in return for its lease commitment, as many lenders require a substantial preleasing commitment before they will provide long-term financing.

Some joint ventures extend only through lease-up and stabilization; other participants intend to be long-term owners. The joint venture equity partner has an inherently riskier position than the debt partner. He may be expected to pick up cost overruns in the development process, and his position is subordinate to that of the lender.

Providers of Debt Capital

The primary sources of debt capital include commercial banks, savings and loan institutions, life insurance companies, pension funds, REITs and bond issues. These are all financial intermediaries; that is, they accept the surplus funds of individuals and businesses and lend them to individuals and businesses with a shortage of funds. These institutions differ in their sources of funds, time frames, risk tolerance and regulatory constraints. These distinctions, in turn, influence both the types and terms of the loans they make. Debt capital providers are also discussed in Chapters 22 through 24.

Commercial Banks

Because a large portion of a bank's deposits takes the form of demand deposits payable on the demand of the depositor, a bank's funds must be more liquid than those of other financial intermediaries. Their need for liquidity leads commercial banks to prefer loans of short duration, such as construction loans. In practice, commercial banks have been the primary source of office real estate development loans, though they are now generally on the sidelines.

Federally chartered commercial banks are regulated by several federal institutions including the Federal Reserve, the Comptroller of the Currency in the U.S. Treasury Department and the Federal Deposit Insurance Corporation. The Federal Reserve regulates banks by controlling the money supply. This is accomplished by adjusting bank reserve requirements through open market operations and by changing the discount rate. The Comptroller of the Currency evaluates the quality of a bank's loan portfolio to determine whether the bank's general reserve requirement is sufficient to protect depositors' money if the loans are not repaid. The Federal Deposit Insurance Corporation, which insures depositors against loss, establishes banks' qualifications for deposit insurance.

Major issues affecting commercial banks concern the quality of the loans they write. In the past, lending officers at some institutions were recognized for the quantity rather than the quality of their loans. FDIC insurance of bank deposits enabled banks to lend on risky projects with the assurance that the federal government would make good depositors' losses. This shift of responsibility from the bank to the tax-paying public came under increasing criticism in the early 1990s as the full dimensions of the bank and savings and loan problem become apparent.

Savings and Loan Institutions

Established in the 19th century to promote homeownership, savings and loan associations historically limited their lending to residential mortgage loans and were prohibited from making commercial property loans. The Federal Home Loan Bank Board (FHLBB) was set up in 1955 to regulate S&Ls and supervise the FSLIC, the industry's insurance fund.

In the late 1970s and early 1980s, interest rates rose and depositors in federal S&Ls began removing their funds in search of higher rates. The Depository Institutions Deregulation and Monetary Control Act of 1980 eliminated the prohibition against commercial mortgage lending at the same time that the FHLBB removed many controls, allowing fundamental changes in ownership and investment that made S&Ls inherently riskier.

Interest rate limits were lifted in 1982, and S&Ls had to seek higher paying and riskier investments in junk bonds, commercial real estate and land development in order to offer depositors more competitive rates. Many S&LS did not have the underwriting skills, experienced personnel or controls to make successful investments in these types of assets. S&L accounting rules also were liberalized at the same time that positions at the FHLBB were cut, so that as S&L financial operations became more complex, the apparatus for supervising them was dismantled. The result was appalling losses.

The Financial Institutions Reform Recovery and Enforcement Act (FIRREA)of 1989 replaced the FHLBB with the Office of Thrift Supervision. The new law sought to improve the supervision of savings and loan associations and banks by strengthening their capital requirements, accounting standards and supervision. The Office of Thrift Supervision was given until the end of 1992 to turn over to the newly formed Resolution Trust Corporation (RTC) all insolvent thrifts; the RTC is charged with completing the disposition of assets within six years. The Real Estate Capital Recovery Association is the industry's principal trade organization. Its membership is open to attorneys, appraisers and accountants.

Life Insurance Companies

Three financial intermediaries that are not depository institutions are major sources of debt for office buildings: pension funds, REITs and life insurance companies. Pension funds and REITs have been discussed above as major sources of office building equity funding. Life insurance companies also invest equity funds in real estate, but the majority of their investments in real estate are in debt rather than equity. In 1990, life insurance companies provided about 26% of commercial mortgage money. Commercial banks provided 46% and savings and loan associations provided 14%.

Until the 1980s, life companies tended to make long-term mortgages (15-30 years) on leased buildings, to match their long-term liabilities. Much of the principal balance was amortized during the life of the mortgage. Losses due to loan defaults were low. A favored investment was office buildings.

During the 1980s, the life insurance industry greatly expanded its product base. It actively pursued pension fund investments by offering guaranteed investment contracts (GICs). GICs pay a stated rate of interest on an investment, plus the return of principal, at a specified time, and can be written for varying terms, usually between three and seven years. The investing public loved the GIC because the word "guaranteed" implied safety. Large sums of money flowed into the life industry coffers through GIC investments, with the total investment in this product reaching over $200 billion by 1991.

Because GICs and other new investment vehicles offered by life companies have a shorter term than the traditional life company liabilities of life insurance policies and retirement annuities, the life companies sought to shorten the average term within their investment structure. A key investment developed to match GIC liabilities was the bullet loan, made chiefly on commercial real estate. Bullet loans typically had terms of five to ten years, with an average term of seven years. They involved little if any amortization of principal and typically were not pre-payable without substantial penalty. On expiration, the borrower had to pay the bullet loan in full. Although some bullet loans were backed by additional collateral or guarantees, most were non-recourse to the borrower, and the only loan collateral was the mortgaged real estate. During the 1980s more bullet loans were written for office buildings than for any other type of real property.

In 1992, some life companies that had taken on substantial GIC liabilities and matched these liabilities with bullet loans experienced a liquidity crunch. Investors cashed out their GICs at a time when the life companies could not cash out the mortgage assets that were supposed to back the GICs because the collateral backing the bullet loans had decreased sharply in value. Money flowed away from GICs because of the low rates of return on fixed income investments. Moreover, the failure of some prominent life companies caused a re-evaluation of the creditworthiness of GIC issuers.

In the 1980s, life insurance lenders focused their efforts on new production. Loan servicing was generally relegated to a back office task. Few loans failed. In the 1990s, loan servicing has found its way to the front office. Few new loans are being made. Many old loans are failing and must be restructured or involuntarily renewed. Due to foreclosures, life companies find themselves with more real estate assets to run than they have ever managed before. Like banks and savings & loan associations, life companies must build asset management departments and acquire expertise in state laws regarding foreclosure and bankruptcy.

Credit Corporations

Some of the most inventive debt financing has been offered by the financial subsidiaries of large, public corporations such as General Electric Capital Corporation, Chrysler Capital Realty Inc. and I.T.T. Credit. Their chief source of funds is commercial paper, sold on the strength of the parent corporations's credit rating.

This commercial paper, with terms ranging from one to several months, carries an interest rate floating above a standard index such as LIBOR, the London Interbank Offered Rate. Loans from credit corporations also are offered at floating interest rates a specified number of basis points above a standard index. An interest rate spread provides the earnings on performing loans, but losses can occur if the loan defaults.

Credit corporations are responsible to their stockholders and the buyers of the commercial paper. But apart from the laws regulating the sale of the securities that fund the credit corporations, there is little governmental review of credit corporation investments. The providers of funds to the credit corporation are expected to be financially sophisticated and therefore not in need of intensive regulatory protection.

Generally, credit corporations have been willing to take on more risk and more varied types of risks than most alternative lenders. Credit corporations have often lent at a higher loan-to-value ratio than more traditional sources of debt. They are regarded by borrowers as a lender of last resort.

Some credit corporations have employed reasonable underwriting techniques and experienced relatively modest losses from borrower defaults. Others have been so aggressive in placing money into real estate that their losses from defaults during the market downturn of the early 1990s have been well above the norm experienced by the more traditional regulated lenders. Still, credit corporations are expected to play an increasingly important lending role in financing office buildings and other commercial real estate for the balance of the decade.

Secondary Market Operations

In addition to the direct primary lenders described above, there is a growing market for secondary mortgage loans. For years, America's largest corporations have accessed the bond markets for their borrowing needs, and single family residential mortgages are routinely packaged and sold as bonds. The bond market for commercial real estate debt, however, is still relatively undeveloped.

Bond Financing

The financing of commercial real estate through bonds, on a non-recourse basis, started in earnest in 1984 as a way of funding a billion dollar debt issue on three major Manhattan office buildings. The bond financing allowed the institutions that bought the bond issue to fund the large principal balance jointly. Few, if any, institutional sources would have been willing to fund the debt independently using traditional mortgage instruments. When the credit crunch of the early 1990s severely reduced the traditional sources of debt funding for commercial real estate, there was a surge of interest in financing commercial mortgages through bonds in small denominations. This financing technique is often referred to as debt securitization.

Bond financing is now touted as a way to increase the flow of funds into commercial real estate from sources that did not provide substantial funds into the industry during the 1980s, and thus are not financially weakened by having invested in an industry that subsequently went bust.

Most mortgage-backed bonds are backed by a pool of mortgages. This diversifies risk and allows for a bond of sufficient principal size to support the costs of forming, underwriting and selling the bond issue. Commercial mortgage-backed bonds usually are secured by credit support beyond the security provided by the real property attached via the lien. Buyers of bonds usually do not have the capacity to examine the risks posed by the real estate security, so they rely on this additional credit support and the bond rating agency's opinion on the creditworthiness of the bond. Securitized bond financing is discussed more fully in Chapter 25.

PART TWO: THE FEE PARTICIPANTS

Life Cycle of an Office Building

The life cycle of an office building begins with the raw land, proceeds through construction, lease-up or sale, an initial operating phase and later operating phases. To prolong its useful life it may be renovated or rehabilitated, possibly more than once. Similarly, it may be resold and refinanced several times in its life. At some point, rehabilitation may no longer make economic sense. New office building technologies or changing patterns of demand may dictate that the building be converted to another use or demolished so the land can be readied again for new construction.

The Land Development Phase

The development process starts with the raw land and an entrepreneur— here referred to as the developer—who believes that the site can be improved with an office building. At this early stage, the developer must obtain the land, explore its suitability as an office building site, obtain approvals to construct the building, and improve the land with utilities and roads so that it is ready for office building construction.

Some developers specialize in the development of raw land by buying the land "wholesale," shepherding it through the zoning and approval process, providing roads and utilities to the site and selling the site, ready for construction, at the "retail" price. In the central city, the equivalent wholesale-to-retail conversion may mean assembling the site from a group of small adjoining land parcels under different ownerships. This may entail buying out or otherwise enticing tenants to move so that existing buildings can be demolished. Unused development rights also may be purchased and assembled, primarily from adjoining sites, to permit the construction of a building larger than the parcel's zoning allows.

At this time, too, the developer begins to secure the necessary government approvals for construction of the building. Increasingly, traffic studies, air and water quality studies and often a full-scale environmental impact study are likely to be required. The land sale acquisition may not be consummated until the preliminary results of these studies find the proposed office building legally permissible, marketable and feasible. A more detailed discussion of this topic is found in Chapter 14.

The Design, Funding and Leasing Phase

At the successful conclusion of the preliminary planning and design stage, full architectural and engineering plans will be commissioned and leasing will begin. Once, financing would have preceded leasing, but now preliminary leasing commitments are a prerequisite for financing. Lenders insist on signed lease documents as evidence of market demand.

Funding a major office building is increasingly complex. The moneys for the long-term or permanent loan and the construction loan generally come from separate sources. Because the loans will cover only a portion of the building's cost, the developer may raise equity funds to make up the difference between the financing and the total project cost.

The developer, with the help of mortgage bankers or mortgage brokers, must arrange simultaneously for the construction loan and the permanent mortgage on the finished building. A mortgage banker or mortgage broker assembles the loan package with documentation on the financial creditworthiness and experience of all parties involved with the project. The package also contains the outside research studies to demonstrate the marketability and feasibility of the building and an appraisal to estimate the total market value of the completed structure.

The Construction Phase

The developer probably will hire a general contractor to construct the building. The general contractor, in turn, will hire, coordinate and supervise subcontractors in the various building trades. The subject of construction is covered in Chapter 16. Leasing will be directed by a leasing broker who may design and execute a complete marketing strategy. Leasing efforts will continue throughout the life of the building as the original leases expire and space is relet to keep the building occupied.

The Operating Phase

Once the building is open, a property manager takes over the day-to-day responsibilities of running the building. He may be part of a separate property management firm, or the leasing broker may also act as the property manager. The completed building requires on-going maintenance and security. Periodically the professional services of lawyers, tax specialists, accountants and appraisers will be called upon. Sophisticated professional property managers not only ensure the smooth daily operation of the building but also view the building as a renewable capital asset for their owners. Office building management is discussed in greater detail in Chapters 26, 27 and 28.

The Refinancing Phase

At some time in the building's life cycle the owner may consider refinancing. Mortgage bankers and brokers will search for suitable financing. Some reasons for refinancing include:

- The bullet loan term has expired.
- Depreciation allowances have gotten low.
- The long-term loan has amortized to the point where most of the periodic payments are principal rather than tax-deductible interest.
- The building has appreciated to the point where the owner wants to realize value by cashing out or refinancing for a larger loan amount.

The Renovation or Gut Rehabilitation Phase

In later years the office building may require renovation or gut rehabilitation. A gut rehabilitation is a complete interior renovation in which the HVAC, elevators, electrical system and plumbing are replaced, tenant interiors are modernized and lobbies are re-done. In other words, the interiors are stripped to the enclosing walls and floors. Some basic building systems may need upgrading or replacing. The quality of the tenancy may have declined. Now building contractors skilled in remodeling take over. This process may occur several times in a building's life cycle, especially if the building is located in a market that preserves its architectural heritage. In time, however, the land on which the building sits may become more valuable than the building itself. The building may be demolished and the site readied once again for a new and higher use in a process called supercession. Rehabilitation and modernization of office buildings is discussed in Chapter 17.

Real Estate Fee Market Participants

Developers

At the development stage many real estate participants are called into play. Foremost is the developer, the entrepreneur who conceives the plan to construct an office building. The developer may be the land owner (an individual, family, institution or corporation), a construction or development company, an equity investor or a speculator.

At one time, the developer's role was all-encompassing. He formulated the idea of the office building project, and its execution reflected his vision. Before 1980, the developer was an individual who had an equity interest in the project. That equity might have been raised from internal sources or by obtaining an office building loan for more than the cost of construction. He might have shared equity with his lenders or might have sold all or part of the equity after completion. Depending on the degree of his equity ownership, the developer would have been paid from fees only, from fees and rents, or from the proceeds of the sale of the finished office building. His time frame might have been short (construction and initial lease-up) or for as long as he owned and managed the building. As a general rule, however, the original developer was the major equity holder and manager of the properties he developed.[3]

Architects and Engineers

The architect's job is to provide an office building design that maximizes the use of space, and thus maximizes revenue, while minimizing costs. His tasks extend over several activity phases. The architect draws up preliminary building massing plans to establish how many rentable square feet the site can hold in a layout that will satisfy tenants' needs and comply with zoning regulations. After preliminary designs are approved, more complete working drawings and engineering specifications are produced. Contractors bidding on the job use these plans and specifications to make construction bids, and prospective managers use them to estimate operating costs. During construction the architect or engineer also may administer the construction process to insure that plans are carried out. After construction architects may do space planning for tenants and even train personnel in the building's maintenance. The construction process is discussed at length in Chapter 16.

---

[3] Anthony Downs, *The Structural Revolution in the Commercial Real Estate Industry* (New York: Salomon Brothers, 1992).

Appraisers

Real estate participants call on appraisers to assess their risks in making decisions regarding investments, transactions, developments, redevelopments, underwriting, condemnation, assessment and taxes. A determination of market value for underwriting or lending purposes is the most common use of an appraisal. Appraisers estimate the value of property rights at a given moment. Most commonly, this is the market value of the fee simple interest in the property, but an appraiser may estimate partial property rights and other kinds of value. A more detailed look at valuation can be found in Chapter 29.

Other studies, such as market and feasibility studies, may also be carried out by appraisal professionals. Market and feasibility studies are less structured than appraisals and address risk issues other than valuation. The market or marketability study will gauge the supply and demand for new office space, addressing such questions as how quickly the new office space will be absorbed and at what rent or sales price. Feasibility studies go a step further by measuring the cost of new office space production and operation against the projected rental revenue stream. They estimate whether the new office building will earn a sufficient return on cost for its developers and investors to warrant its construction.

In 1987, The Appraisal Foundation was organized by eight major appraisal associations in order to make the appraisal profession self-regulating. The purpose of the Foundation is to develop and promote uniform standards of professional appraisal practice and to establish uniform qualification criteria for appraisers. The Uniform Standards, recognized as the generally accepted standards of appraisal practice, have been adopted by all appraisal member organizations belonging to the Foundation and focus on the development and reporting of appraisals in an ethical and competent manner.

Title XI of the Financial Institutions Reform, Recovery and Enforcement Act of 1989 (FIRREA) requires that the financial institutions regulatory agencies and the Resolution Trust Corporation adopt regulations governing the performance and use of appraisals by their regulated institutions. Agencies must establish appraisal standards for federally related transactions under their jurisdiction and prescribe categories of federally related transactions which require the services of a state certified or state licensed appraiser.

Attorneys

The legal life cycle of the office building is documented and often planned by real estate lawyers. All entities will have their own legal representation. Generally, the attorney's role is to identify and eliminate risks for his client by representing the client throughout the process. The representation will include such functions as counseling, interpretation, negotiation and documentation. Real estate lawyers may be generalists or specialists in a substantive area of real estate law such as environmental permit issues, zoning, leasing, tax law or real estate financing. The legal framework of office building investment is discussed in Chapter 5.

Commercial Real Estate Brokers

Commercial real estate brokerage began as a sideline to insurance, stock brokerage, law and other business ventures, but by the 1950s it had emerged as an established industry in its own right. Because leasing the office space is central to the ongoing life of an office building, this task should begin at the earliest planning stages. Increasingly, brokerage agencies participate in the planning of the total marketing campaign. This includes design of the tenant space, establishment of rents, specification of lease and workletter terms and preparation of promotional materials. Nevertheless, the central task of the leasing broker is finding the prospective tenants and negotiating the office leases. The topic of brokerage is discussed at length in Chapters 18 through 21.

The nature of the broker-landlord agreement, historically, has been clear-cut. The broker is the agent of the landlord because the landlord pays his commission. In return, the broker has a fiduciary responsibility to the landlord to obtain the highest price and best terms. Traditionally, the tenant in a real estate transaction is not represented by the broker. Under the law of agency, a tenant is considered a third party who must protect his own interests.

Problems have arisen in the application of these rules. In practice, the broker acts as an intermediary in negotiation between the landlord and tenant. Especially where a cooperating broker brings in a tenant, the tenant may believe that the cooperating broker has an obligation to him. By common law, however, even the tenant's cooperating broker is an agent of the landlord because the landlord pays the broker's commission. Chapters 19 and 21 discuss these legal relationships.

The NATIONAL ASSOCIATION OF REALTORS[R] (NAR), founded in 1908, is the country's largest trade organization, with 750,000 members. Along with its real estate affiliates, NAR promotes professionalism among its members through programs of education, publication and research. It also aids real estate transactions by making sales tools such as computerized listings available to members. NAR promulgates a code of ethics and standards of professional practice.

The individual states require brokers to acquire and maintain state licenses and regulate real estate brokerage practices. Brokers must acquire and maintain state licenses that are issued based on education, experience and examination. Much state regulation deals with conditions for licensing, compensation, the nature of the listing contract and conditions under which a commission must be paid.

Mortgage Brokers and Bankers

A broker is an intermediary who brings participants together for a transaction. A mortgage broker brings together the borrower and the lender in a mortgage transaction. Typically the broker is paid a commission by his principal, the borrower, based on a percentage of the mortgage if a transaction occurs. Less often, the broker will represent the borrower in a search for financing in exchange for a fixed fee, with an additional predetermined performance fee paid as a bonus if the search for financing is successful. The term mortgage banker applies to a lender who guarantees to advance the funds itself if it is unable to place the loan as a broker. Many mortgage brokers incorrectly refer to themselves as mortgage bankers but do not meet the conventional definition since they never advance the funds.

When the mortgage broker is engaged by the borrower he is the advocate of the borrower. He typically will present a property in its best light and not volunteer information which would indicate that the property and client he represents are less than fully creditworthy. Mortgage brokers, however, are constrained by anti-fraud laws from misrepresenting facts. If they want to cultivate strong business relationships with lenders, they must act professionally. The mortgage broker who repeatedly brings poor transactions to lenders eventually will lose access to these lenders. Because borrowers hire brokers in large part for their access to lenders, it is good business practice for mortgage brokers representing borrowers also to protect the lender's interests to some degree, but never to the extent of compromising their fiduciary relationship with the borrower.

The mortgage correspondent is engaged by the lender in markets where the lender does not have its own lending staff and typically is paid a commission for placing mortgage money. However, there is an inherent conflict of interest with the commission method of payment. In his underwriting role the correspondent should represent the lender as an unbiased fiduciary, but the correspondent's compensation is based on the volume of mortgage money which successfully clears the lender's underwriting hurdles. Many lenders in the 1980s did not have appropriate controls over the underwriting done by their correspondents and even allowed these professional brokers to perform the property appraisals. As a result, large numbers of correspondent-initiated loans in the 1980s have defaulted. Many institutions have dropped their correspondent relationships, restructured the reward system for the correspondents or tightened their controls over the underwriting process.

Construction Companies

An office building can be constructed under a variety of organizational arrangements. At one extreme, an organization designs and builds the structure with the architect, engineer and construction contractor all employed by the single entity. At the other extreme, the developer hires the architect, engineer and general contractor separately; the general contractor does no construction work himself but enters into a series of separate contracts with building trades subcontractors. Alternatively, the contractor may do some of the work himself and subcontract the remainder. The type of employment arrangement directly affects the type of contract between the developer and the contractor and the method of payment. More details on construction contracts can be found in Chapter 16.

Property Managers and Asset Managers

The property manager oversees the day-to-day operations of the office building for the benefit of the property owner. He represents the owner in transactions with tenants, vendors, subcontractors and the general public. The manager has a contract with the owner detailing the scope of his services and is paid a management fee. The role of the property manager is expanded upon in Chapters 26 and 27.

Two developments launched the role of property manager. Early building technology limited the size of building structures, and hands-on owner management was the rule. In the late 19th and early 20th century, technology allowed the construction of larger buildings. During the Depression of the 1930s, many of these buildings reverted to institutional hands. These institutions created the demand for third-party management to keep the buildings leased, collect rents, oversee maintenance and make repairs. When the economy recovered, most of these buildings returned to private ownership, but the new owners retained outside management. Over time, the role of the property manager has strengthened as buildings have become even larger and more complex. Professional property managers may be employed directly by building owners, full service real estate companies, government, corporations or financial institutions.

The objectives of professional management go far beyond custodial duties to include optimization of returns, extension of productive life and preservation of capital value. Toward these ends, the professional manager often participates in the initial planning of the building to insure that its construction will facilitate efficient operation. Once the building is constructed, he monitors its financial performance and market position to maximize its capital value throughout its useful life. The asset manager's role is examined in Chapter 28.

The property manager frequently also acts as leasing agent, either exclusively or in cooperation with outside brokers. Some property managers undertake management functions principally for the more lucrative leasing commissions.

Several associations represent property managers. The most important are the Building Owners and Managers Association (BOMA) International and the Institute of Real Estate Management (IREM). Both offer ongoing professional education through conventions, seminars, meetings, publications and periodicals. In addition, they publish reports of rents and expenses by city, property type and building size. These reports are widely used within the real estate industry for planning, forecasting and budgeting purposes.

Real Estate Counseling

Real estate counseling as a distinct real estate specialization is a relatively recent phenomenon. It is an outgrowth of other, more specific functions. The larger the counseling company, the greater the breadth and depth of its capabilities. What distinguishes counselors is not the functions they perform but the contractual nature of their relationship with their clients. The Counselors of Real Estate lists a wide variety of specializations, including:

Acquisitions and dispositions

Alternate uses

Asset management

Corporate real estate

Development advisory

Expert witness

Feasibility studies

Investment management

Land assembly

Market studies

Redevelopment

Site location

Tenant representation

Workouts and financial restructuring

The breadth and diversity of function is one of the defining characteristics of counseling. The other hallmark of counseling services is that compensation is fee rather than commission-based.

The relationship between the counselor and his client resembles the relationship between the lawyer and his client. The counselor is a problem solver who assembles knowledge and applies it to the solution of the client's real estate-related problems taking into account the client's objectives, tax position, risk preference and time horizon. The advice may be dynamic, changing as conditions change. If value is an issue, it will rarely be the only issue. Where the counselor is employed in a transaction function, payment will consist of a fixed fee for service, regardless of the outcome, although there may be an additional bonus for a successful outcome. In property management questions, the counselor will not take responsibility for day-to-day property operations. Membership in the Counselors of Real Estate, formed in 1953, is by invitation only. Members receive the designation Counselor of Real Estate (CRE).

CONCLUSION

This chapter has descibed the tasks, motivations and regulation of the key investment and fee players in the life cycle of an office building. It is difficult to describe the players involved without reference to recent events that are profoundly changing their roles and relative status.

Two conditions are obvious. First, the office market in the early 1990s was oversupplied in nearly every geographic location and building configuration. While analysts debate how long these conditions are likely to persist, there is no disagreement on the seriousness of the imbalance between supply and demand for office market space. Second, the financial condition of many institutions that provide debt and equity financing for office buildings has been seriously eroded. Analysts may debate whether the resulting decrease of institutional money available for real estate is primarily a cause or an effect of adverse property market conditions. The truth is that these factors feed each other. Declining market conditions constrict liquidity, and constricting liquidity worsens market conditions.

The current relationship between office space production on the one hand, and office space and financial management on the other, is not permanent. Real estate production, by its very nature, is cyclical. Nevertheless, even when equilibrium is restored, the relationships among the players in the office building industry may have been permanently altered.

In perspective, the office market is destined for a recovery in which equilibrium will once again be attained between supply and demand. Although improved technology will increase the incidence of the "cottage industry" phenomenon at the same time that the volume of office space required for white-collar need declines, the office building will continue to play a major role in serving the agglomerative needs of business companies. Once a new frictional vacancy rate is established, there inevitably will be a resumption of development, and the office industry will regain its status as the premium type of building. It will be the principal property tax contributor as well and will serve as a basis for the generation of economic benefits for the country.

ABOUT THE AUTHORS

Beth S. Krugman, Ph.D., is vice president, Valuation and Technical Services Division, Landauer Associates, Inc., where she is responsible for real estate consulting with an emphasis on market studies, economic base analyses, valuations and site location searches. From 1975 to 1980, she was an assistant professor in the Department of Urban Affairs of Hunter College, where she created and taught graduate courses in economic and environmental planning. Krugman has authored several reports and studies, including the New York Metropolitan Market Report for the Urban Land Institute's *Market Profiles*. She has an AB in economics from Mount Holyoke College, an MA in city and regional planning and a Ph.D. in urban planning from Rutgers University.

Brian A. Furlong is senior vice president, Valuation and Technical Services Division of Landauer Associates, Inc. He was formerly an independent consultant offering appraisal and consulting services for commercial real estate. He has also served as a development consultant with Miller Klutznik Davis Gray Company, and an adjunct lecturer at the New York University Real Estate Institute. Furlong holds a BA in economics from the State University of New York-Albany and an MS in real estate appraisal and investment analysis from the University of Wisconsin-Madison.

5

THE LEGAL FRAMEWORK FOR OFFICE BUILDING INVESTMENT

by Alan J. Pomerantz

INTRODUCTION—UNIQUE LEGAL ASPECTS OF THE OFFICE BUILDING

An office building is a unique asset. Whereas some types of investments gain their value mainly from inflation or their intrinsic rarity, and others generally decline in value with use, the office building's greatest attraction comes from its business use, and the rent stream that use generates. Generally, it has been considered the most favored type of building for long-term investment.

More than any other asset, the modern office building is an important source of revenue for most municipalities, cities and states. As a result, office buildings are creatively taxed in ways that other assets are not. Generally, taxes are imposed on office building transactions, such as their purchase, sale and financing. The mere right of ownership is often taxed, as is the right of use. Municipal services provided to the office building and its tenants, such as sewer and water service, are taxed. Finally, any profits made by the owner are also taxed.

In addition, since land is theoretically infinite in terms of duration, its ownership structure is more complex and varied than that of most other assets. A modern office building comprises a series of complex estates, interests, rights and responsibilities, each having different characteristics, benefits and risks.

This chapter will briefly review certain legal aspects of modern office buildings in urban centers.

ACQUIRING THE OFFICE BUILDING

Two basic legal considerations arise when acquiring an office building: first, what are the interests or "estates" that are being acquired; and second, who or what entity should acquire them?

The Estates Comprising an Office Building

An office building is generally composed of three basic "estates," each with their own characteristics.

The Land

Land is unique. It is impossible to manufacture; it cannot be moved to another location; and absent some dramatic catastrophic event, it is nearly impossible to liquidate or destroy.

The privilege of owning land is always taxed, except for exempt entities such as government or certain private non-profit uses such as hospitals and museums. The ownership of the land is often a matter of public record and its purchase, sale or financing is frequently a taxable event. In addition, because land does not get used up, it cannot be depreciated for income tax purposes.

The Building

That which is built upon the land differs significantly from the land. The legal, social and structural aspects of office building ownership are historically less important than land ownership. Even though an office building is built on the land and "affixed" to it, it is not considered part of the land, but is viewed for most purposes as a separate estate. Buildings are subject to tax separate from the tax on the land. It is not necessary for the owner of the land to also be the owner of the building. A building can be built on land leased to the building owner.

Buildings are subject to use and aesthetic considerations. They can be made in different sizes, heights and designs. Buildings wear out. They can be renovated or torn down. New ones can be constructed where old ones once stood. They are "wasting assets" and, unlike land, can be depreciated for income tax purposes. In order to maintain their value, buildings require maintenance and repair. They can be damaged by fire, wind, rain, mischief and vandalism, and are often insured against such losses. Although it is difficult to steal a building, materials that constitute the building can disappear.

Space within the Building

Simply stated, the reason to construct an office building is to increase the amount of floor space on which to place people and property. The developer can use the space itself, or rent or sell the space to others. When the space is rented, a third estate, called a tenancy, is created within the office building which is defined by the walls, floors and ceilings. Certain areas of space can be subject to exclusive occupancy rights, while other areas may be shared with the owner, other tenants or the public.

Types of Ownership of Office Building Estates

The land, building and office space can be owned in many different ways. Each type of ownership has different characteristics and the decision of how to own each estate will depend on the goals of the owner, the type of office building, the available financing and the market.

Fee Ownership of the Land and Improvements

Complete, absolute ownership of land is generally called fee simple absolute. Historically, fee simple absolute meant ownership from the center of the earth to the top of the sky and included everything that was or came on the land, such as rocks, minerals, trees, animals, buildings and structures.

Governments have taken away many of the rights previously incident to land ownership. For example, airplanes, weather balloons and communications satellites fly over land without the owner's permission and without paying compensation; quasi-governmental utility companies have the right to string telephone and electricity wires above, on and beneath the land; governments can dig trenches across the land for drainage pipes, water conduits and cable television wires which may not even provide service or value to the land owner. Rights of adjacent landowners to streams and lakes also encroach on absolute ownership.

In addition, federal, state and local laws and regulations significantly limit a land owner's right to use the land and improvements. Such limitations are often contained in environmental laws, zoning regulations and building codes. Certain activities on the land are limited by ordinances restricting noise, burning, mining, manufacturing, farming and hunting. Over time, the common law has also restricted a landowner's right to use the land through legal concepts such as attractive nuisance and unjustifiable force. That is, a landowner may be liable to a trespasser who is injured by falling into an unfenced, empty swimming pool; or to a burglar who is severely injured by a home protection device.

The ultimate limitation on fee simple absolute ownership is the government's right to simply take or use the land and improvements through a process called condemnation. Although the law requires that the government pay "just compensation" to the owner, the owner does not have the right to say no. Fee ownership is no longer simple, nor is it absolute.

Leasehold Estates

A lease, like a sale, is a conveyance. However, unlike a sale, a lease is for a finite period of time and traditionally contains use restrictions. Both the land and the space within the building can be leased.

A lease of land is usually called a ground lease. Historically, ground leases were used for tenant farming. The tenant/farmer paid something of value to the landowner, usually a percentage of the crops grown, and was responsible for every aspect of ownership.

In urban society ground leases have developed into sophisticated documents. Often, a developer will lease land from a fee owner and construct an office building on the leasehold estate. The reasons for using ground leases are complex and varied. Tax and accounting treatment of land ownership is different from building ownership. A company's balance sheet treatment of land ownership may also be different from a tenancy interest. There may be limitations on available financing, or just a resistance to selling land.

A space lease describes the rights, duties and obligations of occupants of a portion of an office building. Generally, a space lease conveys to the tenant for a period of time the exclusive use of part of the building described by the walls, floor and ceiling; and the nonexclusive right to the "common areas," such as the halls, elevators and lobbies.

Condominium Ownership

Condominiums began as "horizontal" ownership regimes or systems which provided a way for a group of individual home owners to control certain common elements built for the benefit of the entire group. Each condominium owner owned in fee its building lot and all the improvements on the building lot, and owned with the other condominium owners an undivided interest in the common areas, such as the roads, tennis courts and swimming pool. The common areas were managed by a condominium association which charged each condominium owner a maintenance fee.

The concept of condominium ownership has been translated in urban centers to high-rise buildings as a "vertical" ownership regime. In a vertical condominium, each condominium owner owns in fee a section of space within the building. However, a vertical condominium owner does not own everything above or beneath its unit since generally there is another condominium on the top, the bottom and sometimes on all sides. Each condominium owner owns a partial but undivided interest with the other condominium unit owners in the land beneath the building and in the building's common elements. There are limitations in certain states on forming a condominium on a ground lease estate.

Each condominium unit in a horizontal or vertical condominium is evidenced by a deed and is a separate tax lot. Each condominium unit owner is solely responsible for the real estate taxes imposed on its unit and its share of the real estate taxes imposed on the common elements. In addition, each condominium unit owner is required to become a member of the association which is responsible for the maintenance of the common areas, the land, the exterior of the building, and the heating, ventilation and air-conditioning systems that service the common areas. Generally, the owner of a vertical condominium unit cannot build on its unit, and its use is restricted in ways similar to the restrictions imposed in an office space lease. However, since it owns its "space" in fee, a condominium unit owner can sell or mortgage its space, subject to the condominium association agreement and restrictions, and the other restrictions imposed on any real estate by municipal, city or state authorities. Condominiums originally were totally residential. In recent years, some office condominiums have been developed, but they have never attained the volume or the popularity of the residential type.

TYPES OF OWNING ENTITIES

Each office building estate can be owned in different ways.

Individual Ownership

Historically, people owned land and buildings. That is still sometimes true. An individual who owns an office building is subject to the risks and benefits inherent in the individual ownership of any asset. Although there is no legal reason why individuals cannot own office buildings, the risk of unlimited liability has created other types of ownership entities which limit risks. Individual ownership of office buildings is rare.

Joint Tenancies

Joint tenancy describes two or more people or entities who own an undivided interest in an asset. There are three basic types of joint tenancies.

Tenants-in-Common. Tenants-in-common describes a legal arrangement whereby two or more entities own the office building. The entities can be individuals, partnerships, corporations or trusts, or any other legal entity. Generally, any tenant-in-common is free to sell or dispose of its interests. Upon the death of an individual tenant-in-common, that tenant-in-common's interest passes to the deceased tenant's estate.

Joint Tenants with Right of Survivorship. The legal structure of joint tenants is basically the same as that of tenants-in-common, except that upon the death of an individual joint-tenant, the deceased tenant's interest passes automatically to the surviving tenants and not to the estate of the deceased tenant.

Tenancy by the Entirety. This is the name given to joint tenancy between individuals married to each other.

Partnerships

There are two basic kinds of partnerships: general partnerships and limited partnerships.

General Partnerships. A general partnership is a combination of two or more entities engaged in an enterprise. The entities can be individuals, partnerships, corporations, trusts or any other legal entity. The nature of the relationships among the partners will be determined by their partnership agreement and state law. Each partner in a general partnership is liable for any acts committed by any partner in the furtherance of the partnership's business enterprise. As with individuals, all of the assets of any partner are available to satisfy the obligations of the partnership. For tax purposes, a general partnership is a "pass-through" entity; the partnership is not a "taxpayer" and the tax attributes are distributed to the partners in accordance with the terms of the partnership agreement and state or federal law.

Limited Partnerships. A limited partnership is a hybrid entity created by statute. A limited partnership is composed of at least one general partner and at least one limited partner. The general partner operates the business, and like an individual or partner in a general partnership, is liable for all of the acts and debts of the partnership. A general partner may be an individual, general partnership, corporation or another limited partnership. Each limited partner invests a specific sum of money or thing of value in the partnership and risks only the amount invested. A limited partnership, like a general partnership, is a pass-through entity for tax purposes. Limited partnerships can be publicly traded.

Corporations

Corporations are also creatures of statute and are restricted or empowered by state law and their corporate charters and bylaws. A corporation has limited liability; the assets invested by the shareholders are the only assets available to satisfy the obligations of the corporation. Generally, real estate corporations are not pass-through entities for tax purposes.

Trusts

A trust is an entity that holds assets for the benefit of another party, termed a beneficiary. Trusts can be simple arrangements created by individuals seeking to benefit their dependents, or complex publicly-traded trust agreements, such as real estate investment trusts (REITS), which are formed for the purpose of acquiring real estate and real estate-related assets. Real estate trusts may be privately owned or publicly owned. Public real estate trusts offer trust units for sale on the various exchanges or over-the-counter. They generally do not pay any income taxes at the trust level but pass through the tax liability to the unit holders.

SPACE TENANTS AND TENANCIES

The relationship between the office building owner and the space tenant is described in the office lease. Office leases have become complex documents dealing with significant financial and performance obligations that extend well into the future. The office lease will generally be the longest commitment a tenant will make and is often the most significant financial obligation it will undertake. It is also one of the most important. Without a place to work, it is impossible to work. The tenant must consider expansion, services, comfort and cost. The office building owner/developer must consider each lease and the effects that each lease will have on the operation of the entire building, other tenants, its ability to sell the building and its ability to finance or refinance the building. Cash flow generated from space leases is often the most important aspect of office building valuation.

Area

The office lease must clearly define the area within the building, termed the demised premises, which the tenant has the exclusive right to occupy, subject to the restrictions contained in the lease. Tenants often require the right to take additional space in the building, an important right if the tenant anticipates expanding its business. An owner's obligation to provide expansion space, however, materially affects the owner's ability to rent the space that is subject to the option.

Tenant Work

An important aspect of the demised premises is its condition and the owner's or tenant's obligation to change it. An owner's commitment to provide work, particularly in the future, will have a material effect on its ability to sell or finance the office building, since the obligation will most likely "run with the land" and require future expense. The tenant, lender and owner must be satisfied that monies will be available to fund future construction obligations. A more complete discussion of the work letter and its effect can be found in Chapters 18 and 19.

The Term of the Lease

The term of the lease commences when the owner is obligated to deliver to the tenant the exclusive right of possession of the demised premises and the tenant is correspondingly obligated to accept the delivery. The term of the lease ends when the tenant is obligated to surrender the demised premises to the owner. Often, the commencement date of the lease does not coincide with the commencement date of the rental obligation since a tenant may be entitled to occupy the demised premises before it is obligated to begin paying rent. This can be particularly troublesome if the rent commencement date depends upon the performance of certain acts by the owner, such as completing construction of a portion of the demised premises or the common areas, and is not readily ascertainable by reference to a clear act or a date. If the rent commencement date is uncertain, a tenant has leverage to bargain for a delay in payment of rent. If a lease termination date is uncertain, a court may impose one or may find that the lease is unenforceable and will be converted into a tenancy at will.

Usually, lease commencement date issues arise when the landlord is obligated to do work for the tenant or the tenant has assumed the obligation to prepare the space at its expense in return for a rent allowance or a free rent period; and the tenant's obligation to pay rent commences when the work is completed. Though common, these arrangements create the obvious problem of determining when the work is done and also raise important legal considerations. In certain jurisdictions, a tenant under a lease who has not taken occupancy may not have the full rights to enforce the lease until it takes occupancy and begins to pay rent. A landlord may have a different duty to a future tenant who is in the demised premises performing work that the landlord might otherwise perform, than to a tenant in possession pursuant to a lease. Issues arise as to whether the tenant is a business invitee, licensee, partner, agent or trespasser. The determination of these issues can be meaningful if damages occur to the office building, or if third party liability arises; and it may also affect insurance coverage and workers' compensation obligations.

Generally, there is no limit to the length or the term of the lease. The longer the lease, however, the greater the need to provide appropriate market adjustments or "bumps" to the rent payment in the lease, and expense pass-throughs, in order to maintain the value of the asset and permit sale and refinancing.

In most states, the law requires that leases for more than a specified period of time, usually one year, be in writing to be enforceable.

Renewal Options

An option to renew the lease is generally an important element to a tenant, since it permits the tenant's business to remain at the location. In most jurisdictions, options to renew will be enforceable even if the right to renew extends in perpetuity. Options to renew are generally strictly enforced with the tenant responsible for exercising the option within the contractual time period. In other words, the option right terminates on the contractual date and cannot be extended without mutual agreement. The property owner is not obligated in any way to provide an extension.

Termination of the Lease

A tenant is obligated to vacate the demised premises at the termination of its lease. Tenants do not always do that. In most jurisdictions, the law deems such a tenant, usually called a holdover tenant, to be a month-to-month tenant and to owe a market rent. This may not be sufficient certainty for a lender or an owner. Therefore, it is becoming common to provide for liquidated damages or rents above market if a tenant holds over, providing a tenant with an economic incentive to vacate.

A tenant may vacate the demised premises prior to the termination date of its lease either by willfully breaching the lease, or rejecting the lease under the powers granted by the Federal Bankruptcy Code to a debtor-in-possession or trustee to disaffirm executory contracts. A tenant who terminates a lease prematurely may be obligated to pay damages incurred by the landlord to re-rent the demised premises. Therefore, it is important for a lease to discuss the landlord's obligation to improve and relet the demised premises if a tenant vacates, and whether the landlord can sue at once for damages caused by the breach, or must wait until the demised premises are re-rented before determining its damages. Generally, agreements imposing penalties on a debtor-in-possession who rejects a lease are not enforceable, and the Bankruptcy Code limits the damages that the landlord can recover.

Types of Tenancies

There are several different kinds of tenancies.

Tenancy from Period to Period. If a tenant agrees to occupy the demised premises for a defined period which is automatically renewed unless terminated by some specific notice or act, the tenancy is called a tenancy from period to period. For example, a month-to-month tenant is one who occupies the premises until the landlord or tenant notifies the other that the tenancy will terminate at the end of a specific month. Tenancies from period to period can be made by oral or written agreement. However, if the initial period is greater than a specified length, applicable state law may require that a tenancy from period to period must be in writing to be enforceable.

Sometimes a tenant remains in possession after the expiration of a fixed-term lease. Generally, if a tenant remains in possession with the consent of the landlord, the tenant is deemed to be a tenant from period to period, the period usually being the time over which the tenant paid rent under the term lease. For example, if a tenant was paying rent to the owner monthly under a ten-year lease, and if the tenant tenders, and the owner accepts, monthly rent upon the expiration of the lease, the tenant will be deemed to be a month-to-month tenant.

Tenancy at Will. A tenancy at will or at sufferance is a tenancy slightly to the legal side of a trespass. The landlord may terminate a tenancy at will by advising the tenant to leave. The tenant may terminate merely by leaving. Neither party is obligated to provide any notice to the other.

Tenancy for a Specific Period. A tenancy based on an oral or written lease agreement for a specific period of time is a tenancy for that period of time. A tenant who remains in possession of the demised premises after the termination of that period is either a tenant from period to period, a tenant at will or a holdover tenant, depending on the understanding and the behavior of the parties.

Holdover Tenancy. A tenant who remains in possession of the demised premises at the conclusion of its lease term without the consent of the owner is a holdover tenant, and not a trespasser. In most jurisdictions, an owner cannot arbitrarily evict a holdover tenant, such as hiring a moving company to physically remove the tenant, since American jurisprudence believes that such behavior is likely to breach the peace. Accordingly, an owner is required to employ judicial remedies to evict the tenant. Sometimes the various state legislatures and court decisions have permitted a tenant to remain in possession for a considerable period of time after the termination of its lease, particularly if occupancy of the premises is essential to the tenant's business and the tenant is paying market rent.

Trespassers. Tenants who enter property without a defensible or "color-able" claim to possession are trespassers. Generally, a landlord is obligated to resort to a judicial remedy to remove a trespasser.

Transfers of Tenancies - Subletting and Assignment

In most jurisdictions, an assignment of a lease is the transfer by a tenant of the entire demised premises to a third party for the entire balance of the lease term. Absent agreement or law to the contrary, the assignee assumes the lease obligation and the assignor is relieved from the lease obligation.

Subletting is the transfer of less than all of the demised premises, or the transfer of the entire demised premises for less than the entire balance of the lease term. Absent agreement or law to the contrary, a tenant sublessor remains liable to the landlord for the tenant's obligations under the lease; and the sublessee, or subtenant, is liable only to the sublessor for its obligations under the sublease.

A tenant may generally assign or sublet its lease without obtaining the landlord's consent, unless this is expressly prohibited. In most states, the landlord of commercial space (unlike a landlord of residential space), can prohibit assignment or subletting without its consent.

If the landlord consents to an assignment or subletting, a breach by the assignor, sublessor, assignee or subtenant will have different effects on the integrity of the lease estate.

Breach after Assignment or Subletting

If an assignment is approved by the landlord, the assignee becomes a tenant under the lease and owes all its obligations as tenant directly to the landlord. Unless otherwise agreed, the subsequent acts of the original tenant/assignor are irrelevant.

As a sublessor, however, the original tenant remains directly responsible to the landlord for the tenant's obligation under the lease. The sublessee renders its performance to its landlord, the tenant sublessor. The sublessee's failure to perform does not relieve the tenant/sublessor from its obligations to its landlord. In addition, even if the sublessee performs all of its obligations to the tenant/sublessor, this does not guarantee its right to remain undisturbed in the premises. For those rights to continue, the tenant/sublessor must comply with its obligations to the landlord under its lease. For example, if the subtenant pays its rent to the tenant, but the tenant does not pay rent to the landlord, the landlord can terminate the lease and evict the tenant *and* the subtenant. The subtenant's rights to occupy the premises are derived directly from and can be no greater than those of the original tenant.

Recently, corporate tenants have found creative ways to circumvent restrictions on assignment and subletting by permitting affiliates to occupy the premises or selling stock in the tenant corporation to a third party to effectuate an assignment.

THE OFFICE LEASE AND THE PERMANENT LENDER

Most office leases provide that the office lease is automatically subordinate to the permanent lender's lien. The law varies as to the effect of a mortgage foreclosure on a subordinate lease. In some jurisdictions, upon a foreclosure the tenant has the option to terminate or keep the lease. In most states, a foreclosure terminates a subordinated lease. If the lease is not subordinated, it survives the foreclosure.

In order to achieve clarity, an office tenant will often enter into a subordination/non-disturbance agreement with the lender. Traditionally, a subordination/non-disturbance agreement establishes the subordination of the office lease to the lender and provides that on foreclosure or transfer of the property by deed in lieu of foreclosure, the new owner will not terminate the lease provided that the tenant performs the terms and conditions of the lease. Often, subordination/non-disturbance agreements will also provide that the permanent lender or new owner will not be liable to the tenant for prior acts of the owner or obligations under the lease, such as "fix-up" costs, prepaid rent or security deposits, unless such sums are actually transferred to the new owner or the obligations are specifically assumed.

THE TRANSFER OF THE OFFICE BUILDING

The transfer of an office building affects numerous property rights and obligations between the buyer and seller, and with third parties such as the building's tenants, adjacent land owners, lending institutions and government agencies.

The Contract of Sale

The contract of sale for an office building is a complex document that must deal with many relationships and contingencies.

Form of Contract

The contract for the sale of real property must be in writing and executed by the party to be charged. Any written document that contains all the essential terms of the agreement will be valid. Contracts for the sale of real estate can be recorded to provide notice to third parties of the pending transaction.

Description of the Premises

The contract should contain a clear and unmistakable description of the interests being conveyed, including the building's address, its metes and bounds (i.e., boundary lines and measures) description and a survey reference. Only by reviewing an exact description of the interests can the full effect of the transfer be understood. For example, an office building may encroach upon streets, rights of way, easements and other valuable interests. Adjacent property owners may have built structures that encroach upon the property being sold. An owner may have previously conveyed or limited certain interests or estates in favor of other parties, such as development or "air rights," rights of way, height restrictions, setback restrictions, sight, air and light easements and joint maintenance obligations. These restrictions and obligations will ordinarily encumber the property and pass with it to the new owner.

The sale of an office building usually includes the personal property affixed to it, or owned and used in connection with the maintenance and operation of the office building. These property interests should also be understood and described.

Mortgage and Financing Clause

It is rare that an office building is unencumbered by a mortgage, or that the purchase does not require third-party financing. Accordingly, the contract should contain a clear description of the terms of any existing mortgage to be assumed and of any mortgage contingency options.

Tenancies

An essential element of an office building is its tenants. An important aspect of a contract of sale for an office building is the status of each tenant. Provisions should be made for the purchaser to examine each lease and for the security deposits to be transferred at the closing. Landlords often have future obligations to tenants, such as options for future space, funding tenant improvement work on option or renewal space, repairs and maintenance on existing space and other monetary concessions. The new owner will usually assume these obligations as a matter of law. In addition, the parties must agree on the treatment of existing tenancies that are in default, and the leasing of vacant space and the extension of existing tenancies, before title is transferred.

Operation of the Building Between Contract and Closing

Often there is a considerable amount of time between the contract and the closing on an office building sale, to enable the purchaser to prepare to take title. During that period, the building must operate, and the parties must agree on the way it will be operated and the risk of loss or damage to the property during the contract period.

Rent Adjustments

Rent adjustments at closing are generally very complex. Future rents that have been collected can easily be adjusted. However, often a tenant is in arrears. If the rent arrearages are not adjusted and the new owner collects only part of the rent, should that rent be kept by the new owner, applied first to current rent, or applied to arrears and paid to the seller? The contract should contain these provisions. Adjustments must also be made if there is pending litigation with a tenant. A large office building usually has numerous leases and there may be tenant problems at the time of closing that did not exist when the contract was executed. At the contract signing, each contingency must be examined and decisions made about their treatment when title passes.

Title Companies and Title Insurance

Title companies perform two valuable services. First, they conduct title searches to indicate all liens and encumbrances of record, and other recorded limitations affecting the office building, such as options to purchase, rights of first refusal, utility easements and rights of way. They can be helpful in obtaining copies of surveys, recorded violations, permits and other matters affecting title, ownership and operation of the office building. Second, they insure their findings. Lenders who finance office buildings almost always require mortgage title insurance.

Title searches are usually done by the purchaser after a contract of sale is signed. Therefore, it is essential that the purchaser define in the contract what will be an acceptable title at closing.

Governmental Regulations

Municipal, city and state government and quasi-governmental authorities regulate office buildings. These restrictions "run with the land" and will always encumber the office building. The broadest governmental restrictions involve land use and zoning. These restrictions often are not liens against the property and therefore must be ascertained from other sources. Modern urban zoning ordinances are often negotiated with a municipality in return for obligations by the owner. Such owner obligations may include maintaining and providing public areas, public transportation in the form of owner-financed buses to rail terminals or escalators to public facilities such as subways, or setting aside an area of the building for a specific use such as for retail or cultural space. The right to occupy an office building is usually subject to a certificate of occupancy which may set forth restrictions on the use of all or portions of the building. The operation of the office building (in addition to its existence) is also regulated by law or municipal ordinances, orders or requirements issued by departments of buildings, fire, environment, insurance, labor and health. Office buildings are sometimes located in national or state historic preservation zones which may severely limit the owner's right to alter the interior or exterior of the building.

Office buildings may be the most highly regulated property in urban society. Complex regulations affect every aspect of office building ownership and operation and must be clearly understood by all parties.

Office Leases

Generally, under all existing office leases, the purchaser of an office building becomes the "landlord." In addition to acquiring all the benefits of the leases, the new office building owner also acquires all of the landlord's obligations, which may include providing tenant improvements, repairing or altering space, providing tenants the option to expand or cancel, paying brokerage commissions, providing building services such as cleaning and maintenance, and being liable for security deposits and rental claims or setoffs (allowances) allowed to a tenant under an existing lease. Each office lease and brokerage agreement must be read and understood as part of the purchase of an office building.

Service and Maintenance Contracts

Often, contracts to service and maintain an office building are automatically transferred to and become the responsibility of a new owner. Such contracts include service to the elevator, heating, ventilation and air-conditioning system, security, cleaning and maintenance. Sometimes supply contracts for oil, gas and light bulbs are also automatically assumed by a new office building owner.

DEEDS

The conveyance of any real property and improvements is evidenced by an instrument called a deed. All deeds must contain the identities of the seller and the purchaser, words of conveyance and a description of the property and interests being conveyed. Most states also require the inclusion of a "trust clause" which cuts off the right of certain parties to file a lien against the property after it is transferred for work done for the prior owner. Instead, such liens would attach only to the proceeds of the sale. Generally, deeds require a certain form of formal execution, witnessing or acknowledgement to comply with state recording statutes.

Types of Deeds

There are three main forms of deeds.

Full Covenant and Warranty Deed

A Full Covenant and Warranty Deed conveys title absolutely and contains the seller's warranties that the seller owns the real estate, has the right to convey it and warrants good title. In most urban centers, which have sophisticated recording statutes and accessible land records, and with the use of title insurance, most sellers resist providing a Full Covenant and Warranty Deed since the warranty of title contained in such deeds can be "insured" by the title company.

Bargain and Sale Deed

A Bargain and Sale Deed does not contain the warranties found in the Full Covenant and Warranty Deed. However, it does convey title absolutely. A common modification of this deed is a Bargain and Sale Deed with Covenants Against Grantor's Acts, which provides that the seller has not encumbered title to the property. This is the deed customarily used when conveying an office building. Providing a covenant against grantor's acts does not usually add any greater responsibility to the seller, since in most transactions the seller will also provide to the title company, and sometimes to the purchaser, an affidavit of title which will contain the same warranties and representations as a Bargain and Sale Deed with Covenants Against Grantor's Acts.

Quitclaim Deed

A quitclaim deed contains no warranties or covenants of any kind. It merely releases any interest which the grantor has in the property. A quitclaim deed is not usually offered or accepted in commercial transactions.

Other Types of Deeds

In addition to the main types of deeds, office buildings can be conveyed by an executor's or trustee's deed if the office building is owned by a decedent or a trust; a referee's deed in a foreclosure action; or a deed executed by a guardian on behalf of an infant or a committee on behalf of an incompetent.

TAXES

The ownership, transfer, financing and use of an office building are generally subject to municipal, city and state taxation.

Ownership

The owner of an office building is subject to an annual *ad valorem* tax based upon the assessed valuation of the land and improvements. In certain states, the municipality or city, as well as the state, may impose a real estate tax. The assessed valuation may be modified when a property is sold to reflect the new value of the office building. An office building owner can usually protest the amount of the assessment by a proceeding called a *certiorari* proceeding. Under that proceeding, an office building owner can request a hearing on the valuation of the office building, in the hope of reducing the valuation and obtaining a corresponding reduction in the tax obligation.

Most municipalities bring water to the edge of the property, and remove used water and sewage from the edge of the property. This service is subject to an annual sewer and water tax regardless of actual use or consumption. The use of water is usually metered and taxed separately.

Transfer

Most municipal and state jurisdictions impose a tax when an office building is sold. This tax is usually assessed on the sale price of the property and any mortgages assumed by the purchaser. Some jurisdictions also impose a "stamp tax" or deed tax on instruments evidencing the transfer, and impose a filing fee on any instruments recorded incident to the sale.

Financing

Some municipal and state jurisdictions impose a tax on the amount of any financing secured by a mortgage on an office building. These taxes are usually imposed at the time that the mortgage is recorded.

Use

Major urban cities often impose a tax on office building tenants for the use and occupancy of the building. This occupancy tax is usually paid annually and is assessed on the value of the lease.

PILOT Programs

Municipalities sometimes enter into agreements with landowners to provide payments in lieu of taxes (PILOT programs). There are various reasons why a municipality will enter into a PILOT agreement. The program usually affects the amount, rate or timing of payments in return for certain concessions granted or given by the office building owner. For example, the owner may agree to a public arcade that is open to the public at reasonable hours. A further illustration is the creation of a public mini-park by the developer in exchange for a PILOT agreement providing for lower than normal real estate taxes.

Profits

In addition to the federal income tax on profits, some states also impose a tax on the profits realized on the sale of an office building. Unlike the federal income tax calculation, state profit taxes are usually calculated by deducting the cost of the building (without depreciation) from the sale price.

CONCLUSION

The modern urban office building is perhaps the most highly regulated and taxed type of property, and is subject to the most complex and varied legal structure ever devised to own and operate real estate. The structure is capable of enormous flexibility and creativity. A clear understanding of the legal estates, the methods of ownership, and the elements involved in each is essential to understanding, developing and owning office buildings.

Office buildings are also inherently more complicated because of the frequently customized nature of office occupancy, in which space is laid out individually for each tenant. Large office buildings lend themselves to more complicated financing in which various levels of debt (according to term and risk) may be securitized through the sale of collateralized mortgage obligations. The tendency of a municipality to impose exactions (such as the contribution by the developer of land elsewhere for low-rent housing) complicates ownership. Leases themselves are enormously complicated documents. Perhaps more than with any other building type, the office building owner must have skilled and experienced legal assistance to avoid the pitfalls that otherwise confront office investment.

ABOUT THE AUTHOR

Alan J. Pomerantz, Esq., is a partner at the law firm of Weil, Gotshal & Manges, where he heads the firm's real estate department. He holds a BA from the City College of New York, a J.D. from New York University School of Law and a post-graduate degree with a concentration in the European Common Market from the University of Amsterdam. Pomerantz has published numerous articles on real estate-related topics. He has served as program chairman at the Practicing Law Institute, and is a member of the faculty of the Real Estate Institute of New York University. He has lectured extensively on real estate and real estate financing in the United States and abroad.

PART II

THE PUBLIC INTEREST

6

THE ECONOMIC BENEFITS AND PUBLIC COSTS OF OFFICE BUILDINGS

by Judith S. Reynolds

INTRODUCTION

Private office building development is a public concern. There are public-private connections in the physical, cultural and economic spheres that continue to evolve as the 20th century draws to a close. Architecture defines the space that people occupy, whether it is space in which to reside, to work or to visit. Office structures, because of their height, bulk and general prominence, play a large part in establishing the character of the commercial crossroads that are at the centers of the built environment. The distinctive office skylines of New York, San Francisco, Boston and Chicago immediately identify those cities; they are their most prominent visual characteristic and they give meaning to the city as a concept. Small cities and towns too have their core areas where office buildings are located. These notable expressions of human architectural and cultural awareness are such that the public feels justified in having some voice in their design and, at the very least, the right to complain when they fail to express the appropriate cultural standard.

The public's attention is drawn to an office building in two ways; the first is the way in which it functions; the second is the nature of the building—how it reflects the mentality that created it. A building is a human creation; as such it is an expression of human ideals. Office buildings are primarily useful structures—that is their reason for being—but they are also an expression of a people's level of culture, their appreciation of beauty, their tolerance for the banal. This is one major aspect of the general public interest in the development of office buildings.

The physical, cultural and economic aspects of office buildings are strongly intertwined. In the physical or spatial spheres, office buildings concentrate many employees within a confined space and add to street congestion, infrastructure costs and public service concerns. This physical concentration produces significant visual and environmental impacts. Height, size and architecture can enhance or detract from the spatial arrangement of the environment. The placement and bulk of office buildings affect sunlight, shadows, air flow and protection from winds. In the cultural context, there is an important direct societal connection between people and office buildings. They function not only as places in which to work; they are also part of the community as a whole and part of the reason people live, work, shop and visit areas where office buildings are located. Office building locations and design affect pedestrian traffic, tourism, crime, vagrancy and a sense of community.

The concentration of office buildings in the centers of cities has traditionally functioned to allow necessary and desirable interaction between urban workers in all types of businesses and service industries. There is still a great demand for this kind of interactive proximity, although the advent of the widespread use of computers, improved telephone communications and rapid delivery services has made it feasible to relocate a significant portion of office-based employment in suburban locations where lower land costs, the relative absence of congestion and easier commutes are attractive to landlords and tenants alike. Suburban office building development has its own distinctive characteristics that link it to a cultural identity; these include easy highway access, park-like settings and low height and density. Thus it is not only metropolitan governments that have a vested interest in new office development, but also suburban and town jurisdictions.

The public interest in office development is increasingly economic. City governments, faced with the exodus that began after World War II of middle class residents and their tax dollars to the suburbs, have had to bear more of the burdens of welfare and health care for the indigent, increased demands for police and fire protection and the deterioration of aging infrastructures. Cities have had to develop means to provide services that they no longer can pay for out of federal income tax dollars.

Governments at all levels function more or less as distillations of public opinion; where the people are concerned with light and air, public safety and access for the handicapped, so too, generally, are their government servants. Unfortunately, government bureaucracies, as the ultimate expression of the division of labor, sometimes represent impediments, stultification and maximum inefficiency (and occasionally greed) more than they represent the direct democratic expression of the people's concerns. It is between these two extremes that the proper intersection of the public and private sectors in office building development must be located.

HISTORICAL PERSPECTIVE

There is an important link between publicly and privately built office buildings that bears on the regulation of the latter. The United States, in the first years after the Revolution, set out to create an image befitting the new Republic and its democratic ideals. The classical structures of Greece were the models for the nation's eighteenth and early nineteenth century federal banks, post offices, libraries, courthouses, administrative headquarters and custom houses. Capital investments were made for lengthy periods and quality construction was thought to be economically prudent. Public architecture of a high quality was believed to have the potential to strengthen the attachment of the people to their government. National pride was served by grand buildings; these were to become the common property of the nation. Later, the classical Greek model gave way to the

Their distinctive office skylines immediately identify cities such as New York, San Francisco, Boston and Chicago (pictured). (*Photo by Jon Miller/ Hedrich-Blessing*)

Italian Renaissance model, the French Second Empire model and the Beaux Arts model, but the emphasis on quality of design and construction was sustained.

Private office development has not always achieved the ideal standard that the country established for its public buildings. The international style, so well expressed in many dramatic skyscrapers, degenerated into commonplace ugliness in the office structures built strictly for their utility in the 1950s and 1960s. The Modernist trend in office building construction sought to express its technically proficient age, but was so misinterpreted and overworked that eventually the public became dissatisfied with it. Widespread public criticism, together with the historic preservation movement of the 1960s, helped to motivate the more interesting and better-constructed buildings of post-modernism. An emphasis on quality in materials, equipment and construction, as well as design, was revived by the interest in historic buildings. The public sector had intervened, not only to save historic structures from demolition, but also to discourage the sterile environments produced by too much utilitarian modern architecture. Post-modernism has been an effort to break up the tedious box that office buildings had become by adding back the classical elements in new forms. Now American culture seeks a new architectural expression for office buildings.

Changing Patterns of Metropolitan Area Land Use

After World War II, the development pattern of cities changed when most new residential construction began to take place in suburbs. Center cities began to evidence widespread neglect and deterioration. Municipal authorities turned to the federal government for help. Center-city deterioration was initially addressed, in the 1950s and 1960s, with sweeping federally funded urban-renewal programs. These, in hindsight, were generally a massive overreaction that resulted in acres of land being cleared without consideration either of what replacement buildings would be built or of such basic market economic forces as supply and demand. Urban renewal had become a socially and economically bankrupt policy in the United States by the mid-1970s. More project-specific federal programs replaced urban renewal in the drive to rebuild and preserve urban cores. Community Development Block Grants and Urban Development Action Grants financed many worthwhile projects. The historic preservation movement was supported with federal legislation; substantial tax incentives became available for preservation and restoration of landmark buildings. On the whole, these federal programs had a definite revitalizing effect; much inner-city new development took place and many older structures were preserved or restored. Streets and public spaces were rebuilt as well; residents and tourists returned to downtown areas. However, most of these federal subsidy programs were eliminated in the 1980s.

A local source of subsidy for infrastructure and housing was needed. Office buildings, regarded as symbols of wealth and even excess, became, in many cases, the targeted source for financial aid for deteriorated neighborhoods. Cities began to look to office building developers to pay for deficiencies in the overall fabric of community, reasoning that if the city had both poverty and an area of prosperous office development, there should be some redistribution of resources.

Today, in most cities, developers are offered incentives in return for the exactions required of them, but there has been an attitude change: growth is no longer as welcome as it once was. Managed growth, and sometimes, no-growth, have become the watchwords. Urban areas have progressed to a point where a price must be paid for growth, and government's new responsibility is deciding how to allocate costs among the beneficiaries of growth.

A New Philosophic Approach to Zoning

How did zoning, that reliable, prescribed set of land use controls become so transformed that it now requires office building developers to help pay for new growth? In the late 1960s, the concept of the Planned Unit Development introduced a greater flexibility into the zoning process, and this greater flexibility became part of the grounds for negotiation between governmental jurisdictions and developers. PUDs allowed both the jurisdiction and the developer to benefit, and they were legally defensible as an extension of state and local governments' rights to regulate the use of land on the grounds that the process was ordered and carried out according to specified guidelines. The key to the process was an individual review that granted extra heights and densities within the context of an overall plan. Developers had complained of the rigidity of zoning by right; the public sector had seen a way to benefit. Zoning gradually became a set of negotiated rights.

The opening up of the zoning process coincided with the citizen participation movements that began in the 1970s. A new set of concerns emerged, issues on which the public could take a strong stand and which allowed citizens to participate in the development process. Organized groups, sometimes in concert with, and sometimes in opposition to, government officials, began to exert leverage over private developers to curtail development that threatened community and environmental resources. Legislation was written and passed that empowered citizen groups to ensure that local governments protected landmark properties, archeological resources, wildlife habitats, wetlands and coastal areas, and neighborhood and community configurations. The courts supported these efforts by expanding government's jurisdictional power to include the protection of such interests.

Suburban office developers have traditionally paid for their right to develop. Suburban jurisdictions, often bedroom communities lacking any infrastructure except what residential developers install, or any commercial or industrial tax base, have only been able to provide needed services to their residents by requiring developers to pay for infrastructure and public amenities. Frequently the demand for new office development in the suburbs is in direct conflict with insufficient roads and streets, insufficient public utilities such as sewer and water, and public concerns about open space. More recently, suburban developers have also had to contend with the new emphasis on the environment, particularly on the protection of wetlands and other ecological systems.

The simple zoning regulations of the early twentieth century have grown into a proliferation of complicated public controls. Most cities and suburban jurisdictions of the 1990s have extensive planning objectives within which new office development must fit. The types of controls that affect office building development, in addition to the traditional zoning regulations and building codes, now include rigorous handicapped access requirements, special-use districts (controlling landmark preservation, shopping facilities, theatres, the arts, parking and public transit), regulations protecting view corridors, neighborhood and community resources, protection for archeological resources, seismic requirements, planned-unit development specifications, transferrable development rights, incentive zoning, linkage payments, impact fees, proffers, and outright moratoria and quantity limitations.

Large office projects require voluminous impact studies exploring their effect on a wide range of physical, social and financial relationships. A new group of professionals has come into being to meet the needs of governmentally-decreed land economics concerns: planners, traffic engineers, architectural historians, utility engineers, environmental experts, land use attorneys and numerous others.

An intensified level of interaction between the public and private sectors emerged during the 1980s. Where city governments control sites, they are participating directly in partnerships with private office developers in an effort not only to regulate the characteristics of office projects, but also to earn their own share of profits and income. This new codevelopment trend is controversial in the context of the traditional and legal separation of government roles from private property rights.

ECONOMIC CONTRIBUTIONS OF OFFICE BUILDINGS

Concentrations of office buildings form the nuclei of urban development; this was not so before World War II when center cities were formed around manufacturing, retailing and related enterprises. Office employment has become the predominant type of employment in the United States. Office buildings are an embodiment of investment wealth drawn from a wide variety of sources including property developers, pension funds, insurance companies, real estate investment trusts and foreign funding resources. As the repository of this investment wealth, office buildings have become the most prominent transforming element of the modern city. Although they are subject to cyclical swings in value and occupancy, office buildings are generally regarded as secure investments, not only producing regular income flows, but also advancing in value over time.

It is significant that these sources of employment and wealth now are frequently developed outside the center city. The communications revolution has allowed office functions to be flexibly located, resulting in the emergence of separate office markets in formerly suburban locations. Joel Garreau defines an "edge city" in part as one having five million or more square feet of leasable office space and more jobs than bedrooms.[1] He reports that two-thirds of all American office facilities are now in "edge cities" and that 80% of them have emerged only within the past 20 years.

PUBLIC COSTS ATTRIBUTABLE TO OFFICE DEVELOPMENT

The costs to the public of office development are both monetary and social. Those considered the most onerous are urban congestion, traffic jams, strained transportation facilities, air pollution, higher levels of taxation, the loss of affordable housing and the reduction of the natural environment. Large-scale and highly visible investments in office development contrast sharply with severe urban problems such as homelessness and over-crowded housing, increasing crime, and drug and alcohol addiction; the co-existence of these two types of trends produces an atmosphere of incongruity and inequity.

Large office buildings create particular problems of fire and police protection because of their density of occupation. This density requires intensive public transportation, street, tunnel, and bridge maintenance, electrical supply and telephone communications. Interruptions in any of these services or a fire or police emergency within the confines of a skyscraper or other large office development can be disastrous. In addition, the congestion of large-scale office development causes human anxiety that is a health and social liability. Skyscrapers are regarded by some as hostile environments that stack people vertically, placing them at the mercy of high-speed elevators and windows that cannot be opened. Air pollution and the removal from a natural environment add to these anxieties.

---

[1] Joel Garreau, *Edge City* (New York: Doubleday, 1991)

TAXATION AND FISCAL POLICY

Office development is interactive with tax and fiscal policies of federal and local governments. Federal income tax policies between 1981 and 1987 helped to create the enormous increase in new office construction that took place in most major cities in that period. Changes in interest rates, as well as capital gains treatment, tax rates, allowable depreciation rates and limitations on deducting excess losses all affect the desirability of investing in new office construction or rehabilitation of existing office structures. The relative attractiveness of the tax and financial policies of the United States has drawn much foreign investment in office building development, particularly since the middle 1970s.

More than 20% of the total average annual state and local expenditures in the 1950s and 1960s went to install new public facilities and systems. This new infrastructure was required by the surge of population growth and formation of new households that took place after World War II. By the 1970s this figure had declined to 10% of total average annual expenditures, in part because fewer new installations were needed, but also due to the lack of adequate revenues. The decline was partially offset by federal aid. In the 1980s the figure declined to less than 10% in the face of a growing economy and the withdrawal of federal subsidies. This reduction explains the deteriorating condition of much public infrastructure in the United States. In many cases, bridges, roadways, tunnels, sewer and water lines are not receiving adequate maintenance, especially in the large Eastern cities.

The United States is becoming increasingly urban; although large cities are growing only slowly or not at all, small cities have greatly increased in population. These cities are frequently too small to take advantage of economies of scale and are, as a result, very expensive to manage. At the same time that large cities are facing the deterioration of their aging infrastructure and small cities are growing rapidly, the ability of cities to increase property taxes to raise revenues for infrastructure needs has been greatly limited by the entrenched resistance of their citizens to such increases. Tax revolts directed against government expenditures in general have focused mainly on limiting increases in property taxes. Like city expenditures, property tax revenues rose sharply in the 1950s and 1960s, but by the end of the 1970s had fallen to a level below 5% of personal income; this low level has continued and has been inadequate to provide traditional government services.

Cities have been forced to turn to sources of revenue other than property taxes, such as user charges, which are charges collected directly from users of specific services. After the 1970s, user-charge revenues rose from approximately 20% to approximately 30% of locally financed expenditures for public infrastructure.[2] Cities also borrow through bonds, but this increase in debt results in an ever growing demand for more revenue to pay back investors with interest. Many older cities are increasingly unable to match revenues with the cost of providing such basic services as fire and police protection, refuse removal and street cleaning, to say nothing of the sharp increases in social welfare and medical costs.

Still, property taxes remain an important source of revenue for all jurisdictions—cities build convention centers, skyways and parking garages to engender new office development that will increase their tax bases. They lease land and participate directly in development, not only to profit directly, but to increase property tax revenues. Office building owners generally pay the major portion of commercial ad valorem taxes and sometimes pay at higher tax rates than those for other types of property. Furthermore, ad valorem taxes are typically the single largest expense borne by office building owners and tenants.

CONSTRAINTS ON DEVELOPMENT AND DEVELOPER CHARGES

Growth management, which includes efforts by government to control when, where and how office building development takes place, has become a significant area of public governance. Government efforts to manage growth are a response to the increased interest and participation of widely varying factions of citizens, including the urban poor, in what constitutes the proper management of maintenance and change in their own communities. This broader base of public participation in the development process has replaced, in many cases, the former coalitions between government bureaucrats and influential developers and their financiers. Local governments now give heed to well-organized groups of citizens that are influential in directing and controlling new development. Citizen activists serve on public commissions and boards along with the traditional development community representatives.

There are convincing economic arguments favoring control of office development. Uncontrolled development results in excesses that are wasteful of vital resources and that weaken the market for existing office buildings. The "boom and slump" cycles of office building development tend to be less drastic in cities where controls have been instigated.[3] There are also social reasons for controls on office development that revolve

[2] Dick Netzer, "Public Finance Context" in *Private Supply of Public Services*, Rachelle Alterman, Ed. (New York: New York University Press, 1988) p. 39.

[3] Michael Bateman, *Office Development: A Geographical Analysis* (New York: St. Martin's Press, 1985) pp. 117 and 155.

around its negative aspects, such as urban congestion, loss of affordable housing and small retailing, and the loss of neighborhoods.

Social scientists disagree as to whether economic growth and development favor the community as a whole and whether therefore the market should dictate the investment and development decisions that are made. Those who oppose a market-oriented emphasis believe that neighborhood and community goals should be balanced against the exchange value goals of developers and financiers.[4] The reaction of San Franciscans that produced linkage payments and strict limits on new construction resulted from the rapid growth of office building development in the period between 1960 and 1980 when the total amount of office space in the city doubled, going from 35.6 million square feet to 71 million square feet. In 1980, in the three-mile square financial district there were 53 million square feet of office space and 200,000 employees.[5]

Public Policy Implications of Exactions

Exactions of various kinds are supported by the increasingly powerful organized citizen efforts to control office and other real estate development. The term "exactions" encompasses a wide variety of preconditions and obligations that developers are charged with as the *quid pro quo* for project approval. Exactions are at the heart of the redefined role of government in the development process. Exactions are, in essence, privatization of functions that government has traditionally carried out. The trend toward privatization is radically changing the relationship between the public and private sectors. Government as a supplier of services does not always perform at maximum, or even average, efficiency; in some cities, certain commonly expected government services, such as street cleaning, are now supplied by private companies. Of course, any services, utilities and facilities not provided by government should reasonably result in reduced land values.

Exactions are considered "for the public good"; they are benefits exacted for the public, not in general, but in a way related to the particular project that must bear their price. Exactions fall into four general categories:

1. Those for infrastructure such as rights-of-way and utility lines
2. Those for necessary public facilities such as schools and fire stations

---

[4] For a comprehensive treatment of the position favoring democratization of the urban development process see Joe R. Feagin and Robert Parker, *Building American Cities: The Urban Real Estate Game* (Englewood Cliffs, N.J.: Prentice Hall, 1989).

[5] Manuel Castells, *The City and the Grassroots: A Cross-Cultural Theory of Urban Social Movements* (Berkeley: University of California Press, 1983).

3. Those for desirable public amenities such as plazas, arcades and art galleries
4. Those for "linked" benefits such as low- and moderate-income housing, job training programs and hiring agreements

The developer might provide these exactions directly or pay for them in cash, depending on the jurisdiction. Exactions can be stipulated by regulation or ordinance or can be negotiable. Stipulated exactions can be arbitrary, as in the case of impact fees, or voluntary, as in the case of incentive zoning. Some jurisdictions apply exactions to all new development; others impose exactions only when additional density or height beyond stipulated norms are requested.

Incentive zoning permits developers to exceed specified densities and heights if their projects include certain specified amenities such as shopping arcades, roof-top observation decks, daycare centers and art galleries. Frequently the nominal densities permitted by the zoning are not economically feasible, forcing developers to seek the bonus densities and as a matter of course to supply the required exactions. Additional densities and heights can also be obtained in some jurisdictions through the purchase of transferable development rights from sites that are then protected from further development in pursuit of historic preservation or environmental objectives. Exactions are used to remedy perceived inadequacies in the economic and/or social fabric of communities.

THE LEGAL BACKGROUND OF LAND USE CONTROL REGULATIONS

Under the laws of the United States, the public and private sectors are meant to be separate and distinct. Property rights are protected by the Constitution, but state and local governments are given the right, as a police power, to regulate the use of land.[6] The Fifth and Fourteenth Amendments to the Constitution through their due process clauses limit the powers and procedures of government. These constitutional limitations require certain principles of due process in the actions of governments, including clear standards, equal treatment of all, adequate notice of actions to be taken, decisions based on the merits and a clear connection to a legitimate public purpose, i.e., one related to the public health, safety and welfare. The police power of government jurisdictions is intended to promote the public good; public policy must adhere, in its land use planning and control manifestations, to these principles.

---

[6] The United States Supreme Court interpreted the police power of the constitution to include zoning in the 1920s.

Exactions versus Takings

The Constitution decrees that owners of private property taken by government must receive just compensation. What constitutes a taking becomes highly uncertain where complex land use regulations are concerned. Whereas a measurable loss in value was at one time indicative of a taking, the courts, including the Supreme Court, began in the 1970s to reflect a trend toward expansion of the police power concept. Furthermore, society, through judicial interpretation, was deemed to have an interest in private property that went well beyond the maintenance of order and the provision of services to include historic and archeological resources, open space and even redress of imbalances created by new development. Still, developer exactions must remain within the purview of these expanded police powers, not deny due process, and not constitute a taking.

The granting by the Constitution of land-use regulation rights to the states has tended to create widely differing and innovative forms of land-use legislation. No central administrative authority reviews and coordinates state and local land-use laws. The reviewing authority becomes the courts; once tested in the courts, land-use laws become more solidly grounded.

The expansion of developer exactions has proceeded step by step to an ever-broader base. The concept of developer exactions began in the 1920s as part of the instigation of subdivision law. In connection with the early Maps and Plats Acts, street or road dedications were sometimes required. Eventually developers were required to pave rights-of-way, following specific standards, and to provide utility easements and sites for parks, schools and sewage treatment facilities.

In-Lieu Fees, Impact Fees and Linkages

The in-lieu fee developed as an extension or broadening of these required dedications, on the basis that the sites developers could provide were not necessarily adequate or appropriate. From in-lieu fees, development impact fees could be justified as required to pay for capital improvements necessitated by the new developments. Impact fees provide governments with greater flexibility; they can be applied to more general facilities serving a wider area. Linkage exactions go a large step further by requiring developers to fund housing, employment and other social services, but they have been defended as extensions of impact fees.

Exactions generally are not covered by state enabling statutes, which are mostly restricted to zoning. Local governments tend to regard exactions as land-use control regulations and valid exercises of the police power. They have been challenged in court on the basis that they are, however, taxes, which would be subject to stringent and specific statutory requirements.

State courts have, for the most part, upheld exactions as a police-power regulation.[7]

Where land use exactions have been struck down as illegal, the weak link has often been the lack of a sufficiently direct connection between the public purpose for which exactions are sought and the developer's project. A case in point is that of the Municipal Art Society versus the City of New York. This 1987 decision stated that New York City had illegally sold bonus density rights when it required the buyer of a Columbus Circle site to pay millions of extra dollars for improvements that were not directly connected to the developer's project.

The Rational Nexus Standard

The courts have, over the past 20 years, developed a "rational nexus" standard by which the more extreme developer exactions can be deemed valid or invalid. A two-part analysis characterizes this standard. First, there must be some real evidence that the development in question creates a specific need and that the exaction will be proportional to that need. Second, the funds exacted must be designated to provide some benefit to the development.[8] Thus a requirement for a developer to contribute land for rights of way must both be proportionate to the share of traffic created by the project and must serve the developer's project.

CONCLUSION

In the United States the public/private intersection has changed radically since the 1950s and 1960s, when development of new office buildings was considered desirable by most jurisdictions. During that post-war growth period, new suburban development required the installation by developers of infrastructure facilities; this became the precedent for what was to come. Developers supported the concept of zoning and subdivision regulations as the basis for an orderly and dependable development process. Later developers also supported the concept of Planned Use Development. Incentive zoning was first instituted in New York City in 1961. Although the history of exactions and controls is not new, the balance has clearly changed; a wider popular base of citizen input is influencing the direction of office building development in the United States.

---

[7] Julian Conrad Juergensmeyer, "The Legal Issues of Capital Facilities Funding," in *Private Supply of Public Services*, p. 55.

[8] Fred P. Bosselman, "Downtown Linkage: Legal Issues" in *Downtown Linkages* (Washington, D.C.: The Urban Land Institute, 1985) pp. 30-31.

This set of inroads into traditional property ownership rights goes against the grain of laissez-faire capitalistic ideology which dislikes anything more than a modicum of government interference in the private development process. The private development sector is still strong and has not capitulated to the grassroots movement that wants to limit and control office building development. It seems inevitable that the emerging public/private sector nexus will have to be the product of negotiation.

ABOUT THE AUTHOR

Judith S. Reynolds, CRE, MAI, is a partner in Reynolds & Reynolds, Inc. An appraiser and consultant, she has worked in commercial property valuation in Washington, D.C., for 25 years, developing a strong interest and expertise in the valuation of historic properties and preservation easements. Her book *Historic Properties: Preservation and the Valuation Process* was published in 1982. She has served as editor-in-chief of *The Appraisal Journal* and on the Executive Committee of the American Institute of Real Estate Appraisers. Reynolds holds a BA in international studies from Trinity College and an MA in European history from The Catholic University of America. She has a particular interest in American cities and towns.

site plan ordinances. In California and New Jersey, for example, zoning ordinances which are not consistent with the master plan may be declared inoperative or illegal.

The comprehensive plan is the official statement of a municipality which sets forth its major policies concerning desirable future physical development. Generally, the comprehensive plan discusses not only the physical development of the municipality, but other factors which affect the quality of life such as preservation and conservation of valuable resources, social considerations, economic development, community facilities, housing, circulation and utilities. The plan is based on an analysis of local and regional trends, requirements mandated by courts and the legislature, and citizen goals and objectives. The comprehensive plan documents community goals and objectives and provides implementation strategies to achieve the stated objectives. The primary purpose of the plan is to provide advisory and elected officials with a guide upon which to base their land use decisions. The plan serves as the factual and policy basis from which regulatory tools such as zoning, subdivision and site plan ordinances, and impact fees or exactions are derived. These in turn are used to implement the plan. Good comprehensive planning requires consistency between the plan and implementation ordinances since the ordinances can create windfalls and wipeouts. In many states, consistency is required by statute.

Planning Methods

Zoning is the division of land uses in a community into categories by area and use. The power to zone is often granted to local communities by the state. A zoning ordinance must be reasonably related to the public health, safety, morals or welfare. This means that the ordinance must promote valid public purposes and the methods selected by the ordinance must be reasonably related to the goals and purposes of the ordinance. The ordinance must not result in a "taking" of property and, as noted earlier, it must be consistent with a comprehensive plan. Finally, the ordinance must not violate other constitutional provisions, such as equal protection.

Zoning ordinances usually regulate use, intensity (i.e., density and floor area ratio), height and bulk. This usually includes building size, shape, density and placement for each zone. Zoning ordinances typically control uses by establishing permitted uses, which are allowed as of right, and conditional or special exception uses, which are allowable uses subject to stated conditions that ensure compatibility and appropriateness. Nonconforming uses and structures are uses and structures existing prior to the zoning ordinance and not in conformity with its provisions. Many ordinances allow their continuation unless they are destroyed or damaged to a certain percentage. Some ordinances require that nonconforming structures be amortized and discontinued over a certain period of time. In other words, the use must be terminated after a designated number of years and the nonconforming site becomes subject to the new zoning.

There are several procedures available for evaluating and approving applications which do not conform to the zoning ordinance standards. It must be emphasized, however, that whenever possible, the application should not include any zoning variances. The primary reason is because variances require higher levels of proof or justification, often difficult to secure. A better approach is to seek a zoning amendment and submit the application as a permitted use meeting all provisions of the ordinance.

Variances from the zoning ordinance requirements are granted by a quasi-judicial body, the board of zoning appeals or adjustment. Amendments or rezonings are changes in the zoning ordinance and are enacted by the legislative body, often on recommendation of the planning commission. Variances are usually granted only where there is hardship caused by some peculiar aspect of the property such that it cannot be used for the purposes for which it is zoned. Variance requirements usually mandate a finding that the hardship was not brought on by the applicant (self-imposed), and that the proposed use will not cause substantial detriment to the neighborhood or the character of the neighborhood. Personal hardship is not valid grounds for granting a variance.

Typically, bulk variances (exceptions to the physical standards such as setbacks, coverage and height) are handled differently than use variances (permission to locate a use normally prohibited in the zone). Generally, it is easier to prove the need for bulk variances than for use variances. Where a distinction is made, some courts will allow a use variance only upon a showing of hardship or special reasons, but bulk variances may be granted on a showing of practical difficulties.

Zoning Flexibility

Prospective office building investors or developers should attempt to convince local authorities that flexibility built into zoning or site plan regulations benefits both the community and the developer. The municipality benefits since the project can be tailored to meet specific site characteristics, avoiding constrained areas such as wetlands, flood hazard areas and steep slopes, and to provide more open space. Developers benefit by reduced site costs and more marketable projects.

There are a number of devices to provide flexibility in the zoning ordinance. Floating zones are zoning provisions that are intended to be located on the zoning map only after an application is made and the project meets certain requirements such as minimum area, required utilities and traffic mitigation. They are typically used for large scale developments where special development controls are applied to the particular parcel. Floating zones give the community and developers flexibility in dealing with each other.

A commonly used form of floating zone is the planned unit development (PUD), which requires submission of a comprehensive conceptual development plan at the beginning of the process. Depending on local legislation, PUDs can allow mixed uses, increased density and the right to waive zoning requirements such as setback lines and lot coverage requirements in order to achieve greater flexibility and better design. Greater density or intensity of development than normally provided as of right may be tied to providing certain amenities such as mass transit facilities, more open space, lower income housing or recreation facilities. PUD approval involves simultaneous rezoning, subdivision and site plan approval, thus providing significant savings of time and money. Another benefit of the PUD provisions is that they allow developers and communities to work together to achieve separate, but mutually desirable, goals.

Flexibility is also achieved through clustering or lot averaging, where buildings are permitted to be located closer together and large areas of the site are preserved. Zero lot line zoning permits structures to be located on lot lines to provide more open space within the lot.

Another important zoning device to achieve open space, farmland preservation and protection of critical areas is transferable development rights (TDR). The TDR separates ownership rights from development rights and allows an owner whose right to develop on a property may be severely restricted to transfer the development right to another property or to sell the right to someone else. The local ordinance designates the sending district from which development rights may be sold and receiving districts, where the additional density or intensity of development may be built.

Subdivision and Site Plan Controls

Subdivision ordinances provide standards for the subdivision of property to ensure that all new developments have roads and utilities and that stormwater management and environmental areas are properly considered. Soil erosion and sedimentation control, landscaping and aesthetics are also considered. Whereas zoning regulations control location and land use patterns, subdivision and site plan regulations control the quality of development by providing design standards for individual lots.

Impact Fees or Exactions

Development exactions (e.g., requirements for open space, parks, affordable housing) may affect development patterns and significantly increase the cost of development. The principal issue that arises is the extent to which the municipality may impose requirements on builders for the right to develop. Usually, requirements will be upheld (even if off-tract in some instances) where the dedication is required to offset impacts on utilities or facilities created by the subdivision or site plan. Exactions on developers

may include requirements for dedication of land, construction of improvements, or payments in lieu of improvements. Impact fees and linkage fees
may be required to pay for services not directly associated with a specific
development but recognized as placing indirect burdens on the community
(e.g., a day care center or fees to pay for off-tract, low cost housing).

As exactions become less closely linked with specific development, their
validity may be called into question. States have used three tests to decide
cases: the reasonably related test, the rational nexus test and the "specifically and uniquely attributable" test. The reasonably related test permits an
exaction if there is any relationship, direct or indirect, between the requested improvement and the proposed project. The rational nexus test is a
middle ground test that requires a balancing of the community's needs
with the developer's rights. The "specifically and uniquely attributable"
test is the most stringent and limiting test and requires that the dedication
or fee be specifically and uniquely attributable to the subdivision or site
plan.

Whenever possible, developers should strive to have exaction formulas
specifically set forth in the ordinance. This allows for more accurate
forecasting of costs and prevents the placement of discriminatory burdens
on the applicant at the time of application approval. Some concern has been
expressed that exactions have become so widespread as to constitute a
public taking from the land owner and a discriminatory or arbitrary
process against the developer.

Planning Considerations in Office Building Development

Office development is often considered a positive, attractive use by local
governments. It provides additional local property tax revenues and does
not directly generate additional school children. In addition, it is often a
good transition use because it produces few negative impacts, with the
exception of traffic. Finally, office development can provide attractive, high-
profile, prestigious buildings or the low-density campus atmosphere which
add to a community's image.

Site design considerations for office development typically focus on
building orientation and location on the lot, public safety, visual quality,
circulation and landscaping. The location and construction of parking and
sidewalks are important considerations, as is appropriate landscaping to
screen parking or utility structures and to enhance open spaces. Increasingly, office developments are required to provide public spaces, day care,
health and recreation facilities and onsite employee services. However, the
astute office builder can tie these requirements for amenities to increases in
the floor area ratio.

Land use considerations for office development focus on the compatibility of the office project with adjacent properties in terms of use, scale and

intensity. Adjacent developments should complement each other in use and should be of similar scale and intensity. Since office developments usually have a high number of employees per square foot (1 per 250 square feet is not uncommon), they require large areas for parking unless the office site is served by public transit. How this parking is designed, including location and landscaping, is a critical element in the site plan review process.

Other considerations include the impact of the development on community facilities and services. In certain situations, office development may generate the need for additional road capacity and traffic control devices, police and fire equipment, expanded utility services, and additional housing, schools and recreational facilities.

The fiscal impact of the project is also an important consideration and can be a major selling point in securing approval. The number of jobs generated by the office project has both positive and negative connotations. Most municipalities welcome the additional employment opportunities. On the other hand, the new jobs also generate additional housing demand and in many jurisdictions, a mandatory lower income housing obligation.

An employee cafeteria extends into a man-made pond at Spiegel Corporate Headquarters in suburban Downers Grove, Illinois. In landscaping the site, its prairie setting was preserved. *(Photo by Jon Miller/Hedrich-Blessing. Courtesy of Skidmore, Owings and Merrill)*

Finally, the environmental impact of the office project will certainly be examined. Environmental considerations include groundwater protection, air quality protection, wetlands protection, coastal and inland water protection, endangered species protection and protection of historic/cultural resources. These are typically addressed in an environmental impact statement (EIS) prepared by an engineer or planner.

The federal groundwork for the preparation of an EIS was set forth in the passage of the National Environmental Policy Act (NEPA) in 1970. This act requires the preparation of an environmental statement for any major federal action which significantly affects the environment. The statement must include the following:

1. The environmental impact of the proposed action
2. Any adverse environmental effects which cannot be avoided
3. Alternatives to the proposed action
4. The relationship between short-term uses of the environment and long-term effects
5. An irreversible commitment of resources

Since 1970, many states have adopted environmental impact statements similar to those outlined in the federal legislation. Many municipalities also have environmental impact statement requirements. Some municipalities require the preparation of an EIS for only certain types of development; others apply the requirement to all proposed developments. In certain situations, the EIS requirement may be waived. For example, a strong argument for a waiver could be made for the reuse of an existing building with no new impervious coverage.

OFFICE DEVELOPMENT FROM THE DEVELOPER'S PERSPECTIVE

Basic Inputs

Assembling a development team is crucial to the development of a sound land use plan. The team is typically comprised of a land use attorney, architect, site engineer, planner, environmental expert and traffic engineer. These experts prepare necessary studies and participate as expert witnesses at public meetings before local boards. A coordinated planning process for an office project will combine the skills and expertise of each member of the development team to create a comprehensive development plan. Generally speaking, the attorney acts as "quarterback," directing and focusing the team on its stated objective of securing approval and ensuring that all testimony is consistent and on point.

The first part of the development process is the site analysis, a detailed analysis of all physical characteristics and any environmental features on the property. Features such as topography, soils, floodplains, vegetation, wetlands and streams are critical to the site design since their layout and orientation on a site can affect potential access, circulation and the extent of development feasible.

Regulatory agencies may also be involved if permits are needed to allow a development to encroach on any of these natural features. The local zoning regulations must also be carefully analyzed to determine what can be constructed "as of right" or without any deviations from municipal zoning requirements. With these inputs, conceptual site designs are typically undertaken to show various ideas and layouts for the proposed development.

At times, designs are undertaken that deviate from the zoning requirements. The extent of such deviations can range from minor exceptions or waivers for relief from design requirements to more serious variances such as relaxation of bulk controls or allowing a use normally barred in a district. Deviations invariably complicate the review and approval process and, if possible, should be avoided. For example, variances require notice to surrounding property owners, which produces large, often hostile turnouts at meetings.

Information relating to infrastructure, specifically on the availability of water and sewer service, is also incorporated into the conceptual design phase. Securing adequate sewage treatment capacity to meet the needs of the office project is critical to the project's feasibility. This information may be obtained from municipal utility plans, including wastewater and stormwater management plans, or may require discussions with applicable utility authorities. Options that can be reviewed for sewage treatment include septic tanks in exurban areas and on-site treatment plants.

In addition to local approvals, permits are normally required from county and state planning and environmental agencies, as well as utility districts. Federal regulatory permits may also be needed in certain cases. Indeed, freshwater wetlands and their buffer areas are extremely important in terms of maximum yield and effect on design. For example, wetlands and required buffer areas between wetland boundaries and areas disturbed for development limit the area of a site which can be developed. Consequently, the site yield may be reduced and the site design may be affected due to the configuration of wetlands, buffer areas and other environmental constraints.

Design Considerations

Office development design considerations are driven by tenant or prospective tenant needs, location, site characteristics and municipal planning objectives as expressed in the local ordinance. This review of site design concerns is not exhaustive. Municipal officials, planning boards and community residents also verbalize concerns throughout the approval process at public meetings and these concerns also have to be addressed.

The major design considerations for an office development site include the following.

Intensity

The intensity of the office development is typically controlled in the municipal zoning code. Density, usually expressed as a floor area ratio (FAR) standard, limits the total amount of floor area that can be constructed on a site in relation to the size of the tract. If the FAR in an office zone is .5 and a particular site in that district is 40,000 square feet, a total of 20,000 square feet of gross building area could be constructed. FARs for suburban office developments typically fall within the .25 to .50 range. In urban centers, FARs may be 2.0 to 10.0 or greater. A pro forma analysis done in the conceptual phase of the design typically points to a minimum amount of square footage required to make the project financially feasible. If that minimum is higher than the maximum FAR, a variance may be needed. As noted earlier, this type of variance may be difficult to secure without showing hardship, change of circumstances or other special reasons. The intensity of the development represents a balance of local planning objectives, project feasibility and surrounding land uses.

Access and Circulation

Access to the office site is a primary design concern and a critical and often controversial part of any office development. Different types of office buildings and different tenants require varying degrees of accessibility and visibility. Proximity to highways and mass transit are important in determining the patterns of commuters and the amount of off-street parking needed. Potential linkages into the existing circulation system of the community are other primary considerations in developing the office site. Access for emergency services, such as fire and police protection, is also important. Pedestrian circulation should be carefully considered in site design. Parking areas, transit stops, open space areas and separate buildings within office parks should be connected with pedestrian paths. Pedestrian paths which connect with existing or planned walkways at the perimeter of the site are helpful in promoting a pedestrian-friendly circulation network and integrating separate sites into a coordinated entity. Connecting walkways to adjacent or on-site retail services may also help to reduce midday traffic generation.

Traffic Generation

Trip generation, and how the cars get to and from the site, can be counted on to provide the most controversy at any hearing for office development. The projected number of trips generated by the office development and the capacity of the surrounding road network must be considered in determining the size of the building, access to and circulation within the site. The number of trips determines the extent and type of improvements, controls, traffic signals, ramps and acceleration and deceleration lanes. The developer must be able to prove to the municipality and perhaps the county or state (in the event the site abuts a county or state road) that additional traffic generated as a result of the office building can be handled by the existing road network or as a result of planned improvements.

Traffic generation is estimated by a traffic engineer and is based on the size of the project (in terms of square feet or number of employees), the location of the office site (urban locations generate fewer automobile trips) and the availability of readily accessible mass transportation as an alternative to automobile usage. The Institute of Transportation Engineers' *Trip Generation* (5th edition, 1991) contains trip generation rates for a variety of office uses, including general office buildings, corporate headquarters buildings, single tenant office buildings, research and development centers, office parks and business parks. This data source for trip rates is frequently used by transportation engineers in projecting peak hour traffic generation for office developments.

Parking

Providing sufficient parking is critical in the marketing of office buildings to prospective tenants and assuring municipal officials that parking will be accommodated on-site. Parking configurations at office developments vary from traditional on-grade off-street parking lots to structured parking or parking decks. Providing some covered parking may be an effective marketing tool, particularly in attracting tenants from older buildings. Suburban municipal ordinances typically require one parking space per 250 square feet of office floor area, although more parking may be needed for medical offices and less may be needed for corporate office space which typically devotes more floor area to each employee than standard office space. As areas become more urban and mass transit is available, parking ratios drop. As little as one space per 1,000 square feet of office floor area may be required in areas well served by mass transportation systems. Low parking ratios are used in many urban areas as disincentives to automobile usage. While parking decks are expensive to construct, they may be the only alternative in a municipality that requires a certain proportion of the site to remain as open space.

Other concerns related to parking areas include adequate lighting and the provision of handicapped parking stalls. Clean air requirements can have a major impact on the entire question of on-site parking. Applicants can be expected to develop and implement transportation strategies designed to discourage peak-hour, single occupancy automobile trips. These strategies could include flexible work times, incentives for car or van pooling and even parking charges.

Sewer and Water Availability

The availability of sewer and water systems to handle the demands of any project is critical in determining both overall feasibility and the size of a project. It may also affect timing and requirements for off-tract contributions to expand or improve sewage facilities. First, the site must be analyzed to determine whether it is located in existing or planned sewer service and water areas. Connecting into existing systems with adequate capacity is the ideal situation. Alternative systems may have to be explored if such a connection is not possible because of inadequate capacity or the absence of any system. On-site septic treatment might be permitted for low-density office uses in exurban areas. On-site treatment facilities such as chemical treatment plants are another possibility.

Where public water is not available, test wells may have to be drilled to determine the feasibility of using well water. Checking with local and regional regulatory agencies early in the conceptual process is critical since some types of alternative systems may not be permitted. In addition, securing permits for sewage treatment and water service systems also consumes time and money. The type of systems used and the timing of hookups can significantly affect the size and phasing of office projects.

Stormwater Management

Stormwater runoff resulting from the addition of impervious surface must be managed through detention or retention basins or recharge areas so as not to increase the volume or rate of flow on a site. A retention basin is used for the permanent storage of runoff, while a detention basin is used for temporary storage. A typical requirement is that the amount and velocity of flow remain the same after development as before. Stormwater detention and retention systems should be designed with safety, aesthetic and maintenance considerations in mind. Minimizing erosion and pollutants in runoff are also key factors. In urban areas, stormwater runoff is generally handled by storm sewer systems.

Landscaping

Landscaping is an important aesthetic feature for office developments and can also serve to connect and integrate various buildings within an office park setting. Maintaining existing vegetation where possible is advantageous to keep stormwater runoff to a minimum. Landscape plans, prepared by a certified landscape architect, are usually submitted as part of the site plan and are reviewed during the approval process.

Environmental Considerations

Environmental considerations have become increasingly important in the site plan approval process. Natural features of the site, including topography, wetlands, flood plains, soil and geologic conditions, endangered or threatened plant and animal species, and coastal areas all require special attention in the design process. Air quality and water quality are coming under increased levels of regulation. The federal Clean Air Act has design implications for large-scale office developments, which may be required to reduce single-occupant automobile commuting.

Regulations on both state and federal levels are in place to protect most of these features and permits are often needed for proposals that violate applicable regulations. For example, wetlands permits are needed to cross wetlands and provide buffers between wetland areas and proposed developments. In addition, historic sites and sites contaminated with hazardous materials (which fall under the Comprehensive Environmental Response, Compensation and Liability Act at the federal level and various statutes at the state level) are also subject to local, state and federal regulations. Knowing which permits are necessary before submitting the actual applications is important. In fact, smart developers will make unofficial contact with the agencies that issue permits to determine their requirements and reflect their comments on the plans.

Emergency Protection

Fire protection is a concern that needs to be incorporated into the layout of the site, and around and within individual office buildings. It is also a feature in marketing the safety of an office building. The primary objective, however, is to meet applicable fire code standards, which in many states are mandated by the state, particularly with respect to protection within individual buildings. Meeting with the local fire and police departments as part of the design phase prior to the actual submission of an application is recommended.

Americans with Disabilities Act (ADA)

A landmark civil rights ordinance, this act requires that all commercial and public accommodations, including stores, hotels, office buildings and transportation facilities, be readily accessible and usable by persons with disabilities. The ADA will have a significant impact on office building design and subsequent planning and zoning activities. For instance, all public meeting places must be accessible. Under ADA, site plans for new office development will be checked for accessibility of public entrances, sidewalks and parking. A building is considered accessible if it has no barriers to individuals with disabilities. ADA compliance can also affect the exterior design of buildings, particularly with regard to doors, ramps and signage. On the interior, the location and configuration of restrooms, hallways, fire exits and doors may have to comply with ADA design requirements. These features of the ADA might make a centralized location for public transportation, signage, barrier-free restrooms and information designed for the use of visually impaired persons necessary in future developments.

The Approval Process

Site plan approval is needed for the design and external layout of an office building. A site plan submission will address those areas required by the municipality in the local site plan ordinance. These include details that relate to access, circulation, parking, lighting, landscaping, utilities, drainage, signage, environmental constraints and building relationships. The submission requirements are often summarized in a checklist which the applicant submits with the plans to demonstrate that all requisite elements have been provided. If specific pieces of information are not provided, waivers may have to be requested. Dimensional or bulk variances are usually specified on the site plans. All requirements of the zone are summarized and the extent of conformance with individual standards is typically presented in a table on the site plan. In some cases, site plan approval is accompanied by applications for subdivision. They are often handled simultaneously.

Site plans are usually required to be on file at a central location (often the municipal building) in order to be available for public inspection. They are also reviewed by municipal officials and technical experts, who submit written reports on their findings. Public hearings are held for all types of approvals, including proposed rezonings and variances as well as proposed site plans. In conjunction with the approval process, the developer will present various studies and expert witnesses to testify in support of certain aspects of the proposal. Obtaining approvals is usually a time-consuming process. The time needed to secure approval can be significantly reduced if: the plan meets all local requirements; no variances are needed; the applicant has reviewed and addressed the comments of local officials, if possible, or is prepared to present evidence as to why they can't be followed; and the presentation is made by experts in a careful and coordinated manner.

Studies undertaken for review by the municipality typically include the following.

- **Fiscal/Economic Impact:** Fiscal impact compares the service costs generated by the development with projected property tax revenues. The consumer expenditure impact of employee income streams (new jobs) on local businesses, including the multiplier effect, can be presented in an economic impact study. These two studies can be used to point out some of the project's major benefits.
- **Rezoning Request:** A rezoning request presents support for a proposed change in zoning by examining the local zone plan, ordinance and comprehensive plan, the surrounding land uses and suitability of the area for development under the existing and requested zoning. The request may also have to include changes in circumstances or testimony to support the change.
- **Variance Request:** A use variance report should satisfy the required proofs that the proposed use advances the purposes of planning, does not significantly impair the intent and purpose of the local zone plan and ordinance, and does not cause any substantial detriment to the public good. The proofs required for the granting of other types of variances are typically not as stringent. Usually, undue hardship or a showing of practical difficulties is required.
- **Traffic Impact:** The most critical study deals with traffic impact. This study should address how many vehicles the project will generate and the capacity of the surrounding network to accommodate the traffic. This study will also determine off-site and off-tract transportation fees and/or improvements.
- **Environmental Assessment:** An environmental assessment report, prepared by an environmental planner, summarizes the potential impacts of the office development on the environment and determines what mitigation is needed. Upon reviewing this assessment, the local board or municipal officials may determine that a comprehensive environmental impact statement is warranted. An EIS can be a major time consuming and expensive study, depending on the type of project proposed.
- **Community Impact:** In addition to all other impacts, municipalities may seek to determine what impact an office development will have on the community. These impacts include (in addition to the ones cited above): police and fire needs, demand on recreation facilities, image of community and impact on way of life.

Overall, the benefits of the office development should be emphasized throughout the approval process in public hearings and submitted studies.

Adding jobs, taxable valuation and amenities to a community are positive impacts. Holding informal public meetings for neighborhood groups or attending local board meetings to keep the lines of communication open with respect to current or future plans can be beneficial in maintaining a positive image in the community.

CONCLUSION

The preconstruction phase of development, spanning the period from the conceptual phase through the approval process, can be quite complicated and time consuming. Careful planning to address all anticipated concerns of the community and coordination with a competent and experienced development team can remove many of the standard roadblocks in the process. A willingness to work with a community and its local boards toward a concept which is beneficial to both the developer and the public is the ultimate goal. The benefits of carefully planned and well-conceived office development can be enjoyed by the public and private sectors alike.

ABOUT THE AUTHORS

Harvey S. Moskowitz, Ph.D., AICP, PP, is president of Moskowitz, Heyer & Gruel, PA, community planning and development consultants, and has been a practicing planner for close to 40 years. He has a Ph.D. from Rutgers University and is the author of many articles, books and publications relating to development and planning. Moskowitz has served as a director of the American Planning Association and as a member of the New Jersey Board of Professional Planners.

Susan G. Blickstein, PP, a licensed professional planner in New Jersey, has a master's degree in city and regional planning from Rutgers University. She works with the firm of Moskowitz, Heyer & Gruel, PA, as a planning consultant involved with the preparation of community master plans and development regulations, and she is a consultant to major office/mixed use developers. Blickstein also lectures in the Department of Urban Studies and Community Health at Rutgers.

Janice E. Talley, PP, is a licensed professional planner in New Jersey and an associate with Moskowitz, Heyer & Gruel, PA, community planning and development consultants. She works as a planning consultant to developers and municipalities in both rural and urban areas in New Jersey. Talley holds a master's degree in city planning from Georgia Institute of Technology. She recently co-authored an article published in the *Journal of Urban Affairs* analyzing the impact of historic district designations on minority commercial areas.

8

COMMERCIAL
PUBLIC-PRIVATE
JOINT VENTURES

by Lynne B. Sagalyn

INTRODUCTION

The 1980s witnessed a proliferation of new-style real estate projects defined by their special public-private status. Variously referred to as partnerships, joint developments, codevelopments or just public-private deals, the common theme was enterprise. Public agencies had gone into the business of real estate in any number of ways—as developers, lenders, equity investors, land lessors and in selected cases, operators.

The diversity of these nonregulatory roles reflected the public's broad agenda for development and a freedom to experiment with new ways of achieving those goals. It also reflected the fiscal tenor of the times. With the shutdown of the federal urban renewal program in 1974 and the cutback of urban categorical aid programs in the early 1980s, local governments had to innovate and improvise in order to meet their city planning and economic development objectives. At the same time, pressures at home pushed them to search for new sources of funds after a rash of tax-cutting referenda (beginning in 1978 with California's Proposition 13) made raising taxes or going to the voters for approval of new bond issues a chancy political call.

In that context, commercial real estate development became a most strategic resource with which to prime the private-investment pump, capture new sources of long-term public revenue in addition to property taxes, finance needed infrastructure and public amenities, generate jobs, revitalize downtown business districts or recast the uses of dormant industrial waterfronts. To many public officials, especially those in cities striving for a comeback, office development was the engine driving investment growth and became the centerpiece for attracting private capital.

The broad definition accorded "public-purpose" projects provided a rationale for every type of public agency to become involved in commercial real estate development: municipal real-property departments, redevelopment authorities, transit agencies, county governments, port authorities, school districts, quasi-public development corporations, even the U.S. General Services Administration, the U.S. Navy and the U.S. Postal Service. The task for some was to initiate development projects, using as incentives the established tools and techniques of public finance that had evolved since the 1950s in cities' quest to redevelop their downtowns.

For those in strong real estate markets, the situation presented an opportunity to use publicly owned land in a new way, as a capital resource for financial gain and social benefit. While the level of financial returns expected from private development on these lands rarely was perceived as the solution for balancing distressed budgets, long-term revenue streams from commercial projects could provide some margin of discretionary spending, especially for the special-purpose, quasi-governmental agencies which typically acted as public developers on the behalf of cities.

Because the joint-venture concept is so malleable and the public's goals quite broad, the "partnership" characterization, mistakenly, has come to encompass nearly any type of informal public-private relationship, whether or not it involves the public in risk-taking typical of development projects. For the purposes of this discussion, public-private joint ventures will be defined as those in which a public entity has put resources such as land or money at risk through a formal, legally binding agreement and, as a result, is actively involved in the development, construction, financing or operation of a privately owned project as a decision-making partner.

The objective of this chapter is to present an overview of public-private development ventures as they evolved in the 1980s. It focuses on the structures and forms of public participation with particular emphasis on the financial and political factors which shaped cities' decisions to enter into business alliances with developers. The intent is to place the large and varied repertoire of financial techniques used to structure public-private ventures in context by relating them to:

1. The strategic objectives sought by public officials,
2. The practical problems of joint development, and
3. The institutional arrangements for implementing these projects.

CHANGING RATIONALES AND ROLES

Public-private partnerships have a long and varied history as a mode of governmental operation in the United States. In the field of public works, they have been the rule rather than the exception, though the reasons for adopting the public-private format have varied over time. In the 19th century, partnerships resulted from the pragmatic response of state and local governments to promotional ambitions and needs in their economies. They took several forms: land grants, charters and franchises to private companies; investments in privately held stock companies; and financing for canals and other internal improvements, in addition to subsidies and other forms of assistance designed to stimulate economic development.

In their next phase, from the second half of that century through the early 20th, public-private arrangements in local economies resulted from the demands of big-city growth which imposed new requirements on local governments for the provision of water and sewage systems, subways, bridges and highways. Though initiated by private enterprise, these infrastructure systems called for large public capital investments which often were beyond private companies' means (or their willingness to bear the risk entailed); the consequent response of government was some form of mixed enterprise or responsibility for implementation.[1]

The aggressive expansion of governmental assistance for economic development characteristic of the 19th century gave way before the end of that period to dramatically curtailed public action, and, in some cases, to explicit prohibitions on the lending of public credit for private enterprise. Following the economic depression of the 1930s, these legal constraints were increasingly relaxed or avoided, the result of which was a substantial revival of publicly assisted economic-development activity.[2]

With the passage of the federal urban renewal program in 1949, public-private relations in the field of real estate similarly entered a new phase. Under this program, which funded the physical clearance of slums and land assemblage for the rebuilding of downtowns, cities worked with developers at arm's-length as required by federal guidelines. After shut-down of the program in 1974, cities quickly dropped the cumbersome federal regulations and embraced a new strategy that brought them into face-to-face negotiations with developers. After a long tenure as regulators and donors, cities became dealmakers and co-investors in private development projects.[3]

---

[1] See Ann Durkin Keating, "Public-Private Partnerships in Public Works: A Bibliographic Essay," in *Essays in Public Works History* 16(December 1989), pp. 78-108; Carter Goodrich, "American Development Policy: The Case of Internal Improvements," *The Journal of Economic History* XVI(December 1956), pp. 449-460; Joel A. Tarr, "The Evolution of the Urban Infrastructure," in *Perspectives on Urban Infrastructure*, ed. Royce Hanson (Washington, D.C.: National Academy Press, 1984), pp. 4-60.

[2] See Martin E. Gold, "Economic Development Projects: A Perspective," *The Urban Lawyer* 1(Spring 1987) pp. 199-215.

[3] Bernard J. Frieden and Lynne B. Sagalyn, *Downtown, Inc.: How America Rebuilds Cities* (Cambridge, Mass.: MIT Press, 1989).

This change in roles was one of substance as well as style. In their agreements with private developers, public officials made commitments that went beyond traditional public works. They promised to build parking garages, skyways, parks, even department stores—as publicly owned elements of private projects. The new role marked a change in expectations about the public sector's separateness from the private sector. The federal rules of urban renewal had prohibited the physical integration of publicly funded improvements with privately owned structures because such linkages threatened to breach the fiscal integrity of public support. Public subsidies had been kept separate from private ownership through disposition policies which favored the sale rather than the leasing of land. With the cutback of federal support, however, the sharp dichotomy between public and private activities gradually eroded, and pragmatism, not prescribed rules, began to shape city development practice.

The new style of practice placed a high premium on public entrepreneurship and private market feasibility. Cities custom-tailored financial assistance to fit local project needs. Loans replaced grants as the way to deliver subsidies, with public dollars stretched farther through cost-sharing arrangements with developers. And in bargaining with developers, public officials negotiated direct financial stakes in a project in the form of profit-sharing arrangements. For select public-private projects, cities had become risk-takers.[4]

These new strategies proved to be workable and powerful alternatives to direct federal aid for city development, so much so that they led the way for the most current phase of joint enterprise—strategic development of publicly owned land for public gain. With the powerful growth of investment in downtowns in the early 1980s, big cities like Boston, Los Angeles, San Francisco and New York—which once had to buy developer participation in revitalization projects with deep subsidies—began to sell development opportunities, rights to build hedged with complex responsibilities to produce and obligations to perform. These cities negotiated with developers for a sophisticated package of returns which included inflation-protected revenue streams, profit-sharing dollars and public improvements, as well as commitments for job-training programs and minority hiring.

The economic rationale for this form of public development— tied as it was to strong real estate markets—was not confined to big cities where high-density, high-value land markets stimulated thoughts of significant gains for public treasuries. Some suburban and county governments were early entrants into this business, as were transit operators and port

---

[4] See Lynne B. Sagalyn, "Explaining the Improbable: Local Redevelopment in the Wake of Federal Cutbacks," *Journal of the American Planning Association* 56(Autumn 1990), pp. 429-441.

authorities.[5] In both locales, the logic of aggressive public action was often irresistible because it offered a timely means of tapping real estate development to finance targeted capital investments or boost fiscal capacity in the operating budget. Based on their proprietary interests (as opposed to their regulatory powers), local governments moved with the market pendulum from giving financial assistance to capturing the benefits of rising land values.

STRATEGIES AND STRUCTURES FOR PUBLIC-SECTOR PARTICIPATION

The ways in which government intervenes in real estate markets to influence private investment decisions cover a wide spectrum of policy approaches, from relatively passive policies to aggressive public behaviors. At the passive end of the continuum are carrot-oriented regulatory positions (incentive zoning and transfer of development rights) and programmatic assistance (tax abatements) through which local government provides noncash subsidies targeted to attract certain types of private investment or offers market-based incentives to stimulate the provision of desired public amenities in private developments. In both instances, implementation is uniform, the benefits of public assistance available to all who meet qualifying conditions on an entitlement.[6]

At the other end of the continuum (the focus of this discussion) are aggressive strategies of public intervention which rely upon bargaining and custom-tailored negotiations with private firms over the terms and conditions of development. Selective processes of competition rather than prescribed incentives determine access to development opportunities by private firms. Public-private ventures, by definition, are singular policy

---

[5] For example, as early as 1976, the City of Fairfield (California) participated in a private regional mall project, netting in excess of $1 million above its land acquisition costs and a share in the center's annual net cash flow as well as any future refinancing or sale transaction. The Fairfax (Virginia) County Board of Supervisors in 1987 approved a controversial deal with a private development partnership designed to deliver—at no cash outlay to the taxpayers—a new $83.4 million government center on 100 acres of existing county land.

[6] See Jerold S. Kayden, *Incentive Zoning in New York City: A Cost-Benefit Analysis*, Land Policy Roundtable Policy Analysis Series Number 201, Lincoln Institute of Land Policy, 1978; Judith Getzels and Martin Jaffee with Brian W. Blaesser and Robert F. Brown, *Zoning Bonuses in Central Cities*, American Planning Association Planning Advisory Service, Report Number 410; Terry Jill Lassar, *Carrots & Sticks: New Zoning Downtown* (Washington, D.C.: Urban Land Institute, 1989); on tax abatements, see R. Andrew Parker, "Local Tax Subsidies as a Stimulus for Development: Are They Cost-Effective? Are They Equitable?" *City Almanac* 16(February-April 1982), pp. 8-15; Daniel R. Mandleker, Gary Feder, and Margaret P. Collins, *Reviving Cities with Tax Abatement* (New Brunswick, Rutgers University, Center for Urban Policy Research, 1980).

interventions. Comparisons across projects and cities do, however, reveal commonalities in the public sector's strategies and ways of organizing joint ventures as well as financial principles underlying its deals with private developers.

Strategic Decisions

In implementing a joint venture, a public entity faces five fundamental tasks:

1. Selection of a developer
2. Determination of the terms and conditions of the development opportunity
3. Negotiation of a disposition and development agreement
4. Resolution of problems and conflicts which inevitably arise throughout the development process
5. Monitoring of performance responsibilities and payments of project revenues due over the life of the agreement[7]

From a strategic perspective, some of the decisions a city must make in the early stages of planning a joint venture are key, as these decisions subsequently come to shape both the agenda for negotiations and the tools available for managing the joint-development project.

Selection of a Developer

One such decision concerns the process for selecting a developer. The choice is typically between an auction-type price competition or a development-prospectus competition through which a parcel is offered for disposition and a developer selected on the basis of comprehensive responses to a request for development qualifications (RFQ) or a request for developer proposals (RFP). For nearly all public-private joint ventures, the RFQ/RFP approach has been the preferred option over the auction bid approach.[8] Selection of a developer based primarily upon general qualifications (RFQ) without a subsequent second-stage submission of competitive development proposals (RFP), as a rule, has not been sufficiently effective. Not only does it provide too little information about the developer's plans for the site, it quickly eliminates the public sector's options and weakens its position in the negotiations over program and business terms which follow.

---

[7] For a detailed discussion of the steps involved in joint development, see Robert Witherspoon, "Codevelopment: City Rebuilding by Business and Government," Development Component Series (Washington, D.C.: Urban Land Institute, 1982); also *Downtown Development Handbook* (Washington, D.C.: Urban Land Institute, 1980), pp. 149-182 in particular.

The task of developing the RFP is formative; it sets the stage for future implementation of the project. Whether the RFP is short and open-ended or long and detailed regarding a project's land uses, design guidelines and business terms, development of the RFP requires the public entity to assess its specific objectives for the project with an eye on the following:

1. Defining broadly the character of the private development
2. Identifying public roles and types of assistance available
3. Structuring a set of project-specific planning conditions and business points to which developers must respond
4. Providing an orderly and clearly understood procedure for evaluation of proposals

The level of specificity for each of these elements is often a matter of market conditions. For example, when the market is weak and the site untested, attracting the attention of qualified developers may require a detailed prospectus and thorough feasibility study (a priori); conversely, when the market is strong, less documentation may be needed but correspondingly more attention should be paid to other matters, in particular, detailing terms and conditions for the contemplated business deal. Differences in market dynamics, site characteristics, the nature of public objectives for a project and the legal alternatives available for designating developers all factor into this decision and make generalizations about the "best" approach inappropriate.[9]

Lease versus Sale Disposition

When land for the public-private venture is publicly owned, a second key strategic decision is the choice of whether to sell or lease the parcel. Sale disposition can generate substantial revenues up-front for use in other public projects; it eliminates the risk of future non-payment;[10] and under

---

[8] Empirical studies of auction dispositions for housing in Boston and New York revealed critical limitations—low levels of rehabilitation investment and ultimate property-tax recidivism. In both cities, the evaluations led to new disposition policies which eliminated the highest bidder standard and substituted negotiated sales procedures and criteria that permitted the city to maximize the noncash public benefits from development or link site usage to other city-planning objectives. While the disposition of city property for housing raises a distinct set of policy issues, cities perceive a common need for affirmative control to maximize public interests when key priorities are at stake. See Christine A. Flynn and Lawrence P. Goldman, *New York's Largest Landowner: The City as Owner, Planner, and Marketer of Real Estate*, Report for The Fund for the City of New York, 1980; H. James Brown and Christopher E. Herbert, "Local Government Real Estate Asset Management," unpublished report for Lincoln Institute for Land Policy Seminar, September 1989.

[9] See Witherspoon, "Codevelopment," p. 18.

[10] Alternatively with a lease, the infusion of cash can be duplicated with prepayment of rent and the risk of nonpayment can be nearly eliminated with the purchase of a riskless government security, as was the case for Copley Place, a large-scale, mixed-use project in Boston.

certain conditions it promises higher dollars for the public treasury than lease arrangements. In terms of controlling land use, restrictive covenants can be attached to property deeds as a condition of sale as was done under urban-renewal dispositions. As an instrument for managing public-private development, however, leasing affords cities many more strategic advantages.

First, because the lease contract is such a flexible vehicle, it readily accommodates divergent interests. By tying the price and conditions of possession to specific responsibilities and standards of performance, cities can design agreements which match developers' financial needs with their own diverse, politically driven needs. Other disposition approaches cannot always package the public agenda—inflation-protected revenues and profit participations; control over the extent and timing of development; specifications for quality design, public amenities, open space, housing uses; and hiring targets for local residents and minorities—in a single transaction.

Second, through lease dispositions, cities can gain access to decisions typically left to developers and maintain control over the private provision of public amenities in, for example, large-scale mixed-use projects. Such control gives cities additional levers for managing the risks of public-private development, restrictive covenants having proven to be notoriously difficult to enforce. Exercising affirmative control in this way, cities link their business interests (as land proprietors) with their planning objectives (as regulators);[11] in this there are political benefits as well as financial gains.

Politically, leasing is an institutional arrangement for capturing new long-term revenues whose spending can be directed through channels of decision-making outside municipal budget processes.[12] Boston's Redevelopment Authority (BRA), the city's most independent line agency, is an illustrative case. Capitalizing on the downtown building boom which began in the early 1980s, the BRA chose to lease its large commercial-development sites, under financial terms designed to augment its already formidable planning responsibilities and political powers. In the case of Rowes Wharf, a mixed-use development on one of the last remaining waterfront sites downtown, the RFP specified the following firm financial parameters:

---

[11] Whether this "two-hat" problem creates a conflict of interest is the topic of a collection of articles in Terry Jill Lassar, *City Deal Making* (Washington, D.C.: Urban Land Institute, 1990).

[12] See Lynne B. Sagalyn, "Leasing: The Strategic Option," The Lincoln Institute for Land Policy and A. Alfred Taubman Center for State and Local Government, Harvard University, Working Paper (forthcoming). As a practical matter, leasing is a "prime-sites-only" strategy. For the large inventory of surplus sites—functionally obsolete school buildings and fire stations, small and odd-sized pieces of land in out-of-the-way places, and abandoned utility easements—dispositions typically are handled more efficiently by a sale.

Boston's Redevelopment Authority chose to lease Rowes Wharf and other large commercial development sites under financial provisions that enabled the agency to become fiscally independent of City Hall. *(Photo by Nick Wheeler, Wheeler Photographics. Courtesy of Skidmore, Owings and Merrill)*

1. A land lease, with no subordination of the BRA's fee interest or annual lease payment
2. Minimum base rents of not less than $600,000 for the residential portion of the site, $700,000 for the commercial portion
3. Rent escalations on terms competitive with the private market
4. For the commercial portion, additional percentage rent from refinancing or sales transactions
5. An "as-is" disposition in which the city would incur no expenses in development for the parcel and give no tax abatements[13]

---

[13] In terms of uses, the proposal requested residential condominiums (approximately 425,000 square feet) and office and retail space (approximately 240,000 square feet), a boat terminal, open space along the water edge reserved for pedestrian, water-related and boat terminal uses, and parking below grade; overall gross FAR was not to exceed 4, or 665,600 square feet. Boston Redevelopment Authority, *Design and Development Guidelines: Rowes/Fosters Wharf*, 1982. See also Stephen P. Hayes, "Converting Public Property into Public Policy: The Disposition of Government Real Estate by the Boston Redevelopment Authority in the 1980s," thesis for a Master of Science in Real Estate Development, MIT, September 1991.

By the late 1980s, growing revenue streams from this and other dispositions had made the agency fiscally independent of City Hall.[14]

For public agencies, the experience of joint-venture development in the 1980s validated the concept's strategic appeal: Projects got built in less time than under the earlier, cumbersome urban-renewal procedures which required arm's-length relations between public agencies and private developers. Further, having a say in decision-making throughout the development process proved to be an effective (if trying) way to manage the implementation of complex projects. The process of negotiating for a package of social as well as financial benefits also afforded city officials a way to meet their political needs. The agreements, however, were highly complicated transactions.[15] And as a practical matter, the time, expense and expertise required of the public sector to negotiate and implement public-private projects (whether through lease or sale dispositions) precluded their widespread or uniform use.

Offering—A Development Opportunity

More than simply land per se, what cities are selling (and developers buying) is a development opportunity—rights to build hedged with complex obligations to perform and responsibilities to produce. In concept, this development opportunity is similar to the option commonly used in private land transactions, the critical difference being one of mandated performance.

Meeting the terms of the disposition and development agreement (DDA) requires developers to make up-front payments for land or infrastructure improvements and to follow through with affirmative behavior including nonmarket actions such as the construction of housing simultaneously with office development. While some flexibility is built into the DDA's performance schedules, generally the agreement is not so elastic that developers can buy a market position years in advance and wait until the time is right to build. Also, it is standard practice for cities to protect their interests by incorporating anti-speculative covenants and conditions limiting transfer by a designated developer.

The terms and conditions that make up the "pricing" of this development opportunity are complex, in no small part because planning

---

[14] The majority of lease-revenue dollars came from just three large-scale projects: Charlestown Navy Yard, Marketplace Center, and Rowes Wharf. See Sagalyn, "Leasing: The Strategic Option."

[15] See Robert H. Frelich, "Public/Private Partnerships in Large-Scale Development Projects," in *Managing Development Through Public/Private Negotiations*, eds., Rachelle L. Levitt and John J. Kirlin (Washington, D.C.: Urban Land Institute, 1985), pp. 15-21 at p. 20 for a brief statement of the types of legal considerations to be included in a partnership agreement.

ambitions and political considerations drive city officials to achieve multiple objectives. In the 1980s, cities used their proprietary, financial interests in land to extract three distinct types of benefits:

1. Land values were transformed into long-term revenue streams
2. The dollar worth of land was traded for in-kind capital contributions in the form of developer-provided infrastructure, open space, or public amenities
3. The rights to develop were phased and linked to commitments to build housing, restore historically sensitive structures, or hire city residents.

In this regard, the agenda cities have had for large-scale public-private projects is different and broader than those of specialized port authorities or quasi-autonomous transit agencies, which typically manage their real estate assets with an eye on maximum financial returns.

A case in point is Los Angeles' disposition of the land underlying California Center. The 8.75-acre site was the only big parcel of land left in downtown when in 1979 the Community Redevelopment Agency solicited development proposals. After two moribund decades, the market in downtown L.A. was hot, and the agency was intent upon capturing the benefits of its landowner position by offering the parcel on a long-term lease basis.

The RFP called for a mixed-use project of 3.5 to 4.4 million square feet with a substantial (30%) allocation to housing uses; a major public-benefits package including a new, free-standing structure for the Los Angeles Museum of Modern Art; and an adjacent 1.5-acre central park, as well as other pedestrian open spaces to be provided, owned and maintained by the developer. These "products" were not substitutes for direct financial returns—which the RFP made clear should reflect prevailing market practices and include provisions for inflation-protected rents, escalations pegged to rising property values and profit-sharing participations. Rather, they were linked elements which would be priced as part of the development opportunity.

In weak real estate markets where public-private development initiatives aim to catalyze additional private investment, the public agenda is no less ambitious. What differs are the terms and conditions of the public's financial involvement, with assistance more than benefit-capture as the overriding force shaping the price structure of a public-private deal.

Financial Assistance

After the federal-aid cutbacks, cities had fewer direct grant dollars from Washington with which to fund their projects, but they still had wide recourse to indirect federal subsidies through the issuance of tax-exempt bonds until the 1986 Tax Reform Act curtailed their use for private-purpose projects.[16] While pushed to rely heavily upon local resources, cities have a long list of incentive tools from which to fashion their assistance packages: tax-increment financing, special assessment districts, tax abatements, dedication of sales or special-purpose taxes, eminent domain, land write-downs, land swaps, land leases, second-mortgage financing, loan guarantees, loan subsidies, capital improvements and leases for office space, as well as value-creating tradeoffs based on zoning bonuses.[17]

Packaging assistance is pragmatic. The objective is to create combinations of incentives that make a desirable real estate investment financially feasible for both the public and the private participants. Feasibility here, by definition of the public's involvement, means overcoming serious obstacles and problems—land assembly, negative neighborhood externalities, excessive or premium costs, heavy up-front capital investments—that inhibit private development, renovation or redevelopment. Through diverse and numerous means, the public-assistance package reconfigures the risk/ return relationship of private investment by following one or more of these financial tactics: reducing capital costs, absorbing the demands for new infrastructure, lowering operating costs or reducing debt-service burdens.

Because service-sector employment has been the engine of economic growth in the 1980s, office development has been seen by public officials as market-driven, in need of little, if any, aid. There are important exceptions to this generalization, notably policy initiatives aimed at shifting the location of new development within a city. New York's "Outer Borough" strategy in the early 1980s was designed to increase the attractiveness of development sites outside Manhattan (and keep back-office employment from migrating across the river to New Jersey). Under this policy umbrella, the city and state governments provided an extensive package of financial incentives—as-of-right tax abatements and moving allowances, waivers of occupancy taxes, cut-rate electricity and selective sales tax exemptions—for the MetroTech project in Brooklyn, an 8.1 million square foot, 16-acre complex of nine office buildings and two academic buildings. Similarly, it supplied incentive packages to other office-based projects in Brooklyn, Queens, the Bronx and Staten Island.[18] Another indirect rationale for

---

[16] See John E. Petersen and Cathie G. Eitelberg, "The Tax Reform Act of 1986: Major Provisions Affecting the Tax-Exempt Securities Market," A Special Bulletin of the Government Finance Officers Association, Washington, D.C., 1986.

[17] For a detailed discussion of individual public financing tools, see Gary E. Stout and Joseph E. Vitt, "Public Incentives and Financing Techniques for Codevelopment," Urban Land Institute Development Component Series, 1982.

[18] See Thomas J. Lueck, "'Other Borough' Strategy Bucks Difficult Times," *New York Times*, Real Estate Section, March 10, 1991, p. 1; Forest City Ratner Companies, *Metro Tech Center* (promotional brochure); for a critical evaluation of the strategy's problems, see N. David Milder, *Expediting Development Projects in the Outer Borough Downtowns*, a report of the Regional Plan Association, New York, March 1988; New York City Public Development Corporation, Fact Sheets.

assisting office development comes from its role as the most stable program element of mixed-use projects, whose higher-risk retail, hotel or residential components are often not feasible without some form of public financial support.

Though the terms and conditions of public aid are custom-tailored to meet the needs of individual projects, in their business deals with developers local governments structure assistance within the framework of several general policy principles. First, public aid should be delivered through cost-sharing mechanisms. Second, investment of public dollars requires a return for risk-taking apart from increased collections of property taxes through some form of loan recapture or profit participation in future project revenues.[19] Third, the timing and conditions of public commitments should be linked to specific private obligations and responsibilities to perform. In each instance, the public sector seeks to create binding ties, mutually dependent commitments and business interests which establish incentives for the completion of an economically viable project. Big up-front subsidies can carry risky projects through the first uncertain years, but they cannot turn weak projects into successes. Beyond the task of making development feasible, the hard art of crafting public-private deals is finding ways to assure the efficacy of public investment in joint-development ventures.[20]

OPPORTUNITIES AND EXPECTATIONS IN THE PRIVATE SECTOR

Public-private development remains an area of opportunity for private developers. While some of the downtown "mega-projects" of the 1980s are not feasible in the depressed office market of the 1990s, publicly sponsored projects are still moving off the drawing boards into construction. Also, a large inventory of publicly owned sites exists for smaller projects— infill, residential and neighborhood commercial development in particular— according to an experienced advisor to local governments. "The assemblages are occasionally large and well located. Infrastructure is often

---

[19] Lynne B. Sagalyn, "Public Profit Sharing: Symbol or Substance?" in *City Deal Making*, edited by Terry J. Lassar (Washington, D.C.: Urban Land Institute, 1990), pp. 139-153.

[20] For practical insights, see Robert Wetmore and Chris Klinger, "Land Leases: More than Rent Schedules," *Urban Land* 59(June 1990), pp. 6-9; Robert Wetmore, "Lessor Beware! A Land Lease is Usually a Partnership," *Urban Land* 47(October 1988), pp. 20-23; David E. Dowall, "Applying Real Estate Financial Analysis to Planning and Development Control," *American Planning Association Journal* 51(Winter 1985), pp. 84-94; Lynne B. Sagalyn, "Measuring Financial Returns When The City Acts As An Investor: Boston and Faneuil Hall Marketplace," Real Estate Issues 24(Fall/Winter 1989), pp. 7-15.

already in place. And if the offering agency has a realistic view of the market, the price may be right."[21]

These offerings stem from enduring economic and political rationales. Whether pursuing long-term objectives to manage public land assets strategically for financial gain, or trying to prime the local economy by playing a counter-cyclic role, or seeking redevelopment of neighborhood areas, landowning government agencies aim to use their property assets to carry out an agenda. To do so, they seek development partners who will supply expertise and private investment capital.

Strategic Commitments

Public-private development projects require an extraordinary amount of staying power from private developers. Described as "high-risk" and "not for the timid," the "game" entails long-term commitments of time, energy and money in anticipation of future payoffs—profits, enhanced market position, prestige—which remain uncertain. Furthermore, because the public agenda commonly includes design excellence, public access and other social goods, the implementation process is lengthy. The roles played by the public sector in initiating these projects, brokering regulatory approvals, shepherding environmental-impact and community-review processes and providing financial-aid packages ease the way through the inevitable hurdles these projects encounter. The complexity of these joint ventures, however, creates its own burden; it is a special risk inherent in the development opportunity.

The lengthy development process means that even the most promising of projects can get caught in a cyclical downturn after hundreds of thousands of up-front dollars have been spent. Alongside the roster of success stories is a graveyard of stalled and aborted projects waiting for the next cycle. In one notable case, New York officials and the developers of the prized South Ferry site agreed to kill the "unrealized six-year-old project which was meant to embellish the harbor-front skyway with a new pinnacle, rejuvenate lower Manhattan's ferry terminals and add a substantial cultural dimension to downtown life." More than just a new architectural trophy, the project was expected to deliver substantial public amenities and generate $375 million (net present value) for the city. The decisive factor: In a depressed office market, no major tenant commitments could be lined up.[22]

If risky and complex public-private projects are not sure winners, they are often unique deals. The opportunity of building on a large site—often unique because of its prime downtown location near large concentrations of

---

[21] Robert Wetmore, "Bidding for Public Property: Guidelines for Developers," *Urban Land* 50(May 1991), p. 8.

service-sector employment or on the waterfront—represents a singular opportunity to buy a long-term market position. This was especially so for out-of-town developers in the 1980s seeking to establish a market presence; they accounted for a highly visible proportion of RFQ/RFP submissions on major public-private projects across the nation.

One way to do this was to take on difficult "mega-projects" that could not be duplicated, at least in the near term—high-stakes projects made more feasible because they were supported by special financial incentives and positioned to go through the development process with a public partner. Developers did not see these projects as being competition-proof; rather what they might have was a quasi-monopoly in a locational sub-market for a substantial period of time. The play entailed great uncertainty, but therein lay the opportunity for above-average returns and, hence, the rationale for strategic commitments of private capital.

Another strategic attraction of public-private development resides in the competitive advantage of building high-density projects at transit stations, in the suburbs as well as downtown. This is especially the case along expanding proven systems with extensive existing or committed networks, such as those in Washington, D.C., Toronto, Atlanta and Miami. The physical link between office buildings and rail lines translates into potentially higher absorption and rental rates, reduced parking requirements and long-term value appreciation. In turn, station location and design determine critical real estate elements of a project such as retail frontage, rentable retail space, pedestrian traffic, internal project circulation and project cost. Transit-related development imposes construction requirements of greater cost and complexity than would be found in other projects, including the provision of an envelope for access before the actual construction of the building, structural spanning and substantial public access/easement requirements. And as with other public-private projects, it carries its own special risk: "[I]t may be many years before the [transit] system reaches its full potential since this type of development often involves uncertain timing and financial commitments for extensions and new lines before the benefits of an integrated system are fully achieved."[23]

[22] David W. Dunlap, "New York City Scraps Plans for South Ferry Office Plaza," *New York Times*, January 4, 1991, p. B2; New York City Public Development Corporation, Fact Sheet for South Ferry Plaza, January 1990. The list of big-city public-private projects stalled out by 1990 includes: in New York, Riverwalk, Times Square Redevelopment, Columbus Circle Coliseum site, Renaissance Plaza; in San Francisco, Yerba Buena Gardens; in Boston, Commonwealth Center, Boston Crossing, One Lincoln Street, and the South Station air-rights development.

[23] Michael C. Clark, "Risk and Reward: The Developer's View," in *ULI/UMTA Policy Forum on Joint Development of Rail Transit Facilities* (Washington, D.C.: Urban Land Institute, 1986), pp. 90-93, at p. 92. For case studies of several projects, see *Joint Development: Making the Real Estate-Transit Connection* (Washington, D.C.: Urban Land Institute, 1979); and Jeffrey R. Algatt and Ann Lenney, "One Reading Center, Philadelphia: Playing the High-Risk Development Game," *Urban Land* 44(January 1985), pp. 8-10.

More so than with other types of development, the risks of public-private development are political. Gauging the level of political commitment to carry through with a project and government's financial and personnel ability to deliver on agreements permeates a developer's assessment of project feasibility. The joint-venture process is neither inexpensive nor painless. With the cost of submitting a response to an RFP at $50,000 upwards to several hundred thousand dollars, the cost of buying into a development opportunity represents only the first of many more hard-dollar commitments before construction can begin. Costs rapidly escalate from delays (both anticipated and unanticipated) during the early planning stages of a joint-venture project, some of which result from the action or inaction of government officials and agencies.

Shared Decision-Making

The public interests at stake in joint-venture projects draw governments into the management of development and details of decision-making typically left to the private sector. As cities share more of the risk with their elaborate aid packages, they ask for more control. When they take charge of developing parts of a project, as was the case for the mixed-use Town Center project where the City of St. Paul built a park on the third level of the retail mall, shared control is the most practical way to proceed. While it was possible to settle some of the big issues in advance (as the public authority in charge of the project tried to do in its marathon negotiations), there was no way to anticipate all the details far in advance of actual work. Further, the demands of mutually dependent construction schedules overlapping in time and space ruled out the hands-off control style of urban renewal. For the city to cut a straightforward deal, prepare and transfer the property and then merely monitor the developer's performance until the project was done according to plan would have been out of the question. The deal in St. Paul was an implied agreement to share both design and management decisions throughout the development period and to cope with problems by renegotiating earlier understandings if necessary. Frequent trips back to the bargaining table were required to get the project over unexpected obstacles.[24]

The ground lease form of property disposition similarly creates an ongoing business relationship. For the developer, leasing minimizes the up-front capital investments and makes more efficient use of taxable deductions. For the government agency, retaining ownership of the land allows the public to benefit directly from the fiscal returns of urban growth

---

[24] For a more detailed discussion of this and other cases, see Frieden and Sagalyn, *Downtown, Inc.*, pp. 140-142.

through lease payments and percentage rents and then, at the end of the lease term, to capture the residual value of the built improvements. Alongside these mutual benefits, however, lies the potential for conflict and tough lease negotiations, especially if the RFP does not include a pattern lease document setting out the agency's terms and conditions which would affect the developer's bid.

Structuring a ground lease which is acceptable to a long-term lender is the developer's major concern. In strong markets, government often will not subordinate the land and, for reasons of both business and policy, officials want participation in project revenues above a base fixed rent. To control its exposure to the political as well as to the business risks of having a proprietary interest in a private investment, the public sector seeks tight lease conditions and, through participation formulas, protection against charges that the developer is earning a "windfall." Both positions present problems to institutional lenders, who seek protection from the potential loss of control through foreclosure by the government fee owner.[25] Negotiating solutions involves sharing information that is normally kept private as the process draws the public agency into the details of financing arrangements and opens the door to the developer's books. As each side tries to find compromises that meet the needs of their different constituencies, there is room to maneuver, but the formal agreements that are struck are lifelong. Expecting to revamp the signed lease at a later date is not a feasible position for either a developer or a government agency.

The practical problems of implementing public-private development preclude anything but an active, if not aggressive, role in project decision-making for the public sector. Attempting to cover up-front all conditions that might arise in the course of development would not only extend the process interminably, it would be unrealistic. Reconciling initial differences, finding efficient cost-sharing arrangements, coordinating public and private construction schedules, recasting the deal when crisis threatens the project and managing the process within the bright light of public review calls for flexibility in response to new economic and political events that continually confront complex public-private projects. For developers, participation in the venture means making changes in their normal manner of doing business—giving up degrees of freedom—in order to adjust to the demands of working with a partner who is politically accountable.

---

[25] In the case of percentage rent, lenders hesitate because they fear the reduction in the amount of income to be capitalized when a large percentage of the income stream is committed to a ground lessor. In the event of foreclosure, the valuation impact would be substantial unless the lessor had agreed to subordinate the percentage provision in the lease. For a detailed case discussion (1101 Connecticut Avenue, Washington, D.C.) of these issues, see *Joint Development*, pp. 76-81.

CONCLUSION

The turn to public-private ventures in real estate came from local governments' efforts to manage the development process with greater control than that afforded by arm's-length relations or regulatory strategies. Its effectiveness has made it a legitimate strategy for stimulating local economic development, implementing complex redevelopment projects and financing selected items of capital infrastructure. City governments, public authorities and other special-purpose agencies have strong incentives to continue along this course with developers who now better understand, from observation and experience, how to play by the new rules.

Public-private development agreements are complex. They reflect many tradeoffs made during negotiations in which the public's broad agenda gets reconciled with its limited resources and the demands of private investment. Similarly, the roles adopted by the public sector—broker, facilitator, lessor, builder, lender, investor—reflect the multi-faceted nature of the problems (bureaucratic, financial, political) to be addressed as well as the conditions in local real estate markets at the time those roles become defined.

Because they can be molded to fit the particular situation at hand, public-private ventures have become a preferred vehicle by which cities (1) deal with the feasibility problem of excessive cost and financial risk which inhibits private investment in areas of public priority; (2) overcome problems of implementation common to the command-and-control strategy of urban renewal which stymied redevelopment efforts throughout the 1960s and 1970s; and (3) benefit financially from their proprietary interests in publicly owned land. In each instance, the public-private alliance affords government entities flexibility in seeking a combination of fiscal returns (increased property-tax assessments, lease-revenue streams, profit-sharing dollars) and public goods (design amenities, infrastructure improvements, resident job-hiring). If this is an impressive set of benefits, the challenge of implementation, in turn, commands the unusual combination of powerful motivation and modest expectations.

ABOUT THE AUTHOR

Lynne B. Sagalyn, CRE, Ph.D., is a professor in the finance division of Columbia University's Graduate School of Business and is coordinator of its real estate program. She was previously on the faculty of the Department of Urban Studies and Planning at MIT. A frequent author, her most recent book is *Downtown, Inc.: How America Rebuilds Cities.* She is a member of the Urban Land Institute, the Counselors of Real Estate and the American Real Estate and Urban Economic Association. Sagalyn received her Ph.D. from MIT and a Master of City and Regional Planning from Rutgers University.

PART III

OFFICE MARKET SPACE ANALYSIS

9

CYCLES IN OFFICE
SPACE MARKETS

by Anthony Downs

INTRODUCTION

Activity in office space markets moves in a cyclical manner. This chapter examines why this is so and what forms such cycles take. It first examines recent movements in total United States office construction. Next, it analyzes forces influencing the demand side of the market, then those influencing the supply side. Finally, it examines how the forces influencing supply and demand interact to produce a three-phase office development cycle.

ACTIVITY LEVELS IN U.S. OFFICE SPACE MARKETS

Activities within office space markets consist of (1) additions to supply in the form of new construction or conversions of non-office space to office uses; (2) removals, which occur mainly through obsolescence, demolition, or the conversion of office space into other uses; (3) tenant movements that generate brokerage activity and/or changes in the space occupied; (4) sales; and (5) financing and refinancing of both existing and new buildings. During most of the period since 1945, additions have vastly outweighed removals, so the total supply has expanded almost continuously. Therefore,

The views stated in this chapter are solely those of the author, and not necessarily those of the Brookings Institution, its trustees or its other staff members.

this chapter concentrates mainly on factors that influence additions to the total supply, with some discussion of sales, financing and refinancing activities.

Since 1945, additions to the office space market have occurred in surges interspersed with periods of very low additions. In the period just after 1945, memories were still strong of the vast oversupply of office space in the 1930s that followed a building boom in the 1920s. This inhibited developers from building new office space and financial institutions from funding it. Hence most changes in office space supply initially were conversions of former loft and manufacturing buildings to office use. These occurred mainly on the fringes of large central business districts, as in Chicago and New York.

By the 1950s, a few New York entrepreneurs started building large new office buildings downtown. In the late 1950s and the early 1960s, they and others began to build similar structures in other major downtowns, notably Chicago and Los Angeles.

Other spurts in total new office construction occurred in the early 1970s, the late 1970s through 1981, and from 1983 through 1989. These are shown in Figure 9-1. The last was by far the largest surge of office building in U.S.

FIGURE 9-1

NEW OFFICE SPACE CONSTRUCTION, 1972-1991
Index of Square Feet, January 1972 = 100

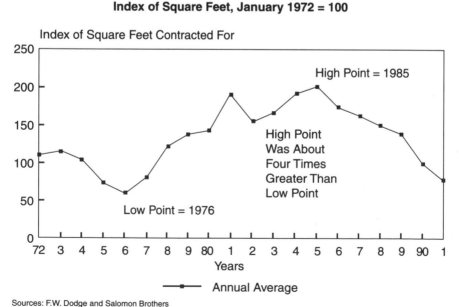

Index of Square Feet Contracted For

High Point = 1985

High Point
Was About
Four Times
Greater Than
Low Point

Low Point = 1976

Years

 Annual Average

Sources: F.W. Dodge and Salomon Brothers

history. It accounted for the creation of a substantial fraction of all U.S. office space in existence as of 1991. These movements in construction levels are influenced by factors on both the demand and supply sides of office space markets.

FACTORS INFLUENCING THE DEMAND FOR OFFICE SPACE

The demand for office space is influenced by four major factors: (1) growth in the overall size of the labor force, (2) shifts within the labor force toward or away from occupations that take place in offices, (3) technological changes that influence the amount of space required per office worker, and (4) cyclical movements in overall economic prosperity that influence the rate of growth of space demand from office tenants. Each factor is analyzed below.

The Size of the Labor Force

The U.S. civilian labor force grew rapidly in the 1970s, with average increases of 2.4 million workers per year, or 2.6% compounded, from 1971 through 1979. This growth slowed in the 1980s to an average of only 1.8 million per year, or 1.5% compounded.[1] These movements are shown in Figure 9-2. This surge in the 1970s was caused by the entry into the work force of the many young people born in the baby boom from 1950 to 1965. In addition, there was a marked increase in the percentage of women working outside the home. Both of these forces will increase more slowly in the 1990s than in either previous decade. The number of people aged 18 to 34 will actually decline in this period.

The Share of Workers Employed in Office Space

There has been a long-term movement in the composition of employment within the U.S. toward office work and services and away from agriculture and manufacturing. This has caused the demand for office space to grow faster than the growth in the overall size of the labor force. From 1970 to 1988, the total number of employed civilians rose 46%, but the number employed in finance, insurance and real estate—the most office-intensive occupations—soared 102%. Those employed in all types of services increased 82%. In contrast, the number employed in manufacturing went up

---

[1] Data from U.S. Bureau of the Census, *Statistical Abstract of the United States* (Washington, D.C.: U.S. Commerce Department, 1991 and other years) table on Employment Status of the Noninstitutional Population Aged 16 and Over.

FIGURE 9-2

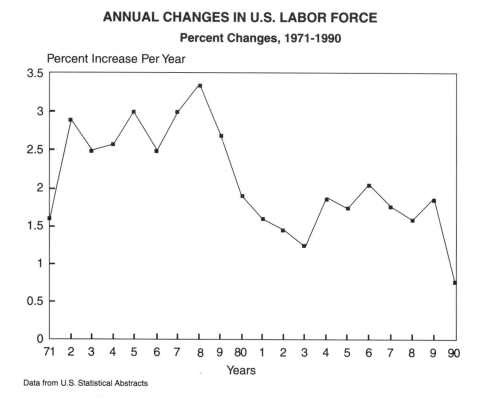

ANNUAL CHANGES IN U.S. LABOR FORCE
Percent Changes, 1971-1990

Percent Increase Per Year

Years

Data from U.S. Statistical Abstracts

only 2.7%.[2] Annual changes in office-based employment from 1972 through 1990 are shown in Figure 9-3.[3]

Moreover, there is a "self-reinforcing" character to movements in the office development industry.[4] Many activities associated with commercial real estate development occur in offices. Firms engaged in such activities include mortgage lenders, banks, insurance companies, lawyers, architects, planners, investment counselors, and construction and development

---

[2] Data from U.S. Bureau of the Census, *Statistical Abstract of the United States for 1991* (Washington, D.C.: U.S. Department of Commerce, 1991) p. 400.

[3] Salomon Brothers' economists made subjective judgments about what share of each major type of employment occurred in offices, and then applied those estimates to data concerning various categories of employment derived from U.S. Census Bureau data cited earlier, obtained from various annual volumes of the *Statistical Abstract of the United States.*

[4] I am indebted to David Shulman of Salomon Brothers for pointing out this aspect of office employment.

FIGURE 9-3

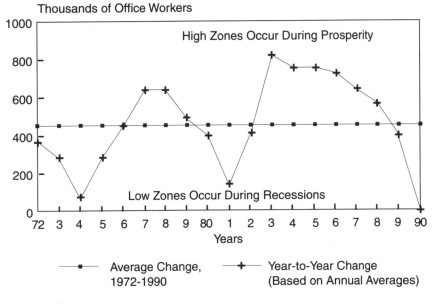

ANNUAL CHANGES IN OFFICE EMPLOYMENT
Year-to-Year Job Changes, 1972-1990

Thousands of Office Workers

High Zones Occur During Prosperity

Low Zones Occur During Recessions

Years

■— Average Change,
1972-1990

+— Year-to-Year Change
(Based on Annual Averages)

Source: Salomon Brothers

firms. One estimate concluded that 25% of the office space in downtown Dallas was occupied by firms associated with the real estate industry.[5] Hence when commercial real estate development is booming, its prosperity stimulates demand for the space its practitioners are creating. This tendency was accelerated in the 1980s by the long super-boom in new commercial real estate development.

Conversely, when new development activity is declining, shrinkage in office space occupancy by the same types of firms aggravates the loss of demand from other sources. This deepens overall cutbacks in office occupancy. This is now happening in the 1990s. For example, the closing of many savings and loans and banks in the financial crisis of the early 1990s notably reduced office space demand in many communities.

---

[5] Estimate made by the Trammel Crow Company and stated orally at a meeting of the Federal Reserve Board on December 3, 1991, by Don Williams of the Trammel Crow Company.

The Amount of Space Required Per Office Worker

In the 1960s and 1970s, the introduction of air conditioning into office buildings caused an expansion of the total space demanded per worker because air conditioning equipment took up a great deal of room. In the 1980s, the use of computers, telecommunications equipment, and other office machinery similarly expanded the space needed per worker. On the opposite side, the use of office partitions and space planning has reduced the amount of space allotted per worker. It is not clear just how future technological trends will affect office space use. Moreover, those trends are likely to be dominated by purely economic considerations—especially pressures on firms to reduce expenses by cutting their total space.

Changes in General Prosperity

The most important cyclical forces affecting changes in office space demand are those stemming from the general economic cycles inherent in the U.S. economy. In fact, the general business cycle causes cycles in both office space demand and overall commercial real estate development activity. This section focuses on its impact on office space demand.

During periods of rising overall prosperity, the square foot demand for non-residential space of all types increases. This occurs for two basic reasons: more activity by each firm and more expansive consumption of space per worker as "business living standards" increase with prosperity. If vacant space of the desired quality is available in existing buildings, this demand is satisfied by such space. Rising demand will not drive up rents until the amount of existing space is reduced to where competition among space users seeking expansion becomes acute.

If existing space is not available, this demand causes a sharp rise in rents on existing buildings. They eventually become high enough to make financing of added space feasible. This in turn stimulates the planning and construction of more new space.

In general, during periods of general business recession, increases in the demand for space of all types slow down or become negative. Businesses find their sales falling off and their expenses still rising. Their profits fall, so they try to reduce expenses. This causes them to defer expansions into additional space and sometimes to cut back on their use of existing space. In such periods, businesses also compress the amount of space they use per worker. They reverse the increases in "business living standards" that took place during rising general prosperity. They may also sublease space they are not using, which causes competition among owners of existing space to rise, thereby putting negative pressure on rents. Additional competitive pressures arise as space turnover decreases.

The approximate timing of recent U.S. general business cycles is shown in Figure 9-4. It depicts both overall U.S. unemployment rates and annual

FIGURE 9-4

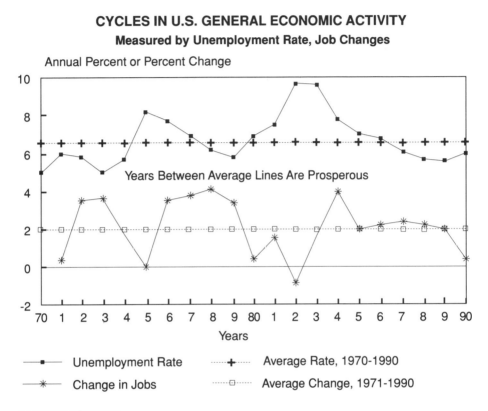

CYCLES IN U.S. GENERAL ECONOMIC ACTIVITY
Measured by Unemployment Rate, Job Changes

Annual Percent or Percent Change

Years Between Average Lines Are Prosperous

Years

———■——— Unemployment Rate   ······+······ Average Rate, 1970-1990

———*——— Change in Jobs   ······□······ Average Change, 1971-1990

Data from Labor Department

percentage changes in the total number of persons employed from 1970 through 1990.[6] Both these variables are considered "coincident indicators" of business cycles; that is, they move in close coordination with the business cycle itself. The upper part of this graph shows the average unemployment rate of 6.7% for this entire period as a straight horizontal line. The lower part shows the average percentage increase in jobs as a straight line. Consequently, years in which both variables lie between these two average lines are highly prosperous because they have below-average unemployment and above-average job increases. These boom periods include 1972-1973, 1978-1979, and 1987-1989. At the other extreme, years in which both variables lie outside this middle zone indicate economic adver-

---

[6] *Statistical Abstract of the United States*, tables on Employment Status of the Noninstitutional Population Aged 16 and Over.

sity because they have above-average unemployment and below-average increases in jobs. These recession periods include 1975, 1980-1983, and 1990. Several other periods show mixed conditions, with one variable better than average and the other worse. These mixed periods include 1971, 1974, 1976-1977, and 1984-1986.

Thus, Gross National Product and general economic activity in the U.S. move in a cyclical manner. Yet the cycles are not at all regular or fixed in length or amplitude; both vary greatly from one cycle to the next. Experience shows that this cyclical movement of the general economy is by far the most powerful force influencing office space demand and therefore office market activity as a whole.

The Cyclical Movement in Office Space Demand

The demand for office space rises during periods of general economic expansion and its rate of increase slows or becomes negative during periods of general economic contraction or stagnation. However, the amplitude of these cyclical movements is also influenced by the other three causal factors discussed. If these other factors are moving in ways that increase the demand for office space, that will accelerate upward movements or dampen downward movements stemming from the general business cycle. This happened in both the 1970s and the 1980s. Increases in the labor force due to the baby boom and more women working, plus technological needs for more space, plus faster relative growth of activities occurring in offices—all accentuated the increase in demand stemming from the general business cycle. Conversely, if these other factors are moving in ways that decrease the demand for office space, that will dampen upward movements or accelerate downward movements stemming from the general business cycle. This is happening in the 1990s.

CHANGES IN THE SUPPLY OF OFFICE SPACE

Five major factors influence changes in the supply of office space: (1) current and expected levels of rents and vacancy in the existing office space inventory, (2) the availability of financing, including both the amount of capital available for commercial real estate development and the terms under which it can be obtained, (3) the willingness of city governments to provide both the infrastructure needed for major office developments and financial incentives for their creation, (4) federal and other tax law changes that favor or hinder commercial real estate development, and (5) current and expected costs of land acquisition and construction on sites suitable for office space uses. These first four factors are discussed here. (The fifth is omitted because variations in cost elements are influenced by general economic forces.)

Current and Expected Levels of Rents and Vacancy

The Concept of the "Equilibrium Vacancy Rate"

Levels of rent and vacancy in office space markets are determined by the balance of supply and demand in the local market at any given moment. A certain minimum level of office space vacancy is necessary to maintain sufficient flexibility for expansion and movement among tenants so that they are not strongly competing for the same space. This minimum "frictional" vacancy level is considered the equilibrium vacancy rate. In theory, when vacancy equals this level, there is neither an upward pressure on rents due to strong competition among tenants for the same space, nor a downward pressure on rents due to strong competition among space owners for tenants.

If current demands for space exceed or are nearly equal to the total current supply, taking the *quality* of both demand and supply into account, then vacancy will fall below the equilibrium rate. Rents will be driven upward by competition for space among users. Such competition will eventually push rents above the level that makes construction of additional space profitable; so developers will start building more space.

On the other hand, if the current supply of space exceeds the demand for it by a sizable amount, then the vacancy rate will rise above the equilibrium rate. That will cause competition among landlords to capture tenants, driving effective rents downward. (Effective rents are defined as gross rents less the loss from rental concessions, the excess of tenant installation costs over normal building standards and miscellaneous costs such as moving or lease assumptions.) Rents will eventually fall below the level at which construction of additional space is profitable. This will cause a cessation of new construction projects.

The Size of the Equilibrium Vacancy Rate

This rate was traditionally considered to be 5% in office space markets. However, this is no longer regarded as correct, for three reasons. First, the equilibrium vacancy rate varies among different markets. Some are more dynamic than others; they contain a higher fraction of rapidly growing or rapidly declining types of firms, or are experiencing faster population growth or decline for other reasons. Dynamic markets have higher equilibrium vacancy rates than more static markets.

Second, this vacancy rate is specific to different quality grades of office space. Many tenants seeking Class A space (the most modern space with the highest quality amenities) will not be satisfied with lower quality space, even if the latter is less expensive. Hence there can be a shortage of Class A space at the same time that there is a surplus of Class B and lower quality space, and an overall surplus in the market.

Third, because of the massive overbuilding of office space in the 1980s, the average overall vacancy rate for major U.S. metropolitan areas exceeded 19% from 1985 through 1991. It is not likely that this average vacancy rate will fall all the way to 5% before the construction of new office space begins again. Hence the equilibrium vacancy rate in the first half of the 1990s will probably range from 8% to 12%, depending upon specific conditions in local markets.

Influences on the Balance of Supply and Demand

The relationship between current space demands and the existing inventory of space in any period is determined by (1) the amount of inventory at the beginning of the period, (2) the level of demand at the beginning of the period, (3) changes in demand during the period, and (4) changes in supply during the period. At any given moment, the amount of inventory and the total amount of demand at the beginning of the period have already been determined by previous conditions. Hence changes in both the demand for and supply of space are the most dynamic and crucial factors influencing the balance between supply and demand during the current period. This means the key variables are the rates of space absorption on the demand side and new office construction on the supply side.

There is one key exception to this generalization. It occurs when there is a massive surplus of office space in a market for an extended period of time. Then, even if demand rises sharply in some period and vacancy rates therefore fall, the remaining inventory of vacant space is large enough to prevent rents from rising—or even to stop them from falling. This was the case in most large U.S. metropolitan areas during the last few years of the 1980s and in the early 1990s. Under such conditions, demand must rise sufficiently faster than supply so that net declines in vacant space occur. In order for rents to be affected, this must continue until the vacancy rate is driven below the equilibrium vacancy rate.

How could such a large surplus of supply arise if the self-equilibrating mechanisms described earlier are operating? This can happen when expected future rents and property values differ sharply from current effective rents and property values. Thus, in the late 1980s, when effective rents in office buildings were falling in most markets, investors and developers continued to build new space because they expected future rents, and therefore future property values, to rise. In view of the clear evidence of high vacancy—a rate over 19% continuously from 1985 through 1990—this expectation was foolish, if not completely irrational. However, it is an error to believe that institutional and other investors always behave rationally.[7] These expectations were wrong. Moreover, they generated

---

[7] For a discussion of this point, see Anthony Downs, "What Have We Learned From the 1980s Experience?" *Salomon Brothers — United States Real Estate Research*, July 1991.

behavior that further aggravated the oversupply of space, causing rents to move in exactly the opposite direction from what the investors and developers had expected. Other factors contributing to the creation of this surplus are discussed below.

The Availability of Financing for New Office Space

Interest Rates

Commercial mortgage interest rates exert a key influence on the financing of office space development. They tend to move in close relationship to the general structure of interest rates, which is in turn influenced by the general business cycle. Interest rates rise gradually during general economic expansions as the economy moves closer to full capacity production. Then they rise when monetary authorities decide it is time to slow down economic activity because of imminent or existing inflation. This usually leads to a contraction in general economic activity. The most interest-sensitive activities fall first. Since office construction is highly interest sensitive, it tends to decline during such periods. Movements in interest rates from 1960 through 1992 are shown in Figure 9-5. The graph uses

FIGURE 9-5

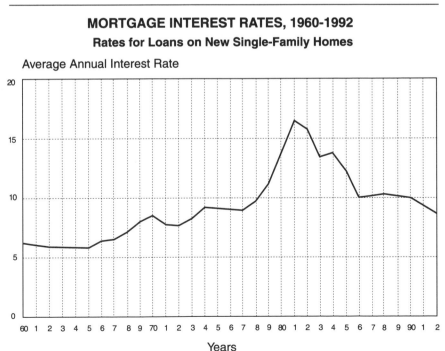

MORTGAGE INTEREST RATES, 1960-1992
Rates for Loans on New Single-Family Homes

Data from U.S. Statistical Abstracts

interest rates on new single-family homes, since no comparable data are readily available for commercial interest rates for that entire period. However, both types of rates move in roughly the same manner.[8]

After a general recession has set in, overall borrowing demands decline and interest rates gradually begin to fall. In fact, monetary authorities deliberately reduce short-term rates in order to stimulate the next expansion, and long-term rates usually follow soon afterwards. This increases the feasibility of financing additional office space construction. Of course, that feasibility also depends upon the level of rents that developers can expect to achieve from marketing the new space.

Absolute Credit Availability from Banks and Thrifts

Prior to 1983, periodic "credit crunches" in banks and savings and loans affected the availability of capital for real estate development. The underlying cause of the credit crunches was regulatory ceilings on the interest rates banks and thrifts could pay depositors for funds. When market interest rates available from other institutions—such as money-market funds and Treasury securities—exceeded those ceilings, depositors withdrew funds to earn higher yields elsewhere. That caused an absolute shortage of lendable funds in banks and thrifts, and most developers could not obtain financing at almost any price. Such credit crunches occurred in 1966, 1970, and 1975. After 1982, these institutions were deregulated and ceilings on their deposit rates were removed. They started paying high enough rates to keep from losing deposits. This ended absolute shortages of funds, though the price of borrowing—mortgage interest rates—varied more than it had in the past.

In fact, banks and savings and loans were flooded with deposits in 1983 and 1984. Because they were able to offer depositors both competitive interest rates and federal deposit insurance, they lured billions of dollars away from money market funds and other investments. Moreover, savings and loans were given new powers to invest in non-residential properties as well as housing. These changes stemming from financial deregulation were key factors causing both banks and savings and loans to overinvest in financing new office space construction from 1985 through 1990.

Other Forces Raising Investment Fund Availability in the 1980s

By a peculiar series of historic accidents, at the same time that U.S. banks and savings and loans were being flooded with funds available to finance

---

[8] Data from *Statistical Abstract of the United States*, tables on Money Market Interest Rates and Mortgage Rates.

office development, several other events were occurring that generated among other institutions a similar appetite for financing new office space.[9] Passage of the 1981 Tax Act extended extraordinarily favorable tax benefits to investments in the construction of new commercial real estate. This stimulated massive expansion of the real estate syndication industry, based upon offering income tax shelter to high-bracket earners. A second event was the deregulation of major financial institutions in many foreign nations, which permitted them to invest in U.S. real estate in amounts never before allowed. A third trend was a huge expansion in the funds held by U.S. pension funds for investment, and their managers' desire to diversify out of a sole reliance on stocks and bonds. A final factor was the loss by U.S. commercial banks of several major past targets for their lending. These included less-developed countries abroad, large corporations that shifted to raising funds through commercial paper markets, and farmers depressed by the agricultural recession of the early 1980s. So banks had unprecedented amounts of money to invest and fewer places than ever before in which to place it.

The Resulting Super-boom in Office Space Development

These forces resulted in an immense flood of investment funds pouring into commercial real estate markets after 1983. At the same time, the total demand for office space was rising strongly because of the demographic and technical factors described earlier. This coincidence in time of soaring office-space demand and unprecedented amounts of investment funds looking for somewhere to go generated the greatest office-space development boom in American history—and probably in world history! It started around 1978 and continued through 1989, temporarily interrupted by the recession years of 1982 and 1983.

There is some controversy about whether this super-boom in office space construction was primarily demand-driven (by rising user needs for space) or supply-driven (by rising pressure from investors to find an investment vehicle). Most likely it was at first driven by a combination of these two forces. But after 1987, it became dominated by supply-side forces. By then, user space needs were amply accommodated, as indicated by vacancy rates consistently above 19% from 1985 through 1991. But investor pressures to place money led to both careless underwriting and a grossly over-optimistic view of future rent, occupancy, and property value levels. This generated the massive overbuilding that dominated property values from 1990 onward. (It had already dominated effective rents for at least two years prior to 1990.)

---

[9] For a detailed discussion of this subject, see Anthony Downs, "The Fundamental Shift in Real Estate Finance From a Capital Surplus in the 1980s to a Capital Shortage in the 1990s," *Salomon Brothers Bond Market Research — Real Estate*, February 1991

Of course, a lack of available financing can influence levels of activity in office markets negatively. After the Comptroller of the Currency initiated a major bank credit crunch in early 1990, it was extremely difficult for developers and investors to finance new construction, purchase or refinancing of major office buildings. This lack of financing, along with the heavy impact of a huge oversupply of existing office space, severely depressed levels of new office construction from 1990 forward.

The availability of financing is a critical factor influencing levels of activity in office markets—and under some conditions can become the dominant factor. Strong availability can stimulate high-level development, and low availability can choke off almost all new development—as in the early 1990s.

Government Policies Affecting Office Space Development

Local government policies making land available for office space development were partly related to urban renewal programs in the 1960s and 1970s and to specific local government tax and other incentives. Urban renewal programs often involved the clearance of slums near downtowns, providing sites that could be developed in part with new office structures. Federal financing of land acquisition and clearance made such projects possible in most of the communities that created them.

Local governments tend to offer more incentives for real estate development within their borders during periods when their economies are suffering from a lack of prosperity, but not from severe depression. The latter inhibits such incentives because local governments cannot then afford them.

Federal tax policies have substantially influenced the willingness of equity investors to put funds into the development of new office space—both favoring and hindering such development. The most important law in recent times favoring development was the Tax Act of 1981. It encouraged syndication firms to create new space almost regardless of whether it had any occupants. The most important law hindering development was the Tax Act of 1986. It removed most of the construction incentives provided by the Tax Act of 1981.

THE PHASES OF THE DEVELOPMENT CYCLE

The office space *demand* cycle has two phases: (1) expansion, and (2) contraction or stagnation. However, the office space *development* cycle is based upon the interaction of both supply and demand forces in the market. This cycle has three phases: (1) boom, (2) overbuilding, and

(3) gradual absorption. These three phases follow in the same sequence in every cycle. But they have differing lengths in different cycles, depending upon both demand and supply factors like those discussed previously.

The Boom Phase

This occurs in the middle and toward the end of a period of expansion in the general economy. At that time, increasing general prosperity has stimulated rising demands for space among all types of office users. These users have absorbed all the available vacant space of the quality they desire. Competition among them for space has put upward pressure on rents, which have risen above the level necessary to make new development feasible. At the same time, increased prosperity has not yet driven interest rates so high as to prevent such development. So sources of financing are available for office developers, and lenders are encouraged to support new projects by strong demand forces. As a result, many developers start creating additional office space through construction of new buildings. This leads to a period of high-volume new office space construction. Boom phases occurred in the late 1960s, the early 1970s, the late 1970s, and from 1985 through 1989.[10]

The Overbuilt Phase

This arises at the end of a general expansion period when the economy slides into a recession. Increases in demand for office space slow sharply; total demand may even decline. At the same time, the new space started during the boom phase is increasingly becoming available. This happens because there is a substantial lag between the initiation of new office-space development and the appearance of that space on the market. The resulting combination of slower or no growth in demand, plus increased supply, causes big increases in vacancy rates. This puts downward pressure on rents as space owners compete for tenants. So developers stop initiating additional projects. Thus, the overbuilt phase is marked by rising vacancy rates, stagnant or falling effective rents, and a sharp decline in new office space construction. Overbuilt phases occurred in 1970-1971, 1974-1976 and from 1987 onward.

---

[10] Booms in *actual construction* lag somewhat behind booms in *contracting for construction*— which is shown on an earlier chart—because of the long periods required to convert contracts into actual structures. Thus, each office building boom actually occurs somewhat later than each office contracting boom, sometimes by two or three years.

The Gradual Absorption Phase

This phase begins when the general economy has started climbing out of a recession and has begun expanding significantly. Demand for office space gradually rises along with general prosperity. At first, this increased demand is accommodated by the excess space that was started in the boom phase and came "on line" in the overbuilt phase. But since new building has virtually ceased, continued growth in demand gradually soaks up more and more existing vacant space. This stabilizes rents and eventually begins to put upward pressure on them. Thus, this phase is essentially a transition between the overbuilt phase and the next boom phase. Gradual absorption phases occurred from 1976-1978 and from 1980-1983. Another one will probably occur in the mid-1990s.

CONCLUSION

There is little doubt that levels of activity in office space markets—especially new construction—move in cyclical fashion over time. Their cyclicity arises mainly from the close relationship of office space demand and supply factors to the general business cycles inherent in the U.S. economy as a whole. As long as the economy exhibits cyclical movements in general levels of activity—which it has done for 200 years—office space markets will reflect those cycles as well.

However, the cycles in office markets do not have a rigidly fixed duration or amplitude; in fact, both dimensions vary tremendously. That variation is also closely linked to the diversity in length and severity of cyclical movements in general economic activity. Thus, because the general economic expansion of the 1980s had an unprecedented length, so did the boom phase of the office space development cycle. Unfortunately, that length contributed to the creation of a massive oversupply of office space and other commercial real estate space that will overshadow activity levels in most U.S. markets for at least the first half of the 1990s.

Even so, by closely observing the many factors influencing office space activity levels, participants in those markets will be able to anticipate when an overbuilt phase will end, to be inevitably replaced by a gradual absorption phase, and ultimately by another boom phase.

ABOUT THE AUTHOR

Anthony Downs, CRE, Ph.D., is a Senior Fellow at the Brookings Institution in Washington, D.C., a private non-profit research organization specializing in public policy studies. Before that he was for 18 years a member and then chairman of Real Estate Research Corporation, a national consulting firm. Downs has served as a consultant to many of the nation's largest corporations, to major developers and to government agencies at all levels. Downs received a Ph.D. in economics from Stanford University, and is the author or co-author of 15 books and more than 300 articles. He recently completed a study of traffic congestion called *Stuck in Traffic* and is working on a study of urban growth management in the United States.

10

OFFICE SUBMARKET DELINEATION IN TENANT LOCATIONAL BEHAVIOR

by R. Thomas Powers

INTRODUCTION

Clusters of office buildings within a market area often constitute a distinct submarket. Submarkets may be delineated by geographic boundaries or by tenant definition. Among the factors that could lead to the identification of an area as a submarket are government actions, the emergence of an alternative, competitive submarket, and tenant perception. Most often an office submarket emerges because of location advantages. For example, a submarket may have excellent access by means of several different modes of transportation, or it may be situated close to important tenant services such as banks, restaurants and quality shopping. Occasionally, a major developer can "force" a submarket to emerge before its time—Las Colinas, Texas and Reston, Virginia are examples. Both are master-planned communities in which major institutional financing was obtained, thus creating a town (and a submarket) very quickly. However, the basic ingredient in office submarket delineation comes from recognition of the submarket by users and consumers, and their desire to be at that location.

In order for real estate professionals to do an efficient job of selecting where to develop office space, leasing that space and maintaining a submarket's competitive edge, it is important that they understand how office submarkets evolve and are delineated; what factors enable a submarket to prosper; and why some submarkets fizzle after only a brief popularity.

HOW OFFICE SUBMARKETS ARE DEFINED

At the outset it would be helpful to define what constitutes an office submarket. This is similar to defining an aesthetically pleasing office building: everyone has a different point of view. Any definition must include both a functional and a conceptual component. An office submarket might best be defined as a geographic area which efficiently combines the locational needs of the user (tenants) with the convenience demands of consumers (the user's employees and customers), while offering economically competitive rents.

The exact boundaries of an office submarket can rarely be defined. For example, a major land use in an area may define a submarket, as the Galleria Mall along Loop 610 in Houston "identifies" that office submarket. Other major land uses that can support the identity of an office submarket may include a university or a government complex. A long used "local" name may define a submarket—Tyson's Corner in Northern Virginia is one example. Occasionally, a significant business event which takes place in an area may identify a submarket—Wall Street is an office submarket synonymous with global securities trading. There are submarkets defined by specific rent gradients within urban cores (downtown Los Angeles), by ethnic perception (the downtown Miami submarket vs. Brickell Avenue), or by a major amenity (golf in Arvida's Park of Commerce in Boca Raton). The convenience of road access and the terrain are additional identifying factors. Practically every urban area in the United States has office submarkets which exist in plan and perception but can not be exactly defined spatially.

Does it matter if a submarket cannot be precisely defined? Generally not, because the growth of a popular office submarket is almost always restricted by other factors before marketing abuses can occur. One restricting factor is land availability. The lack of available land could be due to government restrictions, existing natural features such as difficult terrain, or land prices too high for a new building to come on line and compete on an economic basis. Sometimes developers attempt to stretch the geographic limits of a popular submarket. For example the popular Boca Raton, Florida, office submarket was "grown" by an aggressive developer to include a portion of Delray Beach. The added building was a dismal failure because the developer simply could not get "Boca" rents in Delray Beach. A key point is that even though a submarket may not be explicitly defined, the market imposes intuitive, reasonable limits on a popular submarket's boundaries. The real estate professional must understand and respect those limits.

Office Submarket Identification Categories

The criteria used to identify an office submarket can differ among urban areas; the criteria can also differ within an urban area. The core of an urban office market area is almost always designated as the "downtown" submarket or central business district (CBD). It is usually characterized by the highest density development, supports specialized users and typically demands the highest rents. The CBD historically has been the most sought-after office submarket. The popularity of a downtown location may cause several adjacent submarkets to emerge. New York, Atlanta, Los Angeles and other mature urban downtowns support two or more distinct office submarkets. When such multiple submarkets occur, they are usually characterized by extremely specialized users—a financial district vs. a corporate headquarter district vs. a legal district.

During the 1990s, industry professionals will also need to recognize "second-cycle" office submarkets and "air rights" submarkets as emerging possibilities for downtown locations. A second-cycle submarket emerges as older buildings are removed to make way for newer, higher-density development. Air rights submarkets emerge as a result of the more efficient utilization of space over existing structures, such as construction of a new office building over an existing parking deck.

In the suburbs there is often a very different set of office submarket delineators. A more diverse group of users characterizes the suburban submarket. Such users have many locational criteria in common; among the most important are ease of access, rent level sensitivity and proximity to consumers—both employees and customers. Competition for users among suburban office submarkets is fierce. A submarket must have not only some, but all of the elements tenants desire in order to be competitive. Those office submarkets which came on line in the 1980s without these elements will pay a stiff economic penalty in the '90s.

Perhaps the easiest office submarket to identify is the exurban (beyond the suburbs) small town submarket. Here submarket overlap rarely occurs; competition is mild; and the developer can often determine geographically where the submarket will be located. Users and consumers are more at the mercy of the developer in exurban areas, principally when the developer has the financial backing to create a submarket. However, the needs of users, consumers and developers can be more easily meshed in these types of submarkets.

Identifying Office Submarkets by User Type and Function

During the 1970s the single most significant office submarket delineator seemed to be the peripheral, high-speed highways or urban beltways. Washington, Atlanta, Houston, Boston—almost every major U.S. city felt their impact. The attribute of a beltway location was that it best satisfied the needs of users and their customers and met the economic criterion of competitive rents. Competitive rents were especially important as so many interchanges were opening at virtually the same time that land availability and price was not an initial issue for users.

Another factor facilitating the emergence of suburban office submarkets during the 1980s was the changing nature of the user base. Small businesses were comprising more and more of the user market, and their space needs, the amount of rent they were willing to pay, and the priority they put on a convenient location for themselves were quite different from the needs of the major regional and national corporations that so much of the office space had been built to accommodate. If researchers like MIT's Dr. David L. Birch are on target, small business formations will remain the backbone of the U.S. economy in the 1990s. These small businesses are likely to relocate or add branches in a way that does not conform as readily to time-tested economic development and industrial location theory as do the location choices of large corporations. Office submarket identification increasingly must encompass this unpredictable business location trend as well.

Meanwhile, the extraordinary consolidation within basic industries such as technology, financial services and transportation companies will change forever the way those industries think about office space utilization. This consolidation means they will be employing fewer people; as a result they will need less space and will be releasing space back into the market as they abandon excess locations.

Major user activity centers are often important in identifying an office submarket. Technology companies usually prefer to be located in close proximity to a university. Examples include Forrestal Center in Princeton, New Jersey; Research Triangle Park in Raleigh, North Carolina; and the Stanford Research Park in Palo Alto, California. Almost every major university has fostered or could support the emergence of an office submarket. Large medical complexes, often situated in university settings, provide similar support. Government complexes are notable for spurring the emergence of office submarkets. Often developers will offer to build government complexes and move the government entity into the complex in order to foster the ancillary demand for office space that government activity generates. This "instant submarket" delineation is especially prevalent in exurban locations, such as St. Lucie West, Florida.

A transportation complex may define an office submarket if that transportation complex is high speed, in a high value-added environment. Access by high speed air (helicopter) and water (hydrofoil) vehicles will increasingly identify urban submarkets in America's largest cities in the 1990s.

HOW OFFICE SUBMARKETS EVOLVE, GROW AND GAIN USER ALLEGIANCE

It is the aggregate collection of user and consumer perceptions that identifies a submarket. Office submarkets do not spring up overnight and rarely does a developer build a building in hopes of creating a submarket. The positive response by users to a building and then to a core of buildings causes the developer(s) to continue to construct buildings. This in turn creates the critical mass of users, consumers and economic rents which then identifies the submarket.

Most people think of modern office submarkets as evolving on previously vacant land. That evolution is clearly the most common and is referred to as the horizontal office submarket. These submarkets rim major urban areas, are characterized by low-to-moderate densities, and support low- to mid-rise buildings in campus configurations. They often are strategically placed along major highway arteries and, in fact, excellent access is an integral locational attribute, although such a submarket may quickly develop other uses, such as business services, retail, restaurants and clubs, hotels and the like, which further enhance that submarket's growth and appeal.

Different types of office submarkets began to emerge in the 1990s. Second-cycle vertical office submarkets are one of them. Older buildings are demolished and new, higher density buildings take their place. In an economic sense, this is called "successive utilization." In select cases, the vertical office submarket will be (perceptually) identified by a single building, such as the World Trade Center submarket in New York and the Sears Tower submarket in Chicago. The major force working against a proliferation of this type of submarket is the mismatch between convenience and users' economic means. Because vertical submarkets are more expensive to create and maintain, pressure by users and customers to keep office space affordable will be the controlling factor in both horizontal and vertical submarket growth in the 1990s.

Rarely does one think in terms of office submarket shrinkage, especially in the United States. Still it happens. Witness the decay of select urban submarkets in older northeastern and midwestern cities. Such shrinkage has a cycle and creates a submarket all its own. First, tenants gravitate toward the horizontal submarkets (suburbs); rents decline at the core; functional and particularly economic obsolescence sets in. Submarket shrinkage first occurs within the user base and shortly after in the consumer base. It may be 10 to 15 years or longer before any spatial shrinkage of the submarket occurs. In fact the office submarket may never experience spatial shrinkage; it may revert instead to the higher density second-cycle vertical office submarket described earlier. Whether the submarket physically shrinks or reverts to second-cycle use ultimately depends on the competitiveness of the horizontal (suburban) office submarket.

Once an office submarket gains momentum and notoriety, how it maintains this competitive advantage is simple to understand but difficult to achieve. As a submarket evolves, an astute developer or marketer will create user and consumer awareness through creative, aggressive marketing programs. Examples of submarkets where this has occurred include the Aventura submarket in north Miami and Los Colinas in north Dallas. Marketing programs created an image that made users and consumers want to be located there. As long as rents remain competitive such submarkets flourish. However, widespread overbuilding and economic recessions separate the strictly image-driven submarkets from those with sound user and consumer locational attributes and economics.

Office Submarket Cycles: The Agents of Change

The real estate industry prides itself on being entrepreneurial, attracting pioneers and risk takers. While this is certainly true, it is odd that government, a force which tends to restrain market competitiveness, is the single most significant agent shaping the location, form and substance of office submarkets within the United States.

Most government influence comes from local (city, county, regional) institutions in the form of zoning regulations. Zoning is the single most important agent affecting land values by designating (or changing) the permitted use or density of a property. Government also influences office submarkets through transportation planning, environmental regulations, water and sewer plans and the like. Even the length of the governmental approval process has an impact on the ability of a fledgling office submarket to compete with more established submarkets. While the industry bemoans more government involvement, the 1990s is likely to be the most governmentally restrictive development period in the history of the industry. Increasing environmental pressures and concurrency requirements similar to those in Florida will compel more government involvement, which in turn will tend to slow the pace of development.

Economics (prices and rents) is usually the second most important agent influencing the evolution and growth of office submarkets. Economics is related in part to government policies. In addition, the comparative economics of different submarkets will affect the success of each. Land economics (price) is an obvious starting point. Clearly, office submarkets can collapse even if the land purchase was not overpriced; however, there is no history of success by the initial developer in submarkets where land prices escalated too fast relative to solid alternative locations.

The economics of comparative rents within and among submarkets is of utmost concern to the user. Comparative rents are very important in identifying emerging submarkets or restructuring existing ones. In theory, the rent a user pays reflects certain characteristics about the asset, the submarket, the user, the user's customers and sometimes even the developer. Table 10-1 lists major characteristics which define an office submarket.

Each characteristic shown in Table 10-1 affects the competitive economics of the submarket. To a great degree, those aggregate characteristics are the economics of the submarket. And to the extent that one office submarket has a greater abundance of these characteristics, that submarket should grow and prosper more rapidly and maintain its competitive advantage longer than the competition.

QUANTIFYING OFFICE SUBMARKET COMPETITIVENESS

It is sometimes mandatory, and always useful, to quantify the degree to which an office submarket is competitive with other submarkets. Such quantification can lead to better locational decisions. Such a quantification scheme, or comparative indexing model, does not have to be overly complex. Still, the more pertinent quantifiable factors that are addressed, the better the comparative understanding of submarkets that will be achieved.

TABLE 10-1   Characteristics Identifying An Office Submarket

I. **Asset Characteristics**
   Desirability of the Location
   Quality of Construction
   Quality of User Services
   Availability of Consumer Services
   Architectural Qualities and Features

II. **User Characteristics**
   Current Profitability of the User's Business
   Outlook for Business Profits
   Nature of the Business
   Inter-Tenant Synergies

III. **Market Characteristics**
   Comparative Economics of Competitive Submarkets
   Strength of Local Sublet Market
   Job Growth Within Office User Categories

IV. **Developer Characteristics**
   Developer's Reputation
   Market Creativity and Aggressiveness

Source: Thomas Powers & Associates

It is important to understand that utilizing a quantitative approach neither guarantees success nor limits liabilities. Models are simply tools to assist the professional in considering as many market factors as possible, in as objective a manner as possible, when comparing submarket attributes. Nothing ultimately substitutes for common sense and the application of the professional's years of experience in the industry. However, model output coupled with experience and common sense should reduce the risk associated with identifying competitive office submarkets.

There is nothing new about the theory or mathematics of what is presented here. What may be new to the reader is the application of two specific modelling techniques in identifying and comparing office submarket attributes. These techniques may be used to measure competitiveness within a submarket as well, assuming the submarket is of sufficient maturity and size.

The Gravity Model

The first technique utilized is based on the Gravity Model. Like the Newtonian laws governing force and mass, competitiveness (delineation by market acceptance) between office submarkets may be related to laws governing the intervening distance between and makeup of office submarkets. The Gravity Model as used here is essentially a spatial indexing model that can be adapted to measuring interoffice submarket competitiveness by creating an index. Properly utilized, the model can also rank submarkets according to user-consumer preference; rank undeveloped locations for likely success as a submarket, and so forth. The major shortcoming of this model is that it does not provide significant explanation for why users and customers choose such a location.

The Gravity Model may be specified as follows:

$$M_{ij} = \frac{(V_jL_j)}{(R_j)} \frac{(R_i)}{(V_iL_i)} / D_{ij}$$

Where i is "from" and j is "to":

M_{ij} = computed index quantifying the degree of competitiveness between submarkets i and j

V_i and V_j = office market vacancy rates (expressed as %) at i and j

R_i and R_j = office market rents ($/sq. ft.) at i and j

L_i and L_j = labor force availability (unemployment rate) at i and j

D_{ij} = the intervening distance between comparative submarkets

Table 10-2 illustrates a theoretical data base (I) for five submarkets. Vacancy, rent, labor and "push" and "pull" components are given. The push out of a submarket would increase with rents, labor shortages or space shortages, unless some prestige factor keeps the tenant in the area. The pull into a submarket would increase with vacancy (space), labor availability and bargain rents.

Based on the distances shown (II) and the interaction of the competitive submarkets (III), the spatial index can be computed using the gravity model provided. The closer the calculated value of M ij is to zero, the more similar the submarkets being compared. It is up to the industry professional to apply local knowledge and experience to judge how close to zero the submarkets can come without being negatively competitive.

It is well beyond the scope of this chapter to dwell on the empirical application of this model to measure office submarket competitiveness. However, the reader is referred to Anderson (1979), McFadden (1987), Miller (1967) and Niedercorn (1969) for a thorough discussion of the application

Table 10-2   Theoretical Data Set Illustrating An Application of the Gravity Model

	Vacancy	Rent	Labor	Push (R_i) $\overline{(V_iL_i)}$	Pull (V_jL_j) $\overline{(R_j)}$
I					
Submarket 1	20.00	100.00	90.00	0.06	18.00
Submarket 2	10.00	120.00	100.00	0.12	8.33
Submarket 3	5.00	90.00	110.00	0.16	6.11
Submarket 4	20.00	80.00	120.00	0.03	30.00
Submarket 5	25.00	120.00	90.00	0.05	18.75
II					
Distances	—	1.00	3.00	2.00	1.00
Distances	1.00	—	1.00	2.00	3.00
Distances	3.00	1.00	—	1.00	2.00
Distances	2.00	2.00	1.00	—	1.00
Distances	1.00	3.00	2.00	1.00	—
III					
Interaction	—	4.21	1.03	7.58	9.47
Interaction	19.64	—	6.67	16.36	6.82
Interaction	8.93	12.40	—	44.63	13.95
Interaction	2.73	1.26	1.85	—	5.68
Interaction	8.73	1.35	1.48	14.55	—

Source: Morton O'Kelly, The Ohio State University Department of Geography

and economic contents of the Gravity Model.[1] Where multiple submarket competitiveness is being indexed and compared, the closer the calculated value of "M" is to zero, the more similar that submarket is relative to the alternative comparative submarket.

Regression Analysis

Another comparative office submarket identification technique consists of applying regression analysis in a more variable-rich manner than the Gravity Model will allow. The application of this more sophisticated modelling technique does not guarantee a more accurate result. However, it does allow the analyst greater opportunity to apply varied sensitivity analyses to the problem; playing such "what if" scenarios can build greater confidence into the ultimate decision about comparative submarkets.

A simple regression model may be specified as follows:

$$A = a + bx + se,$$

Where: A = the dependent variable

a = the constant term in the regression equation

b = the beta coefficient quantifying the importance of "x"

x = the independent variable, i.e., the historic measure

se = standard error of the equation

Generally, the more complex the problem, or the more sensitive the desired explanation, the more variables that will be utilized in the regression, although there are limitations. The major limitation to multiple variable input is colinearity among independent variables. The following case study illustrates how regression analysis can be used to identify the "best" future submarket among several alternative sites.

Sawgrass International Corporate Park Case Study

Sawgrass International Corporate Park is a 612-acre office park located in western Broward County (Ft. Lauderdale), Florida. While marketed as a planned office park, in reality its size and success make it an office submarket. Today, Sawgrass is one of the most successful office parks in the state; in 1980 it was merely a developer's dream situated close to Everglades National Park.

---

[1] Complete references for the works cited can be found in the bibliography for Part III at the end of this book.

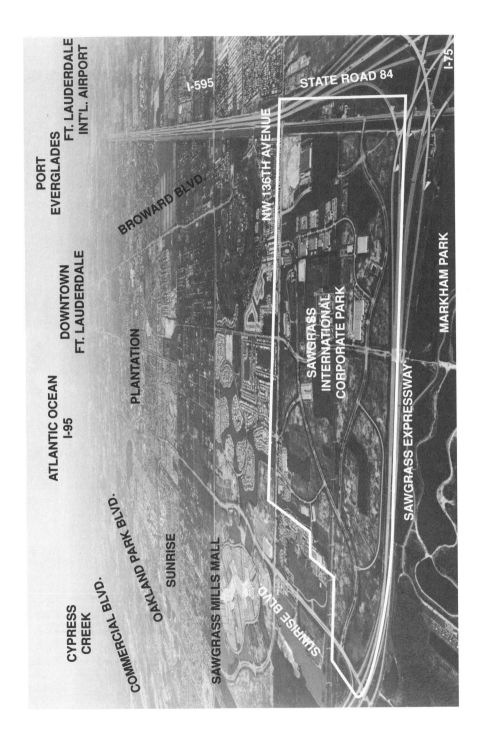

The developer, The Stiles Corporation, sought a large parcel of land to assure development control and a long-term development position. It considered six major sites, all located in South Florida (Dade, Broward and Palm Beach Counties). The property selected had few visible attributes, was hindered by limited access and was not close to any of the existing office submarkets in South Florida (see photograph on facing page). But the developer was looking ahead to the 1990s and beyond.

Why did the developer choose this site over the others under consideration? The regression technique discussed earlier could be utilized as one tool in the decision-making process. The independent variables utilized in the comparative location research and upon which the regression model was built included:

- **Proximity to a major airport:** This was measured in miles. Since South Florida has three competitive airports, ranking the "quality" of each airport was important. This ranking was based on the number of daily nonstop flights from each to the major U.S. business destinations of New York, Los Angeles and Atlanta.
- **Proximity to quality housing:** This component consisted of several variables: number of rental housing units within a five-mile radius in projects less than five years old; and number of for-sale housing units in a ten-mile radius priced between $75,000 and $125,000.
- **Proximity to quality shopping:** This component had two variables: (1) number of miles to a major mall; and (2) number of miles to a significant community shopping center (125,000 square feet minimum). The major mall was double weighted to assure its position as the more important feature.
- **Accessibility:** This was measured by the linear miles of existing and planned (within five years) interstate highway located within a ten-mile radius of the site; and by the number of miles of existing and planned major arterial highway located within five miles of the site.
- **Submarket competitiveness:** This component had three variables. The first variable measured the number of square feet of existing and planned office space in the area (assuming a Floor Area Ratio, that is, the percentage of the site that the building covers, of .30). The second variable measured "tenant desirability" by averaging effective market rents and the vacancy rate in existing office space[2]; (the lower the blended number, the more competitive the area). The third variable quantified the likely future competitiveness of the area. It consisted of computing the difference between the current square foot selling price of developed office land and the square foot price of raw land zoned for office use in the six submarkets.

---

[2] Note: The analysis shown here was done after-the-fact but it does document that the developer made the optimum choice relative to the possible locations.

- **Quality of life:** This somewhat subjective component consisted of a ranking of three variables: schools (average SAT scores at the area high school); business (interviews with industrial recruiters); and residents (interviews with knowledgeable residential brokers). This variable was weighted at only 50% of its value due to its subjective nature and the need for the analyst to interpret the interviewees' insights.

After collection, all data within submarkets were normalized into logarithmic functions and an additive score for each individual submarket was computed. The average of these six submarket scores, along with each of the individual submarket additive indices, became the "set" of dependent variables. Hundreds of regressions were run using multiple combinations of the independent and dependent variables. Not surprisingly, accessibility tended to be the best predictor of the future likely strength of the Sawgrass submarket location; land prices also proved to be statistically significant.

The application of regression analysis to business/industrial location analysis is discussed in detail in Isard (1969) and Rogers (1967).

CONCLUSION

The accurate identification of office submarkets is, and will remain, as much art as science. Still, rigorous analysis is fundamental to reducing location risk for the developer, the lender/investors and others whose livelihood depends on the quality of office submarket location decisions.

In a world of perfect information gathering and analysis, the speculative office space construction oversupply of the 1980s would not have happened. But there is nothing perfect about the dissemination and use of information within the real estate industry. What remains maddening, and sobering, about the 1980s is that so much of the product built early in the cycle was well located, prudently priced and in demand. It was the construction excesses during the latter part of the cycle that proved to be the downfall of so many once vibrant office submarkets. The moral, if there is one, is that all the sophisticated analysis in the world will not stop development where such development is capital and not demand driven, i.e., where risk prudence takes a back seat to capital availability. Surely the lender must impose higher underwriting standards and serve as a brake against an imprudent pace of supply.

Looking ahead, it is likely that the configuration of office submarkets in the 1990s will change more rapidly than was true in the past. Poorly situated office submarkets that emerged in the 1980s will reach functional obsolescence long before the physical plant wears out. In such cases, adaptive reuse will be in order. A downtown building might be retrofitted for elderly housing. Some well-located "see-through" buildings could be adapted for rental housing, and not just for low-to-moderate income families. In some instances a major downtown building could become its own urban neighborhood; a mix of uses within the vertical shell would spread the leasing/sales risk and broaden market response for the currently empty office space. It is clearly a time to be creative; the aging of the baby boomers, coupled with their changing lifestyle preferences, may offer opportunities for such creativity.

The 1990s have also ushered in the sobering reality that office asset prices and values can go down. There is too much handwringing over the current cycle of property deflation. Now is the time to begin taking advantage of price normalization and to utilize the flexibility this deflationary cycle offers. Office space originally renting at $30 per foot is going for $15; vertical structures that cost $125 a square foot to build are being purchased for $60 a square foot. It is clear that such price changes create enormous adaptive reuse opportunities for select properties. It is entirely likely that such flexibility will change the very nature of many existing office submarkets — likely for the better.

ABOUT THE AUTHOR

Thomas Powers, CRE, is president of Thomas Powers & Associates, a real estate research, advisory and investment services firm located in Fort Lauderdale, Florida. He was formerly executive vice president of the Goodkin Research Corporation; served as senior analyst with the Federal National Mortgage Association (Fannie Mae); and worked at the Program on Neighborhood and Regional Change at the Massachusetts Institute of Technology. Powers holds a graduate degree in regional economic development from East Carolina University and studied international economics at George Washington University.

11

OFFICE MARKETABILITY STUDIES

by Richard Kateley

INTRODUCTION

Office marketability studies are used to make "go/no go" decisions about a specific property. The study may be for either an existing or a proposed building.

The analysis addresses three questions:

- The rent or sales price the office building can achieve
- The period of time it will take to rent or sell the property
- The most appropriate building type, size and quality

The marketability study is a practical, pragmatic decision tool. It is data driven and detailed: the more data and the more detail, the better. Therefore, this chapter will emphasize the types of information collected and analyzed, the manner in which data and findings are displayed, and the typical sources to which the analyst can look to obtain reliable information. This chapter also stresses the critical importance of informed judgment and experience in bridging the inevitable gaps in data and interpreting the information that is available.

TYPES OF MARKET STUDIES

This chapter focuses on the site-specific marketability study. However, this is one of a broad array of office market analyses. The most general and widest ranging market study compares more than one city or metropolitan area. These evaluations are frequently prepared for firms that are seeking multiple office development or acquisition opportunities and want to rate and rank a large number of geographic areas in terms of attractiveness. Alternatively, a corporate office space user may be considering a move and need a study that compares cities along such dimensions as labor availability, housing costs and general quality of life.

A second type of office market analysis focuses on the dynamics of a single metropolitan area and describes the economic base, past and current development trends, and various indicators of the strength of the office market. This overview type of study may also feature in-depth descriptions of the office submarkets and their assets and liabilities. Neither the comparative office market study nor the metropolitan office market overview deals with specific properties or sites. Rather, they concentrate on aggregate conditions and economic fundamentals.

Finally, the site-specific marketability study addresses a particular parcel of land. Even within the category of site specific studies there are important variations. The analysis may be of a vacant property where the question of marketability refers to a hypothetical structure. In the second instance, plans for the office building may have been drawn and the analyst can then work with precise descriptions of building size, square footage and design. Last, a marketability study may be conducted for an existing structure. In this case, the analyst has a real building to deal with and a track record of leasing and occupancy.

Because the term "market study" covers so many alternatives and levels of detail, it is extraordinarily important that the analyst and the user of the study be in complete agreement about what is, and is not, included in the investigation. In other words, the relationship between client and analyst is best spelled out in detail, preferably in the form of a written contractual agreement, so that misunderstandings resulting from the numerous ways the term "marketability" is used can be avoided. The scope of services provision in the contract assures that the level of research and data collection fits the needs of the user of the study and protects the analyst.

All market studies for office development or investment rely on the same fundamental economic base information. Whether comparing cities, describing an entire metropolitan area, or focusing on a specific parcel of land, the office market analysis must be grounded in an understanding of the local economy, employment, disposable personal income and demographics. Therefore, all market studies begin with a description of the features of the economy that have long-term implications for growth and activity. Because the demand for office space responds to growth in certain employment categories, job formation is a critical aspect of the economic base analysis.

There are clear limits to a marketability study. If the study is site specific, it can't be used to make decisions about other, alternative projects outside the submarket. Market studies also have a relatively short shelf life. Because they look at the near term—the time it will take to build and lease the office building—they are quickly out of date. A more substantive limitation inherent to the market study is that it does not address financial feasibility, including critical determinations on development cost and forecasted net operating income. However, the market analyst's findings are critical inputs to the assessment of financial viability that is described in Chapter 12.

A well-formulated and complete office market analysis has six components:

1. Analysis of the demand for office space in the submarket
2. Analysis of the supply of space within the market area
3. Assessment of the assets and liabilities of the site and its environs
4. Evaluation of other office properties with which the office building must compete
5. Allocation of demand from the defined total market to the specific property
6. Conclusions (based on 1-5) on achievable rents or sale price, the time needed to complete rent-up or sale, and recommendations on the best building for the property.

The study typically begins with an introductory description of the entire metropolitan area and a more detailed analysis of the dynamics of the submarket as depicted in Chapter 10. In this chapter, it is assumed that the market analyst has already evaluated the metropolitan area and its submarkets. The focus here is directly on the six key site-specific issues that comprise "marketability" and how they are defined and measured. The chapter ends with a discussion of data sources and the use of new research tools such as Geographic Information Systems (GIS).

ANALYSIS OF SUPPLY AND DEMAND

Supply and demand for office space at a particular location are a complex function of metropolitan area, submarket and building specific variables. Following is a discussion of how demand and supply are defined, measured and analyzed in a site-specific marketability study. First, a note of caution: Many "market studies" consist largely of chamber of commerce promotional material, or basic data on the metropolitan area economy, population, major employers and the like. Although this kind of information is of value in a short overview designed to orient the reader, it is of limited use in actually drawing conclusions about rents and the time required to lease an existing or proposed office building.

Demand for Office Space

Demand for office space is a natural outgrowth of increases in "office-prone employment" and of the desire of some space users to replace their existing quarters with new space. New demand and replacement demand can also be expressed in terms of net absorption, defined as the difference between the aggregate square footage of space occupied this year as compared to last.

Both the employment growth and the net absorption approaches to determining demand for space are useful and complementary. Table 11-1 shows a typical chart of historic absorption and indicates how it varies from year to year. It is critical to distinguish between absorption and leasing activity. Leasing activity refers to the square footage of office space that is signed and committed in a given year. It includes space that a tenant now occupies and decides to remain in. Leasing rates do not factor in the vacancy that is created when a tenant moves from one building to another and leaves empty space behind. Net absorption, on the other hand, measures the amount of additional space actually occupied each year and thereby serves as an indicator of true demand. There can be negative absorption, too. A market may have *less* space occupied as well as more.

Demand, as measured by space absorption, is calculated by a building-by-building analysis of occupancy. For a submarket, absorption is aggregated from the individual properties in the submarket. The analyst may

TABLE 11-1   Historic Absorption and Vacancy Rates

Year-End	Total Net Rentable Area	Space Absorbed During Year	Vacancy Rate
	(000s sq. ft.)	(000s sq. ft.)	(%)
1978	64,933	2,857	6.4
1979	65,591	2,518	3.5
1980	69,556	3,409	4.1
1981	71,762	322	6.6
1982	75,297	1,419	9.1
1983	80,010	2,364	11.5
1984	82,462	2,417	11.2
1985	84,755	2,206	11.0
1986	88,197	1,779	12.5
1987	92,572	2,755	13.9

Annual Averages:
   1978-1982 2,105,000 sq. ft.
   1983-1987 2,304,000 sq. ft.

Source: Heitman Financial

have to do the arithmetic (subtracting last year's occupied space square footage from this year's) or, as is the case in many markets, large brokerage firms, financial institutions, or trade journals may compute the net absorption rates.

The analyst will compute three-year, five-year and ten-year "average absorption" rates to get a sense of the typical demand dynamics in the market. Exceptional years, where there is very high or very low absorption, need to be explained by local professionals who are familiar with the market's past development cycles. While there is no *a priori* reason to assume that absorption will always change in the future as it has in the past, the market's "track record" is the baseline against which the analyst must work.

The analyst should also consider the types of space being absorbed and the kinds of tenants that are active in the submarket. Although the total numbers are important for historical analysis, it is helpful to know if the absorption is comprised of a few large users or many small tenants. Similarly, the kinds of tenants—accountants, financial institutions, associations, corporate users, and so on—moving or expanding need to be known. It is also essential to be cognizant of large firms or industries which are contracting.

The analyst will obtain insights into the composition of absorption from leasing brokers, tenant representatives and building managers. While these "data" will be incomplete and impressionistic, they can be very important in judging future absorption. For example, if most of the big law firms have moved in the last two or three years, creating strong positive absorption, it is not likely that absorption will continue to be strong unless a new type of tenant is involved.

While absorption is frequently used as a proxy for measuring the demand for office space, it does not tell the whole story. As noted above, changes in the number of jobs that occur in office settings—office-prone employment—is the underlying determinant of the need for space. Increases in the number of workers housed in office environments should translate into demand for space. Unfortunately, the correlation between the two is not perfect.

Using employment data to calculate office demand is tricky, and involves the following steps. First, as shown in Table 11-2, the analyst must obtain employment projections by industry type. The Federal Bureau of Labor Statistics categorizes every business or economic enterprise and groups them into similar classes by Standard Industrial Classification, or SIC, codes, expressed in numbers of employees. This government system is widely used by market analysts and others seeking to understand economic growth and business activity.

The second step is to determine, for each industry, the percentage of workers likely to be employed in office space (as opposed, for example, to retail or industrial settings). The proportion will be defined differently for different metropolitan areas. The category "Wholesale and Retail Trade" may, using national norms, have only a small percentage of its employment in office space. But in a city such as Chicago, headquarters of both Sears and Montgomery Ward, the percentage will be much higher.

As a way around the difficult and judgmental task of calculating office-prone employment, many analysts instead rely solely on the SIC code's Finance, Insurance and Real Estate (FIRE) employment category. An increase in FIRE employment is held to translate into an increase in demand for office space. While this is clearly a crude assumption, it is frequently employed.

Another analytic hurdle in using employment data to measure office demand is that employment numbers available from the Federal Bureau of Labor Statistics and from state offices of employment security are reported only for county or metropolitan areas. These statistics can be used to describe employment changes for all of Dallas or Des Moines, for example, but they are not available for the relevant office submarkets within a city or metropolitan area. Therefore, the analyst must allocate future job increases to each submarket. In the simplest case, that means deciding what proportion of new office employment will be "captured" downtown versus in the suburbs and what proportion will be captured by Class A, B or C buildings. In more complex cases, say in very large markets such as Houston, Atlanta or Los Angeles, which may have as many as ten office

TABLE 11-2   Average Annual Net Employment Gains (Losses) by Industry, 1975-2000

	Average Annual Jobs Created				
Industry	1975-1978	1979-1982	1983-1990	1990-1995	1995-2000
Construction	4,100	(6,900)	3,000	900	900
Transportation, Communication and Public Utilities	800	(5,400)	3,800	1,800	1,500
Wholesale and Retail Prices	18,200	(3,400)	10,900	8,700	6,600
Government	(1,800)	(7,200)	(900)	1,400	1,400
Manufacturing	10,800	(55,800)	6,100	(1,300)	(1,800)
Finance, Insurance and Real Estate	5,700	7,800	5,600	4,900	3,200
Services	16,600	26,000	26,100	22,800	15,800
Net Employment Gain or Loss	54,000	(44,900)	54,600	39,200	27,600

Source: Department of Commerce, Bureau of the Census

submarkets, the task of allocating new demand is a challenging one. As a result, employment data are generally useful only in describing the general context or overall pattern of office space demand.

The recommended approach is to merge the top-down methodology of defining office demand using employment growth and the bottom-up technique of defining demand as the amount of space actually absorbed. However, for the analysis of a specific building, the net absorption statistic is by far the more useful because it documents the ebb and flow of space use in the market area in which the subject property must compete for tenants.

Supply of Office Space

The supply of office space is much easier to define and measure than demand. As in the case of absorption or employment change, it is important to have historic patterns for the submarket. Table 11-3 is an example of an office space supply table that shows the inventory of space by year, new additions and vacancy. These data are now publicly available from national and local brokerage firms and from proprietary data vendors who specialize in office markets.

Office space within a submarket is usually classified into three tiers—A, B, and C—depending on location, age, quality of construction, mechanical systems and image of the building. Space inventories should separate the different classes of space because they appeal to different tenancies.

The supply of office space consists not just of existing buildings, but also those under construction, those that are planned, and those that have space available to sublet. Information on planned buildings and those under construction can be obtained from city government offices and by interviewing knowledgeable local real estate professionals. Buildings are then grouped by the year they will open which gives the analyst a clear picture of what the short and intermediate term future hold for new space

TABLE 11-3   Supply/Demand Projections

Year	Constructed During Year	Total Inventory End of Year	Absorption	Year-end Vacancy Amount	Percent
1987	4,167	92,572	2,750	12,855	13.9
1988	850	93,422	2,200	11,505	12.3
1989	4,895	98,317	2,100	14,300	14.5
1990	4,960	103,277	2,100	17,160	16.6
1991	2,780	106,057	2,000	17,940	16.9
1992	1,325	107,382	2,000	17,265	16.1

Source: Heitman Financial

availability. For those buildings that are "planned," the analyst will need to use judgment to decide which will actually proceed at the time intended.

Historic construction, current vacancy, and the under-construction and planned additions to the inventory together comprise the supply side analysis. Trend analysis will show the analyst whether the current and projected supply situation is normal or represents an important increase or decrease in new space.

Vacant space should be carefully evaluated by the market analyst. Is it in a few large blocks or many small rental areas? Is the vacancy rate the same for A, B and C space or for other breakdowns of building types? Another caution: Leasing agents may claim that there isn't enough high quality or large block space available for some prospective users. Assertions like these need to be investigated, not just accepted.

Important to this analysis is the issue of sublet space, i.e., space that is vacant but does not appear in the vacancy numbers because it is being paid for. But it is also being marketed, frequently at very low rates, and therefore should be counted in the inventory of available space. Sublet space can be estimated, and the analyst must consult local experts in order to judge its impact. Generally, however, large amounts of sublet space act to reduce net effective rents for smaller tenants who are willing to take this space "as is" in return for advantageous lease terms.

Merging Supply and Demand Analysis

The juxtaposition of the historic record of absorption and vacancy provides the analyst with a reasonably clear insight into the submarket's supply and demand dynamics. If, on average, a submarket has absorbed 100,000 square feet of space annually, and there are currently 100,000 square feet vacant, then the market is nearly balanced, all other factors being equal. When the amount of vacant space (and space under construction) greatly exceeds the average absorption, the situation is frequently described in terms of "years of excess supply." If a market that absorbs 100,000 square feet a year has 500,000 square feet vacant, it is characterized as having a five-year supply.

It is critical to note that this type of analysis proceeds entirely based on (1) past history and (2) averages. Both are notoriously bad predictors of the future. Although there is no direct connection between the metropolitan area employment measure of demand and the performance of the specific submarket, the overall demand numbers should be used by the analyst to help make a judgment about the likelihood that future absorption rates will remain as they have been in the past. There may be a clue in the aggregate numbers about an upturn or a downturn, or a change in the employment mix that may presage an increase or decrease in overall office-prone employment.

It is more useful, however, for the analyst to interpret the absorption and vacancy numbers in light of specific submarket factors. What kinds of tenants are represented in the market and are they likely to grow? Are there specific government programs that will spur development? Is the direction of growth changing in a way that will affect the submarket positively or negatively? Only careful work in the submarket, usually based on interviews with knowledgeable local professionals, can unearth these factors. Aggregate demand numbers and historic absorption clearly have their place in defining the baseline, but they need to be interpreted in light of particular local events and socioeconomic and even political trends.

It should also be remembered that area data and submarket numbers characterize aggregates. It is a logical fallacy to make inferences about individual buildings from aggregates (the so-called ecological or contextual fallacy). Similarly, it is a mistake to judge the marketability of a site-specific project based just on the submarket supply and demand analysis. In order to come to an opinion of the market acceptance of a particular office building, the analyst must consider its individual assets and liabilities and its competitive position.

SITE ASSETS AND LIABILITIES

The submarket analysis is an "in the field" exercise. The market analyst must literally walk the market, visit the competitive projects and generally understand how the area, and the site, are perceived locally. This part of the market study calls for data creation as well as data collection and analysis. The analyst may collect impressionistic information but where possible it is prudent to be more quantitative. It may be sufficient to conclude, for example, that there are shopping opportunities "close by." But in other cases, it may be necessary to actually measure the drive time from a site to nearby residential enclaves if the project's viability depends on that kind of proximity.

Maps and the aerial display of data are critical elements of market analysis. Understanding the site in relation to current and future development and in relation to a host of physical, environmental and geographic features is absolutely essential. The ability of the analyst to configure and display information in map-like form (called Geographic Information Systems, or GIS) greatly enhances office market analysis.

Site features—positives and negatives—that affect marketability are many. They are grouped into (1) physical issues, (2) visibility and access, and (3) the condition of the surrounding area. While the specific issues will be different for a suburban or downtown site, the following features are always evaluated.

(1) Physical Features

Size:
: Given zoning and building code ordinances, is the site large enough to build on? In many situations, bonuses in the form of variances from site planning and density requirements can be obtained from the local jurisdiction.

Shape:
: Is the site regular in configuration, or irregular in a way that may affect its development potential? Oddly shaped parcels may restrict access, limit density or adversely affect locally acceptable design.

Topography and Soil:
: Are there any topographical features that enhance or detract from the property? Soil testing is not the province of the market analyst, but features of the site that would affect the project's marketability should be noted.

Environmental Status:
: Is the site "clean"? Contamination from previous users and contamination from adjacent users via infiltration must be tested. While this is not an issue that the market analyst addresses, any indication that environmental problems exist must be explored. In the case of an existing building, the effects of asbestos may be evaluated in terms of impact on rentability. A remediation program will affect leasing rates and timing.

(2) Visibility and Access

Visibility:
: Is the site visible from major thoroughfares? Low visibility may have an impact on rents.

Access:
: Is the property easily accessible to pedestrians, cars, cabs and limousines, and service vehicles? One-way streets and complicated expressway off-ramp systems may deter future tenants.

Adjacent Uses:
: Are there immediately adjacent physical or aesthetic negatives, such as an unattractive building next door (for example, a structured parking deck) or views that are blocked by adjacent high rises, that could affect

marketability? Similarly, positive adjacencies (a park, for example) enhance rents and speed leasing time.

Prestige
Address:

Is there any special advantage to the street address, or, for suburban office buildings, the subdivision or business park name? Many markets have outgrown the concept of the 100% office location, but in others the image of address, such as Park Avenue in New York, is still strong.

Future Site
Protection:

Is the site protected from future adjacent or nearby uses that could compromise attractiveness? Solar easements and views are the most frequent issues, but parking and other low-density adjacent uses can also be affected.

(3) Environs

As important as the site itself are the locational advantages and disadvantages of the site's position within the submarket. Among the most important issues to be considered by the analyst are the following.

Overall
Submarket
Image:

What is the image, or status, of the submarket? Is it high-end? Does it have a dominant character, as for example, the financial district? Are there local, historic forces that mitigate for or against the submarket? An area's image can change, but it happens slowly.

Amenities:

Are there nearby conveniences and services such as restaurants, shopping, health clubs and eating clubs. Are they within walking distance? It is important to actually walk the surrounding area to determine if there are physical or psychological boundaries or "dividing lines" that may limit access to amenities.

Access to Mass
Transit and
Parking:

Nearby inexpensive parking and walking distance to mass transit may be critical depending on submarket conditions. In some markets, attached covered parking will be the norm. If driving to the site will be important, the actual drive times to residential areas will need to be established. For larger potential users (in number of employees), the availability of mass transit is usually important.

Proximity to Other Uses:	Proximity to courts, government agencies, and special uses such as financial institutions need to be determined.
Security:	Is the surrounding neighborhood safe? Are there cabs at night? Safety and security are increasingly important in suburban areas as well as inner city office districts.
Public Policy Impacts:	Is the site in an expanding section of the submarket or is the direction and velocity of growth changing? Are zoning changes imminent? Where will future growth corridors occur? They can be affected as much by public policy, infrastructure and public facilities programs as by private market forces. City or other governmental officials can explain capital improvement and other programs that may affect the site environs.

Site and surrounding area attributes are based in part on the market analyst's judgment and in part on empirical data. Distances to important destinations around the property can be walked and quantified. Amenities can be quantified as well, by literally counting restaurants, convenience shopping opportunities, health clubs and other facilities.

The dominant users of space in the submarket will in part determine the desirability of the site. If the area is oriented to government offices, utilities and large corporate tenants, it may have less appeal to boutique service firms that want a different "atmosphere." These intangible, qualitative aspects of the site and its environs are critical to the future rentability of the space, the type of tenants obtainable and the lease rates it will achieve.

COMPETITIVE ANALYSIS

Site and locational attributes are meaningful by themselves, because they are either positive or negative. However, office buildings compete against a finite number of other office buildings for tenants and many of these factors must be judged in relation to the competition.

The analyst's first task is to precisely define the submarket in terms of the specific office projects—existing, under construction, proposed—that are or will be comparable to the building being studied. For a brand new project, the competition will be other Class A buildings that have available space. If the study is for the purchase of an existing office structure, the competitive alignment must be identified in terms of properties of similar location, age, design and quality.

A useful tool in evaluating the competitive position of the site is to prepare a matrix such as that displayed in Table 11-4. In this example, the subject property is contrasted to buildings judged to be in direct competition for tenants along a number of the dimensions discussed above. By making forced choice ratings of each office building, on a one to five scale, the analyst can create a quantitative measure of the attractiveness of the site. This matrix should be reviewed by knowledgeable local real estate professionals to assure that it is accurate.

PREVAILING AND FORECAST RENTS

Once the competitive alignment is established and the relative attractiveness of the site and location are determined, the analyst is prepared to address the question of lease rates. Unfortunately, historic data on lease rates are hard to obtain and frequently are not very reliable even when available. The rents that will be achieved by the analyzed building are a function of (1) submarket vacancy; (2) new supply coming on line; and (3) current leasing packages. High vacancy translates into downward pressure on rents. Large additions to the supply mean that downward pressures will intensify. Therefore, the vacancy projections made earlier (comparing absorption estimates with supply estimates) play a crucial role in determining future rents. Of course, rents go up as well, and a supply and demand analysis that projects a balanced market will support lease step-ups.

Unless the subject building is dramatically superior to the competition, it is unwarranted to expect that the property will get better than "market" rents. The analyst must be prepared to spend significant time in thesubmarket determining exactly what lease terms and conditions prevail

TABLE 11-4   Competitive Alignment Matrix

| | Site Attribute | | | | | |
| | | | Proximity To | | | |
Properties	Access	Parking	Shopping	Courts	Mass Transit	Total
A	2	4	4	3	5	18
B	4	3	3	5	2	17
Subject	3	2	3	5	3	16
C	3	1	4	5	3	16
D	2	2	5	1	2	12

5 = Excellent
1 = Poor

Source: Heitman Financial

and what kinds of deals are being done. Rent is itself a complicated term, and how it is computed locally, and especially how net effective rents are quoted, must be determined. Various concessions (such as abatements, free rent, moving allowances, expensive tenant improvements and lease buyouts) complicate the task of comparing one lease transaction with another. Effective rent, not gross rent quotations, becomes the comparative measure.

Rental increases over the course of the initial leasing of the property, or at the time leases must be renewed in an existing building, are projected based on the analyst's best estimate of the supply and demand balance in the market in the future. There is no substitute at this point for good judgment. The analyst has to balance current rental rates against future increases or decreases. The vacancy rate offers the best indication of how competitive the market will be, but it is just a clue. As a result, it is prudent to provide future rental changes as a range (such as $10-$12 per square foot) rather than as a point estimate ($11). Past performance may be a guide to the pattern of rent increases. Alternately, the future rental rates may be described on the basis of different scenarios, a "worst case/best case/most likely case" presentation that factors in some of the qualitative aspects of the market that will affect the increases the building can achieve. Table 11-5 shows rental projections, expressed in ranges, for two leasing scenarios.

Absorption

Experience shows that, despite what developers would have one believe, one can't beat the market in terms of rental rates. However, the speed with which the building is leased is a variable that the market study must address. There are two complementary approaches to measuring

TABLE 11-5   Projected Rents

Year	Contract rent (net)	Scenario I		Scenario 2	
		Average Concession package	Average Effective rent*	Average Concession package	Average Effective rent*
	($/sq. ft.)	%	($/sq. ft.)	%	($/sq. ft.)
1989	22.00-24.00	30	15.40-16.80	25	16.50-18.00
1990	22.00-24.00	25	16.50-18.00	20	17.60-19.20
1991	22.00-24.00	20	17.60-19.20	15	18.70-20.40
1992	22.00-24.00	15	18.70-20.40	15	18.70-20.40

*Over the length of the lease.

Source: Heitman Financial

absorption for a specific building. The first is to analyze the absorption experience of other recently built properties that are comparable to the subject property. If, on average, they leased, say, 20,000 square feet a month, then that is a benchmark against which the property can be measured. The second approach is to do a simple "shift/share" or capture rate analysis. For example, if there are five buildings competing for tenants then it may be assumed that each will capture 20% of the market. The annual absorption and leasing rates (collected in the first phase of the analysis) can then be divided into fifths to calculate each building's share. However, the share allocated to each building need not necessarily be proportional. For example, the analyst might conclude that a particular building's market share should be greater because of its location or because it has design features or amenities which are not present in the other properties.

Neither of these methods—the use of comparable building absorption rates or the market share capture rate—is foolproof. But together they provide the analyst with the likely range, or probable band, of absorption. The precise estimate will depend on the amount of pre-leasing, special attributes (pro and con) of the building, and the owner's willingness to trade off between achieved rent and speed of absorption.

Recent academic research has focused attention on macro or metropolitan area analysis of office absorption, but these techniques do not apply to the evaluation of a specific property. Assessing competitive strengths and weaknesses and allocating a share of new office demand remain judgmental. Many developers and investors are quick to assume that their building will "outperform the market." The lessons of the overbuilding in the 1980s suggest that the methods outlined above are critical to making objective judgments about office performance.

Design Recommendations

If the market study is done for a to-be-built property, it may contain recommendations that the analyst believes will maximize leasing performance and rents. Developers and their financial partners, as a rule, tend to build too much space and spend too much on the space. There is a possibility of creating a Class A building on a Class B site, or the opposite. The market analyst, based on the information collected in the analysis, may make recommendations in the following areas:

- **Size of project:** The building might be smaller or larger, or perhaps built in phases rather than all at once. It is not axiomatic to build to the full zoning maximum.
- **Orientation on the site:** Changing the orientation of the building to better "meet the street" or to face anticipated competition may be required.

- **Floorplates:** Consistent with sizing recommendations, smaller or larger floor sizes and floor configurations (many corner offices) may be more marketable.
- **Amenities:** These include parking (above code requirements), a restaurant, convenience shopping, a health club, among others. Landscaping and site planning recommendations may also be made.
- **Level of finish/quality of construction:** If market demand is present for new but "vanilla" space that can be leased less expensively than the competition, it may make sense to downgrade the level of finish.

If the marketability study is done for the purchase of an existing building, the analyst is more limited in the scope of recommendations. However, the rehabilitation of common areas, changing entryways, facade improvements and other changes may be possible and may contribute to the building's success in attracting and retaining tenants.

DATA SOURCES

The marketability study is based on experienced judgment as well as quantitative information and data. The assessment of achievable rents and

Higher density mid-rise office buildings in a suburban setting may have parking needs that require large open land areas and reduce the amount of landscaped open space. *(Photo by Bob Harr/Hedrich-Blessing)*

the pace of absorption are particularly dependent on the analyst's ability to synthesize often disparate findings into a logical and coherent pattern. The evaluation of the site and its environs is also heavily judgmental, and based on the opinions of local professionals as well as those formed by the analyst.

But good judgment is also based on good data. Fortunately, office market information is more and more reliable and comprehensive. Following are sources of the types of data required by the market analyst.

Office Space Supply

Information on the existing inventory of space for submarkets is produced by large real estate brokerage houses and by proprietary vendors. Vacancy numbers vary across inventories because firms start from a different universe of properties. It is essential that the inventory distinguish Class A, B and C space by careful definition.

Space under construction can be obtained from local brokers and other real estate professionals, including appraisers. In a small market, or one with little activity, financial institutions also provide this information. Planned buildings can be identified by city officials from building permits issued, or by the research staff of local real estate brokers. Not all planned buildings proceed, and their timing is subject to change.

Estimates of sublet space vary by market. There are no consistent guidelines for reporting sublet space, so the analyst must exercise care in using available figures.

Office Space Demand

Employment data, by industry and by SIC code, are available from the Bureau of Labor Statistics, *Employment and Earnings*. States provide employment data and projections, usually from the office that handles unemployment compensation. Some localities, using state data, publish estimates of "where workers work" that are extraordinarily useful. Federal data and census data report occupation and employment based on "where workers live."

Data on net absorption (and leasing activity) are created by the major national brokerage firms and by independent consulting and research organizations. The quality of data from the first source is variable; most of these firms are strong in some markets, weaker in others. For-profit data providers are also spotty in their coverage, so it is best to inquire locally as to which of the available sources is most reliable.

The chamber of commerce, utility companies, area economic development agencies, major banks and other organizations make data available on general economic trends, major employers, infrastructure and capital projects, and other aspects of the economy that influence overall demand for office space. Typically, these data are at the metropolitan area level of aggregation and are not directly useful for a site-specific analysis.

Geographic Information Systems

Geographic Information Systems is a growing industry that provides data, software for manipulating the data, and in some cases, specialized hardware (plotters, mapping devices). The common thread in GIS is that the information can be "geo-coded," that is, it has a finite physical location that can be expressed by longitude and latitude. A property (515 Main Street), a building (Southdale Mall), an individual shopper's address, a hospital— anything that can be geo-coded—can then be displayed in aerial format. Geographic Information Systems allow the analyst to illustrate and relate points over physical space and to produce maps showing density as well as distance.

GIS is most helpful with retail and housing analysis, where the census creates a massive data base. Data bases that relate to site-specific office marketability analysis are less well developed. As noted, census data on employment show where people live, not where they work. Until a GIS data base provider is able to get access to data on where people actually work, the demand side of the office analysis will not be greatly enhanced. On the supply side, GIS data bases that inventory office buildings permit the analyst to map different configurations of buildings (to create a submarket or to define a competitive alignment) and are extremely useful. GIS also "digitizes" maps. Purchase of a map data set for a locality allows the analyst to create any level of scale or detail that is needed for the analysis. Thus, a first map may show the subject site in relation to the entire downtown, and a second will "zoom in" to show the site in relation to the two or three blocks surrounding it.

Information on GIS is available from a wide array of consulting firms. A national clearinghouse for GIS-related data and software is GIS World, Inc., located in Ft. Collins, Colorado.

CONCLUSION

Office marketability studies answer the question: How will an office building in this location perform? Market performance refers to the speed with which the building will lease and the rents it will command. For an existing building, maintaining tenants and keeping rent levels are the relevant issues.

The analysis comprises extensive data collection plus analysis and informed judgment. Successful market studies require that the analyst and the ultimate user of the study—developer or investor—share a common vision of the scope of the study and the level of detail.

ABOUT THE AUTHOR

Richard Kateley is executive vice president and director of research at Heitman Financial Ltd., a full-service real estate advisory firm. He coordinates the firm's research, works on new products for pension funds, and provides market briefings to clients. Prior to joining Heitman, Kateley was president and CEO of Real Estate Research Corporation, a national consulting and appraisal firm. He authored the well-known industry forecast, *Emerging Trends in Real Estate*, and has published more than 20 articles in professional and trade journals. He has a BA from the University of Texas, an MA from the University of Chicago, and was a Fulbright Fellow.

12

FEASIBILITY ANALYSIS FOR OFFICE BUILDINGS

by John D. Dorchester, Jr.

INTRODUCTION

Feasibility analysis plays a crucial role in office building decision making. However, "feasibility" and "feasibility analysis" are among the most misunderstood and misused terms and processes in the real estate industry.

In broad terms, feasibility analysis develops a "go" or "no go" recommendation for each alternative under consideration. While market analysis supplies some critical ingredients needed for feasibility analysis, the latter supplies the analytical process leading to a decision. For an investor, feasibility analysis assists in differentiating properties and identifying those which can meet investor objectives. For the developer, feasibility analysis makes it possible to test each potential site and related development program and make an optimum choice. For the space user, feasibility analysis provides a means of selecting between buy or lease choices, and among specific implementation programs associated with each. For any investment decision, feasibility analysis provides a systematic analytical process for applying data to decision making. The analyst uses the analysis framework to determine whether stated goals can be accomplished through the course(s) of action tested.

This chapter defines feasibility analysis and examines the concepts contained within its meaning. Next, it looks at business applications for feasibility analysis to establish a framework for more detailed examination

Research assistance for this chapter was provided by Frederick A. Rendahl.

of feasibility analysis processes. Finally, it relates feasibility analysis to other important topics contained in this book.

Feasibility analysis should be recognized as an extension of market research fitted to a particular decision maker and a given decision framework. It is neither an isolated process nor an answer to a question in itself. Feasibility analysis gains its value from proper understanding, reasonable processing and careful final application within the larger system of which it is an integral component.

CONCEPTUAL MISAPPLICATIONS

Common misuses of the concept of feasibility analysis are illustrated by the following examples:

1. A mortgage banker submits a package for a potential mortgage commitment. It contains a section called "Appraisal and Feasibility." The appraisal indicates a market value estimate higher than what is required to cover the debt sought and the submission concludes that "the loan is feasible."
2. A developer asks a real estate counselor for a feasibility study for a proposed office building. All that is needed, it is explained, is a calculation of the internal rate of return from the developer's pro-forma income and expense projections and a statement that the result is acceptable to the general investment market.
3. An appraiser is asked by a bank to estimate the market value of a proposed office building. The appraiser does not talk with the potential borrower. The report sets forth a market value estimate and concludes that the value estimate and associated analyses indicate that the building is "feasible."

Each of these examples suffers from a similar flaw: a failure to recognize that "feasibility" must be applied to one or more scenarios associated with specific, identified objectives.

DEFINITIONS AND CONCEPTS

James A. Graaskamp's definition of a feasibility project is one where "...the real estate analyst determines that there is a reasonable likelihood of satisfying explicit objectives when a selected course of action is tested for fit to a context of specific constraints and limited resources."[1] The elements of

---

[1] James A. Graaskamp, *A Guide to Feasibility Analysis* (Chicago: Society of Real Estate Appraisers, 1970), p. 4.

Graaskamp's definition are implicit in other definitions and should be examined individually:

1. **"Reasonable likelihood":** Feasibility does not require an absolute certainty, and one would be an impossible expectation. Feasibility does, however, rely upon an acceptable probability that estimated outcome(s) of a decision will occur.

2. **"Explicit objectives":** Investors have differing objectives. Without identifying these objectives, feasibility cannot be determined because there is nothing to test. Sometimes broad market objectives are identified rather than those for a particular investor; if the situation is explained and the objectives are explicitly set forth, this limited use of "feasibility" should be applied with caution.

3. **"Selected course of action":** Ultimately, feasibility says: "It is feasible to do a particular thing in order to accomplish specific objectives." To reach this conclusion, the analyst identifies a series of possible ways in which to meet identified objectives, tests each, and eventually identifies one (or more) that are most likely to accomplish stated objectives.

4. **"Specific constraints":** Constraints may be internal or external. Both internal and external constraints tend to differ among investors. They cannot be ignored or wished away. During feasibility analysis, selected courses of action are tested against these constraints to determine probabilities that the objectives can be achieved.

5. **"Limited resources":** Even if money were no object, prudent analysis and decision making require recognition that financial resources should be considered scarce, and their use should be optimized within the context of the investment decision. Human resources are also a major consideration. These include quality and quantity of personnel for the tasks to be accomplished, and a series of more subjective factors such as experience and psychological suitability to the risks and requirements of alternative courses of action.

Comparing these elements of a feasibility analysis with the misapplications discussed above, it becomes clear that feasibility concepts and definitions are important to both the counselor and the client. When properly applied, they offer opportunities for cogent communication, focused analysis, and better reasoned decisions.

BUSINESS APPLICATIONS FOR FEASIBILITY ANALYSIS

Because it tests courses of action, feasibility analysis is appropriate whenever a new capital expenditure is required or a decision must be made regarding an existing investment. If only one course of action is available, there is no decision to be made. In this rare situation there would be no need for a feasibility analysis. In all other cases, however, feasibility analysis assists and guides the decision of what to do. Even the decision to do nothing is an implicit decision that this is the most feasible course of action to accomplish the decision maker's objectives. Feasibility analysis normally requires consideration of all alternate courses of action.

To illustrate, appraisers have long applied three approaches to estimates of market value. Each is based upon the principle of substitution, which can be restated as "alternate courses of action." The cost approach considers construction of a new building. The sales comparison approach considers acquisition of another property. The income approach considers alternative investments, whether in real estate or elsewhere. Each of these options has numerous sub-options. During feasibility analysis, specific alternatives are identified, analyzed, tested, and weighed for their ability to accomplish stated goals.

By helping the client (or employer) identify objectives, constraints, assignable resources and decision criteria, the real estate counselor develops a contextual framework for the feasibility analysis. The basis for a decision is broadened, reasons for the decision are more focused and risk is reduced. The process includes identification of crucial facts and assumptions, validation of those assumptions for which facts can be found, and clear understanding of those unresolved assumptions upon which decisions might be made. While *uncertainties* (the probabilities of unforeseen events occurring) are ever present, *risks* (the probabilities that foreseen events will not occur) can be better identified and dealt with through this process. Thus feasibility analysis is applicable to all investment decisions.

THE FEASIBILITY PROCESS

In office building feasibility analysis, the marketplace, the office building product and the client are all components of the decision process. The role of the counselor is to assure that all three are brought together in a framework which allows independent analysis of each while recognizing the importance of each in the final decisions made.

Role of the Marketplace

The marketplace can be viewed in direct or indirect terms. Directly it is those properties and market conditions which influence or are influenced by a given property. Indirectly it includes the rest of the world, particularly those components which offer broad investment alternatives or constraints.

While market analysis involves identification and quantification of markets and submarkets related to supply and demand issues, feasibility analysis considers data developed from market analysis to identify alternatives, weigh probabilities, and deal with external constraints. Market analysis supplies the "raw materials" of facts and forecasts from which feasibility determinations can be developed.

It is the underpinning of the actual marketplace that makes feasibility analysis so important in decision processes. Decisions are made to achieve future outcomes for selected courses of action. At decision time, no one can know the future. However, by better understanding the marketplace, the counselor's feasibility analysis is built on a solid foundation in which specific risks can be isolated and considered and a far greater range of alternatives can be weighed. Without this base, feasibility analysis is merely an exercise.

Market considerations will include demographic, economic, social and political/governmental issues. For feasibility analysis it is particularly important that distinctions be made among the following:

1. **Demand vs. absorption:** Broadly speaking, demand is purchasing power which is, or is likely to be, demonstrated for a given product. Absorption is that which has been sold or rented. Absorption is an evidence of demand, but is not a complete substitute for a demand estimate. Absorption can only occur within a given supply. Although absorption can affect future demand (by removing or deferring potential demand units), it cannot independently reflect potential or latent demand, and may evidence consumer (tenant) willingness to accept less than what is desired if a supply of what is desired is not available. Absorption is also thought of as the net addition to the total inventory after adding what has been rented or sold and subtracting what has been removed by demolition, fire or abandonment.

2. **Forecasts vs. projections:** Forecasts are estimates of the future. They may be made through various processes, and both the source data and estimation process should be identified and analyzed to use their results. Projections are extrapolations of the past. Graphically or mathematically they are extensions of known historical data into the future. Projections may be used in forecasting, but the process should be distinguished because projections have an inevitable result which derives from the way in which they are made.

3. **Precision vs. accuracy:** With the advent of computers, analysts can now make approximations to more decimal places than ever before. Mathematically, however, there is a limit to accuracy which is inherent in any data set. Even more important, the seeming persuasion of mathematical precision should never be confused with an accurate result. Perfect math may give results that are unrelated to or unreliable within a given decision process.

4. **Market opinion vs. "the right answer":** Widely held market opinion, even if wrong, has substantial impact on specific decisions and ultimately on the market at large. Proper market research will identify and

isolate differences between market views and research results, and will provide a basis for understanding market situations more accurately. Feasibility analysis requires the analyst to examine these conflicts and assess their effect on the identification of alternatives and establishment of probabilities for each course of action, as well as their impact on final objectives. Oddly, some decisions can be made correctly for the "wrong" reasons, but doing so still requires detailed research and analysis. In the long run, the analyst will make more correct decisions based on adequate research and for the "right" reasons.

In preparation for feasibility analysis, market research looks to the marketplace for comparable/competitive properties, legal and political factors which offer opportunities and constraints, economic data signaling areas of stability and/or change, financial data from which alternatives can be identified and measurements can be drawn, attitudes and activities of others who are (or are potentially) active, and other factors. Good market research identifies a property's niche and the dimensions and characteristics of its market. The range of issues and the need for continuity in their treatment are reasons why market research and feasibility analysis are closely related and should be closely orchestrated.

Role of the Office Building

The real estate product is both a physical and an economic subject for the feasibility analysis. The nature and status of both land and building are critical to the analysis.

Understanding the office building requires more than just a "bricks and mortar" approach. Although physical aspects are crucial, it is the building's ability to produce income (or utility) over time, weighed against the cost of doing so, which is of paramount importance. Accordingly, physical examination should raise important physical issues, but it should also identify those factors which bear upon capital and operating costs, risk, longevity, alternatives and market acceptance.

The following examples illustrate incorrect or incomplete consideration of the physical product, as well as numerous errors in the feasibility process:

1. **Overbuilding:** The corporate or business "monument" whose creation cost far exceeds any reasonable expectation of return (other than ego or prestige) is common. If ego or prestige is a stated goal, then the overimprovement may be highly successful. Too frequently, however, replacement of an individual removes that decision criterion, leaving a property which cannot provide a fair return on investment. Proper feasibility analysis should raise the alternative of hold for a period of time and then sell. This alternative would measure the apparent margin of overinvestment, and provide a basis for a reasoned decision.

2. **Layout:** The design of many office buildings is based on the assumption of a specific occupancy. Specially adapted buildings frequently cost more to produce, and then more to prepare for market upon sale, than buildings with more flexible design. The physical design issue should be raised in feasibility analysis, and the financial and other objectives should be analyzed after quantifying and analyzing this marginal cost. Even so-called standard buildings require knowledgeable scrutiny: If parking meets zoning requirements, do the spaces provided meet market needs?; Are bay and corridor sizes appropriate for furniture layout, traffic movement, and logistical support?; and many more questions of this nature.

3. **Special design:** An unusual exterior design or site layout is frequently undertaken "because it was drawn" rather than because market research indicated a preference for it. Feasibility analysis questions whether market research has accurately captured the market attitude toward styles, designs, building materials, layout, siting, and other factors. Coupled with astute market analysis, feasibility analysis permits a tailoring of project design for specific market segments and better optimization of investment costs and returns.

In the purchase and sale of office buildings, there is much to consider beyond the transaction itself. Feasibility analysis requires the identification of alternative courses of action beyond those most likely to be chosen. Testing courses of action which intuitively appear infeasible provides a clearer view of those eventually chosen, assures that important alternatives are not overlooked, and sometimes provides a new insight into the entire decision. The process also provides a place and framework for consideration of the investment decision and the management of its consequences.

The Role of the Client

Feasibility studies focus on the client as well as the property in identifying alternatives, constraints and resources. Frequently the counselor's first task in feasibility analysis is to acquaint the client with decision-making processes and the role that feasibility analysis plays. Key elements which must be considered include:

1. **Client objectives:** There must be an explicit, written statement of what is to be accomplished through the investment. The feasibility study will eventually identify ways in which the objectives can be met, what is involved with each alternative and how likely the forecast outcomes are. Identification of objectives requires skill on the part of the counselor and open, confident participation by the client.

2. **Client alternatives:** Alternatives available to the client should be viewed in the broadest sense. The purchase decision, for example, may have as viable alternatives:

- Do nothing
- Buy another building
- Locate in another neighborhood or city
- Rent with options
- Acquire the entity that owns the building
- Invest elsewhere
- Do something else

Alternatives are even available in the structuring of the purchase contract, financing arrangements and the like.

3. **Client resources and constraints:** The counselor cannot assume that the office building investment is the right one for the client or that it can be made without other significant effects on the client. Examples of constraints include:

- Effect of diverting available cash into the office building investment and away from the business which will occupy the real estate
- Insufficient experience in property management or the associated decision whether to procure professional management
- Absence of a long-term financial strategy in which the office building investment is only a part
- Inadequate reserves to carry the investment through economic downturns, rent loss during renovation or other difficulties
- Inadequate contingency reserves for cost or time overruns
- Psychological factors, including effect of the new risk position upon the individual(s) involved

It is important that the counselor communicate regularly with the client during the feasibility analysis process. It is not uncommon for clients to develop new insights or to change their objectives. It is not unheard of to complete the perfect analysis only to learn that the client can no longer proceed with the investment!

Decision Criteria

To achieve stated objectives the client must eventually say "go" or "no go" for each alternative identified. A goal of the feasibility analysis is to test each alternative and to produce results which can be easily considered and weighed in making these decisions. The factors to be considered and the results they must achieve to be acceptable are referred to as decision criteria. A few of the more common ones are:

1. **Internal Rate of Return:** The IRR is one of the most common decision criteria and can be used in a number of ways. One way is to require that the most probable IRR for an investment exceed an established minimum consistent with the general risk associated with that type and class

of office building. A discussion of IRR methodology can be found in Chapter 29.

2. **Absolute cash required:** This criterion identifies the total or maximum cash requirement at any given point in the investment. For example, a building requiring a $10 million capital outlay for its purchase may also require $2.5 million to achieve stabilized occupancy and establish reserves. A decision criterion setting an $11 million maximum cash outlay requirement would find this investment alternative infeasible.

3. **Time to market:** Development of a sizable office building may require several years for completion and occupancy. For an investor that must measure performance regularly over the period that the project is nonperforming, the sheer time needed to complete the project might disqualify the alternative.

A Brief Summary

It can be seen from the foregoing discussion that feasibility analysis is an ingredient within a larger decision-making process, and is a logical extension of market analysis. Principal steps in feasibility analysis include, but are not limited to, the following:

1. Identification of client objectives in writing
2. Identification of constraints
3. Identification of resources
4. Establishment and testing of alternatives
5. Identification of decision criteria
6. Application of decision criteria to the decision
7. Report to client, including recommendations

To be successful, feasibility analysis must provide an analysis framework which clearly sets forth what the client wants to accomplish; acceptable alternatives and the risks and rewards associated with each; and the likelihood that the objectives will be accomplished through the avenue chosen. Where assumptions or "acts of faith" are required, they are identified and their likelihood and possible outcomes are evaluated. The decision is made by the client, based on the research and findings of the counselor.

A FEASIBILITY ANALYSIS APPLICATION

The following example illustrates some basic principles which distinguish the role of feasibility analysis in decision making.

The Analysis Situation

Two + Two, a medium-size accounting firm, is considering development of an office building for its own use. The 100-person firm currently rents 25,000 square feet in a 150,000 square foot suburban multi-tenant building. The current space is cramped and cannot provide for expected future growth. The present lease expires in six months and there is a one-year extension option. Approximately 5,000 square feet of expansion space is available in the same building. Current gross rent is $15 per square foot or $375,000 per year. Pass-through charges of $250,000 bring total annual occupancy charges to $625,000, or $25 per square foot. The building manager has told them that current market rental value for their space, and for the expansion space, is $17 per square foot plus pass-throughs. Market research indicates that vacancy rates have been steady at 12 percent over the past two years.

Two + Two has been approached by Deal & Son, a local developer, with a proposal for a new building in Deal's office park. Deal offers two alternatives:

1. A turnkey build-to-suit building will be delivered to Two + Two for cash upon completion of construction. The building will contain 40,000 square feet and total cost is guaranteed to be $6,600,000 or $165 per square foot. The building and required occupancy permit will be delivered no later than the date of expiration of Two + Two's lease, extended by exercise of the one-year option.
2. Deal will construct a 40,000 square foot, free standing single-tenant office building for Two + Two and will lease it to them for a base term of 15 years with two five-year renewal options. Base rent will be $16 per square foot of floor area, fully net, with annual CPI increases over the term of the lease. Two + Two will have approval over plans and specifications and Deal will guarantee occupancy upon expiration of Two + Two's extended lease.

Two + Two's 14 partners are divided over what to do, but favor development of a freestanding building. They unanimously agree that they need counseling advice.

The Client Interviews

Two + Two engages a counselor and a meeting is set. The counselor quickly realizes that there are substantial differences in the clients' goals and objectives. Many of the older partners favor a new building because it will provide a personal investment avenue or they believe a new building is more prestigious and will enhance the firm's market image. Younger partners are concerned about the personal financial load a new building may create, the commitment of capital which may take away from other business growth opportunities. In addition, they fear it may make new partnerships more difficult or less attractive. Other concerns include the hidden costs of owning and managing a building, the problem of internal versus agency management, and the loss of accounting business from the owner of their current building.

The counselor asks Two + Two's managing partner to provide, on behalf of the firm, a statement of the general goals that are to be met. The counselor works with the managing partner to assure that the statement is understood by all the partners, that it expresses the view of the firm and that it is in a form that permits the counselor to assist Two + Two in making its decision. During this period the counselor also continues gathering other facts about the client. These include future growth prospects and plans, the firm's opportunity cost of capital, capital resources and constraints, and other financial matters. The counselor also begins evaluating the firm's experience in real estate negotiation, its appetite for taking on the risks of a new building, its preparedness to carry through with ownership and management of a building and other "off balance sheet" considerations.

When the goal statement is completed, Two + Two's managing partner sends the counselor a letter (Figure 12-1). Two + Two's goal statement includes the following items:

1. Provide a minimum of 30,000 square feet immediately and guarantee control of another 10,000 square feet by no later than the expiration of the current lease's extension option.
2. Require no more than $750,000 in capital from the partnership exclusive of moving costs or tenant improvements.
3. Require an initial occupancy cost as either a tenant or owner not to exceed $20 per square foot.
4. Enhance the firm's image.
5. Retain the accounting business of their present office building's owner.
6. Arrange for additional space to total 40,000 square feet in existing building as leases expire.

These goal statements are simplified for illustration purposes; the first three actually include specific decision criteria. In practice many prefer to take a matrix approach to this step, identifying each goal, associated decision criteria and a weighting of the importance of each.

The Analysis Period

Market research for any feasibility analysis should be tailored to assist the counselor in identifying alternatives, analyzing them, and judging their relative ability to meet client objectives. Two + Two's counselor, after additional client discussions, identifies five alternatives to test:

FIGURE 12-1

Two+Two

MEMORANDUM

To: Bob Counselor, CRE
From: Ted Two, Managing Partner
Subject: Goals and objectives, proposed office

After considerable debate within our management committee subsequent to our meeting with you, we developed the following primary goals and objectives for our new office:

1. We will require a minimum of 30,000 square feet of office space immediately and a guarantee of another 10,000 square feet no later than the expiration of our current lease's one year extension option.

2. We can provide no more than $750,000 in cash equity from the partnership exclusive of moving costs and tenant improvements. This will come from a group of senior partners rather than from the practice. We are uncertain as to how to equitably structure the ownership positions and will appreciate your assistance.

3. Our practice can afford an initial occupancy cost of not more than $23.50 per square foot per year. We understand occupancy cost to include a net return on our investment plus real estate taxes and operating expenses.

4. If affordable, we believe that relocation to our own "Two+Two Building" will have substantial positive influence on our image and future business; hence it is a highly desirable option.

5. Because we provide a wide scope of services for Will Oldmoney, our landlord, we ideally want to reach a solution which will not offend him or lose his business.

Until our meeting we didn't realize how little our partners had communicated with one another about our needs or possible solutions. The issues you have helped us face are helpful and most appreciated.

1. Stay at the current location
2. Purchase the building Deal will develop for them
3. Rent the building Deal will develop for them
4. Rent in another building
5. Create a joint venture to own Deal's building

Market research must be performed to evaluate each of these five alternatives. An implicit sixth alternative—to do something else—must also be tested. Research frequently uncovers alternatives not obvious at the inception of feasibility analysis.

From the limited data given above, it is apparent that some alternatives may establish conflicts among Two + Two's goals. Certain alternatives can be determined simply while others may require assumptions and higher degrees of risk. Examples of considerations in determining the feasibility of the above alternatives include:

1. **Stay at the current location:** This alternative should accomplish goals 3 and 5, but may be infeasible if the additional 10,000 square feet are not available. At present, the option cannot satisfy goal 1. A new alternative might be identified: to buy out another tenant's position in the present building. New research would be required to identify buyout prospects, replacement space and other new variables. This alternative requires new discussions with the present building's management (or owner) and the possibility of sophisticated negotiation on behalf of Two + Two. This alternative is the most conservative and least costly, but requires further analysis concerning how to obtain the added space.
2. **Purchase the Deal building:** This and the other alternatives involving new construction present a series of risk factors not normally a part of rent alternatives. For example, can Deal deliver on time and within cost? What will the quality of the building be? What will its actual occupancy cost be? Although the building is intended to enhance the firm's image, a poorly executed building could have the opposite effect. At the same time, a successful project not only meets most of the objectives, but could have a strong effect on business profitability. Research and analysis will also uncover additional alternatives: purchase of another existing building or dealing with another developer. Each should be weighed in evaluating Deal's deal. Risk analysis and establishment of probabilities are especially important to the younger Two + Two partners who may still have problems with this alternative. Several constraints may make this alternative infeasible, including availability and cost of outside capital.
3. **Lease the Deal building:** Although at face value this appears to be a clear and simple alternative, it contains many of the same uncertainties and risks as alternative 2. In addition, there is the issue of the vacant future expansion space. Can Deal actually carry the cost of this space at no cost to Two + Two? Will the firm have additional carrying costs for

insurance, maintenance, cleaning and the like because of the additional space? What will additional operating costs be? How will the assessor consider this vacant space and what happens to ad valorem tax pass-throughs to Two + Two?

4. **Rent in another building:** Although this alternative violates goal 5 (unless the building owner has other buildings) it may be necessary if other alternatives are less feasible and if Two + Two is to progress. The process of identifying goal 5 places special responsibilities on the plan of action to accomplish each alternative, even including a move from the current location. A relocation may be made more plausible by working with the current owner to assure little, if any, interruption in building rents; a full understanding that the current owner cannot expect their accounting firm to flourish with constrained space; and the like. Thus, even conflicts among goals can be mitigated through feasibility analysis.

5. **Create a joint venture:** Through their direct or indirect market activities counselors often can provide alternatives which may not be available to clients. Most accounting firms have individuals who are familiar with joint venture arrangements, but they may not have the ability to negotiate such arrangements or to bring together those who might become outside investors. In a case like this, decision makers need to determine whether they want to serve as a general partner, or whether another should be found.

To assist the client, the counselor proposes two methods for testing the developer's proposal: (1) determining the justifiable land and building cost[2] to produce a building that meets Two + Two's maximum rent requirement; and (2) determining the rent required to justify the developer's cost proposal. These tests will give the firm a better understanding of the investment potential of Deal's proposal and the likelihood that the proposed building will meet current investment requirements.

Figure 12-2 summarizes the steps taken to analyze justified cost given the firm's allowable rent (or "revenue" to the building owner). The firm previously established a $20 per square foot per year limit, but in discussion with the partners, the counselor learns that they intended this number to be the base rent figure, not gross rent. After further discussion, the maximum gross rent for the initial occupancy period is set at $23.50 per square foot per year, $1.50 per square foot below the firm's current total occupancy cost. Total building operating costs (including ad valorem costs and tenant improvements) are estimated at $10.50 per square foot per year. With a 40,000 square foot building, the landlord's net income (allowable

---

[2] A justifiable cost is a cost low enough to produce a market return on the cost to the owner and to produce affordable rent to the tenant.

FIGURE 12-2

REVENUE TO JUSTIFY COST

(Per Square Foot Per Year Data in Parentheses)

Allowable Occupancy Cost	$940,000 ($23.50)

-

Less: Operating Expenses	$420,000 ($10.50)

=

Income Attributable to Land & Building	$520,000 ($13)

/

Risk Adjusted Capitalization Rate At Two + Two's Cost of Capital	10%

=

Justified Cost, Land & Building	$5,200,000 ($130)

occupancy cost less operating expenses) attributable to the land and building is therefore $520,000, or $13.00 per square foot per year.

Additional discussion with Two + Two's managing partner establishes that the firm's average cost of capital is about 10%. If this return is warranted after consideration of various risk elements (differentials between those risks associated with building ownership and the risk contained within the firm's 10% expectation), net income of $520,000 divided by 10% results in a justified land and building investment of $5,200,000. If the decision criterion is to accept the investment only if the justified land and building value at full occupancy is equal to or exceeds the proposed $6.6 million cost, this alternative will be rejected as infeasible.

The second test, illustrated in Figure 12-3, first identifies the proposed land and building cost, then produces the income necessary to support this cost. Gross cost of $6.6 million multiplied by Two + Two's average cost of capital (10%) shows that $660,000 net income must be produced from the building to satisfy land and building costs. Operating expenses of $10.50 per square foot per year times 40,000 square feet add another $420,000. With a single-tenant building and no vacancies (although 10,000 square feet will probably not be used initially), no separate vacancy and collection loss allowance is necessary. With $660,000 required for land and building costs and $420,000 for operating expenses, $1,080,000 is required to support the investment, or $27 per square foot per year.

Required annual revenue based on a cost of $27 per square foot is $3.50 per square foot higher than the established maximum rent of $23.50 per square foot. If the decision criterion is not to accept this alternative unless rent is equal to or less than $23.50 per square foot per year, the alternative must be rejected as infeasible. Based on the intended initial occupancy of 30,000 square feet, the effective rent would be an even higher $36 per square foot. If the firm does not realize $1,080,000 per year in cash or an equivalent economic contribution, Two + Two will further subsidize the building by accepting a rate of return lower than the 10% rate it established. If a minimum 10% rate of return is another decision criterion, a lower return will be rejected and the alternative will be deemed infeasible.

Of course, Two + Two could suggest to Deal that the transaction be made at its desired rental ceiling of $23.50 per gross square foot. By subtracting

FIGURE 12-3

REQUIRED REVENUE BASED ON COST

(Per Square Foot Per Year Data in Parentheses)

Cost	$6,600,000 ($165)

X .

Risk Adjusted Capitalization Rate At Two + Two's Average Cost of Capital	10%

=

Net Operating Income	$660,000 ($16.50)

+

Operating Expenses	$420,000 ($10.50)

=

Effective Gross Income	$1,080,000 ($27)

+

Vacancy and Collection Loss	$0 ($0)

=

Required Gross Income	$1,080,000 ($27)

the estimated operating expenses of $10.50 per square foot, as set forth in Figure 12-2, the net rent to Deal would be $13 times 40,000 square feet, or $520,000. Deal would then receive a 7.9% return on its investment ($520,000 divided by $6,600,000) rather than the 10% it presumably wanted. It then remains to be determined whether Deal would be interested in a 7.9% investment.

Two + Two also had the alternative of exploring with its current landlord whether the additional 10,000 square feet of space could be obtained in accordance with Two + Two's space expansion schedule. The most plausible alternative might well be for the firm to remain where it is and to take additional space as it becomes available on lease expiration, even if this was accomplished at some inconvenience to the tenant. At the same time, the accounting business of the landlord could be retained. If this alternative proves infeasible, it will probably be necessary to determine whether space of 40,000 square feet can be found in an existing building in the market area.

At this point the counselor can review these intermediate results with the client and continue working toward an optimum decision. Each result provides an opportunity to reevaluate the criteria for the alternative being analyzed and those established for other alternatives. If image and ownership are paramount, and if the cost differentials are affordable, the client may justify the apparent rental income premium or cost surplus of the new building proposal in some other way. This is common for many institutional and headquarter buildings. In such cases, the feasibility analysis helps focus on the basis for the decision and the marginal cost of choosing the alternative.

For some decision criteria, specific performance measures can be articulated for the real estate or related investment considerations. It is more difficult to quantify criteria that relate to the client's overall business, psychological effects, or other subjective matters. Experienced counselors must call on their business training and experience to differentiate elements of the final decision which are based on real estate reasoning from those with other bases.

In performing the feasibility analysis, a counselor takes an organized, systematic approach to developing each of these lines of reason, testing each alternative, weighing the market evidence necessary to quantify and qualify data needs, identifying and assessing risks and uncertainties, and ultimately making client recommendations. The final written and/or oral report assesses the strengths and weaknesses of each alternative, identifies the probable ability of each to meet client objectives, and make recommendations. Well-performed feasibility analysis logically leads to a "go" decision for a specific alternative which includes an understanding of associated risks and uncertainties, an identification of what is expected to be accomplished, and sufficient data and analysis to permit both the making and the management of the decision.

No attempt has been made to present here an ultimate solution to Two + Two's expansion problem. Rather, the objective has been to emphasize the importance of developing clear alternatives from which the client can choose what, in its judgment, is best for it. Moreover, it is common during a feasibility study for additional alternatives to surface which in turn could influence the final decision.

CONCLUSIONS

It is not uncommon to see reports, including appraisals, which refer to a "feasibility analysis section." Frequently these conclude that a building or a development project is feasible without identifying a particular investor or the goals to be accomplished. Although such reports are used by decision makers, they are outside the more specific function of feasibility analysis discussed here.

Properly performed by the counselor and understood by the client, feasibility studies also provide a framework for the management of decisions once they are made. Decision criteria which involve performance, including internal rates of return, cash flow expectations or requirements, limits on time involvement and the like can be monitored and to some extent managed. They become focus points to judge success of the decision and to assure that, through good management, success is achieved. Where performance cannot be achieved, these criteria can also signal when and why new courses of action may be required.

Feasibility analysis requires a variety of market, analytical and interpersonal skills. The experienced counselor will apply many analytical techniques in assessing alternatives, and will frequently find new alternatives for identified constraints. Thus, feasibility analysis should be viewed as both a decision making requirement and an opportunity: a requirement because it makes the decision and its outcome more certain; an opportunity because it is a creative means of finding optimum solutions to client problems.

ABOUT THE AUTHOR

John D. Dorchester, Jr., CRE, MAI, is president, Real Estate SCIENCES International, Inc., Winnetka, Illinois, a firm specializing in large-scale land development and project analysis, market research and feasibility analysis, investment counsel, environmental issues, litigation support, GIS and other computer modeling, and assistance in client decision making. He is a former national president of the American Institute of Real Estate Appraisers and has been a member of The International Assets Valuation Standards Committee since 1981, serving as chairman in 1986-1989.

PART IV

OFFICE BUILDING DESIGN AND DEVELOPMENT

13

OFFICE PLANNING AND DESIGN

by Ronald A. Harris

The public frequently is unaware of the extensive work involved in the planning and design of an office structure. Seemingly like magic a new building appears on the scene, completed and ready for tenant occupancy; tenants then move in and begin paying rent.

But the process of creating a new building that will be a successful investment is clearly more complex than that. The rent charged must exceed the cost of operating the facility and the debt service on the loan taken out by the developer to build it, and must also provide a return on the cash equity. The goal is to produce an immediate capital profit to the developer and an on-going return on the developer's investment. Any mistakes or errors of judgment in the planning process can have a long-term effect on the success of the project not only operationally and visually, but also in terms of its profitability.

It is therefore extremely important for the developer to pay close attention to all aspects of the planning process—starting with the initial idea to build an office structure on a given site in a given location. Every decision made by the developer involves a complex process of relating cost to value, i.e., will the renting public pay sufficient rent to justify the selection of superior facade materials, interior finishes and mechanical systems? If more money is spent, will it be readily recouped in added value?

Every owner or developer approaches the planning process from a different viewpoint, depending on his knowledge, expertise, experience and in-house staff capabilities. Owners or developers with experienced in-house personnel may begin the planning process themselves, while those just entering the industry or undertaking larger, more complex ventures for the first time may employ advisors to assist them. The advisor most often turned to in the planning stage is an architect.

But whether he utilizes his own staff or directs the activities of an architect, the owner must establish his overall policy aims and strategies before he begins the critical development planning activity. Prior to embarking on a project, an owner or developer begins by assessing his resources and capabilities, including his personal finances and network within the real estate community. By matching those assets to the potential business opportunity, he can establish his strategy, as well as an appropriate timetable for achieving his overall goals and objectives.

SITE PLANNING

Developers may already own a site or may have one that they would like to acquire in order to build a structure. The first consideration is zoning and other local building and environmental regulations. Armed with the existing legal survey description of the land and a tax assessor's parcel number or a site address, the local zoning and building and environmental regulations can be easily obtained through the planning department of the city or county in which the site is located. If the site is zoned for an office structure, nothing further is required at this stage. However, if the existing zoning does not permit office use, a variance would be required. The developer then must investigate if such a variance is obtainable, and what investment of time and cost would be needed to get a variance approved. This should include the appeal process in case the original submission is rejected.

There are other restrictions or formulas that determine the type and size of building allowed. In many cities, the total area that can be built is subject to a floor/area ratio. This is based on a formula restricting the total square footage of the building to a multiple of the total square footage of the site. For example, if the floor/area ratio was 10:1 and the site was 30,000 square feet, the maximum size of the office building would be 300,000 square feet. Alternatively, the allowable size of the building may be related to a parking requirement and the number of parking stalls could determine the size of the structure. In some cases, size could depend on both the floor/area ratio and the parking requirements.

Additional local restrictions that may be imposed include setback or open-space requirements, design control, exterior appearances, and other special programs. In San Francisco, for example, a developer building an office building in the central business district (CBD) must either include a given number of residential units on the site or pay for the city to build this same number of residential units in another location. On one project, the city of San Francisco allowed the developer to build hotel rooms in lieu of the residential units. These are generally referred to as exaction requirements, and they are becoming more common.

These requirements affect not only the design of the structure, but also the total cost of the development. The developer may apply for a variance in cases where he believes they are too restrictive, too costly, or would be difficult to incorporate into the design program. The developer needs to understand the rules, as any of these exactions might make the project uneconomic or infeasible.

The developer must also insure that all the necessary utilities— electricity, gas, water and sewer, and telephone—are available to the site. In most communities these services are readily available, but there can be limitations. Sewer moratoriums, for example, are commonplace in growth areas. It is worthwhile to call all the utility companies to verify that their facilities are available before proceeding with the development process.

One final item of increasing importance is the soil conditions on the site. Before the architect or structural engineer can do their design work, they need to know the condition of the ground on which the structure is to be built. Special soils engineering firms perform the necessary test borings and provide the soils report on the property. This is the developer's first external cost, as all the work to this point can have been done by his staff. Soil testing does not have to be done until the developer has acquired the property and is fairly certain that he is going to pursue the project. Many contracts of sale to purchase a site are subject to a satisfactory soils test by the buyer because of heightened concerns about toxic waste and noxious gases.

Several other items must be investigated—some before and others after the site planning process takes place. A great deal of the necessary information can be supplied by the architect, although generally this research will add to the cost of his services. If the developer already has the architect on the development team, it would be natural to have the architect obtain the appropriate information. He will eventually need to verify it.

PRELIMINARY FEASIBILITY STUDY

Several analytical studies are made during the office planning and design program. An owner or developer must be satisfied that his project will be marketable when it is completed—that tenants will like his project and be willing to lease space in it at a given market rental rate. He must also verify that the project is feasible and meets his goals and objectives. At a minimum, an owner or developer will conduct informal, in-house marketability and feasibility studies before actually beginning the project.

Once the developer has determined the size of the structure he can build on the site, he must perform a preliminary feasibility study. This is a quick basic analysis to determine if the project looks economically feasible. Later, the developer may order a more formal marketability and feasibility study through an outside advisor, usually at the insistence of the mortgage lender. From the estimated size, a projected construction cost can be estimated—a basic dollars per square foot calculation of the hard construction cost. The cost of the land should also be known at this stage.

The final ingredient in the total project cost is the soft costs. These include the architect's fees (including his related professional consultants for soils engineering, structural engineering, mechanical engineering, graphics and landscape design), interim interest on construction financing, insurance during construction, marketing costs and other costs incurred during the planning and construction phases. Fees paid to other advisors and fees paid by agreement to the developer himself may also be included. A rule of thumb is that soft costs equal 25% of the hard costs of construction, but these costs can easily run to 35% or more, because of excessive leasing commissions, advertising and promotional costs, and added interest charges resulting from an extended initial leasing campaign.

An analysis of total project costs is illustrated in the following example:

Land	$ 1,500,000
Construction Costs: 300,000 sq. ft. x $70/sq. ft.	$21,000,000
Soft Costs: 25% x construction costs	$ 5,250,000
Estimated Total Project	$27,750,000

If a developer wanted to be more conservative, a contingency factor could be added to the above. A 4.5% contingency factor would add $1,250,000, increasing the total estimated project cost to $29,000,000.

Step two is to estimate the financing that might be available for the project, the equity that the developer would then have to invest and the annual payments needed to service the loan. If a lender were willing to lend 70% of the total cost, the developer could borrow $20,000,000. He would have an equity investment of $9,000,000 (using the conservative $29,000,000 projected total cost), and if the annual loan contract was at 11% constant including 10% interest, it would cost $2,200,000 per year to service the $20,000,000 loan.

Step three is to estimate the operating results—how much rent will be received and how much it will cost to operate the property on an annual basis. Both of these categories will vary from year to year, but for the purposes of this initial estimate of the projected results, the developer would look at a one-year stabilized condition. The anticipated revenues can be estimated from the developer's knowledge of market rents. Assuming that the average annual rent for this quality of office space is $24 per square foot, and applying this to the previous example:

300,000 sq. ft. x $24/sq.ft.	$7,200,000
Less: Vacancy (5%)	(360,000)
Effective Gross Income	$6,840,000

Table 13-1 sets forth a summary of the total estimated project costs and the total estimated operating results. In Table 13-2, the analysis continues with the testing of economic feasibility. Two basic conditions are tested — the projected cash flow return on the developer's equity and the value related to costs. The object is to determine whether the final value will exceed the cost of building the structure, as this represents the developer's paper profits.

It appears that the initial cash-on-cash return on equity will be 13.6%. The developer can then determine if it is worthwhile to proceed. It should be noted that a 13.6% return on equity is not particularly attractive, as the actual return may be lower for a variety of reasons. Due to variables in the forecasts, actual costs could be more; equity could be less; income could be higher; and operating expenses could be lower or higher.

The increase in value over projected total costs is moderately favorable. By spending $29,000,000, the developer has created a value of $36,000,000. If everything went according to plan, the developer would have created a $7,000,000 paper profit, which, if the property were sold, could be converted to cash or another form of asset.

TABLE 13-1   Preliminary Feasibility Study

Total Estimated Project Costs	
Land–30,000 sq. ft. x $50.00/sq. ft.	$ 1,500,000.00
Construction Costs–300,000 sq. ft. x $70.00/sq. ft.	21,000,000.00
Soft Costs–25% x construction costs	5,250,000.00
Estimated Total Costs:	$ 27,750,000.00
Contingency–4.5% x costs	1,250,000.00
Total Estimated Project Costs:	$ 29,000,000.00
Projected Loan–70% x $29,000,000.00	(20,000,000.00)
Developer Equity	$ 9,000,000.00

Total Estimated Operating Results	
Income–300,000 sq. ft. x $24.00/sq. ft.	$ 7,200,000.00
Less: Vacancy–5%	(360,000.00)
Effective Gross Income	$ 6,840,000.00
Less: Operating Expenses–50% EGI	($ 3,420,000.00)
Net Operating Income	$ 3,420,000.00
Less: Debt Service on $20 million at 11%	(2,200,000.00)
Cash Flow	$ 1,220,000.00

**Table 13-2   Preliminary Feasibility Study
Tests of Economic Feasibility**

Return on Investment		
Projected Stabilized Cash Flow	$ 1,220,000.00	
Owner's Equity	$ 9,000,000.00	= 13.6%

Value Related to Costs		
Net Operating Income	$ 3,420,000.00	
Value at 9.5% CAP Rate [1]	$ 36,000,000.00	
Total Projected Project Costs	(29,000,000.00)	
Projected Value Created:	$ 7,000,000.00	

[1] The overall rate at which the property can be re-sold is dependent on a wide variety of events, including but not limited to money market conditions, state of the overall economy, status of the local real estate market, demand for investment property, and overall rates obtained from recent comparable sales.

DESIGN CONCERNS

The architect should be hired early in the planning process, certainly no later than after the preliminary feasibility study. The architect will verify zoning and other pertinent regulatory considerations in order to establish a more definitive building size. At the same time, the architect will lay out how the building envelope or footprint might fit on the site and will begin to consider a preliminary building design.

At this stage, many factors need to be considered, in no logical order of preference. One is the density—whether the building will be a low, medium or high rise structure. The location of the site, land values, zoning, market conditions, even the site itself will dictate this choice. If the development will include parking, how this is located and how it relates to the building structure is important. The architect must also start thinking about the building shape. This becomes more complex for a multi-use project, as all of the different elements of use must relate to and interact with the others.

More accurate construction costs become critical. If the preliminary feasibility analysis projected a construction cost of $70 per square foot, the architect must design a building that can be constructed within this cost range. If actual construction costs are $100 per square foot, the economics of the project are adversely affected.

A discussion of design concerns cannot overlook the relative efficiency of the design. The efficiency factor is the ratio of usable area to the gross area, and it should be at least 80%. Then, by use of a load factor, a building can achieve a 90% or better rentable area. The more rentable area, the more income is available to cover the cost of operation; that increased income is carried to the bottom line to provide a higher net operating income (NOI). Increased NOI not only makes the project more valuable, but also provides a greater return to the owner.

Market and Economic Criteria

The architect needs other input to meet the design objectives. The type of tenants expected, and what tenants are looking for in new buildings will affect the design process. Will this office building serve large space users or will most of the tenants be renting small or medium size office areas? Will tenants be using open office layouts, or will they require large numbers of private offices—all with window access? The aesthetics of the project are also important to prospective tenants, as people prefer to occupy attractively designed buildings, and have been known to pay more rent per square foot for the privilege.

The developer will undoubtedly call on his leasing agents or consultants to develop this tenant profile information for the architect. Leasing agents are very aware of the marketplace, and what is needed to attract tenants. Leasing agents can also provide data on general supply and demand considerations, as well as realistic market rent levels. Based on their advice, the space in a specific building could be designed to meet a certain niche in the market, or to meet the needs of a large space user. Full-time leasing brokers are knowledgeable about the rental rates that various types of tenants will pay, and can deter the developer from designing space to rent for $24 per square foot for a market that is accustomed to paying only $18 per square foot.

As a result, the leasing consultant not only provides critical information to the architect, but its analysis of the marketplace assists the developer in revising his economic feasibility by converting preliminary estimates of rental income to more dependable, documented facts and figures.

Construction Timing

The amount of time required for construction determines when the building will be available for occupancy, and also the length of time that interest must be paid on construction financing. One of the components of construction time is the type of construction. Since the developer would like his office building to open at an optimum time in the marketplace, determining the length of time of construction will allow him to analyze the best time to start construction. It is desirable, of course, to come on line when there is a substantial demand in the marketplace for office space. Conversely, the developer does not want to complete his building in the midst of an oversupply of office space, a recession or both.

It must be remembered, however, that market conditions can change rapidly, often due to external economic conditions other than supply and demand. Since the lead time for completing a major office project can be up to four years, it is often difficult to predict what conditions will be that far in the future. The developer must make his best judgment of what market conditions will be, because once the project starts, it is virtually impossible to stop, and the completed building is at the mercy of these conditions.

DESIGN CRITERIA

This section will address specific design considerations for an office building. Certain areas of design are particularly critical to both the leasing and the operation of an office building.

Floor Plans

While the footprint of the building will dictate actual floor sizes, there are two very important considerations related to the location of the core area. Even if the program is to rent full floors, there may come a time when these floors must be subdivided for small tenants. Thus, when a public corridor is added, the width of this hallway is an important consideration. Generally, this corridor will be a minimum of four feet, but it can be wider, especially if it makes the individual office areas function better. The best quality office buildings have public corridors that are a mimimum of six feet, and frequently are wider.

On a subdivided floor, the ideal dimension from the exterior window line to the public corridor wall in tenant areas should be 28 to 30 feet. This allows for a 10-to-12 foot window office, a 4-foot interior hallway for circulation, and another 10 to 12 feet for interior private offices or work areas. The importance of locating tenant entrance doors in relation to fire exits must be emphasized. Any tenant entrance more than a given distance from a fire exit may require the entire corridor to be sprinklered for fire safety. If the whole building is sprinklered, this is not a problem. There have been instances where a developer felt that his rental market was for 5,000 square foot tenants, and thus located only one entrance within the prescribed distance to a fire exit. Later, when he could not lease enough 5,000 square foot spaces and subdivided the space, it was necessary to extend the corridor length to add additional tenant entrances; the new entrance doors were too far from a fire exit, and sprinklers had to be added at great expense. This, in turn, affected the building load factor, as there was more common area and less usable area on these floors.

It is important to pay attention to the floor layouts in an office building in the design phase. Once the building is built, any miscalculations about these programs cannot be easily corrected. To the extent that the design incorporates flexibility, the developer can better accommodate tenant requirements when the space market changes.

Structural Considerations

It has already been noted that the type of structural frame used affects the length of time of construction and related costs and may be dictated by the soil configuration. This section looks at other structural design considerations.

Additional considerations come into play for tall or complex structures such as high-rise office buildings or multi-use projects. If elements must be "stacked," for example, what section in a hotel/office complex goes on top? There can also be window washing concerns. For example, straight window runs require different window-washing apparatus than multiple facades of differing heights. While the foundation is larger, structural elements diminish the higher up one builds, resulting in more rentable square feet on the floor. Finally, where should important building services such as waste removal and mail services be located? Mail slots and waste removal facilities both require penetrations that run the full height of the building. Moreover, the elevators used for waste removal should be located near the building exit where the waste will go out. The number of entrances and building security are additional concerns as the structural frame is developed.

Elevations and Building Enclosing Wall Materials

Elevations refer to geometrical projections of a building on a plane perpendicular to the horizon. The building enclosing wall materials are variously referred to as the building skin, or in the case of steel or concrete framed buildings, curtain walls. The elevations and the enclosing wall materials together account for the visual image that the building projects to the general public. Regardless of the type of building frame used, the enclosing walls are generally prefabricated away from the site, usually in some type of sections. They can be precast stone, marble or granite, or some form of metal such as aluminum. Each section has pre-cut openings for window installation, and in some instances boxes in portions of the building's mechanical systems.

The architect also selects the enclosing material to incorporate in his or her design. The question always arises whether the material selected is guaranteed. It is important to look at the financial stability of the suppliers, and the expectation that they will remain in business, so that the owner will have enforceable guarantees if things go wrong in later years.

Fenestration is the design, arrangement and proportioning of windows. Some are flush with the curtain wall and act as part of it. In other instances, windows are set back from the columns of the precast facade panels in a reveal effect. They can be different sizes or shapes, depending on the overall design concept, but whatever is selected should be uniform throughout the structure. Once an architect decided that the windows should all look uniform from a distance. To accomplish this he made the windows near the top of the building taller so that perspective caused them to appear uniform. This caused the owner many problems in later years because the floors had to be of commensurate heights to accommodate the windows. As a result of this design element, specially sized partitions and doors, among other items, were required. If window sizes are uniform, window coverings can be a uniform size as well, and the building will not have to keep multiple sets for replacement or for cleaning.

Mechanical Systems

To this point, only exterior design criteria have been discussed. Major interior design issues include the building's mechanical systems.

Vertical Transportation

Elevators are the principal vertical transportation system. The issues to be decided are how many, how complex, and what make they should be. Further, in the case of high-rise buildings, it must be determined how many banks of elevators are needed, and how people will be moved from parking facilities under the building to the tenant floors above ground.

When there is parking under the structure, for security reasons there should be one system to move people to the lobby level, and then a separate system for the upper floors. This can be either an elevator or an escalator. Escalators are an excellent means of transport when the elevator lobby is above street grade or when there are several floors of shops.

Elevators may be either hydraulic or electric. Hydraulic elevators are best for low-rise buildings of up to four floors, because they are simpler and easier to maintain, but slower. Electric elevators are recommended above that height. Electric elevators can be as sophisticated as required, with high speeds and computer-driven operating programs.

Other areas of design concern are the interior finishes in elevator cabs, including floor covering, wall finishes and lighting. At least one freight elevator should be planned to run the full height of the building and to stop at every floor. The freight elevator must also be tied to the waste removal process because that is the only effective way to bring trash from each floor down to the area from which it is collected.

Electrical Systems

The electrical engineer will establish criteria for the electrical systems to insure that there is sufficient load available to handle all of the building's mechanical and lighting system needs, as well as any tenant requirements. This electrical load must be distributed throughout the building's various ducts, with sub-panels where necessary to serve individual tenants.

Cabling systems should be amply sized and housed to handle increased communication requirements in the future.

Electrical requirements in office buildings are constantly increasing due to technological advances. Selecting an energy-efficient lighting control system can help to lower operating costs. A computer-operated lighting control system can be programmed to turn lights on or off automatically at certain times. For exterior areas, photo-sensitive cells can be used which automatically turn lights on when it gets dark and off again when it gets light, avoiding the need for constant reprogramming. Lamps throughout the building can be changed to take advantage of new, more efficient bulbs that give equivalent output while using less energy.

Similar energy management controls are available for mechanical systems. In addition, there are energy management systems that integrate the controls for the lighting and the mechanical systems. A so-called "smart building" is capable of constantly adjusting electrical and mechanical systems to run more efficiently.

Plumbing Systems

In addition to the piping systems for mechanical equipment, there are plumbing requirements for the public restrooms, sprinkler systems, and for tenants to tap into plumbing lines for such uses as kitchen sinks, cafeterias, medical facilities, private bathrooms, and even in some cases, private showers. All plumbing should be vertically stacked for economy, uniform access and drainage. There should be shut-off valves at all locations so that the entire water supply does not have to be shut down for minor repairs. Related to this, the truly outstanding developer will insist that public bathrooms be amply sized, equipped with shelves and coat-hooks, with full-length stall partitions and an increased volume of air circulation over ordinary standards.

Consideration should be given to including a building wide sprinkler system. This is relatively inexpensive to install during initial construction, but is costly to add later. There is no question that sprinklers provide a more effective fire safety program than any other single item.

Heating, Air Conditioning and Ventilation Systems

The installation of a heating, ventilation and air conditioning (HVAC) system represents one of the major costs of any office building, and it is vital that the developer does not stint in this area. If sufficient capacity is not available at the start, or if the system is badly installed or not balanced properly, the building will experience tremendous problems later, which may be insolvable or at best expensive to correct. Air turnover has become a major design concern, as it has been found that recycled air frequently contains more pollutants than the outside atmosphere.

Equally as important as capacity are proper zoning and appropriate heat loads. The sun rises in the east, travels in the south, and is warmest in the west. Only the northern exposures escape direct sunlight, and buildings need to be zoned accordingly. Large office buildings usually have two systems: a central interior system and a separate perimeter system that specifically addresses the heat load situation. Another effective system in certain circumstances is the use of individual heat pumps. These allow more direct control, and if a heat pump has problems, it is easily replaced, thus reducing the time that a space would be without heat or air-conditioning. A qualified mechanical engineer will design what is optimum for the specific property.

The zoning of HVAC systems can be refined even further, with separate zones created for individual floors or even subfloors. This can make it easier to meet specific tenants' HVAC requirements, particularly if the tenant needs to utilize the system after normal operating hours. Separate system zoning facilitates using only certain elements of the system, and makes it easy to determine the time and cost of usage so that the tenant can be billed for this additional service.

Partitions and Finishes

The first partitions to be installed are the corridor walls on floors designated as multi-tenant floors. Fire code regulations establish the fire rating required for these walls.

There are many more considerations regarding the interior partitions demising the tenant areas and those used by tenants to create their interior office layout. Probably the most critical are sound control ratings. A sound control rating is based on a decibel scale and is measured on a room-to-room reading. Often, actual installation does not provide the levels described in sales brochures, so it is advisable to set up a mock office in the actual building and do the testing on site under actual conditions as part of the bidding process.

There are two basic types of partitions: fixed and demountable. Sound control and construction considerations apply to both. The choice is based on several criteria, with cost being one of them, flexibility being another, but volume also plays an important part due to the large number of lineal feet of partitions in a major office structure. A key consideration is whether the partition extends to the underside of the concrete or metal ceiling deck. This enables improved sound control over partitions that only abut the hung acoustical ceiling.

Whatever the selection, these partitions need to be finished with paint or other covering such as wallpaper, fabric, veneer or similar treatments. Frequently, they are factory prefinished. The wall systems are then completed with doors, door closures, door handles and a locking device. Setting up a good keying system with grand master and master keys will pay many dividends later during the building's operations.

Other Required Facilities

There are a number of other design considerations. Some—such as security, life safety programs, waste removal and mail handling arrangements—apply to all buildings. Others, such as parking, landscaping and building amenities, apply only to some buildings.

Security planning begins with the number of exterior entrances that must be protected. Security is easier to provide if there are fewer entrances, but this is not always possible. Modern technology has provided great assistance in security coverage with video cameras and card access entry systems. Life safety systems, including a sprinkler system, fire doors, fire stairs, fire alarms, smoke alarms and other basic equipment should be incorporated into the design parameters.

Every building must dispose of waste. During the design process, thought should be given to minimizing the distance and the time it takes to move trash from the floors where it is created to the place from which it is picked up and removed from the building. Consideration should also be given to installing trash compaction equipment to reduce the bulk amount of waste. Both elements will help reduce future operating costs.

Mail handling involves both delivering mail to the tenant and picking up the mail that the tenants send out each day. The designer should consult with the U.S. Postal Service to obtain its suggestions. Many large buildings have a mailroom on the premises, and this needs to be provided for in the original design.

Building codes often contain specific accessibility requirements for the handicapped, including such features as entrance ramps, special stalls and other items in restrooms, door handles, and the location and configuration of elevator buttons. The Americans with Disabilities Act (ADA), which went into effect in January of 1992, mandated additional accessibility features that must be incorporated into office building designs. In many instances, older properties are required to retrofit to meet these standards. All architects should be knowledgeable about these requirements, which can add substantially to the construction costs of an office building.

Not every office building includes parking in its structure. Parking may be on-grade outside the building or located in a separate structure adjacent to the main office building. In some cases, local governmental agencies require that parking be provided, while in other cases they limit or deny parking. If parking is provided, the developer must deal with such issues as the allocation of parking to tenants and policing of assigned spaces, security in parking areas, and how the parking operations will be managed. Should the parking be leased to an outside operator or self-run?

Should it be self-park or a valet arrangement? Because parking is generally a cash business, accounting and controls are essential.

Buildings also vary in the amount of landscaping they have to design, install and maintain. Landscaping includes both the exterior grounds and the interior greenery used to make public areas more attractive. Whether the plants are inside or out, the major considerations are the availability of water and the selection of plants that will thrive in their specified locations.

Finally, the building design must include the amenities and facilities that have been identified for inclusion as a result of an investigation of what tenants are seeking. A frequently sought amenity is supporting retail and restaurant facilities. Many newer buildings offer child care facilities or a health club to help attract potential tenants. Since these all have special requirements, they must be addressed in the design phase.

CONCLUSION

This chapter has briefly described the major points that must be included in the design and planning of an office building. It demonstrates how

Attractive landscaping and employee amenities such as this terrace overlooking a pond appeal to potential tenants. *(Photo © Jane Lidz. Courtesy of Skidmore, Owings and Merrill)*

critical the design phase is for the developer. Thoughtful, well-planned design affects not only the structure itself, but the costs to operate and maintain the office building, as well as the return on the developer's equity investment.

ABOUT THE AUTHOR

Ronald A. Harris, CRE, CPM, a principal with Cantrell, Harris & Associates, San Francisco, has more than 35 years of experience in the real estate industry, primarily in the areas of consulting, property management and development. Harris is a member of the Counselors of Real Estate. He is also a member of the Institute of Real Estate Management, serving as president in 1985. An emeritus member of IREM's national faculty, he helped write and taught the institute's course on the development, leasing and management of office buildings. He co-authored and edited IREM's book *Managing the Office Building*.

14

ARCHITECTURAL OFFICE DESIGN: FROM PROGRAMMING THROUGH CONSTRUCTION

by Henry H. Brennan

INTRODUCTION

Beauty, it's said, is in the eye of the beholder. With office buildings, however, the concept of beauty is considerably more complicated. One complicating factor is the architect's need to satisfy the aesthetic and technical demands of more than one beholder. The architect must first respond to the needs and demands of the owner/developer who engaged his services. At the same time, the architect must also strive to suit the ultimate judges of his work, the tenants or end users of a facility, a constituency he may never meet and whose make-up and preferences he will know best through past experience. The building must fit into the context of its surroundings, and all this must be accomplished within the constraints of site, zoning and economic realities that can dictate the basic footprint the design must follow.

This chapter describes the role of the architect in the office building development process. It addresses criteria for selecting an architect, pre-design questions to be answered, design issues, the owner's and contractor's responsibilities in the design process and the roles of the design team members.

HOW TO SELECT AN ARCHITECT

From an owner's perspective, one key to creating a well-designed building is to select the right architect. The architect's impact will be felt in many ways, usually going far beyond the creation of design concepts and blueprints. The architect's skills and expertise can mean the difference between a building that merely looks good and one that has lasting value with the capacity to perform well in a highly competitive marketplace for years to come. The architect's design skills, technical capabilities and responsiveness will also determine how smoothly a project proceeds, from the early planning stages through final construction. A good design firm must not only be capable of capturing the owner/developer's vision, but it must do so in a manner that ensures constructibility within budget parameters and schedule constraints. Following are some of the criteria for successfully managing the selection process.

- **Relevant experience:** The most critical issue is the architect's experience with the type of office building planned. The owner/developer shouldn't have to pay for the architect's learning curve. Some factors to consider include the architect's experience and successful track record working on buildings of a similar size and complexity, as well as a comparable level of quality, as the one being proposed.
- **Design/technical capabilities:** Does the firm have the resources and technical skills to handle the project? The firm's capabilities must match the scope and technical complexity of the project.
- **Compatibility:** Are the firm's design philosophy and method of working compatible with the owner/developer's work style? Some owners want to be intimately involved in the planning and design process, while others leave the design to the professionals they have hired. It is important to select a firm that can work comfortably under the conditions established.
- **Budgets and schedules:** Can the architect work within budgetary and schedule constraints? The owner/developer should pick an architect with a track record of achieving quality design within established budget parameters and schedule requirements.
- **Responsiveness/service:** Is the firm responsive to client needs and can it provide the level of service expected? While reference checking will answer this question in part, there are other factors to consider. For instance, is the firm too busy with other work to give the project the attention it deserves? Will the people being interviewed work on the project? Will the firm's principals be available and involved in the project, and how will the owner/developer interface with the key staff members who will work with the owner on a day-to-day basis?
- **New technologies:** Does the architect have experience with the latest building technologies and how they relate to both tenant needs and operating requirements? Such expertise is especially critical as projects

get bigger and more complex. Does the firm utilize the latest computer-aided design and drafting (CADD) technology?

The office building's architectural, HVAC, electrical and plumbing information stored on CADD discs is also useful for building tenants and their consultants during interior planning and design for tenant fitout. On projects that involve consultants in remote locations, the use of modem connections for the transmission of CADD-based data also allows the design team to communicate in a rapid, coordinated fashion.

- **Construction interface:** Does the architect work well with contractors? If the owner/developer plans to use a construction manager, does the architect have experience in working under this type of construction arrangement? It is also important to know the architect's performance record on phased or fast-track construction projects.
- **References:** How satisfied are past clients and contractors with the architect's work? It is important to obtain honest appraisals from four or five people who have worked with the architect on projects of a similar type, scope and complexity. They should also be able to provide insight into the performance of the individuals who will be assigned to the project.
- **Outside consultants:** Who will the architect use as outside consultants for such things as mechanical/electrical design and structural engineering? If this is done in-house, is the firm's engineering staff capable of handling the job?
- **Fees:** Architects are in a highly competitive marketplace. The architect's fee is an important consideration, but fees alone should not determine the selection of a firm. Fee differentials between competing firms are a minor component of total project costs.

The final decision will be based not only on references and objective qualifications, but on an owner's subjective sense as well. How well a firm communicates with the owner/developer, how carefully the architects listen to the client's concerns and preferences and how they incorporate those messages into workable solutions are criteria not easily measured by resumes and photos of a firm's finished projects. In the final analysis, the owner/developer must believe in the architects hired and have confidence in their ability.

THE DESIGN PROCESS

Some owners and developers say that they establish all the criteria for an office building's design and make all the decisions, then the architect turns these elements into design drawings and construction documents. If that is indeed the case then they are being shortchanged. The architect can and should play a much more significant role.

Pre-Schematic Design

Architects can make their most important contributions in the pre-schematic design phase of a project. This is when the basic programming and planning decisions are made and the greatest control can be exercised over project design and budgets. It is at this point that the best opportunities exist for saving money or ensuring that it is spent wisely.

The design team's activities during the pre-schematic design phase include gathering and evaluating all the existing and proposed data, such as programming, surveys, environmental reports, soil borings, traffic studies, utilities and all applicable regulations (zoning codes and other local, state and federal regulations) that will govern the design and construction of the project. Once this data has been accumulated and evaluated by the owner and architectural/engineering team, the goals for the project can be finalized. The initial master plan, site design and conceptual design work are done quickly in sketch form to study the potential alternative solutions that best meet the design objectives.

After a thorough review of these alternate studies, a single design proposal is selected and packaged in a presentation format which includes site plans, floor plans, elevations, sections, perspective renderings and perhaps a block model to illustrate the design concept. The drawings together with a project description and net and gross area calculations are used to establish the initial project cost estimate and schedule. The owner/developer can use this package to assist in attracting tenants, to submit to local agencies for zoning and other necessary approvals and for presentations to potential lenders.

Program

The programming phase of the project precedes design. In this phase the architect, working with the owner/developer, develops a list of project objectives, such as building size, type and quality of target market, budget, project image, basic floor size requirements and building systems. The program will vary from site to site, large versus small site, suburban versus downtown, large tenant versus small, financial tenant versus general office, and Class A versus Class B marketplace. If the tenant is known before design commences, it is possible to include the tenant's special requirements in the base building design, resulting in project cost and schedule savings.

Site Constraints

A thorough site analysis is undertaken to document all existing conditions and determine how they affect and may shape the proposed development. A site's physical constraints are defined by its location, size, shape, topographic contour, surface features, adjacent developments, vehicular and pedestrian access, mass transportation availability, subsurface soils, utilities and environmental conditions. Existing site conditions are generally documented through surveys, soil boring reports, and traffic studies and reports.

Zoning Considerations

Zoning regulations will dictate basic design parameters. Key zoning issues include density and height limitations, setbacks, parking and open space requirements, and in some cases ground floor retail uses. Floor area ratio (FAR) is generally dictated by site zoning. The total building area is calculated as a multiple of the site area (i.e., FAR of 10 with a 40,000 square foot site will permit 400,000 square feet of building area), generally excluding mechanical, basement and parking areas.

The impact of zoning on design will vary from location to location. In New York City, for example, zoning requirements often create a need for complicated setbacks, forcing the architect to design space from the outside in. Height restrictions play a key role in many markets. In Washington, D.C., most commercial zones limit building heights to a range of 90 to 130 feet, necessitating specific types of structural systems and floor-to-floor heights to maximize the amount of usable space. Height restrictions have also been imposed in many suburban markets to reduce the impact of large-scale development.

Development incentives are another zoning-related issue that can greatly influence a building's design. For instance, by incorporating public plazas, interior public space, subway entrances and other civic improvements in their buildings, developers frequently are permitted to increase the allowable floor area ratio. All these factors must be identified and incorporated when beneficial into the pre-schematic planning for a project.

Parking

Parking needs, which are determined by zoning, by the availability of mass transit and through market demands, play a crucial role in a building's design. Zoning laws and market conditions can require as much as five parking spaces per 1,000 square feet of office space, or none (in the case of New York City). Most typical for a suburban location and in some urban markets is three parking spaces per 1,000 square feet of space, which in a parking structure is equal to the area of the office building. For most urban sites, parking requirements are between one and two spaces per 1,000 square feet of space.

Though rarely looked upon as a focal point of a development, the garage size and cost can have a major impact on the overall design. While this is

Herald Square, a mid-rise office building in Washington, D. C., that totals 230,000 square feet in 11 stories, is built to the maximum allowable height of 130 feet. Unique exterior lighting incorporated into the building's design highlights its place in the uniform Washington skyline. *(Photo © Maxwell MacKenzie. Courtesy of Brennan Beer Gorman/Architects)*

not to say that the design of an office building must be sacrificed to accommodate the parking element, the visual appeal of the project depends upon successfully integrating the two elements into a unified design.

The appropriate parking solution is determined by such factors as site size, shape and contour, height and density restrictions, land values, design criteria for the building, marketing strategy and the demands of a large pre-lease tenant. The most common type of parking is on-grade. Where the size, configuration and contours of a site are adequate to provide the required parking, on-grade is the least costly alternative. Where space is not available, structured parking must be considered, generally involving three types of garages.

1. Above-grade structured parking is a freestanding deck of two or more levels. The least expensive type of parking after on-grade, it provides optimum efficiency in terms of area, structure, circulation and ventilation.
2. Below-grade parking is more expensive since it requires added site excavation, structure and mechanical systems. However, underground parking may improve the overall development by removing cars and the supporting structure from view.
3. Composite parking offers the greatest economic and aesthetic challenge for the project team, but often it provides the only solution for small, expensive sites. It is a combination of below and above grade parking, with the office building above. Like underground parking, it is more expensive since it has less efficient area and structure. Furthermore, composite garages usually require ventilation and sprinkler systems, as well as more expensive exterior facades to integrate with the office structure.

The design of the parking must be viewed as an essential element of a project's overall success, making it an important initial planning consideration. The structure must be visually integrated with the overall building design to create the desired image for the project. Because of its cost factor, efficiency in the garage design is as critical as efficiency of the office building itself.

Problems related to site conditions, zoning constraints and parking clearly must be solved within the context of an owner/developer's marketing objectives and budgetary parameters. An architect's innovative conceptual design might overcome a host of site difficulties and make a powerful aesthetic statement, but if it fails to address fully the owner/developer's needs, the design must be viewed as a failure.

MEETING TENANT NEEDS

For a project to be successful, it must include a design strategy for meeting the needs of potential tenants. Using the owner/developer's marketing objectives as a guide, the architect must establish design parameters that will provide the foundation for the project's ultimate success.

Satisfying user needs was easy when the majority of buildings were owner occupied. Today, fewer corporations want to own real estate and the design challenges are much greater. Even if a developer is building for a major tenant, he must look at the needs of second generation users and take into account the possibility of future multi-tenant use.

Given this reality, building design must be oriented toward suiting the widest range of prospective tenants. Meeting tenant requirements often means that base building design must be created from the inside out; interior space must offer both flexibility and efficiency, at reasonable cost.

The design of the typical office floor is an important starting point in office building design. The two key components are the usable office space to be occupied by the tenant and the building core. The core includes the base building's functional elements, such as passenger and service elevators, stairs, mechanical and electrical risers, distribution and equipment rooms and the lavatories. On multi-tenant floors, the core includes the circulation corridors required to access each tenant suite entry, exit stairs and the other core elements. On single tenant floors, the circulation system is generally included as part of the tenant's area.

Floor Configuration

Floor configuration is one initial planning concern that can dictate the shape of the entire building. In general, the simpler and more regular the floor shape, the more easily it can be adapted to the tenants' needs throughout the life of the building. Rectangular shapes best meet the planning needs for typical offices and work stations that make up tenant space. They work more efficiently than curved, diagonal or irregular shapes. The exterior building design can accommodate rectangular forms without becoming monotonous by using combinations of rectangular shapes or offsets to create interest. The key is to keep exterior form as an important part of the whole design without compromising the interior function.

The depth of space provided on each floor is another critical factor for potential tenants. For maximum flexibility, in a typical center-core building the depth from the core to the outside wall should be between 35 and 45 feet. This depth works well for executive space, multi-tenant users and smaller floors. For larger floors and open floor operations, 45 feet is ideal. This space should be column-free to allow maximum freedom in placement of walls and furniture systems.

On smaller sites that dictate a smaller footprint, a side core may be the only way to provide a satisfactory amount of space from the core to the outer wall. On suburban sites with large floors, atriums or irregular shapes are often used to introduce daylight into interior spaces.

Planning for Future Needs

Planning the core space requires architects to predict both future tenant needs and emerging technology. The challenge is to dedicate sufficient space and system capacity to serve a range of potential users, without taking away usable space or adding unreasonably to initial construction costs. Often, relatively inexpensive steps taken initially can greatly reduce future costs of adapting the building to tenant needs.

A high-rise office building in an urban setting, 101 Hudson in Jersey City, N.J., comprises 1,500,000 square feet in 42 stories. Typical office floors (31,700 square feet at mid-rise levels) provide 45 feet clear span tenant space from core to exterior. Facing page: Central core includes: 1. passenger elevator lobby; 2. exit stairs; 3. service elevators and lobby; 4. toilet rooms (note enclosed high-rise elevator bank surrounds women's room); 5. mechanical and electrical rooms; and 6. multi-tenant corridor. Notched corners provide the potential for 12 corner tenant offices. *(Photo by b & h photographics, Robert D. Golding, photographer. Photo and floor plan courtesy of Brennan Beer Gorman/Architects)*

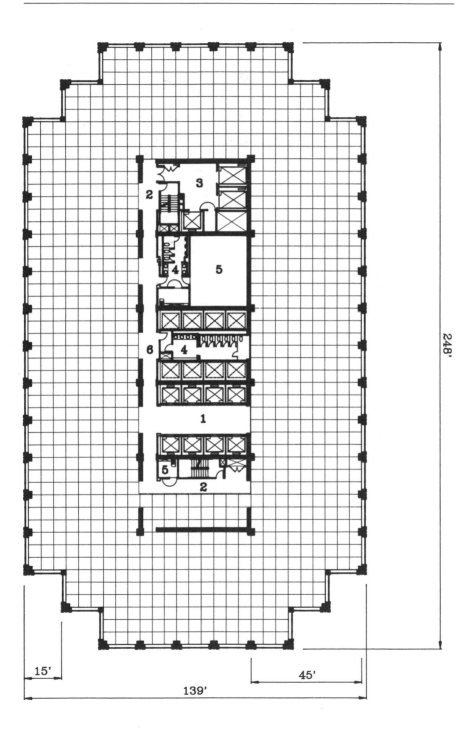

Electrical

Financial district users require a large amount of electricity and sophisticated communications systems to run computers and other equipment. To accommodate these potential tenants, it is relatively simple and inexpensive to provide adequate room for future electrical risers, switchgear and vault space.

It is easier to provide additional air conditioning capacity for the heat generated by added electrical equipment when the building is built rather than to retrofit it later. A good compromise is to install an oversized condenser pipe that tenants can tap into to increase air conditioning output as needed. The oversized pipe adds little to initial costs, takes almost no additional space and eliminates the later expense of replacing or adding pipes. It is also critically important to provide an HVAC system that gives tenants the flexibility of convenient and inexpensive off-hours air-conditioning on each floor.

Mechanical Areas

The roof and mechanical rooms can be designed with sufficient space to add cooling towers or other mechanical equipment in the future. In many locales, mechanical space is not counted as part of the zoning envelope and therefore does not reduce useable area. Conversely, the added mechanical area is often considered rental space, thus increasing the rentable area within the allowable zoning envelope.

Floor-to-Floor Heights

Floor-to-floor heights must also be determined by balancing greater flexibility against increased costs. To create a column-free, 45-foot area between the core and exterior walls, heavier, deeper beams must be used to span the space.

The approach used to distribute electrical and communication systems may also have an impact on floor-to-floor height. Unsightly power poles that feed wires from the ceiling down to workstations in large open spaces or the inconvenience of accessing power from the floor below, are unacceptable for new buildings. One alternative method is to distribute these systems through the steel deck supporting the concrete floor. However, the electrified deck has limited capacity for high-tech tenants and is more costly to add to a reinforced concrete structure.

For greater capacity, a separate raised floor from six to 18 inches in height can be added. This increases floor-to-floor height and adds to the cost of construction. However, it creates a more competitive product in certain marketplaces and higher potential rents will offset the increased construction costs. A compromise is to provide a nine foot clear ceiling height at each floor, allowing the tenant the flexibility to add a raised floor system.

Both the exterior of the building and the interior public areas must incorporate materials and technology that can survive the test of time, both physically and aesthetically. Materials should be selected that age well and will minimize maintenance requirements. Designing a building for the broadest possible range of tenants requires extra effort and an understanding of tenants' needs. But the payback can be substantial.

DESIGN FEATURES

From the very beginning of a project, an owner/developer is faced with decisions on where to devote the most money for building features. Many design considerations are beyond anyone's control. But in the realm of selective spending, there are some important guidelines to follow.

As with most things, first impressions count in building design. Especially in a speculative building, it is wise to invest money in those elements that create a good first impression. Some of these include:

- **Exterior appearance:** The first thing a tenant and his clients see is the building exterior. This fact should be reflected in an exterior design that relates contextually to the surrounding environment and creates an appealing image. With today's superior technologies, curtain wall, i.e., non-load-bearing, construction can often be blended with granite and other classic materials to provide a timeless statement of quality.
- **Streetscape:** Particularly in urban settings, the design of streetscape areas is critical. The use of rich materials on the lower floors, combined with decorative entry canopies and carefully designed windows, can have a tremendous impact. Where retail space or public plazas are mandated by the marketplace or by zoning requirements, they must be carefully integrated into the building design to enhance the visual image sought by the owner/developer. In suburban settings, the issue is often more a matter of thoughtful landscape design to create a complementary visual appeal.
- **Lobbies and public spaces:** In the competitive office market, the key to positioning a building may lie in the lobby. Creating dynamic lobbies is no longer a matter of choice; prospective tenants are demanding exciting public spaces. From an owner/developer's perspective, care and money should be put into the lobby because it helps form an impression of the quality level of the entire building.

The key factors in lobby design include the use of materials such as granite, marble or rich woods; impressive detailing and finishes; use of art that makes its own visual statement; dynamic and functional lighting; attractive concierge/security stations; and efficient pedestrian flow patterns. To help offset the cost of higher quality finishes and detailing, lobbies today are often smaller in scale.

- **Vertical transportation:** Elevators are another important factor in conveying an immediate sense of quality and convenience. An efficient delivery system is essential, with high-speed elevators and state-of-the-art controls to enhance performance. While such systems have higher initial costs, they provide a payback in terms of greater tenant satisfaction. The quality of the elevator cab finishes should complement the finishes in the building's lobby.

- **Typical floor core elements:** The tenant floor must be consistent in design and quality with the other base building areas. Public areas are as important as the building's main lobby. The elevator lobby and tenant corridors on individual floors must continue the theme established in the entry lobby and elevator cab interiors. Key details include finishes, light fixtures, and directional and individual tenant graphics. The lavatories present a number of design considerations as well. The architect starts by providing an adequate number of fixtures to meet the needs of the tenants, with entry screening for privacy from the corridor. The creative use of colors and materials on floors, walls, counters and partitions is also important, with an eye toward durability and ease of maintenance. Adequate ventilation and balanced lighting must also be provided. Finally, quality accessories must be conveniently located, including mirrors, hooks, shelves, trash receptacles, soap, towel and paper dispensers.

- **Mechanical/electrical systems:** High quality, flexible mechanical/electrical systems are imperative to meet users' technical requirements. Sophisticated tenants are demanding systems that can easily be adapted to meet changing technological needs, are economical to operate, and permit easy off-hour use.

- **Amenities:** An owner/developer's need to satisfy market demands is an overriding factor in building design. The discretionary amenities most commonly incorporated into a building because of competitive considerations or to satisfy the requirements of a large pre-leased tenant include retail services, dining facilities, fitness centers, day care facilities and interior landscaping. The new office buildings that stand out, and the older buildings that are internationally recognized for their enduring quality, integrate most of these items into their design.

Energy, Hazardous Materials and Life Safety Issues

In recent years, several other factors have come to have a major impact on building design. These include the energy crisis that began in the early

1970s; the banning of asbestos products and the removal of asbestos and other hazardous materials from existing buildings; and life safety concerns.

Since the oil crisis of 1973, energy conservation has been a major component in the design of office buildings. The architect is concerned with the ability of the building envelope to keep out cold in the winter and heat and sun in the summer. Increased fuel costs have made energy-efficient building envelopes more cost effective over the life of the building.

Government regulations now dictate many of the design elements used to conserve energy. The use of double glazing for all windows, reductions in the amount of glass and increases in the insulating value of walls and roofs, have dramatically reduced the amount of heat loss/gain within office buildings. In addition to double glazing, glass is available with tinted and reflective surfaces to reduce the heat gain from the sun, and with special gases in the void between the glass panels to reduce heat loss from within.

The selection of heating and air conditioning systems is a major part of energy conservation. The use of more efficient equipment, heat recovery systems, free cooling with outside air or condenser water, and cogeneration all must be evaluated, measuring upfront cost against the long-term payback. Many utility companies provide rebates for using more efficient equipment or simply for reducing electrical consumption. Con Edison in New York, for instance, gives a rebate for using absorption chillers in lieu of electric centrifugal chillers, since the reduced electric load puts less de-mand on its power-generating facilities.

Tenant demands and government regulations have quickened the pace of asbestos removal in existing buildings. Prospective tenants are also more knowledgeable about life safety issues and have such factors as fire control systems and sprinklers on their list of criteria when evaluating an office building. Some elements that used to be discretionary for the owner/developer are now mandated by building and fire departments, insurance companies and tenants.

Both energy efficiency and life safety issues have added substantially to construction costs in office buildings. The design challenge is to anticipate these external forces and minimize costs that might be incurred later through upfront planning.

The mandate for the early 1990s is the Americans with Disabilities Act (ADA), passed in 1991. The ADA requires that public and tenant areas in office buildings provide for accessibility and usability by physically im-paired persons. Building owners are required to comply within reasonable limits in existing buildings. In the case of new office buildings, the legislation will not have a major impact, as well-designed buildings incor-porate most of the ADA provisions through compliance with accessibility codes already on the books. However, like asbestos abatement, energy conservation and life safety, ADA will have a considerable impact on the cost of renovating existing buildings.

Owners must carefully consider security issues as well. Security is more difficult to plan for without knowing the tenant make-up of a building (especially in multi-tenant situations). In most cases, landlords provide all security outside the tenants' demised premises. However, some large tenants will provide their own external security arrangements, at their own expense.

In most urban markets, Class A facilities offer security provisions in entranceways and public spaces. This usually takes the form of a reception station with video equipment and personnel who monitor all activity 24 hours a day, seven days a week. In smaller buildings and in some suburban markets, economics often lead owners to implement electronic measures, including card entry and sophisticated personal recognition/identification systems, and elevator controls that prevent off-hour access.

Whether they address space needs, aesthetics, safety concerns or government regulations, design considerations must be geared toward meeting the needs of tenants, both current and future. Building owners/developers have become sophisticated about what features will provide the greatest payback. They realize that the answer rarely lies in one "must have" feature or amenity, but rather in a design that offers overall consistency, flexibility, efficiency and attractiveness.

In the final accounting, what makes a timeless design? Simply put, it is an architectural statement that has been defined by the context of the site, yet is somehow unique. It is a final product that has not been driven by fads, but has been achieved through a series of intelligent decisions based on value.

THE PROJECT TEAM

To most owner/developers the actual design process is less important than the results. But knowing how architects function and what can realistically be expected of the design team during each phase of the project will help make the owner/architect relationship more productive.

The project team is made up of three major components: the owner/developer, the design team and the construction team. The owner/developer functions as leader of the overall project team, designating a representative to act on his behalf throughout design and construction. This project manager must be qualified to lead the team and make decisions on a timely basis.

It is the owner's responsibility at the outset of the project to provide the architect and consultants with all the data needed to design the building. This includes a building program; traffic studies; borings and soil investigation reports; and site surveys showing metes and bounds, contours, utilities and existing structures on the site.

Construction Team

The construction team, led by the general contractor or construction manager, is responsible for the building's construction, including coordination of all the subcontractors for the project. The general contractor or construction manager works directly for the owner and interfaces with the architect during construction to build in accordance with the construction documents.

In many major office building projects, the contractor or construction manager is hired on a negotiated basis early in the design phase and thus becomes a key member of the project team, assisting the owner/developer and architect in cost estimating and scheduling during each phase of design. The early involvement of the contractor on the project is critical for phased or fast-track construction. For more on the role of the contractor or construction manager, see Chapter 16.

If the decision is made to bring the contractor on board early, it is best done at the start of the schematics phase, after the scope of the project has been defined but while there is sufficient time in the design process to take advantage of the contractor's preconstruction services. Since the major decisions affecting the cost of the project are made in the initial design phases, accurate cost estimates during these phases will enable the owner to make wise design decisions.

Cost control efforts in the schematic design phase may lead to design changes in order to meet the project budget. By the design development phase the major design decisions should be set. At that point, further cost control is accomplished through value engineering—the refinement of systems and finishes to achieve design objectives at the lowest appropriate cost. The contractor has the opportunity to participate in these decisions using his prior experience in the marketplace. Only minor value engineering should take place during the construction document phase. If the proper decisions were made initially, the project can proceed not only on budget but on schedule. Major changes during design development or construction document phases can have an adverse effect on the design schedule and delay the start of construction.

Design Team

After the architect has been selected and the scope of services to be performed has been determined, the owner and architect negotiate a contract that establishes basic compensation, defines the design team and establishes the terms of the work to be performed. Other consultants necessary to complete the project design, especially the major engineering consultants, are then selected jointly by the architect and the owner/developer, to ensure compatibility. As leader of the design team, the architect normally contracts directly with the various consultants and is responsible for scheduling and coordinating the work of all the design disciplines.

Structural Engineer

The structural engineer is responsible for designing and preparing the construction documents for the building foundations and superstructure. During the early design phases of the project, the structural engineer evaluates existing site soils information and alternate structural systems for the project. This enables the owner/developer to select the most cost effective system to meet the program requirements.

Structural System

Office building structural systems to be evaluated for a high-rise office building can include a variety of structural steel and reinforced concrete systems. The selection of the final system should be based on the following considerations.

Flexibility:	Is the structure adaptable to changes or modifications of tenants over the life of the building, including loading, openings, and compatibility of the floor system with distribution of power and communication wiring.
Floor Loading:	Live load on the floor is the weight of occupants, furniture and equipment. Minimum building code standard for office buildings is fifty pounds per square foot live load plus twenty pounds per square foot partition loads. Some tenants are demanding heavier live loads either throughout the building or for specific spaces such as storage, files, library, vault or computers.
Efficiency:	The ability of the structure to meet the longer spans desired by many tenants in office buildings today.
Depth of Structure:	Required depth of structure relative to span, floor-to-floor height and overall building height.

Stiffness:	The ability of the structure to withstand lateral forces such as wind and earthquakes. This is more critical in high-rise buildings.
Fireproofing:	The cost and how easily the structure meets fireproof requirements.
Constructibility:	Adaptability of the selected structural system to the construction methods standard in the office building's region.
Scheduling:	The time it takes to erect the structural system can affect move-in dates for tenants and construction costs.
Cost:	The various systems must be evaluated to select the lowest-cost structure meeting all of the criteria set down for the project.

Steel is generally the preferred structural framing system for tall office buildings because of its flexibility, its capacity to achieve long spans efficiently, its ability to withstand earthquake loads and its speed of erection. There are exceptions, however, specifically in locales where concrete is the normal method of construction and is, therefore, less expensive. Concrete also requires less floor-to-floor height which affects cost and can also be critical in cities that have set fixed limits on height, such as Washington, D.C.

Parking Superstructure

If the project includes structured parking, the same analysis must be made. However, the factors influencing the selection of a structural system for a parking garage are different. The ideal garage is a clear span of approximately sixty feet to maximize efficiency. In cold climates, garages must be able to withstand deterioration caused by freeze-thaw cycles and the salts carried by cars during the winter months.

A good structural system meeting these criteria is post-tensioned concrete, which can achieve the long spans with minimal deterioration. However, cost or adaptability to the structural systems selected for the office building may dictate use of one of the other systems, i.e., steel, reinforced concrete or precast concrete. Care must be taken in the design to accommodate building maintenance and operation for all garage structures.

Foundations

Building foundations are the least understood of the building systems because they are not seen and are frequently subject to forces beyond man's control. The most often used and least expensive foundation system is spread footings. The size of the footings depends on the column loading and the ability of the soil to support that loading. In sites with poor or unusual soil conditions it may be necessary to go to deep foundations such as piles or caissons. A thorough soil investigation, including borings, must be undertaken at the beginning of the project since the soil condition can have a major impact on the building cost.

Mechanical/Electrical Engineer

Mechanical/electrical disciplines include HVAC (heating, ventilating and air conditioning), plumbing, life safety and electrical. These are normally available within mechanical/electrical engineering firms, but since each is so critical to the success of the project, the firm's ability must be carefully evaluated in each category.

In the initial design phases, mechanical/electrical engineers provide evaluations of building systems to assist the owner/developer in selecting the optimum systems. These include the following.

HVAC

Several considerations determine the selection of heating, ventilating and air conditioning systems. One is the availability and cost of fuel (i.e., oil, gas or electric). The decision will be based on both the relative cost of operation and the dependability of supply. The mechanical engineers will also evaluate the sizes, types and quantity of boilers needed to generate building heat, and will consider the possibility of using city steam, if available, as an alternate heat source. (City steam is the excess steam from the manufacture of electricity which is sold by the local public utility to developers and channeled through a piping system to buildings in the central business district.) Finally, they will evaluate heat delivery systems to determine whether baseboard radiation should be used at the building perimeter or other systems integrated with the air conditioning.

The air conditioning system is a significant cost component in an office building and a major user of both floor and ceiling space. Selection of the air conditioning system is therefore critical to the design process. The choice of chillers, cooling towers and air handling equipment varies greatly depending upon the system selected. Central systems include electrical centrifugal, absorption or turbine chillers and their supporting cooling towers to generate chilled and condenser water.

Cooled air can be delivered from a central mechanical room to each floor through air shafts or from the central chillers through chilled water pipes to individual fan rooms on each floor. From these shafts or floor fan rooms the air is distributed throughout the entire floor via ducts located in the ceiling plenum. Another popular system is a Package Direct Expansion (DX) unit located on each floor. DX units contain compressors, coils, fans and controls necessary to provide air conditioning for the space and are linked to the building cooling towers with condenser piping. The DX system eliminates central chillers and provides tenants on each floor with individual control. This is an advantage during off-peak hours, but is generally more expensive to operate.

Zone control is generally provided through variable air volume boxes to the various zones on each floor, including interior zones and each exposure of the exterior zone. These systems can also be used to heat the perimeter zones. A higher number of zones will add to the initial cost but provide greater comfort and flexibility for the user.

Since the greatest temperature changes are experienced at the perimeter of the building, hydronic (hot and chilled water) delivery systems can provide heating and cooling most efficiently at the exterior wall. For example, a four-pipe fan coil system features individual units at each office or approximately every ten to fifteen feet, providing every office with optimum comfort and control. This is also the most expensive of the systems initially. Alternatively, perimeter heat pumps may be used together with DX systems, but these require more maintenance than central chillers.

Plumbing

The plumbing issues in the design of an office building are not as complex as some of the other elements. However, well-planned lavatories in the core of each floor are an important part of the tenant's perception of the building. In addition, wet stacks have to be provided to permit tenant flexibility in locating toilets, sinks and other facilities requiring sanitary services within their space. All of the necessary connections to the public utilities must be provided for water, sanitary sewage and storm sewage, as well as drainage for the site.

Life Safety

The requirement that sprinkler systems be included throughout office buildings has added cost to the building and piping to the ceiling plenum. Other life safety systems required today include smoke exhaust, stair pressurization, sophisticated fire alarm systems and elevator controls.

Electricity

Lighting, power and communication systems reflect the most dramatic change in tenants' requirements. A minimum of five watts per square foot must be provided to each floor—two for light and three for power for the normal office user, plus additional power for such special requirements as computer facilities and data processing equipment. It is not unusual in high-tech office buildings to find an average of eight to twelve watts per square foot needed to satisfy the sophisticated tenant. Transformer vaults and electrical switch gear rooms, as well as the vertical risers and floor distribution systems, must be sized not only to meet tenants' current requirements, but to accommodate the anticipated increase in the use of office equipment.

Building Management

Sophisticated automated systems are available to control many building functions, including energy management, life safety, elevators and security systems. As with other building elements, selection of the appropriate system is based on market demand and cost and payback criteria. Many "smart buildings" are more hype than reality. Due to initial cost, few buildings are designed to fully utilize the systems available, except in some large, high-tech tenant occupancies.

Communications

The growth in telecommunication systems has generated even greater space demands on the vertical and horizontal distribution systems in office buildings. It is difficult to anticipate the precise systems a tenant will demand today, much less in the future, but it is possible to plan sufficient space within the floor and shafts to accommodate these systems.

Lighting

As the typical tenant's power requirements have grown, their lighting needs have been reduced through the use of more efficient lighting fixtures. Accepted design practice, as well as the energy codes in place today, have held lighting design to under two watts per square foot.

Special Consultants

In addition to the principal consultants (structural and mechanical/ electrical), other consultants may be needed depending on the size and complexity of the building and the disciplines available within the architect's in-house staff. These include civil engineering, landscaping, vertical transportation, acoustics, exterior wall, window washing, special lighting and graphics.

Civil Engineering

For larger sites more typically found in suburban locations or cities with large parking requirements, civil engineers may be needed to develop off- and on-site utilities, grading, special site structures, roads and parking areas. They also interface with public works departments and other governing agencies within the local community.

Landscaping

On both large and small sites, landscape architects play an important role in helping to create an exterior environment that will be attractive to potential tenants and the surrounding neighborhood. In addition to landscaping of all types, their work includes plazas, site furniture, fountains and other exterior amenities that will animate the site and create the proper foreground for the building and its occupants.

Vertical Transportation

In larger, high-rise office buildings, the vertical transportation system is a major cost component and an important factor in the tenant's perception of the building's quality. Speedy, comfortable elevator service is taken for granted by tenants and buildings that cannot provide it will not be competitive. The normal criteria for elevator service include twenty-five to thirty-second waiting intervals, and a load factor of fifty percent of the car's capacity during peak hours. Ideally, no more than twelve floors should be serviced by one bank of elevators, minimizing travel time.

The number of elevators servicing each bank is determined by the population within that zone. The population figure should not be based only on the anticipated initial tenant's requirements but should take into account a broad range of tenant occupancies over the life of the building. Executive floors may be sparsely populated and allow 250 square feet per person, while general administration and back office space may have a much higher density. An allocation of 150 square feet per person is not unrealistic in a tight market where tenants want to make the most effective use of their space.

Acoustics

The most critical acoustical consideration is the ability to close out unwanted noises from the work space. Double glazing has become standard in window design not only for its energy efficiency, but for its ability to reduce street noises.

The increased size of mechanical systems throughout the office building (in the central mechanical rooms, mechanical rooms on each floor and equipment in the ceilings) has increased the amount of sound generated from mechanical equipment that must be isolated acoustically from the work space. This is done through proper selection of equipment, vibration isolators, insulation and the design of wall and floor enclosures surrounding this equipment to isolate the sound.

Exterior Wall

The complexities of exterior wall systems have made the exterior wall consultant an important part of the design team for large office buildings. It is recommended that a wind tunnel test be conducted for a high-rise office building to establish the lateral forces placed on the building's superstructure and to determine the water and air pressure that will affect the building facade. The actual effect of wind over the surface of a high-rise building is often greater than the criteria established in most building codes. These forces must be analyzed to design a building with a skin that is water-tight and will minimize air infiltration. The exterior wall studies include evaluations of manufactured metal and glass curtain wall systems, as well as the more traditional masonry, stone and precast concrete facades.

Window Washing

Since most large office buildings are designed with fixed glazing, exterior window washing is required to clean the exterior walls and maintain the facade. These systems are especially complicated in cities such as New York where setbacks in the tower are the norm rather than the exception. In order to work properly, the systems must be designed in conjunction with the structural supports and exterior wall design. Therefore, the design of an appropriate window washing system must be considered early in the planning stages rather than as a maintenance feature added after the building is completed.

Lighting

Lighting consultants are often retained to provide special lighting in areas such as the lobby and the exterior building and site lighting. It is critical that the building look as good at night as it does in the daytime.

Graphics

Graphics design includes exterior signage and identification as well as interior signage and directories. Ideally, a basic theme is established for the graphics and carried through all areas of the building. The first job of good graphics is to communicate a message simply and clearly. Its further objective is to look good and complement the architecture.

Cost Estimating

During all phases of design, cost estimating is provided by the architect or by an outside consultant retained by the architect, except when it is provided by the construction manager or contractor as a member of the project team.

SCHEMATIC DESIGN

There is often a considerable gap between completion of pre-schematics and the initiation of schematics, due to the time required to obtain site approvals, tenant commitments and financing. Once the owner/developer has completed this process, the architect/engineers begin the schematic design phase.

The architect/engineers and owner/developer re-evaluate the design assumptions made during the pre-schematic phase and make whatever adjustments are necessary to satisfy the requirements of local agencies and potential tenants. Architectural plans and elevations are developed in greater detail to clearly define the building design. Engineering studies are made to establish the optimum systems for structural, mechanical/ electrical and vertical transportation. The drawings and written documents produced by the design team now provide sufficient information to establish a realistic cost estimate for the project. If the estimate at this point exceeds budget objectives, the design may need to be adjusted to achieve a balance between design and projected cost.

DESIGN DEVELOPMENT

Once the schematic design has been approved, design development documents are prepared that fix and describe the design including the structure, building systems and finishes. Evaluation of constructibility, the necessary sequencing of construction trades and long lead items are identified at this juncture. The drawings and written documents prepared during this phase are re-evaluated once again with an updated cost estimate to establish that the project still meets its targeted objectives. If the project is over budget, value engineering is undertaken until these objectives are achieved.

CONSTRUCTION DOCUMENTS

Construction documents are prepared to communicate the materials and methods of construction necessary to build the project. They include all of the drawings and specifications required by each of the design disciplines to satisfy local agencies in order to obtain permits and to provide the documents necessary for bidding and construction. The architect and its consultants assist the owner/developer in obtaining all the necessary agency approvals.

After approval of the construction documents, the architect assists the owner/developer in obtaining bids or negotiated proposals and in awarding and preparing contracts for construction. In the case of phased construction, the owner/developer may authorize bidding and/or negotiation of portions of the work prior to completion of the construction document phase.

SERVICES DURING CONSTRUCTION

Normal architectural/engineering services provided during construction include checking shop drawings, material samples and technical data submitted by the contractor and his subcontractors and suppliers for compliance with design intent. The design team also makes periodic visits to the job during construction, and is readily available to answer questions and provide clarifications to the contractor as needed. Full time on-site representation by the architect/engineer is not normally part of basic services, but is recommended on major projects and provided as an additional service.

CONCLUSION

With an ever-changing marketplace as the driving force behind office building design, the entire process has become increasingly complex. A host of technical considerations must be integrated into the program if a building is to be successful. The role of the architect and the design team has expanded to help the owner/developer deal with these issues. Architects are required to be more than creators of aesthetically pleasing designs; they must be team leaders as well, managing a broad, multi-faceted design effort.

While technology may have changed the way the process unfolds, it has not altered the basic tenets of good design. There are some well-designed buildings from 25 years ago that have adapted successfully to current technological and market demands. The new buildings created today will have to be measured in a similar manner 25 years from now.

What can owners and architects do to ensure timeless design, and the long-term success of a building? The key factors have been a constant for quite some time—quality of design and materials and the building's flexibility to accommodate change.

ABOUT THE AUTHOR

Henry H. Brennan, AIA, is a founding partner of Brennan Beer Gorman/ Architects and Brennan Beer Gorman Monk/Interiors, headquartered in New York. Since the formation of the firms, Brennan has directed the development of numerous major office projects as well as the renovation/ restoration of internationally known landmark hotels and offices. The firm's international practice includes a mixed use office/hotel/residential project in Bangkok, Thailand.

15

THE OWNER'S VIEW OF OFFICE DEVELOPMENT

by Michael T. Lutton

THE MARKETABLE CONCEPT

Office buildings are created when there is a demand for the product. The demand may come from a specific user who needs a location to house its business or from an entrepreneur who spots a lack of available space and identifies the need for new speculative space.

User-driven segmentation

Single-tenant buildings incorporate the characteristics of the business that will occupy them. Unlike speculative buildings, they may contain health facilities, conference rooms, cafeterias, executive dining rooms, laboratory floors and other types of specific uses at the behest of their sole tenant. Because of these special uses, most build-to-suit, single-tenant occupancies are under a long-term lease to maximize the value of these non-standard improvements particular to the tenant.

Speculative multi-tenant buildings are designed for maximum flexibility to accommodate a wide array of businesses. Unlike single-tenant buildings which are dictated by the user, speculative buildings are built to reflect the personal desires and preferences of the developer.

Office buildings are divided into three categories: low-rise, mid-rise and high-rise. Low-rise buildings (one to three stories) are usually part of a complex of buildings and are generally situated in suburban locations, where low density allows for drive-up parking, lower construction cost and typically lower operating expenses. These buildings appeal to users who desire the convenience of bypassing parking garages, elevators and lobby security. They also are attractive to corporate users who believe a campus-type environment is more consistent with the company's image.

Mid-rise buildings (four to twelve stories) are the most common type of office building in this country. Found in both urban and suburban locations, mid-rise buildings appeal to users seeking an upgraded image from the low-key ambiance of the low-rise. These buildings offer the efficiencies of the high-rise without the critical mass and the numerous problems high density creates.

High-rise buildings (thirteen floors and higher) dominate the urban skyline and support the continuing evolution of U.S. cities. They provide the tenant not only with an office, but usually with all of the other amenities he needs to be comfortable. Because high land costs make high-rise Class A urban buildings expensive to develop, economics dictate that their density be great.

Low and mid rise buildings are often part of a complex of buildings situated in suburban office parks. These buildings appeal to users looking for convenience and a low-density ambiance. *(Courtesy of The Irvine Company)*

How Demand and Supply Issues Affect Marketability

Demand and supply are measured by vacancy and absorption rates. Vacancy is usually measured by how much net absorption has occurred in a given quarter (i.e., the amount of gross space leased less expirations and tenant defaults). As the vacancy in an area decreases, rental rates begin to rise. When vacancy rates approach single digits, rental rates approach amounts sufficient to offer a developer an adequate return on his investment. This simple equation is what determines whether a building should be constructed.

Other issues that should be examined when evaluating market conditions affecting demand include the following:

- **Sublease space:** Because this type of space typically is not tracked accurately, the vacancy factor can be substantially incorrect, affecting the absorption of the planned project. Sublease space can also lead to depressed rental rates, as the master tenant frequently offers the space at a rent that is substantially below market prices.
- **Class A vs. Class B space:** It is important to determine what percentage of the vacancy is in Class A buildings. The overall vacancy factor may be 16%, yet in Class A buildings it may be only 5%, resulting in an immediate need for new space. Functionally obsolete space is less desirable and does not compete against Class A space.
- **Major user build-to-suit:** Demand for a build-to-suit building by a single user depends on the tenant's credit rating and the value of the lease. Vacancy rates are not a factor in the analysis as long as the building can be secured by the credit of the tenant requesting the build-to-suit.
- **Financing concerns:** Lenders may be reluctant to issue construction loans on specific types of buildings due to short-term market adjustments or regulatory requirements. Even if construction financing is available, a prior long-term commitment may not be obtainable.
- **Major employer base:** Even if vacancy rates are in the single digits and rental rates are high, it may be a disastrous time to build because a major employer in the area is suffering through a down business cycle or a restructuring of its industry.

All of these factors need to be evaluated carefully by the developer before a decision to build is reached. Any of these and other issues can turn a seemingly good opportunity into a horrendous business mistake.

Tenant Trade-offs

A major question that must be asked before an office development can be considered is where employees live. Employers must identify where their labor is coming from in order to offer a convenient location. Employees' desire to work close to where they live has greatly influenced the rapid rise of the suburban office niche. The desire for a shorter commute has led to large mixed-use projects that may incorporate office buildings, hotels, health clubs, restaurants, day care centers and even entertainment complexes. The full-service complex offers all the advantages of the high-rise urban environment without the congestion and commuting time. Suburban developers who address these quality of life concerns enhance their opportunity for success; there is a clear advantage for the prospective tenant to stay in the suburban location. Recent rental rate comparisons have shown that tenants will even pay higher rent to be closer to home. The growth of the suburban marketplace is indicative of the depth of this demand.

Supply of Office Space

In order to measure supply, a developer must do the following:

1. Measure the total square footage in the marketplace
2. Measure the total vacancy in the marketplace
3. Measure the total sublease vacancy in the marketplace
4. Differentiate the supply and vacancy into competitive and non-competitive space

After the vacancy rate is determined, the net absorption for the last quarter must be extrapolated into a projected annual absorption. Dividing that number into the total square footage of vacant competitive space gives the number of years of supply in that market. Basing the formula on an actual full year or longer rather than extrapolating on the basis of a quarter results in a more accurate estimate of a year's supply.

After the existing supply of office space has been determined, the total unleased square footage of buildings under construction must be added to the total square footage, which is divided by the annual net absorption figure once again. It is critical that all vacant space and space under construction be analyzed before the decision is made to build. Projects proposed by other developers could also affect the lease-up of the project being analyzed.

After existing supply, space under construction and proposed projects have been evaluated, the analyst can begin to evaluate the impact of supply factors on rental rates. These rates will not rise if there is a continuous supply of space in the marketplace. Rates only rise if space is absorbed and development is curtailed. The decision to build office buildings other than build-to-suit projects should only be made after the developer is confident that demand will outstrip supply.

THE DEVELOPMENT PROCESS

The development process is governed by the entrepreneurial drive to satisfy a need and make money in the process. It requires a long-term commitment of both time and resources. A developer must have a mission statement that describes what he does, where he does it, and most of all, how he does it. When establishing a development firm, the individual will usually focus on one or two disciplines, i.e., retail, industrial, office or residential. Each of these areas has distinctive nuances that require a degree of product specialization.

Office developers typically concentrate on a specific type of product. A small developer may concentrate on low-rise suburban development because this product type does not have heavy capital requirements. Mid-size and large developers may tackle large, mixed-use projects that may require years to develop. Due to the challenging nature of large-scale development, the developer's reputation is critical to obtain the necessary government approvals and potential infrastructure requirements. A municipal government is less likely to do business with a developer who has not successfully executed similar projects. Confidence in and respect for the developer provide strong motivation for government officials.

Recognizing one's limitations and understanding local attitudes toward the proposed project are necessary to a developer's success.

Market and Feasibility Analysis

Whether it is performed in-house or by an outside consultant, the developer must have independent verification of the market, i.e., supply and demand, for a product. In most large urban and suburban areas, major real estate brokerage houses track market conditions on a quarterly basis. A review of several local market surveys will quickly reveal trends affecting that particular area. More site-specific market surveys can be obtained through appraisal and brokerage companies.

Once market conditions have been researched and verified, rental rate and absorption numbers can be inserted into a feasibility analysis. The analysis should take into account market condition, absorption, rental rate and rate growth, project cost, rental rate concessions, operating expenses and any other costs—both one-time and ongoing—that would affect financial performance.

An analysis should be performed to verify that the project will satisfy the developer's investment criteria after allowing for a reasonable contingency. This analysis should be used to set the limits for project investment. By understanding total cost and return, an analyst can "back into" the maximum price he can afford to pay for the land. Appraisers call this the land residual method of estimating total value and land value. Once this number is verified, site acquisition can begin.

Site Selection

Office development is predicated on location, location, location. A good site is flat, is easily accessible, is not on a fault line, is above the flood zone, and does not interfere with public access or neighbors' use. The closer the site is to a usable, buildable condition, the less money the developer must spend to have it prepared.

Once a site is identified, it must be checked for permitted uses. If the site does not have the proper zoning entitlement for construction of the desired product, what is the process for getting the entitlement? Sites should not be purchased without entitlement unless the developer is reasonably assured that it is obtainable.

Before entering into a land purchase, the developer should have a civil engineer check the metes and bounds, identify easements that may affect development and verify acreage. The engineer should also prepare a topographical map showing the various elevations on the site and any unusual characteristics. In addition, prior to purchase a soils engineer should check the soil for any toxic contamination or groundwater and evaluate the quality of the existing soil. Depending on the type of building, the soils engineer may make specific recommendations to the structural engineer about how best to support the product's foundation.

Site Planning

Once the economic and site feasibility studies are completed, the next step is preparation of the site plan. Through the market evaluation process, the developer has discovered that the marketplace desires a particular floor size and by providing this, he gives his product an edge over the competition. The developer discusses his vision of the project with the architect. It is the architect's job to incorporate the market considerations into the site plan envelope, while complying with local government and Uniform Building Code requirements.

The ultimate success of the project will depend on how well the building meets the market's desire. Once several studies are ready for review, the developer checks the site plan for a variety of things that could hinder marketing of the project. Ingress and egress, loading, security, utility enclosures and locations, HVAC location and type, floor to ceiling height and the number of required elevators must all be discussed and agreed on, as they bear on the site requirements.

Once the building's "footprint" has been determined, the architect can proceed with the elevation studies that lead to the design of the building's shape and exterior appearance. Here again, marketing considerations dictate the type of exterior finish.

Preliminary Financing Concerns

When the developer has completed the feasibility analysis, located the site, and developed a site plan and elevation, his next step is to identify his source of debt and equity. Underwriting conditions for loans of all kinds change according to market conditions. The only common thread throughout evolving financial times is the lender's wish to see the developer/owner at risk with real equity (cash money or convertible security). Equity can come from private sources such as individuals or private foundations, or from public institutions. Life insurance companies and pension funds also invest heavily in commercial real estate.

Once an equity source is identified, construction money can usually be found. An equity source is betting, along with the developer, that he will get a certain return on his investment and that the total cost will not exceed a given amount. The investor focuses on the developer's track record and the project's ability to meet pro forma forecasts. This is particularly important because the investor is usually the guarantor of the construction note and downside risk. Obligations are usually the investor's concern. Every cost in excess of the investor's anticipated cost erodes the investor's return, thereby diminishing the success of the project.

An investor will typically try to persuade the lending institution issuing the construction loan or permanent loan to make the loan non-recourse. This limits the investor's liability to the amount of his investment so he is not liable on the loan. Most equity investors form partnerships with the developer, who typically provides the development services as his "sweat equity" in return for his partnership percentage. The investor reserves the right to reduce the developer's ownership interest if additional capital is required.

Depending on the equity source and collateral, developers can sometimes obtain an acquisition loan for a percentage of the acquisition price. This "bridge" loan is used on an interim basis to fund the acquisition. Most acquisition loans are either paid off out of the construction loan or rolled into the loan by the lending institution. Lending institutions will make bridge loans only if they feel confident about market conditions. Construction loans vary in term according to the length of the construction period or the security on the loan. Some lenders will allow the loan to be considered a "mini permanent" loan of five to ten years if they feel there is adequate collateral.

Developers attempt to secure "take out" financing or permanent financing either at the project's initiation or when occupancy nears stabilization. The permanent loan is used to pay off (take out) the construction lender and is long term in nature. The loan is based on certain debt coverage ratios of the project's net operating income, and the project's performance should easily support the loan. Various types of construction, bridge and permanent financing are discussed more fully in Chapter 22.

Appraisal

The appraisal process is critical to the developer because it is the basis for all money borrowed against the property. A raw site appraisal will evaluate the property in an unfinished, unimproved state and offer no opinion as to the site's best use, but instead defer to the existing entitlement. Finished site appraisal takes into account the infrastructure in place and its value to the site. Bulk value, upon completion, takes into account the replacement cost of the improvements in place without regard to the economic value of the leases. This is a pure measurement of costs.

Sophisticated appraisals of office buildings take a set of assumptions on rental rate growth, operating expenses and escalations and capital replacement requirements, and analyze the project on a ten-year discounted cash flow basis to determine the project's real value at stabilized occupancy. The value of an office building is based on the value and security of its leases and what someone is willing to pay for it.

Zoning and Other Approvals

When new areas for development are considered in the general or master plan, most states require that an Environmental Impact Statement (EIS) be completed. The report evaluates the proposed development's impact on transportation, government services, water, sewer waste management, and habitat, and issues negative or positive findings on these and other concerns. EIS reports are the vehicles by which growth control movements typically support or protest growth modifications. Citizens' concerns with rapid growth stem from their desire to maintain or improve their quality of life. The study also gives the developer an opportunity to communicate to the citizens of the community the positive impacts of the development.

Density varies in different cities due to the conditions each city places on development. For any development project, the first consideration is the allowable buildable area that the entitlement permits. Density is measured by coverage. The density of a suburban one-story office building might be .40 of an acre due to setback requirements, parking requirements and easements. The governmental jurisdiction might permit a developer to increase the site's density in return for building a parking garage, a trade-off that would have considerable economic impact. Another measure of density is floor area ratio (FAR), measured by square feet of land. A high-density project would have a FAR of 20 to 1. In other words, the developer could build 20 square feet for every square foot of land. The density, or FAR, dictates land prices. The impact of parking, circulation, public areas, setbacks and so on determine the ultimate density of the site. Other factors that affect density include height restrictions, ingress and egress and traffic concerns, view corridors, public area shadowing and a variety of other local restrictions.

The job of the developer and architect is not to maximize density, but to build a project that enhances the community while providing an adequate return to the developer. Many commendable projects did not maximize their allowable density, either for market or cost considerations. The developers were concerned with the public's perception of the project.

Before the developer can obtain financing, request a permit or begin construction, he must have a legal parcel. A recorded parcel map describing the parcel or parcels to be encumbered by the lender is a requirement. The map is prepared by the civil engineer and recorded by the title company. Once the parcel is legal, the civil engineer can provide grading plans to the city or county to obtain a grading permit. This allows the developer to finish the grading and cut the pad for the site.

Final Design and Financing Arrangements

After the site plan has been completed, the architect creates partial elevations. Once the concept is approved, conceptual or design development drawings are prepared. This set of plans incorporates the type of mechanical systems to be used in the building, a section of the exterior wall, and all other pertinent information necessary to complete preliminary pricing and proceed with ordering long lead items. When the developer is satisfied with the development specifics, he authorizes the architect to proceed with the working drawings that will ultimately be used to construct the building. Most developers employ a contractor at the design development stage to do preliminary pricing and value engineering. Once the drawings are approved, the developer will attempt to close his construction loan, in order to proceed with the project.

Most construction loans are set up on a voucher or draw request system. Ten percent of the cost of the total work in place and stored materials is held in reserve until the contractor has completed all construction, including the "punch list" of final items to be completed. Monthly payments are based on the percentage of work completed, less previous payments and the reserve amount. The contractor submits the complete draw request to the owner and the lender's representative for review. Once the percentage of work has been verified, the lender will fund the loan. Typically, funding is once a month and includes allowable development fees to be paid to the developer. During the construction and lease-up period, it is the owner's responsibility to fund capital shortfalls. Operating capital deficiencies are usually projected in the pro forma, so the equity investor knows how much cash he will put into the project until its rental stream stabilizes.

Construction

The development of the drawings dictates whether the job will be successful once construction begins. The toughest part of office development is the conceptual effort put into the initial analysis and design. Construction is the easiest part, if the developer has put a good team together.

Most general contractors today are brokers. They do no direct construction, but instead coordinate activities between the architect and the various construction sub-trades. The general contractor will negotiate a fee or bid a project based on a contract with the owner/developer. The general contractor then contracts with each sub-trade to perform the work on its behalf. The timing of each task is delineated in the project schedule prepared by the contractor and evaluated by the owner, architect and lender. The schedule is attached to the contract and specifies such things as shop drawing turnaround times between the architect and contractor, long lead item delivery and when various items must be ordered. The larger the building, the more lead time is required. Items not ordered on a timely basis can delay completion and occupancy. This not only increases interest cost, but also delays rental revenue. Adherence to the architectural/ construction schedule is crucial to the successful construction of the project.

Contractors typically enter a lump sum bid, then make every effort to hold costs under that amount. The contractor is usually responsible for any costs exceeding that lump sum. A guaranteed maximum amount (GMAX) contract allows the contractor to use amounts not spent in certain categories to offset overruns in other categories. With a cost-plus contract, the contractor works at his cost plus a negotiated mark-up. All of these types of contracts have risks and rewards, and the accuracy of the cost estimates depend on the quality of the plans and specifications that the architect has produced. Both the GMAX and cost-plus contracts call for a negotiated fee to cover the contractor's general and administration overhead. The combined fee and overhead is what should be evaluated.

DEVELOPMENT ISSUES AND STRATEGIES

Following are some additional issues that the owner/developer must address.

Options on Land

With a land option, the developer buys the time he needs to decide if the development is feasible by offering the landowner a fee in order to tie up the property exclusively for a specified period of time. The developer controls the property and knows his ultimate cost without having to commit to purchase. Should the developer not acquire the property, the landowner is compensated by keeping the negotiated fee.

Joint Ventures with Landowners

Joint ventures with a landowner are generally beneficial for the developer, as the landowner can contribute his equity in the land to the development joint venture in return for a percentage ownership. The advantage is that the joint venture owns the land without having to purchase it, freeing up capital for other uses. If the property is debt free, it can be used as security for a loan to fund pre-development costs.

Joint Ventures with Finance (Equity) Partners

Joint venturing with a financial partner provides the developer with a source of capital whose perspective is usually long term. The financial partner puts up most of the equity and funds development cost in return for an ownership interest and a preferred return on its money. Equity partners are particularly desirable for large scale multi-phased development.

Relationships Between the Developer and the Development Team

The developer's credibility is only as good as the team he has put together. The team must act professionally and responsibly at all times to be credible to the community and the lender. Relationships between consultants, community leaders and contractors must be disclosed to all parties concerned.

Credit Potential of Developer

Many projects require more equity than the developer has available. The lender may require credit enhancement to make the loan. Types of enhancement often requested include:

- **Letter of credit:** These must be issued by a bank in good standing. The letter of credit is held in escrow, to be paid to the lender only in the event of a default by the borrower.
- **Cross collateral:** The developer pledges equity in another development as additional collateral to secure the loan. The danger of cross collateral is that if one project fails, it could cause the developer to lose the other one as well.
- **Personal guarantee:** The developer pledges personal assets as additional security on the loan. This is a dangerous act if there is a prospect of a down market.
- **Bonding:** In this instance, the lender requires a bond that insures completion of the project regardless of the developer's financial condition.

Market Activity and Positioning

The market reacts quickly to events and so must the developer. If the rental market is dropping, the developer must determine how to react quickly, as his responses to market conditions will have long-term impacts. If the market is soft and two years away from a rent spike, the developer will benefit from offering tenants short-term leases so they will be in a less advantageous position when the market turns up. Because office buildings are long-term investments, the developer must carefully watch and plan around the cycles of the rental market.

Cash Conservation

Cash conservation is the key to good yields. In the long run, money is made in the office business by renewing tenants in place. When a tenant vacates, the owner loses rental income for several months, must pay a commission to find a replacement and must spend on capital improvements for the new tenant. In most instances, a new base year will be required, resulting in the loss of expense recovery. The economic impact of losing a tenant, particularly in a down market, is devastating and sometimes irreversible, leading to the economic failure of the project.

Project Planning and Budgeting

Each product should be economically modeled and goals and objectives established. Annual project budgets should be prepared and reviewed for results monthly. Development cost through the project's completion to asset management should be accounted for in each budget, in order to insure that nothing is lost in the transition.

PARTICIPANTS IN THE DEVELOPMENT PROCESS

An architect is employed based not only on his design and technical capabilities, but most important, on his firm's ability to work in a team environment. The developer asks the architect for a schedule and fee proposal based on an agreed-on scope of work. The developer employs a civil engineer to determine site requirements so that the architect can recommend, and include in his proposal, the necessary electrical, mechanical, acoustical, structural and curtain wall engineering. The developer will want to maintain control over the civil, soils and environmental engineers due to potential liability and conflicts of interest.

The developer interviews marketing teams and gathers their perspectives on the market and the building features in demand. The marketing team may tell him, "We need six watts of power per square foot, floor loading to support legal files, and full glass is a must. In addition, central HVAC, bay depths of 38 feet or less for multi-tenant layout from the core, and 20,000 square foot floors sell best." The brokers ask for high-speed elevators if structural requirements preclude the use of a split bank of elevators. The developer asks for his competitors' average load factor (the difference between rentable and usable space) and is told it is 11%. After hours of conversation, the developer prepares his list of requirements to develop a high-quality, marketable building to discuss with the architect. The architect, in the meantime, has reviewed the governmental, building code and other issues affecting the site. Taking into account the developer's requirements and any governmental restrictions, he begins work on the site plan.

After the site plan is finished and checked for accuracy, the developer asks the architect to lay out some hypothetical floors to see how tenants will fit in the building. Once flexibility is assured, the site plan is checked again to ensure adequate access for pedestrians, cars and service vehicles. The architect reviews the elevation schemes with the developer, who approves the building's geometry and exterior wall plan. The architect gives the plan to the structural engineer to review and devise the structural plan, as steel will be one of the building's major costs. Upon review and re-review, the site and building core are evaluated to remove wasted space, provide sufficient room for HVAC and lighting, and lessen the amount of structural steel necessary.

Once the site plan, building footprint and elevations are reviewed, the architect is told to prepare a design development plan. At this stage, the developer and architect will proof the building systems, identify long lead items and begin to schedule and price the building. Some developers employ the mechanical and electrical subcontractors at this stage to negotiate a design/build price, in order to take the risk out of these two complex systems. The developer will also employ a general contractor to estimate the job based on the daily refining of scope and to help make value engineering decisions. When the design development plan is complete, the contractor will provide the developer with a cost estimate based on the scope of work specified in the architectural drawings or on a suggested revised scope that will accomplish the same objectives at a lower cost.

The developer then asks for a commitment from his construction lender and is given the go-ahead. The developer authorizes working drawings to begin and negotiates a guaranteed maximum contract with the contractor based on the scope of work defined and redefined in the design development plan. It will be the contractor's responsibility to keep the architect within the agreed-on scope of work. The project team meets weekly to review progress and pricing. Value engineering changes are made by the project team. However, changes that affect marketing are made only by the owner and his marketing team.

The architect, in conjunction with the owner and his consultants, submits the plans to the city in packages. Long lead items, such as elevators and electrical gear, are processed first, in order not to delay construction. The timing for submitting drawings, ordering long lead items, and authorizing overtime to stay on schedule is critical.

The contractor sends the owner approval packages to release scopes of work (e.g., steel, HVAC, electrical and miscellaneous trades) as defined in the GMAX contract. The contracts are let and the project proceeds in an orderly process. City inspectors sign off on each sub-trade. The architect responds to requests for clarifications from the field. The owner monitors costs, approves the monthly draw request, increases his marketing effort, and begins to organize the transition from development construction to asset management. Warranty information and shop drawings are turned over to asset management, as are maintenance contracts negotiated with the installing contractor during the building shell and core purchase. The preleasing activity starts during construction and is administered by the property manager. Elevator service to the preleased floors must be arranged to avoid interference with the contractor. There is a push to obtain the Certificate of Occupancy, so the first tenant can move in. The certificate is based more on life safety requirements than on the state of the tenant improvements.

The contractor, when processing the monthly draw requests, submits lien releases to assure the owner and lender that the subcontractors are being paid for their work. Without the releases, the project could be liened by the subcontractors for work not paid, which would affect the project's financing.

The last step in the project is miscellaneous site work and landscaping. The owner must push at the end to get the architect's final punch list completed. The architect reviews the contractor's work and requests repair where the work is not consistent with plans and specifications. The sooner the contractor is off the site, the quicker the owner can begin actively marketing the project. It is time to make it a performing asset.

CONCLUSION

The office building developer must be a risk taker, analytical, well-versed in construction and most of all, a good communicator. He must know how to organize and direct a team under tight control and yet allow a certain amount of artistic freedom.

All of these traits will not help the project succeed unless the land is well located and is acquired on good terms. The project must be of high quality and considerate of its neighbors and community. It must appeal to the eye from a distance and feel comfortable at street level.

Developers are responsible for creating the communities where people live and work. They must think long term, maintain a historical perspective and always be aware of the impact their project will have on the next generation.

ABOUT THE AUTHOR

Michael T. Lutton is vice president of The Irvine Company, which is developing the nation's largest master-planned urban environment on 64,000 acres of land owned by the company in Orange County, California. As president of the Irvine Office and Industrial Company, a division of The Irvine Company, Lutton is responsible for all office-related development, leasing management and sales on Irvine Company land and Bren Investments' off-ranch portfolio. Lutton has lectured extensively for the Urban Land Institute and the National Association of Industrial and Office Parks, and he is a member of both organizations.

16

THE CONSTRUCTOR'S ROLE IN OFFICE DEVELOPMENT

by Ted Rhoades

INTRODUCTION

The Various Roles of the Constructor

The troika generally responsible for the design and construction of a building is the owner, architect and contractor. This terminology invokes the image of a linear process wherein the architect (and consultants) completes the construction documents, following which the project is put out for competitive bidding among general contractors. This technique is still common, particularly in the public sector. However, most speculative office buildings, and in many cases suburban buildings and institutional offices, involve a construction professional in a very different role, either as construction manager or as design/builder. In this chapter, the generic term "constructor" is used to describe all three of these roles in order to avoid confusion with the traditional general contractor's role. Each of these roles will be examined in detail.

As General Contractor

The general contractor is the construction firm that is typically hired on the basis of a competitive bid utilizing completed construction documents. The general contractor assumes responsibility for completing the construction in accordance with the contract documents. The construction price is a fixed amount; the general contractor lets all subcontracts, and keeps any cost savings or makes up any overruns. The relationship of the owner-architect-general contractor team is shown in Figure 16-1.

As Construction Manager

The construction manager is typically retained by the owner early in the preconstruction phase, generally soon after the architect is hired. Through the design phase, the construction manager acts as an advisor to the architect and owner, providing a variety of services aimed at keeping the project within the owner's budget and timetable. When the drawings and specifications are complete enough to permit construction to begin, the owner has the option of asking the construction manager to provide a guaranteed maximum price (GMP), with trade contracts running to the construction manager or directly to the owner.

For most large office buildings in the private sector, the owner will require a GMP and all subcontracts will run to the construction manager. Under this arrangement, the construction manager assumes the role of a general contractor during the construction phase, but with differing contractual arrangements. It is unusual in the private sector for the owner to let the subcontracts directly, but this is not uncommon in the public sector.

When there is no GMP and the subcontracts run to the owner, this is often referred to as "pure construction management." In this case, the construction manager monitors and coordinates the work of the subcontractors throughout the construction period as the owner's agent, but the owner takes the associated risks. This arrangement is most often seen in the public sector.

FIGURE 16-1

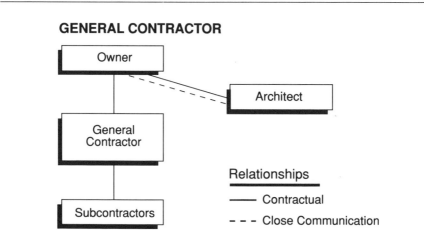

GENERAL CONTRACTOR

For the purposes of this chapter, the role of the construction manager is defined as that of an advisor/contractor, who provides a guaranteed maximum price and retains all subcontractors. The construction manager's relationship to the owner and architect is illustrated in Figure 16-2.

As Design/Builder

A design/build arrangement is often favored by owners who can define the intended result but have little time or resources to oversee the day-to-day process of design and the division of responsibility between the designer and builder, including the unproductive conflicts that can result. The most common form of design/build arrangement is for the constructor to retain the design firm and to execute the contract with the owner.

At its best, design/build can produce a satisfactory product at less cost and in a shorter time than any other process; at its worst, the owner can lose design control and be saddled with an unsatisfactory building that meets neither its short-term nor long-term needs. The ideal result is achieved when the designer produces the best design that meets the owner's needs, while the constructor optimizes the cost of each design element.

The design/build relationship between the owner, architect and constructor is illustrated in Figure 16-3.

Advantages and Disadvantages of Each Role

Figure 16-4 summarizes the relative advantages and disadvantages of each contractual relationship. The most desirable contracting method will

FIGURE 16-2

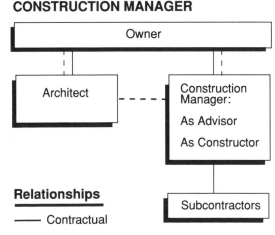

CONSTRUCTION MANAGER

depend on the owner's priorities. If the owner seeks the earliest possible completion at the lowest cost, design/build is the best option. For an owner uncomfortable with the possible loss of design control to a design/builder, but with insufficient staff or resources to select and work with an architect/ construction manager team, the best solution may be to hire an architect to complete the design and then retain a general contractor to handle the construction. But for the experienced owner who wishes to create a sophisticated, cost-effective product, retain full design control and operate under a guaranteed maximum price, hiring a construction manager is the option of choice.

THE CONSTRUCTOR AS GENERAL CONTRACTOR

Relationship to Owner and Designer

The general contractor typically is selected as a result of competitive bidding following completion of the drawings and specifications. Consequently, there is no relationship between the general contractor, owner and designer during the design period. During construction, the designer normally assists the owner in administering the contract with the general contractor by reviewing payment applications, shop drawings and other submittals, advising on claims, resolving technical questions and visiting the site at intervals. A widely used description of the designer's duties is contained in Article 4 of American Institute of Architects (AIA) Document

FIGURE 16-3

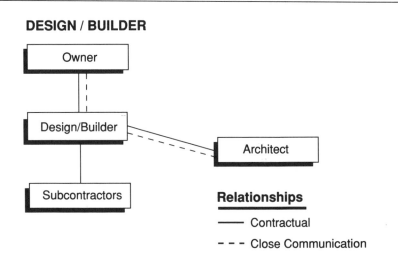

A201-1987. Some owners with adequate staff resources may undertake some of these duties, but it is fishing in dangerous waters for the owner to assume any of the designer's professional liability for design errors and omissions.

The relationship between an owner and a general contractor is sometimes characterized as inherently adversarial. In a contest between bidders who must offer the lowest price in order to be awarded the contract, the winning bid will represent the cost for exactly what is shown on the bidding documents—no more and no less (assuming no error was made). Inasmuch as a perfect set of construction documents has not yet been prepared and likely never will be, the stage is set for the general contractor to claim additional money and often additional time for even the smallest change or clarification of the documents. Further, since the general contractor has no particular relationship with the owner beyond the contract terms, with the only rewards for good performance being the profit made and the opportunity to bid again on future work, the incentive to perform as part of a team may not be strong.

Many general contractors take pride in their work and care about relationships. On private work, good performance as a general contractor can lead to negotiated engagements with a satisfied owner; indeed, many constructors routinely receive 50% or more of their construction manager work from clients previously served.

FIGURE 16-4

KEY:	1	2	3			
	Least or least likely		Most or most likely			
Result or Feature				**Role of the Constructor**		
				GC	**CM**	**D/B**
Lowest construction cost				1	2	3
Earliest completion				1	2	3
Owner say in sub selection				1	3	2
Owner administrative cost				2	3	1
Design control by owner				2	3	1
Quality of result				1	3	2
Owner liability for design errors and omissions				3	2	1
Owner liability to trade contractors				3	2	1
Owner pays actual, not estimated, cost				1	3	2

Selection of the General Contractor

When to Select

The project should be put out for bids only after the drawings and specifications have been completed, so that all competitors will be bidding on the same scope of work. The bidders will price only the work specifically shown in the bid documents, with any uncertainties, ambiguities or omissions setting the stage for future claims.

Prequalification

Public owners usually are required to accept bids from any bidder who can furnish performance and payment bonds. Private owners, however, can and should preselect the contractors from whom they will accept bids. Prequalification may be a formal process utilizing AIA Document A305, *Contractor's Qualification Statement*, or an informal process based on the owner's personal knowledge of qualified contractors, their local reputation or other criteria.

The owner should have the following information before adding a contractor to the bid list:

- How long the contractor has been in business
- Names and backgrounds of the top executives
- For a specific project, names and experience of the key personnel to be assigned
- Names of projects similar in scope and complexity, including brief description, contract value, time to complete and an owner and architect reference for each
- Whether and under what circumstances contractor has ever failed to complete a project
- Any significant outstanding claims, arbitration proceedings or lawsuits
- Financial strength (balance sheets for the last three years)
- Expected work load for the period of the project
- Trade and bank references

For any given project, between three and six qualified bidders should be identified. A bid list containing more than six names tends to be self-defeating, particularly for larger, more complex projects, because as the list gets longer, the quality of the contractors on the list deteriorates, and the most qualified contractors may be discouraged from bidding.

Obtaining the Best Price

Assuming that the owner has prequalified a reasonable number of bidders, timing is an important consideration. If the owner puts a project out for bids at the same time that one or more other projects are out for bids, likely by the same contractors, the owner's chances of obtaining a good response are improved if the bidding period is extended. This will permit the bidders to concentrate their maximum effort on each project.

Some other strategies that will help the owner in obtaining the best price include the following:

- Allow sufficient time for bidding; the architect can help in this determination.
- If alternate prices and unit prices are needed, ask the bidders to submit them 24 to 48 hours after the base bids are submitted. This allows the contractors to concentrate on assembling the best possible base price, as well as enabling them to prepare the best possible alternate and unit prices, since they will by then have identified the low bidders among the subcontractors. If the alternates and unit prices are submitted with the base bid, they must be prepared without this information, forcing the contractors to use the highest adds and the lowest deducts received in order to submit their bids on time.
- Notify the winning bidder within ten days of the bid submission, with work to commence within the following ten days.
- Request bidders to state the date on which they expect to achieve substantial completion, rather than imposing a date in the bid documents. This puts the schedule into competition, and could be a deciding factor if bids are very close.
- Do not ask the contractors to assume the liability for risks beyond their reasonable control.
- Cultivate a reputation for fair dealing and prompt payment of bills.
- Retain an architect with a reputation for quick responses to shop drawing and other submittals, requests for clarifications and change orders—and the ability to admit that sometimes he or she might have made a mistake!
- Use reasonable payment terms; pay invoices within 10 to 15 days of receipt; pay interest on late payments; and release amounts retained on payments promptly.

Engaging the General Contractor

When the bids have been received, the owner should open them privately in order to retain maximum flexibility in the actual award. Normally, the award should go to the lowest bidder. There are, however, factors other than a low base bid to take into account:

- The low bidder's situation may have changed since prequalification; e.g., a financial reverse may have occurred; a large project may recently have been secured which would curtail necessary resources; or key individuals may be unavailable.

- The low bidder's schedule may be longer than another bidder's, so that the price differential is more than erased by the cost to the owner of the added time.
- The combination of the base bid plus accepted alternates may determine the true low bidder.
- While it may be prudent to bond the low bidder, the next bidder may have a stronger balance sheet and performance record, possibly rendering bonding superfluous; the premium saving may then make the second bidder the true low bidder.

Finally, the thoughtful owner will inform all bidders of the base prices and any alternate prices received, without necessarily identifying which contractor submitted each price. Accepted alternates should be incorporated into the contract amount. If the owner has not made a decision on certain alternates, these may be identified in the contract as open alternates, along with acceptance dates beyond which they are inapplicable. Unit prices should also be incorporated into the contract.

The Owner-General Contractor Agreement

Model Agreements

There are just two model stipulated sum agreements on the market for non-engineering projects, both published by the American Institute of Architects. They are:

- AIA Document A101, *Standard Form of Agreement Between Owner and Contractor, where the basis of payment is a Stipulated Sum.* This document is to be used with AIA Document A201, *General Conditions of the Contract for Construction.*
- AIA Document A107, *Abbreviated Form of Agreement Between Owner and Contractor, for Construction Projects of Limited Scope where the Basis of Payment is a Stipulated Sum.*

The latter document should be scrutinized carefully before use, as a number of important issues covered in A101 and A201 are either not covered in A107 or are covered incompletely by comparison. If an owner prefers a cost-reimbursement type contract with a guaranteed maximum price, AIA documents A111 (with A201) and A117 may be used. It is strongly recommended that the current issue of each of these documents be used.

Some owners prefer to use their own contract formats. The standard AIA documents provide an excellent guide and checklist for preparing these customized contracts because they reflect standard industry practices. However, use of the standard documents, coupled with desired modifications, can save contractors and owners an immense amount of time by eliminating the need to "reinvent the wheel."

Risk Allocation

Standard agreements published by the AIA, which are widely used for building construction and whose provisions have withstood numerous court challenges over many decades, allocate risks to the party (owner, architect, contractor) that is best able to control each risk or is best able to sustain its financial consequences. These agreements assign responsibilities as follows.

The owner is responsible for:

- Providing adequate project funding and paying to the contractor the amounts properly due in accordance with the contract terms
- Providing a site ready for construction
- Providing construction documents sufficient for the efficient and expeditious completion of the contractor's work
- The added cost and time to the contractor due to *force majeure* events such as unknown conditions and other events that are beyond the contractor's reasonable control, including acts of the owner and architect, acts of God and unusual weather conditions
- Timely response to the contractor's requests

The architect is responsible for:

- The complete design of the building, including meeting all building code and other legal requirements
- Liability for design errors and omissions
- Timely approval of shop drawings, payment applications, change orders and other contractor submittals

The contractor is responsible for:

- Performing in accordance with the contract documents
- Completing the work for the contract amount and within the contract time
- Providing insurance coverage adequate to protect itself against specified claims arising from its operations and for which it is legally liable
- Timely payment of subcontractors

Scope of Work and Change Orders

On any project, the owner should typically expect the contract amount to increase by 5% on account of change orders. About half of these change orders will result from scope changes ordered by the owner during construction. The other half will result from errors and omissions in the plans and specifications, coordination problems, force majeure events, unknown conditions, delays and other unanticipated events beyond the contractor's control that are reimbursable under the contract.

It is incumbent on the owner and contractor to be as precise as possible in defining the scope of work on which the contract amount is based. The basis of many disputes is the lack of agreement on exactly what scope of work is included in the contract amount, particularly when the gray area of "intent" of the documents is raised.

Finally, the contract should allow the contractor to perform work under change orders and be reimbursed for it as the work proceeds even though the change order amount has not been finally determined.

Time Commitments

In virtually all contracts, time is declared to be "of the essence," the most important single element of the contract. It means that the owner will suffer damage if the time commitment in the contract is not met. It must also be clear that the contractor too will suffer damage if events beyond its control prevent it from meeting the contractual time commitment. This latter concept is one of the most contentious in the industry, turning on the issue of just what delays the contractor could reasonably have anticipated and therefore allowed for in fixing the contract time and amount. Some owners allow the contractor a time extension only for defined delay events, but disallow any claim for additional cost arising from such delays. The standard AIA and Associated General Contractors of America (AGC) contract forms do not contain such one-sided risk transfer provisions, and it is not in any owner's interest to sanction them. In the end, the owner will pay anyway through higher bid prices, through "corner-cutting" by un-principled contractors, or through the bad reputation that will attach to that owner.

Some contracts provide for liquidated damages, i.e., an estimate as-sessed against the constructor of the damages an owner may sustain because of unexcused delays in completion. Such a provision sets an adversarial tone and guarantees that the owner will receive frequent requests for time extensions. Smart contractors rarely have to pay such damages because they can include a projected liquidated damage sum in their lump sum competitive bid if the owner has set an unrealistic completion date. Alternatively, they can document through letter writing more than enough legitimate delay claims that liquidated damages will never be paid. Liquidated damage provisions create ill will and rarely lead to completion of the work one day earlier than it would have been completed absent such a provision.

THE CONSTRUCTOR AS CONSTRUCTION MANAGER

Relationship to Owner and Designer

The construction manager relationship is the most widely preferred format in the private office construction sector. The owner, architect and constructor enter into a team relationship with the common objective of meeting the owner's cost, time and quality goals, with each party retaining primacy in the areas for which it is best suited. For a successful project, the owner must provide the architect with a clearly defined program (which the architect may in fact assist in preparing), and must articulate the building budget and expected completion date. The owner must also remain closely involved with the design and its relationship to the program. Ideally, the architect produces the best design that meets the owner's program, and the construction manager examines each design element to determine the most cost-effective way to achieve the desired result.

Selection of the Construction Manager

When to Select

The construction manager should be selected before the design process begins in order to be of maximum value to the team. The construction manager may be selected either before or after the architect is retained. It is important that the owner select a compatible team, allowing whoever is hired first—the architect or the construction manager—to advise in the selection of the other.

The Selection Process

Since the owner does not select a construction manager on the basis of a low bid, the selection criteria must be subjective. Information the owner will want to obtain includes:

- The projects previously constructed by the construction manager that are similar in scope, complexity, size and quality, references for each, and the role of the construction manager (advisor/constructor, agent or general contractor)
- The names and backgrounds of the construction manager's top executives and the experience of the key personnel to be assigned to the project, including length of service
- The construction manager's financial strength, including balance sheets for the last three years, trade and bank references, default record, any

significant outstanding claims, any arbitrations or suits in progress and bonding capacity (even though the owner may not ask the construction manager to provide bonds)
- Current and projected workload

If the architect has already been retained, he or she should assist the owner in drawing up a list of potential construction managers and participate in evaluating the proposals. Particular emphasis should be placed on the construction manager's past success in working as an advisor/constructor, as this is as much an art as a science, requiring a pro-active and imaginative approach to a project. (If the construction manager is hired first, it can play the same role in the architect selection process.)

The selection process will be greatly enhanced to the extent that the owner can provide more information about the project, including general scope, approximate size, location, time frame, names of other players involved to date, financing arrangements and type of contract expected. Questions should be encouraged, and a site visit and preselection conference often prove valuable.

The construction manager's expected fee for services should be a factor in the selection, but only to the extent that the fee is not exorbitant. The primary consideration is whether the preferred construction manager will perform in the owner's best interests, as demonstrated on previous engagements. Any fee differential can disappear quickly if the construction manager is diligent in suggesting viable savings alternatives and completing the project on or ahead of schedule.

Engaging the Construction Manager

Once the owner has identified the construction manager, there are two options. The first is to enter into an initial agreement covering the preconstruction consulting phase only, to be followed later by a construction agreement when the guaranteed maximum price has been prepared. Or the agreement may encompass both the consulting and the construction phases, with the guaranteed maximum price and the date of substantial completion to be added by later amendment.

Defining the exact scope and timing of the construction manager's involvement through the design period is difficult, so it is customary to reimburse the construction manager during this time for actual staff time (direct personnel expense times a multiplier) plus out-of-pocket expenses. Alternatively, the construction manager may be paid a monthly retainer. If a cap has been placed on the cost of these services, the contract must provide for its adjustment if the scope of services is modified or if there are delays not caused by the construction manager's negligence.

The fee for services during the construction phase is usually established when the construction manager is engaged. It is customary to establish the fee initially as a percentage of the estimated cost of the work, then convert it to a dollar amount at the time the estimated cost of the work is computed as part of the guaranteed maximum price.

Selection of Subcontractors

It is not uncommon during the preconstruction phase for the construction manager to utilize (with the owner's approval) carefully chosen sub-contractors in the major trades, most often mechanical and electrical, to assist in the preparation of estimates, schedules, savings programs and life cycle studies. These same subcontractors may later be engaged to perform the actual construction if their final prices are within the line item amounts established for their work, or other contractors may also be invited to bid.

As the time approaches to prepare the guaranteed maximum price, or to let certain contracts for early-start work in advance of the GMP, the construction manager should prepare a list of qualified subcontractors in each trade from whom it proposes to solicit bids. This list may be based on the construction manager's knowledge of these subcontractors from past experience, or it may result from a formal prequalification process. It should then be reviewed by the architect (and its consultants as appropriate) and the owner. If additional names are suggested, the construction manager may, at its discretion, add these names to the list. If deletions are suggested for good reason, the construction manager should withdraw such names. It is treading on dangerous ground for an owner to force a construction manager to utilize a subcontractor against whom it has a valid objection. That subcontractor's possible later non-performance leaves the owner open to a claim.

When subcontractors are prequalified, the low bidder should be awarded the work, barring adverse intervening circumstances such as a recent financial reverse, loss of key personnel or recent award of a major project.

After the documents have been put out for subcontractor pricing, bidders conferences for the subcontractors are advisable to answer questions that may arise because the bidding documents are not yet complete. Each bidder should price a complete installation, spelling out any assumptions made in arriving at the price. When the bids are received, the construction manager will need to analyze each one carefully for completeness and make any necessary adjustments so that they are of equal scope and the true low bidder can be ascertained.

The Owner-Construction Manager Agreement

Model Agreements

Both the American Institute of Architects and the Associated General Contractors of America publish standard documents for constructors to use in providing preconstruction and construction services. These are:

- AIA Document A111, *Standard Form of Agreement Between Owner and Contractor, where the basis of payment is the Cost of the Work Plus a Fee with or without a Guaranteed Maximum Price.* This document is to be used with AIA Document A201, *General Conditions of the Contract for Construction.* A111 and A201 cover construction services only; a separate preconstruction agreement is required.
- AIA Document A117, *Abbreviated Form of Agreement Between Owner and Contractor for Projects of Limited Scope where the basis of payment is the Cost of the Work Plus a Fee with or without a Guaranteed Maximum Price.* This too covers only construction services. A117 is a condensed version of A111 and A201, but careful scrutiny is recommended as a number of important issues covered in the former documents are either not covered in A117 or are covered less completely.
- AGC Document No. 500, *Standard Form of Agreement Between Owner and Construction Manager (Guaranteed Maximum Price Option).* This document covers both preconstruction and construction phase services. When the guaranteed maximum price is prepared, it (and the date of substantial completion) is added via AGC Document No. 501, *Amendment to Owner-Construction Manager Contract.* This document is much shorter than the combined A111 and A201, and deals with fewer subjects and in briefer form.
- AIA Document A121/CMc and AGC Document 565, *Standard Form of Agreement Between Owner and Construction Manager Where the Construction Manager Is Also the Constructor.* Published in 1991 as a collaboration of the AIA and the AGC, this document is tailored specifically for use when the construction manager is the advisor/constructor. It should be used in conjunction with A201. It is highly recommended for use in this type of engagement.

AIA documents using the suffix "CM" or "CMa" following the document number are *not* intended for use by construction managers serving in an advisor/constructor capacity. Rather, these documents are designed for use under agency-type construction manager engagements and by trade contractors retained directly by owners. AIA Documents B801 and B801/CMa, as well as AGC Documents 510 and 520, are also intended exclusively for agency use.

Once again, it is strongly recommended that the current issue of any of the model agreements be used. Both the AIA and AGC update their documents at roughly ten year intervals, reflecting changes in relationships, technologies and liabilities that need to be addressed. The local chapters of each organization can supply current documents. As previously noted, use of these standard forms greatly facilitates the contract process.

Risk Allocation

The agency format is not recommended for private owners. By retaining the construction manager as an independent contractor, the owner greatly reduces the exposure to risk. Prior to establishment of the guaranteed maximum price, however, the construction manager assumes no liability for the budgets and schedules it prepares; these are prepared strictly for the information and guidance of the owner. Once the guaranteed maximum price and the date of substantial completion are agreed to, the construction manager assumes the normal contractor's risks of overruns and delays (except as excused by the terms of the agreement). Responsibilities continue to be allocated in the construction phase as set forth earlier.

Fee Arrangements and Incentives

A key difference between the construction manager and the general contractor is the owner's ability to reward the construction manager, as a member of the project team, for meeting the owner's project goals. The most common method is through a "savings clause," under which an owner shares with the construction manager any difference between the actual cost of the work plus the construction manager's fee, and the guaranteed maximum price (as adjusted by change orders). Sometimes the sharing of such savings depends on the construction manager's achieving the date of substantial completion (as adjusted).

The construction manager's base fee should be converted from the initial percentage of the estimated cost of work to a dollar amount at the time the GMP is accepted. If it remains a percentage, then the construction manager earns more fee to the extent that it expends more of the owner's money, and loses fee to the extent that it doesn't—hardly the incentive the owner should provide. When the base fee is fixed, and particularly if savings are shared, the construction manager has the incentive to minimize costs, thus satisfying all parties.

Cost, Schedule and Design Control

Early in the preconstruction phase, the construction manager converts the construction portion of the owner's budget into a target estimate, against which all subsequent estimates are measured. The construction manager also develops a schedule of activities of the owner, architect and construction manager (and other players, such as financing sources and governmental units) for the design and construction periods as required to meet the owner's completion target. This target schedule is continuously refined as events actually unfold. It is not unusual for the project team to meet weekly during the design phase. At these meetings, recent developments (design changes, savings ideas) are evaluated, the current status of the budget and schedule against the targets is reviewed and recovery strategies are devised as needed. It is of the utmost importance to establish a definite process, to adhere to it, and to keep accurate records of all decisions.

Throughout the design phase, the construction manager evaluates each design element for constructability and possible lower cost alternatives. Each alternative presented must be accepted by both the owner and architect, or it is rejected.

It is important that the team understand each member's roles. The rule is that each member retains primacy in its own areas of greatest competence and all decisions are arrived at openly. More than one set of good intentions has foundered when these simple rules are not observed.

Recouping Cost of Scope Changes

Once the guaranteed maximum price is agreed to, the basic process is the same as that described in the section on the general contractor. The construction contingency customarily included in the guaranteed maximum price is not meant to cover the cost of scope changes; rather, it is for the construction manager's exclusive use to cover possible costs of unexpected events that are not the basis for an increase in the contract amount.

Role of the Construction Manager during Design

Preparation of Estimates and Schedules

In order to prepare reasonably accurate early estimates and schedules, the construction manager must rely on its experience with comparable buildings, adjusted for any known differing conditions. It is important for the owner to know as early as possible whether the project is going to be feasible, and to be kept apprised at regular intervals of the progress toward meeting the established cost, time and quality goals. A process must be established and adhered to for such updating and reporting. Each successive update of the estimate and schedule must reflect the full extent of the most current information.

As a general guideline, budget updates should be prepared as often as new information becomes available. Full scale re-estimates should be prepared at the conclusion of the schematic design and design development documents. Updated budget reports should be prepared in an easily understood format. A simple method is to divide the project into building

FIGURE 16-5

Major Construction Company
99 Summer St Project
Date: 12/7/92

BUDGET CONTROL REPORT

Budget Parameters	Demolition, Excavation & Foundation	Structural Frame	Roofing & Waterproofing	Exterior Wall	Interiors	Vertical Transp'n	HVAC Plumbing Fire Protection	Electrical	Sitework	G.C. &. Fee	Contingencies	TOTAL
Budget Estimate Dated 1 Sept. 92	1,936,000	4,979,000	1,749,000	5,109,000	11,724,000	147,000	5,737,000	2,801,000	5,300,000	3,553,000	3,012,000	46,047,000
Accepted Revisions:												
1. Revise the Finish Floor Level	(8,000)	15,000					(3,000)		(28,000)	(1,000)	(1,000)	(26,000)
5. Revise Structural System		60,000								2,000	2,000	64,000
6. Revise Skylight/Clerestory Detail		(10,000)	(75,000)	5,000	5,000		(6,000)	3,000		(3,000)	(3,000)	(89,000)
7. Change Transformer/Primary System	10,000							(35,000)		(1,000)	(1,000)	(22,000)
9. Reduce the Parapet Height			(10,000)	(45,000)						(2,000)	(2,000)	(59,000)
Total with Accepted Revisions	1,938,000	5,044,000	1,664,000	5,069,000	11,729,000	147,000	5,728,000	2,769,000	5,272,000	3,548,000	3,007,000	45,915,000
Pending Revisions:												
2. Add an Underslab Drainage System	20,000						5,000			1,000	1,000	27,000
4. Revise Ground Level Earth Support	20,000	(65,000)			(10,000)					(2,000)	(2,000)	(59,000)
Total with Pending Revisions	1,978,000	4,979,000	1,664,000	5,069,000	11,719,000	147,000	5,733,000	2,769,000	5,272,000	3,547,000	3,006,000	45,883,000
Rejected Revisions:												
3. Revise Glazing Materials				(6,000)	(12,000)					(1,000)	(1,000)	(20,000)
8. 12" CMU in lieu of 14" Cavity Wall	(10,000)			(125,000)						(5,000)	(6,000)	(146,000)
Total of Rejected Revisions	(10,000)	0	0	(131,000)	(12,000)	0	0	0	0	(6,000)	(7,000)	(166,000)

systems. A sample budget report is shown in Figure 16-5. Note how the alternative systems, designs and materials are tracked.

Similarly, the schedule of activities of the owner, architect, construction manager, governmental entities and others should be continuously tracked. A sample schedule update is shown in Figure 16-6.

Value Engineering Studies

Value engineering is a sophisticated analysis of the true cost of a building system or component, taking into account all costs incurred during its life cycle, including amortization of initial cost, operating and maintenance costs. Other considerations might involve gain or loss of rentable space, or the consequences of earlier or later completion of construction. The owner has to determine which cost—first or last—is more important.

Constructibility Reviews

One of the most important roles the experienced construction manager can play is careful attention to constructibility issues. In reality, this is quality control, and it should be an ongoing activity. These reviews should focus particularly on details related to a watertight building envelope; new, unproven products; simplification of details for easier fabrication and installation; lack of coordination between architectural, structural, mechanical and electrical drawings and specifications; and reasonable tolerances.

Early Purchase of Long Lead Items

In order to meet a completion date or simply to speed up the construction, the construction manager should identify items for early purchase. The construction manager may, for example, on the owner's behalf, order the steel some months prior to starting foundation work. Other early-order items might be major pieces of equipment or major items for which a price rise is about to occur. Such items should be identified in the construction manager's schedules.

Fast-tracking of Construction

Another major advantage of bringing the construction manager on the team at an early date is that construction can begin prior to design completion. For the earliest start, the architect can be directed to complete the construction documents in a sequence that will allow construction to start long before interior details are worked out, for example, and before a guaranteed maximum price can be prepared. This latter point may give

FIGURE 16-6

MAJOR CONSTRUCTION COMPANY   PRECONSTRUCTION SCHEDULE

DATA DATE: FEBRUARY 28, 1992   PROJECT: INGALLS BUILDING

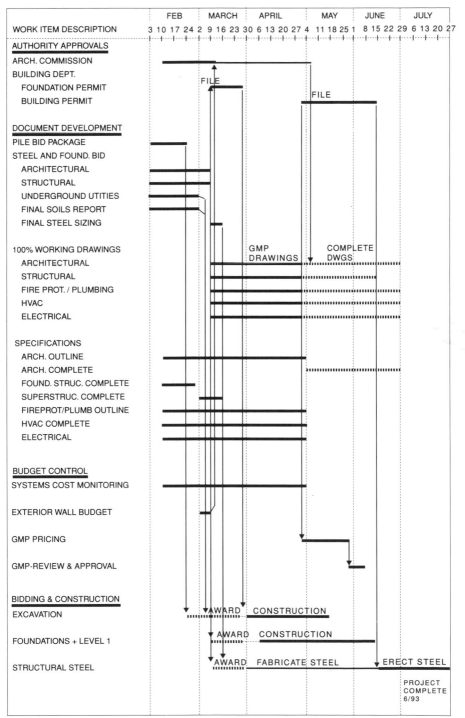

pause to owners and lenders, making it important for the construction manager to make accurate estimates and carefully monitor design.

Provision of Guaranteed Maximum Price

Most owners and lenders require the price to be guaranteed at the earliest feasible moment; too early can be misleading and too late can be a disservice. Accompanying the construction manager's guaranteed maximum price should be a statement of the basis for the price—the design documents used and the assumptions made by the construction manager in a good faith attempt to provide as complete a price as possible. For items not designed, allowances can be established.

Role of the Construction Manager during Construction

In the construction phase of the project, the construction manager takes on the mantle of a general contractor, but continues to function as a contributing member of the building team. The work proceeds on an open-book basis (that is, the construction manager's job records are open for the owner's inspection at all times), with the construction manager reimbursed for the actual cost of the work performed, subject to the terms of the contract.

During construction, most owners request periodic progress updates. This should consist of a concise summary of the following:

- **The financial status of the project.** This should include not only the status of money expended and commitments made to date, but a forecast of the balance to be expended. The forecast, in order to have validity, must be based on sound engineering judgments rather than being an accounting exercise. The simplest format is a one-page statement of the variances between estimated line item amounts and indicated outcomes.
- **The progress of the construction.** This report, also on one page, should show variances between planned milestone dates and actual completion dates, with reasons for any delays, and recovery plans if delays are on the critical path and would delay project completion. The owner may also desire an updated schedule with each progress report.
- **The status of changes.** This report should list changes in three categories: approved change estimates, and the change order number assigned; pending change estimates, i.e., changes which have been submitted but not yet approved by the owner and architect; and approximate change estimates, i.e., potential changes with preliminary estimates of cost only, and not yet submitted. The summaries of these three categories are incorporated into the financial status report. Thus the owner has advance notice of potential cost increases and can take appropriate action to mitigate such costs.

- **Problem areas.** This summary highlights existing and potential problem areas, such as potential industry strikes that would affect the project or the need for information from the owner in key areas.

It is standard practice for the construction manager to provide a one-year repair warranty, with the one year clock starting on the date of substantial completion, as certified by the architect. Certain specification sections may require longer warranties; the construction manager should obtain such warranties from the manufacturer, supplier or subcontractor and pass them through to the owner.

THE CONSTRUCTOR AS DESIGN/BUILDER

Relationship to Owner and Designer

Owners turn to a single source for the design and construction of projects for administrative simplicity and to transfer liability for non-owner-originated scope changes arising from design errors and omissions to the design/build team.

Few firms in the building field employ both designers and constructors because of difficult liability issues, state laws and other factors. Thus the design/build team normally consists of a contractor plus an independent design professional retained by the contractor. A successful design/build team will comprise two firms that have worked well together in the past and have built up a level of trust and respect.

It is essential for the owner to provide the design/build team with a clear statement of its needs, including scope and budget, time and quality goals. With the close relationship formed between the constructor and designer, these goals can often be achieved more readily than through any other project delivery method. This method can also, if not properly managed, lead to a highly unsatisfactory result for the owner. Thus, great care must be taken in structuring the relationship so that the team's goals are congruent with the owner's goals.

Selection of the Design/Builder

Prequalification

In addition to the usual criteria for prequalifying constructors and architects, the owner needs to make sure that a compatible design/build team is selected. If a "request for proposal" is sent to qualified constructors, it is important for the owner to ascertain whether the constructor and its architect have previously performed design/build work, and the history of all projects on which they have worked together, whether in a design/build relationship or otherwise.

Selection Process

The owner may choose not to issue a "request for proposal" to a number of firms, but may select the constructor, or both the constructor and architect, without competition. Usually, however, the design/build team is allowed to form itself. The owner may also establish a competition in which pre-qualified teams prepare preliminary drawings and an estimate of cost and time for the project. Since this is a costly process, it is common for each submitting team to receive a fixed reimbursement or an honorarium for their efforts. The drawback is that the owner is kept out of the design process until the competition is concluded. Whatever the method of selection, it is vital to select a compatible team.

Engaging the Design/Builder

As in the engagement of a construction manager, the services of the design/build team are divided into two parts—the preconstruction and construction phases—with the duration of the first phase indeterminate due to factors beyond the team's control. When the guaranteed maximum price has been agreed on, the construction fee and contract time can be fixed.

The Owner-Design/Builder Agreement

Model Agreements

Both the American Institute of Architects and the Associated General Contractors of America publish owner-design/builder agreements.

- Document A191, *Standard Form of Agreements Between Owner and Design/ Builder.* This document is divided into two parts. The intent is for the parties to determine the scope and feasibility of the project in Part 1, Preliminary Design and Budgeting, and thereafter enter into Part 2, Final Design and Construction.
- AGC Document No. 400, *Preliminary Design-Build Agreement.* The intent of this document is for the design/builder to complete the design and prepare a guaranteed maximum price. If the GMP is accepted, construction is added to the scope of work in a further agreement.
- AGC Document No. 410, *Standard Form of Design-Build Agreement and General Conditions Between Owner and Contractor.* More comprehensive than No. 400, this document provides for both design and construction services, to be performed under a guaranteed maximum price.

- AGC Document No. 415, *Standard Form of Design-Build Agreement and General Conditions Between Owner and Contractor (Where the Basis of Compensation is a Lump Sum)*. This agreement is the same as No. 410, but is structured for a stipulated sum.

Again, use of the current edition of standard documents is highly recommended.

Risk Allocation

In addition to assuming the risks normally associated with construction, the constructor in a design/build relationship assumes the additional risk of losses arising from design errors and omissions. Thus the constructor, in its contract with the architect, needs to be indemnified by the architect against loss, expense or damage arising from the architect's professional liability, backed by adequate professional liability insurance. However, the constructor and the architect need to decide who will bear the additional construction costs arising from the normal design deficiencies and coordination problems.

Fees and Incentives

The design/builder's compensation during the design phase can be the actual cost of the services performed or a stipulated sum, with a means of adjustment if the work extends beyond a certain date or if the scope of work has been increased. In the construction period, the fee is normally the agreed-upon percentage fee multiplied by the estimated cost of work that was computed when the guaranteed maximum price was prepared.

The constructor's fee normally is higher in design/build engagements, in recognition of the added administrative burden and risk it has assumed by employing the architect.

Incentives may be structured exactly the same as in a construction manager engagement. The design/builder may, in turn, offer an incentive fee to the architect if the constructor shares in savings with the owner and the architect has met certain goals.

Cost, Schedule, Design and Quality Control

The owner must decide to what extent it wishes to be involved in cost, schedule, design and quality control issues. One option is for the owner to give the design/builder a program, a budget and a time frame, then step back until it receives a guaranteed maximum price. At this point, the owner may find that what it has bought bears little resemblance to what had been envisioned. However, so much time has passed that the owner may have little choice but to proceed with the inappropriate design. This process is "cost-driven."

The other option is for the owner to stay closely involved with the design/build team during the design phase, reviewing at frequent intervals the design progress, the updated budget, and any alternative materials or systems or deviations from the program being proposed. With this approach, there will be no surprises when the design/build team presents its guaranteed maximum price. This process is "need-driven."

Responsibility for Scope Changes During Construction

Responsibility for changes in scope during construction is divided between the owner and the design/builder, unlike other contracting formats in which changes are completely the owner's responsibility. Under design/build, the contract amount is changed only when the owner orders a change in the scope of the work. Scope changes arising out of design document errors and omissions are not grounds for an increase in the contract amount. The constructor will likely include a design contingency fee in the guaranteed maximum price to cover such eventualities.

Other Features

Another unique feature of the design/build arrangement is that the owner has no architect to administer the constructor's contract. It therefore must fill this gap, either in-house or from outside.

THE CONSTRUCTOR'S ROLE IN TENANT FITOUT

Control of the Process

In an office building in which the owner is also the tenant, the tenant fitout can be incorporated into the original contract amount and date of substantial completion. If the base building work starts before completion of the tenant design, this work can be added to the contract via change order. Since the base building work will likely still be underway, the constructor can easily integrate the additional work using the same subcontractors. The alternative, using an outside contractor or the owner's in-house staff, can create interference and may void certain base building guarantees, particularly in the electrical and mechanical areas. Finally, if the tenant fitout work is parceled out piecemeal, the base building constructor will find it difficult to complete its work in a systematic and economical way.

The issue becomes considerably more complex when the owner develops the building on speculation. Tenant spaces will be leased erratically over a period of time, usually starting before the base building is completed and continuing beyond completion, possibly for a year or more. Individual tenants may wish to engage their own contractors. A further complication arises when the constructor has included in the contract amount an allowance for tenant work, sometimes expressed as a single amount or as a series of itemized trade amounts. Alternatively, the constructor may have included in the contract a series of unit prices applicable to the standard tenant items, or have bought from each subcontractor its portion of the standard tenant work. Sorting out these numbers as tenant work progresses can present difficult accounting problems.

Regardless of the project delivery system chosen, the key to a project's success is the ability of the owner or developer to assemble a competent design and construction team and to foster an atmosphere of trust. *(Photo by Abbott-Boyle, Inc. Construction Photographers. Courtesy of Turner Construction Company)*

The next two sections set forth the easiest methods to understand, track and control the fitout process. They apply to speculative office buildings with multiple tenants.

Performance of the Work

The base contract work should be for completion of the shell and core only. For as long as the base building (shell and core) work is in progress, all tenant work should be undertaken by the on-site constructor and the on-site mechanical and electrical contractors.

For tenant work that starts after base building completion, the owner and tenants should have the option of retaining the original constructor or engaging another firm. This not only provides flexibility for the owner and tenants, but allows the original constructor to decline if it has other, more desirable, opportunities. This division also eliminates the problems of interference and voiding of guarantees.

Basis of the Work

The constructor should prepare for the owner's use a unit price for standard tenant finishes as stipulated in a tenant work letter, specifying for example, the lineal feet of partitioning of a particular type per 100 square feet of tenant area, the number of doors per lineal measure of partitions, and so on. The owner will use these figures in negotiating with tenants how much tenant work will be included in the rent and how much will be directly at the tenant's expense.

For tenant work that commences prior to completion of the base building, the original constructor can either undertake the fitout as change orders to the contract or work directly for the tenants. If the owner wishes to control the work, separate change orders should be issued for each tenant's work; the constructor must then keep track of costs allocable to each tenant change order.

The developer may want the constructor to include a tenant allowance in the base contract to simplify arrangements with the lender. In this case, the contract is adjusted as follows: The change order authorizing each tenant's work is figured on the basis of the total cost of the work, and from the total is deducted the amount of the tenant allowance in the base contract that is allocable to the area occupied by each tenant.

For tenant work performed by the constructor after base building work is completed, the prearranged fee should be higher than for tenant work performed earlier, as the volume of work performed is now relatively small. The estimated indirect and overhead costs will also increase in relation to the direct cost of the work for the same reason; in addition, there now are no base building personnel spending only part of their time on tenant work.

Some constructors have special tenant divisions to estimate, schedule and perform tenant fitout efficiently and cost effectively. This averts the possibility that base building personnel and resources will be diverted from their main task of completing the base building on schedule, and is therefore a highly recommended process.

Use of unit prices submitted by the base building subcontractors as the basis for pricing tenant work presents several problems: the low subcontractors may not have submitted the lowest unit prices; the date or dates when the unit prices may be utilized is not known, so prices must be inflated; and finally, few tenants buy standard partitions, doors, fixtures, and so on. This practice is thus not recommended.

CONCLUSION

Just as there are many varieties of office buildings, so there are many varieties of project delivery systems. A key to a project's success is the ability of the owner or developer to assemble a design and construction team that itself benefits from the successful completion of the project. Success is defined as meeting the owner's objectives of cost, time and quality, each of which will be of benefit to the owner in the marketplace. Ultimate success, however, will be measured by the degree to which the building satisfies the needs of its users.

It is not enough to hire a constructor on the basis that "anybody can build a building"; a constructor who gets a lot of repeat business from savvy owners, who has earned a fine reputation, will move mountains to maintain it. That constructor will be aggressive, creative and pro-active throughout the project. An owner should look at the buildings the constructor has built recently, examine the quality, talk to the architect and engineers. Performance, not talk, is what counts.

Finally, each member of the team should have well-defined responsibilities in the area that they have reasonable control over, or are best able to assume liability for. The owner should avoid confrontations, keep in touch and settle disagreements promptly, without engaging in paper warfare. Arguments are a non-productive use of valuable time; trust is the key to a productive partnership.

ABOUT THE AUTHOR

Ted Rhoades, following a 40-year career with Turner Construction Company, the nation's largest building contractor, formed Ted Rhoades Consulting, Wayland, Mass. In 1989, he led a team that studied New York City's capital project management system and made recommendations to the mayor for improvements. He is the author of a book on construction contracts and has chaired a committee of the Associated General Contractors of America that worked with the American Institute of Architects to create a new contract document known as AIA A121 CMC/AGC No. 565. He is also on the panel of arbitrators of the American Arbitration Association.

17

RENOVATION, REHABILITATION, RESTORATION AND REMODELING OF OFFICE BUILDINGS

by Daniel P. Coffey

INTRODUCTION

In the 20th century, improvements in building technology and parallel advances in communications and machine technology have intensified functional and economic obsolescence in office buildings. Major causes of functional obsolescence include inadequate floor plate sizes and configurations, electrical systems that are unable to cope with the requirements of rapidly changing computer and communication systems, and inadequate air conditioning systems. However, the most insidious form of obsolescence is economic, related to the changing character of office demand.

Unlike Europeans, who have tended to respect their older buildings, American investors in the past were preoccupied with newness, viewing older buildings as candidates for the wrecker's ball. Office buildings were considered to have a short life cycle due to obsolescence and physical deterioration. Lenders too were reluctant to finance more than cosmetic remodeling. By the late 1960s, however, Americans' attitudes about the long-term utility of older buildings began to change.

The author acknowledges the contributions of John R. White on the investment, valuation, financing and marketing issues and for the 333 East 38th Street case study.

These changing attitudes are traceable in part to the ornate design of older buildings with their grand classical, gothic and art deco design. But the economics are equally appealing. Investors can rent rehabilitated space for 60% to 80% of new building rents and still obtain a market return on their equity investment. Tenants can occupy good quality space at a lower cost while enjoying the stylish grace of architectural styles that are effective counterpoints to the facelessness of many newer buildings.

This chapter looks at the many issues that are involved in evaluating and investing in older buildings for office use.

DEFINING THE TERMS

In making decisions about the future of an older building, a clear understanding of the terminology is important to avoid confusion and misrepresentation. The four "R"s of working with older buildings are renovation, rehabilitation, restoration and remodeling. In addition, adaptive re-use, which can occur in any of the four "R"s, is the conversion of a building from its original function to a new use. The following discussion presents the commonly accepted definitions of these terms. In practice, however, they are too often used imprecisely. It is wise for developers, brokers and appraisers to describe exactly what extent of capital improvements and design changes have been or will be made to a building to eliminate confusion over nomenclature.

Renovation

A renovation results in an essentially new building within the framework of an old one. It typically meets new building code requirements. Complete tenant evacuation during construction is necessary, although floor by floor renovation is sometimes possible. This term often is used interchangeably with rehabilitation, but should not be. Its goal is a building that is like new, rather than one that is fully repaired. A minimum renovation usually includes replacement of the entire elevator, HVAC, plumbing, fire protection and electrical systems as well as revamping of exits, fire separations and structural systems to meet new construction codes. Roof replacement and repair or replacement of exterior enclosure elements such as walls, windows and doors also are frequently part of a renovation.

In a total renovation, major elements such as elevators, stairs, duct shafts, lavatories, mechanical rooms, building entrances and even lobby locations are added, relocated or reconfigured for functional, efficiency or marketability reasons. The former Goldblatt Department Store in Chicago is an example of this type of renovation and adaptive reuse. The renovation also included stripping back to structural steel a blank brick wall and adding a new facade and entry plaza on the building's north side.

The real estate market frequently uses the term "gut rehabilitation" to describe a total renovation in which the entire interior except for the floors is ripped out to make new tenant space. A renovation of this nature requires tenant evacuation. The rent loss during the construction period is generally capitalized as part of the development cost.

Rehabilitation

Rehabilitation is generally considered to be less substantial than renovation even though it usually involves repair of all of the building's basic systems and elements of construction. Repair may include replacement or strengthening of deficient or damaged structural elements. Repair of leaks and damage to roofs and exterior walls, windows and doors also are typically included. Frequently, moving parts of elevators, mechanical, electrical, plumbing and fire protection systems are overhauled, rebuilt or replaced.

During a rehabilitation, the building's systems are brought into general conformance with local codes and ordinances. Occasionally, special rehabilitation and landmark sections in local codes make it easier to achieve conformance. Such sections typically allow for the possibility of "grandfathering" pre-existing deficiencies or "archaic," non-conforming construction systems and techniques through a series of tradeoffs. Installation of sophisticated life safety alarm systems or automatic fire suppression systems are commonly requested tradeoffs. Generally, local building code officials and fire marshals are slow to allow non-conforming conditions but are willing to discuss methods for diminishing risk. On occasion, local codes and ordinances can be re-interpreted to allow for variances.

For example, a re-interpretation of a local electric code saved nearly two million dollars on an $11 million project. Under the prior interpretation of the code, any work performed on a non-conforming existing system eliminated its "grandfathered" status and mandated the need to replace *all* attached circuits and elements in the electrical system. With the concurrence of local officials, "work" was redefined to exclude the act of disconnecting circuits that were no longer necessary. Unneeded and unused circuits were disconnected from the old service while usable circuits were kept in place. A new service was then installed for all new electrical requirements. More than two-thirds of the original electrical system was retained.

Many building codes contain a "percentage of replacement cost" clause for older buildings that sets a threshold above which they must conform to codes intended for new construction. Though such thresholds are occasionally contradicted by rehabilitation and landmark clauses in the same code, they are often troublesome and enforced strictly by code officials who feel they are being pressured by the development team. On occasion, in order to stay below such thresholds, outside professionals, contractors and appraisers are required to certify or give an opinion that the cost of work is within the percentage criteria. Escalation of the value of a 1923 dollar to current value is one technique that has been used successfully. Consideration of the cost of replacing "priceless ornament and "irreplaceable" decoration can also be used to avoid the threshold. As with any subjective interpretation, the owner, architect and contractors should endeavor to meet the intent of the code as it relates to health, safety and welfare. A substantial unsafe condition should always be eliminated.

Restoration

A restoration project attempts to restore a building to its original condition or to its condition at a certain date. Decisions are generally made based on historic data, early photographs or original architectural documents. An example of restoration is Colonial Williamsburg, Virginia, which has been reconstructed to a specific era in the town's history.

The issue of restoration is often related to and confused with issues of preservation and landmark designation and certification. Certification or approval by landmark agencies of the work done in improving a structure is a complex but generally optional step. It is undertaken for reasons ranging from obtaining tax credits to obtaining a marketing advantage. Certification is occasionally required by local ordinances or by conditions of sale.

Landmark requirements rarely call for restoration, which requires proof of authenticity of the original or period condition. Instead, landmark agencies tend to favor conformance with the federal guidelines stated in the "Secretary of the Interior's Standards for Rehabilitation of Historic Structures," discussed below. These standards call for preserving and rehabilitating all elements of merit that do not distract from the historic integrity of the structure. For instance, a classically detailed office building built in 1895 with a remodeled but well designed 1930s art deco lobby could be rehabilitated and receive certification despite the generally incongruous appearance of lobby and exterior.

Rehabilitation of Historic Structures

A certified historic rehabilitation qualifies for a tax credit of 20% of the rehabilitation cost. Guidelines are contained in the "Secretary of the Interior's Standards for Rehabilitation of Historic Structures." As with most building codes, the final interpretation of requirements may vary with location and official. Typically, however, interpretations are consistent. Each certification and interpretation creates a constantly evolving consensus on what is acceptable.

An evolving consensus was confronted in combining the 1871 Page Brothers Building and the 1921 Chicago Theater into a single mixed-use building consisting of offices, retail and performing arts theater. Both buildings were listed on the National Register of Historic Places. To make the project feasible, a complex financing structure was devised involving government grants and loans and investor equity capital.

It was decided that the six-story cast iron and masonry facades of the office building would be restored while the entire interior structure would be removed, replaced and made one story higher. Simultaneous with this development strategy discussion, the Park Service was re-interpreting its guidelines in response to numerous historically insensitive "facadectomies." The rules changed midstream as a new consensus was being formed. It became policy that anything "holding up" historically significant building fabric must also be retained even if it is otherwise insignificant. The two landmark buildings could have become a parking lot had it not been for careful research and helpful landmark officials trying to work within the rules without establishing the wrong precedent. A new and acceptable interpretation evolved from research showing that the history of the Page Building was one of constant change, including frequent replacement of internal structural elements. This tradition of change was continued in the rehabilitation as the architects replaced the wood floors and joists with a new fire-resistant reinforced concrete structure that reduced the total number of columns by more than one third, filled in a small light-court, provided for a new core, added a floor and increased the rentable area by more than 30%. The project won an award from the National Trust for Historic Preservation.

Remodeling

Remodeling, often used interchangeably with the terms modernization and refurbishment, implies a cosmetic change to reflect current tastes or usage. Remodeling is the least complex, costly and time consuming of the four "R"s. It involves cleaning and redecorating finishes, furnishings and minor equipment. Typically floors, walls, ceilings, lighting and signage are redone to improve or update the appearance of the building's common areas, such as lobbies, corridors and lavatories. Cosmetic changes to a lobby or the interiors of the elevator cabs is considered a remodeling. In the office building market, remodeling is generally done with selective changes over a period of time with minimal disruption to tenants.

Conversion or Adaptive Re-use

Frequently the best way to extend the useful life of a building is to convert it to a different use. A conversion nearly always requires a substantial rehabilitation or renovation; otherwise, the stamp of the prior use is evident and the marketability of the converted space may be compromised, resulting in rents that are too low to achieve the desired rate of return. Older, multi-floor department stores with floor sizes ranging from 40,000 to 100,000 square feet, as well as the large lofts and manufacturing buildings which proliferated from the 1910s through the 1930s, often are adaptable to office use due to their large floor sizes; high ceilings; good column spacing; fireproofing; and heavy floor load capacity. However, the small number of windows in relation to floor space in such buildings can present problems.

Hotels are sometimes converted to office use. However, because their structural steel or reinforced concrete frames have been engineered for subdivision into small rooms, the column spacing is often irregular or too short. Even when interiors are completely removed, it may be difficult to design suitable office space layouts. Generally, hotels lend themselves better to conversion to small offices since the close column spacing problem is minimized. Occasionally, obsolete apartment buildings are converted to office use. These too lend themselves best to small offices because of the column space deficiency.

Another consideration in adapting a building from one use to another is the structure's weight-bearing capacity. Building codes require that offices have a greater floor load capacity than hotels or apartment buildings. In the case of the 1916 Alexander Hotel in St. Petersburg, Florida, which was being rehabilitated as an historic structure and converted to office use, the structure of wood joists resting on wood corridor bearing walls was inadequate for office floor loads. The architects replaced the walls with a new steel frame that allowed the joist span to be shortened and the structural capacity increased. As an additional benefit, a minimal number of columns replaced the space-obstructing bearing walls, allowing greater flexibility of office layouts.

The Adaptability for Reuse

The rehabilitation developer must make a basic decision about whether a depreciated and obsolete structure is suitable for rehabilitation. The first step is to review the structural integrity of the foundation and structural frame. A field inspection by an architect and structural engineer and examination of the original building plans, if still available, can assist in making this review.

Developers, working with their architects, must decide whether the existing core is in a suitable location on the floor for sub-division into office space. The depth of the space from the core, the availability of the windows and the column spacing all affect the building's marketability and rent levels. Important questions include the degree to which windows, exterior facade and enclosing walls must be repaired or replaced. These represent critical cost differentials.

Decisions of this magnitude cannot be made without a feasibility study. Multiple questions must be addressed: i.e., development cost; real estate tax treatment; rent levels; and the anticipated rent-up time. It may become apparent to the developer that the depreciated structure is incapable of re-utilization and its current use has been superseded. The site may be worth only its land value for a new, presumably higher and better use, less the cost of demolition of the old improvements.

In recent years, some obsolete office buildings have been converted to residential condominiums. In an oversupplied office market, investors in depreciated office buildings may install new elevators and mechanical systems and permit residential tenants, with architectural assistance, to complete the space within their own demising walls. In New York, many older office buildings with small floor plates have been successfully converted to residential use, attracting tenants with their distinguished architectural style. Most older office buildings have windows that may be opened and comply with basic codes. Thus obsolete office buildings may have viable alternative uses.

VALUING THE SITE AND OBSOLETE BUILDING

Developers frequently seek an appraisal prior to acquiring a site improved with a building that can be rehabilitated or converted to office use. This analysis may be of the land value only, or it could include a pro-forma forecast of the probable net operating income (NOI) and the value of the completed project. An appraisal will be required by a lender who is considering making a construction loan, a mini-perm loan or a long-term permanent mortgage on the project.

The process of determining the value of a land site improved with a largely depreciated and obsolete building can be difficult. The developer feels that the real estate should be priced at less than the land value since the building is an encumbrance that detracts from the land value. The seller naturally wants to realize the full market land value, plus the value of the reusable improvements such as the foundation walls, frame, floors, roof and enclosing walls.

The answer may lie somewhere between these two extremes. The appraiser will estimate the land value by looking at the recent sales prices of comparably sized and located land sites. Appraisers may penalize sites slightly because of old improvements. The appraiser will then estimate the depreciated replacement cost equivalent to the market value for the building. If the property is empty or nearly so, the appraiser characteristically will heavily discount the replacement cost because of the uncertainty of the utility of what remains and the potential difficulties of financing the rehabilitation.

The developer or lender may also ask the appraiser to prepare a pro forma estimate of the capitalized value of the NOI from which he will subtract the combined value of the shell and estimated rehabilitation costs in order to arrive at the residual land value. The developer's objective is to have a land value substantially in excess of what was paid for the land and depreciated improvements. This often is a primary measure of the profitability of the initial investment.

THE IMPORTANCE OF MARKET ANALYSIS

The market for rehabilitated office space began to expand in the early 1980s during the height of the development frenzy, as rents rocketed to historic highs in new buildings. White collar service firms—in fields such as law, accounting, finance, real estate, advertising, public relations and publishing—were expanding, but few of these tenants could afford the extremely high rents being asked. As their leases expired, enterprising developers lured these tenants to rehabilitated buildings with the promise of tenant installations generally equivalent to new buildings at rents that were 30% less. In New York, hundreds of tenants moved from the high-priced Grand Central and Plaza districts to Park Avenue South and lower Madison Avenue, where commercial rents in rehabilitated loft buildings were more affordable.

Knowledge of trends is not enough. Through micro market analysis, developers can identify the types of tenants who are looking for both low rents and the comforts of new building interiors with reliable elevators. Successful rehabilitation developers do not acquire a property without consulting knowledgeable office brokers on the overall layout of the building, the types of tenants who could be induced to move, the rent levels and the absorption period.

WHO SHOULD OCCUPY

The issue of occupancy depends on a combination of market factors and building characteristics. A building in a good location that is generally suited to a particular type of tenant will eventually be filled with that type of tenant. Identification or targeting of tenant type depends on the arrangement of a building's floor plan as well as its size and configuration.

Certain buildings tend naturally to accommodate certain types of tenants. Regardless of age, such buildings will have high occupancy and solid rental rates if they are in a reasonable location, are in good condition and are targeted to the appropriate tenant market. Similarly, serviceable but mistargeted buildings will have high vacancies and be forced to accept lower rental rates.

The following three-part approach to analyzing the architectural plan of an existing building can help owners better target and retain tenants in older buildings.[1] The three elements of this approach are:

1. Plan configuration
2. Opportunity potential
3. Efficiency

Plan Configuration

The first step is to categorize the office building by plan configuration type based on the location of the service core, the shape of the plan and the placement of windows on the exterior or interior of the building. Types of plan configurations can be divided into nine basic categories:

1. Point Block
2. Distorted Corner
3. Multiple Corner
4. Separated Interior Core
5. Exterior Core
6. Atrium/Courtyard
7. U-Shape
8. Modular/Additive
9. Hybrid

Each plan configuration type has advantages and disadvantages for tenants. The point block plan, for instance, provides for flexible, readily dividable space around the center core and is useful for full-floor or multiple tenants. A multiple corner plan can accommodate more prime offices for tenants with many partners, such as law firms. A separated interior core plan generally affords large amounts of deeper space that is good for single-tenant operations and banking tenants.

Opportunity Potential Factor

Step two, a procedure for matching a tenant to the space, involves the use of graphic representations and mathematical formulas based on proximity to an exterior window or an alternate view such as an interior atrium or courtyard. This method is called the "opportunity potential factor." To determine the opportunity potential factor, the architect tallies the total quantity of usable area in 20 foot deep rings away from the interior or exterior glass line of an existing building. A factor of 1, 2 or 3 is assigned to each ring based upon its distance from the window (1 is assigned to the ring closest to the window). The sum of the factored areas is then divided by

---

[1] This approach was developed by the author in the early 1980s as assistant to Gerald McCue, FAIA, former dean of the Graduate School of Design at Harvard University.

the total usable area of a floor to determine the plan's opportunity potential factor. A value of 1.5 gives a generally optimum mix of windowed and interior offices for the average professional service firm. A lower value typically is better for multiple small tenants on a floor, whereas a larger value is better for operations and data processing uses or for tenants that need large quantities of library, computer, storage or file space.

Efficiency

The third step is an analysis of the usable area that results from single versus multi-tenant corridor layouts. The market tends to gravitate to reasonably efficient ratios of gross to rentable to usable square footage. Buildings with higher ratios often must "write down" the multi-tenant loss factor to be competitive. For buildings with very high ratios resulting from small floor plates or badly placed or spaced service cores, single floor tenants are often the only way to achieve a reasonable degree of efficiency.

Examples

Two examples of renovation projects that utilized these techniques of studying plan configuration type, developing a quality potential factor and analyzing general plan efficiencies are the Templeton Mutual Center in St. Petersburg, Florida, and the DePaul Center in Chicago, Illinois.

In St. Petersburg in the mid 1960s, Florida National Bank built a six-story building of nearly 100,000 square feet for bank and captive law and accounting tenant occupancy. Emptied as a result of bank mergers and tenant flight to newer, more efficient office buildings, the building was vacant and, due to its abandonment by several developers in the mid 1980s, had gained the reputation of being infeasible. The three-step analysis described above was performed for a local developer. It showed that because of the split, exterior core plan configuration, multi-tenant common corridors caused greatly decreased plan efficiencies. The exterior cores also reduced the amount of window space and the span between windows and resulted in a quality potential factor of nearly 2.0. All three characteristics pointed away from the small professional firms that characterized the primary tenant market in St. Petersburg.

The architect recommended that an optimum use would be a single tenant per floor or for the entire building. With multiple tenants, rehabilitation costs, which are based on gross square footage, would be excessive in relation to usable office area. The eventual result was a much lower original purchase price for the developer and a specifically targeted marketing effort that obtained the Templeton Mutual Funds Headquarters and Operations Group as sole occupant of the building.

Because its core plan was less efficient for multiple tenants, renovation and marketing of this St. Petersburg office building focused on attracting a sole tenant. As part of the renovation, a leaking, deteriorated curtain wall system (top) was replaced with a new system of tinted reflective insulating glass (above). *(Top: Courtesy of Daniel P. Coffey & Associates. Above: Photo by Barry Rustin Photography)*

The company's computer, conference, filing/storage and other operational support functions were ideal for the deeper interior spaces. At the same time, the operations staff still had reasonable views from their open plan, interior offices. Executive suites and offices were clustered in corners. The pre-existing plan was well configured for its new use. The tenant and developer are both satisfied and the building is fully occupied.

A second example is the DePaul Center/Goldblatt Building renovation in downtown Chicago. The building, an 11-story, 2 basement, 650,000 square foot former department store, had been vacant for nearly 10 years, and despite its landmark status, was on the verge of being demolished. In its current form, the building had no identifiable tenants.

With only two windowed facades and 140 x 360, 50,000 square foot floors, the building's quality potential factor was extremely high, approaching a "cavelike" 3.0. The single tenant efficiency ratio was reasonably good. However, the location of decrepit elevators and other core elements was poor, and the building contained a combination of central and perimeter cores. Analysis indicated that the space was best suited for single-floor tenants with a high need for interior, windowless space. However, the cores required complete reconfiguration and replacement to increase efficiency and allow better layouts. To mitigate the size of the floors and reduce some of the excess windowless areas, the architect proposed small 2-story atriums within the structural grid.

As a result of this analysis, DePaul University decided to renovate and convert the white terra cotta building, constructed in 1911, into a mixed-use center containing university offices, classrooms and library, speculative offices and retail space. Deep space on the six DePaul floors is used for classrooms and library stacks. The speculative floors were soon leased to the City of Chicago for back office and operational uses.

FINANCING RENOVATION, REHABILITATION AND CONVERSION

In the past, lenders have regarded older buildings as second class real estate and have been reluctant to assume the risk of financing full-scale renovation, rehabilitation or conversion. As a result, the quality of such efforts frequently has been compromised, increasing the probability of poor operating performance and a lower than expected return on investment. More recently, this attitude has changed. As tenants have sought the high-quality space and lower rents offered in renovated, rehabilitated or converted older buildings, lenders have begun to take a more positive attitude about financing them.

Assuming that the developer has a solid concept, a comprehensive architectural plan and a good location, successful financing often depends on the quality of the mortgage application. The application must incorporate a market analysis which details the types of tenants that will be sought, the rent levels, the distribution of space size and the probable absorption rate. The developer must also provide the lender with realistic cost figures for the rehabilitation. At the same time, the lender should allow the developer to capitalize the net operating income lost during the construction period, plus developer fees, real estate tax charges and construction loan interest.

An important element of the mortgage application is the pro forma, a line item estimate of the probable gross income; the time required to achieve normal occupancy; the probable real estate taxes; and all operating expenses, including a reserve for capital replacements and tenant installations. The NOI should be a fair estimate or the borrower's credibility may be questioned. The total cost and probable net income will serve as a basis for the lender's decision on the amount and terms of the loan. The developer and his financial partners must demonstrate they will have substantial cash equity in the deal.

It is generally more difficult to obtain permanent, long-term mortgage financing in advance of the construction work on a renovation or rehabilitation project than it is on a new building. Leasing commitments, in the form of signed leases or strong letters of intent for 60% or more of the space, are generally required. In rehabilitation projects, this is not always possible. In these instances, if the developer has a good track record, he may obtain a mini-perm loan, as described in Chapter 22. He may, however, be required to personally sign the bond or note accompanying the mortgage, adding another element of risk. These mini-perms are generally from three to seven years in duration. A minimum of five years is usually necessary for a rehabilitation to achieve operating maturity. At that point, the developer can seek a long-term replacement loan.

UPGRADING OR ADAPTING A BUILDING FOR OFFICE USE

After identifying the best match of tenant to a building, the owner must analyze what changes must be made to the building to make it suitable for office use. This analysis is important for accurate budgeting of the improvements, an element critical to the financing, feasibility and completion of a project.

Every building has unique conditions and concerns. There are, however, standard categories of elements that are of fundamental concern in an office building. These categories are:

1. Structural system
2. Life safety systems
3. Exterior systems

4. Conveyance systems
5. Mechanical and electrical systems
6. Code compliance and Americans With Disabilities Act
7. Toxic substances

Structural System

In evaluating the need to upgrade or improve a building, the first step is to determine the integrity and capability of the structural system. In other words, will the building continue to stand up? The initial analysis determines the type of structural system and the materials of which it is made.

In the 19th century and early 20th century the primary structural materials were masonry bearing walls, cast iron, heavy timber and occasionally wrought iron. Around the turn of the century, steel was introduced and systems began to move away from wall and joist to post and beam framing. The determination of material is an important consideration when major work is contemplated. Cast iron and wrought iron are generally not weldable and require great care when repairing, reinforcing or attaching things to them. Cast iron is also brittle and reacts poorly to impacts and vibration. Masonry bearing walls are generally unreinforced and may require significant strengthening in an earthquake area.

A second important structural factor is the condition of its pieces. Beam and truss connections to walls at the edge of roofs may be dangerously deteriorated if the roof or roof drains have been poorly maintained. Careful inspection for differential settlement of the structure is also important. This analysis usually starts with review of the exterior walls for cracks followed by a review of the basement walls and floors. These are where settlement problems tend to be most visible.

Another important structural consideration with older buildings involves the floor construction. Through the early 1920s, a clay tile arch floor and fireproofing system was used in iron and steel structures. Each beam and column was wrapped with a clay tile cladding. Between each pair of beams, more tiles were laid on forms to create a self-supporting flat or slightly curved arch structure. Cinder concrete fill was then added on top. The result was a very heavy, fireproof structural system and floor. Drawbacks of this system are its heaviness, thickness and general instability. Each part of the arched floor tends to act as a keystone; as a result, the loss of a piece or creation of a hole—for example to insert new duct or large pipe shafts—can cause a whole bay of a floor to become less stable.

Floor construction techniques used since the 1920s are generally more easily modified and adapted. They typically consist of flat or ribbed reinforced concrete slabs or metal decks filled with concrete. Depending on the concrete thickness, both tend to be naturally fire resistant. Under most circumstances steel beams, columns and floor decks require spray-on fireproofing to meet fire resistance requirements of the building code.

Life Safety Systems

Fire safety issues are one of the major reasons that building codes were developed. No other work performed on an existing building is as closely reviewed as that related to fire safety.

Fire Exits

Exit stairs are an important consideration. Their placement and separation determines the amount of area required for the public corridor of a multi-tenanted floor. A building should have a minimum of two exit stairs. Many older buildings have exterior fire escapes attached to the building. These are not desirable and are acceptable to most code officials and fire marshals only because they are already in place. The amount of work being done to improve a structure often dictates whether fire escapes can remain. A complete renovation will usually trigger a requirement for replacement.

Placement of exit stairs is another issue. Most building codes contain remoteness, travel distance and dead end corridor tests intended to ensure that occupants of a building can get to an alternate stair exit even if the primary route is blocked by fire. Stairs should be remote from each other so that an impediment to an exit path blocks only that path. Many high-rise codes require that the exit stairs be pressurized to prevent smoke infiltration.

Eliminating exit stair deficiencies can add considerable expense to a project. A new stair may be the only solution. An exterior addition containing a stair tower is recommended when site availability and floor plan permit. This maintains usable area in the building and eliminates costly demolition and insertion of beams and stairs.

Fire Protection Systems

Fire protection systems include sprinkler systems, smoke and heat detection devices, fire hoses and valves, standpipes and even hand operated fire extinguishers. These systems come in various forms and degrees of sophistication and complexity. This variety provides considerable advantage when doing work in an existing building because most older buildings have some form of code deficiency that is very costly to correct. Code officials often allow variances when fire protection systems are in place or will be added as part of the work. Occasionally, in return for the variance officials will request an increase in hazard class or system sophistication by one step above what is required under the code. Such increases in the fire protection systems generally are significantly less costly than full code compliance and may result in insurance savings in the operating budget.

Exterior Systems

Elements of the exterior enclosure of a building include the roof, windows and walls.

Roof

No other system can cause as much damage as failure of the roofing system. Water penetration causes damage ranging from peeling of paint to deterioration of the structure. Water damage is often intensified in climates that experience rapid and frequent freeze-thaw cycles.

Problems frequently occur in parapet walls and roof valley areas and in roofs with insufficient slope. Roof drains that are inadequate, improperly located, stopped up or damaged are another source of leakage. It is also important to remember that roofs do not last forever. The building owner must know when a roof was installed and what warranties are in place. Roofs typically last between 15 and 20 years. They should be replaced if considerable work is being done on a building because of the high probability of damage during construction.

Windows

The exterior wall is the second source of water infiltration problems in many older buildings. As with a roof, periodic maintenance, repair and occasional replacement are required.

A key evaluation of an existing window is whether it leaks and whether it has adequate energy characteristics. Leakage is usually related to the original design, the installation or unrepaired damage. Damage can be caused by sealant failure or a lack of adequate maintenance such as periodic painting. In some cases repair is possible; in others, complete replacement is necessary.

The window framing members, if replaced, should be of a thermally isolated type. A thermal break prevents heat gain and loss through the frame. Yet the area of greatest energy consideration is the glass. Double paned, insulating glass reduces heat gain and loss and can also be effective in reducing noise transmission. The type of glass is a second concern. Most older buildings have clear glass which provides good visibility but limited protection from heat gain and solar glare. Tinted glass and reflective glass installations, introduced 20 or more years ago, may be candidates for upgrading or replacement.

The decision of which glass to use when replacing windows is an aesthetic as well as an energy-related decision. Clear glass is always called for when historic properties go through the landmark certification process.

An example of a cost effective window wall replacement that improved the building's appearance as well as reduced energy consumption is the

Templeton Mutual Center renovation in St. Petersburg, Florida. An ugly, deteriorated, leaking, energy inefficient curtain wall system was replaced with a new system of tinted reflective insulating glass with custom frames and trim.

Exterior Walls

Exterior walls are either load bearing or self carrying. Load-bearing walls, often found in buildings constructed prior to World War I, support the beams and floors of a building. More modern and taller buildings are typically clad with a self-carrying exterior wall that is hung from the structural frame.

As the exterior wall ages, sun, wind, water and temperature produce stresses that cause it to fail as an enclosure system. Water is the primary enemy. It is often driven forcefully against the wall by the wind and enters through a wall in a pressurized condition. Some water will penetrate even the most sophisticated exterior walls. A key factor of a well-designed wall is the controlled draining of depressurized water.

Even in "modern" buildings such as the stainless steel-clad Inland Steel Building in Chicago, water penetrated to the plain steel supports and eventually caused enough deterioration to require replacement. In older buildings of reinforced concrete, reinforced masonry or terracotta, metal reinforcing bars and support clips were often made of carbon steel, which rusts. Rusting steel expands and can cause a wall to crack and spall. For this reason, stainless steel and epoxy-coated steel are often recommended for repair and renovation of existing walls.

Conveyance Systems

Elevators can be found in nearly all office buildings. Elevator systems are of two types: hydraulic or traction. Hydraulic elevators are the slower of the two. Elevator speed affects the ability to answer an elevator call. Door speed, number of stops and travel distance also affect waiting and travel times. In improving an existing building, it is essential to review and limit the number of stops per bank of elevators.

Important considerations when repairing or replacing elevator systems include the depth of elevator pits, the floor to floor heights and the elevator penthouse overrun. Increased speeds can cause need for deeper pits and taller overruns. Speeds can also be limited by the floor to floor height. It is important to remember that speed going up or down is controlled by the amount of acceleration and deceleration that can be endured by elevator passengers. When heights and distances are insufficient, high-speed equipment cannot achieve significant advantage.

Elevator location is another major factor in evaluating older buildings. Typically, modern elevator banks have no more than four elevators in a row.

A bank might have up to eight elevators in two rows of four with doors opening opposite each other. Many older buildings have lengthy rows of six, eight or ten elevators serving all the floors of a building. In the renovation process, these long banks of elevators typically are divided and assigned to clusters of floors, creating high-rise, mid-rise and low-rise banks of elevators that serve only a few floors. This allows better service for tall buildings.

Mechanical and Electrical Systems

Mechanical and electrical systems age and deteriorate at their own paces. Both require continuing maintenance or the rate of deterioration escalates. Current office needs have tended to overburden most older systems due to increasing automation and computer usage. Office buildings often have insufficient power capacity and distribution to serve current tenant needs. If power is added, the cooling and ventilation system often cannot keep up with the heat that is generated.

Controls for existing systems often lack sophistication and energy saving options. Another important consideration for existing buildings is the federally mandated phase-out of the use of chlorofluorocarbons (CFCs), which deplete the ozone. CFCs are key to most cooling plants. The elimination of these chemicals will cause replacement of much equipment in the next decades. It is important to weigh this factor into decisions whether to repair or replace older systems in existing buildings.

Code Compliance and the Americans with Disabilities Act

In working with existing buildings, a continued concern is that ordinances and codes are written primarily for new construction. Most codes and code officials recognize this difficulty and allow for variances and trade-offs in the interpretation of inherent discrepancies. Key concerns mentioned earlier include trade-offs such as sprinkler systems and special interpretations through rehabilitation and landmark clauses and sections.

The Americans with Disabilities Act affects older buildings in an entirely different way since it is not a "codified" act. Rather it is a civil rights act that will eventually develop standards of acceptable practice through the creation of consensus and precedent in the courts.

It is currently too new to have created a consensus. It has however, mandated that buildings become accessible. Many states, including Illinois and California, have required accessibility through their building codes for many years. These codes and standards have been supplemented with the American National Standards Institute (ANSI) standards for accessibility. Most recently, organizations such as the Building Owners and Managers

Association International (BOMA) have issued recommendations. To date, compliance with all of these existing standards offers uncertain protection. In some cases, compliance is physically or financially impossible. An analysis and program for upgrade and general accessibility can offer protection for an existing building. A defense for a property owner not executing a plan of action can be "excessive economic hardship." To qualify for this defense, a thorough analysis of needs and costs is essential.

Toxic Substances

Toxic substances such as polychlorinated biphenyls (PCBs) and asbestos are another important concern that arises in working with and improving existing buildings. Toxic substances can be found in nearly any building but typically have been used in buildings and building improvements that date from the 1940s through the early 1970s. An exception is the presence of oil and fuel tanks, which may be found in even older buildings. PCBs and other chemicals are occasionally found in older office buildings but are more often found in electrical transformers or abandoned fuel tanks.

Asbestos was for many years a common building material. This fire protective material was used as insulation on pipes and boilers, in walls and ceiling panels, and as a binding agent in vinyl and asphalt floor tiles and roofing materials. It was even occasionally used as the binding agent in plaster walls. Asbestos does not have to be removed unless it is in a "friable" condition which allows the fibers to escape into the atmosphere. Expert analysis and federal and state standards determine the friability of the asbestos.

Another problem substance that is frequently discovered is lead. Lead was often present in paint. Similar to asbestos, paint containing lead does not always have to be removed unless it is flaking or is being disturbed.

It is always recommended that asbestos, lead, PCBs and other toxic or hazardous materials be assessed in a property being considered for improvement or purchase. Complete removal of such substances is recommended when major improvements are undertaken.

THE CASE OF 333 EAST 38TH STREET

An example of the successful combination of conversion and renovation occurred at 333 East 38th Street, New York. The 12-story fireproof loft and storage facility was formerly occupied by United Parcel Service. In 1988, Stephen L. Green, a noted rehabilitation developer, entered into a long-term net lease for the land and building of 49 years with renewal options. The owning syndicate required the developer to provide as security a letter of credit from a commercial bank. The amount was reduced as higher tranches of capital cost were reached in the belief that the fee owner required less security as the conversion to a competitive office building was completed.

When it was acquired, the storage building was only partly occupied. The property was appealing because it had good quality brick and limestone enclosing walls, excellent fenestration with light on all four sides and large (36,000 square foot) floor plates. Moreover, the 13-foot ceiling heights permitted suspended acoustical ceilings of 8 feet, 10 inches with recessed lighting fixtures, column spacing was a tight but reasonable 22 feet, and an on-site, subterranean garage provided 150 parking spaces.

One problem was the need to install four new passenger elevators to supplement the building's two small elevators, and to remove the massive freight elevators used in the storage operation. A new lobby with revolving door entrances was created from old loading docks. Because of suspected leakage problems with single-pane glass factory-type windows, and to conserve energy, the windows were replaced with insulating glass and new frames. Additional improvements included new decentralized HVAC systems, new electrical cabling, plumbing and lavatories. Tenants were offered an interior installation valued in 1990 at $35 a square foot, which rivalled new buildings. It included floor covering, suspended acoustical ceilings, recessed fluorescent lighting, standard partitioning and adequate electrical outlets.

By 1992, the building was 100% rented, mainly to full floor or larger tenants. Asking rents started at $23 a square foot and increased to $32 a square foot on the upper floors. This was $10 to $15 a square foot less than midtown office buildings four to eight blocks away. Some of this differential in rent can be attributed to the property's more remote location, several blocks from a subway station. The rule of thumb nevertheless held, namely, that a rehabilitated office building can be profitable with rents at approximately 70% of new building levels.

The renovation cost an estimated $12 million before the costs of tenant installations, architect's fees, real estate taxes and interest charges during construction. The developer obtained a soft loan for carrying charges while the plans were drawn and construction contracts let, as described in Chapter 14. The developer subsequently converted the loan to a construction loan and increased the amount. After five years, the developer has the right to a five-year extension as a mini-perm loan, provided that a defined occupancy rate and rent level are obtained.

CONCLUSION

The improvement of existing buildings through renovation, rehabilitation, restoration and remodeling probably offers the brightest opportunities for office developers and investors in the foreseeable future. Adaptive re-use of

At 333 East 38th Street in New York, a 12-story loft and storage facility was successfully renovated and converted into offices (top). The modern new lobby (above) was formerly loading docks. *(Photos by Jaime Ardiles-Arce. Courtesy of JCS Design and S L Green Real Estate Inc.)*

office and other building types is another promising area. All of these categories of improvement require skill and effort and do not come without considerable risk. Investors must protect against surprises by insisting on competent, experienced teams of architects, engineers, contractors and leasing brokers.

The primary reason to undertake such projects, despite the hazards, is their favorable economics. In the belt-tightening mood of the 1990s, tenants will favor quality space at the lowest rents. For the investor, the quality level selected for the renewal process will be determined by the market. However, in general, the higher the quality of the effort, the higher the return on investment. What will make these investments especially attractive will be an improved lending climate in which mortgage lenders will assign higher priorities to financing such efforts. The wise investor will respond strongly to the profit potential.

ABOUT THE AUTHOR

Daniel P. Coffey, AIA, is a principal of Daniel P. Coffey & Associates, Ltd., Chicago, a full-service architecture and interior design firm that has done numerous projects involving older buildings. Coffey has a bachelor's degree in architecture from the University of Illinois, Urbana, and a master's degree in architecture from Harvard University, and is a former Fulbright-Hays scholar to Germany. He has been a member of the Urban Land Institute, the National Trust for Historic Preservation and the Landmarks Preservation Council of Illinois. Coffey is a frequent speaker at professional conferences and has served as a guest instructor or project critic at the University of Illinois, Urbana and Chicago, Notre Dame, Yale and Harvard.

PART V

SPACE MARKETING AND INVESTMENT SALES MARKETING

18

SPACE MARKETING IN OFFICE BUILDINGS BY EXCLUSIVE AGENTS OR OWNERS

by James E. Bell

INTRODUCTION

There is a common thread that links the diverse functions involved in the development and operation of an office building. That thread is marketing. Beginning with building design, site planning and amenities selection, continuing through the daily operation and management of the building, the most commonly asked question should be: "How does this activity enhance the successful marketing of the project?" Without marketing, there are no tenants or customers. Without tenants, a building amounts to nothing more than bricks and mortar. Without marketing, there is no linkage between the physical product and customer needs and wants.

The purpose of marketing within the context of an office building is to produce rental income, and as a by-product, to create investment value. From the construction phase until the final act of sale or disposition of the property, the owner of an office building must constantly be concerned with the marketing of his property in order to maximize the value of the asset. Unlike other real estate disciplines which relate primarily to specific phases of ownership, the marketing process needs to be ongoing, flexible and interactive.

MARKETING VS. LEASING

For the office building developer or investor, is there a difference between "marketing" and "leasing"? Are they not in reality the same tenant-procuring activity? Contrary to popular conceptions, they are in fact two separate activities with distinct but complementary purposes.

The difference between marketing and leasing was best described by Buck Rodgers, former vice president of worldwide marketing for IBM. Marketing, according to Rodgers, is "the process of relating profitably to the business environment." It is having what customers want. "Selling [or leasing in this case] is the art of persuasion," or the process of getting customers to want what you have available to sell or lease.[1] In other words, marketing is a proactive process, rather than reactive. Marketing is understanding the market, anticipating what customers will want, and taking the total actions necessary to be in a position to satisfy that demand. Leasing is the art of making the deal and necessarily has a narrower focus.

Office building ownership is a long-term economic endeavor that can extend over many years before reaching a profitable conclusion. This chapter discusses the role of marketing and leasing during the different phases of the office building life cycle.

MARKET TIMING

With the long lead time involved in developing a new office building, a great degree of skill, or at least an abundance of luck, is required to anticipate the correct market timing. Anticipating what market conditions will be 18 to 36 months in the future when the new building will be ready for occupancy is one of the most difficult challenges facing a developer. With increasingly volatile markets, foreseeing the next 6 to 12 months is a difficult enough task.

While few building developers have the ability to accurately foresee market conditions several years in advance, most can recognize a trend in the market either upward or downward. Thus, a key market timing decision usually becomes whether to lease space at today's lease rates or wait to see if lease rates will improve later. If the developer waits, those higher lease rates may be partially or totally offset by increased capital costs and carrying charges. A decision to proceed with renting is often forced by the pressure of interest rate charges, which does not give the landlord or the developer the flexibility of ideal market timing.

For a new building, the most momentous event involves obtaining the major tenant. Does the developer secure the major tenant today even if the

---

[1] Quoted from an unpublished speech by permission of the speaker.

lease rate is less than pro forma rent, or does he wait and run the risk of the market deteriorating further? Deciding is a matter of experience and judgment and, in some cases, intuition. There is no solution other than to approach the decision armed with all of the necessary market information and to weigh the possible consequences of being wrong. Only the office building owner, the professional risk-taker with a vested financial interest in the outcome of his decision, is in a position to make these critical choices.

MARKET RESEARCH

Marketing begins with a thorough understanding of markets and customers. Market research can help lay the foundation for success by raising key market issues. For example, is this the best time to build? What rents can be achieved? What concessions are required? Who are the prospective tenants and where will they come from? What size of tenants are in the market? How much construction allowance must a developer provide to complete tenant improvements? Which amenities do tenants prefer most?

There is no doubt that the years of experience and the professional instincts of a seasoned leasing agent or broker are among the best sources of market information. However, a well thought-out and focused program of market research can yield valuable insights that may not be apparent to the professional marketing person.

An abundance of market data is available from the major real estate brokerage firms and professional real estate associations such as BOMA (Building Owners & Managers Association International) and SIOR (Society of Industrial and Office REALTORS®). Many of these statistical reports are available free of charge and provide good general indicators of market activity. However, they suffer from the weakness that they are too broad in terms of product segmentation and geographical markets to be of great value in determining a marketing plan for a particular building.

The building owner must seek additional sources of local information, possibly retaining the services of real estate research specialists. In selecting a consultant, preference should be given to the one who has the most extensive experience in the immediate market area where the building is located, as well as with the type of office building and the types of tenants desired.

A number of real estate research companies have developed data bases through which they monitor building tenancies and occupancy patterns. They have the ability to isolate and analyze specific product segments such as high-rise buildings versus low-rise buildings, newer versus older buildings, and migrational patterns of different types of businesses (for a more detailed discussion of SIC code analysis see Chapter 11). Real estate brokerage companies also have collected massive databases to identify prospective tenants by name, address, amount of space, type of business and other characteristics, greatly expediting the tenant canvassing and solicitation process.

One of the best sources of market information, and one that is readily accessible, is the landlord's existing tenant base. Every building owner should periodically survey his own tenants, if for no other reason than to become aware of unhappy tenants before they are lured away by a competitor. During the process, a great deal can be learned about which building features or services are most needed or liked. The owner should listen carefully to what tenants are saying. Comments such as "the floor layout is not very efficient," or "there are not enough restaurants nearby," or "the elevators are too slow," should cause the owner to start asking hard questions. How can these problems be overcome with existing tenants and how will they be corrected in future buildings?

Emphasizing Strengths

Market research helps to differentiate the owner's product from that of the competition. To the typical tenant, all office buildings tend to look alike. Differences need to be pointed out and positive aspects emphasized. Many advantages are not obvious. For example, are floor layouts more efficient due to core configuration or column spacing? Layout efficiency equals savings to the tenant. Is the owner a long-term holder of real estate? This can be an advantage to the tenant who does not want to deal with frequent changes of ownership or property management. What level of security services is provided to tenants (e.g., 24-hour manned security or automated card key access)? With rising crime rates, there is heightened tenant sensitivity to security services. All strengths and advantages need to be identified and specifically communicated during the leasing process. In the case of a to-be-built office building, it is especially important that the desired features be identified as early as possible so they can be designed into the new building. (See Chapter 11 for a discussion of the locational and functional advantages that should be considered in the initial planning stages). A list of the strengths or advantages of the property serves as a basis to prepare the material needed for future promotional and leasing activities.

MARKETING MATERIALS

A variety of marketing materials, also known as collateral materials, is needed to support the office marketing and leasing efforts. Marketing materials serve both to catch the attention of prospective tenants and to communicate important information and messages. Production of these materials often requires the services of a professional, such as a public relations firm or advertising consultant. Many such firms specialize in office building marketing programs.

Following are the most commonly used types of office marketing materials.

- **Building brochures:** The brochure contains basic descriptive information and pictures. Its purpose is to convey the primary marketing messages, to emphasize the project's unique features and to point out the specific benefits to tenants choosing this particular building. Creatively designed, the brochure will spark tenants' imagination. It should be attractive yet functional, containing sample floor plans wherein a prospective tenant can sketch a preliminary layout. It should contain the leasing agent's name and phone number. The brochure can be designed to permit pages to be inserted which provide additional descriptive information on the owner, the area, news clipping reprints and other supportive material. A key insert contains the specifications for the finishing of the tenant's space, or as it is commonly called, the work letter.
- **Space availability bulletin:** This should be produced and updated on a frequent basis, such as monthly or quarterly. It provides a floor by floor listing of specific vacancies, along with the asking rental rate and related information such as when the space will be available and tenant improvement allowance. This is a handy reference tool for brokers to match a prospective tenant with a specific available space.
- **Mailing lists:** Historically, most office lease transactions occur when existing tenants relocate within the immediate market area. This means that a mailing list comprised of the names and addresses of tenants located within a short distance of the building will constitute the primary target market. A direct mail list is essential for exposing the building to as many prospective tenants in as short a time as possible.
- **Lease proposal forms:** A lease proposal needs to be more than a standard form. The owner should develop a format that can be customized each time it is used. It should be personalized and delivered to the prospective tenant inside an attractive folder embossed with the building's trademark or logo. The proposal cover can be as important as the contents in making a good first impression.
- **Signage:** Little needs to be said about the importance and necessity of signage. As with other marketing materials, the simplest and least expensive approach is not necessarily the most effective one. It is often necessary to employ a signage consultant to achieve the desired look. A billboard sign may suffice, but a monument sign may project a better quality image. Municipal codes may restrict the size and placement of signs. Allowance should be made for adding the names of several tenants in the future, often a negotiating point in securing major tenants. In short, a signage program should be well-thought-out from the beginning to provide maximum benefit.

- **Audio/visual presentations:** An increasingly common leasing tool is the audio/visual presentation. A simple version is a five to seven minute video or slide presentation that provides marketing highlights. In recent years, audio/visual presentations have developed into an art form, with sophisticated miniature modeling and extravagant photography and lighting effects, often housed in a specially designed leasing center or pavilion. Whether there is a relationship between the amount of money spent and the leasing effectiveness of the audio/visual presentation is a subject of ongoing debate. However, there is little doubt that some kind of audio/visual presentation is now standard equipment in the marketing of major office buildings.
- **Advertising:** Advertising is usually overrated as a method for leasing office space. Radio or television advertising is costly and inefficient. The primary target market is typically more localized. Print advertising in newspapers and trade journals can be helpful if it is focused locally. However, the owner or developer should ask what he hopes to accomplish with the advertising. Name recognition is an achievable objective; generating inquiries from prospective tenants typically is not. A beneficial type of advertising is "tombstone" ads, announcing major leases or other events of importance such as architectural awards, since these enhance the project's and owner's recognition and image.

THE MARKETING TEAM

Many functional specialties must be combined to carry out the marketing of an office building, beginning with pre-construction activities and continuing through building operation and maintenance. However, the task of carrying out the marketing and leasing plan falls specifically on a group of people called the marketing team. Their assignment is to implement the marketing plan in a manner which results in successful leasing and continued occupancy of the building. Many developers create the marketing team early in the planning process. Their contributions to marketing strategy are often crucial, involving recommendations on product design, timing, strategy and procedures. The members of the marketing team then become effectuators by carrying out the strategy they helped to create.

Leasing agents are the central characters in the marketing plan. However, there are a number of other individuals whose supporting services are indispensable. Included are the landlord's attorney, financial analyst, space planner and property manager.

Leasing agents are the driving force. They are the catalyst that makes deals happen. One of the owner's earliest and most important decisions is determining whether to handle the leasing function in-house with leasing agents on staff, or to grant an exclusive listing contract to an outside real estate brokerage company.

The choice of in-house versus outside leasing agents is based on many factors. Among these should be a self-assessment of the owner's marketing strengths and weaknesses. The owner and the marketing team should balance and complement each other. For example, some owners are experienced negotiators while others may do more harm than good negotiating directly with a prospective tenant. Responsiveness also is a critical characteristic which all deal makers should have in abundance.

In-House Leasing Agent

The in-house leasing staff is the sales force for the building. Ideally these individuals have a record of success in real estate brokerage and possess the necessary sales skills and self-motivation. Unlike a real estate broker, who works on commission, an in-house leasing agent typically receives a base salary and may earn performance or incentive pay.

An in-house leasing staff offers a number of advantages:

1. Their sole purpose is to lease the owner's building.
2. It is easier for the landlord to direct day-to-day marketing and leasing activities.
3. The in-house leasing agent can negotiate with prospective tenants on a "principal to principal" basis without an intermediary or middleman.
4. A full commission can be paid to the procuring outside broker without the need to pay an additional commission to a listing broker.
5. An in-house leasing staff avoids the rivalry that can result between brokerage companies when one is selected over another as exclusive rental agent.
6. If a landlord owns several large buildings, an in-house leasing staff is a more effective way to establish a major presence in the marketplace and increases the likelihood of seeing all of the prospective tenants in the market.
7. The landlord retains the flexibility to hire an exclusive broker to assist if the workload increases beyond what the in-house staff can handle.

There are also a number of disadvantages inherent in the in-house approach:

1. Finding and hiring qualified and experienced office leasing personnel can be difficult. Outstanding brokers can earn more money by staying in commission-based brokerage. The top performers normally are not interested in leaving brokerage for a salaried position nor are they generally interested in working exclusively for one owner.

2. Unless the landlord has a sufficiently large portfolio of properties, there may not be enough work to keep the in-house leasing staff busy all the time. During slow periods, the in-house leasing agent becomes an underutilized overhead cost.
3. The production of marketing collateral material may be slightly more costly because all of these costs will be borne by the landlord. With an exclusive listing, the real estate brokerage company may be willing to contribute monies toward brochures, signs and other marketing support materials.
4. The owner's marketing staff may lack the extensive market knowledge of the exclusive agent, who may be more aware of what is happening in the marketplace.

Selecting motivated individuals is essential for an in-house leasing staff. It follows that a compensation system must reward such individuals based on their performance. The standard arrangement is a competitive base salary plus the chance to earn a bonus based on performance. Under a good bonus program, in-house leasing agents may be able to make as much money working for an owner as they can acting as exclusive agent or broker.

Where leasing compensation systems tend to vary significantly is in the bonus program. The following questions need to be considered before a bonus program is structured:

- Should the leasing staff be able to earn larger bonuses than other in-house support staff such as asset managers, attorneys, or even the director of the marketing department? In general, the answer should be "Yes, if they perform."
- Should leasing bonuses be awarded strictly on the basis of a pre-set formula, or should they be determined subjectively, considering such non-measurable factors as effort or attitude? Usually a combination is best, with the weight on performance.
- Formula-based bonuses tend to motivate in-house leasing personnel to perform like commission-based brokers. This can strongly stimulate leasing volume but may result in the achievement of less than optimal rents. Thus, senior management must have the say-so on rents that depart from the official schedule.
- Is there a large amount of vacant space that is eating away at profits? How much renewal leasing is there versus new leasing? Generally, renewals should pay less than new leases.

The leasing agent's task is one of the most critical functions and should be rewarded as such. This means paying good bonuses to the big producers. It may also mean paying bonuses that rise in direct proportion to the amount of space that is leased. This type of direct incentive will nearly always have a strong, positive effect on the leasing activity.

Exclusive Leasing Agent

There are as many compelling reasons for hiring an exclusive agent as there are for having an in-house leasing staff. The decision depends on the capability of the landlord, the size of the leasing task and the availability of capable agents.

Following are some of the advantages of hiring an exclusive agent to lease an office building:

1. A good agent is already fully trained and equipped with the tools of the trade. Most undergo a period of apprenticeship when they join a brokerage company and gain experience working in cooperation with other brokers in the office. They typically are seasoned sales professionals who have received specialized training in office leasing within a specific geographical market.

2. Large brokerage companies have resources and support systems that are not available to a single landlord. These include centralized data bases of market information and names of prospective tenants, multiple listing systems, research departments, advertising or public relations support and national accounts programs.

3. The opportunity for networking with other brokers and agents is enhanced. Daily communication among agents within an office facilitates the process of matching vacant space with prospective tenants. In addition, most major brokerage companies have regional and national networks of offices that share information on space availability.

4. Brokers are experts in their market area. It is difficult for an in-house leasing agent to be as well versed and knowledgeable as an exclusive broker who spends his entire business day in the local market. This enables the agent to provide market insight and advice as a part of his service. Brokers also systematically canvass the office tenant market as a means of finding tenant prospects.

5. Hiring an exclusive agent may not cost any more, and may cost less, than having an in-house leasing staff. The landlord will likely pay a leasing commission on most lease transactions whether he has an in-house leasing staff or not, because most lease transactions are brought in by outside brokers. Moreover, a creative owner can often stimulate competition between brokers and thereby negotiate more favorable fees and terms under the listing.

6. The task of staffing is made much simpler. The landlord interviews several top brokers and makes his selection. Individual abilities can be matched with the task at hand. If the landlord makes a wrong choice and the agent is not performing as expected, a change can be made relatively quickly, unlike having to terminate the in-house leasing agent and find a replacement.

7. Brokers are totally performance-oriented. Unless they make deals, they do not get paid.

Hiring an exclusive leasing agent is not without its drawbacks, however. Some of these include:

1. Any agent worth choosing will be pursuing other opportunities in other buildings simultaneously, and not working exclusively on the landlord's behalf.
2. An agent is not as motivated to maximize rent as he is to make the deal. The owner must be alert to agents who are not necessarily acting in the owner's best interest by favoring the tenant's position on lease terms over the owner's.
3. Occasionally there are potential conflicts of interest and divided loyalties, for example when an agent represents two properties which directly compete. The landlord must be careful to screen out these situations ahead of time.
4. Some brokers are more proficient at "pitching a listing" than they are at carrying out the marketing plan. The owner should be aware that some brokers' strategy is to "control the property" with minimal effort and hope that outside cooperating brokers will bring in the tenants.

On-Site Leasing Agent

Most large office buildings employ an on-site leasing agent to handle walk-in prospects, telephone inquiries and existing tenant renewals. This function is frequently combined with the on-site property management office. If an exclusive listing broker is retained, the individual assigned to on-site duties may be the broker himself or a trainee. Where a large amount of vacant space is involved, it is essential that an on-site leasing agent be available at all times.

Property Manager

If a landlord could retain 100% of his tenants, no new leasing would be necessary. A good property manager is an integral part of the marketing team. In the context of property management, marketing is known as tenant relations. Good tenant relations makes the task of negotiating lease renewals a great deal easier. The question of who is responsible for negotiating lease renewals, the property manager or the leasing agent, must be decided by the landlord. There is no standard approach and the landlord needs to consider the same types of questions raised earlier. However, it is of paramount importance that the landlord make it entirely clear who has specific responsibility for renewals, or this task may well be neglected.

Attorney

A common landlord's lament is that there are not enough good deal making attorneys. Finding one and making him or her part of the marketing team is just as important as having the right leasing agent. Attorneys can make or break deals, and often do. A good leasing agent will not allow an attorney to take over the negotiating process. There are specific issues which the attorney should be asked to resolve, and the balance of the negotiations should be left to the leasing agent or owner. Generally, the leasing agent is in control of all the business terms of the lease and directs the negotiations.

Space Planner

The space planner, whether an in-house person or an outside architectural or space planning firm, should be selected based on his or her ability to enhance the deal-making process. This means not only preparing the space plans, but helping the tenant to conceptualize his space requirements and making suggestions that will satisfy the tenant's needs while saving tenant improvement dollars. It is especially important that a prospective tenant's desires not get out of control and create an overly expensive build-out and an uneconomical lease transaction for the landlord. Thus, it is critical to ascertain the tenant improvement costs and determine how much of that cost the landlord will bear.

Financial Analyst

Frequently it is helpful to assign a financial analyst to evaluate the impact of a specific lease proposal on the economics of the entire building. The best asset managers provide that service as a routine part of their responsibilities. Sometimes managing agents may do this analysis as well. Large lease transactions can have huge financial consequences not only in terms of the rental income, but also outlays for tenant improvements and commissions. These need to be weighed against the likelihood that the tenant will continue to be present in future years. Analyzing financial statements is not as simple as it used to be, with the proliferation of mergers, leveraged buyouts and bankruptcy workouts. The services of a financial analyst, as well as those of the chief financial officer himself in many instances, are beneficial in evaluating a proposed lease transaction.

THE OFFICE LEASE

The office lease, by virtue of practical limitations on the enforcement of its provisions, tends to favor the tenant. After the lease term commences, the tenant assumes the position of power; he has possession of the premises. Although the lease has rights and remedies for both parties, the tenant receives de facto protections under the law in many states which go beyond what the lease provides. Most attorneys will acknowledge that, regardless of what the lease says, a court of law will hold most landlords to a higher standard of conduct than the tenant. Even though the tenant may default, it is likely that the landlord will find it difficult and expensive to regain possession from any tenant that is unwilling to cooperate. Borderline compliance and legal maneuvering such as making partial rent payments, curing a default after the cure period has expired or filing for bankruptcy protection will commonly forestall the lawful eviction of a non-performing tenant at great cost to the landlord. It is therefore of utmost importance that the lease provide clear rules and definitive time frames governing non-compliance of both tenant and landlord.

Standard lease forms are available from organizations such as the American Industrial Real Estate Association.[2] While a standard form lease will no doubt need to be revised or amended by each landlord to suit his own purposes, and in accordance with applicable state law, it has the advantage of being readily recognizable and generally accepted by many attorneys as a good format from which to begin negotiations.

It is often advisable for a landlord to develop a customized lease form, particularly if he has multiple buildings or a large number of leases. Another argument for using a customized lease form is that regardless of which form is used, sophisticated tenants will negotiate it heavily, so the landlord might as well start with a form with which he is totally comfortable and negotiate from that base.

At a minimum, every lease form should include a section at the beginning entitled "Basic Lease Provisions" which provides a summary of the key terms and conditions. It is senseless to make someone sift through the entire lease looking for the key business points. Future administration of the lease will be greatly simplified for both the landlord and tenant if these provisions are clearly delineated.

SELECTING AN EXCLUSIVE LEASING AGENT

Following are some of the major issues to consider when selecting a broker or agent to handle leasing on an exclusive basis.

---

[2] *Standard Office Lease - Gross* is available from the American Industrial Real Estate Association, 345 So. Figueroa, Suite M-1, Los Angeles, CA 90071, (213) 687-8777.

- **Track record:** The landlord should look at the agent's track record. How many leases has the agent negotiated in the immediate market area? How many leases has the agent done with this particular landlord? Perhaps the best gauge of the agent's ability to bring future tenants to a project is how successfully he has done so in the past. A good agent will already have brought prospective tenants to the landlord's building on a continuous basis, not just after he gets the listing.
- **Relations with other agents:** Is the agent respected and trusted by other agents? Even though an agent may be a prolific deal maker, if he has alienated other agents in the past, it can have a negative effect on his ability to do business in the future. A good indication is the percentage of the agent's transactions that have been made alone versus those done on a cooperative basis.
- **Listing agent vs. tenant representation broker:** It is becoming common for agents to specialize in one or the other. A good listing agent knows how to make a landlord feel comfortable with the job he is doing, but may leave the task of searching for tenants to other agents. A tenant rep broker may be needed on the team since he is more likely to have access to and/or control of tenants. (See Chapter 19 for a discussion of tenant rep brokers.) The landlord should be aware of potential conflicts of interest such as when a listing broker also is the exclusive representative of other buildings or tenants.
- **Number of agents:** How many agents are on the team? What other agency relationships do they have? It is common for two or more agents to share an exclusive listing. More than two is often unworkable. However, with two on the team, a landlord can select individuals who complement each other in terms of market knowledge, personal skills and specific responsibility for tasks of the marketing team. For example, one agent may be more proficient at stirring up tenant interest, while the other is more skilled at negotiating and closing the deal.
- **Corporate resources and stability:** Does the brokerage company provide services? Are they a member of a nationwide network of offices? How many brokers are there in the local office? How many of these people work specifically in office building leasing? Do they have a history of high personnel turnover?
- **Marketing plan recommendations:** Before hiring a broker or agent, the landlord should solicit a proposed marketing plan and specific leasing recommendations. It may not be the plan the landlord ultimately adopts, but broker input is invaluable in developing a workable leasing strategy. Moreover, it is helpful to have the agent commit himself in terms of objectives such as the amount of leasing to expect, rental rates that are achievable and other leasing targets.

The Listing Agreement—Standard Provisions and Issues

The brokerage company will prefer using its standard form listing agreement. This agreement is usually satisfactory for one-time leasing assignments or small leasing jobs, but needs significant expansion and modification for larger marketing programs.

Following are several of the issues that need to be addressed by the landlord in negotiating an exclusive listing agreement.

Term

This will be dictated by how long it will reasonably take to get the space leased. Generally a shorter term is better from the landlord's perspective, although he should be careful not to let this dampen the enthusiasm of the broker. It is easier to extend the listing agreement as a reward for good performance than it is to cancel the listing agreement for poor performance. Regardless of the length of the listing agreement, the landlord may want to insist on a 30-day cancellation provision that can be exercised if the broker is not performing as expected. Institutional owners/investors may need the right to cancel a listing agreement upon 30 days notice for any reason whatsoever, although this is not likely to be exercised if the broker is performing well. It is unfortunate but true that occasionally the best way to re-motivate and re-energize the efforts of a brokerage team is to raise the possibility of the listing being canceled or not renewed.

Rent

Usually it is preferable to merely state "upon rent and terms acceptable to landlord." There are too many variations in lease terms and conditions that may or may not be acceptable to the landlord to attempt to state them on the listing agreement. However, some states may require a specific asking rent in the agreement in order for it to be enforceable.

Owner's Obligations

The owner may be responsible for paying a commission for any lease executed during the term of the listing agreement, unless it is specifically stated otherwise. This can include renewal leases as well as new tenant leases. It can also encompass lease transactions in which the agent played little if any role. That is the meaning of an exclusive listing, and is fair and equitable as long as he is living up to his obligations under the listing agreement. It is not possible, nor should an owner expect, that the broker will be the driving force in every lease that is consummated. Also, in most states, the owner is obligated to fully disclose any information regarding hazardous materials that are present on the property.

Broker's Obligations

A broker or agent will not guarantee the successful lease-up of an office building. However, a broker should be expected to guarantee that he will carry out a marketing program that has been approved by the owner which, if correctly implemented, should result in leases being consummated. It is always advisable to attach a copy of the marketing plan to the listing agreement. The agent's performance should be judged not only in terms of how many leases are executed, but relative to the leasing plan he promised to implement.

Commissions

The schedule of commission rates will vary by the local market and by the brokerage company. It is often wise to agree to the broker's standard listing commission if it is not unreasonable, even if it is higher than another brokerage company may charge. The old adage generally applies that "you get what you pay for." The larger question, however, is whether it is necessary or advisable to offer a full standard commission to the procuring broker if he is someone other than the listing agent. This is driven by local market conditions and has become an increasingly acceptable practice in many areas of the country. It effectively doubles the incentive to the outside broker as compared to the standard 50/50 split with the listing agent. While this may seem expensive, it is a small price to pay if it results in faster and more successful lease-up of the project. However there is considerable ongoing debate as to the effectiveness of this as an incentive.

When are commissions paid? The standard method in many areas is to pay half upon lease execution and half upon lease commencement. A variation that helps to protect the landlord is holding the second half of the commission until the tenant has actually started paying rent or the free rent has expired. The listing agreement may also include a provision that the broker will rebate or credit back part of the commission if the tenant goes bankrupt within a few months of occupying the space. The risk of a tenant bankruptcy can be reduced by a careful prior credit investigation of the tenant. However, owners frequently accept tenants with marginal credit just to get the building rented. While the rebate is not an unreasonable request for the landlord to make, it is important that the broker not be coerced into accepting terms under which he will be less than fully motivated to perform.

Exclusions

If the landlord has had interest from prospective tenants prior to granting an exclusive listing, it is customary to exclude these prospective tenants by name from the listing agreement for a limited period of time. What constitutes a reasonable period of time is subject to negotiation, but 60 to 90 days is typical. This is especially important if the owner is switching exclusive brokers since the owner may be obligated to pay both the old broker as well as the new broker if a lease has been a long time in the making.

LEASING STRATEGY AND POLICIES

The key ingredients for a successful marketing strategy are the three "A's": achievability, accountability and adaptability. These concepts should be kept in mind when putting together the marketing and leasing plan. The plan should include the following important elements.

- **Market analysis:** The current competitive environment provides the framework for setting objectives and developing the action plan.
- **Leasing goals:** These need to be challenging yet achievable; there is little value in setting impossible targets. On the contrary, unrealistic goals may inhibit the leasing team by discouraging pursuit of otherwise makeable deals.
- **Preleasing:** For new office developments, this is the top priority since without it many buildings would not be built. How much preleasing is required is a function of the market, the owner and the lender's requirements. Preleasing establishes momentum and helps establish the building's image in the marketplace by the nature of the precommitments it secures. The market perception of the building may soar or sink based on the first tenant to be announced. After the abject experience of the 1980s, lenders have increasingly insisted that a building be substantially if not totally preleased as a condition for making a mortgage loan.
- **Target prospects:** The landlord must identify the likely potential tenants by type of business, using SIC (Standard Industrial Classification) codes, and by geographical target areas. They must compile lists of prospective tenant names and create priorities by degree of likelihood.
- **Action plan and schedule:** This should itemize the key marketing tasks and who will be responsible for each. This checklist of action items should cover everything from putting up signs to designing brochures and collateral material, scheduling open houses and mailing invitations, identifying prospects and canvassing buildings.
- **Adaptation to changing market conditions:** The marketing plan should be constantly revised and redirected based on lessons learned along the

way and new market realities. If it is not working, it must be changed. If deals are lost, the landlord should find out why so that the next time the results will be different.

Lease Economics

Minimum acceptable economic terms of the leases are governed by the landlord's financial objectives but tempered by the realities of the marketplace. The highest possible rent is desirable but not always the overriding factor. Also important are the goals of leasing the building quickly, attracting image conscious and credit worthy tenants, and minimizing future tenant turnover and the future costs of releasing.

The landlord must spell out clearly to the marketing team the minimum acceptable lease terms and conditions. He must let the marketing team know which ones are more important and where there is room for negotiation. It is important for the leasing agent to know where there is flexibility and where there is not.

A standard method must be established for analyzing the economics of a proposed lease transaction. There are several common methods that are used.

- **Effective rent:** Starting with total rent over the lease term, any concessions such as free rent, above-building-standard tenant improvements, lease assumption costs and moving allowances are deducted and the remainder is divided by the number of months and the amount of square footage. This provides a concession-adjusted average effective rental rate (either gross or net, depending on what is quoted) per square foot that can be compared to the minimum acceptable rental rate per square foot established by the landlord.
- **Present value of future cash flows:** The shortcoming of the effective rent analysis is that it does not account for the timing of income and expenses incurred during the life of the lease. For example, spreading the free rent concession over the term of the lease may improve the net present value to the landlord. Increasing the frequency of scheduled rental increases, such as annually rather than every 36 months, helps to boost both the average effective rent and the present value. The present value method is most useful in comparing several alternative rent schedules to determine which gives the greatest economic value to the landlord. It is also valuable for the tenant to know what his discounted effective rent is.
- **Value added approach:** Does the proposed lease add value to the building? Does it increase or decrease the value relative to the last appraisal or landlord's estimate of the building value? It is common in multi-tenant buildings to utilize computer software to measure the impact of a single lease on the entire building's future income stream and thus its investment value.

- **Downside risk:** What happens if the landlord does not make the deal? Even though the proposed lease may not meet the minimum acceptable terms and conditions, it may still be worth doing. The alternative of having continued vacancy may be worse. This can be projected based on how long it may take to find another tenant and whether the market is likely to get better or worse in the interim. Landlords accept many less-than-perfect deals as the best alternative at a given moment. This is because the true effective rent to the landlord keeps falling every month that the space sits vacant.

Certain terms and conditions of a lease can have sizable economic consequences which are difficult to quantify. For example, how do you measure the economic impact of granting an option to renew or of granting the tenant a participation in the future equity of the building? Contingent events such as these are often left to subjective evaluation in order not to overcomplicate the quantitative analysis of lease economics.

Directing the Leasing Team

In directing the leasing team, the following concepts should be kept in mind.

- **Point responsibility:** While office leasing is a team effort, each member of the team must be the "point person" for specific tasks. For instance, leasing agents should be assigned responsibility for canvassing specific buildings, contacting specific tenants and pursuing specific deals in the marketplace. Success and failure should be recognized on an individual basis. The old axiom holds true that "if everyone is responsible, no one is responsible."
- **Making it happen:** The leasing team should constantly take the initiative to instigate activity. The landlord should avoid unnecessary procedural restraints and encourage initiative and aggressiveness in the pursuit of a deal.
- **Time is the biggest deal killer:** Patience can be fatal to a deal. Nothing good happens for the landlord during the time a deal takes to get signed. The only things that typically grow during an extended negotiation process are attorney's fees, tenant concessions and the risks of being blind-sided by a competitor.
- **Personal qualities that succeed:** A leasing team is known by the calibre of its individuals. Respect in the marketplace is generated by a reputation for responsiveness, thoroughness, integrity, imagination and "win-win" attitude.

Negotiating the Lease

The negotiating process becomes cumbersome when too many people are involved. The tenant may be represented by a broker, and the landlord may have an exclusive agent. This creates a communication chain stretching from owner to owner's agent to tenant's broker to tenant, with ample opportunity for miscommunication. Brokers play an important role, but there comes a time in many lease negotiations when it may be better for the owner to work directly with the prospective tenant. This is especially true in the case of larger or more complicated lease transactions. Good-faith intent by both parties is best expressed face to face so that the myriad of details does not end up killing the deal. It is important that the owner retain control of the negotiating process and not relinquish it to the brokers and attorneys.

The landlord has other issues besides rent that are especially important to him, as does the tenant. There are two sides to each of these issues. The following discussion takes the landlord's point of view.

Credit Worthiness

Special attention should be paid to the prospective tenant's financial statements. It may be better not to do the deal if the tenant is unstable. The tenant's creditworthiness also affects how the lease economics are structured. Is the security deposit sufficient? It may be better to spread out the free rent than to give it all up front and find that the tenant cannot pay the full monthly rent when it comes due. If substantial tenant improvement dollars are to be expended by the landlord, he should request a letter of credit from the tenant to cover his costs in the event the tenant fails to perform under the lease.

Rental Increases

Regularly scheduled rental increases are usually preferable to flat rent throughout the lease term, even though the average effective rent may be the same. With flat rent, the tenant faces a hefty rental increase at renewal time, posing a major psychological obstacle to renewing the lease. On the other hand, starting the rent too low during the first year can result in the tenant paying above-market rents during the latter years of his lease term, creating a disgruntled tenant who feels he can get a better rental rate elsewhere.

Tenant Improvements

A standard office work letter can help the landlord keep his costs for tenant improvements under control. It provides the tenant with building standard improvements to his space such as doors, hardware, lighting, ceiling, electrical outlets, partitioning, carpeting and wallcovering. Quantities are also standardized according to the tenant's size and dimensions. The alternative approach is to provide a standard dollar allowance per square foot. While this is quite common and has the advantage of appearing simpler, it raises the issue of competitive bidding to achieve maximum value per dollar of construction expenditures. It can also cause problems later when the tenant discovers that the standard allowance falls short of covering the cost of what he needs, and he has to pay the difference.

Parking

This is a limited resource that the landlord must allocate with great care, keeping in mind that what is given away today cannot be offered to a prospective new tenant tomorrow. This applies not only to the number of spaces but to the location and type of spaces as well. Reserved parking is a special privilege which should be held out as an inducement to attract key tenants.

Operating Expense Increases

The American Industrial Real Estate Association's standard lease form calls for the tenant to pay a pro rata share of operating expense increases over the base year amount. Base year expenses are typically the actual operating expenses during the first year of the tenant's occupancy. An alternative approach is to specify estimated first year expenses in the lease. The landlord should be prepared to document the prior year's actual expenses in order to justify his estimate of base year expenses. Tenants will negotiate hard on this issue, which goes hand-in-hand with rent.

Subletting

Tenants' rights to sublet should be strictly limited. The greatest risk for the landlord is that a major existing tenant could put up a large amount of space for lease and compete with the landlord for tenants. If subletting is permitted at all, the landlord should be entitled to receive all sublease profits, or at least a sizeable enough share to discourage the practice. The landlord's consent will normally be required on all subleases but cannot be unreasonably withheld.

Option to Extend

Options by their nature are entirely for the tenant's benefit, since they tend to encumber the space and limit the landlord's future ability to lease it to others. However, they are necessary for most large tenants and therefore must be structured in a manner that minimizes their future impact on the leaseability of the building. For example, an option to extend the lease should provide for early notification by the tenant to give the landlord ample warning. Extension options should always provide that rent may be adjusted upward, usually according to a predetermined formula such as a cost of living increase or market rate increase.

Expansion Option

This can be very costly because it may force the landlord to keep space vacant until the tenant decides he needs it. If so, the cost should be factored into the net effective rent calculation for a truer picture of the economics of the deal. There are better alternatives that accomplish the same purpose for the tenant. A right of first refusal on adjacent space gives the tenant a preferred position when the adjacent space becomes available. A right of first offer is even better for the landlord, since it grants only the right to be the first tenant to make an offer to lease if space becomes available. The landlord can also agree to relocate the tenant to a larger space if the tenant expands by an agreed amount, such as 50% or more.

Signage

Building-top signage rights are frequently used to help capture the major tenant. These rights should not be assignable to subtenants. Lower signage on the building such as "eyebrow" signage or monument signage is also an effective inducement for many identity-conscious tenants. The landlord should be careful about granting exclusives or other limitations that tenants may request to keep out their competitors.

Authorization

Not enough attention is paid to verifying the authority of the individual signing the lease. The landlord should request a corporate resolution as evidence of the signer's authority. This simple precaution can prevent the tremendous amount of aggravation that can ensue later from a question of the lease's validity.

There are many techniques of lease negotiation that have proved successful. Regardless of the technique chosen, the landlord should always:

(1) have a clear understanding of what he absolutely needs, (2) be prepared to walk away if he does not get it, and (3) never close the door. In a tough competitive office leasing market, the landlord who is not prepared to lose a deal cannot effectively close the deal. When a tenant senses that the landlord is desperate or will make the deal at almost any cost, the deal gets tougher to make. If the landlord has to walk away from the negotiating table, he should always restate his minimum requirements and indicate where there is room for further discussion. If he has done a good job up to that point, it is likely that the tenant will come back for at least one more try.

PUBLIC RELATIONS

Does the landlord need a public relations plan? Yes. Does he need a public relations firm? Not necessarily. A public relations plan is an essential part of the office marketing and leasing plan. A well-designed plan can enhance the marketing effort; a poor one can waste time and resources. The first step is to determine the scope and objectives of the public relations effort. For example, if there will be a sizable investment in collateral materials, open houses, advertising or promotional activities, it may make sense to retain a public relations consultant. If the landlord is simply producing a brochure and granting an exclusive listing to a broker, a public relations consultant may be unnecessary.

A public relations program enables the owner to establish and maintain a positive image and credibility in the community and in the marketplace. Being a good corporate citizen is an integral part of corporate marketing. This can involve contributions to the arts, sponsorship of special community events or dedication of space to community use. In a competitive market, being concerned only for one's own building is shortsighted and, in the long run, costly because of the eventual loss of support from both community and tenant bases. A positive image makes it easier to obtain entitlements and permits from governing agencies, enhances the acceptance of the company's leasing agents and provides further support for the building's long-term value.

Being a good landlord is something that must be demonstrated on a daily basis. This includes having a reputation for fairness and responsiveness, and a concern for quality and long-term value. The essence of good corporate marketing is to understand one's own values and principles and then become well known for them in the marketplace.

CONCLUSION

Office space marketing is the activity through which the office building owner infuses investment life into the steel, glass and stone physical structure, and makes it a viable income-producing enterprise. Each step in the marketing process, from initial research through building design and lease procurement, is directed toward the realization of a single objective: a fully-leased building. However, signed leases do not in themselves generate and sustain income. The true objective is to create a customer base for the building that can be sustained and replenished by continuing the same marketing processes that initially created it.

The owner plays a central and indispensable role in this process. Marketing is perhaps the least delegatable function in office building development and operations. Unlike mechanical design or maintenance functions, which can be assigned to sub-contractors, the marketing function requires the inspiration and leadership that only the owner can provide. The success of the enterprise will reflect the extent to which the owner understands and is responsive to the needs of his customers or tenants. When parts of the marketing function are delegated or sub-contracted to outside agents or brokers, the owner must strive even more to remain close to his customers.

ABOUT THE AUTHOR

James E. Bell, CRE, is senior vice president/portfolio manager at TCW Realty Advisors, Los Angeles, California. He has more than 20 years of real estate experience including real estate brokerage, development and investment advisory services. He was previously asociated with The Irvine Company, one of California's largest developers, as vice president of marketing and leasing. Prior to joining The Irvine Company, Bell was involved in commercial brokerage with Coldwell Banker. Bell holds a BA from Augustana College and an MBA from the University of Southern California. He is a member of the Counselors of Real Estate and the National Association of Industrial and Office Parks, and is an associate member of the Urban Land Institute.

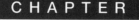
19

TENANT REPRESENTATION BY ADVISORS AND BROKERS

by Peter E. Pattison

INTRODUCTION

This chapter looks at the office building from the perspective of the tenant and his advisors—a viewpoint significantly different from that of the group of real estate professionals who are called upon to maximize the value of the property.

Owners and developers buy or build office buildings and in doing so they take two sizable risks: (1) the control and management of the development process and related costs to completion; and (2) the marketing or leasing risk. Owners take these risks with the expectation of achieving the highest rental rate and best terms possible—the maximum profit.

Office buildings are produced for tenants who need business housing. Next to personnel costs, occupancy costs are the biggest expense most businesses incur. Accordingly, users want to pay the least amount possible and extract the most favorable terms.

Owners are usually highly experienced, having produced office space year in and year out. The tenant, on the other hand, is usually inexperienced since a relocation typically occurs only once in a senior executive's career. This is a compelling reason for most prospective tenants to seek the best possible counsel to help them work through the many pitfalls of leasing or purchasing space.

TENANT ADVISORS

Because of the complex issues facing prospective tenants, typical large transactions require a comprehensive group of tenant advisors to help the tenant through the myriad of questions, contrary facts, market assessments and programming issues with which he is suddenly confronted. These advisors can be divided into three broad groups:

1. A real estate advisor who may be an open agency broker or a tenant representative. A real estate advisor deals with the lease negotiations and the real estate market.
2. Interior architects, space planners, programmers, engineers and other consultants whose task is to deal with how the tenant functions in the premises and the resulting physical layout.
3. Real estate attorneys.

Real Estate Advisors

The primary advisor for most tenants in their consideration of leasing or purchasing office space is the real estate advisor. In smaller transactions, a real estate advisor is often the only outside help required by many firms who rely on building owners for architectural and engineering services and use in-house counsel. For larger transactions a more extensive team is normally required. The remainder of this chapter focuses on larger tenants who need more comprehensive services.

Over the past 45 years the vast majority of tenants have used open agency brokers ("brokers") as real estate advisors. Brokers act as middlemen to bring together a willing buyer and a willing seller. They give advice and counsel to the tenant, but in almost all real estate markets in the United States they are paid by the owner of the office building. A broker gets his authority to offer properties from the owners of properties under consideration. This authority entitles him to offer all properties to the prospective tenant whom he in fact represents. The broker's payment is contingent upon successful completion of a transaction, at which time the broker is paid a commission as the procuring cause. The definition of "procuring cause" is enormously complicated and varies from jurisdiction to jurisdiction, but in general, the broker must produce a tenant and propose terms which may be modified but usually are acceptable to both parties.

At one time, brokerage commission rates were set by local real estate boards, but the U.S. Attorney General stopped this practice in the 1970s. Commission rates now are proposed by brokers and are subject to negotiation. The Attorney General had assumed that an open market would drive rates down, but his ruling has had the opposite effect in markets where brokers determine the success or failure of buildings. Open market brokers set rates where they want and usually prevail because they have become powerful market forces. Their ranks include such legendary figures as Charles F. Noyes, Leon J. Peters, Robert Byrne, Joseph Bernstein, John Dowling and John Cushman.

The Broker's Conflict on Representation

Historically, it has always been paradoxical that tenants' interests were represented by brokers who were paid by the parties they negotiated against. This issue was seldom confronted head on in periods when market pricing and terms did not vary dramatically from building to building. With the rapid escalation and following de-escalation in rental rates and the diversity of lease terms over the past 15 years, however, more and more tenants have engaged brokers or consultants as their advisor to obtain the best representation and to avoid any conflict of interest. Even more serious is the situation where the tenant is not fully informed about how the broker gets paid or the total amount of the proposed commission. It is essential that all parties to a lease transaction identify their allegiances at the outset.

The alternative to the open agency broker is the real estate consultant or tenant representative ("real estate advisor"). Real estate advisors are paid by the prospective tenant—a practice common in other international jurisdictions. This practice was pioneered in the United States 35 years ago by James D. Landauer, and until the mid-1980s the Landauer firm was the principal tenant advisory group in the country. Other major advisors who followed Landauer were Henry Hart Rice, Peter Pattison (the author), and in recent years, brokers turned tenant representatives such as Julien Studley and John Cushman.

Real estate advisors are compensated in various ways, but usually they are paid an agreed-upon monthly retainer for a stipulated period with a bonus payment upon completion of a successful transaction. Because the bulk of the fee is usually certain and a smaller portion is contingent, compensation tends to be significantly less than a brokerage commission, usually 25%-50% of the customary brokerage fee on large transactions. In the case of smaller transactions the fee is comparable to a commission because most real estate advisors calculate the time and effort involved and price their services accordingly. It often takes as much time to do a 20,000 square foot transaction as it does to do a 100,000 square foot transaction.

While historically brokers have performed the bulk of transactions, since 1980 the number completed by real estate advisors has increased steadily. Today most major transactions are handled by real estate advisors. In addition, investment brokerage firms have started to offer real estate advisory services on a fee basis, and major real estate brokerage firms now offer tenant representation services as an alternative to commission work. It seems likely that the future will see more and more transactions undertaken by real estate advisors, with an increasing number of brokerage firms performing an advisory role.

Qualifications and Experience for Real Estate Advisors

A good real estate advisor must be experienced in the real estate marketplace. This experience begins in many ways—as a canvasser, at a listings desk, in building management, in appraisal. Whatever the genesis, most real estate advisors go through an apprenticeship that centers on exposure to market conditions and negotiating smaller transactions. Getting to know the market is fundamental to giving good advice. Some markets can be learned in a relatively short period of time (6 months to one year), while other markets (major cities such as New York) require many years of experience. Historically, most good real estate advisors begin their careers by cold calling and knocking on doors, talking to potential users, learning about their needs and trying to match them with existing inventory. With persistence, the advisor completes a small transaction, then another. Suddenly the neophyte has a few successes behind him and he is ready for the new challenge of larger space users or more complicated transactions. The path is arduous—20 turndowns for each sympathetic listener or prospective client. However, most successful real estate advisors would not trade this experience for an easier path. Like military basic training, this experience is hard to get through but can never be replaced.

While there is no better way to become known in the marketplace than by cold calling and knocking on doors, other forms of self promotion can prove valuable. Joining business associations, doing charitable work, attending social gatherings, joining college and school associations all provide a basis for talking about one's work, listening to the problems of others, and perhaps discovering an opportunity to provide real estate advisory services. In the past, making one's experience known was sometimes enough to get a major assignment. However, in most markets today numerous brokers and real estate advisors are competing fiercely for the same assignments and most prospective tenants find themselves overwhelmed by would-be real estate representatives offering similar services.

Getting the Assignment

Thirty-five years ago it was common to acquire assignments at the country club, and being in the right place at the right time was sometimes all that was needed to secure a major assignment. In those days, the difference between a favorable deal or a bad deal was 25¢ to $1.00 per square foot with a long-term fixed rental rate. Today rents are seldom fixed over a long term, and usually escalate either on a stepped basis or subject to some form of index. Sometimes the difference between an average and a well-negotiated transaction will determine whether a firm can make a profit or remain in business. Numerous firms in recent years have folded because of badly conceived and negotiated office space leases. Proper real estate representation has gotten to be very serious business indeed. No longer are office leases assigned to office managers, to be signed and blessed by senior executives only upon completion. Top management now routinely is involved in major office lease decisions and is instrumental not only in deciding by whom and how they will be represented, but also in the process of negotiating terms.

To obtain an assignment, brokers and real estate advisors must contact the prospective tenants. In large brokerage firms, numerous canvassers and brokers continuously call every logical tenant. Smaller brokerage firms do some canvassing but rely more heavily on networking. Whatever means is used, the real estate advisor can only obtain an assignment when he knows which tenants are in the market. The real estate advisor must tell his story, differentiate himself from the many others seeking the business and explain why he or his firm will achieve the best possible results for the client. If he is persuasive, he has an excellent opportunity to make the short list—usually two to four firms—asked to submit a detailed proposal or make a formal presentation to a real estate committee or senior management. Formal presentations and proposals are a fairly recent phenomenon in the real estate advisory business, and are a further indication that major lease and occupancy commitments are taken seriously at the highest levels of management.

Often the selection of a real estate advisor is based not only on his qualifications, but also on the chemistry between the advisor and the client. Clients hire people with whom they feel comfortable. After the presentation has been made, no feeling is more exhilarating than being asked to return to discuss contract terms. Real estate advisory contracts tend to be short and to the point. They should specify the amount of compensation and terms of payment, termination and a clear description of the tasks required and the tasks not covered in the agreed-upon fee.

Interior Architects, Planners, Engineers and Other Consultants

When a tenant relocates to new premises, he must evaluate his space needs for the present and the future. A relocation is an opportunity for the tenant to evaluate how his business is organized, to analyze work flow, spatial and circulation requirements, adjacencies, communication relationships and proposed project standards, i.e., the size and function of offices and work stations. This work is almost always carried out by an architectural or space design firm, because a relocation to new premises requires constructing a building within a building to the exact specifications of the incoming tenant.

Most space planners work directly with the tenant, although their efforts are closely coordinated with the real estate advisor and the real estate attorney. While the architect is the main advisor in this phase of the work, he is often assisted by mechanical, electrical and structural engineers; construction managers; special consultants for such things as acoustics, lighting and telecommunications; as well as relocation advisors who coordinate the actual physical move. The space planner works closely with the real estate advisor in analyzing the cost of building the tenant's premises and allocating these costs to the owner/developer for a cash payment or customized work letter. This project cost analysis is extremely important, as the capital cost of a relocation can be very expensive.

Real Estate Attorneys

The real estate attorney is usually retained early in the process to give the prospective tenant insight into the legal problems that might emerge and to respond to the lease documents initiated by the owner's attorney. The lease documents should reflect all the terms, issues and agreements of the lease negotiation, and any legal issues that should be settled prior to the final agreement of terms, such as liability, subleasing rights and guarantees. Other clauses such as bankruptcy, condemnation, fire damage and user rights are usually left for negotiation after the first draft of the lease has been submitted.

THE TENANT REPRESENTATION PROCESS

The following section sets forth the process of tenant representation, describing how the various advisors carry out their roles and how these roles are coordinated to achieve the best possible results. For purposes of illustration, the process described is comprehensive. Not all transactions have so many steps or go into as much detail. It is the role of the real estate advisor to determine the level of service necessary in a specific situation.

Formation of the Real Estate Advisory Team

The real estate advisory team usually consists of: (1) a senior executive or principal who oversees the assignment and typically engages in the real estate negotiations; (2) a project executive whose principle job is to ensure that all of the required tasks are undertaken, set up meetings and schedule events, and manage the day-to-day tracking of the project; (3) a financial executive who prepares estimates, budgets and long-term projections; and (4) if necessary, a junior associate who carries out market research, conducts tours and performs the small but necessary tasks associated with a major transaction. Outside the real estate advisor's firm, other team members who need to be put in place normally include a programmer/space designer, real estate counsel, engineers, a construction consultant and perhaps a telecommunications consultant.

Programmatic and Structural Issues

The real estate advisor prepares a short list of firms specializing in space programming and design for the client's consideration and review, and screens the firms on the client's behalf. He assists the client in interviewing the candidates and making the final selection.

The advisor prepares, with input from the client, a detailed statement of tasks for the planner. He also prepares a schedule and a set of contractual terms and conditions for the planner's employment. The real estate advisor typically negotiates the contract terms and conditions with the selected planner, and reviews the tasks and timing of the project with him, to make the best use of his involvement and the information he has been hired to develop.

The real estate advisor also meets with the client to gain a full understanding of its strategic and economic objectives. He advises the client on the costs and benefits of the various transaction structures that may realistically be obtained, including a straight lease, a lease with equity, a joint venture, an outright purchase, a lease with cash flow participation, a condominium interest and other alternatives. He then integrates the objectives and expectations expressed by the client into the transaction structures he believes to be achievable, and assists in deciding on the preferred type of transaction to be pursued.

Market Review and Solicitation Process

Upon being retained by the client, the real estate advisor begins to prepare a complete inventory of space available in the market that he believes would meet the client's needs. This compilation includes all existing buildings with the necessary space, sites upon which a building may be developed, and projects that are already under development. For each alternative, he prepares a profile that includes an assessment of the appropriateness of the facility, a review of the owner/developer of the project, a summary of the terms and conditions being quoted and an assessment of what terms and conditions he believes may be obtained through negotiation.

The real estate advisor reviews each alternative with the client and planner to determine its appropriateness in terms of layout; floor size; clear spans; mechanical, electrical and structural characteristics; ratios of usable, rentable and gross areas; amount of usable and rentable space per person; and other characteristics. He then eliminates those alternatives that are clearly inadequate or deficient in key respects, and develops a short list of options that can be implemented successfully.

Armed with his detailed statement of space needs and criteria and the short list of buildings, sites and projects that may meet the client's requirements, the real estate advisor prepares a detailed memorandum setting forth the economic and strategic terms and conditions he believes will provide a successful solution for the client. This document serves as the basis for a proposed strategy and for the negotiations that are subsequently undertaken.

Financial Projections

The client is provided with detailed financial projections based on the terms stated in the memorandum. The real estate advisor meets with the client and typically makes a formal presentation of the terms and projections he has detailed. After a thorough review and client input, the real estate advisor makes any changes necessary.

For each short-listed alternative, he provides the client with a further refined set of financial projections based on (1) the "asking" terms and conditions set forth by the owner, and (2) the terms and conditions he believes can be achieved. After the client has approved this, the advisor prepares a detailed Request for Proposal (RFP) for the buildings, sites and projects on the short list, setting forth the proposal format, time frame and type of transaction he would like to pursue.

Selection and Negotiation

When proposals have been received from the short-listed parties, the real estate advisor prepares an analysis of the economic and strategic features of each proposal for review with the client. He furnishes the client with long-term (i.e., 20 year) projections of the occupancy costs they may expect to experience under each proposal, including rental expense, escalations for increases in operating expenses and real estate taxes, the cost of amortizing any tenant work not funded by the other party, and the cost of expansions which may reasonably be expected over time. These projections take into account the benefits that may accrue to the client by virtue of any equity, cash flow or other type of participation that may be proposed as a part of each transaction.

Based on this analysis, the real estate advisor then recommends that one or several of the proposals be pursued as a "preferred" option, with one or more backup alternatives. He meets with top management to present his recommendations and typically is asked to assist in developing an internal consensus and resolve to enter negotiations to implement the selected alternative.

Now the real estate advisor begins the process of negotiation with the selected owner, keeping the client apprised of his progress to ensure that all terms and conditions remain consistent with the client's objectives. As negotiations progress, he furnishes the client with updated financial projections reflecting terms currently under negotiation, together with revised statements of the current status of the transaction terms. He coordinates the negotiations and preparation of budgets with the project team, to ensure that the terms relating to tenant work and other features are handled correctly. He works with the planner to review costs to ensure that these either are dealt with in the transaction or are understood by the client to be part of their expenditures.

As the terms under negotiation begin to converge upon those he believes are acceptable, he begins to prepare a memorandum of understanding among the parties setting forth the precise terms and conditions that will subsequently be committed to documentation. This memorandum is carefully reviewed by the client and serves as the focus of negotiations by the parties as the transaction nears resolution.

When an agreement has been reached, the real estate advisor arranges for the detailed memorandum of terms and conditions to be signed by all parties or transcribed into a letter of intent if required by counsel. As documentation proceeds, he works with the client and its counsel to resolve any issues that arise and ensure that the documents accurately reflect the bargain struck during negotiation.

Implementation

With the signing of the lease documents, responsibility for the project implementation shifts to the owner and the other advisors. The real estate advisor continues to be available to the client to ensure that the other parties live up to the terms and schedules that were negotiated. Often he is asked by his clients to attend project meetings, review budgets, change orders, and other project memoranda, and counsel them throughout the implementation process. Typically, his involvement continues through the move into the completed space and a review of the initial cycle of rental escalation billings.

PRINCIPAL ISSUES FOR NEGOTIATION

Terms and conditions vary from transaction to transaction, but the main elements in contention between the landlord and the tenant are the following:

1. Rent
2. Area to be leased
3. Lease term
4. Provision for increases in operating expenses and real estate taxes (escalation clauses)
5. Amount of cash or construction items that the landlord will provide to the tenant
6. Strategic rights to increase or decrease space, to cancel or extend the lease term, and to sublet

7. Other inducements which may be offered by, or extracted from, the landlord
8. Liability issues

Rent

The annual rental rate is typically quoted in dollars per square foot multiplied by the rentable area of the premises. This rate is usually expressed in dollars per annum, but in some cities it is quoted as dollars per month. Rates historically have been quoted in gross dollars, that is, the rate includes base operating expenses and an agreed-upon real estate tax base. However, in larger leases rates are often quoted in net dollars, with each tenant paying his proportionate share of operating costs and taxes.

From the end of World War II to the mid 1970s, most rental rates were fixed over a long term of 15 to 20 years. This worked well in a period of low inflation, but the high inflation rates of the late 1960s and the 1970s led most owners and landlords to fix rates for shorter periods and to increase them at programmed intervals, e.g., in years 5, 10 and 15 of a long-term lease. Today, landlords attempt to provide for an increase in rental rates in year 10 or 15 of the lease to the greater of current rents as escalated or fair market value. However, tenants often resist this, preferring to have known rates and to take advantage of favorable market conditions. Rates are the primary point of negotiation because most tenants use rates as a measure to compare their lease transaction to those of friends and competitors. Consequently, many landlords, while trying to achieve higher total dollar rents, artificially "push" rates down by adjusting the rentable area of the premises.

Rentable Area

The aggregate total rent is calculated by multiplying the dollar rate by the rentable area. Measurement techniques have therefore become extremely important as owners and landlords have "grown" buildings dramatically over the last 15 years.

Perhaps the only space measurement in an office building universally agreed upon is the gross floor area, which is obtained by measuring from the outer dimensions of the building with no deductions. Before World War II office building rentable area was defined as the area inside a tenant's demised premises, but after World War II, with the evolution of the modern office building, rentable areas were calculated by measuring the gross area, deducting vertical penetrations and then adding back a proportionate share of common facilities such as air conditioning and electrical rooms. This technique is still recommended by the Building Owners and Managers Association International(BOMA), but many cities prefer instead to use "add on" factors. This number is obtained by calculating gross floor area, deducting elevators and stairways to get the usable area of the floor and then multiplying that number by a common area factor of 1.15 to 1.25. For example, a gross floor area is 200 x 200 or 40,000 square feet. From this is deducted elevators, stairs, risers and ducts having a total of 3,000 square feet, so the usable area is 37,000 square feet. This number is then multiplied by a factor of 1.25 to obtain a rentable area of 46,250 square feet. Measuring techniques and the definition of rentable area have become a major point of contention in many lease negotiations.

Area to be Leased

The size, shape and location in the building of a tenant's premises all are subject to landlord/tenant negotiation. In most high-rise buildings landlords command a premium rental rate for upper floors. The tenant's principal concern is to lease space that works well for his operation and proposed tenant installation. Tenants also want the best views, adjacencies to elevators and contiguous floors. On the other hand, the landlord's concern is to be certain that any space in the building not leased by the tenant is still marketable at projected rental rates.

Lease Term

Most leases vary in duration from 5 years on a short-term lease to 25 years on a long-term lease. The ideal lease for a landlord is long term with periodic increases at fixed rates or adjustments to market. American tenants have resisted these one-way adjustments, favoring leases with fixed rates and the right to cancel at year 10 or 15 for an agreed-upon penalty payment. Smaller leases usually run for shorter terms and have no cancellation rights. The length of the lease has a strong influence on the amount of capital dollars contributed by the landlord; shorter leases have a smaller contribution because of the abbreviated amortization period.

Escalation Clauses

Virtually all leases contain provisions for increases in operating expenses and real estate taxes known as escalation clauses. In addition, landlords in favorable markets often want to include a Consumer Price Index (CPI) or other index, or a portion of the index, to further adjust rates upward so that the capital portion of rent is not diluted. Capital indexing has never been fully accepted by most American tenants and CPI clauses tend to appear and disappear in leases depending on market conditions. Real estate advisors are often able to eliminate CPI clauses, but never escalation clauses. It is the real estate advisor's task to see that these clauses are fairly and properly drawn.

Operating expense escalation clauses are calculated in one of two ways: (1) actual operating expense increases, or (2) increases in accordance with an index, usually the Porters' Wage. A properly drawn actual operating expense clause requires careful definition of expenses that can be included and expenses that are excluded such as leasing costs, capital improvements and executive salaries.

Porters' Wage clauses originated in New York and were common 10 to 15 years ago, but they have become increasingly controversial and are not generally used throughout the country. When the clause was first conceived in the early 1950s, porters' average hourly wage was basically the same as the cost to operate the building expressed in dollars per square foot. A penny for penny increase was fair and generally was accepted by tenants. With the passage of time, however, landlords used this clause as a hidden profit center by increasing the 1¢ for 1¢ to 1¢ for 1.5¢ or 1¢ for 2¢. In addition, in New York City the Porters' Wage (including fringes) is more than double the average operating cost of a building, resulting in distorted increases favoring landlords. In addition, some landlords have made extremely aggressive assumptions regarding the calculation of fringe benefits included in the Porters' Wage index. Therefore, an appropriate lease clause should specify the method used to calculate these benefits. Most well-represented tenants insist on an actual operating expense clause or an index that is equitable.

The tenant must be concerned about two important issues in real estate tax clauses: (1) to be certain that the base year is a full assessment, and (2) to avoid dramatic increases in taxes if the building is sold during the term of the lease. Many municipalities give partial assessments during a building's lease-up period. The first year of a lease term, therefore, is not necessarily an appropriate tax year on which to base increases. The resolution of this problem is complex and often very technical, but well-negotiated leases place the burden of a stable base year on the landlord and not the tenant. In addition, tenants have to protect themselves if major improvements are performed during the lease term, or sale of the building or another capital event precipitates a large increase in taxes. This has become one of the most contentious areas in lease negotiations.

Construction

Landlords typically finish the base building including the core area on tenant floors with electrical and mechanical systems ready for distribution in the tenant area. The balance of the floor is left unfinished so it can be customized for each tenant in accordance with the tenant's plans. Most leases provide for the landlord to do a certain amount of tenant work (workletter) or to make a cash contribution toward work undertaken by the tenant. In new projects, the amount of the contribution usually covers the bulk of the work. Workletters provide for partitioning, doors, floors, ceilings, lighting fixtures, HVAC and electrical distribution, telephone and electrical outlets, and miscellaneous other items such as structural reinforcing and stairwells.

The value of the workletter or the cash allowance fluctuates dramatically—from $15 to $100 per square foot depending on market conditions and such variables as the condition of the space, the rental rate, the length of the lease term and the strength of each party's negotiating position. Negotiation for workletters is therefore a complex undertaking and requires the real estate advisor and the space planner to be fully familiar with costs, different operating systems and the pros and cons of different building standard materials and systems. It is also invaluable to the tenant for his advisors to have expertise in the construction process so they can set up controls for cost, quality and schedule.

If the landlord undertakes the buildout work in accordance with a workletter, he is responsible for completing the work on a timely basis. The lease term commences upon completion of the work. If the tenant accepts a cash allowance instead, it is necessary to negotiate how long he has to complete the work before rent commences. This is almost always a contentious part of the negotiations, as the landlord wants the construction period to be as short as possible while the tenant wants it to be as long as necessary to complete the work. Nothing is more unpopular to a tenant than paying rent before beneficial occupancy. Other issues surrounding tenant work are the approval of plans and alterations, the tenant's right to select his own contractor, and use of building systems such as construction lifts, rubbish removal and temporary electricity. Failure to address these issues can be very costly to the tenant.

Strategic Rights Concerning Space Needs

Long-term planning in most companies is based on 3-to-5-year projections while leases run for 10 to 20 years. Most prospective tenants, therefore, have enormous difficulty assessing their needs over a lease term. Strategic rights to add space or decrease space, to extend or cancel lease terms are often critical to allow tenants the flexibility they need to deal with future uncertainty. While rights to add or modify space commitments give flexibility to tenants, they are major hindrances to landlord leasing programs, and are highly controversial and hard fought. Nevertheless, rights to acquire additional space during the term of the lease or to modify commitments are usually obtained by tenants taking more than one floor or occupying more than 40,000 square feet of space. If the landlord is forced to provide such options, the agreement is usually subject to constraints on the amount of space, timing and flexibility. It is usually not difficult for a tenant to secure the right to extend or renew a lease at fair market value. The right to cancel is more difficult to obtain and is usually subject to significant penalty payments.

Equally important issues are the rights to sublease or assign the lease. The right to sublease is strategically important to tenants while its limitation can be enormously valuable to landlords. It is always best to confront the issue and work out an arrangement that is satisfactory to both parties. Other strategic rights include the ability to name the building, the right to appropriate signage and the right to restrict other tenancies that the tenant deems not to be in its best interest.

Other Inducements

Equity

When a prospective tenant would be the major occupant in a property, it is not uncommon for the landlord to make a portion of the equity or cash flow available to the tenant. Landlords always ask that a tenant pay for an equity position, but under certain market conditions an equity position may be obtained at no cost. There are no fixed rules as to the amount or nature of tenant participation, but one common formula is to grant the tenant 1% of the equity for each 2% of the space it has under lease.

Rent Abatement

Another inducement for tenants is a rental abatement at the commencement of a long-term lease. This is in addition to the period of free rent meant to cover the construction of the tenant's premises. A common procedure in soft markets is for the landlord to maintain the asking rents while granting generous free rent periods at the beginning of the term. This feature is often treacherous for tenants who take the short-term benefit but find themselves saddled with non-competitive rents in the later years of the lease. This situation is referred to as "mortgaging" a firm's future. Recent changes in accounting rules have discouraged this practice.

Liability Issues

Liability issues include personal and corporate guarantees, condemnation, fire damage, inability to perform, defaults and so on. All issues in a lease have an economic impact and should be assessed on this basis. However, liability issues are generally negotiated by counsels for the landlord and the tenant.

This brief summary is not meant to be an all-inclusive list of key issues in a landlord/tenant negotiation. It does, however, highlight some of the main issues vital to the tenant's welfare that must be addressed if the tenant is to be properly represented.

CONCLUSION

The theme of this chapter has been to demonstrate that the interests of tenants in office buildings are usually very different from the interests of the building owners. The battle to gain strategic advantage with respect to rent and other lease terms is continual. This diversity of interests and rapidly changing market conditions have created a situation in which more tenants are seeking the best possible real estate advice and counsel. They are no longer willing to settle for representation by the building agent or a broker who may not achieve the best possible terms for them. More and more over time tenant representation will become a separate discipline. Agents will represent owners, tenant representatives will represent tenants, and both will be paid by their respective clients. In this next decade, real estate firms will have to confront this issue and adjust accordingly.

ABOUT THE AUTHOR

Peter E. Pattison, CRE, is executive managing director of Edward S. Gordon Company. Until 1992, he was president and chief executive officer of Pattison Partners, Inc., which he founded as Peter Pattison Associates in 1973. Pattison Partners, Inc., developed real estate for its own account and represented major institutions with a variety of real estate problems, principally relocation and development. Prior to that, Pattison was chief operating officer and director of Uris Buildings Corporation, where he developed and leased more than 15 million square feet of office space. Pattison is a graduate of Yale University and is a member of the Counselors of Real Estate.

20

BUYING AND SELLING EXISTING OFFICE BUILDINGS

by Bernard H. Mendik

INTRODUCTION

The inventory of existing office buildings at a given moment accounts for as much as 90% of the total inventory in a good market, and even higher in a bad market. The balance of 5 to 10% represents those office buildings in various stages of development and lease-up. As a result of the extended economic life of real estate, the buying and selling of existing office buildings is a major facet of the real estate industry. The vast bulk of sales transactions and financings occur in the mature existing inventory, generally considered to be office buildings that are three or more years old. These have far greater impact in the aggregate than sales and financings related solely to development projects.

Buying an existing office building requires a great deal of expertise — one can argue even more than what is demanded to build a new one. With an older building, the investor is buying the building with all of its flaws, which must be identified. He must determine what needs to be done to upgrade the building, how much it will cost, and how that will affect the price he can afford to pay and still make a profit. Because the building has leases in place, the buyer must determine when and whether these leases will be renewed and how they fit into the pattern of the building. Because he is reconstituting a building, he must master many businesses in addition to real estate. His tasks may include redefining the space, redecorating, and making the building more accessible, more secure and more attractive to tenants.

The mathematics of developing a new building appear simpler but in actuality there is equal or greater risk. True, there are countless imponderables in buying an existing office building but the developer of a new building faces the difficulty of estimating the rental absorption of the space. The builder knows what his costs should be, then must apply his skill and management expertise to stay within his budget. The builder faces a greater hazard in projecting what the situation will be in the marketplace when the building is ready to be rented. The time lag between conceptualization and when the building actually comes on the market and is rented—usually three to five years—is long enough for the real estate cycle to move to a new phase. Demand may have long since vanished. A major advantage of purchasing an existing building is that it lowers the investor's risk. An existing building has a rent roll already in place, and the worst that can happen is a diminution of that rent. The owner doesn't come into the market with a building that sits vacant because it can't be rented.

PURCHASE CRITERIA

For real estate professionals, buying and reclaiming an old office building rather than constructing a new one involves what can best be described as "romance." The romance is in increasing the value of the property through value enhancement. Value enhancement may be described as the act of creating added value over the price paid for the real estate (beyond the effects of inflation) by a combination of improved marketing to increase occupancy and rent levels; building modernization to bring the building to competitive parity through higher rents; and the obtaining of financing at the lowest interest rate and lowest amortization requirements.

Perhaps the single most important purchase consideration is a complete understanding of the itemized rent roll, in terms of the size and credit-worthiness of the tenants; the rent level compared to similar buildings; and the lease terms. The very heart of a purchase lies in knowing what the investor can do to increase the rent roll, and how much money it will cost in improvements to achieve the increase. The principle is always the same: will the cost of obtaining higher rents be recaptured in higher value? After all, the continuing increase in profitability over the market norm is the greatest measure of success. In order to achieve this, however, first of all the investor must purchase a building that meets certain criteria.

Location

One of the first requirements is a good business location with stable tenancies. The building does not need to be in a prime area, but it must be in a location that has "upside." For example, in the late 1970s the area around Penn Plaza in New York was considered to be a tertiary location—

unlike a prime area such as Grand Central or Park Avenue in Manhattan. But an enormous number of white collar workers commute into Penn Station from New Jersey and Long Island and from there disperse to workplaces throughout the city. A real estate investor with vision could see that an attractive building adjoining Penn Station would appeal to large corporate tenants, whose middle management employees would substantially shorten their commute by coming directly into the building. Though the area was considered almost the boondocks at the time, it had the potential, given an improved environment, to be an excellent location.

The primary locational criterion is the assurance that there is an upside potential in land values and ultimately in rents. How can an upside be recognized? In or near central city locations, it may be a shortage of land for

Although the area around Penn Plaza in New York was considered to be a tertiary location in the late 1970s, an astute investor could see that Two Penn Plaza, adjoining busy Penn Station, had the potential to be an excellent location. *(Courtesy of the Mendik Company)*

competitive new construction that drives the market. It might be a distinct transit improvement or a major public improvement to the area made by the municipal government. It may be as obvious as the installation of a major sewer system in a suburban location. The professional investor has an instinct for upside situations that defies description. There is no disciplined format in office building acquisition that totally answers the question of whether the location has upside potential. The most successful investors appear to recognize it through the caliber of the existing tenancies and the tenants' prospects for success in their business.

Physical Condition

The physical state of the building is also of prime importance. The building must have structural integrity in the quality of its reinforced concrete or structural steel frame. The enclosing materials and roof must be in reasonable condition. It is always possible to rearrange the interiors, but not the frame and not necessarily the cladding materials or fenestration. Investors look for buildings that are in basically good condition, but either have a very low rent base from old leases or have not been managed properly or are slightly run down. But because the buildings must be financed before they can be fixed up, they must have a certain character as a building. The building's flaws must not only be correctable, but they must be correctable within the economics of the investment, that is, any capital outlay beyond the purchase price must be recouped in equivalent or greater value.

The most desirable building is one that is free-standing, with light on all four sides. The maximum light and air in an intensely developed central city area can only be obtained if the office building occupies an entire block. Tenants usually want their executives on the perimeter and if a tenant has many executives, a building with four windowed sides provides enormous flexibility. Next most desirable is a block front building that has three sides with light. If a building has only two sides with light, the tenant pool is restricted to companies with fewer executives, lawyers or accountants who need window space. Since interior space is less valuable on a square foot basis than exterior space, such a building has a lower value. Nevertheless, contiguity is an urban way of life and, in exchange for lower rents, tenants accommodate to lesser light in central city locations.

Floor Space

Large corporate tenants such as IBM and AT&T have minimum criteria for floor space. Their departments take up entire floors, and they lose efficiency if they must split a department on two floors. For this reason they prefer floors that are 30,000 square feet or larger and often will not take a floor that has less than 23,000 feet. If they need to split departments over several floors, this consideration goes into their analysis of how much rent they're willing to pay. Investors typically try to buy buildings with floors of at least 25,000 square feet, and prefer buildings with 30,000 to 60,000 square feet. In many central city locations, office buildings have become obsolete because their floor plate is too small to permit leasing to large tenants.

Floor Layout

The most efficient floor layout is a large rectangle. With a rectangular floor plan, the elevators are usually in a central core, which is the most efficient location. With this layout, the entire office can be built around the elevators; only a small corridor is needed in front of the elevators, so a minimum of usable space is lost. The bathrooms, pipes, and slop sinks are also placed in the central core, and all the space around it is freestanding.

Another layout factor is column spacing. If the building was designed with the columns too close to the window line, the size of the offices that can be constructed is limited, and the offices will be long and narrow. If the columns are well placed, there is greater flexibility. Offices can be large, with the corridors between them. The layout of the corner office is important because that is the chief executive's office, and he may choose not to rent space in a building if he considers that office inadequate. With badly placed columns, the owner has to make compromises on the space design, and compromises mean less rent and lower occupancy. This can be sufficient reason not to purchase a building.

Windows

Top executives almost always insist on good ambiance, comfort and prestige. The office doesn't necessarily have to be very large, but it must have a good view. But no matter how spectacular the view from the windows, if the windows are small and elevated, tenants won't be able to see out without getting up from their chairs. This lowers the value of the building. Enlarging the windows is costly and this cost must be factored into the calculation of what the building is worth. Furthermore, windows can't be replaced until a tenant goes out of business or vacates the space for several weeks, creating further complications. A building with deficient windows has a lower value even though it may have an excellent location and views.

Physical deterioration of the building frequently produces leaks and inoperable fenestration, and the cost of window replacement is substantial. Every investor must determine in advance of purchase whether window replacement will be required.

Elevators

Elevators make a significant impression on prospective tenants on two levels. First, the elevator cab should be clean and well-appointed, with dim lights, attractive materials and clean carpets. Second, the elevators should be fast and efficient. Doors should open and close quickly. Timing should be computer-coordinated so there is never a long wait and two cars never stop on a floor at the same time. A perception that elevators are slow or poorly coordinated, even if it is not accurate, is a major irritation factor for tenants.

Another irritant to office tenants dependent on vertical transportation is too many floors on the same elevator bank. Any bank serving more than eight or so floors loses image and the rent level may suffer. Tenants are smart. They compete for the best floor location in this respect. Of course, if the tenant is on the first floor of a particular bank on ascent, he is on the last floor on descent. Nevertheless, arriving assumes more importance than leaving in a tenant's mind. Sometimes, it is impossible to split a bank into two or three banks simply because multiple floor tenants may be inconvenienced.

The waiting period for elevators has been significantly reduced because tenants demanded better service. Unduly lengthy waits for elevators is probably the cause of more tenant antagonism than any other factor. Tenant complaints frequently require the replacement of elevators at considerable capital expense. If the replacement can also result in a lesser number of floors per bank, a major problem that otherwise affects rent levels and tenant quality can be eliminated.

Electrical Requirements

Advances in communications technology have required more space to accommodate augmented wiring and cabling. Owners of older buildings with large floor areas almost inevitably must increase their buildings' capacity to serve larger tenants' communications needs, or run the risk of their becoming technologically obsolete. The electrical augmentation is a twofold process. The first step is to provide riser space within vertical columns to distribution points on all floors, commonly called electrical closets. However, from the distribution point, the power must then be relayed in a series of underfloor ducts or raceways to various locations on the floor. While this is not the most significant capital expense for the professional investor, it is probably more important to the tenant than any other facility or service, because speedy and effective communication is essential to carry on the tenant's business.

HVAC

Air conditioning and ventilation are a constant source of complaints, even in new buildings with the most modern systems. As soon as there are windows to contend with, there is a heat loss factor and the need to accommodate to constantly changing outside temperatures and humidity. In addition, people have different body temperatures and different comfort levels. Since it is too costly to air condition every room individually, the best solution is to create zones that incorporate several offices, but are as small as possible and can provide maximum flexibility.

Some owners accommodate top executives by putting package units in the ceilings of their individual offices that can be operated manually. Tenants can then also control their air conditioning level after hours and on weekends. If an owner is unwilling to absorb this cost, he might make it available to tenants as an option that they pay for.

Certain types of companies, such as law firms, accounting firms and advertising agencies, have employees who sometimes work around the clock or on weekends. These companies don't want to pay for overtime air conditioning in a zoned building. To appeal to such tenants, an owner might consider putting package units on the required floor or using individual air conditioners to supplement the zone units. To do this, the owner must determine whether there is enough power to make these changes, or whether he will need to upgrade. When considering whether to purchase a building, an owner should calculate the costs of HVAC changes that might be necessary over the next five or ten years and include these costs in the analysis of the building. Where supplementary HVAC units are installed to accommodate a tenant's work habits, the tenant must either pay the direct cost or pay more rent.

The Rent Roll

An existing building comes complete with tenants. The prospective buyer must look at the rent roll in relation to his objectives for the building. In a building with large floors, the most desirable situation is to have only one tenant on each floor. It is less efficient to divide floors into small offices because more corridor space is required. Since each tenant pays for his proportionate share of the corridor, a smaller tenant gets a less efficient space count. A tenant who occupies a full 30,000 foot floor gets a higher percentage of usable space than a tenant who leases one of ten 3,000 square foot units.

Is the owner's objective to have all full floors? Mostly full floors? Does he want to attract large corporate tenants who require multiple floors? If a prospective tenant needs half a million square feet, he isn't interested in renting fifty floors of 10,000 feet each; that's inefficient. But he might consider ten floors of 50,000 feet each or fifteen floors of 30,000 each. The owner must determine what types of tenants he wants to attract and how many floors he wants available to accommodate them. Then he must analyze all of the leases on every floor to determine how long it will take to clear floors as leases expire, how much rent loss he will incur by keeping part of a floor vacant for one or more years in order to have full floors to rent, and whether it is worth it. This requires a complicated mathematical analysis for a large building with many tenants. Fortunately, modern computers make it possible to complete this type of analysis on an entire building quickly.

Competitive Rent Levels

Rents in the building must be no higher than the market rate. If they are above market rent, when the leases turn over, cash flow will be reduced. Ideally, investors look to purchase buildings with below-market rents and leases that are coming up for renewal in the next two or three years. This gives them time to improve the building so that when the leases come up for renewal, they can increase the rent and keep the tenants because they are competitive with other buildings the tenant may want to move to.

If the leases that are coming up for renewal are above the current market rate, the owner will not be able to renew them at the rate being charged at the time of purchase. This reduces the value of the real estate. Even if the owner fixes a building, he is going to lose cash flow. That must be factored into the analysis of whether to purchase a piece of real estate. If the market is going down, and the potential of the building is marginal at the time of purchase, it is better not to buy the property.

The prospective buyer will want to make a careful analysis of the competitive market in order to get a sense of how many of the tenants in the building may be looking for new space. Many owners conduct their own surveys; others rely on the surveys done by real estate brokerage firms. These firms maintain computerized data bases and issue quarterly reports that include vacancy rates, how much space is available and what rental values are. This data must be weighed against the owner's personal experience in the marketplace. In addition, it must be looked at in the perspective of the overall economy, not only local, but national and international.

Lease Terms

Some clauses in an existing lease may be unacceptable to an owner. For example, tenants may have free rights to sublet. In this case, the tenant rather than the landlord may profit in an up market when he wants to get out of a lease, even though the landlord has taken all the risk in making the investment. Most landlords restrict subletting for this reason. Usually, they include an option letting them cancel the lease and re-lease the space themselves rather than letting the tenant sublet it. In other cases, the landlord agrees to share the sublet profit with the tenant in an agreed-on proportion.

Another problem can be inadequate escalation clauses for such pass-through costs as taxes and operating expenses. On a long-term lease, this can result in the landlord losing rent each year as expenses go up and he cannot pass the increased costs along to the tenant. To avoid this, he must have a good sense of the city's economy and how much taxes are likely to increase over three to five years. He also needs to have a good estimate of future inflation, which affects operating costs such as labor and supplies. If a lease does not have an adequate provision for escalation, the tenant's rent will actually decline over time. The potential buyer must factor this into the purchase decision.

FINANCING THE PURCHASE

The Existing Mortgage

The prospective buyer needs to analyze the mortgage on the building and determine whether it can be prepaid. If the mortgage is held by a pension fund, the fund may want to retain its investment in the building rather than reinvest the money elsewhere. In this case, it may not give the owner the option of prepayment. Buying the building with that mortgage may not suit the investor's investment philosophy for that building. On the other hand, if the mortgage on the building is very large and the investor can put in very little cash because he can assume the existing mortgage, it may suit his needs.

Some investors prefer to buy buildings that are relatively clear of mortgages, reasoning that real estate is a long-term investment, and over the long term, there are going to be up and down markets. The less leverage an investor has, i.e., the lower the loan-to-value ratio, the more flexibility he has and the lower the likelihood of his having difficulty making the mortgage payments on the building. If the mortgage payment is overly burdensome, in a down market the investor may be in jeopardy of losing the building. Even though an investor may love everything else about a building, if it has an enormous mortgage that he cannot pay off, he may not buy it.

Obtaining Financing

When a developer puts up a new building, he generally goes to a commercial bank for a construction loan. Later, he will replace the construction loan with a permanent loan which is typically committed by the lender in advance of construction. But the building is generally 80% to 90% mortgaged, with only 10% to 20% of equity, because the developer doesn't want to tie up his resources in one building. There is a risk of whether he will be able to rent the building when it is completed and what the cash flow will be.

When a buyer purchases an existing building, it already has a cash flow, or will have one shortly. He can attract co-investors because he can demonstrate to them that over three to five years the building will probably increase in value. If the buyer has a track record, he can show investors other buildings he has purchased over the years, and how he has increased both their intrinsic value and their cash flow. Investors enable the owner to put equity into a building without risking his own resources. He has less of an interest in the building, but he also has less risk. It also gives him a broader base of financing because the more investors who invest successfully in his buildings, the more sources of financing he has to draw on in the future. Then, when bank financing is available at a low enough rate and favorable terms, he can always finance the building, but he is under no compulsion to do so.

When the buyer obtains a mortgage in connection with his purchase, he will attempt to create positive leveraging by obtaining an interest rate that is lower than the rate of return on the net operating income, free of mortgage interest. For example, a building with $100,000 net operating income (NOI) was sold for $1.0 million, or a 10% return. The buyer obtained a $750,000 mortgage for 9% interest or $67,500 per year. The equity income was reduced to $32,500 by the mortgage payment but the buyer now has only a $250,000 cash equity, or a 13% return.

How an investor will finance a building depends on the individual circumstances of the investment. Sometimes he will re-finance the building mortgage to take out the original equity; other times he will take out only a portion of the equity. When an existing mortgage amount is refinanced through the existing or a new lender, the excess of the new mortgage over the old mortgage is tax free to the investor and means that his equity investment in the office building has been reduced by the excess.[1] But

---

[1] Although the proceeds of any financing are treated as "tax free," the actual result is a tax deferral. Upon any subsequent sale or other disposition of a building, the outstanding amount of any mortgage generally is treated as part of the amount realized which, under certain circumstances, can cause an ultimate tax liability substantially in excess of any cash received.

generally, he will not finance it so heavily that he doesn't have capital to put back in if there is a turndown in the market or if he needs to renovate the building or upgrade it technologically. He needs to continually upgrade to keep his buildings competitive with new buildings coming on the market. The wise owner reinvests capital in his buildings to ensure that they are well managed and are technologically superior, in order to retain his tenants.

Sometimes the owner must borrow to maintain or upgrade his building. It the building is not mortgaged or has a low mortgage, it is generally easy to borrow 10% or 20% of the value of the building, even in a down market. Buildings that are over-financed, however, often experience serious difficulties when their mortgages come up for renewal. The successful professional investors, as distinguished from the speculators, prefer lower loan-to-value ratios and do not depend on heavy positive leveraging of the investment to make profits.

THE IMPORTANCE OF RELATIONSHIPS

Working with Leasing Brokers

It's important for building owners to maintain a good relationship with leasing brokers. One way to do this is to make sure they are paid promptly. Another is to have a reputation for being reasonable, for knowing the market, for running good buildings and for being deal makers. Brokers like to bring tenants to such owners because they are confident that they're going to put the tenant in possession, and they're going to get a renewal and a commission the second time around. Because the broker hopes to obtain repeat business when the tenant needs to expand or move into additional locations, he wants to place his clients in good buildings with good landlords who are financially stable.

Working with Sellers

To be successful in buying buildings, the investor must have a good reputation among sellers. The seller must believe that once a price has been agreed on, the investor will go through with the transaction. The buyer must have the experience and technical ability to analyze the deal and come to a swift decision. He needs to have the financial and institutional resources to be able to consummate the deal quickly. Such a reputation must be earned over time. When a building comes on the market, the broker will approach the buyer that he knows is reliable and meets these qualifications. That kind of reputation gives the investor a tremendous edge over other potential buyers.

Market Knowledge

Most investors who reclaim older buildings do it within their own market, because they need to know their market more thoroughly than a developer who builds a new building. There is a narrow band of what the developer must know about the marketplace. He must know what the needs are in that market, who his potential tenants are, what his costs will be and what rents he can charge. So it is not that difficult for him to operate in multiple markets. The investor who reclaims older buildings needs much more information about his market. In addition to knowing who his competition is, he must know who the brokers and lawyers are in that market. A regular and informal exchange of information with others in his business— economists, lawyers, tenants, architects, developers—is vital. He needs to find out who already occupies space in his building and to be concerned about lease renewals. In addition, he must compete against the new buildings that are also coming on the market, which are usually designed to attract tenants from older buildings such as his. It takes a long time to really learn a market in enough depth to be able to invest successfully in older buildings.

Tenant Retention

The bottom line of managing a building successfully is retaining tenants. The money an owner loses from a vacancy is never recaptured. The owner who doesn't put capital back into his buildings because he is concerned solely with immediate cash net profits ultimately will not do as well because he will have more vacancies and turnover. It is important to cosmeticize a building immediately after acquisition. A change in lobby decor is always helpful. Plants, flowers and improved lighting attract tenants and visitors.

Replacing tenants is costly, so the owner's first rule is to take care of tenants in possession so they will renew their leases. When an owner purchases an existing building, he must identify the large tenants that he wants to renew and find out whether they are satisfied with the building. They may have had problems with the previous building management. If the new owner has a good reputation in the marketplace, he often can persuade an unhappy tenant to give him a chance to remedy the problems. Whether or not the owner will try to renew current tenants will depend on his overall objectives for the building in terms of size of tenants, competitive conditions in the marketplace, and current market rents and concessions.

Sometimes it is not possible to retain a tenant, for example if the tenant needs to expand and no additional space is available. But most of the time an owner can retain a high percentage of tenants by understanding what they want. First, tenants want the building to be well maintained, with elevators, windows, heating, air conditioning and so on in good condition.

Next, they need to feel that building management is responsive to their needs. Even if it is not one of the city's trophy buildings commanding above-market rents, there is no reason not to give tenants superior service. This must be accomplished on a daily basis. All of the building staff must be trained to be aware of the details, such as making sure ashtrays are emptied and there are fresh flowers on the reception desk. Any problems must be reported to the building manager and corrected quickly. Management should be responsive to building inspectors and correct any building violations immediately.

Some owners prefer to maintain control over vital services for their property by owning subsidiary companies. Some own management firms that manage all of their real estate. They may have their own cleaning company to control the quality and cost of cleaning. They may also own a security company to ensure the quality of their security staff. These are examples of a vertically integrated real estate operating company, which has a virtually full-line operating capability.

The inexperienced investor does not always fully comprehend that the facts about the building's tenancy on an itemized rent roll are likely to change rapidly and unexpectedly over the period of their lease terms. Many factors prompt unforeseeable changes in the rent roll. Tenants may go bankrupt during a recession. Others sell a portion of their business and want to retrench. Still others are in an expansion mode and require added space. In actual experience, there is unusual volatility to a rent roll. For the astute professional investor, especially in an ascending market, unexpected tenant turnover and tenant expansion may provide a basis for a significant increase in the level of rents and perhaps even allow a higher occupancy level.

Image

For most tenants, the image of the building is an important concern. It must be a place that gives visitors and clients a positive impression of his company. The first impression of the building is its entrance so the entrance has to have "a touch of class."

What does the lobby look like? Does it have attractive materials and finishes? Is it well maintained? Plants and flowers are a positive touch. If there is a fire station, post office, subway station or other public facility in the lobby, it must blend in with the rest of the space. And everything should be clean and polished—even if it is old.

Elevator corridors contribute to the image of the building. Tenants who have a full floor for the first time frequently prefer to do their own decorating. But it pays for the owner to review their plans and make decorating suggestions. He may be able to help the tenant achieve a more attractive result at the same or only a slightly higher cost. If the tenant is on a very tight budget, the owner may contribute toward the decoration of their corridors and elevator bank. This has several benefits. It contributes toward good tenant relations, and it results in a space that is in keeping with the image of the building, thereby enhancing the building's value. The elevator corridor is a small space, usually only 1,000 or 1,200 square feet, so the additional cost to do a first class job is small.

REASONS FOR SELLING REAL ESTATE

What prompts an owner to sell real estate? The answer is different, depending on whether the owner is a private owner or an institution. Institutions sell real estate to meet year-end capital or tax requirements. They may have losses as they approach the end of the year, and prior to 1986 when the tax law changed, they would sell a piece of real estate to get a capital gain to offset the capital losses.

Private owners also occasionally sell for tax reasons. But most often a private owner sells a property for personal reasons, rather than because it is an advantageous time to sell. He may need money to buy something else, or have other opportunities, a partnership may break up, or someone may die and the estate has to be liquidated. Normally, the major owners of real estate do not sell real estate. They are not sellers; they are buyers, accumulators, because real estate is bought for the long term. Occasionally, professional investors tire of a building. This is especially true when they feel the capital gain potential has been exploited to the maximum. Sometimes institutions sell office buildings to demonstrate to their management or to other funds for whom they invest capital the total yield possible with a continuing investment program in real estate. Total yield is the combination of income and capital gain realized on sale, expressed on a discounted basis and called an internal rate of return (IRR). Chapter 28 covers the IRR concept at length.

Sometimes an owner is forced to sell by investors who view the property simply as an investment and see an opportunity to take a large profit. Rather than sell, however, most owners prefer to refinance a mortgage and take the tax-free proceeds from the refinancing. For example, consider a building that is purchased for $100 million, is financed for $80 million, and has a $10 million cash flow. Because of inflation, cash flow from the rents increases from $10 million to $20 million. The building can now be mortgaged for more because the cash flow supports a higher mortgage and there is increased value because the rents have gone up. If the mortgage is due or can be prepaid, the owner can then shop for another mortgage. Now, instead of an $80 million mortgage, he can borrow $160 million, giving him the difference—$80 million in borrowed money, which is non-taxable at the time—in his pocket, and he still owns the asset.[2]

In a declining market, the reverse occurs. Buildings that cost $100 million and were mortgaged for $80 million are revalued at $60 million.

Banks refuse to remortgage at the original price, and the investor must put up more equity, or risk foreclosure. This occurred in the late 1970s and early 1980s, and again in the late 1980s and early 1990s.

CHANGES IN BUYING AND SELLING METHODS

The method of buying and selling real estate has changed dramatically in the past 30 years. Before the recession of the early 1970s, real estate buyers and sellers were generally a small, closed group. A perspective on the development of the techniques of office building brokerage can be found in Chapter 21. The brokers that professional investors worked with were often independent agents with whom they were well-acquainted. The brokers would give the potential buyer only a brief description of the property, including location, size and a non-technical description of the mechanical systems. They would provide a simple report of income and expenses such as heat, oil, electricity, maintenance and repairs. Management, accounting and legal fees were not included, nor were allowances for vacancies or for tenant work. If the buyer made an offer the seller liked, the seller might open his books and show the actual expenses so the buyer could do his own projections.

These projections did not include inflation factors because there wasn't much inflation. Rents were stable, with a minor yearly increase that would just cover the increase in operating costs and taxes. In the 1950s, if a buyer purchased a building that would show a profit of 10% to 12% based on current income and vacancy factors, he would have no difficulty obtaining a mortgage on it because mortgage rates were substantially lower than the net income stream. If he bought a building for 10% and could mortgage it for 6% or 8%, he could increase the yield to 12% or 15% simply by financing the building.

The Borrowing Process

The institutions involved in financing very large buildings were sometimes, as they are today, insurance companies. More often, however, especially for smaller office buildings, the lenders were savings banks. The chief operating officer of the savings bank had the authority to make lending decisions. He, the broker and the buyer were in close contact. People knew who they were dealing with and commitments were verbal. Once the buyer and seller had agreed on the price and basic terms, they would meet with the lender and go to contract on the property based on the verbal understanding that they would get a mortgage.

---

[2] See footnote 1.

After the 1970 recession, the borrowing process became more sophisticated. Rents were depressed, owners weren't putting money back into their buildings, and the banks had to put in more money to salvage the real estate. In the late 1970s inflation changed borrowing methods even more dramatically. Tax rates climbed steeply, as did oil prices. This increased the cost of operating buildings and made it more difficult to predict how a building would do in the future.

Institutional Investors

Institutional investors are those large financial organizations such as insurance companies, pension funds and publicly-owned investment companies that are subject to either federal or state regulatory authority and to SEC requirements. Institutional investors may invest for their own account or invest on behalf of others for fees.

The large-scale institution in the form of an insurance company or pension fund was a potential competitor as well as a potential equity investor with the professional investor. In many cases, the insurance company would become a co-venturer with the investor in the purchase of an existing office building. The insurance company would either provide any necessary first mortgage financing or use its clout to obtain a first mortgage from another institution. Unlike insurance companies, pension funds generally purchased for their own account 100% of the equity without resort to mortgage financing.

By the late 1970s, real estate was starting to attract institutional investors because the transactions were getting very large. Values were escalating, and instead of buying buildings for $5, $10, or $20 a square foot, investors were buying buildings for $40, $50 and $60 a foot. At $40 a square foot, a 750,000 square foot building costs $35 million. These large transactions became too complex for owners to have to deal with a large group of small investors; they required large, institutional investors. These institutions had been in the marketplace building up their portfolios. They were selling some of their older properties and buying new ones, both for their house accounts and for the accounts they managed for other investors such as pension funds. They were excellent sources for both equity capital and mortgage money with equity participation.

Increasing Market Sophistication

At the same time, MBAs were entering the real estate business because they recognized its profit potential. Employed by insurance companies and banks, they brought a new sophistication to the marketplace. The computer was replacing the calculator as a tool and made it possible to use a new technique, called internal rate of return (IRR), to analyze real estate. When it came time to sell a piece of real estate, investors had to adopt these new procedures used by the insurance companies. Sophisticated software packages enabled them to project estimates of increases in income and expenses over as long a period as they wished, factoring in the inflation rate for rents, taxes and other expenses. They could make assumptions about renewal rates and replacement costs, including lost rent, fix-up costs and brokerage commissions, and offset these capital costs against their cash flow. And with the computer, they could do "what if?" calculations, varying their assumptions.

The premise, of course, was that the inflation rate estimates were correct. In the late 1970s and early 1980s, however, owners couldn't enter an inflation rate high enough to compensate for what actually happened. From 1977 to 1982, rents increased by 300% to 400%. If an owner started in 1978 with rents of $12.50 a foot in a midtown New York office building, by 1981 he was getting $40 a foot. So the value of his real estate increased three- or four-fold. The first large transaction that used these new tools and selling methods was the sale of the Pan Am Building by Landauer Associates, described in Chapter 21.

The Economic Cycle and its Effect on Prices

After the Pan Am deal, most large sellers proceeded in a similar manner by hiring investment banking houses. These firms published slick brochures with a thorough description of the building and sophisticated income projections. The competition they generated caused prices to escalate. Both buyers and sellers thought that inflation would go on forever. Cap rates, a multiple of the value of the real estate, were moving down and inflation was moving up, but the inflation rate never kept pace with the declining cap rate and increasing multiplier so that multiples of value were rising proportionately higher than the increases in inflation.

In a period of two or three years from the late 1970s to the early 1980s, some rents quadrupled, but the value of the building increased six or seven times because there was more investment capital competing for real estate investments. Foreign investors in particular were willing to buy real estate for lower returns. Inflation of real estate's basic value and increased competition among buyers caused prices to rise. The result was that many buildings were bought in the 1980s for what later looked like too high a price. The economy entered another recession in the early 1990s, and rents suffered large declines while operating costs continued to escalate, causing property values to drop.

CONCLUSION

The office market has in the past 20 years become increasingly dominated by major institutions; they are naturally attracted to business buildings and business tenants. Yet, there will always be a place for the professional investor. The institutions need the wisdom and counsel of the investor who has the complete pulse of the market and who can make wise decisions on what will be, in the long run, the best investment in terms of income and capital gain. Co-venturing with an institution assures the investor of the requisite financing and enables him to concentrate on the fundamentals for value enhancement.

The full-time investor must also surround himself with the technical support staff required to investigate office properties for purchase. No longer is instinct sufficient. The most sophisticated types of computerized investment analysis must be mastered and used. The independent judgments of skilled and experienced market research consultants have become a necessary addition to the investor's arsenal. In many cases, the lender will force an outside market study on the investor, but in other cases, the investor himself will recognize that he may not have all the answers.

The goal remains the same—value enhancement. In trade jargon some call it the "romance of the deal." It is the quest for profit that motivates the investor to make the correct decisions on the original purchase, the modernization or replacement program, the improved treatment of tenants, the appropriate financing and the ultimate decision to sell. But this is only a goal. How can it best be implemented?

The investor must have a superior management staff to achieve the highest IRR over an extended period. Generally, investors prefer to organize and operate building maintenance and operations, building renovations, and tenant relations, directly themselves, if they have a sufficient critical mass of real estate to justify the staffing cost. If managing agencies are engaged, they must be selected with extreme care, and their performance monitored closely thereafter.

Oddly to some, the professional investor will not indulge in over-financing at any stage of the real estate cycle. He will resist the temptation to recapture his total investment tax-free by re-financing in the up phase because he realizes that there must be enough equity income for continuing property modernization in the down phase. Speculators are a breed apart. They believe in over-financing to the extent that the equity income is substantially consumed by debt service costs. Many believe in "milking the property," the process of extracting all net operating income at the expense of long-term capital replacement programs and even of daily maintenance. Their view is decidedly shortsighted and ultimately self-destructive.

Real estate must be puchased, managed and sold within the framework of long-term ownership goals. No matter how long the professional investor plans to retain a particular office property, he will cosmeticize, replace capital equipment, modernize the property and serve his tenants. He will not stint on what is required to maintain competitive parity with similar or new buildings. His success over the speculator can be very simply measured in his IRR, that is, his capacity to retrieve not only his original capital investment, but a higher level of net operating income performance and a higher profit on sale.

ABOUT THE AUTHOR

Bernard H. Mendik is chairman of the Mendik Company and has been an owner and developer of office, commercial and residential properties since 1957. The company is owner/manager, directly or in joint ventures with individuals and institutions, of a real estate portfolio valued in excess of $2.5 billion with more than 12 million square feet of office buildings, primarily in Manhattan. The company also holds commercial properties in Westchester and Connecticut. Mendik is chairman of the Board of Governors of the Real Estate Board of New York and chairman of the Board of Trustees of the New York Law School.

21

OFFICE BUILDING SALES MARKETING PRACTICES

by John R. White with Thomas W. Adler

THE ORIGIN OF OFFICE SALES TRANSACTIONS

As recounted in Part I, office buildings as a distinct use grew in identity and size as the population and economy grew and urbanized after the Civil War. The earliest developers tended to retain their buildings for long-term income, in many cases willing them at death to their heirs. Transactions were the exception rather than the rule. When an office building owner decided to sell, it was usually through direct contact with other owners of similar properties.

Historically, private sales, with or without an intermediary, were the primary means of disposition. Auctions were never a popular sales technique in the office building field, although this has recently begun to change.

THE EARLIER MARKETING TECHNIQUES

The 20th century brought advances in building construction that permitted the design and development of significantly larger office buildings. Use of steel skeleton and reinforced concrete frames coupled with improvements in vertical transportation enabled builders to construct high-rise "skyscrapers" on large urban lots. As office buildings grew in size and mechanical complexity, so did the practice of real estate brokerage. The Flat Iron and Woolworth office buildings in New York were the forerunners of a massive clustering of office towers in the central business districts of American cities. With them came significant advances in the art of marketing such buildings for sale.

After World War II, both owners and brokers became more knowledgeable about their increasingly complex properties. More relevant information about the property was made available to brokers and buyers. Physical descriptions of the building and its mechanical systems were more detailed. Due diligence investigations of an office property's finances and physical features continued to be a difficult exercise for the buyer because of the business occupancy by large and small companies, the varying nature of the lease terms and the complexity of the mechanical systems.

The sales material provided by the seller was called by various names. In its simplest one-page form, it was called an offering or listing sheet, often referred to by brokers as sales particulars. A more extensive multi-paged presentation was termed a sales brochure. In most cases, the term "offering prospectus" was used when a public offering was contemplated.

Knowledge of the financing of office buildings became an important factor and brokers who were knowledgeable about sources of debt capital had a better prospect for success than those who were uninformed. Buyers were willing to pay commissions to brokers who knew where to find the lowest interest rates and highest loan amounts. Brokers could also facilitate sales by obtaining an informal mortgage commitment prior to the sales effort.

Contents of the Sales Offering

Use of one-page or two-page offering sheets continues to this day, especially for smaller urban and for suburban office properties. Table 21-1 sets forth an example of the usual information provided in such sales offerings. Only the basic data is presented and many essential details are lacking. The revenue and expense statement probably originated with the owner, although brokers sometimes altered the numbers if, for example, they felt expenses were understated, or if particular line items of expenses were omitted. The gross revenue represented by the seller was reduced by the 5% vacancy the building was experiencing. This information was usually sufficient for a buyer to make a decision whether to pursue the purchase. If he was interested, he would require further details from the seller on itemized rents, mechanical systems, service contracts in force and the like.

The proposed financing presumably was obtained by the broker, probably from a local savings and loan or commercial bank, contingent on attracting a buyer. The constant quarterly payment provided for amortization initially at 2% of the principal amount of the loan. However, since the payment was constant, the amortization increased each year equal to the reduction in interest as it was calculated on a progressively declining amount. The cash price of $700,000 represented a 10% return to the buyer after the vacancy allowance.

This financing illustrates the principal of positive leveraging. The office building, despite its age, yielded $220,000 per annum before mortgage debt, or a 10% return. Through the broker, the buyer obtained a loan at 8% interest. The buyer must pay amortization out of the net operating income, which is a cash drain and therefore reduces cash flow. Amortization is

TABLE 21-1   Typical Real Estate Offering Sheet

Location:	2500 Broad Street, N.W. corner of McElroy Avenue, New York, N.Y. Walking distance to rapid transit and new Jersey ferries.		
Plot Size:	100′ on Broad Street x 150′ on McElroy x irregular. Plot area 15,850 square feet.		
Zoning:	C-4, permitting office buildings of four times the plot area.		
Description:	An 8-story office building of 65,000 square feet built in 1923, with floors varying from 6,000 to 9,000 square feet. Two self-service elevators. Extensively rehabilitated in 1987. Now 95% rented.		
Rents:	At 100% Occupancy		$ 655,000
	Escalation Income		$ 100,000
			$ 755,000
	Vacancy Allowance		$ -37,000
			$ 718,000
Expenses:	Real Estate Taxes	$110,000	
	Operating	280,000	
	Management and		
	Leasing -7%	45,000	
	Tenant Work	25,000	
	Replacement Reserve	18,000	$ 498,000
Net Operating Income:			$ 220,000
Proposed Mortgage Financing:	$1,500,000 at 8% interest, payable in four quarterly installments for interest and amortization of $37,000. Due in 10 years.		$ -150,000
Equity Income:			$ 70,000
Price:	(All cash of $700,000 over mortgage)		$2,200,000

Subject to prior sale and withdrawal from the market without notice. While every effort has been made to obtain accurate information, no representation about the accuracy is made.

nevertheless considered a savings because from a balance sheet perspective, it reduces the mortgage liability and, all other things being equal, increases the net worth of the investment. Considering amortization as a savings, the positive mortgage leveraging produced a return to the buyer before amortization of $100,000, or a 14% return on $700,000 in cash equity, and 10% after the amortization payment.

Note that the expenses include provisions for tenant installation and lease renewal expenses (outfitting of the space and brokerage expenses). Provision must also be made for the replacement of mechanical equipment within the building. If the seller has not made these additional deductions, the broker will do so. The professional broker knows that a buyer wants an accurate estimate of these expenses in order to know what the equity net operating income will be.

The Exclusive Sales Agency in Office Marketing

An exclusive sales agency is created when the seller, acting as a principal, engages the services of an agent on an exclusive basis for a limited period of time. The exclusivity provision prevents the seller from dealing with any other broker directly during the period of the agency. The seller usually retains the right of withdrawal or cancellation at any time. The agent is required to use reasonable care, have undivided loyalty, practice full disclosure, keep information confidential and account for his actions.

Variations on the basic exclusive agency contract are almost endless. One common provision, known as co-brokerage, permits the exclusive agent to list the office property for sale with other brokers on an open agency basis. This allows more widespread distribution of the sales offering because the exclusive agent cannot be presumed to know every potential buyer for the property. With a co-brokerage arrangement, the exclusive agent and the co-broker usually split equally one full commission. When a property is particularly difficult to sell, the exclusive agent, usually at the seller's insistence, may promise to pay the lion's share, e.g., 60% to 75%, of the total commission to the successful broker. Sometimes the exclusive agent is empowered to promise a full commission to the successful selling broker. In this event, the exclusive agent will receive an override commission, usually 50% of the commission.

Who pays the promotional costs associated with an exclusive office agency? In large-scale agencies, the seller usually agrees to pay for the offering materials and associated mailing costs, travel and miscellaneous out-of-pocket expenses. The seller generally also pays advertising costs, although advertising is not considered as effective for commercial as for residential properties. In smaller agencies, responsibility for marketing costs is determined by negotiation, but these costs are more likely to be paid by the broker.

Limiting Conditions of Open Sales Agencies

If the broker can negotiate only an open, i.e., non-exclusive, sales agency, the seller tends to impose severe restrictions on the broker's conduct of the agency. Sellers include all the standard disclaimers intended to protect against commission claims or lawsuits. The offering to brokers is almost always made subject to prior sale by the seller directly or by another broker. This protects the seller against another commission claim if another broker simultaneously produces an offer at or above the negotiated price.

An especially vexatious right reserved by the seller is the right to withdraw the property from the market at will and without prior notice. This withdrawal automatically terminates the broker's open agency to offer the office property for sale, even though he might have a buyer at the seller's price at the time of termination. Further, the seller customarily states that while every effort has been made to provide acccurate information to the buyer, the seller is not liable for any misrepresentation or omission of any material fact. These reservations and limitations imposed by the seller make the broker's role as an intermediary infinitely more difficult, but it is a price the broker has to pay to obtain the non-exclusive agency.

Simultaneous Engagement of Brokers

Direct engagement of many brokers on a non-exclusive basis can be an effective sales method when dense market coverage is required. Saturation often produces good sales results. For example, intensive sales efforts must always be made to sell a vacant building. The owner often appoints an exclusive sales agent to administer the sale and deal with the open agency brokers engaged locally or regionally. Other owners perform the sales administration function themselves by dealing directly with the brokers. Sales commissions are tax deductible and cost the business owner only 68% of the sales cost under current tax laws. Moreover, it pays for the business owner to reduce the holding cost by expediting a fast sale. Since time is money, the commission cost after taxes is not necessarily onerous to a seller, even in cases where he must pay a full commission to the selling broker and a half commission to an exclusive agent.

Net Listings of Office Buildings

Sometimes sellers offer an office property for sale net of brokerage liability. In such cases, brokers are expected to receive their commission from the buyer. It is essential that the broker inform a prospect upfront that the property is being offered on a net basis and the buyer must pay the commission. Net listings have in the past provoked unethical and some-times illegal practices by brokers. A common breach of propriety occurs when the broker fails to inform the buyer of the net listing and attempts to make a secret profit by persuading the buyer to pay an exceptionally high price with the intention of pocketing the difference between the net listing amount and the negotiated price.

The broker must have a contractual understanding in writing at the outset so he has a legal basis for a commission claim if the buyer reneges on a net price transaction. Some states, notably New York, require buyers' agents to enter into a contract with the buyer on the purchase of residential property and to disclose to sellers their agency status in the representation of the buyer. Commercial properties are not covered by this statute but the buyer's agent is well advised to have such a contract as well. In many states, net listings are understandably illegal. Dual agencies, in which the broker represents both buyer and seller, are generally permissible when full disclosure is practiced, but they continue to be controversial. Those opposed to dual agencies hold that an agent should clearly represent only one party to a transaction to avoid any possibility of a conflict of interest.

It is not an easy livelihood to be an open agency broker, whether on a net or gross listing basis. Brokers should strive always for exclusive agency contracts where they are assured of an exclusive right to offer the property for a prescribed period of time and are not subject to competitive pressures from other brokers and limitations on their basic agency rights imposed by the client. This is both a more professional way to conduct a brokerage practice and the most effective way for a seller to proceed.

Ethical Conduct in Transactions

The discipline known as ethics is basically a group of moral principles or set of values.[1] Ethics is closely linked to morality, a positive doctrine concerned with the highest standards of personal conduct. Ethics is a continuing effort to distinguish between good and bad.

Few persons are totally beyond temptation. There is always a tendency under competitive pressure to temporize in the interest of expediency. Education programs at the university and trade association level are the best way to raise the practitioner's consciousness about the need for ethical conduct. Lofty expressions couched as ideals or statements of ethical conduct by trade associations have their place but are frequently ineffectual. Business ethics cannot be taught in traditional ways. The best device is to expose students and business persons to real ethical dilemmas through case studies where they must confront the issue and decide what constitutes ethical conduct.

Many of the shoddy and unethical malpractices occur in brokers' relationships with their customers, the buyers. Misrepresentation of the

---

[1] John R. White, *The Real Estate Development Manual* (Warren, Gorham & Lamont, 1990) Chapter 2.

offering is commonplace, for example by shading operating expenses, excluding certain types of expenses or making unsupportable estimates of future rents. Brokers must present the full, truthful facts to a buyer as they know them. They cannot hide behind the agency which has been awarded to them. The third-party buyer is entitled to the same full disclosure and candor as the broker's client.

The most easily misunderstood breach of propriety and ethics occurs where conflicts of interest exist between the sales agent, the potential client or even potential buyers. Conflicts of interest generally are defined as circumstances where the best interests of one person can only be advanced at the expense of another person. A common conflict occurs when an agent holds undisclosed competitive agencies to sell an office building while seeking to obtain another agency from a seller. Another conflict results when an agent, acting secretly as a principal, buys and sells office properties similar to what the seller was offering for sale.

The most serious ethical breach occurs when one party does not disclose to the other that a conflict exists. In one instance, an agent engaged by the seller to offer an office building for sale did not disclose to his client that a potential buyer had engaged the broker's company to make an appraisal of the same property.

Full disclosure by both parties of conflict circumstances is not always sufficient to eliminate the conflict. The outstanding agent will always consider whether outsiders would perceive a conflict even though the parties agree the conflict has been resolved by disclosure. The real estate office inventory is huge. Why risk a perception of conflict? There is sufficient other business for both parties. By adhering scrupulously to an ethical code of conduct, the broker will build a far better reputation.

Real Estate Counselors as Transaction Intermediaries

A modern technique is the use of a real estate consultant as the marketing agent or consulting intermediary. The sales consultant's role is similar to that of the agent. Both are usually employed exclusively for a fixed period. The major difference is that consultants require a fixed, upfront, nonrefundable retainer which they keep regardless of whether the transaction is effected. If the transaction is made, consultants may or may not subtract the retainer from their incentive fee, depending on their contractual arrangement with the seller.

Consultants may take an active role by marketing the office property directly rather than through brokers. They also may be authorized to employ open-agency brokers on an agreed-on commission basis. In this case, the brokers' efforts are subject to a prior sale negotiated by the consultant.

Alternatively, consultants may act in an administrative capacity. Rather than directly offering the property for sale to buyers, the consultant will engage brokers on an open agency basis, usually at or close to a full commission at locally prevailing rates. The consultant in effect becomes a representative of the principal, supervising the sales campaign in the principal's place. Frequently the consultant will have discretionary authority to set the price and terms of the engagement.

The consultant's compensation is normally a set fee, payable at established intervals during the marketing period. What a consultant receives depends not only on the size and complexity of the assignment, but on the scope of services provided for the seller. It is not unusual for them also to receive a "success" or incentive fee for their professional efforts. All the usual marketing costs for brochures, advertising, publicity and travel are normally borne by the seller.

The Counselors of Real Estate, an affiliate of the NATIONAL ASSOCIATION OF REALTORS®, is the professional association for real estate counselors. The Counselors of Real Estate promotes the use of the CRE (Counselor of Real Estate) designation for accredited members as a way of distinguishing them from others in the industry who refer to themselves as consultants or advisors.

Advances in Office Sales Marketing

Two events occurred in the late 1970s that would have a profound effect thereafter on the marketing of office buildings. The first event was the introduction of computer software that enabled a comprehensive analysis of revenue and expenses by line item. The second event was a radical change in the way office properties were marketed.

The new software accepted a variety of facts and assumptions concerning the annual rates at which rents, taxes and operating expenses would increase. It was possible to make a 10-year or longer projection or forecast of the probable net operating income on an annual basis. In cases where rents were expected to increase dramatically, that is, at a significantly higher annual rate than real estate taxes and operating expenses, the disproportionate increase in net operating income was startling.

Consultants, bankers and appraisers aided software companies in formulating the way in which essential lease data and operating expenses were fed into the computer. These original programs were not especially user-friendly. It was years before the evolving personal computer market produced software and hardware that enabled the average person to understand and use the computer as a working tool, and more particularly as a marketing tool.

Brokers and consultants were quick to seize on the potential for improved property analysis and improved communication of the essential data to buyers. It was the beginning of a new era, both in understanding an office property's future potential and in the sharply increased capacity of the broker to communicate that potential with full credibility. From a marketing standpoint, the intermediary gained a substantial new tool for attracting buyers by being able to set forth the assumptions on which projections were based in regular prose, not in arcane computer language. In the process, brokers and consultants experienced a sharp elevation in their standing with office property owners.

As both software and hardware improved, it became easy to do a series of sensitivity analyses for the seller, and once the property was offered, for the buyer as well. If one or more of the basic assumptions were altered, a different pricing would result. If the vacancy factor was decreased to 5% from 7%, there would be increased net operating income to capitalize into a selling price. If it was assumed that real estate taxes would remain stable for five years during a 10-year projection period, with 5% per annum increases each year for the last five years, the NOI and the value would change to that extent as well. Correspondingly, any decrease in rents or increase in the operating expense projection would cause a decline in the net operating income.

Perhaps the most sensitive of the assumptions on which a forecast is built is the discount rate, that is, the interest rate at which future income amounts are discounted to reflect the interest lost until the time of collection of each year's net operating income. The techniques of discounting income over a prescribed period and the selection of a terminal or exit capitalization rate for the presumed stabilized income are presented in Chapter 28 on valuation analyses. Brokers found it essential to master the rudiments of income capitalization and became proficient in the computer software programs that facilitated a more intelligent analysis of the office property's potential. Today's informed brokers are equally comfortable discussing an office property's internal rate of return (IRR) over a prescribed period as they are in using an overall rate of return. The IRR is fully explained in Chapter 28.

The 1990s saw a return to the use of a divisor for capitalization purposes simply because the excesses of the 1980s prompted investors to rely on current rather than future income. Discounting of future net operating income, based on a theoretical growth rate in rent levels and expenses, was largely abandoned in the early 1990s because of adverse market conditions. Nevertheless, investors and brokers both recognize that value is the present discounted worth of future expectations.

CREATING A CLIENT/CUSTOMER BASE

Astute brokers must over time identify those buyers who specialize in office building acquisitions and cultivate their business friendship as an essential part of office brokerage. The best source of buyer prospects is among the owners of the existing inventory of office space in a broker's geographical area. Brokers must maintain a data base, preferably computerized, which provides essential facts on the size, location, office type and financing requirements for every buyer. These records must be systematically updated because there are frequent personnel changes within real estate investment companies.

Buyers are frequently sellers as well. Systematic personal solicitation of owners to obtain sales listings is equally important. A consistent, focused effort to identify and become acquainted with the players in the office market is an obvious prerequisite to matching the buyer against the sales listing.

Enterprising brokers do not confine their prospects to the owners in their immediate market. Because office brokerage has successively become regional, then national and now global, brokers must constantly strive to become acquainted with those buyers who are willing to consider a purchase in any section of the country. Lists may be purchased, or they may be offered as part of a promotional package by a trade magazine or trade newspaper. These sources are only the beginning of the process of building a buyer base.

Trade associations are an excellent source of contacts. The Urban Land Institute, which is comprised mainly of developers and financiers, is an especially valuable resource for the broker. The real estate investment trust (REIT) industry publishes a membership list which is extremely helpful in identifying prospective buyers. Life insurance companies will make available to the broker, on request, the names of individuals in their regional offices who perform acquisition functions, as will local commercial banks. It is also essential for brokers to become acquainted with portfolio managers who manage pension fund assets and who belong to professional trade organizations such as the National Association of Real Estate Investment Funds. In the '90s, many pension funds are buying directly so brokers must also be aware of the largest corporate and public pension funds and their acquisitions staffs.

It is essential to track every recorded sale or newspaper account of an office property and determine the names of all buyers and sellers involved and the details of the sale. Certainly the best prospects are those that are most active in current transactions. Additionally, many brokers use the *Forbes* magazine list of the wealthiest individuals to attempt to cultivate extremely wealthy persons who are capable of buying even the largest office properties, either singly or in a private syndicate or partnership.

Brokerage is a highly personal business. Outstanding brokers make it their business to become personally acquainted with their prospects. This need only be a business rather than a social friendship; the line can readily be drawn if the broker (or prospect) prefers to keep the relationship on a business basis. Other brokers believe they must also be personal friends to maximize business potential. On some occasions, a personal friendship develops without either party planning it. As a general rule, it is preferable to maintain an arm's length relationship, despite a close business association of trust and respect, so that the broker need not compromise or temporize for purely personal reasons. A sense of propriety is vital to the establishment of an enviable reputation as a business person.

Professional brokers are willing to make periodic personal calls on good prospects rather than merely telephoning. Mixing at trade association meetings, seminars and dinners is essential to sound, mutually respectful relationships. Participation in cultural, civic, educational and religious organizations provides a firm base of important acquaintances. Brokerage has never been an 8 a.m. to 5 p.m. occupation. To be successful, a broker must be willing to devote entrepreneurial hours far beyond the norm for the typical salaried position.

THE ELECTRIFYING SALE OF THE PAN AM BUILDING

The one transaction that changed completely the time-honored techniques of office brokerage occurred in 1980 with the sale of the Pan Am Building. The 2.5 million square foot building, with 59 stories and sky heliport, was completed in 1963. Pan Am initially occupied about 400,000 square feet. Over a period of years, guided by a New York real estate consulting firm, it acquired 100% ownership by patiently buying out the other shareholders and by purchasing the ground-leased land from the Penn Central Company just one day after that company emerged from bankruptcy.

In 1980, its cash position dangerously depleted, and faced with the need to pay off or pay down its massive debt, Pan Am asked its real estate consultant to prepare the property for sale. Pan Am permitted the consultant to undertake a special analysis of the property which by computer would forecast the net operating income for 15 years. Because of the wildly inflationary times, rents had leaped from the $12-$15 level to $35 per square foot on the tower floors. Despite discounting, the value was significantly higher than expected because of the exponential increases in net operating income.

Table 21-2 presents the cash flow projections from 1981 through 1996. The net operating income before debt service and commissions in the first five years rose exponentially from $13,725,000 to $37,601,000, or close to three times. In fact, that increase was reportedly experienced by the buyer, Metropolitan Life Insurance Company.

Creation of a New Marketing Strategy

The consultant conceived the technique of providing at the outset to prequalified buyers the intimate details about the property. A 65-page offering brochure was prepared that included the itemized rent schedule, a comprehensive property description and an equally comprehensive market analysis which established the market environment in which the sale would take place. The intent was to attract institutional buyers by doing their homework for them.

Also lending credibility was a documentation book keyed to the offering brochure that included the three-year audited financial statements, the actual leases, the deed, the mortgage bond and mortgage, the service contracts, survey and title insurance policy. Buyers were invited to use the consultant's computer analysis capabilities to change one or more items in the 10 pages of assumptions that accompanied the projections. The candor of the presentation generated a high level of respect and trust between the consultant and the buyers.

Pricing the sale presented unusual problems. At the time, the market appeared to be escalating monthly, with rents rising sharply and vacancies diminishing. Privately, the consultant felt that the real estate would sell for about $350 million, and so informed Pan Am. It was finally decided to offer the property without an official offering price. The consultant's team told

The sale of the Pan Am Building in 1980 revolutionized brokerage techniques. For the first time, intimate details about the property were provided to a list of prequalified buyers. *(Courtesy of Metropolitan Life Insurance Company)*

prospective buyers that they considered the property to be worth a minimum of $350 million, but invited them to consider paying more in the form of a pre-emptive bid.

Prequalifying the Buyers

Before this sale, it was often left to the broker or consulting intermediary to decide to whom to offer the property for sale. Sellers did not consider the possible adverse ramifications of indiscreet submissions of a property offering to poorly qualified prospects. Such lax control of brokers' offerings tended to diminish the value of the offering in the marketplace.

In the Pan Am sale, it was decided that a public offering of such a large building had to be tightly controlled. The obvious way to accomplish this was to develop a series of lists, in order of submission priority, of prequalified prospects. The main criteria used to establish the relative capacity to purchase the property were:

- Audited net worth
- Experience in marketplace
- Current capital capacity
- Banking and credit references
- Experience with property type
- Management experience

Pan Am approved a three-tiered list of prequalified buyers. It was from the first tier that the final three bidders were obtained.

PROMOTIONAL TECHNIQUES

The centerpiece of any promotional effort is the creation of an offering brochure. The elaborateness of the brochure is a function of the size of the offered property. In the historic Pan Am sale, the brochure had extensive pictures of the property, floor layouts and plot diagrams (Figure 21-1). It is important to emphasize, however, that commercial property is not sold solely because of a slick four-color brochure. It is the content that counts.

Real estate buyers react poorly to an offering brochure that resembles those used in selling cars. Moderate quality paper stock and practical but inexpensive binding are preferred. However, graphics are important since they are the best way for a buyer to get an impression of the physical property and its environs. One of the most important sections of the offering brochure is the market analysis, that is, the status of the competitive market for the property type. The top brokers and consultants present the market as they understand it to exist. They do not paint a more optimistic picture than office market events warrant.

When describing an office building, it is always good practice to obtain from the owner a set of outline specifications that provide the essential detail on construction and mechanical systems. The tenant installation standards (the "work letter" in the lease) should be described. The facade materials, the fenestration and the finishing decor in the public spaces must also be presented. Gross square feet and net rentable square feet, by floor and in total, are essential to a full description.

The presentation of the gross revenue, real estate taxes and operating expenses, and net operating income before debt service or depreciation, is probably the most important section of the brochure. Table 21-2 sets forth how the revenue from all sources and the annual operating expenses for the office building are reconstructed from the audited annual financial statements. There is a provision for replacement of depreciable equipment, principally mechanical. The estimated year-by-year cost of brokerage commissions at prevailing local rates is also included. In recent years, as the office market has become more competitive from oversupply, buyers have been forced to provide for the cost of tenant installation expenses, both for new tenants and to induce renewals. Formerly, it was assumed that

FIGURE 21-1

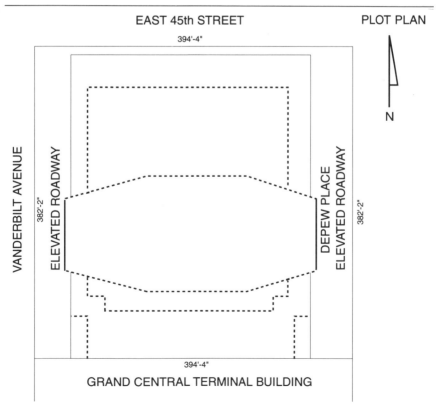

EAST 45th STREET   PLOT PLAN

394'-4"

N

VANDERBILT AVENUE

ELEVATED ROADWAY

382'-2"

DEPEW PLACE

ELEVATED ROADWAY

382'-2"

394'-4"

GRAND CENTRAL TERMINAL BUILDING

TABLE 21-2   Cash Flow Projection – Dollars (000)

Revenue	1981	1982	1983	1984	1985	1986	1987	1988	1989	1990	1991	1992	1993	1994	1995	1996
Base Rents	28,157	28,384	32,621	47,743	58,279	58,432	58,547	66,164	73,232	74,067	74,378	75,796	83,684	105,231	121,119	121,394
Escalation Income	6,749	8,398	9,423	8,497	9,587	13,436	17,722	18,386	20,512	26,203	32,707	39,597	42,132	33,138	31,703	43,057
Cost of Living	173	200	145	84	95	106	119	48	0	0	0	0	0	0	0	0
Percentage Rent	607	655	504	429	446	482	520	562	607	655	708	764	730	669	723	781
Tenant Sales	1,659	1,791	1,935	2,089	2,257	2,437	2,632	2,843	3,070	3,316	3,581	3,867	4,177	4,511	4,872	5,261
Credit Loss	-187	-197	-223	-294	-353	-374	-398	-440	-487	-521	-557	-600	-654	-718	-792	-852
Total Revenue	37,158	39,232	44,405	58,549	70,311	74,518	79,143	87,562	96,934	103,719	110,817	119,425	130,070	142,832	157,625	169,641
Expenses																
Payroll	3,561	3,881	4,231	4,612	5,027	5,479	5,972	6,510	7,096	7,734	8,430	9,189	10,016	10,917	11,900	12,971
Related Labor	784	855	931	1,015	1,107	1,206	1,315	1,433	1,562	1,703	1,856	2,023	2,205	2,404	2,620	2,856
Electric	5,824	6,523	7,306	8,182	9,164	10,264	11,496	12,875	14,420	16,150	18,088	20,259	22,690	25,413	28,463	31,878
Steam	2,365	2,602	2,862	3,148	3,463	3,809	4,190	4,609	5,070	5,577	6,134	6,748	7,422	8,165	8,981	9,879
Elevator Maintenance	514	555	600	647	699	755	816	881	951	1,027	1,110	1,198	1,294	1,398	1,510	1,630
Other Operating	1,006	1,086	1,173	1,267	1,369	1,478	1,596	1,724	1,862	2,011	2,172	2,346	2,533	2,736	2,955	3,191
Water & Sewer	82	89	96	103	112	120	130	141	152	164	177	191	206	223	241	260
Management	474	484	510	574	604	614	626	647	670	687	705	727	753	785	822	852
Insurance	320	345	373	403	435	470	507	548	592	639	690	745	805	869	939	1,014
Real Estate Taxes	8,404	8,908	9,442	10,009	10,609	11,246	11,921	12,636	13,394	14,198	15,050	15,953	16,910	17,924	19,000	20,140
Reserve for Replacements	100	105	110	116	122	128	134	141	148	155	163	171	180	189	198	208
Total Expenses	23,433	25,433	27,634	30,077	32,709	35,570	38,702	42,144	45,917	50,046	54,575	59,550	65,015	71,023	77,628	84,880
Net Operating Income	13,725	13,799	16,771	28,472	37,601	38,948	40,441	45,419	51,017	53,674	56,242	59,875	65,055	71,809	79,997	84,761
Interest	2,790	2,650	2,502	2,346	2,181	2,006	1,822	1,627	1,420	1,202	971	727	469	196	5	0
Amortization	2,430	2,570	2,718	2,874	3,039	3,214	3,398	3,593	3,800	4,018	4,249	4,493	4,751	5,024	321	0
Debt Service	5,220	5,220	5,220	5,220	5,220	5,220	5,220	5,220	5,220	5,220	5,220	5,220	5,220	5,220	326	0
Cash Flow	8,505	8,579	11,551	23,252	32,381	33,728	35,221	40,199	45,797	48,454	51,022	54,655	59,835	66,589	79,671	84,761
Total Leasing Commissions	75	17	1,918	3,282	39	65	24	3,110	478	53	154	264	5,626	7,934	109	130
Adjusted Cash Flow	8,430	8,561	9,633	19,970	32,343	33,663	35,197	37,089	45,319	48,400	50,867	54,391	54,209	58,656	79,562	84,631

increases in rent would provide a good return on installation or refurbishing costs for a new tenancy or a renewal. This is no longer the case. The expense of tenant outfitting must be shown as an annual operating cost, independent of whether the new rent results in a fair return on that added capital cost. This added expense reduces the net operating income available for debt service and equity income. Outstanding brokers will make this calculation for the buyer and provide the necessary documentation as well.

One of the many innovations in the disposition of the Pan Am Building was the use of an audiovisual presentation of the brochure highlights. The narration can be supplied by a professional actor or announcer, or by an articulate member of the sales marketing staff. The presentation should never run more than 12 to 15 minutes and 10 minutes is preferable. The delivery of the message should be crisp and precise; a rambling discourse should be avoided. Ideally, the audiovisual should be shown by appointment in the office of the prospective buyer prior to submission of the offering brochure. It is a cardinal rule of brokerage to make personal presentations. It is considered poor sales practice to mail brochures or audiovisuals because this tends to diminish the quality and exclusivity of the offering.

In preparing a property for sale, exclusive agents should know more about the property than their client, the seller. Outstanding brokers know their chances for success are significantly improved if they in effect "do the buyer's homework." This provides the resourceful broker with a competitive edge over the broker who makes no independent analysis or verification of the salient features of the office property.

The Concept of The Private Auction

In many instances, an exclusive agent or consulting intermediary will manage a private auction for an office property. This technique was used in the Pan Am sale and was the forerunner of many other similarly organized transactions. The process works especially well with larger properties and in a strong seller's market where the agent has tight sales control of the property. However, on an individual case basis, the technique has widespread application.

It starts with private presentations made to the prequalified buyers at their offices. The audiovisual is shown, then a senior sales executive makes a verbal presentation of the property's highlights. The exclusive agent usually allows at least three or four weeks for the buyer to consider the property and to make a due diligence investigation. During this period, the agent may be requested by the prospect to obtain additional information, or to run sensitivity analyses based on altered assumptions.

The agent will then set a date certain for the submission of the first round of bids in writing. It is a matter of ethics that no bids be divulged to a competitor or used against one another. Institutional buyers must be convinced of the exclusive agent's sense of propriety before they will even submit a first round bid. It is then the exclusive agent's responsibility to analyze the array of bids and compare privately their terms and conditions. If, for example, six first-round bids were made, the agent may decide to concentrate on the three highest bidders and designate them for the second round of bids. The agent then notifies the three low bidders that their bids are not sufficiently high to qualify them for the second round.

The final step is to invite the three high bidders to submit another, presumably higher, offer by a date certain, usually within a week. It is improper to suggest to a buyer what price or terms to employ unless the same information is made available to all bidders. All the finalists will have received the documentation book. Between this and the offering brochure, the buyer is well equipped to make a decision to proceed with a bid and on what price and terms.

The Advent of Regional and National Networking

As communications have improved and the office market has become more global, networking, formal or informal, has become an important broker-age function. One important source of networking contacts is trade associations. The Society of Industrial REALTORS®, formed in 1941 as a NATIONAL ASSOCIATION OF REALTORS® (NAR) affiliate, expanded in 1985 into the office building arena and was renamed the Society of Industrial and Office REALTORS® (SIOR). Through its education and other programs, SIOR offers an excellent opportunity for brokers to meet and exchange listings and effect transactions on a multiple market basis.

Another NAR affiliate, the Counselors of Real Estate, addresses the educational needs of those who dispense advice for a fee on a variety of real estate issues, including those involving office buildings. The Urban Land Institute, a real estate trade association not affiliated with NAR, offers brokers and consultants the opportunity to meet developers and financiers who might be buyers or sellers of real estate.

In 1977, a group of brokers specializing in office leasing founded The Office Network for the purpose of making leasing broker specialists aware of the office buildings available for renting. Other similar networks include Colliers International and the New America Network. The trend for large companies to move from major cities to areas that represent growth markets for their products has created an extensive national market for office leasing, especially for regional or state offices of large industrial corporations. Commercial leasing brokers are also in a position to make long-term net leases on single tenant warehouses or light industrial facilities. Many national business corporations prefer to rent rather than to own, so the rental market continues to be active in all commercial sectors.

Within these leasing networks, member brokers often exchange listings of office properties for sale as well. In this way, commercial leasing and sales brokers become better equipped to engage in a national practice. Many large corporations want "bundled" services from one company to satisfy their needs in multiple markets. The national brokerage firms have capitalized on this trend. Through networking organizations and trade associations, the astute broker can accommodate any investment requirements.

MODERN DAY AUCTIONEERING

Brokers can be involved in the auction process by referring prospective buyers to the auctioneer and earning a fee if their customer makes the winning bid. There are times when an exclusive broker will co-broker with an auctioneering company. Finally, many conventional real estate agencies have started auction divisions in order to offer the widest possible range of marketing services.

Since the real estate market is so scattered and diverse, the auction process may possibly disclose the true level of market value, especially when comparable sales are few. Finally, auctions draw attention. The competitive fervor that can occur often results in prices that are higher than anticipated.

One criticism that is frequently leveled at auctions is the low level of real estate knowledge possessed by the auctioneer. Some brokers believe the bid process consists of an uninformed auctioneer dealing with an equally uninformed buyer. Well-managed auction companies engage knowledgeable brokers as auctioneers. There are three types of auctions. The absolute auction promises a sale without reservation at the highest bid price. Buyer excitement and interest is usually heightened under this condition. A variation is the absolute auction with a guaranteed minimum bid price. This eliminates frivolous low bids and enables serious buyers to get to an acceptable bid price. The public auction, with or without a minimum price, with the seller retaining the right to reject the highest bid price is the least desirable technique. Busy investors compare this with a private listing in which an outside party holds an option to match the highest offer. Few serious investors will waste their time under these circumstances.

SYNDICATION'S ROLE IN REAL ESTATE MARKETING

A syndication may be defined as a group of investors joined in a legal entity for a common investment purpose. Originally, real estate syndicates were structured as general partnerships and each partner assumed an unlimited liability for all acts, profits and losses of the partnership. To avoid undue financial consequences for the passive investor, the limited partnership came into being. In a limited partnership, the partnership retains its pass-through income tax status and is not taxable as an entity, but the limited partners' liability is confined to the amount of their equity investment. The general partner is the professional investor who is responsible for acquiring, managing and disposing of the real estate. Frequently the professional investor is able to avoid unlimited liability by incorporation. Thus, a corporation may serve as a general partner.

Syndications may be private or public. Real estate brokers, together with attorneys, create most of the private syndications, subject to the restrictions imposed by the syndication laws in the state in which the property is located. Generally, state laws require registration and approval of the offering prospectus by a regulatory agency for all offerings with more than a prescribed number of investors. However, a syndicate with a small number of investors is usually free of state regulatory control.

In the 1960s through the 1980s, small syndications flourished. These consisted of a relative handful of investors with significant wealth, usually led by a professional real estate investor who could acquire and manage the office property. In many cases, the investors provided the equity capital over first mortgage financing to enable the syndicator/developer to construct substantial office properties, particularly in well-planned office parks.

Enterprising real estate brokers created many of these syndications by first identifying a likely property for sale. The broker would then locate a prospective general partner and interest him or her in the property and in forming a syndicate. In many cases, the proposed general partner had previously committed the interested investors on a standby basis. In other instances, the real estate brokers would also persuade investors to join the syndicate, for which they would be paid a fee by the syndicator.

Brokers frequently control the entire process by obtaining the listing of the office property for sale; arranging a new or refinanced mortgage; obtaining the investors; and then finding a general partner to act as syndicator. Sometimes real estate brokers become the syndicator as well as the general partner. When brokers assume this role, they must be especially careful to disclose to the seller that they will be serving in a dual role, as broker to the seller, as equity respresentative and as the syndicate head of the buying group. Brokers further must disclose to the buyers that they are receiving a brokerage fee from the seller.

A major concern for early real estate syndicates was the lack of liquidity of the units held by the limited partners, i.e., the units were not freely tradeable and lacked any central exchange for pricing purposes. This problem was originally solved by a syndicate organized by Harry Helmsley and Irving Schneider in the 1970s called Investment Property Associates. Their attorneys created a form of limited partnership in which the denominated units of ownership were freely traded over the counter. A further advancement was the creation of master limited partnerships, which were registered on the New York Stock Exchange or the American Stock Exchange, facilitating the creation of a public market for the units.

The volume of real estate syndications increased significantly in the early 1980s as a result of new regulations. The most important impetus came from the 1981 Economic Recovery Tax Act, which permitted accelerated depreciation and hence large non-cash deductions from net operating income. The combination of a large interest component and the high annual depreciation allowance frequently acted to shelter the equity income completely from taxation. Additionally, Regulation D was passed, liberalizing the capacity of thrift institutions to invest in real estate and removing the ceilings from saving deposits. These events provoked an investment climate in which office and other properties were overvalued; fee structures were inflated by syndicators; unrealistic deferred interest accruals were created; and overly optimistic forecasts of future income were made. The volume of public syndicated transactions rose exponentially in the mid-1980s as individuals sought to take advantage of the extreme tax shelter afforded by the 1981 Tax Act. As real estate syndicates grew in size and complexity, they became subject to state laws, usually administered by the Attorney General, and to the Securities and Exchange Commission.

The relative investment desirability of a tax-structured syndication often depended on the relationship between the estimated tax losses and the schedule of capital contributions.[2] In many cases, the equity was paid by the limited partnerships in installments over an extended period of time, while the investors were receiving 100% of the total proposed investment benefits in the form of tax losses. This financing device usually was based on a purchase money second mortgage made by the seller in which the interest was deferred until the mortgage came due. This is appropriate in an upcycle, but in the event of oversupply or recession, or both, the property may be left with a mountain of accumulated debt that cannot be repaid.

Many large public real estate companies engaged heavily in syndication in the 1980s, including but by no means limited to Consolidated Capital Corporation, Fox & Carskaddon Financial Corporation, Integrated Resources, and the Balcor Company. It was not uncommon for the 15 top syndicators to sell over $4 billion of participations per year in the mid-1980s. The large public syndicators accepted as little as $5,000 for investment while insisting on proof of a modest minimum net worth by the investor. By contrast, private syndications frequently require $1.0 million or more. Clearly, the broker has more opportunity to earn fees by raising money

---

[2] Stephen E. Roulac, "The Syndication Business," (*National Real Estate Investor*), August 1983.

privately. Further, the real estate broker or salesperson must have a securities license in addition to his real estate license in order to sell securities for a public syndication.

The syndication business, and along with it the real estate broker, were dealt a cruel triple blow starting in 1986 with the passage of a tax reform act that effectively eliminated most of the excessive tax gimmicks permitted by the 1981 act. The syndication industry could probably have withstood the new income tax restrictions because they eliminated excesses and would eventually have produced more orderly markets characterized by less inflated prices. Unfortunately for syndicators, after the 1986 Tax Act was passed, the various real estate markets began to peak. The stock market crash of October 1987 confirmed the developing oversupply as demand for all types of real estate, and especially office buildings, began slowly to erode. Finally, the recession that started in the third quarter of 1990 and lasted intermittently through late 1992 dealt a final blow to public syndication of individual properties. The public industry is now quiescent and no widespread recovery is expected until the mid '90s.

Inevitably public syndication will re-emerge but with a completely different thrust. The over-leveraged, over-priced, tax-oriented philosophy of the 1970s and 1980s will be replaced by an emphasis on net operating income, with moderate loan-to-value ratios, devoid of the financial hyperbole that characterized pre-1986 offerings. Economics will drive deals in the '90s. For the broker, the immediate outlook in the 1990s will be primarily toward small, private syndications formed by wealthy individual investors. In the aggregate, there are billions of dollars that can be channeled to office building investment. They are attractive investments to business persons because of the business nature of the occupancy and the lack of emotion that characterize business use of office space. Enterprising brokers must cultivate individual wealth and become adept at forming groups of investors capable of purchasing even the largest properties.

CONCLUSION

The stereotypical impression of real estate sales brokers is of indiscriminate mailers of inadequate sales material concerning properties about which they know little and who expect to make sales at a low statistical percent of their mailings. Nothing could be more incorrect.

Modern sales brokers are likely to have an MBA in finance, accounting or marketing. They are well-versed in software packages relating to real estate analysis and have a personal computer as constant support. They have mastered the economics of real estate through trade association courses and university or self-study programs and are knowledgeable about location factors and the physical characteristics of buildings.

Modern sales brokers are adept at performing lease by lease, discounted cash flow analyses, employing various software. Their objective is to know more about the property they are about to offer for sale than the seller does. They are steeped in the law of agency and conduct their business with the candor and sense of propriety that bespeak the ethical person. Their driving ambition may be to invest their commission profits in real estate but they will not do this at the expense of their clients.

They must know virtually everything that occurs in real estate investment and development so they can better serve their clients. Their comprehensive grasp of the fundamentals enables them to relate easily to mortgage bankers, constructors, appraisers and all others in the business. They are on a par with the best securities sales people. Above all, they are conscious of their responsibilities to the community and strive to strengthen their competitive standing through participation in the various trade associations to which they belong.

ABOUT THE AUTHORS

John R. White, CRE, MAI, was with the New York-based international consulting firm of Landauer Associates for more than 25 years, leading the company for 16 of those years under various titles as chairman, president, CEO and director. He is currently chairman of White Realty Group, New York, specializing in asset management, portfolio supervision, acquisitions and disposition. White is a former president of the Counselors of Real Estate and has served as chairman of the *Appraisal Journal* of the Appraisal Institute. He has served as an adjunct professor of real estate at New York University, and has published extensively on real estate subjects, including several books and more than 100 articles. White holds an AB from Harvard University and an MBA from New York University.

Thomas W. Adler, CRE, SIOR, is managing partner of Cleveland Real Estate Partners. He was previously in charge of Grubb & Ellis's national investment real estate services and president of the firm's institutional investment group. After 17 years with Cragin, Land, Free & Smyth, in 1979 Adler co-founded Adler Galvin Rogers, Inc., a Cleveland-based commercial brokerage firm which was acquired by Grubb & Ellis in 1986. Adler graduated from the University of Wisconsin. He is a member of the Counselors of Real Estate and the Society of Industrial and Office REALTORS®, serving as the latter's national president in 1990. Adler is a contributing author to the book *Real Estate Counseling*.

PART VI

FINANCING OFFICE BUILDINGS

CHAPTER

22

THE FINANCIAL STRUCTURING OF OFFICE INVESTMENTS: DEBT AND EQUITY

by Robert A. Steele and
Kenneth H. Barry

INTRODUCTION

This chapter examines the basic manner in which office buildings are financed on a fee simple or leasehold basis; the regulatory limitations on loans; traditional lending sources; and typical terms on conventional loans. It also describes the many different types of mortgage financing, including construction loans.

THE CURRENT OFFICE INVESTMENT PERSPECTIVE

Office markets are based on locational, financial and social market factors that have undergone significant transformation since the early 1980s and the advent of the personal computer. Traditional definitions of central business district (CBD), suburban and other locations have become blurred in virtually all market segments. Telecommunication and computerization of office activities have allowed the growth of new office locations where none existed previously and caused obsolescence of others. The traditional requirement of a central location has become less of a driving force in office space location than financial and quality of life considerations. Lenders must in the future be able to read more accurately the constantly evolving socio-economic motivations for relocation in order to ensure better performance on loans.

Major money center banks are moving computer and back office operations from Pasadena and downtown Los Angeles to Phoenix and Denver; whole companies are moving from New York and New Jersey to Dallas, Texas; others are consolidating in Dallas from scattered locations on the east and west coasts. One reason for these locational shifts is the quality of life advantages for employees in the southwest over the northeast. In addition, companies' costs of operation are lower because of reduced land and infrastructure costs and lower employee pay levels.

The less traditional element that makes these relocations possible is modern telecommunications, which enables companies to locate anywhere there is electric power and a reasonably capable employee base. A nearby college to provide an educated work force is a great plus. Put in a satellite dish, add a networked computer environment, and insurance claims from New York can be processed in Iowa or Ireland with equal facility.

The building boom of the 1980s added another element to the office location equation: a 15%-40% vacancy rate in virtually all market regions

Telecommunications and computer technology have made a central business district location less important in office space location decisions. *(Photo © 1989 by Abby Sadin Photography. Courtesy of Skidmore, Owings and Merrill)*

across the United States. This condition created unparalleled tenant flexibility, and landlord duress. For those few markets with a normal 18-24 month supply of space under current absorption rates, new construction may begin again in the mid-1990s, if financing can be found. But most major markets have a multi-year supply of space, even using optimistic absorption rates. These may see little new construction for the remainder of the 1990s.

OFFICE BUILDING INVESTMENT

Investment in office buildings differs from investment in other property types because of the nature of the real estate. Office buildings, whether large or small, are driven by the relative strength and utility of the location and the management skill and financial strength of the project owner. Lenders are cognizant of these cardinal factors.

Within the office category of real estate, office buildings differ substantially. Central business district (CBD) office projects differ from suburban products. Although the physical structures may be similar, the parking required and the tenant audience may be substantially different. An owner's relative real estate skills and financial strength affect results as well.

For all office building investments, in any market, the owner's ability to manage a building and to attract and retain tenants is the foundation of success. The financial stability of the investment depends totally on these three factors. Success as an investor or a lender depends on the ability to understand, quantify and accept these risk factors.

All office projects have certain basic characteristics that are used in competing for tenants. The conceptual characteristics of location and utility are the core determinants of demand for office space. Unlike retail space, where co-tenancy and critical mass are the determinants of strength and stability, office projects must compete for tenants with the relative prestige of location. There are not necessarily "anchor tenants" that attract other tenants to the location, as there are in retail projects, although the quality of the tenancy in pre-leased space does attract and impress other prospects. But the relative strength of the "address" is the primary magnet for tenants in office projects.

The constraint on a tenant's desire for a specific location is utility and the ease and expense of adapting a given space to specific uses. The tenant's need for larger floor plates may exceed the capacity of a building in the most desirable location. Or the larger floor plate may have been built out for smaller tenants and the cost of reconstructing the tenant improvements may be greater than the landlord can bear. There are a myriad of variations.

From the perspective of financial structure, ongoing tenant stability is critical to the success of an office project. Stability in office property depends on the ability of a specific location to remain prestigious in its market niche and to continue to attract solid tenants. Stability is equally dependent on the building's having sufficient utility to accommodate changes in tenants' space needs over time as the business climate changes.

Location

An unquantifiable portion of "address" is the project's inherent reputation. The project's physical structure may be older, its rents higher and it may not be as well maintained, but if fashion dictates being located in a particular district or at a specific address, that project will attract tenants and others will not. In a competitive lending market, lenders tend to compromise locational standards; they often later regret their lowering of criteria.

In times of excess space or slack general demand for office space, certain projects and districts will still attract tenants because of location and reputation while vacancy rates remain high in seemingly similar projects in nearby locations. In good times, the same location will command higher rents for the same reasons. The lender has to be sufficiently well-versed in market micro-economics to make the best judgments.

Utility

The concept of utility in office space is complex and difficult to quantify. The requirements for specific tenancies and types of tenancies vary greatly over time. At the same time, the type of space offered to the market differs greatly among projects.

Looking at the different space needs of a prestigious law firm for whom image is as important as work quality, a back-office location for a large insurance company with a substantial white-collar employee base, and the "retail" office of a large, Wall Street brokerage house quickly illustrates the diversity of office space requirements. Moreover, space requirements change continuously, even for the same tenant.

A building with a floor plate size and design that can easily accommodate both large and small users will generally offer the best utility. Although some buildings have this quality, most do not. Buildings are typically designed for either large or small users, but not for both. And once a space is built out with tenant improvements, modifying the space for a different use becomes more difficult and expensive.

The utility and adaptability of a space and building in its market niche is critical to the stability of the demand for the property over time. Lenders must become more sensitive to the importance of physical (spatial) utility in their underwriting.

Ownership or Sponsorship

Given the dynamic nature of office building ownership, the third key ingredient for success is an owner who has:

1. A deep understanding of the specific market niche the property serves, as well as the economic forces at work to change that niche
2. The ability to become known and accepted in the targeted community as a responsive and reasonable owner
3. The financial stability to survive periods of substantial change and market illiquidity (the lack of either debt or buyers) and to keep the building competitive during those periods

The most successful owners are imbued with these qualities.

Capital Access Risk

The final element of risk in all office projects is access to capital. The ability of an owner in any capacity (owner, developer, lender, joint venture partner) to quantify the three risk elements of location, utility and ownership is only the first step in structuring an office building transaction. The competition for capital is intense and at times the supply of capital is limited. Access to the financial markets that provide capital to office projects is critical to the equation.

The general capital market in the early 1990s did not allocate a large proportionate share of capital to office buildings of any type. This affected the liquidity of existing property (i.e., the ability to refinance or sell) as well as the value of the property short term. Office lenders in some instances failed to distinguish between financing development properties and the lesser risk of financing existing buildings.

Capital market access is a substantial risk factor for office projects of all sizes and types. Underwriting a perfect project—with perfect sponsorship, location, tenancies and utility—is meaningless unless there are capital sources to finance the project. Capital consists of all forms of debt and equity. The most artful combination assures lesser long-term investment risks.

CAPITAL STRUCTURE AND LEVERAGE

Leverage in capital structures is simply borrowing someone else's capital to acquire (or construct) and own an asset. How much leverage to use depends on the nature of the asset, the market for it, its market value, the availability of capital for the investment, and whether the leverage is positive or negative.

Leverage reduces the amount of equity that an owner is required to invest in a property by an equivalent amount of mortgage financing. Leverage also increases the risk of ownership of a property because if there is insufficient cash flow to service the debt, the property will likely be foreclosed and the investor may lose all his capital.

Positive leverage occurs when the cost of the borrowed capital is less than the expected yield of the asset, free of debt. Negative leverage occurs when the borrowed capital costs more than the investment produces. For example:

Long-term yield expectation	12%
Long-term capital cost of debt	11.5%
Current cash flow	10%
Current capital cost of debt	10.5%

In this example, the asset has positive leverage over the long term but has negative leverage on current cash flow.

The amount of leverage that an investor and property can handle is a function of the property's ability to service the debt from cash flow and of the investor's ability to withstand protracted periods of insufficient cash flow to meet debt service requirements or illiquid market conditions. Illiquid market conditions limit the owner's ability to sell the property for a price sufficient to repay the debt on it.

Conceptually, leverage is the use of any form of capital that is not totally at the discretion and risk of the user and does not include the user's capital. Leverage exists whenever any ownership benefit or contractual right is transferred and there is a risk of loss to the user from that transfer. This includes mortgage debt, limited partners, participating debt, convertible debt and any other form of capital use other than the user's capital.

Leverage is additive to the risks of location, utility and sponsorship already discussed. Leverage in any form increases ownership risk in an absolute sense.

There are two basic types of investors:

1. All-cash investors
2. Leveraged investors

The all-cash investor in office projects is generally an institution, such as insurance companies, pension funds and business entities (public and private corporations with the need and resources to own their office properties). It may also include large private investors.

The leveraged investor in office projects is generally an individual or group and may include institutional investors through a hybrid financing vehicle that will be discussed later. Typically, the leveraged investor has limited capital sources and long-term stability that is not on an historic par with investing institutions.

Individual investors are typically not long-term investors in office pro- jects. They tend to buy and sell (or develop and sell) with market cycles over relatively short time frames. In the life of projects that span a decade or more, short-term investors have more characteristics of speculators than of investors. Speculation in office property is defined as waiting for a specific event or two to occur before selling at a presumed gain. These events may be an opportunistic purchase at a good price, a roll-over of tenants to a higher rent level and presumably a greater value, or perhaps the availability of leverage in a variety of forms due to heated market conditions.

The greater the leverage and the more complex the leverage structure, the greater is the risk. It is difficult to quantify the risk of leverage if market cycles and periods of capital or transactional illiquidity are factored in. Like rain or snow, how long and when a given point in a market cycle will occur is difficult to predict. But the risk remains; markets change.

Capital Market Segmentation

The capital market for office projects can be divided into the following segments:

1. Construction and stabilization period lenders and investors
2. Short-term lenders and investors
3. Long-term lenders and investors

There is some crossover among the various capital categories at different times in market cycles as well as at different points in the effective period of a property's economic life. The objective in any market or economic life cycle is to capitalize a project to reduce leverage risk to the lowest factor possible given the available alternatives, and to address the issues of location, utility and sponsorship with the appropriate structure.

Economic Ownership Stages

An office property may experience the following stages during its long- term economic life:

1. Conception and land acquisition
2. Pre-leasing and pre-development planning
3. Capitalization—debt and equity
4. Construction
5. Initial leasing campaign
6. First tenant cycle
7. Re-tenanting cycles
8. Renovation to address functional obsolescence
9. Market decline due to economic obsolescence
10. Adaptive re-use of structure

11. Economic decline
12. Virtual abandonment
13. Possible supercession with increased land value

The capital structure appropriate for any one of these stages varies widely and depends on market conditions and investor objectives. The rest of this chapter will discuss alternative capital sources and tools and relate them to the various stages of ownership.

THE CONSTRUCTION LOAN

The initial construction period is the most risky ownership period in any real estate project. There are business risks involving land, labor and material availability and timing, cost overruns, and concerns about building inspections, environmental issues, timely completion, tenant occupancy and so on. These and other risks can materially affect the outcome of a project, sometimes to the detriment of the construction lender. These risks are seen not as real estate risks, but as construction risks, by virtually all investors and lenders.

Because of the higher risks during construction, capital costs for the project are generally higher for this time period. Higher capital costs can be expected in both debt and equity forms of leverage.

Construction capital comes from three sources:

1. Commercial banks provide most of the capital for construction.
2. Life insurance companies provide less capital than the commercial banks do.
3. Pension funds and pension advisors have provided construction capital in the past, typically only when the fund has an equity interest in the project.

The Underwriting Process

Commercial banks provide capital to construct office projects under varying credit and valuation restrictions. These restrictions, which can vary depending on economic conditions at the time of the loan, include the following:

1. Borrower Net Worth Strength. Banks tend to prefer borrowers with substantial liquidity relative to the size of their total uncovered borrowings. The borrower should be able and willing to service the construction debt regardless of economic events or delays that occur on the project. It is not unreasonable to expect a net worth requirement equal to the loan size and total assets on the balance sheet of 4 to 8 times the loan size. Recourse, i.e., personal recovery from the borrower's other assets, is nearly always an issue with construction loans; the minimum standard is a completion guarantee and the payment of taxes and insurance on the property. Total recourse is not expected in the 1990s and no recourse was possible as recently as 1989. Personal completion guarantees will be the lender's minimum requirement for the balance of the decade. In most cases, the main borrowing entity and its principals must individually sign the note that accompanies the mortgage.

2. Borrower Skill. The borrower must be able to demonstrate the ability to manage and complete a project. A progression of loan and project size from small to large on the borrower's part is usually necessary to induce lenders to make loans on larger projects. Occasionally the net worth of the borrower's balance sheet will overcome the need for progression.

3. Entitlements and Pre-leasing. The project must have all permits in hand and matters subject to regulatory or political control resolved before the construction loan can close. Typical pre-leasing requirements in the 1990s are at least 70%, and most loans have a breakeven debt service requirement for leasing. At least 50% of the building's leases must be long-term (10 or more years) to strong tenants.

4. Take-out (Permanent) Financing. Most construction lenders view take-out loan commitments with suspicion because of the general ill health of the financial system, as well as of the providers of such commitments. The test is that the property must be adequate collateral for a conventional permanent loan from a permanent lender for the property. Experienced banks are competent at addressing this issue.

An alternative to a take-out commitment is for the bank to issue a mini-permanent loan, that is, a permanent loan for a short term after construction (usually 3 to 5 years) to allow the project time to stabilize and to obtain a permanent loan commitment. These loans can be inherently dangerous for the lender if the market is likely to be unstable because the borrower cannot readily refinance.

Some life insurance company lenders offer take-out commitments to induce a construction loan on projects that they particularly favor. These events are rare occurrences, but they offer a capital source for a few projects.

5. Loan Constraints. Commercial banks typically will underwrite a construction loan of between 65% and 75% of cost. As recently as 1989, loans could be obtained for as high as 85% to 90%. The loan-to-value ratios were in the range of 70% to 75% of value on aggressive valuations. Loan-to-value ratios in the 1990s are in the range of 55% to 60%. Most commercial banks, however, are not eager lenders in the 1990s economic environment.

6. Lenders. The major U.S.-based money center banks and large Japanese, Canadian, French and British banks are the logical lenders for large projects (over $15 million) in the 1990s. Smaller regional and local banks may be lenders for smaller projects. Their pricing will be higher than that of the money center banks, and loan constraints may be more stringent. Some life insurance companies package a construction loan and permanent loan together, but the minimum project size is $25 million and the project and sponsorship must be top quality.

Pension advisors, pension funds and life insurance companies typically are not disposed to handle construction period risks. They are less risk oriented than the commercial banks (as the fees for construction loans indicate), and they do not have sufficient investment officers capable of assuming the task of completing a project. Most of these lenders avoid construction period risks, with the exception of issuing a forward take-out commitment. Their objective is to remain as passive as possible in the lending process and construction loans by definition are not passive loans.

THE PERMANENT LONG-TERM LOAN

Traditionally, mortgage capital for office buildings has been available on a 75% of value basis. The 25% of value "margin of institutional safety" traditionally has been calculated on an artificially determined market value based on market factors such as cap rates and comparable sale indices provided by competent appraisers. The operative limits for mortgage capital are the percentage amount that a lender will lend against the value of a given asset *and* the lender-determined value of that asset.

Virtually all permanent and construction lenders have a stated maximum loan-to-value ratio for office product of 60% to 75%, if the lender is willing to consider the product at all. These lenders have varying valuation criteria that result in a wide range of values for the same asset based on the same property and market information. The result is a wide range of loan amounts that may be available to the borrower.

An alternative method of determining loan amounts (as opposed to values) uses the debt service coverage ratio (DCR). The DCR became widely used in the 1970s as the parity of interest rates, loan amounts and values diverged. The DCR became a substitute limitation on loan amounts and, indirectly, on value.

A nominal DCR ranges from 1.20 to 1.30 for most life insurance company lenders. In other words, the amount of cash flow from the operation of the property available to service the loan must be 120% to 130% of the debt service required by the loan amount and payment schedule.

If a 75% loan-to-value ratio results in a loan with a higher debt service than the property's cash flow can cover, the DCR effectively limits the loan amount. For example:

Net operating income	$1,000,000
Value at 9.5% capitalization rate	$10,526,316
Loan constant (based on a hypothetical 10%, 30-year mortgage)	10.54%
Higher DCR	1.3%
Loan amount	$7,298,204
($1,000,000 divided by 1.3 divided by .1054)	
Loan-to-value ratio	69%
Lower DCR	1.2%
Loan amount	$7,906,388
($1,000,000 divided by 1.2 divided by .1054)	
Loan-to-value ratio	75%

The amount of the loan is an indication of the lender's willingness to assume risk for an office building asset.

Permanent mortgage lenders for office projects tend to be life insurance companies and pension funds and advisors for both large and small projects; for small and medium-size projects, lenders include credit companies and some commercial banks. All lenders use the cash flow model method of valuation for permanent mortgage lending, and capital is more or less difficult to obtain depending on market conditions and project stability.

In the early 1990s, most life insurance companies were not viable office lenders; the exceptions operated on a very conservative basis. Credit companies, regional commercial banks and larger savings institutions were other alternatives for permanent mortgage capital. The life companies are expected to re-enter the office market as equity participants and lenders when the glut of office supply reduces later in the decade.

Underwriting Permanent Mortgage Loans

Issues affecting the underwriting of permanent mortgage loans are similar to those affecting the underwriting of construction loans, with the following differences. Concerning loan constraints, institutions typically will underwrite permanent loans of between 75% and 89% of cost, with loan-to-value ratios in the range of 60% to 65% on conservative valuations. This compares with loans of up to 100% in the past and loan-to-value ratios of 70% to 75% on aggressive valuations.

Loan terms, amortization periods and loan conditions for permanent loans vary by lender and by market segment. Typically, life insurance companies and pension funds are represented by a mortgage banker or advisor, and the loans are processed through them.

Loans made by life insurance companies generally are less expensive than those made by banks or credit companies. Pricing typically is based on an index such as the U.S. Treasury bond or Treasury bill rate for a commensurate period of time plus a spread factor. For example, if the seven-year T-bond rate is 7%, the permanent loan would be at 1.35% to 2% over that rate to adjust the lender's risk for real estate lending. On the other hand, a credit company or bank loan is likely to be based on the prime rate and the spread over that index is typically 2% to 3%. Loan fees are higher than those for a life insurance company loan.

Amortization periods for a typical permanent loan may be as high as 40 years, but most are for 30 years or less. In the 1990s, lenders have shortened amortization periods and 25-year loans are not uncommon. The issue of the amortization period is mitigated by the fact that due dates on loans are seldom greater than 10 years for any lender. Lenders adjust the interest rate risk for longer loan due dates by increasing the interest rate spread over the maturity of the index. In other words, a loan with a due date of seven years will carry a higher spread than one with a due date of three or five years.

Life insurance company loans typically are locked in with no prepayment possible for the first three to five years of the loan term or longer; after that, prepayment is allowed but a penalty is assessed. The penalty, which varies with the lender and with market conditions, has ranged from 1% to 5%. The prepayment penalty usually will begin at the high end of the range and decline over time. Of late, lenders are requiring a "yield maintenance" prepayment penalty based on a mathematical formula designed to protect the lender's reinvestment position by demanding a penalty for the difference between the contract interest rate and the presumably lower interest rate that motivated the prepayment request.

Permanent lenders generally do not allow subordinated debt without prior consent. Some lenders are adamant that no subordinated debt be placed on the property, while others allow the debt under the same underwriting constraints as for the primary debt. A few lenders will allow subordinated debt with a lower coverage ratio than for the primary loan (typically a 1.15 coverage including full first and second debt service) with no maturity shorter than the primary loan term.

CASH FLOWS AND VALUATION

Lenders' office valuation methods range from simple cap rates to sophisticated discounted cash flow models using lender-derived assumptions and discount rates for equating the cash flows over an extended period. The cap rate and office market sales comparison approaches to valuation are generally used as screening devices based on recent results of approved transactions and are only partly based on market-derived data from actual sales. Lenders believe that it is difficult to determine the value of an asset in a changing market and, as a result, tend to extrapolate market-derived information. A typical lender comment is "The last sale may not be the best indication of value...." Unfortunately, in the heat of a competitive market, lenders tend to extrapolate only upward and fail to recognize the imminence of a downward trend.

Lenders use the cash flow analysis approach to valuation in an effort to "control" in a sophisticated computer model all exogenous (market) and all endogenous (property) influences that may affect a property's cash flow over time. Factors considered in the models include effective market rental rates which allow for market-derived rental concessions to tenants; lease terms; tenant improvement costs (current costs for both unleased space and roll-over space as leases expire); and absorption rates (how long a given space will remain vacant and induce a loss of cash flow).

Cash flows are projected for extended periods of time, usually five or ten years beyond the loan term. The theory is that an appropriate exit strategy must be developed when the loan is made so there is a reasonable expectation that the loan will be paid off under any reasonable future market conditions.

The cash flows over time are used for three purposes:

1. To value the property based on present market value, i.e., the discounting of net operating income over a prescribed period at a market cap rate
2. To determine the debt service coverage ratio of the property over time
3. To permit an analysis of sophisticated capital structures other than straight debt alternatives.

Stability of the cash flows is a necessity, and a high proportion of long-term leases is essential to obtain a permanent or construction loan in the current environment. The prospect of market vacancies from short-term leases is viewed as a major risk in an overbuilt market environment.

Some lenders approach the underwriting process for a property on a tenant-by-tenant basis, making extensive investigations of tenants' background and credit to determine their stability and likelihood of remaining for the term of their leases. The tenant-by-tenant and space-by-space approach to developing a property's cash flow is tedious, but it offers the best picture of the property's risks over time within the constraints of the controlled variables. The skill of the lender and borrower in adjusting the variables to fit the market and property circumstances will determine the success of a given loan underwriting effort.

In addition, borrowers are extensively underwritten and investigated to determine creditworthiness. Only the strong and "clean" borrower need apply.

Finally, most lenders are reluctant to return capital to a borrower in the form of refinance proceeds, regardless of the amount of the loan relative to value or cost. Virtually all permanent lenders require that the borrower have real cash invested in a property as a condition to making the loan; the presence of "excess value" is insufficient. In the end, lenders adjust the loan amount to reflect their views of the exogenous and endogenous variables affecting the cash flows in any given interest rate and capital availability environment.

The result of these valuation methods and cash flow assessments is that actual loan amounts in the post 1990-92 recession period have been closer to 60% of value than they have been to 75%. Lenders have been using every available tool to reduce their perceived risk of loss and of not being repaid on time.

In this context, several events have occurred:

1. Leverage availability has been limited.
2. Sale transactions have become rare events, occurring only when a lack of available alternative capital sources has in effect forced a sale.
3. The lenders that are active in the market have been able to pick and choose the best opportunities. The traditional stratification levels of institutional lenders, savings institutions, commercial banks, and credit companies have been blurred, and each lender category has been making loans on office product types that it had not considered previously.

While recent market observations cannot be taken literally for all markets at all times, they have emphasized the importance of liquidity and capital market risk. Even with sophisticated models of cash flow performance, attempts at quantification at best provide only an indication of future events and risk under stated conditions. The lender and the borrower both must develop a greater mastery of cyclical events to avoid the obvious excesses and to know when to anticipate events.

Varying the elements of the models is a way of addressing the issue of variability, but it still provides only an indication under uncertain assumptions. If the general conditions change, the results may change dramatically.

THE APPRAISER'S ROLE

Title XI of FIRREA brought new guidelines and responsibilities for appraisers. What had formerly been referred to as a "full-blown MAI appraisal" became the standard for the industry. Appraisers are expected to be fully cognizant of the market, not only for rental levels, but for concessions, absorption, capitalization rates and discount rates. Their appraisal must completely explore and justify supply and demand factors.

FIRREA requires that the appraiser report three valuations for a development project. The first is an "as-is" value; this is usually land value, but may be more if the project is under way. The other two are the value at stabilization and, most critical, the value at completion. It is easy to see how in the past overzealous lenders, anxious to generate fee income, were willing to pin their hopes on stabilized value and take their chances. It did not work out. Lenders' compromising of prudent underwriting standards proved their undoing.

Appraisers do not establish value; they simply render an opinion of value which should reflect actions of the market. While not discarding the discounted cash flow method, appraisers are relying on it less than in the past. In an oversupplied market, it is difficult to predict with any accuracy what the trend of rental rates, concessions and absorption will be, let alone to forecast growth rates, terminal capitalization rates and discount rates. Instead, the marketplace looks at first year income and expenses and capitalizes its perception of net operating income into value at an overall capitalization rate 100 to 200 basis points over the presumed high point in the market. It is a harsh world.

In such a market, is the appraiser serving as a restraint on the underwriter? The answer is probably yes; however, the underwriter is restrained as never before by regulators, by the lack of available funds and by a very sensitive management.

Licensing and certification are new dimensions in the appraisal field, and eventually all appraisers will be required to have a license or be certified. However, state qualifications for these credentials are not initially high, so the tried and true methods of selecting an appraiser by reputation for skill and integrity will still be the best guarantee of obtaining a realistic and competent appraisal.

HYBRID DEBT AND EQUITY TOOLS

The Standby Loan

Definition: A loan obtained on a standby basis, presumably to be replaced with a conventional permanent loan at current market interest before the construction loan comes due.

Use: To enable placement of a construction loan by assuring the construction lender that a permanent loan is available for the project.

Cost of standby facility: Typically 1% to 3% of the loan amount as an upfront, one-time payment.

Interest rate and terms: Vary, but will be more expensive than a normal life insurance company loan, frequently by 200 to 300 basis points. If it is funded, the lender may require the borrower to let it share in the building's profits. Term is typically the same as for life insurance company loans. The standby lender never expects to fund. In practice, it is caught with the permanent loan more often than is desirable or planned.

Participating Mortgage

Definition: A loan that has as many equity characteristics as debt characteristics, a participating mortgage is used by passive investors (typically pension funds) to participate in the benefits of equity ownership without incurring the direct risk of management or ownership of a property.

Use: From the borrower's side, to increase leverage while reducing or eliminating its equity investment. From the lender's side, to increase yield on investment above the straight mortgage yield available at the time.

Cost of loan: Typically 1% to 5% of the loan amount—a one-time payment.

Interest rate and terms: Typically lower by 1% to 2% than permanent debt rate with a commensurate maturity, including base rate and a participation in the increase in cash flow and value on sale of 25% to 75% over a base amount. The base amount is normally a negotiated figure. Some life insurance company formulas for participating debt are rigid and provide little or no flexibility in tenant roll-over costs and adjustments, and little capital contribution in the event the project requires additional capital.

The investor typically expects total yield of 2% to 4% over the market mortgage rate for a loan with a similar maturity. The difference between the base rate and the yield objective is made up by the participation in increases in cash flow and value.

Participating loan investors are generally interested in cash-short ventures with reasonable near-term upside from renovation-induced rental increases, from tenant roll-overs, or from a substantially pre-leased development property.

Convertible Mortgage

Definition: A loan that is essentially a contingent sale or conditional interest in a property without the attendant risks or problems of direct ownership. Typical investors are pension funds. The amount sold through the loan is typically greater than 90%, but may be only 50%. The loan is a participating mortgage until late in the life of the instrument when it may be converted by a call option to an actual interest in the ownership of the property. The documentation of the investment vehicle is very complex. Ideally, the conversion provision should be in a separate, recordable instrument rather than in the mortgage note or bond. An illustration of a note convertible to 100% ownership is presented in Chapter 25.

Use: To sell conditionally a portion or all of a building while retaining a portion for a set period of time (usually 8 to 10 years) and deferring the tax on the sale for that period of time. The proceeds of a mortgage are tax deferred while the proceeds from a sale are taxable on a current basis. The vehicle permits early capital realization through the loan while potentially locking in a higher price because of market conditions at lower rates resulting from more intense investor demand. The instrument is difficult to work with in adverse proceedings or if the interests of the parties diverge from the original intent of the instrument. Valuation and liquidity issues are difficult to deal with from the investor's standpoint.

Cost of loan: Typically 1% to 5% of the investment amount.

Interest rate and terms: The basic instrument will contain terms similar to those of the participating mortgage, except that the participations are greater (90%) and the instrument contains a provision for conversion to an ownership interest in the property. A purchase of the entire remaining interest may be included in the negotiations. The instrument is non-standard and requires sophisticated parties and legal counsel to effect.

Securitized Mortgage

Definition: The sale of a financial instrument in the capital markets as a security rather than as a whole loan. The instrument sold is actually a hybrid debenture with pass-through provisions for the interest and principal amounts of the note. The security for the debenture is a note and deed of trust on a property or pool of properties. The underwriting of securitized transactions is typically more stringent than that for equivalent life insurance company underwriting. The advantages may be liquidity and lower borrowing costs because of the different (non-real estate) capital market being accessed. Typically, a credit enhancement from a standard rating agency is required on the top portion of the equity unless the debt coverage ratio and loan-to-value ratio are satisfactory to one of the rating services for this source of capital (DCR of 1.5 to 1.8 and LTV of less than 50%). In addition, this type of transaction is difficult to accomplish in amounts less than $100 million. On large-scale securitized mortgage obligations, there may be several tranches, or classes of debt, each with its own seniority, terms and interest rate dependent on the positions and length of the tranche. Securitized bond financing is discussed in Chapter 25.

Use: To access the capital markets at a lower cost and to obtain liquidity that might not otherwise be obtainable. Lower interest costs may be offset by increased legal, accounting, engineering and brokerage/investment banking costs. In a market of ample capital, it is less expensive to borrow large amounts from a major insurance company or pension fund because the origination costs are lower and the interest rate will be competitive.

Bullet Financing

Definition: A medium-term first mortgage loan, usually for five to ten years, generally made at competitive interest rates, and without amortization. Frequently the interest rate will float at a 2% to 3% spread over equal term U.S. Treasuries.

Use: In instances where the borrower cannot obtain or is not agreeable to the conditions of conventional long-term financing. Lenders are attracted to these loans as a matching device with their GICs in which the lender earns the spread on the respective investments.

Bridge Financing

Definition: A short-term loan to "bridge" two events where the risk of the transaction is limited, as opposed to the completion of a significant event such as meeting a leasing requirement stipulating that a certain percentage of the building must be leased before the permanent loan will be disbursed. Sometimes referred to as a gap loan.

Use: To allow the completion of a transaction where no other finance mechanism is available due to time constraints or similar considerations. Mainly used as acquisition financing on a short-term basis where the buyer has been unable to arrange satisfactory permanent financing prior to the closing date.

Unsecured Financing

Definition: Credit-based financing facility based on the credit strength of a borrower.

Use: To provide liquidity in an otherwise illiquid market (to get a loan for a real estate project that is not secured by real estate). Typically the signature strength of the borrower is sufficient to obtain this type of loan, provided it has an acceptable minimum net worth. This type of loan is primarily based on balance sheet considerations rather than on the property's net operating income.

Equity Financing

Definition: An investment made by an all-cash investor.

The ideal timing involves buying low and selling high, but market actions demonstrate anything but this. The market for office buildings in particular seems to be driven by a herd instinct. If offshore investors engage in buying frenzies, pension funds will jump in and compete with them. If one segment of the market withdraws, the rest are quick to follow suit. The market in 1990-92 represented one of the greatest buying opportunities in recent memory. Because of the lack of financing, investment in this market required all-cash buyers.

It is interesting to look at money market influences in an oversupplied marketplace during a recession with falling interest rates. All other things being equal, in a market in equilibrium, overall rates of return would be expected to change as interest rates change. Yet it has been demonstrated that in such circumstances the supply and demand for real estate product has a much stronger influence than the effect of competitive influences in the money market.

In times of tight money, normal mortgages of 65% to 75% of value tend to disappear, and so leveraged buyers disappear. In times of abundant credit, leveraged buyers again become a factor. Somewhere in the overall investment scenario, however, equity yield must result in positive leverage, whether through the cash-on-cash return, the addition of mortgage amortization or appreciation, or a combination of these.

It should be pointed out that leverage is a two-edged sword. If the investor was looking to inflation and appreciation to overcome negative leverage to the cash-on-cash position, with or without mortgage amortization, and inflation does not occur because of an imbalance in the supply and demand of space, the change to negative results is all too apparent.

Equity real estate investment trusts (REITs), another means of raising equity capital, have met with mixed results. The best results have come from well-capitalized, well-managed REITs that have invested in prime properties on an all-cash equity basis. Because by law they must pass through 95% of their cash flow, REITs have become an attractive investment vehicle in the stock market. Typically, these shares are undervalued by the stock market because REITs are not a good vehicle to recognize unrealized appreciation. Unrealized appreciation is the probable increase in value resulting from increases in net operating income, but which cannot be fully recognized until an actual confirmatory sale occurs. The stock market also tends to be influenced by factors that have little to do with the internal performance of a REIT's portfolio. For example, some equity REITS wisely finance the tenant improvements for new or existing tenants out of cash flow from depreciation deductions rather than by borrowing. This reduces the return to the shareholder but strengthens the balance sheet and tends to enhance the value of the properties. The stock market has been slow to realize the soundness of this policy.

There are a number of other vehicles for raising real estate equity capital. The most popular is the limited partnership. Limited partnerships effectively minimize the investor's risk, but they have lost many of the tax advantages they held prior to 1986. Unleveraged partnerships offer the least risk and the best opportunity in the long run for a satisfactory investment.

CONCLUSION

The real estate market in the 1990s is one of the worst markets in decades. Not only are most marketplaces overbuilt, but technological changes have had the dual effect of lowering the need for space and making it easier for business tenants to move their operations to more cost-effective locations. When the lack of liquidity in the lending system, re-regulation and a recession are added to the mix, the result is a situation requiring a long and painful workout.

The opposite side of adversity is opportunity.

Office buildings represent for the large-scale investor the best possible type of property to own over the long term. In the financial structuring of office investments for both debt and equity, investors need to adhere closely to the basics of locational quality, utility of the space, the strength and character of ownership and management, the availability of financing and the structuring of that financing.

This chapter has explored construction loans, short-term loans and permanent loans, and the criteria for their underwriting. The main questions to be asked of the borrower are: does he know the fundamentals and does he have enough at stake to be committed to the project? For the lender, the question is: have enough safeguards been established to underwrite a successful loan?

The appraiser's role has become more important in dealing with office investments. The overbuilt environment and the requirements of Title XI of FIRREA have resulted in the need for appraisers to document carefully each step of the appraisal process. A good appraiser should reflect the marketplace, and the marketplace wants hard-nosed, conservative valuations. This may or may not be a restraint on lenders, who are already closely controlled by regulators, management and the lack of liquidity.

This chapter has also examined various financial instruments and equity sources. Office investments have never suffered from a lack of techniques to solve financial underwriting problems. But the message of the recent past is: "Never ignore the law of supply and demand again."

It is to be hoped that lenders will develop new mortgage officers with a career mentality and a pride in maintaining high underwriting standards. The tendency for lenders to compromise their lending criteria in capital surplus markets must be assiduously avoided in the future. Meeting competition at all costs is a disastrous policy in the long run.

ABOUT THE AUTHORS

Robert A. Steele, CRE, MAI, is president of Parkcenter Realty Advisors, Santa Ana, California. Previous positions he has held include president of MCO Equities, Inc., Los Angeles and senior vice president, Landauer Associates. Steele has served on the Governing Council of the Appraisal Institute and Board of Governors of the Counselors of Real Estate. He is a contributing author to *The Appraisal Journal, Real Estate Issues* and other publications, and has lectured on appraising at the UCLA extension and various professional organizations. He holds a BS from UCLA and an MBA from the University of Southern California.

Kenneth H. Barry is president of Equity Realty Group in Fullerton, California. Other experience includes department head of the Pension Real Estate Investment Department of United California Bank (now First Interstate Bank); retail and land development; and workout and property disposition assignments for the Resolution Trust Corporation, the FSLIC, FADA, and for private developers and property owners nationwide. He holds a BS from the University of Southern California.

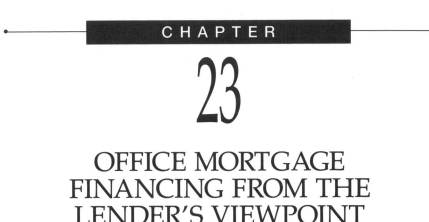

CHAPTER

23

OFFICE MORTGAGE FINANCING FROM THE LENDER'S VIEWPOINT

by Glen E. Coverdale

INTRODUCTION

This chapter discusses "permanent" mortgage financing on improved commercial real estate, as opposed to "construction" financing. This type of financing is also referred to as "long-term" or "fixed rate." None of these terms very accurately describes the mortgage financing typically put in place today upon completion of construction, but they have historic relevance in understanding the topic.

Prior to the 1980s a typical financing scenario for a to-be-built property would proceed something like this: The developer would obtain a commitment from a life insurance company or savings institution to fund a 20- to-30-year loan with a fixed coupon rate. This funding would be advanced upon satisfactory completion of construction according to agreed-upon plans and specifications and possibly the achievement of a specified level of leasing at designated minimum rent levels. Another lender, usually a commercial bank, would provide a construction loan which advanced funds in stages as construction progressed. The funding of the long-term financing provided the funds to satisfy the construction loan.

To assure the permanent lender that the developer would not "walk away" from the commitment if market rates changed in his favor, and also to assure the construction lender that the permanent loan commitment would not be abrogated, the two lenders often entered into a "buy-sell" or "tri-party" agreement. This agreement stated that the construction loan would be repaid directly from the permanent loan proceeds upon satisfac-

434

tory completion of the improvements and fulfillment of any other conditions of the permanent loan commitment. In fact, the construction loan could be written to include all the terms of the permanent loan so that it could be assigned directly without the developer having to execute another set of loan documents.

In recent years the lines of demarcation between "construction" and "permanent" loans have blurred. Construction loans have lately been made without "take outs"[1] and have evolved into "mini-perms" with maturities extending well beyond the date when construction is scheduled to be completed. On the other hand, "long-term" loans today typically have maturities of 5, 7, or 10 years for reasons that will be discussed.

THE ROLE OF COMMERCIAL MORTGAGES IN LIFE INSURANCE COMPANIES' INVESTMENT PORTFOLIOS

For a great many years mortgages have had a significant place in life insurance companies' investment portfolios. For a variety of reasons, that position has been slowly diminishing. American Council of Life Insurance data indicate mortgages amounted to 35.9% of life insurance industry assets in 1970. That share diminished steadily over the next 20 years to 19.2% in 1990. Much of the apparent diminution is definitional. GNMA and FNMA and other securitized mortgage pools are now classified as securities, not mortgages. The remaining mortgage category still includes some single-family residential loans and agricultural loans, but it now consists predominately of mortgages securing loans on commercial properties. The total amount outstanding in life insurance industry mortgages was $270 billion at the end of 1990.

Regulatory Background

To some extent the position of mortgages in insurance companies' investment portfolios has been influenced by regulation. For example, for many years (from the late 1960s through most of 1984) the State of New York limited the mortgage investments of life insurance companies domiciled or doing business in New York to no more than 50% of their total assets. New York's regulations have also tended to set the standards for other states' regulations.

The same regulation limited mortgage loans to 75% of the value of the security at the time the loan was made and required that the payment

---

[1] A "take out" is a long-term first mortgage commitment made before the construction loan is obtained, and which the construction lender relies on to be "taken out" of the loan investment on completion of construction.

schedule fully amortize the loan in 30 years plus up to five years of interest-only payments. The regulation also required that leasehold estates serving as security for loans have an unexpired term of not less than 21 years. More restrictively, the loan payment schedule was intended to fully amortize the loan within four-fifths of the period of the leasehold or 35 years, whichever is shorter.

The New York regulations were recodified in 1984, in the era of deregulation. Restrictions remained on the percentage of assets that could be invested in mortgages, but the 75% of value restriction on individual mortgage loans was eliminated. The new requirement was that the directors and officers "perform their duties in good faith and with that degree of care that an ordinarily prudent individual in a like position would use in similar circumstances." Despite the more flexible regulations, many lenders adhere to the older criteria as a reasonable standard of investment practice.

TRENDS IN COMMERCIAL MORTGAGE LENDING

Forward Commitments

From the 1960s through the early 1980s, lenders would commit a significant portion of long-term mortgage lending before construction began on the buildings which were to secure the loan. This is referred to as a "forward commitment" as opposed to "immediate funding," which refers to an agreement to finance (usually refinance) existing improvements

Immediate Fundings

The term "immediate funding," when applied to commercial mortgage loans, can be misleading. In this context, "immediate" means a closing usually 60 to 120 days after the borrower and lender have reached an agreement.

In the 1980s, as the products life insurance companies sold became more and more interest-sensitive, it became increasingly important for the life companies to match the interest rates and duration of their liabilities (insurance and annuity contracts) with those of their assets (investments) at the time the contracts were sold. This necessitated their making investments that are "immediate" when the funds from the sale are received or are expected to be received. Ideally, the sale of an interest-sensitive product, the commitment of a matching investment and the funding of that investment should all occur simultaneously.

At the same time, the volatile interest rate environment in recent years has also made forward commitments less attractive. If prevailing interest rates at the time of closing differ significantly from prevailing rates at the time of the commitment (usually a two-year time span), either the borrower or the lender may be unhappy or embarrassed by the resulting loan.

Finally, with the high vacancy rates in commercial real estate in the latter half of the 1980s, lenders felt more comfortable lending funds secured by properties that were already constructed and substantially leased at the time the loan commitment was made. As a result, by the end of the 1980s, the forward commitment was no longer in common use.

Shortening of Maturities

Until the early 1970s, commercial loans were typically self-amortizing, or nearly so. However, as interest rates rose, the typical loan with a 20-year maturity and a 20-year amortization schedule was stretched to 25 or 30 years. Some lenders maintained 20-year maturity requirements while extending the amortization schedules to produce a more affordable constant payment, thereby creating a "balloon" payment at maturity for the unamortized balance of the loan.

As the products they sold became more interest-sensitive (e.g., guaranteed investment contracts, Universal Life, single premium deferred annuities), life insurance companies placed increasing emphasis on "matching" investment rates and terms to those of the contracts they sold. Interest rate "guarantees" in these contracts tended to be for shorter terms (3-10 years) than the mortgages then being placed (15-20 years). The interest rate sensitivity of the contracts also increased the importance of maintaining the contracted rate of return on investments for a period certain.

The need to match insurance contracts and investments served to shorten loan maturities in two ways. The lenders desired shorter maturities, typically 3-10 years, to match the periods for which they were guaranteeing rates of return on their contracts. They also needed to prevent the loans from being repaid prematurely to ensure that the initial rate of return would continue for the entire term of the contract. As prepayment restrictions become more stringent, borrowers also became less willing to be "locked in" for long periods of time. They too became more interested in shorter maturities. Further, the "normal" positively sloped yield curve also attracted borrowers to shorter maturities; that is, they could obtain lower interest rates for the shorter terms.

Loans with Equity Features

A counter-trend to the shorter term "permanent loan" was the development of "participating loans" and "convertible loans." These offer the borrower a lower fixed rate of interest and a higher loan amount in return for giving the lender a share in future earnings of the property. The lower fixed interest rate makes the financing more affordable for the borrower. In theory, the lender is compensated for the lower interest rate by the potential for higher returns in later years if the property securing the loan becomes increasingly profitable. Both of these devices are also considered to protect the lender against the erosionary effects of inflation on a fixed income stream.

A participating loan has a fixed rate of interest which may be five to ten percent lower than that on a "straight" loan. In addition, however, the lender receives a percentage of cash flow above operating cost and the minimum debt service. There might also be a requirement that on maturity of the loan, the lender's total return over its life will be analyzed and if a stipulated minimum rate was not achieved, the borrower would pay a lump sum amount to make up the shortfall. This type of provision is referred to as a "look back."

A convertible loan is one in which the lender, in exchange for granting a larger loan and/or a reduced interest rate, is given an option to convert some or all of the loan into an equity position. There are many variable components relating to timing of the exercise of the option, the percentage of ownership, interest rate step-ups and so forth. Usually they are based on a cash flow model of how the property is expected to perform. Examples of convertible loans can be found in Chapters 21 and 25.

These instruments can be attractive to an institution that does not require high levels of income in the early years of its investments. If the institution can look at a total return over an extended time-span, such as 10 years, these instruments can offer returns similar to those on an equity. Notionally, the lender can assign a mortgage rate of return (partially deferred) to most of the investment and an equity rate of return (wholly deferred) to the "top" portion of the loan. The real test is the internal rate of return experienced over the life of the loan.

The quasi-equity form of return illustrates part of the concern some investors have with these formats, i.e. there is some risk that a court might characterize the loan as an equity interest, thus denying the lender the usual legal recourses available on a default or loan satisfaction. With convertible mortgages, the potential legal problem may be avoided if the conversion clause is in a separate document that is not part of the bond or mortgage.

Underwriting

It is important to distinguish mortgage loan underwriting from appraising. While the appraisal process is a vital component of loan underwriting, it is just one part of that process. This discussion will focus on considerations other than the valuation process.

Significant underwriting considerations include:

1. **Quality of the Security**
   Location
   Design

Materials
Workmanship

2. **Quality of the Ownership**
   Experience
   Depth of organization
   Financial strength
   Quality of management demonstrated in other properties
   Maintenance level

3. **Market Conditions**
   Vacancy rate
   Absorption rate
   Economic vitality
   Development activity
   Development restrictions

4. **Loan/Value Ratios and Maturities**
   Debt service coverage
   Pattern of lease expirations
   Proposed loan maturity

Quality of the Security

Probably the most important fundamental in underwriting is dealing appropriately with the quality of the security. It is difficult, if not impossible, to adequately compensate for inferior quality in the security itself by underwriting other aspects of the transaction conservatively.

Quality of the security has a number of facets. There is, of course, the axiomatic quality feature of real estate, location. Whether one says "location" once or three times, there is no denying its fundamental importance. A superior location can ameliorate, but not entirely cure, other underwriting concerns.

In evaluating location, the underwriter should consider not only the factors contributing to the present location rating but should also look to probable trends which may affect location quality in 5 or 10 years. In this country, prime office locations have a history of being mobile. Central business district (CBD) locations may migrate as new construction embellishes previously rundown areas. Major urban renewal efforts sometimes create nodes which "move" downtowns away from the previously most attractive center. (In many instances these "new" centers are located where the original center of the CBD was at the time of the city's early growth.)

Suburban office locations are even more fragile in respect to the duration of their desirability. Locations in well-conceived office parks generally remain attractive longer than freestanding buildings which have fewer surrounding amenities (hotels, restaurants, retail, pleasant landscaping) that can be relied on to anchor the desirability of the location.

Location evaluation should include an estimate of how easily new competition can be introduced which may detract from the desirability of the subject property. The availability of similar sites, the likelihood of new major roads being developed, the extent of zoning and other building restrictions are among the factors that should be considered.

Quality of design, materials and workmanship in the siting and construction of the improvements are other important quality considerations which affect not only the current desirability of the property but also the permanence of its attractiveness. Design considerations should include functionality and flexibility as well as aesthetic elements. Quality of materials and workmanship should be evaluated for durability and ease of maintenance as well as attractiveness.

Quality of the Ownership

Although historically loans secured by commercial real estate have typically been non-recourse, that is secured only by the real estate and not by the borrower's other resources, the financial strength of the borrowing entity is important. The loan is being made to the borrower with repayment secured by the pledged real estate. It is important that the borrower be one from whom the lender may expect trouble-free servicing of the debt. As used here, "borrower" refers not necessarily to the obligor of the mortgage note, which frequently is a single-purpose corporation or limited partnership, but to the ultimate party in interest.

Even though the property securing the debt may be considered more than adequate to enable the lender to recoup the principal amount of the loan, the lender expects and desires to enter into a loan which returns interest and principal as scheduled in a trouble-free fashion. There is a growing tendency for lenders to require some degree of recourse to the borrower over and above the real estate security. The lender is well-advised to scrutinize carefully the proposed borrower's financial strength in relation to the proposed loan, his other obligations and his history of servicing financial obligations.

Evaluating the borrower's expertise and experience in owning and operating similar properties is another significant factor in underwriting a trouble-free loan. Does the borrower have experience with this type and size of property? Is he knowledgeable about the market area? A borrower who has developed apartments successfully in Los Angeles may fail with the same product in Wichita.

There should be sufficient depth in the borrower's management team that an unforeseen loss of a principal or key employee will not create severe operating or financial problems.

An examination of similar properties owned and/or operated by the borrower will yield information about the quality of ownership and management. Are the properties well-maintained? What is the leasing experience? Is tenant turnover low? Is there evidence of good tenant selection? Does it appear that the borrower critically examines proposed tenants for such criteria as financial viability, compatibility with other tenants and contribution to the building's image?

Market Conditions

In addition to factors internal to the loan transaction—the property securing the loan and the ownership and operation of the property—the underwriter will consider external factors which will affect the viability of the proposed transaction. These external factors include the economic vitality of the region, vacancy and absorption rates, development activity and governmental and economic restrictions on future development.

The critical factor is the interplay of supply and demand. What is the outlook for each? The tendency in underwriting this factor is to extrapolate the experience of the previous few years into the next several years. These projections are almost invariably wrong. The momentum of the local economy (to say nothing of the national economy) will not stay on a steady course of growth. It will be subject to spurts and dips. More often than not the underwriting is done during a strong growth period because that is when loan demand is likely to surge. Historically, underwriters have made the tacit assumption that the strong growth in demand is at the baseline level rather than at a temporary peak. When this error is multiplied by a number of underwriters and developers each considering one office building, the result can be oversupply, unexpectedly weak demand and consternation.

This being said, it is extremely difficult to estimate future demand for space except to recognize its probable variability and accordingly to be cautious in outlook. It is somewhat easier to estimate the supply side of the equation by carefully surveying development potential—available sites, buildings that have been announced, credit availability and so on.

Loan-to-Value Ratios and Maturities

The final underwriting consideration is how much margin for error the underwriter should allow in view of the factors already considered—the quality of the security, the ownership and market conditions. These factors will guide his decisions on the amount of the loan, its repayment terms and final maturity.

The pattern of lease expirations should be considered in determining loan terms, especially the maturity date. Ideally, the loan should mature at a time when there is a reasonable expectation that the property will be well-leased and will not have a significant amount of space up for releasing within a short time after the loan maturity. If this can be managed, it will make both the lender and the borrower more comfortable that the loan can be satisfied according to its terms because the property will most likely be financeable at that time.

Determination of the appropriate term for the loan is also necessary in order to determine the interest rate to be charged. Assuming a positively-sloped interest rate curve, longer term loans have higher interest rates.

When the interest rate is known, the underwriter can complete the determination of the value of the property for loan underwriting purposes. In addition to setting an acceptable loan-to-value relationship, normally in the 70% to 80% range for fixed rate mortgages, the underwriter will look at the debt service coverage ratio. This coverage—net income after operating expenses and real estate taxes to debt service—has tended to vary in the 1.20 to 1.50 range based on the quality of the loan security broadly defined and the inflation assumptions used in determining value.

CONCLUSION

Because the valuation process includes dealing with extensive numeric data, the loan underwriter can be in danger of being overly influenced by (seemingly) hard, factual, objective numbers. He must be careful not to slight his weighing of the "softer" information dealing with quality of the security, strength of ownership and management, and market conditions and trends. This information seems more difficult than producing data via the computer, leading the less-experienced underwriter to the tendency to slight his consideration of the qualitative factors and to place too much weight on the computer-generated information.

Having considered a number of factors of importance in office mortgage underwriting and financing, the loan underwriter must keep in mind that the desired result—a mortgage loan with a principal amount and terms that are reasonably satisfactory to both borrower and lender—is probably nearly as much art as science.

ABOUT THE AUTHOR

Glen E. Coverdale, CRE, is executive vice president, Metropolitan Life Insurance Company. He is responsible for corporate planning, quality and strategy, and real estate counseling, as well as for the company's mortgage banking subsidiary. He headed MetLife's real estate and agricultural invest-ment activities for twelve years. Coverdale is active in a number of real estate organizations, including the Real Estate Board of New York, the Realty Foundation of New York, and the Urban Land Institute, and is a member of the advisory board of the Real Estate Institute of New York University.

CHAPTER

24

RESTRUCTURING AND WORKOUTS OF OFFICE BUILDINGS

by Stan Ross and
James R. Giuliano

INTRODUCTION

In a market with widespread office overbuilding, a credit crunch, sluggish leasing activity and other problems such as occurred in the early 1990s, often the cash flows from office development projects or existing properties are not sufficient to service the mortgage debt and meet operating expenses. If office developers or other owners default on the mortgage loans on these problem projects or properties, lenders may foreclose on the properties or accept them from the debtors in lieu of foreclosure.

Lenders have another option, which is to agree to loan workouts that give developers and owners additional time and opportunity to achieve a turnaround of their problem projects or properties. A workout plan has three basic parts:

1. To restructure the loans collateralizing the developer's problem projects or properties. A variety of restructuring plans may be used, depending on the particular circumstances and requirements of the developer and the lenders. There is no standard workout plan; each workout is unique.
2. To realize the maximum value from the development, management and sale of the workout projects or properties.
3. To determine how the developer and his lenders will share in that value.

Usually, the earlier a problem is recognized and acted on, the more easily it can be managed. This stitch-in-time philosophy is as valid for troubled real estate as it is for recurrent chest pains. The first step, then, in evolving a workout plan is the recognition by all parties that a serious problem exists, one that will not self-correct. The second step is to determine, by careful and objective analysis, the underlying causes of the project's shortcomings. Often they will be obvious: the expected market response simply did not materialize; serious construction delays increased costs far beyond the budget; overbuilding and competition from other buildings are ruinous. At other times the causes may be more subtle: the leasing agent is inept or has a conflict; the building's image and reputation are suffering because of a mechanical or cosmetic problem; tenant complaints are not being heeded. Perhaps a project has been free of these kinds of difficulties. It has fully met its developer's expectations. Instead, the problem lies in macroeconomics—real estate values have declined substantially and the property is now overfinanced so that the maturing first mortgage cannot be replaced.

A property's owner will normally be the first to become aware of such problems. While his instinct may dictate otherwise, he should make his lender (and other creditors) aware of them sooner rather than later. Creditors clearly will not be happy to learn of their debtors' problems, but they will appreciate candor and timely notice. Moreover, the borrower benefits from the lender's participating in the early analysis of the problem because a joint decision on the best course of action will be reached more quickly.

THE OWNER'S OPTIONS

The owner of a troubled project has various alternatives:

- Sell the property
- Modify existing debt
- Obtain refinancing
- Allow the lender to foreclose
- Provide a deed in lieu of foreclosure
- File for bankruptcy protection
- Develop a nonjudicial workout plan

If there are personal guarantees for payment of debt, the abandonment alternative may require negotiation as the owner attempts to reduce or eliminate that liability and possibly improve his tax position in exchange for various benefits he might be able to offer his creditors.

Whichever alternative he chooses, the owner will need competent real estate and legal counsel, tax advisers and accountants. In more complex situations involving several properties and different classes of creditors, the owner should retain an experienced workout specialist. For any plan to be adopted, it is essential that the consenting parties believe that it is realistic and based on established facts (rather than wishful thinking), and that everyone's position be understood and given proper weight. The workout specialist should not necessarily be the debtor's advocate but a neutral party whose objective is to establish a fair and reasonable plan. If the parties agree, however, there is no reason why a real estate advisor or accountant cannot act as an advocate for either party.

Bankruptcy

Unless a project is so deeply under water that neither the owner nor any junior creditors have a hope of salvaging equity, a workout should be attempted. All parties will generally have more to gain from a voluntary agreement than from a reorganization under Chapter XI of the Bankruptcy Act or a liquidation under Chapter VII. Bankruptcy proceedings can generate huge expenses and consume vast amounts of time and energy. Control may be lost. In the end, the parties may not agree on a reorganization plan, thus requiring the assets to be liquidated, with the creditors receiving no more and possibly much less than in a workout.

Despite these disadvantages, the owner may prefer to file for bankruptcy for tax reasons. In a voluntary workout plan that includes forgiveness of debt, the owner (if he is not insolvent) may be deemed to have received income equal to the debt reduction, possibly resulting in a taxable gain for which there would be no offsetting cash. By proceeding with the same plan through a court-directed Chapter XI restructuring, the owner may avoid showing such a phantom gain. A second reason for filing is that some creditors will not agree to the terms of a voluntary plan, hoping to be paid off at a higher rate. In cases where at least 50% of the creditors representing two-thirds of the debt will consent to a restructure plan, the debtor will be able to file a bankruptcy petition under what is known as a *prepackaged plan*. This could result in a relatively brief period in the bankruptcy court, perhaps six months compared to perhaps two years where there is no plan at the time of filing. However, some legal authorities caution that prepackaged plans may not always work out as anticipated, especially where groups opposing them are militant.

Even if an owner wants to offer a workout plan, his lender may make the first move by commencing foreclosure. This is most likely to occur when the borrower has fallen into arrears on the loan payments without any explanation or advance warning to the lender. In this event the borrower may have little choice but to counter the lender's action by filing a petition in bankruptcy, which will automatically stay the foreclosure. Generally, however, a lender will not begin by filing for foreclosure unless he feels that negotiations will be useless because there is no equity, or the borrower is acting unreasonably, or is dishonest. Similarly, the borrower will usually not start out by actually filing. The mere threat of doing so is usually a strong enough incentive to bring his creditors to the negotiating table.

Deeds in Lieu of Foreclosure

When a borrower determines that his property is not worth more than its debts and there is no realistic possibility of future operations improving substantially, he still may have something of value for which he can trade; namely, his possession and ownership. Under the U.S. legal system costs and delays are the norm, not the exception, and to wrest title and control from an unwilling owner can prove expensive. Some states, primarily those in the farm belt, allow parties whose titles have been foreclosed upon to remain in possession for a number of months. Accordingly, borrowers can often negotiate a price at which they will cede title and control without resort to their full legal rights. This may include the lender's waiver or settlement of its right to pursue the borrower's personal guarantee of the real estate debt.

LENDERS' CONCERNS

Because of the difficult real estate environment in which lenders have been operating, many have adopted regular procedures for dealing more efficiently with loans that are in default or have been categorized as substandard. Some institutions have formed specialized units, staffed by experienced personnel, to handle these situations.

Lenders generally prefer to deal internally with a troubled real estate portfolio. However, in periods of market distress, they may become overwhelmed by the increased volume of loan restructurings and workouts required by the sharp increase in delinquencies and the consequent need to consider foreclosure. In these periods, they may be required to engage various specialized consultants to assist them in resolving for each troubled loan the basic question of whether to restructure or to foreclose.

Lenders may engage a real estate consultant to act as an advisor in an overall analysis of the delinquent portion of the total portfolio with the objective of identifying those loans on which a quick decision must be made. The consultant may evaluate the status of the loans by a so-called "desk" study after reviewing the most recent appraisals, with or without field inspection of the properties. In some cases, the consultant may be asked to assist in preparing a debt restructuring plan. These consultants have varied backgrounds but are generally experienced developers, appraisers, managers or brokers. Most large accounting firms now employ staff who are accredited and competent in real estate valuation, and are also active in this field.

Loan Restructuring vs. Foreclosure

Restructuring negotiations represent tense moments for the lender and borrower. The borrower's career and business reputation may be at stake.

The lender must balance the professional managerial competence of the borrower against the possibility of a smaller loss if the lender proceeds with a foreclosure action as opposed to a loan restructuring in which, as will be discussed, the lender invariably must make concessions such as interest rate and amortization reductions, or the advance of additional funds to cure real estate tax or ground rent defaults. The lender's natural inclination is to protect its interests by foreclosure, yet this may be the worst possible solution.

If foreclosure is chosen, the lender may face the need to complete construction on partially built office buildings, or to engage in an extensive renovation and rehabilitation effort. In such cases, the advice of an experienced general contractor is critical to determine the capital cost needed to complete or to rehabilitate the office building. Marketing specialists then must estimate the rental value of the space and the time required to achieve normal occupancy, generally in the 88% to 92% range, but adjustable depending on local market conditions. The lender must prepare an internal appraisal or engage a fee appraiser to establish the building's then market value.

A vexatious concern for lenders with real estate owned (REO) office buildings is the need to custom design and construct the tenant interiors as the space is gradually leased. Cost control becomes critical. How much cost can the REO absorb if it is to be returned to viable operation when tenants demand interior installations that far exceed the budget? A complex relationship is required among the lender and space planners, architects, constructors, leasing specialists and building managers. The typical mortgage lender is uncomfortable as a workout specialist and wants to restore its liquidity through re-sale as quickly as possible, sometimes prematurely.

A lender's attitude in dealing with a particular borrower will depend on a number of factors such as their past relationship, the magnitude of the borrower's other real estate problems, the ability of his organization to continue managing the asset properly, and the size and importance of the loan relative to the lender's overall portfolio. If the lender is itself in financial jeopardy or under government supervision, its negotiating posture may be less flexible than usual, since its policies might be dictated by regulators unconcerned with a longstanding lender-borrower relationship.

Most lenders are normally willing to consider a workout plan if the following preliminary conditions can be met:

1. There are reasonable grounds to believe that a workout will produce better financial results than an immediate liquidation.
2. The borrower is honest, is acting in good faith, has divulged all relevant facts, is not merely playing for time in the vain hope that his problem will disappear, and will not divert cash or other assets from the project.
3. The lender has confidence in the borrower's ability to manage the property and such management adds value to the process.

Workout Issues

A basic fear of every secured lender is that after a long period of cooperation with the borrower and perhaps other creditors, no plan can be agreed to, with the result that the lender has lost precious time in gaining control of the asset and faces further delays through a bankruptcy filing. To avoid this possible trap, the lender might reach an initial understanding with the borrower that a foreclosure suit will be started but held in abeyance until either a workout plan is adopted or the agreed-upon deadline for its negotiation has been reached.

A common issue during the workout period concerns interim control of the property during negotiations. Lenders are always concerned that cash-short owners may find other, more pressing uses for the revenues than prompt payment of the property's operating expenses or debt service. If left unchecked, such cash diversions could lead to serious erosions of value for a lender. This does not necessarily mean that the lender will want to assume direct responsibility for operating the property. It may not have the staff for the job; moreover, such control could lead to later charges of mismanagement.

One solution is for the lender to exercise rights that might exist in the documents or petition a court for appointment of a receiver who, acting as agent for the court, collects and pays out funds. Another method used by some lenders is creation of a lock-box arrangement whereby all collections are placed into an account over which the lender exercises control, with withdrawals permitted only to pay preapproved budget items and to make other payments specifically allowed by the lender.

Lenders must be cautious about accepting deeds in lieu of foreclosure, since the borrower's title may be unmarketable at the time of conveyance because of other liens that have attached or because of pending lawsuits for which *lis pendens* have been filed against the property. Typically, a lender will take title in a nominee entity and keep its mortgage lien alive so that it may later complete the foreclosure if doing so is necessary to wipe out junior encumbrances.

The lender, of course, may not be prepared to manage the property; it may seriously underestimate the resources required—in money and management time and effort. These are resources that might be invested more profitably in other endeavors, such as developing new lending opportunities; also, the lender may expose the institution to other obligations such as environmental claims. By contrast, the developer, if he has a successful track record in owning and managing some healthy properties, may be better qualified to manage the office property. So it may be in the lender's best interest not to foreclose and to permit the developer to continue managing the property while a workout program is completed.

The lender's attitude toward a workout may also be influenced by the accounting treatment that a settlement would be given. A basic rule that institutional lenders must follow is Financial Accounting Standards No. 15 (FASB 15): *Accounting by Debtors and Creditors for Troubled Debt Restructuring*. In general, FASB 15 requires lenders to recharacterize a restructured loan if it is determined that neither the borrower nor junior creditors have any substantial remaining equity in the project. Then, even if the lender keeps its loan outstanding and the borrower is still operating the property, the lender must report the restructured loan as if it had actually taken title to the property. This concept is known as an *in-substance foreclosure*. Accordingly, if the lender must treat the loan as though it were foreclosed real estate it may not be as willing to consider a restructuring.

Participation Loans

It is a common practice, especially in the short-term lending field, for a lender that originated a large loan to sell participations in it to other lenders. Where such a loan exists on troubled real estate, dealing with these other participants can prove to be a difficult experience for the principal lender. Normally there will be a written participation agreement setting out the rights of the parties and the duties of the principal or lead lender in administering the credit. Usually the lead lender is not able to do such things as forgive debt, agree to defer payments or release any security without the approval of the participants. Accordingly, in attempting to effect a workout the lead lender should try to keep the participants fully informed and to obtain their consents for each major step taken. To proceed without such approvals could invite later charges of negligence or imprudence, even though the participation agreement gave the lead lender wide discretion. The participants, for their part, may feel frustrated at having to assume passive roles, especially if they feel the lead lender is being too accommodating. Some participants, as a tactic, may disagree with virtually all proposed modifications in the hopes of being bought out at par.

Other Creditors

Many secured creditors become very concerned with bankruptcy filings, not only on account of the delays and expense involved, but also because of a belief that the general tenor of bankruptcy administration is to favor debtors and junior classes of creditors over senior lien holders. For example, the court may confirm a restructuring plan that breaks down the senior loan into secured and unsecured positions, with the latter being the amount of the loan in excess of the appraised value of the property. Further, the unsecured portion may become "impaired," that is, it will be paid over time at less than par or with an interest rate lower than that provided for in the parties' agreement. Where such a plan is confirmed over a creditor's objections, it is known as a *cram-down*.

Under the so-called cram-down provisions of the bankruptcy code, the court may confirm a plan even if some classes of impaired creditors (or equity holders) have not accepted it, provided the plan meets the Chapter XI confirmation standards and is fair and equitable. Except for specific debts that the bankruptcy court determines are not discharged by the plan (such as unpaid income taxes), a confirmed plan binds various parties in interest to it, regardless of whether the claim is impaired under the plan and any creditor, security holder or general partner has accepted it. Except as provided in the plan or the order confirming it, confirmation discharges the debt from all preconfirmation claims and may terminate the rights and interests of equity holders (or general partners).

Under the cram-down provisions, value may not be distributed to junior classes unless the senior nonaccepting class has received full value equal to the claim. A secured lender may be "crammed-down" provided that, among other requirements, the plan is fair and equitable to it. This is the case if:

1. The secured creditor(s) retains the lien(s)...and receives deferred cash payments having a present value as of the effective date of the plan at least equal to the value of the creditor's interest in the estate's interest in the property.
2. The collateral is sold, the lien attaches to the proceeds, and the lien on proceeds is treated either under alternative one or under alternative three.
3. The secured creditor receives the "indubitable equivalent" of its claim. Depending on the valuation issues and cash flow, the strategy of using these provisions in a single asset case may not be feasible.

TYPES OF WORKOUT PLANS

While there can be no standard form of workout plan since the facts of every situation differ and require a specialized solution, all plans will attempt to reach the same basic goals, namely to:

1. Provide the owner with current relief from debt service requirements.
2. Set out steps to be taken to realize value from the assets over an agreed-upon period.
3. Establish how creditors and equity owners will share in that value.

Basic prerequisites for development of any successful plan are full disclosures to the creditors of all relevant facts concerning (a) the debtor's financial picture, including the realizable cash values of his assets and the amounts and terms of his debts and other liabilities, (b) the legal positions of all creditors with respect to the debtor and the real estate, and (c) the present and future values of the real estate that is the subject of the plan. Creditors will not be at all receptive if they believe the debtor is less than open and honest and not fully presenting his situation. Even though the debtor may not be personally liable for debt repayment, a creditor will agree to a forbearance only if he knows that the debtor, assuming he is financially able, is also making some sacrifices for the common good.

The plan, when drafted, must show that by the end of the stated period the creditors will realize greater value than the amount they could obtain from a current liquidation. If not, there is no point to adopting the plan. There are many reasons why a given project may be in trouble. If its difficulties can be cured by more equity capital or by temporary relief from debt service, a workout plan may be the best solution. However, if the problem is caused by long-term declines in value in the real estate markets, then the absence of any clear solution may dictate an early liquidation. The real estate problem should be analyzed objectively by competent, disinterested professionals; and proposals should be based on reasonably provable facts, not blind optimism. But even the conclusion that a plan is not feasible may produce a valuable result since it might accelerate a transfer to the lender without further delay and expense.

Not only must a plan show that an orderly disposition will result in greater values than would a current sale, it must also describe in detail the means by which this result will be achieved. It must show how the momentum necessary to carry out the plan will be created and maintained. For example, if the borrower will continue to operate the property, where will he get the necessary working capital to maintain his going-concern status? How will property deficits be funded? What other cash needs will the borrower have that may not be related to the property? The answers to such questions must be apparent from reading a workout plan.

The plan should also consider income tax effects on the borrower. For example, if debt is to be partially forgiven or the property conveyed to a new entity, with a concomitant tax gain, the means for its payment should be established.

In entering workout negotiations, the developer must decide what he wants to accomplish in the workout. In general, he wants time to achieve a turnaround of his problem properties, the money to do so and the chance to realize a greater return from a workout than from other alternatives. But it may not be possible to structure a workout to meet all of a developer's needs. For example, it may be impossible in some cases to achieve a workout of all of a developer's troubled properties, so the developer may apply triage by negotiating workouts on the properties with the best prospects of recovery and letting the others go into bankruptcy. In some cases, the developer may seek workouts for properties that he wants to save from bankruptcy for personal as well as business reasons.

The Workout Plan

One of the developer's first concerns is to get the cash to meet the properties' operating expenses during the workout. Because the properties' cash flows may be insufficient, or nonexistent, the necessary cash may have to come from sources other than the properties themselves. Financing of the workout must be arranged.

The financing can be structured in various ways, depending on the condition of the properties, the requirements of the developer, the requirements of lenders or other sources of financing, and the circumstances of the particular workout. In some cases, the developer and lenders may negotiate a restructuring of the existing mortgage debt on the workout properties. Possible restructurings include the following.

Temporary Reduction of Debt Service

If the problem is only a temporary cash flow shortage that is expected to be alleviated in the future (for example, reduced income caused by rent-free occupancy for new tenants in the early months of leases), the lender might be willing to accept a lower current rate of interest or abate amortization for a time, with the deferred amounts being paid in later periods or on maturity. In reviewing such a proposal the lender will want to ascertain that the problem is indeed temporary and not the onset of a new, lower rent structure for the building. If it is, the project is likely to be faced with chronic cash shortages and the temporary debt service reduction will not cure the problem.

Permanent Reduced Debt Service or Partial Forgiveness of Debt

Where the cash flow deficiency is determined to be relatively permanent, caused by a significant decline in rents over the entire market, the result will be a decline in value of the real estate. In such cases the borrower's equity may be wiped out entirely. In this case the primary reason a lender would even consider a restructuring rather than foreclosure would be a determination that ownership would be more costly. For example, a foreclosing lender would have to pay for new tenant installations or correct environmental problems, whereas the borrower or a third-party purchaser might agree to fund these additional amounts. The lender may find that in such a case it would be better off reducing the interest rate or even writing off a part of the loan. Where it has already established an accounting reserve, such a decision may be less painful to reach.

Loan Repayment at a Discount

Where there has been a permanent reduction of value, a mortgagee may entertain an offer to accept less than par for its loan and to get quick cash.

In fact, lenders may be more willing to consider this alternative than to forgive part of the debt since a sale will take them entirely out of the problem with no further concern over whether the restructured loan will default again in the future. From a borrower's viewpoint, debt forgiveness or purchase by the borrower of the loan at a discount will create a tax gain that may involve a liability.

Conversion to a Cash Flow Mortgage

This is a fairly common type of restructuring in cases where net revenue does not support the property's debt service. A lender may agree to such a plan when it has confidence in the borrower's ability to operate the property and sees no advantage in assuming possession itself, and when the facts support the case for a rising future value. The basic agreement provides that the lender will receive all cash flow not needed for the property's operations, to be applied to the loan. Generally this will be the same amount the lender would receive if it were the owner. While it is simple in concept, there are many points to be negotiated in this kind of arrangement, such as:

- Whether the borrower will be allowed to deduct a management fee to offset overhead
- Whether capital reserves will be allowed as part of an operating budget
- Whether the borrower's affiliates may be employed and receive payment for their services
- Whether excess cash flow in the period may offset deficits in another period
- How emergency expenditures are to be handled
- Whether the borrower may retain amounts to pay income taxes on the property's earnings

In addition, the developer may be required to make minimum monthly payments to bring the cash mortgage interest rate to a minimum defined level.

Granting the Lender Partial Ownership

While listed here as a separate restructuring device, this is normally used in conjunction with one of the other plans in which a lender agrees to accept less than it is entitled to under its original loan. Again, the appropriate situation is one where the property's future looks much brighter than its current status and the borrower remains in control. The lender is given an equity interest in compensation for its concessions. The ownership position may be given as a percentage of cash flow above a stated threshold or as a provision that the lender will receive a percentage of future sale proceeds. Another variation would be to grant an option to the lender to purchase an interest in the property at a fixed price, exercisable at some future date. One concern that a lender will have with the concept of ownership is that it may be unenforceable on the grounds that a mortgagee is entitled only to the repayment of its debt and can acquire ownership only through foreclosure laws. However, careful legal drafting should overcome that potential flaw.

Dividing a Single Mortgage into Two Liens

Where a lender is willing to remain as a mortgagee but dislikes the unattractive prospect of carrying the delinquent mortgage on its books, a partial solution may be to restructure the mortgage by dividing it into two separate instruments, constituting first and second liens. The property's cash flow must be sufficient to service the first lien adequately at market rates. The second lien could be structured in one of several ways to receive the balance of the property's cash flow, if any. It could have a fixed, reduced interest rate, become a cash flow mortgage or even a "zero" mortgage, with all interest payable at maturity. This type of plan would give the lender relief in the sense that the first lien would be "good" and perhaps capable of being sold or securitized; only the junior lien would remain "bad." While the technique may be criticized as little more than cosmetic treatment, it does help the lender by reducing the ratio of troubled loans in its portfolio.

Giving the Lender Additional Collateral

A lender may agree to forebear if its deferred payments can be secured by other collateral the borrower may have available. Such a plan will not help the lender if the borrower was insolvent at the time the new collateral was pledged and subsequently files a bankruptcy petition or is placed into bankruptcy by another creditor, since the pledge will be considered a preferential transfer and voidable under bankruptcy law. When the developer has multiple problems, providing collateral to a single lender may not be beneficial or fair to the other lenders. Ultimately, the collateral necessary to satisfy all lenders is exhausted and the developer is left without a solution to more global issues.

Raising Additional Capital

A fundamental purpose of workout planning is raising new capital. The most likely sources for that will be those parties that had previously invested in the project through subordinated loans or equity contributions and risk up to total investment loss on foreclosure of a senior position. Unless they had given their guarantees of payment, normally they will have no legal obligation to place additional moneys into a failing property. However, if the workout plan can demonstrate that the new capital would save their positions, they may be willing to advance the additional needed amounts.

Negotiations between senior lenders and junior investors over additional capital infusions need not be completely one-sided in favor of the former. The prospect of new capital is a powerful incentive for the senior to grant some accommodation. Depending on the particular situation, the fresh moneys may be given priority status for repayment.

As the real estate recession of the 1990s grew, so did the businesses of specialists who were capitalized to make investments in troubled real estate. These "vulture funds" look for well-conceived and well-located properties that can be acquired at prices substantially below replacement cost and promise eventual returns of more than twice the norm. They will also acquire defaulted mortgages on such properties directly from the lenders. While such funds can hardly be considered a white knight for an owner seeking to salvage his equity, they can be a suitable source for the lender wishing for a quick exit from his real estate problem.

Example of a Workout Plan

The following is an outline prepared by a real estate company (called the developer here) which, through various corporations and partnerships, held a portfolio of land and improved properties, including several under development and in lease-up. Each property was separately owned by a limited partnership set up for that purpose and encumbered by a first mortgage and sometimes by a junior lien as well. The developer used bank lines of credit to supply working capital. The creditors of the developer included fully secured lenders, lenders relying on guarantees of corporate holding companies controlled by the developer, and unsecured creditors who supplied working capital. Owing to a recessionary environment and overbuilding in some of its markets, the developer experienced significant cash flow shortfalls in its operation and could not adequately refinance its maturing loans or meet certain credit tests in its unsecured lines.

The plan was prepared after a thorough, independent study of the developer's financial situation and of the prospects for the individual properties in light of local real estate market conditions.

> **Duration of Plan**: Four years.
>
> **Liquidation Values:** The plan projected the probable financial results from (a) a forced liquidation of each asset and (b) an orderly liquidation over the duration of the plan, which provided time for lease-up and a return to more normal market conditions. The forced liquidation assumed a sale of property "as is," under the then-existing market conditions. In a few cases (especially the land holdings), an orderly liquidation did not produce substantially higher values, often because of burdensome operating deficits or vast overbuilding in the market. Accordingly, the plan proposed that these assets be turned over to the

secured creditors at the outset, with any deficiency between the debt and appraised value allowed as an unsecured claim.

Asset Management: The developer continued to be responsible for management of the properties, for completing those under development and for selling all the assets in an orderly manner, generally after occupancy became stabilized. The developer was allowed a fee of one percent of gross cash proceeds to offset costs of its administration.

Borrowing Term: Interest on all borrowing accrued at original contract rates and not at any higher default rates provided for in the notes. Maturity dates of all loans were extended to the full duration of the plan, with the developer having the right to repay any loan in whole or in part without penalty.

Prepayment Priorities:

(a) Secured Creditors:

1st Source—Cash flow from the related property's operations, net of operating expenses, and from net proceeds of the property's disposition. Junior creditors' rights were subordinate to those of senior creditors

2nd Source—Value of or cash flow from any additional assets pledged as collateral, upon their liquidation

3rd Source—General assets of the maker of the note

4th Source—General assets of the note's guarantor, if any

(b) Unsecured Creditors:

1st Source—General assets of the maker of the note

2nd Source—General assets of the guarantor of the note, if any

3rd Source—Pro rata share of the collateral pool (see below)

Additional Financing: Secured creditors were asked to provide all additional financing necessary to improve a property under development, such as completion of base building or installation of tenant improvements, and to fund any operating shortfalls. Junior creditors were asked to provide all funds before senior creditors, as well as to make up any debt service shortfall of the senior debt.

Unsecured creditors were asked to provide necessary working capital for asset management purposes, with the proviso that they would receive a $2 priority claim against the collateral pool for every $1 advanced.

The developer agreed to advance a specified amount for working capital, to be recovered from the collateral pool but subordinated to the unsecured creditors' claims; that is, there would be no recovery until all unsecured creditors had been paid in full.

Trade creditors supplying goods and services to the developer or the properties were to be paid on a current basis from working capital or a property's cash flow.

Collateral pool: The net cash flow from operations and sales that were not otherwise committed (the plan estimated these on a quarterly basis) were placed into a pool from which distributions were made quarterly in the following order of priority:

1st—To the trade creditors not paid directly from working capital or specific properties

2nd—Pro rata to the unsecured creditors who advanced current working capital, on a 2:1 basis, with the excess being applied to their prior outstanding loan

3rd—To the developer to the extent of its working capital advances

4th—On a pro rata basis to the secured creditors who had a deficiency remaining after exhausting their prior sources of payment

Bankruptcy Contingency: If the developer filed a petition or was otherwise placed into bankruptcy, the creditors agreed to consent to a liquidation plan similar to this plan unless the developer had not acted in good faith. If certain creditors under a bankruptcy plan received a greater share than they would have under this plan, they agreed to make adjustments with the other creditors to conform to the provisions of the plan.

CONCLUSION

No workout is perfect, meeting all the needs and expectations of the developer, his lenders and other creditors. Every workout is painful, requiring sacrifices on the part of each party in the interests of the common good. Even so, a workout may be a better alternative for everyone than the investor's filing for reorganization under Chapter XI of the Bankruptcy Act. These bankruptcy proceedings can be time-consuming and expensive, fail to result in an agreement on a reorganization plan, and leave the parties with no more and possibly much less than if they had attempted a workout. For a workout to succeed, however, there must be trust and cooperation among all the parties. Considering the potential benefits of a workout, they may have good reasons to cooperate.

ABOUT THE AUTHORS

Stan Ross, CPA, is managing partner of Kenneth Leventhal & Company, a national CPA firm specializing in real estate and financial services. He is recognized for his expertise in solving complex financial and structural problems relating to real estate development and investment transactions. A frequent lecturer at the University of Southern California and New York University, Ross often appears before government policy-making and regulatory bodies. He is a vice president of the Urban Land Institute. Ross is a graduate of Bernard Baruch College.

James R. Giuliano, CPA, is a partner in the New York office of Kenneth Leventhal & Company, a national accounting and consulting firm specializing in the real estate and financial services industries. He focuses his practice in the area of corporate reorganizations, bankruptcies and work-outs. Giuliano has been involved in the restructurings of some of the nation's largest developers. Giuliano received a BS from Babson College, Wellesley, Mass.

CHAPTER

25

ARRANGING CREATIVE MORTGAGE FINANCING

In an entrepreneurial, high risk field such as investment real estate, learning from others' experience is vital to survival. Presented in this chapter are five actual transactions illustrating the creative use of mortgage financing. In each case, the author(s) participated in the transaction as a principal, broker, consultant or financier. A sixth section provides an explanation of securitization financing, which will undoubtedly be an increasingly important financing source in the future.

THE FINANCING OF THE GENERAL MOTORS BUILDING

by John R. White

In the spring of 1981, long-term Treasury bonds were being offered at 13.5%. The Consumer Price Index was at 13%. Although the Pan Am Building had been sold in mid-June 1980 for an electrifying record price, the euphoria was short-lived under the impact of these extraordinarily high interest rates and CPI levels. Investor confidence had rapidly receded and market uncertainty was widespread.

At this inauspicious moment, General Motors, which even then was suffering from foreign competition as well as the high cost of money, decided to offer its headquarters building at 767 Fifth Avenue for sale. It turned to a counseling firm, Landauer Associates, for advice on the disposition. Somewhat reluctantly, because of the suspension of market activity due to the credit crunch, the counselor at Landauer prepared an offering brochure and planned the sale strategy for this premium real estate.

Located between East 58th and East 59th Streets, this handsome 50-story building with its white marble facade designed by Edward Durrell Stone contained 1,637,000 rentable square feet. Because of the 80,000 square foot plot, the building was set back on Fifth Avenue. Together with the Grand Army Plaza facing it to the west, its positioning provided a welcome breath of open space.

Technically the General Motors Building was a leasehold. The land was owned by a major insurance company under a 1,000-year lease that had 980 years to run at a flat rental rate. For all practical purposes, the market regarded the building leasehold as real estate. There would be no obstacle to financing it to the maximum with the extremely long-term lease.

A Strategy for Raising Cash

By mid-1981, it was evident that the sale market for this prized real estate had temporarily disappeared. The consultant was unable to elicit any interest in a purchase. But General Motors wanted to raise cash for its manufacturing facilities. Recalling a secondary mortgage transaction with a separate purchase option it had previously negotiated, the consultant asked GM's law firm, Weil, Gotchal & Manges, to prepare a brief of the various ways in which capital could be raised without a direct sale. The strategy finally conceived was for GM to obtain a loan and to grant the lender an option to buy the real estate at a specified date for the amount of the loan. Title to the real estate would then pass from General Motors to the lender, but GM would be completely free of debt after the option was exercised.

GM wanted the maximum possible loan. The all-cash appraised value of the building was $435 million, inclusive of a first mortgage with a remaining balance of $70 million. Projecting the net operating income for 10 years, the consultant concluded that the real estate could be worth as much as $750 million at the end of that period. GM itself was paying a premium rental of $55 per rentable square foot. It was believed that substantial rent increases would be obtained as the building's leases expired over the 10-year loan period.

The immediate problem was that the cash flow after ground rent and debt service on the first mortgage initially was only $17 million. There was no way a loan could be structured without placing GM in a deficit position. It was nevertheless attractive to GM to obtain a loan significantly higher than the current market value of the real estate. The purchase option on its building was the lure to obtain the financing. Of course, GM would have to accept recourse debt, that is, the company could not use a shell corporation.

Any lender would insist that the loan bear the signature of GM's principal company, a very strong subsidiary, or both.

The consultant determined that a loan of $500 million was plausible, provided that the interest cost, despite the high interest rate environment, was no more than 10% and the loan would have a non-prepayable maturity of 10 years. GM's discounted internal rate of return cost on an after-tax basis would be 8.5%. A loan transaction was structured on an unsecured note basis, that is, not collateralized by the real estate. GM and General Motors Acceptance Corporation would be the note issuers. Since this was a loan rather than a sale, there was no federal or New York City capital gains tax to pay immediately. Furthermore, there would be no local mortgage recording tax since the notes were unsecured. It was decided that the option to purchase the property at no cost (other than the lender's forgiveness of the debt) would be exercised on January 2, 1991, one year prior to the due date of the notes, on one year's prior notice.

An Issue of Control

A possible flaw in the transaction was GM's reluctance to surrender control of the building management to the lender. It was difficult for GM to accept that the future purchase option in return for the loan entitled the lender to manage the property in the interim. The lender's argument for operating control carried special force because both parties had to concede that no lender would have made the loan unless it believed that the real estate would be worth $500 million, and likely considerably more, in 10 years. Why lend if ownership was not contemplated?

GM was concerned that the lender would not manage the building in a first-rate manner. It feared that a recession or depression could adversely affect the office building, causing the lender to reject the purchase option. In this instance, GM would be saddled with the debt, but would still have the real estate.

Another concern of GM was the knowledge that in the first year after the loan was made, the deficit would be $33 million ($17 million equity cash flow less $50 million in note interest). However, this deficit would be reduced considerably as expiring leases were renewed or vacated space was re-rented at what was assumed would be significantly higher levels. By the consulting intermediary's calculations, cash flow would not turn positive until 1989. Thus it was essential to calculate the true cost of the transaction to judge whether GM was justified in proceeding with the borrowing. The calculation was based on loan proceeds less interest cost, operating cash flow deficit, loss of capital gain potential in 10 years' depreciation benefits, and payment of assumed deferred capital gains taxes in 10 years, offset by GM's use of the capital.

After study, GM was persuaded that its after-tax discounted cost was 8.5%. With interest rates then in the 15%-20% range, the cost seemed relatively inexpensive, especially since the loan proceeds were to be used to build a new plant that presumably would produce profits for GM.

The Final Agreement

The final note agreement can be summarized as follows:

Borrower:	General Motors Corporation and GM Acceptance Corporation
Lender:	Corporate Property Investors, AT&T Pension Fund and Kuwait Investment Company
Amount:	$500 Million
Interest Rate:	10%
Amortization:	None
Due Date:	December 31, 1991
Purchase Option:	Exercisable January 2, 1991, at no cost
Debt Status:	Canceled at exercise of option
Market Value of Real Estate:	$435 Million in mid-1981
Estimated Market Value on 1/2/91:	$750 Million
Discounted IRR to Lender/Buyer:	14.5% (20-year projection)
After-tax Cost to GM:	8.5%
GM Lease:	$55 per rentable square foot for 10 years
Management:	Corporate Property Investors on behalf of lender syndicate
Closing Date:	December 30, 1991

The implications of this financing were unique. GM avoided an immediate tax burden at a time when it was critical to preserve its cash. There was no recording tax because the note was unsecured. A short form of option agreement was prepared and filed, which kept the details of the transaction from the public record. The lender was able to obtain management control because the loan was regarded as tantamount to a sale. In retrospect, it was an excellent transaction for both parties. GM obtained inexpensive financing for use in its business of $65 million more than the property's appraised value. The lender received an excellent, tax-free return of 10% while it waited for the exercise option date. During this nine-year period, net operating income continued to rise.

Postscripts to the Financing

There were several interesting postscripts to this unusual financing. An uncommon provision in the ground lease permitted Equitable Life, the lessor, to approve all occupancy leases over a certain square footage. The lender regarded this as an unwarranted intrusion into the financial and operational management of the investment. In 1987, prodded in part by another bidder, the lender paid Equitable $23.5 million for the 80,000 square feet of land underlying the building. This price gave the lender only a 4.25% return on the land rent of $1 million per year, but it ensured the lender complete operating control when the option was exercised.

The lender did in fact exercise its option on January 2, 1991, putting it on a path to a 14.5% or higher IRR over a 20-year period. No one could have foreseen the depth of the general and real estate recession which beset New York as the exercise option date grew near. Office rents rose only modestly over the 10 years, far less than the projection. Net operating income probably was considerably less than the amount necessary to sustain the $750 million value estimate made nine years earlier. Nevertheless, the net income was more than sufficient to support the lender's purchase price of $500 million. Net income was estimated to be $50 million, free of mortgage debt, at the exercise date, compared with only $25 million in 1981. Even with the higher capitalization rates occasioned by the recession and over-supply, the real estate's value at the exercise date was estimated at between $550 and $600 million.

FINANCING 7 WORLD TRADE CENTER

by Jerome B. Alenick

In the 1960s the Port Authority of New York and New Jersey began developing the World Trade Center complex in lower Manhattan. After the 4 million square foot twin towers and ancillary small buildings in the complex were completed, the Port Authority (PA) decided for public relations and political reasons that 7 World Trade Center (WTC) should be built and owned by private developers; the site would be leased to them for 99 years. Since there were no real estate taxes on PA-owned land, the same advantageous PILOT (payment in lieu of taxes) agreement with the City of New York, already in place for the twin towers, would apply to the new building. The site had several other advantages as well. Because of the Consolidated Edison substation in the building base, tenants would be able to purchase high-tension power at substantial savings. No sales tax would be levied on materials used in the construction and completion of tenant space. Tenants also had the use of a 2,000 car parking garage under the World Trade Center complex. In addition, there were many amenities adjacent to the structure, including a 825-room hotel, numerous restaurants including the renowned Windows on the World, 350,000 square feet of retail space, and a vast and comprehensive subway and interstate train facility within the complex.

The Building Concept

Interest in bidding for the site leasehold was keen, and 10 proposals were received by the Port Authority on April 7, 1980. On December 31, 1980, 7 World Trade Company was awarded the lease to develop the one million square foot building. The developer convinced the PA that the financial services companies the building would serve required larger floors than the 25,000 square feet for which foundations were installed. The PA agreed to permit 48,000 square foot floor plates. Over several years, as plans were

No open-ended construction loan could be found for a speculative project of the scope of 7 World Trade Center, so creative financing was required. A stand-by commitment from a consortium of five banks provided the funds to begin construction.

promulgated, the PA consented to a larger building than was originally intended, as it would receive additional ground rent in proportion to the increase in the building's size. This factor was based initially on the square footage occupied by the tenants as the building was leased, to a maximum established by the building size.

The World Trade Center was fully developed by the time 7 WTC was ready to be built, and the PA had no problem allocating all unused floor area ratio (FAR) in the complex to 7 WTC. This was a "cosmetic" compliance with zoning, since the Port Authority, as a state agency, was not governed by city ordinances or codes. In addition, wind tunnel tests showed that a 47-story tower containing 2 million square feet could safely be constructed on the 50,000 square foot site—effectively a FAR of 40.

Pre-Leasing

Since no construction was started for several years after the leasehold was created, the building had no credibility in the leasing market. Construction had to begin in order to convince potential tenants that a projected occupancy date was believable. No open-ended construction loan could be found for a speculative project of the scope of 7 World Trade Center, so a strategy had to be created that would provide the fulcrum upon which a construction loan could be balanced. The economic climate of the mid-1980s provided the answer: a standby commitment. A standby commitment is a promise to lend, on completion of the office tower, an agreed-upon sum at an interest rate far above normal market rates. The purpose is to facilitate obtaining a construction loan while the developer shops for a permanent loan at a market rate.

The Takeout Standby Loan

A consortium of five California-based thrift institutions was created, led by California Federal Savings. The consortium was strong enough financially to give Chase Manhattan Bank, the lead construction lender, and its partners comfort that they would be repaid upon the completion of construction, regardless of whether any leases were signed. The risk that the standby consortium agreed to take in return for a $3 million fee, paid in advance, was remote. In reality, neither the issuers of the standby commitment nor the potential mortgagor, the developer, ever expect to see this type of commitment funded. It is almost a fiction, but a useful one.

The consortium issued its take-out letter and was paid its fee. With this quasi-permanent loan commitment in place, a construction consortium was assembled consisting of seven commercial banks—five from the United States and two from Canada. Tishman Construction of New York served as the construction manager. This firm had built the other buildings in the World Trade Center for the PA. If funding were necessary upon the completion of construction, the standby consortium would receive a rate of 250 basis points over the 30-year U.S. Treasury bond rate. Additional fees would be paid to the thrift institutions to effect funding. The standby permanent loan commitment would be for a term of 5 years on a 25-year amortization schedule.

The Construction Loan

The Chase Manhattan Bank considered the project to be feasible utilizing a $300 million capital budget. It agreed to commit $60 million as its share of the loan—subject to obtaining acceptable participating lenders and to the developer having an acceptable take-out permanent loan in place to repay the construction loan. Other lenders who joined Chase were Citicorp, Norwest Bank, Bank of America, Mellon Bank, Canadian Imperial Bank of Commerce and the Bank of Montreal.

The "Real" Permanent Loan

Throughout 1986, as the building neared completion, a net net lease for the entire building had been under negotiation with Drexel Burnham Lambert. Other leasing efforts had been abandoned. A short time before the scheduled closing of this historic lease, the Ivan Boesky scandal occurred. The lease negotiations were terminated immediately and efforts to release the space were reinstituted.

First a lease was negotiated with an accounting firm for almost 10% of the space in the huge tower. Next, in the fall of 1988, the developer finally consummated a 20-year lease with Salomon Brothers for 1.1 million square feet to serve as their headquarters. Leases were subsequently negotiated with the United States Government, The Hartford Insurance Company and others. By July 1, 1992, the building was 85% leased. Despite the weakness in the New York City downtown market, a lease for more than 100,000 square feet was signed in June 1992 with the Securities and Exchange Commission, demonstrating the building's viability.

In the meantime, a major pension fund, Teachers Insurance and Annuity Association (TIAA) approved, and the developer accepted, a conventional loan of $385 million on September 8, 1987. Upon its acceptance, the standby commitment was terminated. Upon completion of the construction, the permanent loan was closed.

As the New York rental market declined in the late 1980s and early 1990s, severe leasing delays were encountered. As a result the capital costs of the project escalated significantly, requiring the TIAA to increase its loan commitment to $490 million. As a quid pro quo for the incremental dollars, the mortgagee received a 50% future participation in the proceeds over the first mortgage balance of any sale or refinancing as well as a participation in excess cash flow after debt service and operating expenses. The mortgagee agreed to reduce the original interest rate from an adjustable rate that had started at 9-1/4% and escalated to 11% over the years to a pay rate of 9%.

The Future of 7 World Trade Center

Superbly located in the midst of 25 million square feet of Class A office space, 7 World Trade Center has a bright future. With floors of 48,000 square feet, an extraordinary tax structure, one of the world's largest parking garages, adjacent hotel amenities, a vast mass transit hub in the complex, and an aesthetic presence, this two million square foot building has a relatively favorable outlook.

FINANCING AMERICAS TOWER

by Arthur I. Sonnenblick and Jack A. Shaffer

In October 1983, The New York Land Company negotiated a contract with a major owner/developer of New York office buildings to purchase three key parcels on the southwest corner of Avenue of the Americas and West 46th Street. (A Swiss investor acquired a 25% limited partnership interest from New York Land.) The plan was to complete the assemblage of the northern portion of the block front on the Avenue of the Americas and develop a 400,000 to one million square foot office building, depending on the amount of land that could ultimately be assembled.

Although the location was excellent and the leasing market for new buildings was vigorous, the road to completion was to be long and arduous. Not only did the balance of the parcel have to be assembled and rezoning agreements obtained, but financing had to be arranged for the entire cost of the land acquisition as well as construction of the building. To complicate matters further, New York Land needed to acquire more than 200,000 square feet of contiguous development rights from the City of New York, which imposed a requirement that the company redevelop the adjacent High School for the Performing Arts. New York Land did not have the capital to provide the equity for such a large project. Furthermore, New York Land by its own admission had little development expertise. In spite of what appeared to be overwhelming obstacles, the group pressed on.

Finding a Joint Venture Partner

In January 1984, New York Land engaged Sonnenblick-Goldman as its exclusive agent to arrange financing for the total cost of the project. It was obvious from the outset that the funds would have to be invested through a joint venture arrangement and that only an equity investor would be

A joint venture with a Japanese partner provided New York developers with the funds needed to construct Americas Tower. *(Photo by Andrew Gordon)*

willing to provide 100% of the costs. The strategy was to obtain a partner who would commit sufficient funds to acquire the land, and to use the equity in the land to obtain a construction loan for the building. Additional requirements to obtain construction financing were that the joint venture partner have solid construction expertise and be able to act as co-developer since New York Land had no development experience.

In May 1984, Sonnenblick-Goldman met with Kumagai Gumi Co., Ltd., based in Tokyo, Japan. Kumagai Gumi's major business was the construction of dams, tunnels, airports, public works and major office buildings. The company had a strong interest in increasing its construction work worldwide and particularly in the United States. To accomplish this, Kumagai Gumi provided equity money to developers with the understanding that the investment was to be short term. Kumagai Gumi would be taken out of the venture shortly after the completion of construction and its funds returned through a sale or refinancing of the project. As the quid pro quo for providing the equity money, a subsidiary of Kumagai Gumi would become the contractor (at competitive costs), enabling Kumagai Gumi to increase its construction volume.

The Quid Pro Quo

Sonnenblick-Goldman successfully negotiated a joint venture between Kumagai Gumi and New York Land for the development of Americas Tower on the following basis: Kumagai Gumi agreed to fund land acquisition costs (up to and including the entire block, if obtainable) to a total of $80 per square foot of floor area ratio (FAR). As the initial building was to be 400,000 square feet, Kumagai Gumi's minimum commitment was for $32 million ($80 x 400,000). New York Land, however, had already contracted for a substantial portion of the land at an extremely favorable price below $80 per square foot of FAR.

To adjust for this imbalance, the land and building were separated into a fee and leasehold and two partnerships were formed. In the land partnership, the first $14 million of land value (representing the difference between the contract price and the agreed-on land value) was split 40% to Kumagai Gumi and 60% to New York Land. On the balance of the land value, Kumagai Gumi received 49% and New York Land 51%. In addition, the land partnership would subordinate to a construction loan. The leasehold partnership which would build the building paid a nominal rent to the land partnership and was owned 60% by Kumagai Gumi and 40% by New York Land. Kumagai Gumi was to receive a 10% cumulative prior return on its investment. Further, Kumagai Gumi agreed to guarantee completion of the building to a construction lender. Finally, Kumagai Gumi was to joint venture the construction contract with a domestic construction company to be chosen by the venture at a later date.

Since Kumagai Gumi had no interest in being a long-term equity holder, special provisions were included in the partnership agreement to allow for an exit strategy. New York Land had the option to purchase the property after completion at a price equal to Kumagai Gumi's cost, including interest at 10%. Kumagai Gumi had an option exercisable two years after completion that permitted it to require a sale of the property if it wished to recover its equity investment. The joint venture was closed in September 1984 and the partners began the assemblage of the land.

The Project is Expanded

In November 1985, Mr. J. Makita, the 94-year old chairman of Kumagai Gumi, visited the United States and inspected the site of the new development. Mr. Makita was so enthusiastic about the location of the Americas Tower development that he endorsed New York Land's original recommendation to purchase the entire blockfront on Avenue of the Americas and enlarge the building from 400,000 square feet to approximately one million square feet.

Assemblage of the plot and the design work on the new, larger Americas Tower continued. In May 1987, demolition began. A change in the New York City Zoning Ordinance required that any building which did not have its foundation completed by May 1988 would lose substantial development rights. As a result, construction of the foundation commenced in the fall of 1987 even though financing for the building was not yet available. Kumagai Gumi agreed to advance the funds for the construction of the foundation, which was completed in May 1988.

The joint venture agreement provided that the equity advanced by Kumagai Gumi for acquisition of the land would be subordinated to a construction loan to be obtained in an amount sufficient to complete the building. It was assumed that Kumagai Gumi's advances to pay for the foundation would be repaid from the construction loan proceeds. In July 1987, at the request of New York Land, Sonnenblick-Goldman obtained an offer for a construction loan from a bank based in Switzerland in the amount of $235 million. Although this loan appeared to meet the requirements of the joint venture, it was not finalized and Kumagai Gumi continued funding the ongoing construction.

The Project Turns Sour

In August 1988, Sonnenblick-Goldman again sought financing for Americas Tower and received four offers in the amount of $285 million from four different commercial banks. Because of the outstanding location, superior design and Kumagai Gumi's sponsorship, there was intense competition among lenders to make the loan. However, what should have been a happy occasion turned sour. For reasons that were never publicly disclosed, none of the loans were closed and Kumagai Gumi continued to fund the construction with monies provided internally through its own unsecured bank financing.

A year later, again at the behest of New York Land, Sonnenblick-Goldman once more sought financing for Americas Tower. A loan offer in the amount of $270 million was obtained from a life insurance company. Again, this loan was not taken by the partnership. Due to various partnership disputes, in December 1989, a Kumagai affiliate filed involuntary bankruptcy petitions against the project. This resulted in lengthy arbitration proceedings and a one-year stoppage of work on the building before a final settlement was arrived at, providing for the partnership to sell the project to a Kumagai affiliate in January 1991. By early 1992, the building was completed but unrented. Although the joint venture between New York Land and Kumagai Gumi continued in modified form, it can reasonably be inferred that Kumagai Gumi took complete control from the Bernstein brothers.

Rising from the Ashes

In mid-summer 1992, nine years after conception, eight years after completing the joint venture and five years after the start of construction, Americas Tower finally secured its long sought-after major tenant. Price Waterhouse announced it would lease 350,000 square feet and relocate its New York practice office to the building. At the time of this writing, it is expected an additional 80,000 square feet will be leased to Bank Hapoalim.

Americas Tower was conceived as a first class project and was built as such by New York Land and Kumagai Gumi. It deserves its position on New York's "corporate row" as a quality office building. It also illustrates the difficulties faced by the parties in a complicated joint venture. Language and cultural differences may produce misunderstandings in which it is generally preferable for one party or the other to assume majority ownership and operating control.

INTEREST RATE SWAPS AS A HEDGING TECHNIQUE

by Phillip C. Vitali

In the world of floating interest rates, interest rate hedging techniques, and particularly interest rate swaps, have assumed wider prominence in real estate financing. As the use of interest swaps exploded in the late 1980s, the sophistication of these techniques and the permutations available evolved to the point where, using caps, collars and swaptions, almost any combination of anticipated risk may be hedged. However, an interest rate swap remains the most commonly used hedging technique. The primary intent of a swap, to reduce volatility by exchanging an unknown rate risk for a definable exposure, remains constant. Ancillary benefits occurring from a swap can include access to debt markets which otherwise would be closed, increased flexibility and a lower effective interest cost.

The Basic Interest Rate Swap

An interest rate swap in its basic form is a contractual agreement between two parties converting, for a specified period, variable rate interest payments on a stated principal amount ("notational principal") into fixed rate payments. The notational principal may differ from the actual amount of debt outstanding since it is used for calculation purposes and does not change hands. Unlike the market for other hedging techniques, upfront fees for arranging simple swaps are normally de minimus.

The counterparty to the borrower in a typical swap agreement is a large commercial bank, but as transaction size and/or complexity increases, money center banks, investment banks and other large financial institutions become active participants. The broader the universe of sources, the more efficient the market becomes, increasing the probability of exactly matching risks. However, counterparty credit risk needs to be carefully evaluated. Any failure by the borrower's counterpart to meet the payment terms of the swap negates the benefit of the swap and frequently increases the cost of financing.

An interest rate swap holds the most appeal for the office building owner-developer whose priority is to identify and fix the operating costs of a project. The development process is fraught with risks, many of which are out of the developer's control. Transforming a variable rate construction loan into a fixed rate instrument is clearly beneficial during construction and lease-up, the period of greatest uncertainty. Managing interest rate risk improves the odds of success by eliminating one major uncontrollable variable.

Swapping from a Variable to a Fixed Position

For a variable rate long-term loan, similar uncertainties and risks are reduced by swapping into a fixed position. A potential mismatch exists between the relatively flat revenue stream of a leased building and un-hedged debt payments that are subject to fluctuations in short-term rates. This situation can easily pressure expected cash flow levels, especially at times of lease rollover when market forces drive rents, tenant improvement costs and lease-up times. A rising interest rate climate or a poor economy compounds the risk. In a worst-case scenario, debt service costs are escalating while the ability to service that debt is plummeting.

The willingness to borrow on a variable rate basis may provide an owner-developer with the opportunity for not only a larger loan, but also a favorable arbitrage between available fixed rate debt and a floating rate loan, or access to financing in a credit-short environment. A simple swap eliminates neither these opportunities nor the economic risks associated with leasing and the economy. It does eliminate the speculation on interest rate movement inherent in any unhedged variable rate loan. The lure of an unhedged floating loan is the seductive attractiveness of a big pay-off in the form of lower interest costs if the borrower correctly guesses the direction of rates. As with any other speculation, the consequences can be extreme if the gamble is lost. In a business with normally thin margins, unhedged interest rate speculation needs to be evaluated very carefully by the prudent owner-developer.

Caps, Collars and Swaptions

Although a simple interest rate swap protects against an upward tick in rates, the lease terms, tenant credit worthiness or an owner's financial capability may allow for a modest level of rate risk. In such circumstances it is possible to construct an interest rate swap that imprecisely parallels the borrower's risk tolerance. To model the borrower's risk parameters, a swap may be supplemented or replaced by several additional hedging techniques. An interest cap locks in a maximum payment by creating a rate ceiling. If rates float above the ceiling, the borrower's payment remains fixed at the ceiling, and if rates fall, the interest payment declines accordingly. An interest rate collar becomes useful if the borrower believes rates will move in a narrow range. A collar couples a cap with a floor. The floor establishes a minimum pay rate; if the floating rate drops below the floor the borrower pays the difference. The swaption is an option which provides the right to enter into an interest rate swap at a certain rate and maturity date. The complexity of a swaption can be increased by incorporating such features as multiple maturity dates, different interest rates, cancellability, extendibility or amortization provisions. The complexity and high upfront costs of these hedging alternatives generally restrict their usefulness to large individual transactions or to owners who are managing portfolios of debt.

A Creative Swap Example

An interest rate swap took place in the mid 1980s that creatively addressed the question of risk tolerance. The project being developed was a 400,000 square foot office building. The developer had arranged for an institution to be its equity partner. The arrangement provided for an initial investment of cash with a second and final contribution occurring on a specified date four years after the commencement of construction. The funding date was anticipated to correspond to the completion of initial lease-up and the funds were to be used to partially repay outstanding debt. The institutional investor was guaranteed a cumulative preferred return that was to be paid currently and in full until the final contribution was made. From that point forward the equity investor's return was to be paid solely from the cash flow of the property.

Construction and permanent financing in the amount of $36 million was to be provided by a variable interest rate, tax-exempt industrial revenue bond. Additionally, a firm commitment had been obtained from a major bank to purchase and hold the bonds for its own account. The underlying interest rate paid to the bondholder was set at 70% of prime. Since tax reform was under discussion, provision was made in the documents to adjust the rate for any future changes in the bank's tax status as it pertained to this class of investment.

The Swap Contracts

To lessen interest rate risk on the floating rate debt, the developer entered into two interest rate swap contacts with a third party. In this case the counterparty was another large commercial bank. One contract was applicable to the $7.6 million of debt that was to be repaid by the developer's equity partner and the other was applicable to the $28.4 million of remaining debt. The swap contracts provided for the developer to pay interest at a fixed rate and to receive interest at the prime rate. The maturity for the $7.6 million contract was three years and nine months, which coincided with the date of the required debt repayment. The $28.4 million contract was for seven years, which was the expected holding period. Due to the difference in contract maturities, the borrower's fixed rate was 10.18% for the shorter contract and 10.45% for the longer contract.

To parallel the interest rate payable to the bondholder, 70% of prime, the notational amount of each contract was 70% of the stated principal, or $5,320,000 and $19,880,000. The notational amount is the basis used to calculate the payments to be exchanged by the fixed rate and floating rate payors. The developer's annual fixed rate payments totalled $2,619,036 ($5,320,000 x 10.18% plus $19,880,000 x 10.45%). The swap's variable rate payment equaled the notational amounts multiplied by the prime rate. When the aggregate amount of the fixed payment exceeded the variable payments, the developer would write a check to the swap's counterparty for the difference. Conversely, the developer would receive a check for the difference when the swap's variable payment was greater than his fixed payment. In addition to the swap's contractual requirements, the developer remained obligated to make monthly interest payments, at 70% of prime, to the bondholder.

The Effect of the 1986 Tax Reform Act

At the time of closing, the structure of the swap fixed the developer's underlying interest rate on the $36 million of outstanding debt at 7.27%, regardless of any movement in the prime rate. The project was well underway when the 1986 Tax Reform Act was passed and altered the bondholder's tax status by increasing the tax due on income from the bonds. As a result of the higher tax paid by the bondholder, the interest rate on the bonds increased to 77.77% of prime for 1987 and 85.56% of prime thereafter. These changes transformed the swap by eliminating the correspondence between the rate paid to the bondholder and the notational-to-actual principal ratio (70%). In effect the industrial revenue bond regained its variable rate characteristic.

Fortunately, this event was an anticipated contingency. Prior to entering into the swap contract the developer had evaluated three strategies:

1. Enter into a swap with a short maturity (two years) and then rehedge the new variable rate risk
2. Purchase a cap in addition to the swap agreement
3. Determine the level of rate volatility it could afford and structure the interest rate swap accordingly

If this evaluation had occurred a few years later, a swaption would have been another alternative.

The first option was rejected because of the exposure to the interest rate market at a critical point in the development cycle. The second alternative was eliminated on the basis of cost. The third option was elected.

After assessment of the likely impact of tax legislation and the rate volatility the project could support, a structure was created that conformed to the developer's risk tolerance. In the developer's estimation, prime would float in the 8% to 14% range over the life of the swaps. Within that band, the swaps, as structured, created an underlying interest rate that would vary between 8.5% and 9.5%. In the disaster scenario with prime at 21%, the underlying rate would increase to 10.5%. Although interest costs were higher than originally estimated, they were within the projected range. The swap worked as modeled. The project was an unqualified success with construction completed in a timely fashion and an unexpectedly strong lease-up at effective rents exceeding pro forma.

The benefit of utilizing an interest rate swap to hedge a variable rate exposure may be less tangible than a long-term lease with a major tenant or the completion of a project, but it is not any less real. The importance of managing financial risk and sharing interest rate volatility via swaps and other hedging techniques should increase as the integration of real estate finance into global capital markets and the ongoing shift to institutional ownership of real estate assets continue.

FINANCING BUILDING LEASEHOLDS AND LEASED FEES

by John R. White

Traditionally, United States real estate is held in fee simple, that is, the land and land improvements (building and utilities) are the basis for investment. On occasion, an owner would lease his land for long periods in return for ground rent. The land was typically reappraised at stated intervals and a new ground rent set. The landowner (the lessor) permitted the lessee to occupy the land and build on it, subject to the termination date of the lease. To protect its investment in the building, the lessee would normally extend the lease as each term of years ended and accept the probability of an increase in the land rent.

Splitting the Fee Interest

Starting in the 1960s, many sellers split their improved office property ownership by creating a ground lease and retaining the underlying land while offering the building leasehold for sale, subject to the ground rent. In order to increase the value of the respective parts, sellers frequently agreed to subordinate to the leasehold their ground lease position and receipt of the ground rent. This enabled the buyer of the leasehold to arrange a larger institutional first mortgage based on the enhanced value of the collateral. As a quid pro quo, the lessor sometimes also received inflation protection in the form of a limited participation in increases in gross revenue or in net operating income over a stated amount.

The following examples demonstrate the seniority of the positions of the lessor, the lessee and the mortgagee in both a non-subordinated and a subordinated fee.

Net Operating Income in Fee Simple		$ 100,000
Less Non-subordinated Ground Rent	$20,000	
Less Debt Service on $600,000 First Mortgage	$60,000	$ − 80,000
Leasehold Net Operating Income		$ 20,000

In this example, the land owner has a very conservative investment position. If the leasehold net operating income declined to, say, -$10,000, the land owner would not be affected because the first mortgagee must step in to protect its own position by paying the defaulted ground rent.

The Risks of Subordinated Ground Rent

This situation changes radically if the landowner agrees to subordinate his fee position to the leasehold position. The receipt of the ground rent then becomes junior, or secondary, to the debt service requirement on the first mortgage. A willingness to subordinate to the leasehold position exponentially increases the landowner's risk and puts it in the position of being no more than a secondary lien holder. The following illustration demonstrates the added risk:

Net Operating Income in Fee Simple		$ 100,000
less Debt Service on $700,000 First Mortgage	$70,000	
Less Subordinated Ground Rent	$20,000	$ − 90,000
Leasehold Net Operating Income		$ 10,000

The leasehold NOI need only decline to breakeven to threaten seriously the landowner's ground rent payments. If a negative NOI occurs, the landowner (lessor) would have to start a dispossess action against the lessee and terminate the lease. Furthermore, the lessor would have to make the first mortgage payments to protect its land investment and to avoid a foreclosure which might wipe out the lessor's investment. The risk to the lessor has been compounded by the lessee's ability to obtain a higher $700,000 first mortgage because of the subordination of the ground rent. The increased debt service weakens further the lessor's position.

This financing device works well in times of prosperity and increasing real estate values. It has dangerous implications, however, when the market softens. If occupancy is reduced from the market norm, or effective rents decline, or both, the net operating income suffers disproportionately, that is, it is negatively leveraged because of the fixed nature of the ground rent and debt service requirements. Over-leveraging real estate of this nature is not unlike the leveraged buy-outs of large industrial corporations where the buyer accepted the risk of massive debt on the speculation that net operating income would continue to rise and hence enable the investor to pay off at least some of the debt burden out of increased income. Fortunately, in the early 90s, the real estate oversupply, the virtual collapse of the banking system and the recession halted debt accumulation as a financing method.

Long-term investors would not normally be interested in this type of financing because of the over-leveraging. Although this has significant elements of risk to the subordinated lessor, it also has immediate initial benefits to him as a seller in minimizing his capital gains tax since he is only selling the improvements (the leasehold) while retaining the land ownership. The seller also receives the monthly or quarterly rent, although the lessee's obligation to pay the ground rent is secondary to his primary obligation to pay real estate taxes and the first mortgage debt service. And the seller receives an overall price, inclusive of the land value, that may be higher than if he were to sell the fee simple interest intact. The purchasing lessee also benefits because 100% of his building acquisition is depreciable as a wasting asset while the land retained by the then land owner is not.

Financing Leased Fees

The owners of non-subordinated ground leased fees would occasionally resort to land financing by offering the leased fee as collateral for a mortgage loan. Generally these loans never exceeded 50% of the land value, subject to the ground lease. They were unaffected by the leasehold financing. If for any reason there was a default on the leased fee loan, the land mortgagee would foreclose the loan and assume the land ownership while the leasehold position remained undisturbed.

A Successful Secondary Financing

An example of ingenuity by a real estate consultant acting as an intermediary took place at a large Washington, D.C., mixed-use urban complex known as L'Enfant Plaza. The land was leased from the Washington, D.C., land agency and the investment was made in the building leasehold,

The land for L'Enfant Plaza, a larged mixed-use development in Washington, D. C., was leased from a land agency and the investment was made in the leasehold, subject to a subordinated land lease on which ground rent was paid. *(Photo by Joseph S. Romeo. Courtesy of Eastern Realty Investment Management, Incorporated)*

subject to a subordinated land lease on which ground rent was paid. L'Enfant Plaza originally consisted of four office buildings, a Loew's hotel, a 165,000 square foot shopping mall, a large theatre and a 1,000-car parking garage. In this instance, the seller did not want to sell but did want to extract from the property some of the entrepreneurial profit it had made. A convenient way to accomplish this was to obtain a mortgage loan.

The marketing consultant arranged a $5 million convertible second and third blanket leasehold mortgage at a 10% interest rate, in which the lender had the option, within seven years, to acquire a 50% initial interest in the property for a nominal sum. The option was subsequently exercised and the lender, a foreign pension fund, acquired a 50% stock interest which was appraised at the time for $30 million. The pension fund negotiated the purchase of the remaining 50% of the shares several years later at a price considerably less than the appraised value at the time of the exercise of the original option. The overall price paid by the pension fund was far lower than the property's value, demonstrating that leveraged financing can bring benefits in a rising market.

SECURITIZATION FINANCING WITH BONDS

by Brian A. Furlong

A bond is a legal security in the form of a certificate of debt guaranteeing payment of principal and interest as of a specified day. A mortgage-backed bond may be backed by one mortgage lien on one property, or by a pool of mortgage liens against a number of properties. If the bond payments are not made and a default occurs, the bondholders can foreclose on the real estate which backs the bonds.

Investors in bonds frequently do not have the time, skill or inclination to underwrite the risks of the real estate loans which back the bond, or to service the loans after origination. The investors look to others to perform these necessary functions. Typically, a real estate bond is structured and sold to the investing public by a investment bank. If the bond includes one or more new real estate loans, the investment bank will ensure that appraisals are performed, properties are inspected, legal documentation is drawn up and other steps in the loan origination process are carried out. The bond will be rated for credit worthiness by one or more of the four major rating agencies: Moody's, Standard & Poors, Fitch Investors Service, and Duff and Phelps.

The rating agencies often require credit support beyond the lien on the real property alone in order to give an investment grade rating. Credit support may include additional pledged collateral, a guarantee or a letter of credit from an investment grade guarantor. In the case of a bond backed by a pool of mortgages, additional credit quality can be achieved by establishing a blanket lien on the various properties within the mortgage pool, with cross default provisions. This way if one property cannot meet its debt service and the defaulting property has a value below its outstanding mortgage balance, the borrower's investment may be secured by other properties within the pool which have market values that exceed their debt loads.

Once an investment grade rating is obtained, the bond can be sold, with a cost of interest appropriate to the bond rating. The bond buyer may do some of its own investment due diligence, yet primarily it relies on the bond rating agency for its judgment that the bond and its underlying mortgages are appropriately structured and credit worthy.[1]

Using Bonds to Syndicate Debt

Bond financing is an excellent way to syndicate the debt for very large properties. Syndicating the debt expands the universe of possible investors in a transaction which, due to its large size, might be difficult to place with a single lender in a conventional mortgage loan format.[2] Generally, a single commercial mortgage must be quite large before it can be securitized with a rate of interest and a loan-to-value ratio competitive with the cost of funds available from established institutional lenders such as life insurance companies. This is because the commercial loan securitization process is not nearly as streamlined as the underwriting process of the mortgage loan departments of established institutional lenders. Securitization involves fees to the investment bankers, the suppliers of credit support, the rating agency, accountants, attorneys, and the trustee, and these transaction costs will exceed the corresponding transaction costs from traditional lenders on most small deals. In addition, an investment grade credit rating is difficult to obtain on commercial real estate loans, and traditional lenders in the past have been willing to lend more money on small and mid-sized commercial mortgage loans than the principal balance which could support an investment grade rating in a securitized transaction.

Most recent activity in commercial mortgage-backed bonds has involved pools of mortgages. A pool of mortgages is often easier to securitize than a single mortgage, for a number of reasons. First, mortgage pools can

---

[1] The quality of the underwriting review by the rating agency, and the buyer's trust in this underwriting, is the key to the marketability of the rated bonds.

[2] Examples of large debt issues which have been distributed among many lenders using bond financing include the American Express office tower in New York in 1985 and Water Tower Place, a mixed-use retail/office/hotel project in Chicago, which was securitized in 1992.

aggregate sufficient principal to support the front end transaction costs of a securitization. Second, a pool of mortgages can provide investment diversification by location, property type, maturity date and other factors. Mortgage rating agencies are comfortable rating commercial mortgage pools, since they previously had substantial experience in rating large pools of residential mortgages. Finally, the Resolution Trust Corporation (RTC) has been disposing of a large body of commercial mortgages it acquired from failed savings and loans by pooling the mortgages, creating mortgage-backed bonds and selling the mortgages to the highest bidder. The RTC dispositions are "kick starting" the fledgling commercial mortgage-backed securities industry by providing a large volume of activity which allows the rating agencies, the investment banks and the investing public to learn how to efficiently package and price the securities.

Typically, loans cannot be sold in their entirety in a securitized pool. This is because the typical pool of mortgages is of insufficient credit quality, or the information on the loans and the collateral is of insufficient quality, to support an investment grade rating on the entire outstanding principal balance. It is therefore common to pool the underlying mortgages and to establish different classes (called tranches) of securities, with varying rights for receiving the cash flow from debt service generated by the underlying mortgages. A senior class will be established which has a senior lien on the debt service from the underlying mortgages. One or more subordinate classes of mortgage debt will also be formed, and the holders of these securities will receive the debt service left over after the payment obligations to the senior class are met. Investment grade credit ratings are most often assigned only to the senior class of securities, although sometimes the most senior level of subordinate security in a multi-class issuance can also receive an investment grade rating.

The market for whole commercial mortgages has historically been thin, and trading activity has been limited. Most institutions which made mortgages in the past have been content to hold the mortgages to term, and institutions generally preferred to originate mortgages rather than to buy existing mortgages. By originating their own mortgages, institutions received current information on the property plus documentation in the format dictated by the lender. When an existing mortgage is sold the borrower is usually not obligated to provide updated information or new loan documentation; however, this practice is gradually being replaced by full disclosure data.

Creating Liquidity with Classes of Securities

Liquidity can be created by issuing multiple classes of securities. For example, one or more whole loans may not be salable without a steep discount for the reasons already discussed. However, some portion of the debt service receivable under the mortgage agreements might be quite secure, even if the debt service in its entirety is poorly secured and unlikely to be received in full. For an illustration of this, assume that 10 mortgages in aggregate have a principal balance of $100 million and a fixed aggregate contractual debt service of $10 million yearly. It may be that the debt service coverage ratio for a $10 million annual payment is low, and the default risk is high. However, it may be that the properties can easily support $6 million in annual debt service payments, with a high debt coverage ratio and a good loan-to-value ratio to provide a cushion in case of a default on one or more of the mortgages. In this case, the mortgages can be pooled to support a bond issuance, with a senior/subordinate structure. The senior class of bonds can have a face amount of $60 million with a 10% interest rate (as a simple annual rate)[3] for an annual interest payment of $6 million. This senior class of bond will have first call on the full debt service receipts from the underlying loans, which is $10 million annually if the mortgages are paid in full. Once the $6 million is paid to the senior bond holders, any additional receipts from the underlying mortgages is paid to the holders of the subordinate bonds.

Some bond issuances involve intermediate, or mezzanine, tranches of rated securities. For example, the $100 million pool of mortgages discussed here might back a $60 million senior tranche of securities which is rated A, AA or AAA, plus a $10 million intermediate class of securities rated BBB. This intermediate class of securities will have a claim on all funds from the underlying mortgages after the payments are made on the senior class of securities. Finally, a $30 million tranche of securities will be issued which is subordinate to both levels of higher securities. This most junior level of securities will not qualify for an investment grade rating due to the increased risk that it will not be paid in full. Each successive class of security, from the most senior on down, will have a different interest rate commensurate with its payment and default risk.

In this example, the senior bonds are highly credit worthy, even if the underlying loans have a good amount of default risk when considered in their entirety. The senior class of securities may qualify as investment grade, in the opinion of a rating agency. They can then be sold in the bond markets at a price commensurate with their credit risk as estimated by the rating agency. The subordinate classes of bonds can then be sold at some discount or held by the issuer.

---

[3] The interest rate the bond buyers can demand and receive is a function of the credit rating of the bond and the bond's terms, with particular attention paid to the term to maturity relative to the current yield curve. The interest rate for a mortgage-backed bond is usually higher than the interest rate for a corporate bond with the same credit rating. This is because the mortgage-backed bond market is not fully mature; mortgage-backed bonds have a lesser degree of market acceptance by institutional investors; and the rating agencies do not yet have as strong and demonstrable a track record in predicting the default risk on commercial mortgage-backed bonds as they do on corporate bonds.

In sum, securitization is a way to raise capital for real estate by using the bond markets. Many of the buyers of these bonds would not otherwise be providing capital secured by commercial real estate, since they are not equity investors in real estate and they have no loan origination capacity. Securitization can therefore expand the total pool of capital available to the real estate industry, which may be very useful during the credit crunch of the early and mid-1990s.

ABOUT THE AUTHORS

Jerome B. Alenick is executive vice president, Kushner Properties, Florham Park, N.J. In his previous position as senior vice president of Silverstein Properties Inc., New York, he was in charge of financing and acquisitions, negotiating more than two billion dollars of financing over ten years. Alenick is a member of the Bars of the District of Columbia and New Jersey, and has been a licensed real estate broker in New Jersey for 40 years. He served as editor of the *Real Estate Development Manual*, published by Warren, Gorham and Lamont in 1990 and updated in 1991/1992.

Brian A. Furlong See Chapter 4.

Jack A. Shaffer is managing director of Sonnenblick-Goldman Company. He joined the company in 1970, serving as executive vice president of Sonnenblick-Goldman Company of California until 1977, when he relocated to New York City. Before that, he was executive vice president of Dwinn-Shaffer, a mortgage banking firm in Chicago. He holds a J.D. from Northwestern University School of Law and a BBA from the University of Miami. He is a member of the board of directors of Guinness Peat Properties Inc. and is active with the Urban Land Institute.

Arthur I. Sonnenblick is vice chairman of the board and chief executive officer of Sonnenblick-Goldman Company. He is a past president of the Mortgage Bankers Association of New York, and is a member of the Real Estate Board of New York, the Urban Land Institute and the International Council of Shopping Centers. He has lectured at Columbia, Fordham and New York Universities, as well as for numerous professional organizations. Sonnenblick has a BS in economics from the Wharton School of Finance & Commerce, University of Pennsylvania.

Phillip C. Vitali is executive vice president and treasurer of MGI Properties, an equity real estate investment trust traded on the New York Stock Exchange. He was previously with Coopers & Lybrand. Vitali holds a B.S. from Boston College and has earned graduate degrees from Yale University School of Management and the University of Chicago.

John R. White, CRE, MAI See Chapter 21.

PART VII

OFFICE BUILDING MANAGEMENT

26

EXECUTIVE OFFICE BUILDING MANAGEMENT

by George M. Lovejoy, Jr.

DEFINITION OF REAL ESTATE MANAGEMENT

Real estate management requires a wide range of professional and personal skills. The good property manager must have not only the technical skills to deal with sophisticated building systems and accounting concepts, but also the personal skills to effectively handle tenant relations, manage building staff and communicate with building owners.

Real estate management can be defined in terms of the functions performed. These functions can include maintenance, operations, financial reporting, and marketing or leasing. The scope of services provided in each category can vary widely. Virtually every management assignment will include some level of maintenance responsibility to assure the proper condition and functioning of the property and its systems. The oversight of building operations can range from the single function of providing security for a vacant property to the myriad operational challenges of a major skyscraper where thousands of people work each day.

The property manager's marketing or leasing function can vary from support of a third party agent in hosting inspections of the property to total responsibility for the identification, solicitation and negotiation of tenancy.

Mr. Paul S. Goodof, chief financial officer of Meredith & Grew, Boston, Massachusetts, collaborated with the author on the sections covering administration and financial reporting. Mr. Frederick N. Nowell, III, CPCU, partner, Brewer & Lord, Braintree, Massachusetts, collaborated with the author on the section covering risk management.

It is common also to have shared responsibility where the manager handles negotiations with existing tenants, while third-party brokers identify and bring new tenants to the property.

Financial reporting is always a management responsibility. It too can cover a wide range of duties. At its simplest it can comprise merely forwarding approved bills and collected rents for processing by the owner. More commonly, it involves increasingly sophisticated computerized tracking and reporting of operations.

Distinction Between Property and Asset Manager

With the increased sophistication of the real estate field and its participants has come increased attention to the components of managing a real estate asset. Long-term and institutional ownership has changed the focus to issues other than the day-to-day care and operation of the real estate. These issues include attention to "highest and best use." Is the asset in an area where greater economic advantage could be obtained through demolition and new construction, rehabilitation, an addition or simply a facelift? A second example is sophisticated measurement of performance not only in the office building's market but also in competition with other markets and real estate classes. A third is the preparation and execution of a multi-year strategy for the real estate asset. These three examples of more sophisticated responsibilities are representative of asset management. The asset manager is more likely to be responsible for acquisitions, financing and dispositions. The property manager will always have the responsibility for day-to-day management and operations. Where the functions are separate, the property manager will always have less discretionary authority.

Evolution of Property Manager to Asset Manager

There is a natural tendency for the experienced property manager to aspire to asset management. Taking on the more challenging questions of financing, rehabilitation or re-use, acquisition and disposition, portfolio work and the like is a natural career progression. To succeed at this, the manager must hire staff who can do portfolio and property analysis; understand present financing and arrange new financing; obtain municipal permits for and oversee major physical changes; and do analysis, due diligence, negotiation and closing of acquisitions. Perhaps most important, the manager must demonstrate to the client the advantages of obtaining both asset and property management services from one organization. Real estate organizations actively involved in transaction work bring market knowledge and judgment that is difficult to internalize in an institution. This current market knowledge is very important to the decisions faced by the asset manager.

Asset management decisions require the input of the property manager, the asset manager and the owner. The relative role of each will be determined by the availability, the training, the skills and the experience of each.

OWNER VS. AGENCY MANAGEMENT

The real estate manager's opportunities tend to be counter cyclical, with many owners handling their own management in good times and seeking professional help in times of economic stress. As more property is institutionally owned and controlled, there is likely to be more consistency in the use of professional management throughout the business cycle.

The individual property owner often is attracted to the fee potential of owner management. In the case of small properties where the owner lives on the premises or has handyman skills, self-management can be both efficient and cost effective. The more complex the property and its problems, the less likely self-management will be adequate or cost effective. Office buildings in particular require advanced management techniques.

As challenges such as hazardous waste, lead paint, handicapped access and clean air requirements become more prevalent, the resources of professional, well-staffed agency managers become essential. There is a middle ground where an individual owner has a large enough property portfolio to justify establishing a fully staffed and trained management organization. Large successful property owners often internalize the management function; in recent years they have expanded into third party management as well. Some institutions also have established management affiliates to service their property and that of others.

The Competition of Owner Management

For owners who choose to manage their own property, the size and professionalism of their management organization will be driven by the economics. A large number of square feet is necessary to afford the depth of organization and skills provided by the agency manager. The owner manager will need to create an operation and maintenance staff appropriate to the properties managed. This entails selection, hiring and supervision of personnel as well as the accounting and reporting requirements of a payroll. The owner manager will likely subcontract many functions, at least in the early years. As the size of the management portfolio grows, it may justify direct provision of services previously subcontracted. Such services include cleaning, systems maintenance, payroll preparation and building security.

A decision to manage one's property often is accompanied by a decision to create an on-site leasing staff. The advantage of an on-site leasing staff is their total focus on the owner's property, in contrast to third party brokers who have other buildings to service. However, a large portfolio of property is necessary to support this function and to justify the level of compensation necessary to attract accomplished leasing professionals. Because the on-site leasing staff is not active in the total marketplace, it is necessary for it to have access to third-party leasing brokers to obtain market knowledge and to show the property to all potential tenants, many of whom may be exclusively represented. This is best accomplished through fee arrangements that assure third-party brokers of competitive compensation. Often building owners (particularly in oversupplied markets) will offer extra incentives in the form of full leasing commissions, cash bonuses or prizes to outside brokers.

CONTRACTUAL RELATIONS BETWEEN OWNER AND PROPERTY MANAGER

It is customary for the arrangements between the owner and the property manager to be formalized in a contract. Although some organizations have standard contracts, usually each one is tailored to the particular preferences and arrangements between the two parties. The term of the contract can vary from month-to-month to an extended period of time.

Certain matters need to be dealt with in every contract. It is important to have a provision that permits either party to terminate in a manner fair to both parties. If the parties aren't working well together, it is in neither's best interest to perpetuate the arrangement. The property manager makes a significant investment in start-up work in the initial months. Therefore, if the contract is to be terminated in the early months, there should be an appropriate monetary settlement to permit the manager to recover start-up costs. For instance, a provision might call for cancellation rights on thirty days' notice provided the property owner pays a cancellation fee in a specified amount, which would decrease annually over a short number of years. The property manager's right to cancel does not necessitate a monetary adjustment, but the manager should be required to provide adequate notice for the owner to find a replacement.

A second provision of the contract will cover the extent of the property manager's discretionary authority. This will vary with the trust between the parties, the time they have worked together and the magnitude of the responsibility. It is common to require the property manager to obtain specific authority for unbudgeted expenditures in excess of a pre-agreed amount. The property manager is normally allowed to use discretion when confronted with an emergency provided a prompt report is made to the property owner.

The contract will contain a fee arrangement, expressed in cents per square foot or as a percentage of revenues, for management and operations.

This fee is arrived at competitively in the marketplace and needs to be sufficient to provide a profit to the property manager to assure attentiveness to the work. If the property manager is also the leasing agent, there will be a fee for leasing work, competitively arrived at in the marketplace and based either on square footage leased or dollar value and length of the lease.

The contract should include schedules of leasing fees for both an exclusive broker and for sharing with any third party broker. This schedule probably also will include marketing costs and responsibility for their payment. Marketing cost arrangements can vary widely; frequently they are related to the magnitude of the leasing fees. Often the owner will agree to pay up to a budgeted amount for marketing with any expenditures beyond that to be paid by the leasing agent unless otherwise agreed to by the owner. Many property managers like to have exclusive rights in the event of sale of the property; this again depends upon the capabilities of the manager and the strength of his relationship with the owner. If the property manager works effectively to position the property strongly and enhance its value, it is disappointing for the owner to hire another marketing agent. At a minimum, the property manager should receive priority consideration. The property manager normally engages and pays for on-site marketing and maintains staff to insulate the owner from the responsibilities of direct employees. These costs, except for home office management executives, are reimbursable under the contract.

The contract typically will require the manager to prepare an annual operating and capital budget well in advance of the year to which it applies and submit it for review and comment by the owner. This document will usually provide limitations on spending authority and delineate the use and allowable cost of independent third-party contractors. It is customary to conduct periodic competitive bidding for such contractors. The contract will provide for the frequency, content and timing of reports. Also, in these days of careful management of cash balances, the manager should expect to either directly deposit to the owner's account or wire surplus funds with some frequency.

THE IMPORTANCE OF THE ORIGINAL
PROPERTY INSPECTION

Real estate, unlike many other forms of investment, is tangible and therefore requires inspection. An early property inspection is important whether one is considering a property for purchase, doing due diligence, or considering submitting a management proposal. Whatever its purpose, a number of items are common to any inspection. When one is making repetitive inspections, a checklist can be a useful tool to ensure that all the necessary items are considered and an appropriate record is made of the inspection. The inspection is discussed in detail in the next chapter on operations and maintenance.

The property manager should look at remaining warranties. It is customary with new construction, rehabilitation or installation of new systems to have warranties for such items as the roof, the elevators, and the electrical, heating, ventilating and air conditioning systems. Similarly, there may be prepaid maintenance contracts that cover day-to-day maintenance and/or replacement of parts; these can include such items as elevators, heating, ventilating and air conditioning, as well as waste disposal.

The inspector should pay close attention to maintenance and the identification of deferred maintenance. In the case of an acquisition inspection, the deferred maintenance will be an important monetary item in the negotiations. In the case of an inspection by a property manager who is going to take over management, it is important to record the deferred maintenance and advise the owner of the work that will need to be done to put the property in order. In addition, the inspector should be alert to any indication of structural problems, such as cracks in the building, settling or other clues that might indicate a larger problem. If there are indications of such problems, it may be necessary for the inspector to supplement his knowledge by engaging a specialist.

An additional area that should receive careful attention is compliance with ordinances, codes and regulations. Careful attention should also be given to the inspection of the life safety systems and alarm systems. Safety and a safe operating environment for one's tenants should be a primary consideration. The inspector should also check the availability and completeness of building plans. These are often an indication of the care with which the property has been managed and are essential tools in future operation of the building.

Perhaps as important as all the other items discussed is the careful observation of the building staff. Their appearance, uniforms, attitude and professionalism give an important clue as to the standards to which the property has been operated and the attention to detail and care that have been exercised in overseeing the building systems. If the inspector has the opportunity to talk to one or more tenants, that will shed further light on these matters. The inspector should also ask the building managers for a copy of their vendor list. The reputation, quality, experience and professionalism of the vendors are further indicators of the way in which the building is operated.

RISK MANAGEMENT

Risk management is concerned with the exposure of an organization's assets and income to fortuitous, casualty-related loss. It offers a framework for dealing with such risks in an organized fashion. Exposures to loss are identified and are measured in terms of their financial impact. The various methods of risk transfer are considered and a decision is made to eliminate, assume, control or transfer the risk. Insurance is the major means by which the organization may transfer the risk to others.

For office buildings, risk management begins in the construction phase. Plans should incorporate fire protection, earthquake resistance and Life Safety Code standards. During the leasing phase careful attention should be given to lease clauses covering insurance, common areas, and maintenance and repair. Insurance provisions should assure that the tenant carries adequate liability insurance and, in the case of net leases, adequate property insurance on the building. Tenants' insurance obligations must be carefully monitored to ensure that coverage is kept up to date.

The common area provisions should specify what insurance premiums can be passed through to the tenant. Lease provisions covering repairs should specify whether rent is abated in the event of a casualty (thus creating the need for rental value insurance); should describe the extent of hold-harmless releases and subrogation waivers; and should specify the tenant's responsibility for damage to glass, to heating, ventilating and air conditioning systems, and to fixtures and improvements.

Independent contractors pose a special exposure. The construction contract or the manager's purchase order should specify the types and limits of insurance that the contractor must carry.

The manager should reach common agreement with the owner on responsibility for the negotiation and placement of insurance. The management agreement should provide hold-harmless protection for the manager. Agency managers generally seek coverage as additional insureds under the property owner's policies since the manager serves as an extension of the owner in providing management services. Exceptions are workers' compensation insurance where the manager provides coverage for all employees at the property, and the manager's errors and omissions coverage.

The owner or manager should develop a relationship with a knowledgeable insurance advisor. The advisor can provide services such as insurance appraisal, building rate analysis, lease review, monitoring of tenants' and contractors' insurance certificates and supervision of loss recoveries. Premiums for all types of insurance are determined in part by loss experience, and proper safety procedures for building employees, tenants and visitors help to minimize injuries and keep insurance costs down.

TENANT RELATIONS

Good tenant relations are essential to a healthy building at all times, but there are times when an extra effort must be made. For example, when there is a change of management, it is important for the new staff to personally meet each tenant and discuss the impact of the changes on procedures, as well as to convey the interest and concern of the new team. If there are difficulties in the building or a foreclosure or other negative event, it is particularly important for the new team to be visible and attentive to the questions, concerns and needs of the building tenants. Such efforts should be supplementary to, and should reinforce, a strong regular program of tenant relations.

All owners who have had long-term records of success with a multi-tenant property find that a major contributor to that success is a strong tenant relations program. It is the best investment they can make. It creates a bond between the tenant, the building and the building owner that causes the tenant to resist overtures to relocate to another building. If the manager takes good care of the tenant and the tenant's visitors (primarily the tenant's customers), it benefits the tenant's business. That reinforces the space decision and cements the tenant's loyalty to the building.

A good tenant relations program has many attributes. Perhaps foremost is to communicate regularly with the tenant and to establish a close working relationship with the person in the tenant's organization who is responsible for dealing with building staff. The building manager should be readily available and visible. The technique of "management by walking around" is particularly applicable to property management. Some property managers mistakenly believe that if they stay out of sight they won't be faced with problems. Although they may avoid some questions and requests by this method, these are likely to become larger problems if they are not handled promptly.

Another element of good tenant relations for office buildings is management-sponsored promotional events. These can include entertainment events, training in various emergency procedures and holiday-related celebrations. Many buildings put up decorations and provide entertainment at major holidays. Other examples of successful events are a CPR course for tenants, building anniversary parties, a health awareness day or a charity event sponsored by the owner.

Tenants always appreciate extra services. The more of his needs that can be accommodated within the building, the happier the tenant will be, particularly in inclement weather. Some buildings even have the equivalent of a hotel concierge who can arrange for everything from routine office services to tickets for events.

Good tenant relations is also a matter of attitude. A warm greeting, a cheerful hello, calling someone by name, common courtesy—these small things add up to big rewards in terms of tenant appreciation and loyalty.

PUBLIC RELATIONS

A public relations program is important throughout the life of a building. Public relations starts when the building is just an idea and continues through a succession of events to completion and occupancy. Major events that should be publicized include groundbreaking, lease signings, "topping off," completion and a grand opening. Announcements of lease signings continue over the life of the building as do programs to position the building positively in the community and make it attractive to prospective tenants.

An early decision that must be made is whether to staff the public relations program in-house, hire an outside firm, or do some combination of the two. This decision normally is governed by the size of the public relations budget, which in turn is dictated by the level of public relations activity needed. A significant public relations program justifies hiring a highly qualified on-site professional, but more commonly the property manager employs the assistance of a public relations or advertising firm.

Some office buildings have natural attributes that make them easy to publicize and position, while others require more creative work. A prominent location where community events regularly take place or a building with a prominent occupant who gets frequent publicity help to provide a built-in public relations program. In addition, the building can host organized events of many types. Lease announcements can be a continuing positive program. During the original lease-up of the building, lease signings can be announced as they occur; the growing occupancy and the quality of the tenants attracted to the property send a positive message both to the public and to other potential tenants.

A major office building will probably have a brochure and other promotional material available throughout its life cycle. These materials should feature a consistent theme and graphic continuity. The quality of the materials and message will position the building. Promotional materials should include fact sheets, illustrative maps, floor plans and services available.

Good public relations results in good publicity. Good publicity also results from being attentive to the press. Calling the press only when there is something the building manager wants printed will not accomplish this. The relationship with the press must be carefully and continually nurtured by providing advance information, keeping reporters fully informed and meeting with them regularly even when there is no major item to be publicized.

Effective public relations results in consistent, strong positioning of the building through its materials, through its events, through its operating procedures, through the attitudes of the building staff and through the quality of its occupants. All these things together provide an image which is enhanced but not created by public relations.

ANNUAL BUDGET PREPARATION

One of the property manager's most important functions is to develop an operating plan for each property. Such plans may be for a single year, but more commonly they cover a three-to-five-year horizon. By looking at the asset over a multi-year period, the manager can do such things as evaluate the returns from capital replacements and compare them to annual maintenance outlays. Real estate performs best as a long-term asset, and it is best served by a long-term plan. The most effective long-term plans are updated and re-evaluated at least annually.

Once the plan is in place, annual operating budgets that support the plan need to be developed. Income budgets follow the leasing of the property and should include the property manager's best estimate of expenses, such as utilities and taxes, passed through to tenants on either a direct or an escalated basis. Details of all assumptions are helpful to those charged with review and approval.

Expense budgeting is commonly done in one of two ways. The first uses historical expenses incurred and adjusts them based on rates of inflation or

TABLE 26-1   Sample Actual-To-Budget Comparison

	Current Month				Year-To-Date			
	Actual	Budget	Variance	Percent	Actual	Budget	Variance	Percent
Revenue/Income								
Office Rent	500	525	(25)	-4.76	2,250	2,400	(150)	-6.25
Retail Rent	200	250	(50)	-20.00	900	850	50	5.88
Parking Income	150	135	15	11.11	725	750	(25)	-3.33
Other Space Rent	50	40	10	25.00	300	225	75	33.33
Miscellaneous Income	25	15	10	66.67	140	150	(10)	-6.67
Total Income	925	965	(40)	-4.15	4,315	4,375	(60)	-1.37
Operating Expense								
Cleaning	40	45	5	11.11	95	100	5	5.00
Repairs & Maintenance	65	60	(5)	-8.33	170	150	(20)	-13.33
Utilities	50	55	5	9.09	225	250	25	10.00
Roads/Grounds	10	15	5	33.33	60	70	10	14.29
Security	15	20	5	25.00	80	85	5	5.88
Parking Operations	75	65	(10)	-15.38	245	260	15	5.77
Administrative	50	60	10	16.67	200	210	10	4.76
Leasing Expense	0	35	35	100.00	70	60	(10)	-16.67
Real Estate Tax	0	75	75	100.00	75	75	0	0.00
Insurance	15	20	5	25.00	60	60	0	0.00
Total Operating Expense	320	450	130	28.98	1,280	1,320	40	3.03
Cash Flow From Operations	605	515	90	17.48	3,035	3,055	(20)	-0.65

changed circumstances, such as a planned capital investment or a shift in utility rates. This method is suitable for mature properties with professional management and owners who actively participate in the property's operation. For others it carries the risks of failing to challenge the way things are done and failing to seek new economies and operating practices. A preferable approach is so-called "zero base budgeting," in which each expense line item is built from scratch, examining every cost that comprises it. This system forces a hard look at the property operations and services, and allows the property manager to consider alternative ways of meeting the owner's objectives and accomplishing each task.

Presentations to the owner of annual budget information have become increasingly sophisticated, with multi-year actual-to-budget comparisons and extensive narratives explaining any divergences from prior year budgets as well as plans for the ensuing year. Table 26-1 shows a sample actual-to-budget comparison. Many owners require computer disks so they can perform their own "what-if" analyses. Given the dollar volumes at issue, it is not surprising that the annual budget process for large, multi-tenant properties often involves extensive interaction between the owner and manager over several months.

ADMINISTRATION

Accounting

Accounting for property management, like the discipline itself, ranges from simple and straightforward to sophisticated and complex. The accounting needs for a single-tenant net-leased property are markedly different from those for a multi-tenant urban office tower. Similarly, the reporting needs for property owned by individuals can be substantially different from the requirements of institutional owners of real estate. Despite these differences, however, a property manager requires as much information as possible to ensure economic operation and enhancement of the asset's value, and accounting systems should above all address those requirements. The BOMA (Building Owners and Managers Association International) chart of accounts provides detail of typical line items of income and expense for real property (Table 26-2) and most of the standard software packages available for property management incorporate BOMA's basic format. Many managers find it helpful, and in some instances necessary, to expand upon the basics, adding new accounts and descriptions to fit individual circumstances, properties or client requirements. In choosing software, it is essential to obtain systems with sufficient flexibility and adaptability built in to accommodate these modifications.

TABLE 26-2   Summary of BOMA Chart of Accounts

Revenue/Income

Office Rent
  Base Rent
  Pass-Throughs
  Escalations
  Lease Cancellations
  Rent Abatements
  Tenant Services

Retail Rent
  Base Rent
  Percentage Rent
  Pass Throughs
  Excalations
  Lease Cancellations
  Rent Abatements
  Association Dues
  Tenant Services

Parking Income
  Daily/Transient
  Monthly Income
  Annual Income
  Other Services

Other Space Rent
  Storage Space
  Antenna
  Express Parcel
  Shared Services

Miscellaneous Income
  Vending Machines
  Telephones
  Signs
  Late Charges

Operating Expense

Cleaning
  Payroll, Taxes, Fringes
  Contract Services
  Supplies & Materials
  Trash Removal
  Other Expense
  Tenant-Reimbursables

Repairs and Maintenance
  Payroll , Taxes, Fringes
  Elevators
  HVAC
  Electrical
  Structural/Roof
  Plumbing
  Fire and Life Safety
  Other Maintenance
  Tenant Reimbursables

Utilities
  Electricity
  Gas and Fuel
  Purchased Steam
  Purchased Chilled Water
  Water and Sewer
  Tenant Reimbursables

Roads/Grounds/Security
  Payroll, Taxes, Fringes
  Contract Services
  Other Expenses

Administrative
  Payroll, Taxes, Fringes
  Management Fees
  Professional Fees
  General Office Expense
  Other Administrative

Parking Operations
  Payroll, Taxes, Fringes
  Cleaning
  Repairs and Maintenance
  Utilities
  Roads/Grounds/Security
  Administrative

Leasing Expenses
  Advertising/Promotion
  Commissions
  Professional Fees
  Tenant Alterations
  Leasing Costs
  Rent Abatements
  Buyouts

Fixed Expenses
  Real Estate Taxes
  Building Insurance
  Personal Property Tax
  Other Fixed Expense

Amortization and Depreciation
  Amortization of free rent, buyouts, commissions
  Depreciation of building, improvements, equipment

Finance Expense
  Interest, ground rent, financing costs, income taxes

Source: Building Owners and Managers Association International

Income accounting tracks lease administration virtually item for item. Charges for contract rent are critical. An effective tickler system must be established to accommodate rent adjustments required by leases such as CPI adjustments and step rate increases. Pass-throughs and escalations must also be accounted for, in which tenants are charged for their proportionate share of real estate taxes and operating costs, or for increases in those costs over a predetermined base. Because of the economic significance of these types of charges in recent years, many office property owners have provided in leases for monthly or quarterly advance charges based on budgets or on recent actual experience; as a result, tenant-by-tenant reconciliations must be performed once the final figures are known. A further subtlety in recent years is the inclusion as escalatable expenses of the amortization of certain types of capital improvements, many aimed at reducing energy consumption and having a payback. Finally, retail tenants occupying ground or second floors in office buildings routinely have percentage rent clauses, providing movements over minimum rent based on actual retail sales.

If the property manager is new to the building, he should review the historical information to ensure that all billings are up to date. Billings that are not current must be aged and quantified to determine if they can and should be billed. For very old items, the limits for billing may have been passed. Other items may be so large as to place a financial burden on the tenant from which he may be unable to recover. In this case, the manager should make a recommendation to the owner, who should make the decision. Once the billings are up to date, it is a good time for the property manager to evaluate the effectiveness of the rent collection policy, or if no policy exists, to implement one.

Effective expense accounting permits property managers to monitor property operations to assure efficiencies and to identify any problem areas promptly. The broad categories of account classification include: cleaning, utilities, mechanical systems, general operations, payroll/fringes, administrative, capital items, finance items and tenant-recoverable expense. Within each of these categories, managers will choose further detailed breakdowns of operating, capital and finance expenses, with the level of detail dictated by the type of property and the needs of the ownership.

Income and expense accounting is only useful if reporting systems permit the data to reach managers on a timely basis. The status of collections needs to be reported almost daily, and expenses should be summarized at least twice a month. Many institutional owners have cash management programs that require frequent remittance of surplus funds, and proper tracking of both income and expense is as vital to meeting these owner objectives as it is to meeting manager needs.

Through the late 1970s, property managers customarily maintained two commingled bank funds for their business, one for deposit of rental receipts and payment of expenses, and the other for security deposits. With the high interest rates of the early eighties, many owners requested segregated and interest-bearing accounts for both operations and security deposits, as well as lock-box services to speed deposits and increase interest earnings. This trend continues. Managers need to utilize the latest technologies, including on-line balance reporting and transfer services from banks, to keep track of owner balances daily and permit accurate and timely reconciliations.

The accelerating trend to automation, computerization and ready availability of increased amounts of information in business is also true of the property management field. Owners will insist on it, and it provides opportunity to the manager as well through economies of operation and improved efficiency and service. High speed communication and the direct transfer of information enables the owner to have maximum utilization of fund balances through instantaneous knowledge of available funds and wire transfer capability.

Property Operations

Besides handling complex and sophisticated reporting needs, powerful computers are increasingly being turned to property operations as well. They are routinely used in security and life safety systems, monitoring building access and smoke and fire detection systems. In energy management, multiple sensors throughout a building feed data to central processors, and electronic switches and controls may be operated automatically. As a result, building temperatures and air quality can be managed more effectively and uniformly. In addition, because the performance of building system components is checked constantly, problems can be identified considerably earlier than with even the best manual inspection procedures, and often may be remedied at lower cost.

An operating plan for each property must propose staffing levels appropriate to the objectives of the owners and to the contractual requirement of leases. Virtually all agency management contracts provide that personnel hired to operate a building should be employees of the agent and not of the owner; as a result, firms engaged in property management may have significant reimbursed payrolls. Because some employees of the agent may work at more than one property, it is vital to have a flexible accounting system that can allocate accurately all of the payroll and related charges based upon the number of hours worked. In addition, management firms must handle the customary withholding and reporting on a timely basis.

Well-documented systems and procedures are necessary for the protection of the owner and the assets, to guide on-site superintendents in their management of other staff, and to assure compliance with safety and employment statutes. A manual for all personnel should, at a minimum, address:

- Terms and conditions of employment
- Standards of conduct
- Registration for payroll and benefits
- Health, life and other insurance coverages
- COBRA and other statutory benefits
- Vacation, illness and holiday policies
- Maternity and other disability policies
- Policies on sexual harassment
- Policies on AIDS and other infectious illnesses
- Safety policies
- Policies on jury and military service

Operational Reporting to Owner

The first reporting decision to be made is the choice of computerized accounting systems. Generally, this decision is based on the owner's tax or other reporting requirements. Individuals who own real property often prefer cash-basis accounting, which reports income actually received and expenses actually paid. Corporate and institutional owners, on the other hand, usually choose accrual accounting, which accounts for income when earned and expense when incurred, regardless of the status of collections of income or payment of expenses. Other owners require a hybrid of the two, with accruals for income, insurance premium payments and real estate taxes, and cash basis accounting for all other expenses. Finally, some owners require both cash and accrual basis statements because they utilize one for tax purposes and the other for financial statements.

Frequency of reporting is the second decision to be made. To be effective, the property manager should have prompt and accurate status reports several times each month. Most owners seek financial statements and rent rolls monthly, with an analysis of results compared to budget and prior year experience. Some prefer detailed reporting only quarterly, with summary statements for the interim periods.

The content and format of property reports have become more sophisticated over the years. Originally, an income and expense statement, a rent roll and a listing of paid expenses were sufficient to meet the needs of most owners. Increasingly, however, computerization and the need for standardized reporting for entire portfolios by institutions have made it common for managers to provide special operating summaries that permit owners to integrate property operating data into existing computer systems. Many owners ask their property managers to report to them on computer disk, or by direct access (via modem) to the owner's computer. Because the manager's chart of accounts must be able to be converted easily to that of the owner, the manager's accounting computer will generally include a database management system.

As the complexity and detail of financial reporting has increased, the need for accompanying explanatory narrative has grown as well. Variation analysis, explanation of timing differences and rolling revisions to projections are just a few of the items managers routinely include in monthly transmittals that summarize the activity of the property for the period.

MARKETING TECHNIQUES AND RESPONSIBILITIES

No building can be successful without tenants, and a full roster of tenants depends on a good marketing effort. In some companies the leasing function for managed properties is within the management department while in other companies it is in a separate department. In other cases a specialized management organization may depend on third parties for a majority of the leasing effort.

The Lease

One of the important leasing tools is the lease itself. Many owners have a standard form lease. However, with the growing complexity of buildings and systems and the proclivity of national tenants to have their own lease form, it is unusual that a standard lease form can be used in its entirety or with all tenants. Thirty years ago a lease over ten pages long was unusual; today a lease for a major tenant under one hundred pages long is unusual.

The lease document customarily has a series of sections: one dealing with the designation of landlord and tenant, the term, the area and the uses to which the premises can be put; a second covering the premises, the rental and the security deposit; a third on construction items; a fourth covering landlords' covenants; a fifth covering tenant covenants; a sixth covering the arrangements in the event of fire or other casualty or an eminent domain taking; a seventh containing default provisions; an eighth containing mortgage rights; and a ninth covering miscellaneous legalities such as notices of lease or brokerage arrangements. Any major lease will customarily have exhibits as well including a work letter, floor plans, a delineation of services provided, and rules and regulations of the building. In most cases the property manager, even when there is a form lease, will need some legal assistance to complete the documents.

One of the lease exhibits, the work letter, is the road map for the custom design of tenant improvements within the demised premises. The work letter includes a standard tenant build-out section with a detailed recitation of the physical features included in the base building. This is the point of departure for the tenant improvements, and it is important that both parties clearly understand what is included and what is excluded. A typical small tenant work letter is illustrated in Table 26-3.

The next section deals with the tenant finish. This often is in two parts. The first gives tenant finish guidelines, which are the construction standards to be applied to the tenant finish work. These define such things as partitions, ceilings, doors, lighting, electrical system, finishes, flooring, fire protection systems, floor loading, heating, ventilating and air conditioning standards and signage. In addition, there are functional area standards that define for the various areas of the tenant's premises the standards that will be met. These functional areas include the reception

Table 26-3   Typical Small Tenant Work Letter

Standard Features:	Office space shall consist of a professional level mix of open space and closed offices. Open space may be configured with desks or built-in workstations.
Lights:	2 x 2 building standard lights as specified for the entire building.
Ceilings:	All ceilings shall be 2 x 2 lay-in ceilings with a fissure surface.
Carpet:	Shall be 30 oz. quality with choice of solid colors.
Walls:	Shall have two coats of paint over drywall. Demising walls shall go to underside of metal deck, while interior walls will go to ceiling level.
Doors/Frames:	Frames shall be welded metal or knock-down type if required by schedule. Doors shall be solid core oak with finish as determined by current tenants.
Mechanical:	Shall meet code requirements for exhaust and ventilation. Configuration for variable air volume boxes and temperature control shall be unaltered from current locations in ceiling.
Electrical	Electrical panel and transformer shall be unchanged for tenant's occupancy. A ratio of 1 duplex outlet per 150 square feet shall be maintained.
Special Features:	Landlord shall not be obligated to provide kitchens, storage, computer rooms, coffee stations, copy rooms or other non-office facilities unless agreed otherwise.

area, conference rooms, support staff open space, private offices, file and auxiliary areas, employee lounges and lunchrooms. It is important that the tenant and the landlord clearly understand what work is to be done, who is to do it, what the finished result will be and who is to pay for it. This can avoid serious problems when the tenant first moves into the premises—a bad start indeed.

Marketing Strategy

It is important to develop a marketing strategy. The marketing strategy will be based on a market analysis to provide guidelines for tenant prospects and pricing. If the project is not competitively priced, it will not lease, which will lead to tension between the owner and the management firm. The market analysis will help target the market to be solicited. This market should be identified by location, by size and by type of business. Unlike most other property types, office building marketing strategy involves the direct canvass of business tenants on a systematic basis through a combination of "door knocking" and reference to the Standard Industrial Code data, which describes all business tenancies. It is also important in the marketing strategy to qualify tenants. There should be standards for credit, business reputation and space needs. Finally, the marketing strategy should include an understanding between the owner, the attorney and the managing/leasing agent as to responsibility for negotiations in the closing of transactions.

Marketing tools are used to implement the marketing strategy. These tools are limited only by the creativity of those responsible for the marketing, but there are certain common denominators. Marketing centers have become common, particularly in the case of new buildings. These can include sophisticated state-of-the-art film presentations, models of the building and retracting walls that open to reveal a window looking out over the project. They can cost tens of thousands of dollars, or hundreds of thousands of dollars.

Almost every project will have a brochure, with the size and value of the project dictating the budget that can be allocated to the brochure. Many brochures will contain standard fixed information and include pockets for the placement of information that requires updating so the base brochure will last the life of the project.

Mailings are a useful marketing tool, particularly if they are well targeted. Repetitive mailings can convey the momentum of a project to prospective users.

An advertising program usually accompanies a marketing effort, but advertising seldom brings in tenants. It serves rather to position the project in the marketplace and in the minds of prospective tenants. It is important to select carefully the media and the copy to be used. Advertising should convey the same high standards as the other marketing tools. The program should include events and announcements and should be closely coordinated with the public relations program.

Perhaps the most important marketing tool is a canvassing effort that includes a reporting system and regular marketing meetings. Most space is rented through repetitive personal contact. Too much emphasis cannot be placed upon well-trained sales people personally calling on prospective space users. For the sales staff to be effective there must be an efficient written and verbal reporting system so that communication flows in both directions and assures close coordination of the marketing effort. A regular marketing meeting, on at least a weekly basis, seems to impose the appropriate discipline on all parties. These meetings function best with a standard agenda that is followed efficiently and completed in a predetermined period of time.

RELATIONS WITH OUTSIDE CONTRACTORS

As office buildings and their systems become increasingly complex, the property manager by necessity must call more and more on independent contractors with specialized expertise. They are essential support to the modern property manager.

It is important that the manager be sensitive about when legal help is required. The manager must be careful not to practice law on the one hand, yet equally careful not to incur unnecessary legal expense. Some of the myriad of matters that can require professional legal assistance include lawsuits due to accidents; complicated environmental matters; issues of lease interpretation; and complex personnel issues. If the property manager also has asset management responsibilities, legal help may be needed for such issues as zoning, permitting and purchase and sale documentation. Lease documentation and contract review should always be handled by an attorney. An established working relationship with a good real estate lawyer supported by a diversified law firm is ideal.

Every property manager must deal with accountants. In addition to internal recordkeeping, periodic audits will be required for mortgagees, for percentage lease clauses, for owner verification of numbers and other reasons. The property manager can serve his client best by being prepared with thorough work papers for review by the accountants to minimize their cost.

As a result of expanding environmental concerns, property managers increasingly are calling on environmental engineers for both internal and external matters. Issues include air change and maintaining healthy internal air in office buildings; waste disposal and recycling; and the extensive regulations and liabilities associated with polluted sites. These all require the services of a specialized environmental engineer.

The property manager will periodically call in appraisers to perform a variety of tasks. Many leases call for third-party help in setting rents in the event the parties cannot agree. This often involves use of an appraiser. In the case of eminent domain takings, an appraiser is required. Appraisals also are needed periodically in the oversight and administration of mortgages. Increasing amounts of real estate are owned by pension funds, and they require updated appraisals in order to report values to their owners. The property manager should be prepared to make the necessary information available to appraisers and to work with them professionally.

More often than not a property will be mortgaged and the mortgagee is in a sense a partner. The effective property manager will communicate well with the mortgagee, provide timely reports and keep the lender fully informed. The best insurance policy for assuring an orderly workout of any difficulties that may arise is a history of open, frank and full communication.

Municipal and other governmental authorities are always part of the property manager's business life. The property manager must deal with periodic code inspections, safety system inspections and with the taxing authorities, both in setting assessments and in working for reductions when appropriate.

On occasion, highly specialized consultants may be required. They can be in the real estate field or in other specialties. They can be called upon for general matters, such as using a real estate consultant to help in strategic planning or portfolio positioning; or they can be needed for a highly specialized matter such as dangerous machinery vibration or building structural stress. The effective property manager must be able to identify the need for specialized help, and manage and work effectively with that help to attain the required results.

MEMBERSHIP AFFILIATIONS

The real estate field has many professional organizations. With increased specialization, the number of organizations is growing. The Institute of Real Estate Management and the Building Owners and Managers Association International have the most direct impact on the building manager. They both offer valuable data, training, publications, networking opportunities and professional designations. Institutions and individuals seeking property management services increasingly value professional designations in their selection of a manager. The property manager will find it not only an enjoyable experience but enlightened self-interest to actively participate in one or more professional organizations.

OFFICE BUILDING MANAGER OF THE FUTURE

In the future, the need for property managers will continue to increase and respect for the management function will continue to grow. The difficulties in providing new product to the marketplace will result in a greater emphasis on the outstanding care and positioning of in-place real estate. As more property is purchased by institutional and offshore investors, the role of the professional manager will grow in importance and sophistication. The evolution from property management to asset management will continue and the property manager of the future will need to combine effectively both operational and financial skills. The manager will need to meld the competing requirements of increased general knowledge and greater specialization. The manager cannot be expected to be expert in all specialties and will need to call upon, and manage, independent contractors.

The manager of the future must be able not only to manage property but to administer a business enterprise, using the skills of a business executive. He will not only be required to master systems and procedures, but will have to be proficient in computer applications. In short, the manager of the future will have to be well educated, have strong human relations skills, be a good executive and be able to marshal and effectively use specialized expertise, all with a high level of integrity, reliability and competence.

ABOUT THE AUTHOR

George M. Lovejoy, Jr., CRE, CPM, CSM, chairman of Meredith & Grew, Incorporated, Boston, has spent 36 years in real estate management, counseling and brokerage services. He has served as a trustee of three real estate investment trusts and as a trustee or director of seven mutual funds. He has been a member of the Real Estate Studies Advisory Council at Boston University. Lovejoy has also served as president of the Counselors of Real Estate, the Boston Chapter of the Building Owners and Managers Association, the Greater Boston Real Estate Board and the New England Chapter of the Institute of Real Estate Management. He is a member of the Urban Land Institute.

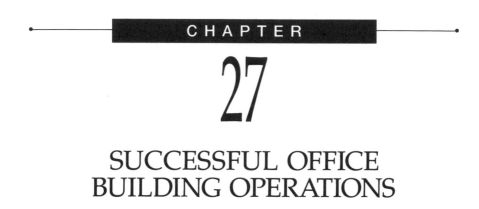

27

SUCCESSFUL OFFICE BUILDING OPERATIONS

by Christopher J. Whyman

INTRODUCTION

This chapter provides an overview of the day-to-day operations of a typical office building from the vantage point of a property manager who has just assumed management responsibility for the building. Systems and procedures will vary depending on the size of the property. In a small building, employees must perform multiple duties, while in a large one, functions may be segregated to ensure greater control. But whether the building is large or small, the principles of good management are the same.

Successful management is not a one-time effort, but is an ongoing daily process. Management success is measured in more than just dollars and cents. Other considerations include tenant comfort, property value appreciation, staff morale and contractor cooperation.

CUSTOMER SATISFACTION

The goal in operating a building is to satisfy the customer. The building manager has several customers. His most important relationship is with his client, the building owner (often represented by the property manager), by whom he is engaged and to whom he owes his loyalty. Other important customers are the building's tenants, their employees and the tenants'

The author wishes to acknowledge the contributions to this chapter of John E. Wooding, RPA, of Eastern Realty Investment Management, Incorporated, Washington, D.C.

customers. These must be satisfied on occupancy questions and on visits to the building. The first step in operating a building is to identify all of the building's customers.

The building manager cannot satisfy the customers' needs if he has not determined what they are. Many managers and owner operators believe they know what an owner or tenant wants—and often they are wrong. The second step is to verify the customers' needs by sitting down with them and asking the right questions. The answers received should be retained as a monthly checklist. After twelve months of operations, the customers should be interviewed again. Negative answers provide an opportunity for managers to improve the services they provide.

The Japanese, in their system of Total Quality Management, have identified three levels of customer satisfaction. These are as follows:

1. Services so fundamental that no one would expect to have to ask for them
2. Services that customers know can be provided, but which may not be offered unless they are requested
3. Services that customers would be delighted to have, but for which they would not think of asking

This third level, known as "Kansei"—the level of service that delights the customer—is the level for which a good building operator should aim.

BASE LINE BUILDING REVIEW

On assuming the management of a new building, the property manager must conduct a base line building review to establish the current conditions. Using the results of this review, a standard operating procedures manual and a tenant manual can be prepared. If these already exist, they must be carefully reviewed and updated as necessary.

Tenant Interview

The first step in the base line building review is for the manager to make an appointment with the contact person for every tenant in the building for an introductory meeting and interview. These sessions preferably should be conducted by someone who is not on the building staff, as tenants will be more open and honest with their comments. The interviewer should work from a prepared list of questions, as well as noting general tenant comments. The areas covered should include restrooms, corridors, entrance lobby, elevator operations, elevator appearance, exterior, building security, security guards, building concierge or receptionist (if there is one), cleaning, parking, building maintenance, heating, ventilating and air conditioning (HVAC), property management office, reactions to special services

FIGURE 27-1

TENANT INTERVIEW

TENANT _____

BUILDING AND SUITE NO. _____

CONTACT _____

PHONE _____

INTERVIEWER _____

Building score _____

Staff score _____

Total score _____

How would you rate the following in the last six months:

Excellent	10
Good	8
Satisfactory	5
Fair	3
Poor	0

CLEANLINESS

NOTES

1. The restroom cleanliness? _____

2. The stocking of restroom supplies? _____

3. The shampooing of hallway carpet? _____

4. The vacuuming of hallway carpet? _____

5. The overall cleanliness of the hallways? _____

6. The condition of wallpaper/paint in the hallway? _____

7. The condition of ceiling tiles? _____

8. The cleanliness of building grounds? _____

ELEVATORS

9. The response time of the elevators? _____

10. The cleanliness of the elevators? _____

11. The cleanliness of the elevator floors? _____

SECURITY

12. The overall security of the property? _____

13. The response time of security personnel when necessary? _____

14. The courtesy of security personnel? _____

15. The operation of the card access system? _____

SUITE CLEANING

16. Nightly suite vacuuming? _____

17. Nightly suite dusting? _____

18. Nightly suite trash removal? _____

19. Nightly suite cleaning overall? _____

PARKING GARAGE

20. Parking garage condition?   _____

21. Parking garage cleanliness?   _____

22. Courtesy of parking garage personnel?   _____

    cashier?   _____

    attendant?   _____

23. Response time of parking personnel when necessary?   _____

HVAC/PEST CONTROL

24. The efficiency of the heating system?   _____

25. The efficiency of the air conditioning system?   _____

26. The air circulation of your suite?   _____

27. The efficiency of pest control?   _____

PERSONNEL

28. The competence of building engineer(s)?   _____

29. The follow-up of the building engineer(s)?   _____

30. The competence of the building manager?   _____

31. The courtesy of the building manager?   _____

32. The competence of the property manager?   _____

33. The courtesy of the property manager?   _____

34. Do you know the name of your building manager?   _____

35. Does the building manager make periodic inspections to your suite? _____

36. Does the property manager make periodic inspections to your suite? _____

37. The competence of the porter(s)?   _____

38. The courtesy of the porter(s)?   _____

39. The competence of the tenant service coordinator?   _____

40. The courtesy of the tenant service coordinator?   _____

41. In general, do you find that we handle your call(s) with efficiency and care?
    Are you confident that it will be taken care of?   _____

42. What is the area of service that we do best?   _____

43. What is the area of service that we need the most work on?   _____

44. How would you rate the property management performance overall?
    (On a scale from 1 to 10)   _____

45. Do you ever deal with our Asset Management and Leasing Department? If so,
    how would you rate their service?
    (On a scale from 1 to 10)   _____

46. Do you ever deal with our Finance Department? If so, how would you rate their
    service?
    (On a scale from 1 to 10)   _____

47. Have you used the concierge service? How would you rate the service? _____

48. Is the mix of retail in the building meeting your needs?   _____

49. If not, what would you like to see in the building?   _____

provided such as Federal Express pickups, tenant get-togethers, entertainment programs in common areas, and finally whether the tenant knows and likes the property manager. Figure 27-1 shows a sample tenant interview form.

Those interviewed should be asked to assign a numerical value to each item indicating their level of satisfaction. This can be turned into a Tenant Satisfaction Index that becomes the benchmark for future surveys, with the goal of constant improvement. The information gathered can also be used as a base from which to initiate a tenant relations/tenant retention plan.

General Property Inspection

The building manager and/or the property manager should make a thorough and detailed inspection of the property to determine the overall physical condition of the building and the effectiveness of its present contractors and building staff. The results of this inspection should be documented in a written report. The building operator will use this information to prepare the annual operating budget, as well as to prepare an operating plan to correct any deficiencies. The inspection will also provide information needed to prepare the capital budget.

The inspection should begin at the top of the building with an examination of the condition of the roof. It must include all mechanical, tenant and public spaces, as well as the exterior and any land, parking areas, gardens or grounds attached to the building. Particular attention should be paid to potential building code and safety violations. Equipment needed for this inspection include a note pad, tape recorder, flashlight, and binoculars. The following types of practical questions should be addressed, as negative answers may be signs of hidden problems.

1. Do the water fountains work? Is the water cold and clear? If not there may be a piping or chiller problem.
2. Do the toilets flush properly? Does the flush valve leak around the handle or vacuum breaker? Does water leak onto the floor at the base of the toilet? Is the flushing slow and sluggish? Any of these conditions may point to main drain problems.
3. Are the electrical closets clean and tidy or are panel covers off and wires hanging loose? Is the closet used for storage?
4. Are the main plant and mechanical spaces dirty? Are there any visible water leaks? Does the equipment sound as though it is functioning normally? Has a space become a catchment area for rubbish, waste or discarded equipment? These signs may indicate careless or unmotivated building staff.

With careful attention to detail on this inspection, the new manager can quickly assess not only the physical condition of the property, but also the quality of the contractors and building staff. He should conduct this type of general property inspection at least quarterly to identify both positive and negative trends in maintenance of the property.

Mechanical System Inspection

This inspection should be carried out by a qualified mechanical property manager who may be on the management agency's staff, a firm engaged as a consultant for this purpose, or by a senior engineer, in the company of the building manager. The inspection should focus on the overall condition of the building's equipment and systems. The starting point is an examination of the building's plans to identify the types of systems in the building. The inspection should begin in the engineer's office with a review of all logs, books, current plant reading sheets, preventive maintenance records and test records of emergency equipment. Reports covering the emergency generator, fire pump, fire alarm and other life safety systems, as well as current air and water test records, should be examined. At this time, the manager should discuss current operating procedures with the building engineer to determine whether they are adequate for the property and to establish the engineer's level of experience and knowledge of the building.

The physical inspection should begin at the top of the building and continue down to the lowest level. The areas that should be covered are the elevator machine room, cooling tower area, main plant, roof and all outlying auxiliary machine spaces including lobby, air handling room, fire pump room and emergency generator room. The main switch gear room and all garage areas should also be checked, as they often contain ventilation equipment, sump pumps, fire pumps and emergency generators.

As with the general inspection, the manager should be alert to code and safety violations. Machine rooms often become a storage area for combustible materials. Storage in machine rooms and electrical closets should be prohibited, as materials stored in these spaces can create a fire hazard or make access difficult. Parts or materials left lying about on the floor can create trip hazards. All fire extinguishers must be checked for condition, pressure and last inspection date. The manager should look for loose exposed electrical wires, missing circuit breaker panel covers, covers missing from junction boxes and burned out lights. It is also important to establish that all V-belt and shaft guards are in place.

As a general guide, it is a good idea to feel all operating electric motors with the back of the hand. If they are too hot to touch, the motor may need to be replaced in the near future. V-belts should be examined for condition, tension and alignment. Water coils, air dampers and outside bird screens should be checked for cleanliness. The condition of all fan blades and housings should be checked. Dirt marks on supply air ducts may indicate air leaks. Pump shaft seals must be examined for leakage.

If the boilers are running, the color, shape and size of the flame should be examined. It should be blueish yellow. If it looks orange and smoky, or white, it probably is not running efficiently and needs adjustment. All piping, valves and pressure vessels such as boilers, water convertors and water storage tanks should be checked for leakage. If the chillers are running, the condenser pressure should be checked and compared to the outside temperature. If the pressure is too high, the condenser tubes may be dirty or fouled. The cooling tower must be inspected for excess water leakage.

If the mechanical room is hot, more ventilation is needed, as excess heat will shorten the life of the electrical equipment. The manager should listen to transformers and switches. If they are humming loudly, these must be examined. A trained ear can pick up a bad bearing, loose or misaligned belts and other problems that a visual inspection alone might miss.

Lease Review and Administration

The manager should thoroughly review all tenant lease files, with emphasis on those items for which maintenance is responsible, such as periodic painting or re-carpeting, overtime HVAC costs, cleaning specifications and the like. The lease files should contain the lease document and possibly a lease abstract, all rent roll changes, general correspondence, lease amendments, escalation information, records of space alterations, miscellaneous billings and a copy of the as-built floor or space plan. From this information, a critical tenant data file can be organized. This file should be set up for fast, easy reference and should contain such information as a copy of the lease abstract and any non-standard lease terms such as day instead of night cleaning, special billing information, whether the tenant is relieved of alteration costs, any concessions made in the lease, unusual operating hours and name of the tenant contact.

A tickler file system should also be set up to show upcoming activity such as a required paint job, when a rent abatement or other lease concession ends, when an automatic rent escalation starts or anything unusual to a particular tenant. Managers with a computerized information management system will enter this information into their data base at the time of this review.

Staffing Requirements

Since no two buildings are alike, there is no formula to determine the number or caliber of employees required for a given building, or even whether any full-time employees are needed. It may be possible for a service contractor to handle all of the work. By carrying out the general property inspection, mechanical inspection, tenant interviews and lease reviews, the property manager should have developed a good feel for the condition of the property, normal daily work requirements and deferred maintenance. Tenant lease requirements and tenant profiles can help the manager make an informed decision about whether the work can be done with an outside contractor, or the number and experience level of permanent staff needed.

SYSTEMS AND PROCEDURES

As the office market grew successively more competitive in the 1980s, and as computer applications and new software programs facilitated better record keeping and maintenance procedures, an increasing emphasis has been placed on carefully monitored written systems and procedures. Not only is the tenant better satisfied with the quality of the maintenance operation, but the owner may gain with improved cost control because of this more systematic approach to real estate management. Many of the systems and procedures are conceived by internal staff. However, there are many requirements for service and repair contracts with outside companies. Whether the maintenance is performed internally or externally, the applied systems are the same.

Information Management Systems

There are many computer software information management systems available. The following is a brief description of the capabilities of one such system.

The software is an integrated real estate program designed specifically to meet property managers' needs. The program consists of three major modules: lease tracking, financial management and property management. The three modules are closely linked, which results in greater efficiency and higher productivity.

The major portion of the program is the lease tracking system. It consists of 15 screens that enable the property manager to input all tenant-related information, including leasing and financial notes which can be placed behind every screen. The system tracks all escalations, such as real estate taxes, consumer price index, operating expenses, common area maintenance and step-up rents. The reports available include rent roll, space analysis, square foot analysis and floor plan layout. The program enables the manager to sort, track and generate reports by any desired category, such as company, lease, floor, retail, office and so on. The lease tracking software interfaces directly with the accounts receivable software and creates billing information to be sent to the tenants, eliminating the need for time-consuming transmittal sheets between departments.

In the financial module, an agency accounts payable system eliminates separate check runs. The system generates checks for all entities, updates the general ledgers for each property and creates the necessary reports. The financial module is linked directly to the purchase order, budget tracking and general ledger systems. The general ledger software is connected with the fixed asset, budget tracking, accounts receivable and job costing software, enabling the property manager to monitor the profitability of the entire operation.

The third component of the system is the property management module. This module interfaces directly with the purchase order and accounts receivable portions of the financial module. The key to the property management system is the work order system. When a staff member receives a call from a tenant reporting a problem, the software allows the staff member to input general information about the problem and create a work order that is sent to other staff members responsible for servicing the tenant. Once the work is completed, the pertinent information can be sent to the accounts receivable module in order to bill the tenant.

Service Contracts

Certain tasks, such as cleaning, security, maintenance and painting, may be contracted to outside service providers. Clear guidelines must be established—and followed—for the administration of all outside services used in the building. Specifications must be established so that all contractors have the same information, and a minimum of three or four bids should be sought.

Before asking a company to bid, the manager should determine whether the contractor's size is appropriate to the job. If the contractor is too small, it may not be able to handle the job adequately; if it is too large, it may not give the job sufficient attention. He should also investigate the contractor's financial status. Is it financially sound? He should obtain current financial statements prepared by an outside accounting firm and review them to assess the contractor's capacity to:

1. Remain in business indefinitely
2. Meet further financial responsibilities in light of its debt schedule
3. Carry the building account from month to month without prepayment requests.

Finally, the manager should look at the length of time the contractor has been in business. If the company has only been in operation for a short time, he should check the past success or failure rate of the principals. He should also obtain business and client references, and should investigate the company's reputation with banks, subcontractors, vendors, suppliers, the Better Business Bureau, and other real estate companies, as well as its general reputation in the community.

Once a contract has been awarded, the manager must constantly monitor the contractor's performance and provide meaningful feedback in face-to-face meetings. The objective is to create a partnership rather than an adversarial relationship, and to work together to constantly improve the services provided.

Purchasing Procedures

Purchasing procedures in a property management organization are as varied as the products and services purchased. However the key to successful purchasing, is, in a word, controls. To protect the organization against expending funds needlessly, controls must be set up and maintained by all managers within the organization. When purchasing procedures are being established, the three basic areas of purchasing—purchasing, receipt and issuance of goods, and payment—should be assigned to different persons whose job responsibilities do not overlap. This control helps to limit potential losses through theft.

Purchasing. In order for any item to be purchased, a purchase requisition or other form must be filled out and authorized by management. Dollar limits can be instituted as well as employee authority levels to aid in the authorization process. The approved purchase requisition will authorize the purchasing agent, or the person requesting the item, to place the order and issue a purchase order. The purchase order system is usually devised by the finance department as it is generally considered to be a financial rather than an operational procedure. Once the purchase order or confirmation order is placed, the order should be traced to assure delivery within the terms of the order.

Receipt/issuance of goods. The receiving clerk takes delivery of the item and verifies the quantity and quality at the time of delivery. The clerk notes on the receiving report any shortages or overages, missing items and items that must be returned because they are incorrect or damaged. The receiving reports are then submitted to the finance department as part of the payment procedure. Items are stocked or issued to the requesting party by storeroom personnel. Accurate records are maintained of "par" items (that is, items used regularly, such as light bulbs, of which a certain amount must be kept on hand), usage levels and other special items or commodities utilized by the organization, such as carpeting or doors used for remodeling, to ensure adequate supplies. These records are generally submitted to management for standing order or deletion on a monthly basis.

Payment. When invoices are received, they are forwarded to the finance department. The finance department then sends the invoice to accounts payable for matching with the accounting copy of the purchase order and the receiving report. When these three documents have been matched, the finance department correlates the quantities received and the prices charged based on the purchase order, and checks the totals of the invoice item by item prior to payment. Any discrepancies are directed to the purchasing agent for resolution prior to payment.

Other issues related to the purchasing process that management may wish to consider for the office building are off-site warehousing, master vendor lists, guaranteed pricing of major items, direct purchase/delivery procedures with vendors, semi-annual credit checks of major vendors, bulk purchases, and specification guidelines by product.

Once the items are purchased, decisions must be made about access to storerooms and storage areas based on the value of the products stored there. If they contain a high-dollar inventory, the number of people who have access, and the times of access, must be limited. If the area houses lower cost items, protection may become more expensive than the value of the items. If storage areas are staffed by regular personnel, it is critical that the procedures be enforced at all times to avoid pilferage. It is also wise to make periodic spot checks to ensure conformance to policy and procedures.

Maintenance Work Orders

Maintenance work should be triggered either through the building inspection process or through tenant complaints. The work to be performed should be recorded on a work order form that is designed to clearly describe the problem—where it is located, what the job is, who is to handle it. The form should also contain space to record how much time was spent, how much material was used and whether the labor and/or materials are billable to the tenants. By documenting how quickly work is being performed, a work order system is a good indicator of the appropriateness of staffing levels and the skill levels of the staff. More important, it documents the level of service being received by the tenants. This information is also important in preparing the annual operating and capital budgets. For example, if unusually large amounts of time and money are being spent on an item of equipment it may be time for major repairs or replacement.

The response time of maintenance personnel can be greatly improved if they have the right information from the outset. It is important, therefore, that the person in the management office who is designated to receive tenant calls and complaints has the intelligence, experience and knowledge of the property to obtain all pertinent information. This person should call the tenant back if work cannot be done promptly to explain the delay. It is a good practice for this individual to occasionally accompany the property manager or building inspector on tenant visits. This will help them to become more familiar with the property and to build a rapport with tenant service contacts.

Preventive Maintenance

Management should have a written preventive maintenance program covering the entire building, including HVAC equipment, all equipment that uses electricity and even such things as door closures, lock sets, ventilation blinds, flush valves and faucets. This should be developed into a manual that makes it easy for the manager to follow the history and progress of the maintenance program and is complete enough for the person assigned to know what must be done. Software for this task is available from any major control vendor, such as Honeywell, Johnson Controls or Powers Regulator.

Each item to be maintained should have a complete checklist of specific tasks to be performed, based on the manufacturer's operating manuals. For a new building, it is important for the building engineer and maintenance staff to meet with the staff of the equipment manufacturers to learn the appropriate maintenance procedures. The instructions in the maintenance manuals should be followed in detail to get the longest life and most economical operation from each piece of equipment. The property manager must determine whether the existing staff is qualified and capable of doing this work. In most cases, he will use a mixture of in-house personnel and contractors.

MECHANICAL SYSTEMS

While there are many types of office building mechanical systems available, they all have three things in common: they must be able to properly heat, cool and ventilate the building.

Heating

The most common sources of heat for an office building are boilers, either steam or hot water, electrical resistance heating, heat pumps, solar energy, steam purchased from the city or power company, and direct fired hot air furnaces.

The fuels used in the production of heat include electricity, fuel oil grades 2, 4, 5 and 6, natural gas, coal and the sun. Ancillary equipment needed for the operation of the heating system may include the following items: fuel oil pumps, condensate tank and pumps, steam-to-water or water-to-water converter fuel oil heaters, temperature and pressure controls, cooling tower, water circulating pumps, steam traps and chemical feeders.

Cooling

To cool a building, normally two types of refrigeration systems are used. The first is the water chiller. This system uses a refrigerant to produce chilled water which is then used for cooling. The second type of system is the direct expansion unit, or DX, system. With this type of system, the refrigerant itself is used as the cooling mechanism. DX units are used in smaller applications, from window units to loads requiring up to 80 tons. Chilled water systems are used when the load requirements are above 80 tons.

The types of chillers available are reciprocating, centrifugal and absorption units. The reciprocating unit is used mostly in DX systems, but can also be used to make chilled water. The centrifugal and absorption chillers are used mostly to make chilled water, but the centrifugal can be used as a DX unit, usually in the lower load ranges of 80 to 200 tons.

These chillers can be powered by electric motors, gasoline, natural gas or diesel engines, or steam turbines. The ancillary equipment needed to operate these machines are chilled water and condenser water pumps and a cooling tower. The chilled water pump circulates the chilled water to the air handlers, which send cool air to the building. The condenser pump circulates the warm condensed water to the cooling tower; the cooling tower cools the condenser cooling water for reuse and is also the rejection point for the heat that is removed from the building.

Most medium and large office buildings use a combination of air and water systems to distribute the conditioned air to the required spaces. Smaller buildings usually use air- or water-cooled direct expansion packed units for this purpose; they generally have as a heat source natural gas burners or electric resistance strip heaters. Heat pumps are also used in these units.

HVAC System Zoning

HVAC systems must be designed to compensate for both internal and external building loads. It is not unusual for the HVAC system for a large office building to be split into five or more zones to handle the various loads. There will generally be one zone for all of the interior space, as the load in this space is fairly constant. However, the spaces adjoining exterior walls and windows are much more sensitive to changing exterior loads and may require from one to four or more zones to handle these conditions. It is not unusual during certain seasons for the load requirements to change from heating to cooling and back to heating during the same day.

Generally, the more zones the system has, the more easily the loading problem can be controlled. A one or two zone air system, or such a system combined with a two-pipe water system is unlikely to be able to deal with heat load conditions. In such a case, it falls on an experienced engineering staff to attempt to manipulate the system to meet the comfort demands of tenants.

HVAC Distribution Systems

The HVAC is distributed via an air system which utilizes a remote air handler and distribution ducts, or a water system which uses pumps and piping. Most large systems use a combination of air and water that can be combined in many different configurations. Generally water systems consist of two, three or four pipes. The two-pipe system delivers hot or chilled water in the supply pipe to a remote air handler, fan coil unit or induction unit; after doing its job, the water is returned to the main plant for reuse via the return pipe. This system is the least expensive to install and operate, but it is also the most inflexible for meeting changing load conditions, as the system can only heat or cool at any one time; it cannot offer heating and cooling simultaneously to different parts of the building.

With the three-pipe system, there are separate supply pipes for hot and chilled water, and in theory heating and cooling are supplied year round. While the system is more flexible in meeting load changes, it is uneconomical to operate, and hot and chilled water mix in the third pipe, which is a common return. The four-pipe system is the most flexible and is economical to operate as there are separate supply and return pipes for the hot and chilled water. The drawback to this system is its high installation cost.

Most large office buildings contain several different air systems. HVAC supply air handlers are used to distribute the conditioned air throughout the building. Return air fans pull air from the building back to the main plant. There, they either send the air, in whole or in part, back to the supply fans for reconditioning and mixing with outside air for reuse in the building, or they discharge it directly to the outside, depending on building conditions and requirements. Other systems include toilet and kitchen exhaust fans, which discharge air from these areas directly to the atmosphere. In addition, there may be elevator machine room fans to cool the elevator equipment and garage supply and exhaust fans to keep auto exhaust in check. In some buildings there is a separate unit for the main lobby. Lobbies usually have different requirements than office spaces because they have higher ceilings, more glass surfaces, doors that open directly to the outside and elevator shafts that act like chimneys.

The supply air handler is the heart of the air distribution system. Air handlers are different from fans. Fans are used to move air from one place to another. Air handlers not only move air; they also have coils that cool and dehumidify, coils that heat and air washers that clean and humidify the air in winter, as well as a method of air filtration. All air handlers have at least some of these components, although some units use electric resistance heaters instead of heating coils. The air handlers may be located in a central plant or they can be located throughout the building, with one or more units on each floor. Packaged units may be used in place of small air handlers. They have the advantage of not requiring hot or chilled water to be piped to them, as they contain a direct expansion cooling system and electric resistance heat.

An example of an air-water HVAC system is the high pressure induction unit. These units are used to condition the exterior office space zone. In buildings where this system is used, there will be a second separate system to serve the interior zone. The induction unit consists of a steel cabinet, water coil, temperature control valve, air filter and an air chamber or plenum equipped with air nozzles. These units are usually located along the exterior walls of the building. Primary air is supplied to each unit from the exterior air handler through a high velocity duct system. The primary air enters the air plenum and is discharged through the air nozzles at a high velocity across the face of the water coil; chilled or heated water is piped and passes into the coil through a temperature control valve. The high velocity air crossing the face of the coil causes the room air or secondary air to be drawn, or induced, over the coil, thereby altering the temperature. The room air is mixed with the constant temperature primary air and flows through the discharge grill at the top of the unit. The primary air, which can be all outside air or a mixture of return and outside air, comprises about 15% and the room air comprises 85% of the total unit output.

The interior zones of a building using perimeter induction units are conditioned by a single duct, constant volume variable temperature system. Because the interior zone usually has a fairly constant heat load, the discharge air temperature is kept at 55 to 60 degrees Fahrenheit year round. Like the induction unit system, this system also uses a central air handler, but it produces a lower pressure, higher volume air supply. The conditioned air is distributed via a low pressure duct system consisting of a main trunk duct which runs vertically for the height of the building and branch ducts fitted with fire and balancing dampers at each floor. The conditioned air is delivered to the office space through ceiling diffuser outlets. These come in several shapes and designs, and some permit air flow to be adjusted. The diffusers can be attached directly to the branch duct or can be connected to it by flexible duct.

ELECTRICAL SYSTEMS

Electricity is supplied from the power company to the main building transformers, which are owned either by the power company or by the property owner. These transformers reduce the incoming power, which in most cases is in thousands of volts, to a usable 480 volts. The power is then sent to the main building switching mechanism, or main switch gear. From there, the power is routed through the main building disconnect switch to various other sub-disconnect switches that make up the switch gear. Some of the 480 volt power is then sent to the motor control center in the HVAC room to be used directly by the air conditioning motors and other large electrical devices. The remainder of the 480 volt power is distributed to step-down transformers located throughout the building, where it is converted to 277 volts for fluorescent lighting, and to 220 and 110 volts for general office and small motor use. Some older buildings also use 208 volt power. The stepped-down power is then sent to the local circuit breaker panels, which are switching protective devices for all of the branch circuits. From there the power is delivered to the end-use receptacles and fixtures.

Circuit breakers should periodically be load tested by a qualified electrical contractor to make sure they will in fact trip on short circuit or thermal overload. Growth in the use of office computers and other electrical equipment and the resulting increase in electrical usage leads to circuit overloading and drops in line voltage. A constantly tripping circuit breaker is a good indication of an overloaded circuit. However, sometimes a breaker that has been installed for many years will not trip when it is overloaded, and a fire can result. For this reason, it is important to periodically check the amperage and voltage draw on the breaker panels. Increased electrical usage can also cause a reduction in line voltage. This can be tested for using a voltage tester. If the indicated voltage is 10% or more below rating, there is a problem, and a qualified electrical contractor should be brought in to correct it.

PLUMBING SYSTEMS

Plumbing systems in office buildings consist of a fresh water supply (cold and hot) and a waste water removal system (sewage and storm water). The most basic supply system is one where the building is tied into the city water main and water is distributed through the building by city water pressure. However, since most building codes limit the water pressure in a plumbing system to 80 pounds per square inch, the city pressure may be insufficient to reach the upper floors of the building.

Several systems have been developed to compensate for inadequate city water pressure. One is the gravity system. With a gravity system, a storage tank is located on top of the building. Water is pumped up to the tank and gravity draws the water throughout the building. Another is the suction tank system. The water supply flows by gravity to the tank, generally located in the basement or on a lower floor, and is pumped up into the building. A third system is the pneumatic tank, where water is pumped into a closed tank which is pressurized with compressed air. Finally, there is the tankless system. This is a variation of the basic city water system, but variable or constant speed pumps are used to boost the water pressure. Some new buildings have installed localized hot water heaters that handle specific areas. However, most older buildings use a central hot water heating source coupled with either a circulating or non-circulating piping system. In the circulating system, there is a supply line and a return line where a pump is installed to keep the water moving, providing instant hot water. This is the system used in most large office buildings. The non-circulating system is equipped with only a supply line. Most building codes limit the length of non-circulatory line to 50 feet from the heat source.

Office buildings have two separate systems for the removal of waste and water: the sanitary drainage system and the storm drainage system. The two systems are separate and unrelated within the building even though they may enter a common city sewer system.

The sanitary system collects the effluent from restrooms, kitchens, water fountains, floor drains and other water-using equipment, and conveys it by gravity flow to the city sewer. The storm sewer is for the removal of rainwater, although groundwater may also be drained into a storm water system. Buildings with underground garages, restrooms or other occupied space located below the main sewer lines have a third subsystem. This is the sump pump or sewer ejection system. Both systems are similar and consist of a steel or concrete enclosed pit or sump that is equipped with pumps. The sump pits collect garage or groundwater and pump it up to the sewer line. The sewer ejector pumps do the same for sewage.

During building inspections, the float rods on the sump pumps should be manually raised until the pumps start. The check should continue until the pumps stop running. They should come to a complete stop and then turn backward for several rotations. This is a backwash feature. If they turn more than several turns, it could mean that the non-return check valve is leaking and some of the water that was just pumped out is flowing back into the pit.

ELEVATORS

There are two types of elevators: electric and hydraulic. Hydraulic elevators are used in low-rise buildings (five stories or less), and travel at 100 to 150 feet per minute. Electric elevators are used in buildings higher than five stories, and travel more than 150 feet per minute.

Electric elevators are powered by an electric motor that turns a grooved wheel which in turn raises or lowers steel cables attached to the top of the elevator, causing it to move up and down the elevator shaft. Electric systems are classified as either geared or gearless. Gearless electric elevators are mostly used in high-rise buildings and have a life expectancy of 60 to 80 years. Geared electric elevators are more commonly used in mid-rise buildings, and can be expected to last for 25 to 35 years.

Hydraulic elevators are powered by hydraulic oil being pumped into or withdrawn from a vertical steel cylinder where a steel plunger attached to the bottom of the car is moved up or down. Hydraulic elevators usually have a life expectancy of 20 years.

The life expectancy of elevator systems is directly related to the level of maintenance they receive. Implementation of a maintenance plan is important also to the smooth, efficient operation of the equipment. After inadequate air conditioning, tenants' second biggest complaint is poor elevator service.

Managers can use their own employees to maintain the elevators, they can have a maintenance contract with the elevator manufacturer or another qualified contractor, or they can use a combination of the two. Regardless of who does the maintenance, there are certain checks that should be carried out on a regular basis. One of these is the speed of the cars. The overall speed of the car depends on several timed functions that the manager can check with a stopwatch. Some of these are:

- **Travel time:** The time required for the car to travel from the starting floor to the next floor should be 3.5 to 5 seconds for gearless elevators and 5 to 7 seconds for geared elevators.
- **Car start time:** The manager should stand inside a car and see how long it takes the car to start moving after the doors have closed. The time should be less than one second.
- **Door operation time:** Center opening doors should open in about 1.6 seconds, and stay open 2 seconds for a hall call and one second for an in-car call.
- **Call button response time:** When a call button is pushed, it should take from 20 to 30 seconds for a car to arrive.

When riding in a car, the manager should check whether the car is level with the floor, how it accelerates and decelerates and the quality of the ride. While making building inspections on random floors, he should push a call button to check car response time, whether hall indicator lanterns and gongs work and whether doors open smoothly. During building inspections, the elevator machine room—where the hoisting machine, motor generator set and controls are located—should not be overlooked.

ENERGY CONSERVATION PROGRAM

In a time of dwindling natural resources and rising operating costs, it is inexcusable for an office building not to have an energy conservation program in place. Even a standard manual program from a utility company is preferable to no program. Because the array of products on the market is so broad and complicated, it is difficult for a building manager to evaluate them. If the building does not have a professional engineering staff, the property manager should consider engaging a competent and reliable engineering firm to conduct a complete energy audit of the building. Such an audit requires mechanical, electrical and computer expertise. The engineering firm will show the present energy status of the building and will make recommendations on alternative courses of action with payback time frames.

There are several low-cost or no-cost steps that building staff or contractors can take to increase the efficiency of existing equipment. The burners on the boiler should be adjusted at the beginning and middle of each season to keep from fouling up the firebox and tubes with soot. It is also essential to have a good water treatment program to keep the water sides of the boiler tubes from scaling up, as both soot and scale are excellent insulators. The condensor tubes on the air conditioning chillers must be cleaned before each season as well as the cooling tower, and the water must be treated to prevent scale. Further, all chilled water, hot water and steam coils should be cleaned on the air sides each season. Even if they look clean, airborn oils and pollution form an invisible film that cuts down heat transfer.

In buildings that are five or more years old, the manager should use the building mechanical plans to locate all in-duct reheat coils and inspect them, even if this requires cutting access holes in the duct work. In most cases, they will be clogged with dirt or original construction debris. The air filters on the HVAC system should be changed at least every six months, and checked to be sure that no air is passing around the filters. Belt drives should be checked for the condition, tension and alignment of the belts and the grooves on the motor and fan pulleys. This can create a drag on the motor, causing it to use more electricity and shortening the life of the motor, fan bearings and belts. It is recommended that all air leaks on fan discharge ducts be sealed and all broken or torn pipe and duct insulations be repaired. The HVAC control system should be checked and calibrated by a qualified contractor twice a year.

CONSTRUCTION MANAGEMENT PROGRAM FOR TENANT BUILDOUTS

Commercial properties (offices, retail and warehouses/light industrial) differ significantly from all residential and hotel properties in one important respect. While residential properties are offered intact, that is with finished space subdivided into rooms, commercial property is originally conceived as a shell and core. All necessary office plumbing and wiring are installed, but the space essentially is customized for each new tenant and occasionally for renewing tenants.

The building manager is required to be a builder of tenant space or a supervisor of construction contractors who specialize in building interiors. A detailed discussion of this process in new buildings is found in Chapter

16. Over time, tenants expand, contract and relocate, so it is essential that the building manager be skilled in the area of tenant installations.

The key ingredient in a successful tenant buildout program is attention to details. With the appropriate concern for details, schedules are met, budgets are realistic and both landlord and tenant can be proud of the quality of the final product. In any property management organization, the implementation of a Construction Management Program (CMP) is essential to successfully and profitably manage tenant buildouts.

The building manager can substantially reduce delays in the construction process by knowing when to bring in the contractor. For tenant installation jobs of over 10,000 square feet, it is generally wise to involve the contractor when the first serious discussions are held with the tenant regarding the buildout of the space. Along with the architect and other design team members, the contractor is a key factor in identifying potential construction problems and long lead time items. He can also be instrumental in reducing construction costs due to overdesign and suggesting cost-saving specification changes before the project begins, reducing the need for change orders.

Firm timelines must be established for the owner as well as the tenant early in the project. The Construction Management Program is dependent upon the timely submission and turnaround of documents by all parties. The faster the contractor has final plans, the sooner construction can begin and the better the final bid price will be. The sooner the space is completed and turned over to the tenant, the sooner it will produce revenue for the owner.

Another key factor in a profitable CMP is knowing when to negotiate and when to competitively bid a project. When evaluating the project, the owner must look at the size of the job, the level of finishes and the tenant's expected schedule. Negotiated contracts can result in construction start dates that are several weeks earlier. But the use of negotiated contracts is wise only if the owner has a sound, trusting relationship with his contractors and subcontractors.

Once the project has begun, unless it involves the entire floor of the building, keeping in-place tenants happy becomes an integral part of the project. Construction is never a quiet task. It is, therefore, critical to keep in-place tenants in mind when planning the project, setting up schedules and selecting methods of construction. Where possible, and within budget constraints, noisy work should be scheduled after normal hours or during slow periods in the workday. Nearby tenants should be briefed on the project and given an opportunity to take part in schedule coordination before plans are finalized. Daily checks by the construction manager or job superintendant to monitor disruptions will also keep existing tenants happy and the work progressing.

CONCLUSION

Operating a building requires a team approach, and all building employees, no matter what their jobs, should be included as fully participating members of the team. Employees should receive training in the best way to accomplish their jobs. They should be coached for continued improvement and should receive regular feedback on their performance and on tenants' responses to their contributions. External contractors too should be treated as team members, and should be helped to understand how their contributions fit into the larger picture.

ABOUT THE AUTHOR

Christopher J. Whyman, CRE, president, CEO and director of Eastern Realty Investment Management, Inc., and its affiliates, has more than 20 years of commercial real estate experience. From 1980 to 1983 he was chief surveyor with the Electricity Supply Pension Fund of England and Wales, where he established the property acquisition and management department. From 1970 to 1980 he was deputy estates manager for Philips Industries, the British part of the Dutch electronics giant. Whyman is both a Fellow of the Royal Institution of Chartered Surveyors and a member of the Counselors of Real Estate. He is a director of the Association of Foreign Investors and a member of the Urban Land Institute.

CHAPTER

28

REAL ESTATE ASSET MANAGEMENT

by John K. Rutledge

INTRODUCTION

Asset management may be defined as the role and functioning of the property owner in the selection, acquisition, management, leasing, financing, and disposition of real estate. Because of the complexities of these responsibilities, a variety of experts and agents may be engaged to carry them out. The asset manager represents the owner and may be delegated discretionary authority to supervise day-to-day management subject to agreed-on budgetary and management policy constraints. Performance of the asset manager can make the difference between superior and mediocre investment results. Usually, but not always, the asset manager contracts with a leasing and managing agency to operate the property for designated fees, subject to the asset manager's monitoring and supervision.

In an institutional setting, the owner may be a pension fund or a personal trust (or perhaps a commingled fund for such investors sponsored by a financial institution). A portfolio manager has responsibility for the entire investment portfolio including stocks, fixed income investments, and real estate. Functionally, the asset manager reports to the portfolio manager concerning that portion of the portfolio which is committed to real estate. The portfolio manager may directly manage the stock and bond investments or may delegate these duties to one or more investment managers.

Very large investors may engage a variety of specialized firms providing investment management and asset management services for different components of the investment portfolio. The portfolio manager allocates capital to the investment and asset managers and monitors their performance.

This chapter addresses the activities comprising office building asset management, whether conducted by the owner or an agent, spanning the term of an investment.

THE ACQUISITION PROCESS

Investment Objectives

The process of investing in an office building flows from an understanding of the objectives of the investor. Those objectives dictate the investment parameters such as property type, size, geographic siting, financing, and the form the investment will take, such as a fee simple equity or a participating mortgage.

A passive investor may seek income, perhaps to meet retirement income needs, or appreciation in anticipation of future income requirements. A speculator may invest anticipating a future sale to a redeveloper or rehabilitator, or may simply expect a cyclical upturn in values or an external event leading to a higher selling price. Tax considerations may motivate a buyer, depending on the most recent tax reform act.

An active investor, on the other hand, may be looking for an opportunity to redevelop or rehabilitate a property or to create value by changing the use of the property.

Perhaps the most basic of all active office building investors is the one seeking a place to conduct business. After all, occupancy is the fundamental basis for putting improvements such as an office building on land. This investor has many of the concerns of other investors but may be more specific concerning locational requirements, existing financing, and the availability of suitable space for his operations. A fully leased building may be unacceptable unless leases expire shortly or can be terminated.

Investor Strengths

An asset should be acquired only if the investor has strengths which can add value to the asset. These strengths may include management capability, construction expertise, leasing talent (or a direct need to occupy), capital, or simply the ability to be patient.

Failure to recognize this principle carries two risks. First, performance of the asset may deteriorate, failing to meet the investor's cash flow and appreciation expectations. Second, the acquisition effort may absorb resources (time and money) and then be unsuccessful. This will happen if weakness, or absence of strength, is fully recognized and factored into expectations of future performance, resulting in an offer that is exceeded by a stronger competing bidder.

Investment Parameters

With an understanding of the investment objectives and strengths of the investor, investment guidelines can be established. An investor may feel more comfortable concentrating in a specific geographic area such as his home city or surrounding region. Geographic diversification may reduce the portfolio risk by allowing investment in diverse local economies (and currencies). If, for example, unexpected events cause oil prices to fall, damaging the economies of energy-producing regions, energy-consuming regions may prosper through lower costs.

It is not necessary to invest in more than a few cities to achieve a significant measure of risk reduction. Diversification efforts may be wasted if chosen cities, though thousands of miles apart, are based on similar industries. Market knowledge and professional contacts must be maintained in each city, and travel and/or local office expenses will be incurred. A critical mass of activity should be reached in each city to assure efficient asset management.

The guidelines on physical condition must be determined. Some investors seek only top quality (sometimes called trophy or Class A) office buildings, while others may be less concerned about image and prefer the higher risk and return that may be offered by properties of lower quality. Willingness to deal with deferred maintenance and, potentially more dangerous, environmental contamination must be decided and understood as well.

Financial considerations include occupancy and the willingness to deal with actual and near term potential vacancy, especially as it may affect cash flow. The existence of debt and its related provisions concerning permitted prepayment, assumability, and the date of any required balloon payment, along with the projected availability and terms of refinancing credit, influence the suitability of a potential acquisition.

Identifying Acquisition Candidates

With thorough knowledge of the investor's objectives, and clear investment guidelines, the asset manager can begin the search for suitable properties for acquisition. The brokerage community thrives on identifying investors and will quickly inundate a potentially active buyer with the complete range of property types, sizes, qualities, and locations, some of which will not even be available for purchase.

Because these unsolicited submissions rarely meet the predetermined guidelines, it is essential to take a proactive, rather than reactive, approach to the search. The network of relationships with carefully selected brokers, developers, other investors, and professionals such as counselors, appraisers, attorneys, and architects must be cultivated and expanded.

Many submissions will be recognized as inappropriate and will be discarded very quickly. Others, though, will more closely meet the stated guidelines and will justify further analysis. Because each property is unique, it is likely that no submission will exactly fit a narrow set of requirements, and a reasoned compromise may be an acceptable choice. Of course, another approach is to continue the search for a property more closely meeting the guidelines.

The Offer

Once the best alternative is selected, an offer can be developed. The process of making an offer and completing the due diligence research can follow a variety of patterns, depending on practices of the parties and local custom. It is desirable to have a commitment by the seller to sell if the due diligence uncovers no problem that cannot be solved by the seller in an acceptable manner. Otherwise, the preclosing research could be completed and the property could then be taken off the market or sold to a later and higher bidder. Consequently, the buyer wants to "tie up" the property before spending significant sums on research.

The amount to be offered may be determined in any one of several ways. Some investors obtain a full appraisal from an independent appraiser. Others complete an internal evaluation based on various assumptions. A discounted cash flow analysis may be completed. Discount rates and assumptions such as future vacancy and rental rates are as varied as the buyers who use them. Replacement cost may be calculated, and sale data on comparable properties, while difficult to obtain, is useful.

Other less quantifiable matters are evaluated. Location is important. General appearance, architectural significance, and reputation of the building are considered.

Analysis of this information will lead to a conclusion on the maximum price that may be paid. Depending on preferred negotiating style, the buyer may submit a first and final offer at the maximum amount or, more likely, will initially offer a lesser amount to provide room for negotiations.

The offer may take the form of a comprehensive contract governing the entire transaction. This document, drafted by the buyer's counsel, specifies the due diligence to which the property would be subjected; the rights of the parties if title, structural, financial, environmental or other problems or misrepresentations are discovered; and the closing requirements. Such a document itself is almost always subject to extensive and time-consuming negotiations. Consequently, some buyers prefer to submit a brief nonbinding letter of intent primarily designed to lead to an agreement on price, to be followed by good faith efforts toward agreement on a complete contract for purchase and sale.

The timing of the offer may depend on the competitive environment. Certain elements of the due diligence process may be easy but critical to the decision to proceed, while the negotiation and documentation of the contract is expensive, and the buyer may choose to begin the due diligence process before the seller is firmly committed to sell. In a highly competitive market, however, tying up the property may be the first priority, provided adequate safeguards are available to the buyer. It is beyond the scope of this chapter to address the legal aspects of the purchase contract, but it is noted that the buyer wants extensive warranties and representations about the property and the seller resists giving them. Negotiating agreement in this area usually takes more time than settling on an acceptable price.

Due Diligence

In addition to defining the rights of the parties, the contract specifies the data and access to be provided to the buyer, time requirements for the seller to supply data (and for the buyer to give notice of problems discovered), deliveries required at closing, indemnifications, termination and escape provisions, earnest money requirements, closing date, and other matters. The importance of this document cannot be overstated. Chapter 21 describes how on larger office properties the data necessary for the buyer to perform due diligence may be substantially provided in advance by the seller's exclusive agent or advisor.

The financial aspect of the due diligence process requires that all leases be reviewed carefully. Deviations from the submission package on matters such as square footage, rental rates and escalations, expiration dates, and other facts should be noted. Options to renew, terminate early, or purchase deserve special attention. Leasing concessions such as free rent, above-standard buildout, and moving allowance may not be detailed in the lease and relevant data should be obtained. The creation of a schedule of lease expirations by year is informative.

Historical operating results and supporting documentation such as invoices should be examined. Title documentation may reveal undisclosed financial obligations such as a ground lease or mechanic's lien. Mortgage documents should be reviewed to assure that financing can be prepaid or assumed as represented by the seller, as well as to confirm the terms of any financing to be assumed.

The first aspect of the physical inspection considers the condition of the improvements. An experienced architect or contractor may be appropriate for a simple building, but a more complex building may demand a team consisting of an architect and engineers specializing in structural, mechanical, electrical, lighting, and other disciplines. Plans and specifications are reviewed and the property is inspected. Compliance with or deviation from plans is noted, deferred maintenance and cost to cure is documented, and deficiencies in design are reported. Pride of ownership may be evident and will provide some assurance concerning the quality of maintenance. A written report should be issued.

Results of this inspection may lead to a decision to terminate the contract and obtain a refund of the earnest money. Less serious findings may be grounds for renegotiating the price.

The second aspect of the physical evaluation concerns the presence or absence of substances considered to be toxic or hazardous. Because few deaths or illnesses resulting from working in contaminated office space have been documented, this is viewed by many as a legal issue, as contrasted to the risk of a structural failure. A Phase I audit is normally required, but the standards of such an audit are still evolving, as are permissible levels of contaminants and indeed even the list of materials considered hazardous.

The substance of the engagement letter or contract with the environmental consultant should be approved by legal counsel. The experience of the consultant is important. The typical consultant carries minimal insurance but will provide higher coverage at an additional cost. The timing requirements in the engagement letter are critical because the related background research on prior use and other matters is time consuming. The purchase contract strictly limits the time available for the due diligence process.

Legal counsel may recommend a verbal report before the written report is finalized. The form and timing of the reporting process should be specified in advance. The consultant usually includes qualifications or limitations in the conclusion, and the buyer may decide that a Phase II audit, involving sampling and testing, is necessary to address concerns raised by the Phase I audit report. The purchase contract may be terminated at this point if contamination is found. If the building appears to be clean, the purchase process may proceed.

It should be noted that the buyer may acquire with the building a liability for future clean-up of previously undetected hazardous substances and that removal requirements may change for known substances. Further, materials such as asbestos acquired with the building may remain the "property" of the buyer even after subsequent removal and transport to a disposal site, burdening the buyer with a permanent liability. If removal is necessary, it may be preferable to require the seller, who already owns and has liability for the material, to complete the removal before the purchase is closed. This way, the buyer never has title to the unwanted substance.

The legal review concentrates on the condition of title and the endorsements such as zoning and survey that should be included in the required title insurance policy. Documents such as easements and ground leases that affect title are reviewed, and the survey is studied for encroachments and for the appropriate certification. Leases and other contractual documents are reviewed for enforceability and closing documents are prepared or reviewed.

In addition to reading all leases, the buyer interviews tenants to determine their individual levels of satisfaction with the property and to get a sense of future plans, particularly as to their interest in renewing the lease upon expiration and their possible need for more or less space than is currently leased. Comfort complaints may be uncovered, and persistent mechanical or structural problems may be revealed. Until the purchase contract is signed, some sellers prohibit buyers from discussing with tenants their future plans on the grounds that it is disruptive to the building management, especially when a transaction does not materialize.

At closing, the seller should deliver a current estoppel certificate from each tenant certifying that the lease is in effect, the date to which rent has been paid, that the owner is not in default under the lease and owes the tenant nothing in connection with lease concessions, that the attached lease copy is the complete agreement between owner and tenant, and other items the buyer's counsel may require.

When the due diligence process has been completed and the closing documents have been reviewed, the final decision is made to close or terminate the contract. Findings may dictate an adjustment to price to achieve the financial performance indicated by the original submission package or by subsequent representations by the seller.

Preclosing Arrangements

Before closing, insurance coverage should be arranged to take effect upon closing and property management plans should be established. The asset manager may have internal property management capabilities or may plan to amend an existing contract adding the new property to others currently managed for the same investor by an independent property management firm. Otherwise a property management firm must be selected and engaged.

Large national firms may bring deep resources to the management of a property. Experts on specialized subjects may be on staff, and corporate relations may be maintained with national tenants. The investor, however, may experience unacceptable turnover at the property level as trainees are hired and subsequently move up through the ranks to other properties or duties. A local firm, conversely, may provide continuity of personnel but lack the depth of resources offered by the larger firm. Tenant relations and the ability to account accurately and promptly for the financial performance of the property are critical requirements.

A property management contract must be negotiated with the selected organization. Authority levels for expenditures, reporting requirements, and indemnifications are usual areas of discussion in arriving at a mutually acceptable contract.

OWNERSHIP RESPONSIBILITIES

Property Management

With completion of the acquisition process, it becomes the asset manager's responsibility to achieve the investor's performance objectives. Typically, the investor is seeking maximum total return. Current income and enhancement of property value, each weighted to reflect the time value of money, are considered and balanced. For example, superior maintenance may detract from current cash flow but assist in maintaining a high level of occupancy at favorable rents over the long term. The competent property manager will understand the goals of ownership and will perform the daily duties toward the achievement of those goals. The asset manager must be clear in communicating those goals to the property manager who in turn requires the authority to function effectively.

Tenant relations are vital to the success of the investment. Regular communications will reveal dissatisfaction and areas of concern which, if ignored, may result in the loss of the tenant and an expensive retenanting effort. A close but professional relationship encourages the tenant to prefer to renew at lease expiration rather than risk the unknown of a new location. Tenant complaints concerning maintenance deserve a quick response, and a good control system provides for accurate tracking of each complaint from the time it is made until it receives attention and is finally resolved. Aggressive maintenance, while expensive in the short term, enhances a building's image and contributes to successful long-term tenancy and financial performance.

Collections and rental delinquencies must be closely monitored and aggressively pursued. Some delinquencies are caused by temporary financial problems, and some form of deferral or forbearance may be justified. A failing business tenant, however, should be removed from the property as quickly as possible so that the space can be leased to a new tenant. Prompt attention and action, along with mutual honesty, are essential.

The asset manager, by carefully reviewing regular (usually monthly) reports from the property manager, can monitor compliance with the operating and capital budgets and can remain current on the status of collections. The property manager should tailor the reports to accommodate any special needs of the asset manager.

Some asset managers find it useful to specify the accounting software to be used by the property manager so that reports can be transmitted electronically. This is especially useful if the asset manager is receiving and consolidating reports from several property managers. The account of the asset manager must be sufficiently important to the property manager, however, to justify installing a new accounting package.

Regular inspections of the property by the asset manager are useful in confirming the performance of the property manager, especially in the areas of maintenance and tenant relations. Most property managers are motivated toward better performance knowing that the "owner" will be visiting. This is also a good opportunity to keep up to date on rental rates, the occupancy/vacancy situation in the market area, new local development activities, and other information useful to the asset manager. Visits also offer the opportunity to meet with other local real estate professionals.

Tenant Retention

Closely related to tenant relations is tenant retention. The loss of a tenant is invariably followed by an expensive transition, especially when vacancy rates are substantial. The next tenant must be found, the space must be upfitted or remodeled, a new lease must be negotiated and documented, and a leasing commission will be incurred. Space surpluses have dominated most metropolitan areas during most of the 1970s and 1980s, and such an imbalance exacerbates the cost of tenant turnover.

Incentives may include the assumption of the tenant's remaining obligation on the not-yet-expired old lease, payment of moving expenses, and above-standard tenant improvements. Free rent, either in the form of delayed commencement of the payment of rent or one or more months each year during which rent is not due, reduces the effective rent, especially in the case of a longer term lease with all the rental abatement occurring in the initial months. The present value of such a lease is reduced even further in a high interest (discount) rate environment.

Rent is lost during the search for the replacement tenant. The costs of transition are compounded during periods of market weakness because of the prospective tenant's position of strength in negotiations, and retention becomes even more important.

As human beings, tenants respond well to recognition and demonstrations of appreciation, and owners and managers have devised innumerable practices for showing the tenants they are important to the success of the property. These expressions reflect the personality of the asset manager consistent with the nature of the building.

Regular visits by the property manager with each tenant provide opportunities to discover and resolve areas of dissatisfaction. They also may reveal a need for additional space or some other situation which could offer an opportunity. It is important to be responsive to the changing needs of the tenant.

The brokerage community maintains excellent data bases of lease expirations and will approach every significant tenant well in advance to solicit the opportunity to represent the tenant in moving or negotiating a renewal. The asset manager will instruct the property manager to begin lease renewal discussions with the tenant at least several months and perhaps even years before the lease expires so that turnover can be minimized. In strong markets with rising rental rates, however, this is less important and may even be detrimental if the market is tight and rents are higher as the lease approaches expiration.

The asset manager should expect, especially in weak market conditions, that brokers will be seeking to represent his tenants in their lease renewal negotiations. Such brokers customarily advise the tenant that the representation will be free because the owner will pay the commission. The owner may refuse to deal through the broker, increasing the likelihood that the tenant will be encouraged to relocate to a building where the owner will pay a commission. It is logical that each party should pay its own representatives or advisors, but the owner often is forced to pay the tenant's broker in a weak market. This is particularly distasteful because the broker's effort is aimed at improving the tenant's deal at the expense of the owner. Good personal relations with the tenant and early efforts to renew are extremely important. The propriety of a broker representing a tenant while expecting a commission from the owner is discussed in Chapter 19.

Leasing

Despite the best efforts to retain existing tenants, vacancies will occur, and the leasing program must be designed to quickly find suitable replacement tenants so that cash flow can be restored and enhanced. If the property is encumbered with mortgage financing, debt service requirements may dictate minimum rental rates. Additionally, the lender may have approval rights on any new lease.

The asset manager may choose to act in a leasing capacity or may contract with an outside agent or the managing agent to fulfill this function. If the property management agent has a leasing capability, this is normally another department within the firm because the duties of a property manager and leasing agent are sufficiently different to preclude assigning both responsibilities to the same individual.

Leasing services are offered by national real estate firms which maintain active relationships with major organizations using large blocks of space nationwide. They also maintain active data bases with information about space users and their current leases. Such a leasing agent may be ideal for a large office building attractive to these prospective tenants. These real estate firms tend to have greater personnel turnover, however, as new employees gain experience and move on up through the organization.

At the other end of the spectrum is the small leasing firm specializing in a limited geographic area or property type. Contacts with users may be top quality but limited in scope, and resources to maintain data bases may be minimal. Within such a small leasing firm, however, the client (asset manager) may receive the attention of senior personnel, probably an owner or partner in the firm, and the frustration of periodically having a new person assigned to the property will be minimized or eliminated. The asset manager must have a good understanding of the property, and its potential, to select the appropriate leasing agent.

In consultation with the leasing and management agents, the asset manager must establish the basic leasing guidelines including the minimum rents to be sought and maximum concessions such as free rent and tenant improvement allowance to be granted. The preferred lease term (in years) should also be decided.

The lease form is important because it will govern the relationship between owner and tenant for the life of the lease and any optional terms. A lease is the conveyance of an interest in the property. It conveys to the tenant the right to occupy and use the space for a stated period of time and for a certain consideration. Consequently, it directly affects the financial performance and market value of the property for the duration of its term.

A standard form of lease is easier for the property manager to administer, and it is desirable to avoid a proliferation of forms within the building, although on occasion a strong prospective tenant will dictate that its own form be used. Even the weakest tenants, however, will insist on some changes to the form. This should be expected, because the form authorized by the asset manager will favor the owner. The lease has legal implications, particularly as to defaults and remedies, and deserves legal review and approval.

The prospective tenant may demand an option to extend the lease or buy the building at some future date. Such options always favor the tenant because the tenant will exercise an option if it is below market at the time of exercise and will negotiate for a better deal if the option is unfavorable to the tenant at the time it would be exercised. Therefore, any option granted to the tenant should be aggressively in favor of the owner.

The leasing agent must have clearly defined duties. The marketing plan should be approved by the asset manager, and the agent is expected to report on his activities in writing at agreed-on intervals. At a minimum, the report includes data on showings, inquiries, brochure mailings, and cold calls. The need to prepare this report, perhaps weekly or biweekly, is an excellent motivator for even the most dedicated leasing agent.

The asset manager must respond quickly to any expression of interest. Prospective tenants are lost for lack of a quick response to questions about the property and prompt participation in negotiations over provisions of the lease. Last month's vacant space has no salvage value, but the operating expenses continue. Responsiveness is vital.

Mortgage Financing—The Portfolio Manager's View

In addition to engaging management and leasing representatives for the newly acquired office building, the asset manager may have financing authority. While the investor may absolutely require mortgage debt to afford to acquire the asset, institutional investors typically are not so constrained. An understanding of the relationship of debt to the investment portfolio is useful. Major investors may include real estate in the portfolio for any of several reasons, but diversification and inflation protection are frequently cited.

Tax-exempt investors such as pension plans must be careful about incurring debt because of the potential for exposing the plan to taxation. While the opportunity may be sufficiently attractive to justify paying the tax, some plan sponsors have a policy of avoiding Unrelated Business Income Tax, or UBIT. Tax law is changed from time to time. Early in 1981, the law was relaxed and, provided certain conditions were met, property debt did not automatically subject the plan to income taxation.

Real estate is a cyclical investment. Tight market conditions induce developers, lenders, and investors to develop, lend, and invest. A surplus of space is then created, vacancy rises, and rents and values fall. Developers and investors are discouraged from creating more space until the vacancy is absorbed and rents rise to a level sufficient to motivate new development. The trough of the cycle is treacherous for the owner of mortgaged, or leveraged, property.

Real estate is a "different" asset class. Recognized academic work by Ibbotson and Fall,[1] as well as others, indicates a low or negative correlation in investment performance between real estate and common stock and between real estate and long-term bonds. This lack of correlation is the basis for the claim of diversification.

Diversification is often cited as a basis for investing in real estate. Figure 28-1A illustrates the growth in a portfolio of assets of a single class, perhaps bonds, with an upward trend (the reward) over time. The volatility (risk) also is reflected. Figure 28-1B shows the addition of an equally risky (volatile) asset class, such as common stocks, to the portfolio. Figure 28-1C shows the addition of a third class of assets, such as real estate. While each asset class carries risk, for which a return is earned, the diversification into asset classes which are not closely correlated results in offsetting cycles and a more steady performance of the portfolio.

Table 28-1 is a correlation matrix. The asset classes which perform exactly the same are perfectly correlated at 1.00. Maximum diversification benefit is achieved with a correlation of -1.00.

Mortgage debt is often associated with real estate. However, a close examination of a mortgage note shows that it is more like a long-term bond. The investor in a mortgage (the lender) receives a fixed payment at regular intervals for the life of the loan as does a bondholder. The obligation of a mortgage borrower to make those fixed payments during the life of the loan

---

[1] Roger G. Ibbotson and Carol L. Fall, "The United States market wealth portfolio," *The Journal of Portfolio Management*, Fall 1979.

FIGURE 28-1

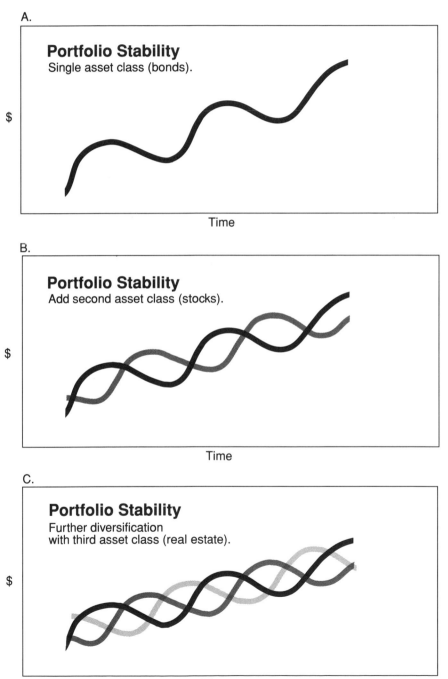

TABLE 28-1   Correlation Coefficients

	Total Returns 1926–1991			
	S&P 500	Corporate Bonds	Business Real Estate	Inflation
S&P 500	1.000			
Corporate Bonds	.2215	1.000		
Business Real Estate	.0282	−.1429	1.000	
Inflation	−.0191	−.1533	.6171	1.000

Source: © Ibbotson Associates, Inc., Chicago

is independent of the performance of the office building, regardless of the procession of the real estate cycle, but the borrower is nevertheless dependent on the net operating income from which the fixed payments are made.

With this perspective, it becomes apparent that a mortgage affects the total investment portfolio, of which real estate is only a part, by acting to offset or neutralize the performance of the bonds in the portfolio. The mortgage is a "negative bond." To the extent that the portfolio is carefully constructed with great attention to asset allocation, a mortgage on real estate upsets the balance among bonds and other classes of assets in the portfolio.

As an investor in bonds, the portfolio is a lender. By mortgaging its real estate, however, the portfolio becomes a borrower. If the mortgage is used to leverage the capital allocated to real estate into a larger real estate investment, the simultaneous result may be the cancellation of the investment performance of a corresponding portion of the bond portfolio. The portfolio is skewed away from bonds and toward real estate. More properly, the mortgaging of property should be done only in close coordination with the portfolio manager and the fixed income (bond) manager. This way, the portfolio manager can ensure that a fixed-income liability is only assumed if the proceeds can be invested in a higher yielding fixed-income asset. The real estate practitioner who focuses on the wonders of leverage and its ability to multiply income and appreciation is insensitive (at peril to his career) to the broader perspective of the portfolio manager.

Mortgage indebtedness may be appropriate when bond rates can be arbitraged. If low-rate mortgage money can be borrowed and the proceeds invested in high-rate bonds of similar maturity, such financing can be attractive to the total portfolio. It is not quite that simple, however, because the analysis requires consideration of the differences in risk, liquidity, transaction costs, and management items such as tax escrows. Additionally, mortgage payments customarily are due monthly while bond interest is paid semiannually, affecting present value calculations.

It must be recognized that debt, while perhaps beneficial to the total portfolio, adds risk to the real estate component of that portfolio. Because real estate performance is not fixed like a bond (or mortgage), positive leverage can turn negative, with declines in cash flow more quickly becoming negative and declines in value of the equity being multiplied. Unless the spread between bond interest rates and mortgage rates favors borrowing against the office building, it may be preferable to sell bonds rather than to obtain a mortgage to finance an acquisition.

Insurance

Certain risks associated with the ownership of an office building can be reduced with insurance. These risks include casualty (fire, wind, earthquake, water), loss of rents resulting from casualty, liability, dramshop (liability related to the sale of liquor), and fidelity (embezzlement by an agent). Other specialized risks may also be present.

Owners of several properties may obtain broader and more economical coverage by purchasing a blanket policy covering the entire portfolio. Such a policy may include coverages not included in the typical policy. For example, earthquake coverage may be included at no additional cost. The owner, asset manager, and all agents and beneficiaries should as classes be named as insureds.

It is common for other parties to provide coverage in favor of the owner. The property manager should provide a fidelity bond covering its employees. Tenants should provide liability insurance covering acts of their employees and visitors along with casualty coverage on their personal property such as furniture and equipment. If the building is leased to a single tenant under a net lease, the tenant may be required to carry the casualty insurance on the building as well. The owner may wish to carry an umbrella policy as an additional layer of coverage to protect against cancellation of the tenant's policy and to cover exposure greater than the tenant's limits of coverage.

A tickler system alerts the asset manager in advance of policy expirations so that renewal coverage can be placed or the tenant or agent can be reminded to provide evidence of its renewal.

Real Estate Taxes

Real estate tax procedures vary widely from state to state and county to county. The asset manager uses a control system to be sure that all taxes are paid before they become delinquent. If the tax is paid by the tenant under a net lease, evidence of payment is obtained and kept on file by the asset manager.

Periodically, the local assessor assigns a new assessment (value) to the property. These reassessments are monitored and appealed when they appear to be high. Important time constraints govern the filing of appeals. Some office building owners are lax in filing tax protests because, under the escalation provisions in the lease, the tenants pay their proportionate share of real estate tax increases. This is highly inappropriate where tax decreases are warranted by market circumstances. When a lease comes up for renewal, the owner may not be able to recapture the full extent of the tax increase in the form of higher rent.

The tax is calculated by multiplying the assessment by a tax rate which is levied by the various taxing bodies such as the school district, municipality, park district, and so on. The tax rate may be in excess of that which is required to adequately fund the respective taxing bodies and may be protested. This protest is usually filed by an attorney and is completely independent of the assessment. Savings which flow from a rate protest are rarely major but may be significant. Protest services customarily are offered on a contingent fee basis.

Inspections

The asset manager, either alone or with the managing agent, inspects the property and surrounding area regularly, observing the physical condition of the property and the quality of maintenance and tenant services. The inspection may also reveal activities by a tenant which may be of environmental concern. While the asset manager is not expected to be an environmental expert, he may note conditions which merit further investigation. The inspection tour offers the opportunity to meet informally with tenants and to gauge their satisfaction with the building and its services. Steps then may be taken to enhance tenant retention efforts.

In touring the building, the asset manager may observe changing tenant needs which may be addressed. Additional amenities and technological applications may be considered. The area tour provides insights on future competition from new properties, changes in traffic patterns, changes in area tenancy, and infrastructure improvements. The asset manager has the responsibility of knowing as much as possible about market conditions affecting the property, and a tour of the area with the property manager is always helpful.

Inspections by the asset manager encourage the property manager to perform his duties effectively. Regular visits may be expected to enhance the quality of maintenance, the frequency of tenant contact, and the level of financial performance. They also allow the asset manager to focus attention on that property and to consider opportunities to upgrade its value.

Capital Improvements

Some capital needs are obvious. A leaking roof may require replacement. A deteriorated parking lot demands repairs. Other items are less obvious. For example, energy usage may be reduced by installing a computerized control system. The property manager may offer recommendations, and ideas frequently come from tenants.

The decision to commit to a capital expenditure may be based on a payback analysis in the case of an improvement which reduces operating costs. Life safety improvements may be mandated, or may be installed to improve tenant retention. Improvements to tenant comfort and general building appearance may also be useful in keeping and attracting tenants and in maximizing rents.

Appraisals

The owner may require periodic appraisals. This is particularly the case for retirement plan sponsors and bank trust departments under the supervision of the Comptroller of the Currency. The asset manager may be charged with the responsibility for obtaining these valuations.

The appraiser is carefully selected. A national designation may indicate the competence of the appraiser, but references should be obtained and checked if the appraiser is not known to the asset manager. Experience in appraising similar property is useful and may be essential if the property is unusual. A discussion of the three conventional approaches to estimating market value can be found in Chapter 29.

The asset manager may choose to engage a different appraiser for each property and to change appraisers after a set number (often three) of periodic appraisals. This policy introduces diversity of opinion to the portfolio valuation process and may avoid a global impact of the bias of a single appraiser. The rotation of appraisers may provide for greater independence as well, because the new appraiser has no vested interest in the previous appraisal.

Alternately, the asset manager may retain a single appraiser for the entire portfolio for an indefinite term. This arrangement may offer greater consistency and continuity of appraisal work at a reduced cost.

Each appraisal is carefully reviewed by the asset manager to assure that it meets the standards of quality expected from the appraiser. The appraisal is an excellent source of information about rental rates and other market data helpful to the asset manager in negotiating leases and in planning for the continued competitiveness of the asset. The asset manager who merely looks at the conclusion of value and then files the appraisal is missing an important benefit provided by the appraiser.

Property Reviews

The asset manager prepares periodic reviews of the asset. A review provides financial data including a comparison of performance to budget, summarizes the most recent inspection, comments on leasing activity, and reports recent appraisal, tax and insurance information. Area trends are also noted in the property review.

The review offers a formal opportunity to re-evaluate the retain/sell position. The decision to retain should be an affirmative one, based on good reasons to keep the building, rather than a decision made by default.

SALE

An investment consists of the cycle of buy, hold, and sell. Most asset managers are quite competent in the various disciplines associated with the holding or ownership phase. The acquisition phase is somewhat more troublesome, as demonstrated by those nonperforming properties that were acquired (or developed and financed) by organizations which intended to avoid mistakes in property selection or development. Asset managers have even less understanding of the disposition end of the cycle, and their policies governing the decision to sell are generally not well articulated.

This may be for lack of practice. As institutions poured money into the real estate market between 1970 and 1989, asset managers were unable to acquire properties quickly enough and had no time or apparent need to sell. Further, selling is an intensive process for which many asset managers are not paid because their fees are based on assets under management rather than acquisition and sale activity. The role of the broker in office property disposition is discussed at length in Chapter 21.

Decision to Sell

The decision to sell is closely related to the acquisition policy and investment objectives of the investor. If investment objectives are clearly stated, then the decision to dispose of the property flows naturally from the achievement of those objectives.

If the objective is cash flow, then sale may be indicated when value increases more rapidly than cash flow and the resulting return as a percentage of value is depressed to an unattractive level. Similarly, obsolescence or other factors may point toward future cash flow at an unacceptably low rate. Changes in external conditions may eliminate the potential for achieving the stated objectives, or the investment objectives may change so that they cannot be achieved with the property, and it should be sold.

As stated earlier, an investment should be acquired only if the investor has strengths or resources which can contribute to the performance of the investment. When those strengths or resources have been exhausted so that the investor can no longer contribute, the property may be more valuable to another investor with greater strengths and that value should be captured through sale.

Finally, in some cases it may become evident that the objectives originally intended for the property cannot be met. If a mistake was made during the acquisition process (a mediocre property was erroneously perceived as an outstanding property), it should be acknowledged as quickly as possible so that the property can be eliminated from the portfolio and resources can be devoted to more promising opportunities.

Policies regarding sale recognize the cyclical nature of the market and incorporate the necessary flexibility to avoid blindly forcing a property out of the portfolio when the market is in the midst of a liquidity crisis and temporarily will not accommodate a transaction. Discipline is essential, however, in the process of regularly reviewing each asset to see if it still belongs in the portfolio. If not, a sale plan is developed.

Sale Plan

The investment manager may be capable of conducting the sale effort with internal personnel. More commonly, however, a broker or consulting intermediary is engaged to act as selling agent. In selecting the broker or advisor, consideration is given to his ability to assist in developing the marketing plan and his capacity to execute it. Experience in the area and with the property type is essential, as is his reputation for integrity and competence.

Some properties are suited for a wide variety of potential buyers, and others will appeal to a more narrow market. The asset manager, with the assistance of the broker as appropriate, decides whether widespread dissemination of marketing materials would be beneficial (and the media to be used) or, conversely, if a short list of most likely buyers can be identified and approached more discreetly.

Pricing must be determined based on a full and realistic understanding of current market conditions. Original cost is irrelevant. If a loss must be taken, that is the seller's problem, and the buyer is not interested in solving it. A fair market value appraisal is helpful in setting a target final price, and an asking price is set somewhere above that target. In an active market, the asset manager will be more aggressive in pricing the property.

While policies vary, one effective institutional selling policy provides for investment committee approval of both the asking price and the minimum selling price (usually but not always the value estimated in a fair market value appraisal obtained to assist in the pricing decision). The selling staff then has the flexibility and discretion to negotiate a sale within that range. Final committee approval of a proposed transaction is routine unless the price or terms fall outside the preapproved parameters.

The asset manager must address the issue of seller financing, known as "taking back paper." Noninstitutional buyers, particularly of smaller properties, may require the financial assistance of a second mortgage to complete the purchase. Because such a buyer may be willing to offer the highest price, the asset manager must be prepared to evaluate an offer calling for seller financing. He considers the risk associated with providing such financing, particularly in view of the amount of senior debt and the projected cash flow available for debt service.

No standards for seller financing exist. It may be a small second mortgage or other subordinate position used to supplement the buyer's limited available cash equity, or it may be a high loan-to-value first mortgage. Terms are tailored to meet the needs of the parties to the transaction. The rate may be high to reflect risk, or low to assist in maximizing the stated sale price. Creativity is usually evident.

If the fixed-income allocation in the total portfolio is satisfied by bond investments, a purchase money mortgage may cause an unintended and undesired distorting effect on the asset allocation and diversification of the portfolio. The addition of the purchase money mortgage, a fixed-income investment, may trigger the need to rebalance the portfolio by selling bonds of a corresponding maturity.

The agreement to terms of a sale is documented by means of a contract for purchase and sale, just as when the property was purchased. This time, however, the interest of the asset manager is reversed. At purchase, extensive representations and warranties were sought from the seller. Now, the aim is to limit ongoing liability to the buyer. Negotiations will dwell on this issue, and again legal counsel is essential to avoid inadvertently assuming obligations best avoided. Toward this end, the seller is advised to fully disclose all information required both by the contract and by law to limit the possibility of a future fraud or other claim by the buyer.

The sale may be closed in escrow, with all documents delivered to the escrow agent and copies to the parties for review and approval. When all requirements of the contract are met or waived, funds are delivered to the escrow agent (usually by wire transfer), the deed is recorded, and documents are delivered to the respective parties.

The functions and duties of the asset manager with regard to this office building come to an end. Investment objectives were determined, a property was selected and its purchase negotiated, it was carefully managed in accordance with the objectives of the investor, and it was ultimately sold with, one hopes, favorable results for the investor. The investment cycle is concluded.

ABOUT THE AUTHOR

John K. Rutledge, CRE, is vice president and director of trust real estate investment management at Harris Trust and Savings Bank, Chicago. He established and manages a commingled real estate fund for pension and profit-sharing plans, and consults with trust customers on a wide variety of real estate investments nationwide. Rutledge holds undergraduate and graduate degrees from the University of Illinois. He is a member of the Counselors of Real Estate and has served on its board of governors and as editor-in-chief of *The Counselor.*

PART VIII

INVESTMENT STRATEGIES FOR OFFICE BUILDINGS

29

OFFICE BUILDING
VALUATION METHODS

by Howard C. Gelbtuch

INTRODUCTION

There are three common approaches to valuation of an office property: the income approach, the sales comparison approach and the cost approach. This chapter will focus on the application of the income approach.

> The relevance of earning power to the valuation of income-producing properties is obvious. Such properties are developed and purchased as investment opportunities; the objective of developers and purchasers alike is to realize a profit on their investment. The greater the earning power, the greater the profit and, therefore, the higher the value of the investment. This is the essence of the income capitalization approach to value and all related theory and techniques. This is not to say that the production of income is necessarily the sole reason for an income-producing property's existence; nor is it meant to suggest that factors not related to earning power cannot influence value. There is no question, however, that the expectation of monetary gain is the major consideration in the valuation of income-producing properties. Indeed, the anticipation of future benefits, either amenities or dollars, is the very basis of the value of any kind of property.[1]

Three broad steps are involved in use of the income approach to valuation. First is a thorough market analysis, discussed in Part 3 of this book. Second

---

[1] Akerson, Charles B., *Capitalization Theory and Techniques Study Guide* (Chicago: American Institute of Real Estate Appraisers, 1988) p. 3.

is the preparation of an estimate of applicable revenue and expense items. Last is the determination of a capitalization rate for the analysis. Underlying this selection process is the principle of anticipation, the perception that value is created by the expectation of benefits to be derived in the future.

The sales comparison approach, in which market value is estimated by comparing the subject to similar properties that have been sold, is based on the theory that the market value of a property is directly related to prices paid for similar properties. Comparable office building sales are most frequently quoted on a price per square foot basis. Although on the surface this approach seems to have the advantage of being easily understood, extreme care should be exercised when comparing square footage amounts to ensure that office building sizes are calculated uniformly. Building areas may be quoted according to their gross square footage, net rentable area or usable area, to name just a few. Office buildings are frequently remeasured upon sale, resulting in a mixture of "old measure" and "new measure," and square footages frequently change with the addition or removal of a tenant.

A comparable sales analysis can also be used to derive capitalization rates and anticipated yields. Again, however, extreme caution must be used to ensure that the income characteristics (quantity, quality and durability) of the comparables are either similar to those of the subject, or are properly accounted for in the adjustment process. For investment properties such as office buildings, comparable sales can serve as a useful check on the valuation of the subject property; the income analysis remains the prime determinant of value.

The most controversial of the three approaches to value is the cost approach. It is best suited to special-purpose properties such as schools, houses of worship, manufacturing buildings and municipal facilities. Because cost and market value may be related when properties are new, this approach is also applicable when estimating the market value of new or recently completed office buildings. As a property ages, however, the difficulty of accurately estimating depreciation reduces the reliability of the cost approach. In depressed markets, prices paid for properties may be compared to their cost when new, i.e., a price of $50 per square foot may represent one-half of replacement cost. Many value oriented buyers, sometimes known as "bottom fishers," are interested in purchasing assets at a small percentage of their original cost. Like the sales comparison approach, the cost approach may serve as a secondary value indicator.

DEFINITION OF VALUE

Market value, the major focus of most valuation assignments, is defined by the Appraisal Institute as follows:

> The most probable price, as of a specified date, in cash, or in terms equivalent to cash, or in other precisely revealed terms for which the

specified property rights should sell after reasonable exposure in a competitive market under all conditions requisite to a fair sale, with the buyer and seller each acting prudently, knowledgeably, and for self-interest, and assuming that neither is under undue duress.[2]

Previous definitions, as well as some courts, have defined market value as the highest price, rather than the most probable price.

The highest price estimated in terms of money that the land would bring if exposed for sale in the open market, with reasonable time allowed in which to find a purchaser, buying with knowledge of all of the uses and purposes to which it was adapted and for which it was capable of being used. [*Sacramento Southern R. R. Co. v. Heilbron* 156 Ca. 408, 104 P. 979 (1909).][3]

Proponents of the latter definition cite the example of an auction, arguably the purest form of market activity, in which an asset (such as real estate) is sold to the highest bidder.

Market value may also be expressed as a range of values or may be concurred in by the appraiser on the basis of values estimated by the client. Concurrence is generally defined as a variation of less than 10% in the probable value that would have been estimated in a full and complete appraisal of the same interests. A 10% variation is generally considered to be a reasonable differential and connotes substantial agreement as to value.[4]

Prospective value estimates are used to estimate value as of a specified future date, such as upon completion of construction or upon assumed stabilized occupancy.

A prospective value estimate is most frequently utilized in connection with real estate projects that are proposed, under construction, under conversion to a new use, or that have otherwise not achieved sellout or a stabilized level of long- term occupancy at the time the appraisal report is written.[5]

---

[2] Appraisal Institute, *The Appraisal of Real Estate*, 10th edition, Chicago, Appraisal Institute, 1992, page 19.

[3] American Institute of Real Estate Appraisers, *The Dictionary of Real Estate Appraisal*, Second Edition (Chicago: American Institute of Real Estate Appraisers, 1989) p. 193.

Also see: The American Institute of Real Estate Appraisers, The Society of Real Estate Appraisers, *Real Estate Appraisal Terminology* (Cambridge, Mass.: Ballinger Publishing Company, 1975) p. 137.

[4] The 10% figure was originally used by Landauer Associates in the first current value balance sheet appraisal performed for client The Rouse Company in the mid 1970s, in which the appraised market value was substituted for the book value in the balance sheet to establish an estimated market net worth. The 10% factor has since been widely accepted. It is considered a tolerance factor, an allowable variation between the company's value and the appraiser's value.

[5] American Institute of Real Estate Appraisers, *The Dictionary of Real Estate Appraisal*, Second Edition (Chicago: American Institute of Real Estate Appraisers, 1989) p. 239.

CLIENT INSTRUCTIONS TO THE APPRAISER

The appraiser should have a complete understanding of the circumstances leading to the request for an appraisal in order to provide a meaningful work product to his or her client. Just as market value may be defined in several ways, leading to confusion or misinterpretation unless the intended definition is clearly identified, the use of the appraisal should not stereo-typically be reported as "for internal purposes."

For example, a new or proposed office building may require two valuations: one upon substantial completion and the other either upon stabilized occupancy or as of a specified future date. Unlike most other property types, the office building initially is completed only through the shell, enclosing walls and core area, including mechanicals. The volume of custom-designed, subdivided space that is rented will determine the time at which "stablized" or normal occupancy is achieved. In a strong market, rent-up may be rapid. In an oversupplied market, it may take up to five years or more to reach normal occupancy, during which period the net operating income may be insufficient to pay the construction loan interest. The appraiser must account for this event in the valuation.

Even if the definition and date of value are clearly agreed upon, confusion can still arise. What if the client and appraiser agree that under certain depressed market conditions, it is reasonable to assume a market-ing period of as much as one year to sell a property. Should this be interpreted as one year *following* the date of value, or a marketing period of one year *preceding* the valuation date? This issue may be particularly important to institutions that have invested in commingled funds, as these institutions are often required to reflect as accurately as possible market value as of the date that unit sales and purchases are recorded.

Appraisals for many clients are subject to regulations under Title XI of the Federal Financial Institutions Reform, Recovery and Enforcement Act of 1989 (FIRREA). These detailed standards require that appraisals conform to the Uniform Standards of Professional Appraisal Practice (USPAP), promulgated by the Appraisal Foundation's Appraisal Standards Board. At the opposite extreme, many large, sophisticated institutional investors such as pension funds and insurance companies not only are *not* subject to FIRREA, but they already have well documented files containing extensive physical descriptions and other material that does not need to be dupli-cated. These investors are frequently more interested in the appraiser's reports on the thinking of informed market participants, rather than in their repeating of macro-economic data.

DIRECT CAPITALIZATION VS.
DISCOUNTED CASH FLOW

Through the mid-1970s, with inflation not perceived as threatening, office buildings were frequently valued by applying an overall capitalization rate, extracted from comparable sales, to a property's stabilized annual net operating income.

By the late 1970s, the United States economy entered a period characterized by high inflation and low vacancies. Interest rate volatility, directly affecting investor return requirements, also increased. The market began questioning the reliability of methodologies for selecting capitalization rates. Soaring rental rates and the increasingly widespread use of personal computers with software capable of analyzing income on a year-by-year and lease-by-lease basis facilitated the transition to a discounted cash flow (DCF) analysis. This approach entails forecasting both income and expenses over an anticipated holding period (usually ten years), then discounting both the annual cash flow and the reversion proceeds from a presumed sale at the end of the holding period at a required rate of return. This rate is interchangeably called a discount rate, equity yield rate or internal rate of return (IRR).

In a perfect world, the value estimated using either the direct capitalization or the DCF techniques would be identical. In the latter approach, capitalization rates are frequently viewed as a result of the valuation, not a cause. Although sophisticated investors rely most heavily upon a DCF analysis, they also tend to have minimum first year return (capitalization rate) requirements. When markets are depressed and the outlook for future revenue increases is pessimistic, buyers may focus more on a return requirement applied to actual income in place, expressed as a first year capitalization rate.

DISCOUNTED CASH FLOW

In estimating future revenues and expenses, the real estate appraiser typically follows the five steps listed here. These steps are discussed in greater detail on the following pages.

1. Catalogue base rentals. Data is entered into a computer on a lease-by-lease basis for existing tenants. A market rent from a rent matrix is assigned to vacant space. Upon lease expiration, a new base rent is

selected from a matrix, expense escalation payments are dropped to zero and a new base year amount is established in the presumed year of re-leasing.

2. Identify other sources of revenue; include utility recoveries, tenant escalation payments, graduated leases and parking revenue.
3. Make a deduction from income for bad debts, collection losses, tenant turnover and vacancy.
4. Project reasonable levels of operating and fixed expenses.
5. Deduct capital items such as leasing commissions, tenant alteration costs and a reserve for future large, one-time expenses.

The result is a year-by-year forecast of net operating cash flow available for distribution.

ESTIMATING CASH FLOWS

The most important ingredient in valuing an office building, or any income-producing property, is forecasting cash flows. The selection of a discount rate and terminal or residual capitalization rate will be influenced by the aggressiveness or conservatism used in calculating estimated revenues and expenses.

Although rent payments are usually made monthly and operating expenses may be paid at varying times during the year, the convention is to present the forecast of revenues and expenses on an annual basis. Year one of the projection reflects the net result of all income and expense activity for the first twelve months.

The annual forecast may be prepared on a calendar or fiscal year basis. A prospective buyer analyzing an office building for purchase in September, for example, may be more interested in the property's anticipated performance during the following full calendar year than in the first twelve months from September because of the time required to perform due diligence, to arrange financing, and to implement a new management strategy if necessary. Nevertheless, some owners may wish to report property performance in conjunction with other business enterprises that operate on a fiscal year basis.

Preparing a forecast is akin to taking a picture at a point in time. It reflects the *anticipated* levels of revenue and expenses including increases or decreases without regard to the past. A look back at a prior analysis that proved to be inaccurate does not necessarily mean it was wrong; property performance merely did not materialize as anticipated. In fact, perhaps the only certainty associated with preparing forecasts is that they will be wrong! Operating expenses, for example, will certainly not increase at exactly 5% per annum for 10 years; however rather than attempt to forecast years of small and large increases, the appraiser attempts to replicate the anticipated average annual increase or decrease over the holding period.

Although appraisers tend to use "projection" and "forecast" interchangeably, care should be taken when applying these terms. To many attorneys, a *forecast* implies the appraiser's best estimate of cash flow performance, whereas a *projection* connotes an estimate of revenues and expenses predicated upon a rate of inflation or deflation dictated by the client to the appraiser and based on past performance. Hence, when appraisals for public offerings are reviewed by attorneys, many insist that they be described as forecasts rather than projections.

REVENUE ESTIMATES

Most computer programs do not require an entry for a lease commencement date. Base rent is usually input in accordance with contractual lease terms as of the date the analysis begins, i.e., January 1, 199X. Step-ups in base rent should also be incorporated into the program. In a depressed office building market, some tenants, particularly those occupying a significant amount of space, may find themselves paying a rent that is above market, and are often able to negotiate away their step-up at some time through the full term of their lease. The appraiser should reflect the likelihood of this event both in the preparation of his forecast and in his choice of discount rate. Most often, tenants who have a contractual obligation to pay rates that are substantially above market rarely pay above market through the full term of their lease.

Similarly, because of market conditions, some tenants' current base rent (without a step-up) may be above market, possibly adding an element of risk about the collectibility of this income. Lastly, the sum of accumulated expense pass-throughs plus base rent may result in a rent higher than could be commanded in the current environment.

The converse may also be true. An old lease, negotiated many years ago but still in effect, may reflect a rental market significantly lower than it is today. This represents an opportunity for a prospective buyer if the lease can be renegotiated.

An option to renew at market rent is generally not accorded any weight in a computerized lease-by-lease analysis unless the rent coincides with the appraiser's view of the market rental value at the time of the option exercise. (The software is indifferent as to the name of the tenant.) However, care should be taken when estimating the option market rent as it may be significantly different for a large tenant than for a small one. The lease agreement may or may not stipulate whether tenant improvements are to be provided or leasing commissions paid. Often the only way these issues are resolved is by negotiation between the affected parties.

Renewal options below market rents provide an economic incentive to renew and the analyst should generally assume they will be exercised depending on the financial strength of the tenant as well as market and economic trends. Options to renew at above market rents (at a previously agreed-on rent now expected to be higher than market at the time of renewal) should, in most instances, not be incorporated into the analysis because the tenant lacks an economic incentive to renew.

Base rent may be calculated according to different formulas incorporating rentable, usable or even gross building area. In strong markets, owners may be able to convert old leases from usable area to rentable area upon turnover, or may be able to incorporate a remeasured (increased) square footage amount; in these instances revenues would increase even if the base rent per square foot remained the same. Many federal government agency leases reflect the General Services Administration (GSA) methodology of space measurement, which is significantly different from that used in the private sector.

The onset in the mid 1980s of historically high rental concessions, particularly in the form of free rent, as an inducement for tenants to lease space, gave rise to recognition of the *effective rent* concept, that is, the rental rate net of financial concessions. Although the effect of any concessions may be discounted to a present value, most market participants prepare effective rent calculations on an undiscounted basis. For example, a five-year lease at $25 per square foot with 6 months of free rent and no other extreme concessions has an effective rent of $22.50 per square foot ($25 less 6 months free on a 60-month lease, or 10%).

Expense Escalations

Few terms are as simple yet as controversial as net leases. Seemingly a net lease is one that contains a clause requiring a tenant to pay all expenses. The Appraisal Institute defines a net lease as follows:

> A lease in which the tenant pays all property charges, in addition to the stipulated rent.[6]

Gross leases are defined by the Appraisal Institute as:

> A lease in which the landlord receives stipulated rent and is obligated to pay all or most of the fixed and operating expenses attributable to the real estate.[7]

The most common type of office gross lease obligates a tenant to pay his pro rata share of increases in operating expenses and property taxes above a

---

[6] American Institute of Real Estate Appraisers, *The Dictionary of Real Estate Appraisal*, Second Edition, (Chicago: American Institute of Real Estate Appraisers, 1989) p. 208.

[7] Ibid., p. 142.

base year, usually the year in which the lease begins. (This is sometimes adjusted, however, so that a tenant signing a lease in December will have a base of the following full calendar year.) Increased operating expenses charged to the tenant may differ from those utilized in the cash flow forecast; property management fees, for example, sometimes can not be recovered but are a legitimate charge against revenues. The best way to ascertain which expenses may be passed through to tenants is to read the actual leases, or at the least, to have them abstracted by a knowledgeable real estate professional or attorney.

Expense stops are sometimes used in place of base years, particularly for new office buildings without an operating history or still in the lease-up stage. Stops are used to estimate operating expenses on a "grossed up" basis as though the office building were operating at stabilized occupancy. In a tenant-dominated market, the expenses used to calculate recoveries from tenants will almost always be greater than actual operating expenses. During periods of strong demand, landlords may be able to lease even fully stabilized buildings with an expense stop less than actual expenses; this differential results in additional income to the property owner.

Many owners of office buildings in Manhattan recover operating expenses using a porter's wage formula. Escalations are based on the increase in hourly wages of unionized building service employees rather than actual operating expenses. If the wage rate per hour exceeds operating expenses per square foot, this clause is more favorable to property owners. For example, a 10% increase applied to a $15 per hour wage results in a pass-along to the affected tenant of $1.50 per square foot. Conversely, if operating expenses were $10 per square foot, and increased by 10%, the amount of expense escalation to the tenant would be only $1.00 per square foot. Commonly known as "penny for penny", there are several variations of this formula known as "penny for penny with fringes" and "penny and a half for penny," among others.

Property taxes are usually recovered separately from operating expenses. In some markets, the base year may be defined as a fiscal year to correspond with the practice of local taxing authorities. In certain markets such as California, during a time of rapidly increasing property values some desirable tenants may be able to negotiate the inclusion of a clause nullifying any increase in property tax pass-throughs, if the assessment increases as a result of a sale of the property.

There are many variations for defining a tenant's pro-rata share—the percentage multiplied by the increase in expenses used to determine the recoverable amount. Many leases stipulate a square footage amount to be used as the numerator with the total building area (usually net rentable) defined as the denominator. However, as tenants move in or out of different sized spaces, the building area changes, affecting the tenant's pass-through calculation.

Many gross leases require the tenant to pay one-twelfth of the estimated increase in operating expenses in advance, i.e., in January the tenant begins paying his or her pro-rata share of estimated expenses for the coming year on a monthly basis. Generally by March of the following year, the preceding year's actual expenses are known and the landlord and tenant "settle up" with one party reimbursing the other for any difference. This differs from the way most computer programs work, in which recoveries match expenses during the year in which they occur.

Just as a lease commencement date is not required input for many lease-by-lease programs, neither is a base year amount required in many instances. Rather than calculate the incremental increase from lease commencement, many programs merely add the current year escalation amount to the recovery amount input by the appraiser for each lease. The appraiser should be careful to ensure that at least one year of actual expenses and their corresponding pass-throughs are input into the program. Otherwise the appraiser runs the risk of mixing actual recoveries with projected expenses.

In the case of net leases, both expenses and recoveries must be entered. Not only is it easier for the reader to follow, but omitting expenses ignores the property owner's inability to recover costs during periods of vacancy or downtime between leases.

Other Sources of Income

Items in this category may include parking; overtime heating, ventilating and air conditioning (HVAC); and in rare instances tenant improvement work if the landlord has his own profit-making construction company. In some markets such as New York City, electricity at some buildings is bought "wholesale" and sub-metered to tenants at "retail" rates, resulting in a profit to the landlord; this may be illegal in other parts of the country. This issue is discussed more fully under "Expense Estimates."

Vacancy and Collection Loss Allowance

When preparing a stabilized estimate of income and expenses, vacancy and collection loss allowances may be combined into a single category. They should be treated separately, however, in the creation of a DCF forecast, particularly if the forecast is prepared using a lease-by-lease program.

In the latter case, vacancy upon lease expiration is generally calculated by making global assumptions concerning the anticipated number of months of "downtime" before each space can be re-let. This timeframe is then applied to the renewal probability programmed by the appraiser to arrive at the actual downtime incorporated into the projection. Imagine a scenario where (a) 50% of the office building tenants are assumed to vacate their space upon lease expiration; and (b) 6 months are required to secure a new tenant for each space. The remaining 50% of the tenants are expected to renew their leases, resulting in no lost time between lease expiration and lease commencement. The program, indifferent as to which tenants will renew (which, more importantly, is beyond the scope of even the most knowledgeable appraiser's ability to predict, especially over the typical ten-year forecast), will apply the following calculation to each tenant.

50% vacate x 6 months vacancy	3 months of downtime
50% renew x 0 months vacancy	0 months of downtime
Weighted average vacancy upon rollover	3 months of downtime

Most software permits the appraiser to override the global vacancy assumptions for specific tenants, making it either longer or shorter. In the case of a space deemed particularly difficult to re-lease, the appraiser may wish to lengthen the anticipated amount of downtime. Conversely, if a tenant has announced his intention to renew, the renewal probability for that tenant might be increased to 100% for the lease already in place.

Some key determinants of renewal probability and downtime are the strength of the office building market; the building's position within the market; the effectiveness of management in retaining tenants (many owners now monitor their retention ratio, that is the amount of square feet renewed divided by the amount of square feet expiring, expressed as a percentage); actual experience of the subject property; and the amount of money invested in, or desirability of, existing tenant improvements (a tenant is more likely to remain in occupancy of attractive customized space).

For some buildings, the appraiser may wish to prepare a scenario where the building does not achieve more than, for example, 90% occupancy over the forecast period rather than the project leasing up to 100% occupancy. (Technically, this can be accomplished by keeping 10% of the building square footage vacant until a date beyond the end of the holding period.) This occupancy level may reflect difficulties inherent in the building, the market, or both. In recent years, the concept of "structural vacancy" has come into vogue. This is defined as:

> ...that vacancy level where rents are in equilibrium. That is, at the structural rate of vacancy, rents will neither rise nor fall. If vacancy rates are above this level then we should expect rental rates to start to fall; below this level we would expect rents to rise. Thus the hypothesized relationship that exists between rents and vacancy is actually between vacancy rates and *changes* in rents.[8]

Factors to consider when estimating a vacancy allowance are generally macro in nature such as area-wide and submarket vacancies and the

---

[8] CB Commercial/Torto Wheaton Research, The Office Outlook Report, September 1991, CB Commercial/Torto Wheaton Research, page A.11.

competitiveness of the subject building, as well as more specific issues such as the desirability of specific office areas within the property.

Collection loss allowances are generally determined by tenant credit-worthiness, economic and local market conditions, and to a lesser extent, the level of existing tenant improvements. A lease to a Fortune 500 tenant may not merit any collection loss allowance, while a start-up tenant in a risky business may warrant a higher than normal allowance. The appraiser should take care to determine who the actual lessee is. In some instances a financially strong parent company may be guaranteeing lease payments, while at the other extreme what appears to be a nationally recognized tenant may be a franchisee or a less creditworthy subsidiary. A stressful national economy can have a negative influence on general business conditions, sometimes causing even strong tenants to experience financial difficulties. Lastly, a highly finished space may provide an inducement for a tenant to continue paying rent, particularly if the tenant contributed to the cost of such improvements; of the factors discussed here, this has the least significance.

With the possible exception of an office building containing long-term leases to extremely sound tenants, it is unwise to assume that all contractual rent payments will be received over the holding period. Therefore, some allowance for collection loss should be incorporated into most analyses. This allowance should be ascribed to expense escalation payments as well. After all, if a tenant is not paying his or her base rent, it is unlikely that he or she will continue making pass-through payments.

EXPENSE ESTIMATES

The Appraisal Institute describes a variety of operating expenses relevant to the operation of an office building, and segregates these into two categories:

> Fixed expenses are operating expenses that generally do not vary with occupancy and have to be paid whether the property is occupied or vacant.[9]

> Variable expenses are all operating expenses that generally vary with the level of occupancy or the extent of services provided.[10]

Key issues related to certain of these expense categories are discussed in the following sections.

---

[9] Appraisal Institute, *The Appraisal of Real Estate*, 10th edition (Chicago: Appraisal Institute, 1992) p. 444.

[10] Ibid., p. 445.

TABLE 29-1   Typical Office Building Expense Categories

Operating Expenses
Payroll
Cleaning
Utilities
Maintenance and Repairs
Grounds and Parking Area Maintenance
Management Fees
Miscellaneous

Fixed Expenses
Real Estate Taxes
Insurance

Capital Expenses
Tenant Improvement Costs
Leasing Commissions
Replacement Reserve

Utilities

Electricity costs may be divided between common area charges such as those for hallway lighting, elevators, and so forth, and tenant electricity costs for electricity consumed within leased areas.

Tenant electricity costs may be measured several different ways. The most common method is an "electric inclusion" basis, whereby electricity costs are passed through to tenants as part of their normal base year calculation. In this approach, electricity costs are treated the same as other fixed or variable expenses.

In certain markets, some buildings are equipped to sub-meter tenant electricity charges. The landlord buys electricity on a wholesale basis from the local utility, and specialized firms periodically read tenant meters located on the premises, then prepare billings to tenants on a retail basis. This frequently results in a profit to the landlord.

Electricity usage may also be measured on a "survey" basis, in which lighting fixtures, computers, copy machines and other electricity-using equipment are counted and their electric usage estimated. Regardless of what standard method is used, surveys are almost always used when a particular office tenant is expected to consume an unusually large amount of electricity.

Management Fees

To provide an incentive to keep the property occupied, management fees are typically calculated as a percentage of collections, or effective gross revenue. The practice varies from market to market, or even building to building, as to whether they are calculated on base rents, base rents plus expense escalations, or even base rents, expense escalations and other income. Equally varied is the determination of whether the management fee is escalatable to tenants.

This presents an interesting dilemma to the appraiser preparing a cash flow forecast, in that the fee cannot be known until the escalations are calculated, and the escalations cannot be calculated until the fee is determined. This is known as a simultaneous equation. Most appraisers run several iterations of their forecast until they achieve a reasonable management fee approximation.

Property Taxes

Municipalities use a variety of procedures when calculating assessed values for property taxation purposes. In California, for example, Proposition 13, passed in 1978, set a uniform property tax rate of approximately 1% on all property. It also rolled back assessments to their 1975-76 level. When properties are sold, the sale price becomes the new assessed value. The assessment of properties not sold increases by 2% per year.

In New York City, most office buildings are reassessed annually, and if warranted, new assessed values are phased in, in equal increments, over the subsequent five-year period. This approach reflects a change in thinking from the early 1980s, when an immediate reassessment upon sale, usually upward, resulted in the sold building being placed at a competitive disadvantage to comparable office buildings that had not sold recently. In Chicago, buildings are generally reassessed every three years, and careful appraisers will check to see when the subject property is scheduled for its next review.

In 1992, in the first litigated challenge to a New York City property tax assessment in more than 10 years, the former owners of a 50-story Manhattan office building, One New York Plaza, successfully argued for a reduction in the building's assessment because they were able to prove that presence of asbestos devalued the structure. A New York appeals court granted the former owners a $23 million property tax refund because the building contained asbestos and had other design deficiencies needing repair.

Tenant Improvement Costs

In most markets, office building owners must to some extent refurbish office areas to tenant specifications. The refurbishment may be in the form of new partitions, lighting, carpeting, and so on, or it may be a "lump sum" dollar amount given to a tenant to spend for improvements. In either case, the costs are most frequently expressed in terms of dollars per square foot. New tenants can usually command a higher expenditure than renewing tenants, although in particularly weak markets, the differential diminishes. For programming purposes, renewal tenant improvement allowances are sometimes expressed as a percentage of new tenant improvement allowances.

Some tenants such as law firms may require an above-average build-out of their space. In such cases the building owner may be able to amortize the excess cost over the life of the lease in the form of additional rent. Appraisers should be cognizant of implied tenant improvement costs when rents are quoted by leasing brokers, and the actual cost expended when examining a rent comparable. Excessive tenant improvement costs can result in increased base rent, while an office leased in "as is" condition with no expenditure required by the landlord may result in a lower rent.

Most lease-by-lease computer programs permit the appraiser to assign different inputs for renewing and non-renewing tenants; a weighted average is then applied in the same manner as to anticipated downtime upon lease expiration, discussed previously.

Leasing Commissions

Like tenant improvement costs, leasing commissions are usually higher for new tenants than renewal tenants. A new tenant may cause a full commission to be paid, whereas a renewing tenant may result in a half commission. In some markets, owners may offer an override, resulting in as much as one-and-a-half times the normal leasing commission. The growing tenant representation business, based on the belief that office building owners are more adept than tenants at negotiating leases, has also affected leasing costs. For programming purposes, commissions are almost always assumed to be paid when earned on the lease commencement date, rather than amortized over the lease term.

For large buildings, appraisers may wish to examine commissions in conjunction with the property management fee. Some full-service real estate firms will manage an office building at a reduced rate, hoping that increased leasing commissions will more than make up for any foregone management fee revenues.

As office rents declined during the second half of the 1980s, the brokerage community in several cities around the country effected a change in the way leasing commissions were calculated. Rather than basing them on a percentage of rent paid over the lease term, agencies moved to a dollars-per-square-foot calculation. Owing to restraint of trade regulations, leasing commissions are usually "suggested" rather than fixed. The Real Estate Board of New York, for example, no longer publishes a commission schedule.

Replacement Reserve

Most appraisers have been taught to incorporate an allowance into their forecasts for the replacement of certain large building components, such as roofs, floor coverings and HVAC equipment. While one intent of this practice is to avoid distortion of an annual income statement by including a large non-recurring expense, appraisers may wish to question whether owners truly set aside funds each year for future capital expenditures. However, even if an amount is not formally set aside, the annual expense must still be recognized.

Large capital expenditures approved by building management and scheduled for implementation within the first few years of the holding period should be recognized, either by incorporation into the forecast or as a lump sum deduction from value. Any change in building operations resulting from this expenditure, such as reduced energy costs, increased occupancy or the ability to charge higher market rents, must also be recognized. Increases in capital expenditures are usually not charged to tenants as part of their normal expense pass-throughs.

WEIGHTED AVERAGES

The use of weighted averages is a useful tool for forecasting tenant improvement costs, leasing commissions and the number of months of vacancy upon lease expiration. The percentage of tenants forecast to renew (or vacate) can have a dramatic impact on cash flow, and therefore on value.

Examine the impact that increasing the renewal probability from 50% to 80% can have on just one component of cash flow, tenant improvement costs.

50% renew x $10/sq. ft.	$ 5 PSF
50% vacate x $20/sq. ft.	10 PSF
Weighted average T.I. cost	$15 PSF
80% renew x $10/sq. ft.	$ 8 PSF
20% vacate x $20/sq. ft.	4 PSF
Weighted average T.I. cost	$12 PSF

Tenant improvement costs under the first scenario are 25% greater than they are under the second scenario. Without adjusting for inflation (or discounting), the $3 per square foot differential amounts to $300,000 for a typical 100,000 square foot office building whose leases roll over only once during the holding period; if each lease expired twice, the aggregate impact would be $600,000 (undiscounted).

Building owners may be prone to overstating historical and future retention ratios, particularly in the case of increasingly uncompetitive older buildings in weakening markets. Buildings with a "franchise," however, owing to an enviable location or striking design, may experience above-average tenant renewals resulting in lower capital costs and less downtime between leases.

The use of weighted averages provides a convenient way to project certain key expenses and events into the future. It does not eliminate the need for the appraiser to thoroughly examine the subject property's historical performance, rent roll or market positioning. Lastly, the weighted average may be overridden, if necessary, to reflect the anticipated lease renewal or non-renewal of a specific tenant.

ESTIMATING GROWTH RATES

When preparing discounted cash flow estimates in the past, appraisers frequently projected that market rent increases would parallel inflation, i.e., if inflation was forecast to be 4% annually, that growth rate was used as a determinant for each succeeding year's market rent. Softness in most real estate markets in the late '80s and early '90s resulted in a rethinking of this approach. Many appraisers subsequently forecasted that market rents would remain level or even decrease for the first few years of their forecasts, a result of supply and demand considerations, before resuming either their upward trend in accordance with inflation, or spiking upward as illustrated in Table 29-2.

Rent spikes are typically used in office markets that are temporarily oversupplied but possess good fundamentals such as Dallas and San Francisco, to allow market rents to "catch up" to where they would have been under a straight inflationary scenario.

Even the appraiser using inflation as a means of estimating future market rents should be aware of this technique's pitfalls and limitations. No appraiser expects inflation, and therefore market rents, to increase at *exactly*

TABLE 29-2   Use of Rent Spikes

Year	Market Rent at 5% Annual Increase	No Growth Followed by 5% Inflationary Increase	No Growth Followed by a Rent Spike
1	$15.00	$15.00	$15.00
2	15.75	15.00	15.00
3	16.54	15.00	15.00
4	**17.36**	15.75	**17.36***
5	18.23	16.54	18.23

* 15.7% *spike*

4% or 5% per year for the typical ten-year projection period. In contrast to calculating when the peaks and valleys will occur, inherent in use of this approach is the assumption that *average* market rent growth will approximate inflation over the holding period.

In addition to revenue items driven by building occupancy, annual inflation rate estimates frequently are also used to project future increases. However, supply and demand remain the primary determinants used to forecast market rent levels. For example, significant inflation will not force up rents in a severely oversupplied market. Conversely, in the 1978-81 market, rents rose even faster than the accelerating inflation rate.

In contrast, office building expenses are generally much more sensitive to inflation than rents. As discussed earlier, property assessments and consequently real estate taxes are subject to various legally mandated treatments in different jurisdictions. Also influencing changes (usually increases) in property taxes are the increasingly dire financial straits many older cities are finding themselves in. For example, the tax rate on New York City office buildings increased by less than .4% annually from 1982/83 to 1988/89, but by approximately 3% per year in the ensuing four years, a rate seven-and-a-half times greater. During the energy crisis in the first half of the 1980s, fuel expense increases were frequently expected to outpace inflation, but that is no longer the case.

There are several measures of inflation, typified by the Consumer Price Index (CPI); perhaps most frequently cited is the CPI for All Urban Consumers, known as CPI-U. Available from the U.S. Department of Labor Bureau of Labor Statistics, the CPI measures the average increase or decrease in the price paid for a fixed market basket of goods and services. Introduced in 1978, it represents the buying habits of approximately 80% of the United States non-institutional population.

Another related indicator is the prime rate, most commonly described as the rate banks charge their best customers. The prime rate is a measure of the short-term cost of funds, and should not be used interchangeably with long-term indicators such as IRRs for a ten-year holding period, or the yield on long-term Treasury bonds. Although it usually moves in unison among commercial lending institutions, the prime rate set by major money center banks sometimes varies for a short time, depending upon the aggressiveness with which banks react to changes in the economy. The prime rate set by at least 75% of the United States' 30 largest banks is published every day in *The Wall Street Journal*, along with several other money rates. In 1981 inflation (as measured by the CPI) was 13.5% and prime was 20.5%. In contrast, in mid 1992 inflation was increasing at less than a 4% pace and the prime rate was 6%.

Also closely monitored is the *Eleventh District Cost of Funds*, published by the Federal Home Loan Bank of San Francisco and used as an index for adjustable rate mortgages (ARMs). It was first published in August 1981, soon after federally chartered savings institutions received permission to offer ARMs. The index is based on data submitted monthly by the district's lending institutions in California, Arizona and Nevada, and is calculated as the ratio of interest expenses in a given month to the average of the ending balance of liabilities for that month and the preceding month. Approximately one-quarter to one-half of all nationwide ARMs are linked to the index; within the 11th district, approximately three-quarters of all ARMs are linked to it.

HOLDING PERIOD

Convention within the real estate industry holds that most forecasts are prepared on a ten-year basis. Residual proceeds are assumed to occur based on a hypothetical sale at the end of the tenth year, usually calculated by applying a capitalization rate to the eleventh year's net operating income. In fact, the length of the forecast period should be governed by the property's lease expiration schedule. If significant expirations were timed to occur in the twelfth or thirteenth year, resulting in a dramatic change in income (either upward or downward), the appraiser would be delinquent in not recognizing the impact of this in the analysis.

At the opposite extreme, imagine a scenario where a property is fully leased to a single creditworthy tenant at a flat net rent for twenty-five years. In this instance, a prospective buyer would be most interested in his initial year rate of return, obviating the need for a DCF approach. At a yield rate of 12%, one dollar of residual value received twenty-five years into the future has a present worth of less than $.06.

There is nothing inherently wrong with using a holding period of ten years. In fact, it is probably an excellent idea to have some uniformity in an industry as fragmented as real estate. Additionally, the use of a ten-year forecast makes it easier to compare the anticipated yield on a prospective real estate investment with returns available from alternative investments such as corporate bonds or Treasury bonds with the same maturity. However, the appraiser should be aware of potential errors that can result from not focusing on a property's lease expiration schedule when performing a valuation.

TERMINAL CAPITALIZATION RATES

Terminal or residual capitalization rates are used to calculate an office building's future value at the end of the holding period by forecasting the anticipated results of a hypothetical sale. This sale is assumed to occur on the last day (December 31 if the forecast is prepared on a calendar year basis) of the holding period, with the future price a function of the following year's income. This residual value is then added to the tenth

TABLE 29-3   Hypothetical Income Stream

Year	10	11	12	13	14
Income	$10,568	$10,034	$12,543	$13,008	$13,975

year's income for valuation purposes. Thus a ten-year forecast actually contains eleven years of revenue and expenses. Remember that the lease expiration schedule should be the primary determinant of the length of the holding period.

There are several techniques used by real estate professionals to estimate the residual capitalization rate. The simplest approach is to first estimate a stabilized year's capitalization rate, then add a premium for the risk associated with forecasting income typically eleven years into the future. The appraiser should check buildings similar to the subject in age and type of income stream to derive an appropriate market capitalization rate. If the appraiser determines, for example, that 9% is the appropriate "going-in" or initial year's rate, he or she might add 100 basis points to compensate for the additional risk of achieving the forecast income in eleven years. The premium added to the first-year rate may also be used to reflect the subject property's aging and consequent depreciation. Care must be taken not to use first-year rates in place of terminal rates.

Another, more technical approach involves preparing a second ten-year forecast (encompassing years 11-20), then discounting these flows at an appropriate IRR (higher than that used for years 1-10 to compensate for the incremental risk of forecasting so far into the future) and solving for the eleventh year residual cap rate. Although this approach may appear more credible than simply adding a premium to the first-year rate, it is doubtful that the market is really this precise in its analyses. Absent any abnormalities in a property's leasing activity or rent levels in the initial or residual year, the "going-out" or residual rate can safely be expected to be higher than the "going-in" or initial rate. One exception may be contract rates in the initial years that exceed market levels.

If the year capitalized for the residual is an unusual year, the appraiser has two choices—either cap an alternate year or adjust the terminal rate. In Table 29-3, the eleventh year is a rollover year in which income is abnormally depressed because of the downtime between old, below-market leases that are expiring and new leases commencing at higher market rents. Clearly year eleven is distorted and it would be an error to base the residual value on that year's income.

The analyst may wish to either extend the projection by one year, or adjust the eleventh year's rate to account for the significant increase in income going forward. Capitalizing the twelfth year income at 10% yields the same residual value as capping the eleventh year income at 8%. While the latter rate may sound low (which it is), it may be justified by future increases in income over the ensuing years.

Unfortunately, selecting a residual year and an appropriate rate may be easier than deciding *what* to capitalize. Most appraisers capitalize net operating income (NOI), usually defined as income before leasing commissions, tenant improvement costs and a capital replacement reserve. Cap rates are frequently expressed as a function of NOI rather than cash flow (NOI less the above three capital items), because excessive lease rollovers can temporarily distort cash flow. However in particularly weak office markets, these capital costs may become so prevalent that they are recognized as an ongoing expense and income is capitalized *after* these charges, rather than these charges being ignored in the eleventh year when calculating the residual value. A variation of this involves the deduction of a stabilized level of capital expenses rather than the actual amount. This approach recognizes the effect of these costs while also accounting for any distortion they may cause.

In projections that include a deduction for debt service, and therefore derive an annual estimate of cash flow to the equity position, an equity cap rate may be used. Depending on the state of the market, this rate may be higher or lower than a traditional cap rate; during periods of stability, one would expect equity return requirements to exceed debt requirements, resulting in a higher cap rate.

Lastly, some appraisers deduct a sales cost from the residual of approximately 1%-3% while others ignore it. The former logically justify its use as recognition of a legitimate charge against future sale proceeds, while the latter opine that estimating a value ten years into the future is so speculative that the impact of a sales commission is insignificant. The former seems founded in better logic than the latter.

INVESTOR RETURN REQUIREMENTS

Real estate competes with other assets for capital. Among the perceived reasons for investment in office buildings are portfolio diversification; a hedge against inflation; control of the investment by an owner/user; easier expansion possibility for an owner/user; promotional value of a signature building; its negative correlation with returns on long-term bonds; and perhaps most importantly, comparatively stable pricing compared to the volatility of stocks and bonds. Table 29-4 illustrates the historical return and volatility among real estate, Treasury bills, stocks and bonds.[11] Real estate's relatively poor performance in the second half of the 1980s and early 1990s caused many investors to re-think their rationale for investing in real

---

[11] Giliberto, S. Michael, Real Estate in the Portfolio: Then and Now, Salomon Brothers, July 8, 1991, page 4.

TABLE 29-4   Real Estate Versus Financial Assets 1978-1990
Annualized Quarterly Total Returns
First Quarter 1978 – Fourth Quarter 1990

	Real Estate	Treasury Bills	Stocks	Bonds	Inflation
Return	10.9%	9.2%	15.1%	9.8%	6.1%
Volatility	3.1	1.3	16.3	9.9	2.1

estate. Nevertheless, once the generic decision to invest has been made, returns available from investments in other asset classes must be weighed. The evaluation process becomes difficult, though not impossible, since daily quotations are available for stocks and bonds, while appraisals of real estate are infrequent and varying.

Over the past several years, the internal rate of return (IRR) has gained greater usefulness and market acceptance as an investment measurement of expected office building performance. IRR is the yield on an investment based on an initial cash investment, annual cash flows from the property and resale proceeds. IRR allows for return on as well as recapture of the original investment. Several techniques are available for the appraiser seeking to reflect the market investor's return requirements.

One approach is to compare returns available from purchasing corporate bonds with a maturity and risk level comparable to that of the real estate investment under consideration. The yield to maturity of a bond investment is identical to the IRR for a real estate investment. Both contain similar payment characteristics in the form of periodic distributions of cash flow followed by a large one-time payment upon termination of the investment. Bonds have an advantage in terms of increased liquidity; real estate has an offsetting advantage in terms of the investor's ability to increase yield if the property outperforms expectations, and to a lesser degree, if there are any tax benefits available. Most important for comparison purposes, the level of risk must be similar. For most multi-tenanted office building investments, the yield available from BBB (Standard & Poor's) or Baa (Moody's) bonds approximates the minimum IRR desired by most real estate investors. Baa bonds are defined by Moody's as follows:

> Bonds which are rated Baa are considered as medium grade obligations, i.e., they are neither highly protected nor poorly secured. Interest payments and principal security appear adequate for the present but certain protective elements may be lacking or may be characteristically unreliable over any great length of time. Such bonds lack outstanding investment characteristics and in fact have speculative characteristics as well.[12]

---

[12] Moody's Investors Service, Moody's Bond Record, February 1992, Moody's Investors Service, page 3.

A second approach involves researching periodically published investor surveys of minimum return requirements for investment in various types of real estate, including office buildings. Several surveys further segregate their findings into specific geographic markets, as well as oversupplied markets. Among the firms publishing these are Real Estate Research Corp. (sponsored by Equitable Real Estate Investment Management, Inc.), CB Commercial Real Estate Group, Inc., Lincoln North & Co., Ltd. (in Canada), Cushman & Wakefield, and Peter F. Korpacz & Associates, Inc. Similar data is also published by the American Council of Life Insurance, and the National Council of Real Estate Investment Fiduciaries, among others.

When comparing IRRs the appraiser should keep several points in mind. First, the returns cited are almost always the minimum return requirements necessary to attract capital to real estate.

Secondly, inherent in most IRR requirements are minimum first-year capitalization rate or dividend requirements. An investment with an 11% IRR and 4% going-in rate is likely to be riskier than an alternate investment with the same yield but a 9% going-in rate. Similarly, the risk of achieving the returns incorporated into the forecast, as measured by the aggressiveness or conservativeness of the projections, directly affects the appropriate choice of IRR. A projection predicated upon double-digit market rent growth is riskier than one for the same property predicated upon nominal rent growth, and therefore demands a higher IRR. The risk is the rate.

Appraisers of office buildings on leased land frequently use a higher IRR than if both the land and building were owned by the same entity.

Some foreigners investing in the United States prefer a *real rate of return* analysis, that is, one that ignores the effects of inflation. This is also a common approach when investing in less developed economies abroad that may be subject to extremely high levels of inflation. Table 29-5 demonstrates the comparison between inflationary growth and real increases.

An IRR rate can be converted to a measure of real rate of return by deducting the inflation component. For example, a 13% IRR with 6%

TABLE 29-5   Analysis of Real Rent Increases

Year	Market Rent Per Square Foot at 8% Compound Growth	Cumulative Increase	Impact of 5% Inflation	Real Increase
1	$20.00			
2	21.60	$1.60	$1.00	$ .60
3	23.33	3.33	2.05	1.28
4	25.19	5.19	3.15	2.04
5	27.21	7.21	4.31	2.90

inflation yields a real rate of return of 7%. In the case of an office building under long-term net lease to a single tenant, the creditworthiness of the tenant may be the primary determinant of the IRR. A purchaser of this property would be akin to a bond buyer, in that the likelihood of receiving the cash flows, and possible residual, is a function of the tenant's ability to pay. In an ideal situation, the appraiser can look to the bond market for a bond issued by the tenant or by a comparably rated tenant for a maturity similar to the projection period, and use the yield to maturity as a basis for selecting an IRR.

CONCLUSION

Valuation is an ever-changing and complex issue. No single measure of return is sufficient to value an office building. Through the mid 1970s, with inflation not perceived as threatening, properties were frequently valued using a capitalization rate applied to a single year's assumed stabilized income. The advent of personal computers and rapid inflation in the early 1980s led to the first lease-by-lease programs with the concurrent ability to prepare forecasts of future revenues. Strong demand for real estate by syndicators, pension funds and foreign investors led to the era of "too much money chasing too few properties." By the mid 1980s prices no longer tracked income. Eventually faced with an oversupply situation, investors became reluctant to make assumptions about the future, and were only willing to pay for income in place by applying a capitalization rate to the first year's income. Back to the future.

Today, most investment decisions incorporate an IRR analysis (for complex properties), a direct capitalization rate used as a divisor and extracted from market sales (for smaller, simpler buildings), and a comparison of the purchase price per square foot to replacement cost (especially prevalent in depressed markets), or some combination of all three. The cost and market approaches have been relegated to a supporting role.

ABOUT THE AUTHOR

Howard C. Gelbtuch, CRE, MAI, is senior director in charge of all valuation activities for Jones Lang Wootton. Previously he was director of real estate advisory services for Coopers & Lybrand, an accounting and management consulting firm. Prior to that he was director of research for Morgan Stanley Realty, Inc., advising developers, corporations, foreign and domestic institutional investors; and senior vice president and head of the real estate evaluation department at Integrated Resources, Inc., where he analyzed and advised on U.S. commercial property acquisitions. He holds a BS in finance from New York University and an MBA in real estate from Baruch College. He has published in various trade journals.

30

OFFICE BUILDING
INVESTMENT ANALYSIS

by Hugh F. Kelly, CRE

INTRODUCTION

Inscribed at one of the world's most storied sites, the Greek temple at Delphi, is the saying, "Know thyself." Juvenal, the Roman poet, maintained that this counsel came from the gods themselves.

Investment analysis differs from the analytical techniques discussed in earlier chapters of this book in its use of specialized, individual criteria for decision-making. Feasibility and marketability studies look outward to market conditions to establish their standards. Such evaluations seek to assess objectively whether or not prevailing circumstances warrant the construction of a new office building or support acceptance of the real estate product.

Investment analysis is more idiosyncratic. The investor's own subjective requirements and abilities are the yardstick measuring the expected performance of the office property under consideration.

While investment analysis is undoubtedly subjective, it cannot afford to be arbitrary. The discipline of office investment analysis requires a sober self-evaluation by the investor in the first place. It also demands a detailed, rigorous investigation into a property's operations and competitive position. Office building investment is not a kind arena for empty displays of ego, nor for wishful projections of a property's unique advantage in a very broad marketplace. In the early 1990s, the investment landscape was littered with the wreckage of office deals based upon such delusions. Investors, like most mortals, are apt to be seduced by the object of their attention. The wisdom of the Delphic saying lies precisely in its recognition that insight into one's true capabilities is rare.

INVESTMENT STRATEGY

Why is it that competing investors, reviewing the identical office property offered for sale, can arrive at widely varying bid prices? Disagreement about factual information relating to the property or to its competitive market may account for some of the spread, but this should tend to be a rather narrow band of price, growing even narrower as the "due diligence" efforts of sophisticated investors become ever more probing. Some further differential is attributable to the requirements of cash flow models that assumptions about the future be incorporated into financial projections. Such assumptions are necessarily judgmental, and will vary from investor to investor. But similar evidence is commonly available to each investor, and expectations about market performance tend to converge as transaction results provide feedback about the outlook of other informed sellers and buyers of office properties.

The most significant reason for the wide range of prices calculated by prospective office investors is their adoption of highly specific investment strategies. Behind the veil of the generic rule, "Maximize profits and minimize losses," are complex choices dictated by strategic stances. These are arrayed along a spectrum of behavior from the very aggressive to the very conservative. The standpoint along this spectrum influences investors' reading of risk, their approach to costs, their selection of product, their deployment of manpower and their plans for the management of the asset once acquired. All such choices have direct implications for pricing levels. Strategic choices always imply tradeoffs. The number of alternatives is vast. But three of the most important options can illustrate the issues involved.

1. Immediate Cash Flow versus Appreciation Potential

It is axiomatic that present value is equal to the anticipated benefits of discounted future income. The certainty and timing of that future income stream, however, can take infinitely varied forms. During rising markets, near-term cash flow is usually de-emphasized in favor of investment structures offering the potential to benefit from improvements in the market. In the early 1980s, many investors looked for office buildings with leases scheduled to expire in the years following the prospective purchase of the property. The expectation was that these older leases would then be readily converted into higher market rents, improving the net operating income of the office building and leading to a higher capital value upon subsequent resale. Comparatively low overall capitalization rates coupled with low cash-on-cash returns were acceptable to investors who could take a patient approach and who had confidence that market rents would remain above the level of prevailing contract rents when the property was purchased. A recently executed, long-term lease was in fact an undesirable feature in such an environment, as many investors believed that such instruments limited the "upside" of the property. This mentality captivated buyers in the rising phase of the cycle.

How the times changed! Strategies relying upon capital appreciation of the property showed more and more disappointing results as the cyclical peak was reached, and investors transferred their preference to the comparatively more assured income derived from existing leases. Economically, this shift of preference was expressed as a higher direct capitalization rate on the initial NOI. Many have read this move as a return to "tried and true" earnings multiples, in contrast to the "more speculative" uses of assumptions in internal rate of return methodology. This misreads market behavior. Direct capitalization expresses implicitly an outlook on the future that is made more explicit in the assumptions generating a discounted cash flow analysis. A higher direct cap rate simply says that the investor foresees less market opportunity to improve future earnings from the office building, that existing contract rents in fact capture most or all of the income potential available in the market. In such circumstances, a newly executed long-term lease with a well-secured tenant is a highly desirable feature and there is little advantage to a lease expiration schedule heavily weighted toward the early years of the holding period.

The reason for claiming that a transaction emphasizing a high initial yield is no less "speculative" goes beyond the understanding that, mathematically, one is reducible to the other. More fundamentally, investment returns for an office building come in the forms of "return on" and "return of" the invested capital. Direct cap rates do not explicitly differentiate between the "return on" and "return of" components, and address only a single year or a hypothetical "stabilized" period. The Appraisal Institute believes that the partial annual return of capital is at least implicit in the overall rate. The "return of" the investment through the eventual disposition of the property is as much entrusted to the uncertain markets of the future as it is under the IRR method of analysis. This subject will be raised again in the discussion of strategic choices relating to risk.

Subjective investor motivations frequently determine the tradeoff between immediate cash flow and appreciation potential. The investor will tilt toward the income side of the equation if the investment is expected to satisfy immediate needs: putting bread on the table, paying for next year's vacation, improving the homestead. If, however, the objective is to build net worth, to create a patrimony, to hedge inflation or to balance an investment portfolio, capital appreciation factors loom larger in the investment decision.

2. Market Share vs. Geographic Diversification

In the United States, it is a bit deceptive to speak of "the national office market" as though it were a well-defined transaction environment. The local nature of real estate clearly is primary for the property investor, with the so-called national market more like the general climate within which the investor operates and specific markets, the weather which dictates the choice of clothes to wear.

In local markets an investor can work strategically toward a strong or even dominant market share. Such a position lets the investor take initiative that enables him to lead the market, rather than merely react. With dominant market share, competitors' activities affect returns at the margin but do not dictate response: the leading player always has more options available than the smaller rival. But when the dominant player introduces change in the form of pricing schedules, operational innovations or new product, the other market participants are vulnerable to income erosion or further loss of market share.

Concentrating investment in a given location is a prerequisite to establishing strong market share, but there are risks entailed in such concentration. Office buildings, like other forms of real estate, are simply residual economic products: they ultimately depend upon activity in a much broader economic arena for their usefulness and therefore their value. For this reason, the largest developers, pension funds, insurance companies and banks practice geographic diversification in their office building portfolios. The theory of risk-spreading is comparatively well evolved, although its short history in the office investment arena makes its performance difficult to assess. But the deliberate policy of diversification is now a mainstream investment strategy.

Like the cashflow vs. appreciation tradeoff, there is a continuum along which the investor operates. Within the office building asset class, the pursuit of market share is not incompatible with diversification objectives. The real limitation is the size of the investor's purse. But for an individual investment, the strategies can be mutually exclusive. Expanding one's position in a given market diverts those investment dollars from efforts to spread risk. Similarly, the deliberate policy of devoting new capital to new markets inhibits the growth of market share.

Investment managers with large stakes in the office building sector are required to make such strategic choices rather regularly. Their tactical investment evaluations often formally incorporate risk-adjusted returns to help in weighing the options. Each investor's sense of the tradeoffs, given the base of their existing holdings, can lead to a decision on a bid price for a property substantially different from that of the competing potential purchasers.

3. The Adaptive Imperative versus Policy Stability

In an ideal world, an investor would rationally calculate the required returns on various components of the investment portfolio based upon factors like liquidity, risk and ease of management. Once the rate of return required for office buildings was determined, the investor would bid for those assets meeting or exceeding the desired standard, and decline to bid on others. However, no such standard of cool rationality actually operates in the real estate business.

It is best to view the pool of real estate capital as being like a lake, with both feeder and outlet streams, and subject to rather dramatic changes in water level. This image may help to explain the periodic changes in the real estate investment climate and to highlight a set of strategic tradeoffs laid out by such shifts. For it happens that economic events can direct a sudden surge of capital toward real estate investment, much as the melting snows of spring fill mountain reservoirs. There are other times when the real estate capital pool is drawn down drastically, leaving the investment landscape parched and sere.

During these periods of capital drought, the water level in the lake drops dangerously low. Recessions in the business cycle often reduce the flow of capital toward real estate, and sometimes necessitate the sale of property at a loss. Occasionally, the incidence of loss is so widespread as to constitute a national deflation in the value of assets like office buildings. This was the case in the mid-1970s bust, and occurred again in the early 1990s. When lenders become concerned that deflation in real asset values is likely to be a persistent feature in the market—owing to endemic weakness in the market for office tenants and lack of investor interest in office building acquisitions—a full-blown credit crunch can ensue, in which the capital pool is drained in a violent whirlpool threatening to suck prices ever lower.

The ebb and flow of capital for real estate investment has historically followed a different rhythm than either the national business cycle of expansions and recessions, or the rise and fall of supply and demand conditions in local markets. Investors, faced with the complicated interplay of several economic trends, are likely to differ in their reading of the probable duration of the trends, the timing of cyclical reversals and the magnitude of the anticipated corrections. When investor judgment concludes that existing conditions are a temporary deviation from a more fundamental market trend, then a strategy of affirming existing investment policy standards is probable and the investor is likely to "ride out the market" instead of accepting an unfavorable price or yield. The longer the duration or, alternatively, the less significant the eventual correction expected, the more likely it is that the investor will modify investment policies

without a consensus of expectations concerning the outcome of economic trends. Their investment analyses are likely to produce widely varying bid prices for property—or, in extreme uncertainty, no bids at all.

Investors are confronted with a troubling dilemma during periods of strong capital flows targeted toward office buildings. There is often enormous pressure to "get the money out," to do deals. Pre-established investment standards, strictly adhered to, may effectively mean being out of the market—and that itself may be an unacceptable alternative. Whether considered from the equity side—as targeted yields, physical quality, ease of management—or from the debt side—coverage ratios, collateral security, borrower's credit history—the range of investment criteria have to be somewhat adaptable, to shift in response to movements in the market. But mere following of the market does not constitute a strategy: it is the abdication of strategy. It is a responsible investment decision to pass on a deal, and the point of tolerance at which an investor sets boundaries is not a matter of simple calculation. In balancing adaptive behavior with investment policy standards, it helps to remember that having the winning bid does not constitute investment success: any fool with enough money can "succeed" in that sense. Success is measured by achieved returns, a difficult yardstick to hold steady as investment pressure builds, and a performance measure which only becomes applicable with the passage of time.

The Lesson Learned

Many additional strategic considerations could, no doubt, be added to this discussion. The three sets of tradeoffs presented here illustrate elements of motivation, portfolio structure and economic expectations that come into play in investment analysis that are typically outside the purview of marketability studies, feasibility studies or market-value appraisals of office buildings. The principal lesson is this: investment analysis requires more than mastery of technique. It could be argued that the reduction of investment analysis to a merely technical exercise in so-called "financial engineering" during the 1980s did much to expose investors to risk as office markets became overbuilt, over-priced and finally over-the-edge. A more comprehensive approach, clearly, is mandated for the future.

THE INVESTOR'S STRENGTHS AND WEAKNESSES

The creation of an apt strategy is, in itself, no small feat. Even this, however, depends on the investor's clear-sighted assessment of his own strengths and weaknesses. An investment strategy for office buildings is likely to be appropriate only if the investor has tallied his basic assets and liabilities in a number of areas, and has done so with rigorous candor. The investor must identify his areas of specialized expertise, and have a genuine appraisal of his financial capacity going into the proposed investment. He must understand that he is but one player among many in this marketplace, and so must have a keen sense of potential allies in his venture as well as a knowledge of his competition. He must also understand that much of what transpires in the real estate marketplace is beyond the control of the industry itself, and he must therefore be alert to a variety of externalities which could affect the performance or even the viability of the investment.

The notion that office building investment requires specialized expertise is sometimes resisted, on the grounds that a basic understanding of the principles of finance provide sufficient analytical tools which can be applied across asset classes with only modest adaptation. Wall Street has traditionally held this point of view. Over time, however, the assembly of an arsenal of specific skills by the office investor can provide an important edge and lead to superior performance. Within the real estate sector itself, the complexity of the office lease (compared, for example, with the comparatively more straightforward warehouse lease) yields its secrets most fully to those with day-to-day operating experience within the property type.

The Issue of Financial Capacity

The concept of financial capacity, for many investors, has unfortunately been limited to the ability to raise the capital required for the initial investment. The use of financial leverage, especially of non-recourse debt, has presumed that once acquired the property will "carry itself," without the investor bearing further obligations for capital infusions. Cash flow projections, even in strong market conditions, repeatedly show instances in which net operating income falls below the level of debt service. Lease expirations are the most common trigger for such credit events, as a rent hiatus occurs, commissions and tenant improvement costs are incurred, and extraordinary capital projects like asbestos abatement may be undertaken. Investors generally anticipate that they will be able to borrow working capital for such needs and that the inclusion of such "downtime" in the projections accounts for the draw on cash, allowing the IRR analysis to include the negative returns in the pricing of the property.

Within the projections, however, it is most unusual to model the effects of market cycles or general business cycles (excepting only an upswing if a market is considered to be underperforming at the time the investment is made). Admittedly, the timing of market cycles is largely unpredictable but their occurrence is among the most normal of economic behaviors. Most analysts would argue that the risks of cycles is a systematic feature of real estate investment, and is therefore compensated for in the discount rate, most specifically in the spread of real estate returns above the "safe rate" represented by the Treasury note or bond of comparable maturity. This argument, however, begs the question of financial capacity. For if a cyclical downturn costs the office building revenue in the form of lower rents, or in the actual loss of rents, this may be the precise time that credit is least available for the necessary marketing program and physical improvements needed to keep the building competitive and to meet existing debt service. In this instance, the owner of the property is faced with a capital call depending upon his own financial resources and failure to meet such a call may mean the forfeiture of his equity.

The issue of financial capacity is relevant to all sizes of office building investments, and to investors of all stripes. The popular limited partnership syndications of the 1980s were largely undone by the reform of the Federal Tax Code in 1986, but were inherently flawed in any event because the partners were typically unscreened in terms of their ability to provide subsequent contributions to the property if needed. As the office markets of the early 1990s were circled by the deep-discount-seeking "vulture funds," another concern emerged. Purchasers acquiring troubled property, whether from the Resolution Trust Corporation, from private creditors in possession, or from distressed equity holders directly, were faced with the probability that the initial acquisition price would be only the first of many capital outlays. With operating losses expected for several years, the vulture funds were, in effect, making an installment purchase of the asset by acquiring the investment on the basis of anticipated recurrent funding. Even the largest institutions, pension funds and life insurers were concerned about the prudence of committing further moneys to office building investments which had already declined in value, eroding their institutional capital base at a time when regulatory scrutiny was becoming ever more intense.

Evaluations of competition are becoming more sophisticated. Analysis of submarkets is increasingly refined, and the delineation of "peer groups" among properties is emerging as a widespread tool. Assumptions geared toward prevailing conditions among properties of a similar age, location, configuration and tenant profile can prove more relevant than conditions measured for all office classes in the marketplace. Care should be advised against the hasty reliance on small peer groups, however. Over time, submarket conditions have shown themselves to be substantially crosscorrecting. Cheap suburban space, for example, is a strong draw for cost-sensitive operations located in the central business district. Conversely, emerging suburban nodes which have been fed by corporate relocations from the urban core may suddenly find their demand drying up if rent differentials narrow.

Beyond Mathematics to Behavior

At this point there may be some understandable frustration on the part of those who conceive of investment analysis as primarily a mathematical exercise. Indeed the common vocabulary of the real estate industry suggests that a numerical value should be the outcome of the process of investment analysis, and that therefore this subject is principally about "figuring." There is no doubt that there is a need for good quantitative methodology. The quantitative disciplines, however, are only one step in a more comprehensive process. Mathematical analysis is, by nature, abstract and reductive, and aims at the manipulability of the data. The complementary step, however, adds the equally necessary dimension of the skills of the investor and the contextual situation defining the investment. These latter elements are often neglected in the investment analysis, and yet may render the assumptions of the "objective" mathematical treatment utterly moot. The principle to be kept in mind is this: the outcome of an office investment analysis is a behavioral, not an arithmetic, result. With that principle in mind, the following are some of the quantitative standards helping to shape that behavior.

Investment Criteria

Capital is a scarce economic resource. Like the other factors in production (land and labor), capital tends to be allocated by its owners to those uses which bring the greatest return. As was seen in the related profit maximization axiom, however, the economic principle can encompass many shades of meaning and application.

Ironically, the first measure encountered is the conceptual opposite of the "maximizing" axiom. Investors begin with a minimum measure of acceptable return on a proposed office investment, a level which must be exceeded if capital is to be rationally allocated to a given property. That minimum level of return is called a *hurdle rate*.

Financial theory offers a variety of equations for deriving the hurdle rate. The common elements in each of the calculations, however, are comparatively few. These are the determination of a base rate (called the risk-free U.S. Treasury rate), plus an added component to compensate for the uncertainty of real estate performance, plus components accounting for the effort of management and the comparative illiquidity of the asset class. There is a fundamentally correct logic to the concept of such hurdle rates, although not a single one of the proposed equations has been proven to fit the behavior of actual office investors. The importance of understanding the equations lies in assimilating the need to account for the conceptual components and establishing a composite rate with which to enter the market.

The nature of a Treasury holding points toward what the other elements of return for the office investor must be. The government certificate is essentially a passive investment, requiring no further attention on the part of the investor and not subject to improvement in value based upon such attention. And the Treasury note is, effectively, a cash equivalent. That is, it can be converted to cash virtually immediately, subject only to its market price rather than its face amount.

The equations developed by financial theorists come in essentially two forms: first are hurdle rates which are built up by addition, "partitioning" the rate into its components, ascribing a rate of return to each component and summing the weighted component to a final required rate of return. The second method for deriving the hurdle rate is to establish the risk-free rate (as above) and then to measure the volatility of the asset class against the Treasury-instrument baseline similar to the calculation of the "beta" rate in the stock market.

While the mathematics of these calculations can be both interesting and useful, it should be pointed out that they are not determinative. Within the real estate investment marketplace there are investors who perform such calculations and those who do not. There are those whose "risk-free" rate is based upon U.S. Government instruments, and those who have access to other high-quality government debt on the international capital markets. There are those whose cost of capital is tax-sensitive, and those who are tax-exempt. All these investors can find themselves at work simultaneously in a single office market, and even in the bidding for a single property. And, if these investors are sophisticated enough both to care about risk-adjusted rates of return and to correctly calculate a hurdle rate on this basis, they are likely to also have a matrix of concerns at play in their ultimate investment decision and are not likely to place an absolute reliance on any single number in arriving at that decision. For example, selection of a bid price may be from a range of values based on varying assumptions.

The examples that follow illustrate how concerns about risk, illiquidity, management capability and costs of capital can enter into the investor's evaluation of an opportunity. But first, a brief discussion is necessary on what makes an investor's investment analysis of an office property different from an appraisal.

Market Value and Investment Value

Real estate appraisers have become the targets for harsh criticism in turbulent markets which have seen office building values first soar sky-high and then drop like hailstones. In the rising markets, valuation professionals were chastised for being "too conservative" for inadequately reflecting the increasingly aggressive assumptions and appetite for risk. In the bear market for property, appraisers were taken to task for maintaining that "fire sale prices" were not the same as market value. No matter what phase the market cycle may be in, there is an element of validity in such criticism of the valuation exercise since, ideally, the appraiser is supposed to reflect the mind of the market, to draw the assumptions and indicators of value from the activity of the market and to simulate the thinking and behavior of the investing community.

In the previous chapter, the role of the appraiser in the office building industry was treated in depth. In particular, the definition of "market value" was seen to be a critical estimate of the most probable selling price at a given moment under rigorously defined conditions. Such conditions sometimes closely approximate the circumstances under which an office building transaction is consummated. Often, though, specific sellers and buyers are motivated by circumstances that are highly individual and which lead to an agreement on price that can vary—sometimes significantly—from the precisely defined market value of the property. This is not a failure of the appraisal discipline, but rather an instance of its limits. The classic market value definition largely assumes the operation of an efficient, well-informed, well-populated market of totally objective buyers and sellers, not the common investment position of highly subjective, differently motivated buyers and sellers. For office buildings, this market is an idealization, not the common investment milieu. So the appraiser is called upon to contrive a proxy environment for valuation purposes that perhaps neither the buyer nor the seller has access to. No wonder that appraisals before (and after!) the fact so often diverge substantially from the actual sales prices.

Investment analysis seeks to arrive at a price reflecting "the value of an investment to a particular investor, based upon his or her investment requirements; as distinguished from Market Value, which is impersonal and detached."[1]

Market value involves an estimate of most probable price, and is found at a point within a range where other prices might also be reasonably estimated. Investment value analysis aims at a related, but distinctly different figure: the price that meets the buyer's investment criteria and which also can be the winning bid.

Market value assumes the transaction is under no duress. Investment analysis attempts to understand clearly the specific motivations underlying the transaction. Through this motivational consideration, one or a few terms or structural elements can frequently be identified as the keys to the deal, and these form the fulcrum upon which the price pivots. Market value looks at "all cash" value or at generally available financing terms. But investment analysis may reveal that the most favorable combination of price to the seller and return to the buyer may depend upon a highly customized transaction structure which is not typical in the market.

That such variables can influence price is not generally disputed. That they can be adjusted by appraisal analysis to a "cash equivalent" level that will indicate market value is a cornerstone of appraisal doctrine. A more controversial assertion is that careful financial structuring can actually "add value" to the property, yet this assertion is at the heart of the concept of

---

[1] *The Dictionary of Real Estate Appraisal.* American Institute of Real Estate Appraisers (Chicago, 1984) p. 167.

"investment value" and is the justification for most of the investment-related jobs that exist in the office building industry.

A prominent entrepreneurial investor in office property acknowledged that he never has a property appraised before purchasing it. "I know what I want to pay for the building, and what I can afford to pay." Still he told a group of real estate loan officers, "I depend on you to know the appraisal value, the market value. Otherwise I am just a cowboy, just guessing about the deal. I don't think I am far off, though, if I can explain exactly why and how my price is different from what you tell me the appraisal number is."

An acquisitions officer for a major pension fund advisor put it differently. "My whole job is to disagree with appraisals. I am supposed to find the more attractive price, earn the better returns and sell at a premium, if I want to prosper. The whole point is to beat the market." To gain advantage, to beat the market—this is the distinction separating the aim of the investment analysis from the aim of the valuation per se.

A CASE STUDY ILLUSTRATION

Although investors are a rather heterogeneous class, highly individuated in strategy and specific objectives, the common goal of superior performance drives the investment analysis of each individual investing entity. It is logically impossible for all the members of the class to achieve above-average performance, to beat the market. But some will succeed, and the question is How? Perhaps reference to a simple, paradigmatic case can show the possibilities.

Access to Proprietary Information

Investment analysis may make use of information not generally available to the public, or even to many competitors in the same office market. This is a distinguishing characteristic of real estate markets when compared with the familiar financial markets in instruments like bonds and stocks. The so-called "fungible investments" trade in markets that approximate perfect information. That is to say, the same information is—in theory—available to all participants, and public trading activity gives constant feedback about whether one's own interpretation of that information is being confirmed or contradicted by others in the market. "Private" information is considered to distort the operation of the market and transactions based upon knowledge withheld from the market as a whole—so-called "insider trading"—are discouraged by law and market rule.

So the first level of using knowledge to investment advantage in office markets is data-related. Data is closely held in the real estate industry, and access to critical information is cultivated by investors. For example, take the case of two investors considering the purchase of a 200,000 square foot suburban office building currently suffering from a 50% vacancy rate. Investor "A" is an experienced local organization which recognizes that the market for such properties is substantially oversupplied, with a 25% vacancy overall, and that achieving a stabilized occupancy level of 90% or better at the subject property will probably take several years of marketing effort (Table 30-1). Investor "B", however, holds a national portfolio of properties and has learned through routine inquiries among its tenants that the Ace Corporation will be consolidating its administrative and data departments, and that Ace's requirements are such that Investor "B" could provide turnkey occupancy at the subject property within three months of acquisition (Table 30-2).

Assume that both investors require an 11% internal rate of return on free and clear cash flow. The depressed condition of the market, and the even greater distress existing at the subject property, will lead Investor "A" to offer far less than the replacement cost of the building. A projected lease-up of the property which anticipates a five-year period before the building is fully occupied indicates that only a price as low as $8.2 million, or about $41 per square foot, can be justified if the hurdle rate is to be achieved.

Investor "B", however, has information which can make a major difference in its offering price. Based on the addition of the Ace Corporation to the tenant roster, at the current market rate (and even accounting for a year's free rent as a concession to Ace), Investor "B" knows that an 11% IRR is achievable even if the price is as high as $10.3 million or $51.63 per square foot, even accounting for somewhat higher operating expenses once the Ace Corporation is in occupancy, and substantial commission and tenant improvement costs in Year 1 of the cash flow projection. Will "B" pay this price? In all probability, no. If prevailing market conditions indicate a value of $8.2 million, this is where "B" will be looking to strike a deal. This is what it will want to pay. The investment value of $10.3 million is what it can afford to pay, while still meeting its hurdle rate. The price is likely to fall in a range between these two numbers.

Certainly Ace will be seeking to extract a deal at terms more favorable than market norms in exchange for signing a long-term lease. The present owners are undoubtedly facing a substantial loss on their own investment at a price of about $8 million, and they can be expected to negotiate strongly that the assumptions leading to such a value are excessively conservative, giving little account of anything but the income in place. The three-way negotiation between the seller, Investor "B", and the Ace Corporation will determine what actual price will be paid by Investor B and what rent incentives will be accorded the major tenant. The key point, however, is that the knowledge that "B" possesses about Ace's needs and intentions gives it a tremendous advantage over Investor "A" in terms of the flexibility on price that "B" can bring to the table while adhering (and in all likelihood nicely exceeding) its minimum investment criteria. Knowledge, in this case, truly is investment power.

TABLE 30-1 Base Case

Years	1	2	3	4	5	6	7	8	9	10	11
Current Contract Revenue (1)	1,525,667	1,552,627	1,580,665	1,189,785	1,595,151	1,319,357	1,602,157	1,498,395	1,539,546	1,898,894	1,852,847
Lease up Tenants Base Rent											
Tenant X	250,000	500,000	500,000	500,000	500,000	250,000	500,000	500,000	500,000	500,000	500,000
Tenant Y	0	0	250,000	500,000	500,000	500,000	500,000	394,375	577,499	577,499	577,499
Tenant Z	0	0	0	0	250,000	500,000	500,000	500,000	500,000	437,687	750,749
Escalation Rent											
Tenant X	0	8,987	18,333	28,053	38,162	24,337	0	11,313	23,138	35,437	48,228
Tenant Y	0	0	0	9,719	19,828	30,341	41,275	26,323	11,805	24,104	36,895
Tenant Z	0	0	0	0	162	10,675	21,608	32,979	44,805	28,552	12,895
New Revenue	250,000	508,987	768,331	1,037,771	1,308,150	1,315,352	1,562,823	1,464,989	1,657,247	1,603,279	1,926,266
Gross Potential Revenue	1,775,666	2,061,613	2,348,996	2,227,556	2,903,301	2,634,709	3,164,981	2,963,383	3,196,793	3,502,173	3,779,113
Less: (Loss)	88,783	103,081	117,450	111,378	145,165	131,735	158,249	148,169	159,840	175,109	188,956
Effective Gross Revenue	1,686,883	1,958,532	2,231,547	2,116,179	2,758,136	2,502,973	3,006,732	2,815,214	3,036,954	3,327,064	3,590,157
Less: Operating Expenses	1,348,000	1,401,920	1,457,997	1,516,317	1,576,969	1,640,048	1,705,650	1,773,876	1,844,831	1,918,624	1,995,369
Net Operating Income	338,883	556,612	773,550	599,862	1,181,166	862,925	1,301,082	1,041,338	1,192,123	1,408,440	1,594,788
Commissions	79,999	0	79,999	0	79,999	0	83,999	0	115,499	120,119	
Tenant Improvements	499,995	0	540,795	0	584,923	0	632,653	0	684,278	711,649	
Net Cash Flow	(241,111)	556,612	152,756	599,862	516,244	862,925	584,429	1,041,338	392,346	576,672	

Value: @10% 8,895,966
     @11% 8,215,532
     @12% 7,595,410

(1) Includes assumed releasing of space upon lease termination.
Subtotals may not add due to rounding

TABLE 30-2 Major Tenant in the Wings

Years	1	2	3	4	5	6	7	8	9	10	11
Current Contract Revenue (1)	1,559,667	1,605,667	1,635,827	1,227,978	1,635,480	1,341,406	1,626,688	1,503,174	1,546,027	1,904,149	1,858,757
Lease up Tenant Base Rent Ace	0	1,500,000	1,500,000	1,500,000	1,500,000	1,500,000	1,500,000	1,500,000	1,500,000	1,500,000	2,342,340
Escalation Rent Ace	0	26,960	54,998	84,158	114,485	146,024	178,825	212,938	248,416	285,312	(315)
New Revenue	0	1,526,960	1,554,998	1,584,158	1,614,485	1,646,024	1,678,825	1,712,938	1,748,416	1,785,312	2,342,025
Gross Potential Revenue	1,559,667	3,132,627	3,190,825	2,812,136	3,249,965	2,987,430	3,305,514	3,216,112	3,294,442	3,689,461	4,200,782
Less: (Loss)	77,983	156,631	159,541	140,607	162,498	149,371	165,276	160,806	164,722	184,473	210,039
Effective Gross Revenue	1,481,683	2,975,995	3,031,284	2,671,529	3,087,467	2,838,058	3,140,238	3,055,306	3,129,720	3,504,988	3,990,743
Less: Operating Expenses	1,450,000	1,508,000	1,568,320	1,631,053	1,696,295	1,764,147	1,834,713	1,908,101	1,984,425	2,063,802	2,146,354
Net Operating Income	31,683	1,467,995	1,462,964	1,040,477	1,391,172	1,073,912	1,305,525	1,147,205	1,145,295	1,441,186	1,844,389
Commissions	360,000	0	0	0	0	0	83,999	0	115,499	120,119	
Tenant Improvements	1,500,000	0	0	0	0	0	632,653	0	684,278	711,649	
Net Cash Flow	(1,828,317)	1,467,995	1,462,964	1,040,477	1,391,172	1,073,912	588,873	1,147,205	345,518	609,419	

Value: @10% 11,160,695
@11% 10,325,965
@12%   9,562,832

(1) Includes assumed releasing of space upon lease termination.
Subtotals may not add due to rounding.

The Local Market Advantage

The local nature of real property can afford real knowledge advantages to investors with in-depth experience in a particular geographic office market. Investor "A" in the preceding example found itself in a weaker competitive position to the broader-based Investor "B". In most cases of a property investor attempting to compete from a distance against savvy local professionals, the shoe is on the other foot. The nuances of the business terms of leases, the most cost-effective property management techniques, the subtleties of micro-market supply and demand variables, the artful dialogue which must occur with government agencies and many other elements of information are the daily routine of the local investor, which allow its analysis to more closely replicate the detailed conditions of market realities. Over the broad extent of the national office market, such smaller advantages are more often the telling difference than the instances where a buyer can exploit a major, closely guarded corporate relocation decision.

The sensitivity of net income to the adroit management of the office property is an essential element in the investor's analysis. Can the property be incorporated in a blanket property and casualty insurance policy? Are mass purchasing opportunities available for materials, supplies or contract services which will reduce the expense items allocable to the individual office building? Are management efficiencies possible, where the investor's slack resources can be utilized at the subject property and income earned without additional property management staff being employed? Does a detailed knowledge of property assessments elsewhere in the jurisdiction suggest the possibility of a successful challenge to the real estate tax bill? In the case of the distressed property in this example, the ability to reduce the effective operating expenses a mere $0.50 per square foot would raise the indicated value nearly a million dollars or nearly 11%. Most frequently it is such operational efficiencies that investors have in mind when they refer to their ability to "create value" through a potential office investment. Table 30-3 uses the Base Case rent and occupancy assumptions, but assumes these decreases in operating expenses.

Knowledge of Facts and Understanding of Systems

These examples have concentrated on *empirical* knowledge, factual information that can have enormous potential value. However, there is something unsatisfying about relying solely on such knowledge for the advantage in office investment analysis. That is because empirical knowledge is merely "case-by-case"; when one investment analysis has been completed, the knowledge is, in a sense, "used up" and the investor gains no special advantage in tackling the next problem. There is, however, a kind of *systematic* knowledge which is also available to the office investor. And

TABLE 30-3 Better Control Over Expenses

Years	1	2	3	4	5	6	7	8	9	10	11
Gross Potential Revenue (1)	1,750,333	2,017,293	2,293,530	2,187,212	2,858,982	2,607,849	3,135,782	2,953,090	3,173,305	3,480,703	3,7≤4,257
Less: (Loss)	87,517	100,865	114,676	109,361	142,949	130,392	156,789	147,654	158,665	174,035	187,213
Effective Gross Revenue	1,662,816	1,916,428	2,178,853	2,077,851	2,716,033	2,477,456	2,978,993	2,805,435	3,014,640	3,306,668	3,5≡7,045
Less: Operating Expenses	1,248,000	1,297,920	1,349,837	1,403,830	1,459,983	1,518,383	1,579,118	1,642,283	1,707,974	1,776,293	1,8≤7,345
Net Operating Income	414,816	618,508	829,017	674,021	1,256,049	959,074	1,399,875	1,163,152	1,306,666	1,530,374	1,7≡9,700
Commissions	79,999	0	79,999	0	79,999	0	83,999	0	115,499	120,119	
Tenant Improvements	499,995	0	540,795	0	584,923	0	632,653	0	684,278	711,649	
Net Cash Flow	(165,178)	618,508	208,223	674,021	591,126	959,074	683,223	1,163,152	506,889	698,607	

Value: @10% 9,855,390
@11% 9,112,294
@12% 8,434,800

(1)Base Case rental assumptions, with escalation rent adjusted for revised operating expenses.
Subtotals may not add due to rounding.

many of the topics treated in this book represent the issues which office investors need to confront each time a potential acquisition is analyzed.

Examples of such systematic knowledge include correct evaluation of user demand. The investor can be misled by reports of "absorption" when "leasing activity" is what is actually meant. To the extent that leasing activity includes lateral movement in the market, it overstates demand. Knowing this distinction helps safeguard against overly optimistic projections for the subject property. Or, in the economic base analysis, the investor should know clearly the difference between "white collar" employment and "office employment," and be able to evaluate demand forecasts based upon this distinction. All too often, investors have been quick to see "services and financial" sector employment as a proxy for office jobs, not realizing that health care workers, teachers, social services employees, repairmen and hotel workers are all subsumed under the "services" sector.

Beyond precision in concepts, systematic knowledge can entail a more highly integrated understanding of how variables in the investment analysis relate to one another. Returning to the paradigm case of the troubled suburban office property, suppose that a close investigation indicates that the "frictional vacancy rate" in this market is 15%, and a careful projection of supply and demand conditions indicates that this rate will be achieved in the fourth year of the holding period for the proposed investment. Less assiduous research has given rise to a common assumption that rents will not rise as long as vacancies remain in the double digit realm, or until the seventh year of the projection. Advancing by three years the point at which market rents would begin to rise toward the rent necessary to make new construction feasible has the effect of adjusting the investment value of the property upward to $12,758,000 at an 11% discount rate. In other words, such an improved analysis of the relationship between vacancy rates and rents (if accurate), would be more valuable than even the insider information that a major tenant was lined up to occupy the vacant half of the property (Table 30-4).

This is far from an academic exercise. In fact, the most vital question facing office investors in the early 1990s concerned the timing of a cyclical recovery. It is clearly true that many, if not most, office properties found their values declining below their replacement cost. It is equally clear that, upon the resumption of a new building cycle, costs to construct exert a powerful upward pull on rents. Hence the dynamic relationship between market analysis and cash flow projections is especially critical in contemporary investment analysis. In the spring of 1992, the National Council of Real Estate Investment Fiduciaries specifically charged its valuation and research committees with the task of drawing up guidelines to improve that relationship.

TABLE 30-4 Accelerated Market Recovery

Years	1	2	3	4	5	6	7	8	9	10	11
Current Contract Revenue (1)	1,525,667	1,552,627	1,580,665	1,196,035	1,620,151	1,455,356	1,849,157	1,897,769	1,983,462	2,417,643	2,284,985
Lease up Tenants											
Base Rent											
Tenant X	250,000	500,000	500,000	500,000	500,000	250,000	721,999	721,999	721,999	721,999	721,999
Tenant Y	0	0	250,000	500,000	500,000	500,000	500,000	445,166	780,666	780,666	780,666
Tenant Z	0	0	0	0	288,833	577,666	577,666	577,666	577,666	499,916	844,332
Escalation Rent											
Tenant X	0	8,987	18,333	28,053	38,162	24,337	0	11,313	23,138	35,437	48,228
Tenant Y	0	0	0	9,719	19,828	30,341	41,275	26,323	11,805	24,104	36,895
Tenant Z	0	0	0	0	162	10,675	21,608	32,979	44,805	28,552	12,895
New Revenue	250,000	508,987	768,331	1,037,771	1,346,983	1,393,019	1,862,490	1,815,447	2,160,080	2,090,675	2,445,016
Gross Potential Revenue	1,775,666	2,061,613	2,348,996	2,233,806	2,967,134	2,848,375	3,711,647	3,713,216	4,143,542	4,508,318	4,730,000
Less: (Loss)	88,783	103,081	117,450	111,690	148,357	142,419	185,582	185,661	207,177	225,416	236,500
Effective Gross Revenue	1,686,883	1,958,532	2,231,547	2,122,116	2,818,777	2,705,956	3,526,064	3,527,555	3,936,365	4,282,902	4,493,500
Less: Operating Expense	1,348,000	1,401,920	1,457,997	1,516,317	1,576,969	1,640,048	1,705,650	1,773,876	1,844,831	1,918,624	1,995,369
Net Operating Income	338,883	556,612	773,550	605,799	1,241,808	1,065,908	1,820,414	1,753,679	2,091,534	2,364,278	2,498,131
Commissions	79,999	0	79,999	0	92,426	0	120,105	0	129,919	135,092	
Tenant Improvements	499,995	0	540,795	0	584,923	0	632,653	0	684,278	711,649	
Net Cash Flow	(241,111)	556,612	152,756	605,799	564,459	1,065,908	1,067,656	1,753,679	1,277,338	1,517,537	

Value: @10% 13,845,667
      @11% 12,757,191
      @12% 11,766,262

(1) Includes assumed releasing of space upon lease termination.
Subtotals may not add due to rounding.

A Playing Field Without Shifting Advantages

Financial power varies considerably from investor to investor. Required rates of return are likely to spread across a rather wide range, dependent upon numerous factors but certainly tied to the investor's own cost of capital. The lower the cost of funds for the investor, either as a borrowing rate or a reinvestment rate, the lower its hurdle rate since the equity return is based upon the spread between sources and uses of money. During the 1980s there were many instances in which the shifting of financial power cast the role of market leader on several classes of office investors. The tax advantages of the 1981 Economic Recovery Tax Act, by raising the after-tax incentives for real estate investment by individuals, prompted a flood of capital into the office industry and bid up the price of property accordingly. The corrective action of the 1986 Tax Reform Act sliced the income tax benefits available out of the equation, changing the hurdle rates for real estate syndications dramatically.

On the debt side of the investment market, the flow of funds to insurance companies from the sale of Guaranteed Investment Contracts swelled the amount of new mortgage debt issued by life companies to more than $25 billion in 1986, helping to keep values high even as the syndication business was collapsing. Again, as long as the insurers were receiving a spread between their GIC rate and the interest rate on the matched mortgage loan, they were motivated to close deals. Equity investors cooperated enthusiastically. And with the decline in the exchange value of the dollar versus the yen which followed the Plaza Accord[2] in 1985, the Japanese found U.S. office buildings readily available at what seemed like excellent rates of return, compared with the basic cost of capital represented by the 4.5% discount rate in their home markets.

Access to capital, and its relative cost, is a fundamental pillar of investment analysis. The sensitivity of the analysis to the rate of return can hardly be overstated. The lack of liquidity for real estate that struck the market in 1990 turned a condition of serious oversupply into a capital crisis for the office industry. Conversely, the reduction of a single percentage point in the rate of return in the paradigmatic case of the suburban office building would represent approximately a $680,000 (or 8.5%) increase in the investment value of the property—*even holding all material facts relating to the property constant.* No wonder, then, that the financial structuring of office investments, and especially the exploration of creative financing tools (the so-called *zai-tech*, or financial engineering) formed the core interest of the industry and of university programs in real estate for much of the decade

---

[2] The Plaza Accord was an agreement in September 1985 by the central banks of the seven largest industrial nations to coordinate mutually interventions in the currency markets and to re-align the values of their respective currencies so that imbalances affecting international trade could be rectified. The effect of the Plaza Accord was to significantly weaken the dollar.

TABLE 30-5

Discount Rate	Terminal Cap Rates		
	9.0%	9.5%	10%
10%	$9,579,143	$9,219,576	$8,895,966
11%	$8,839,599	$8,511,143	$8,215,532
12%	$8,165,943	$7,865,662	$7,595,410

past. The even broader range of indicated value suggested by the matrix in Table 30-5, which does no more than measure sensitivity to changing discount rates and terminal capitalization rates, presses even more strongly the point that there is a tremendous plasticity to the investment decision, and that the selection of investment parameters must rely upon more than a superficial spreadsheet test of reasonability. The stakes are simply too high.

THE STRUCTURE OF DECISION-MAKING

The investor, in undertaking the analysis of a given office property, may elect to view the transaction opportunistically. That is, the investment may be approached as a stand-alone decision. More typically, however, the experienced office building investor will be weighing a number of issues which form the context for the decision. Factors such as the location of the property in a central business district or a suburban business park will be considered material, and will rely upon the investor's outlook for down-towns or for "edge cities" as preferred economic locations. Strategically, the investor will be measuring the effect of adding the office building to an existing real estate portfolio, and to his broader investment holdings. Is he presently satisfied with the balance of his portfolio? Overweighted already in offices? Adding to his core assets, or seeking to raise his overall returns by accepting a higher risk investment with strong appreciation potential over a ten-year period? How will this investment affect the balance sheet, and the price of stock and dividends, if the investor is organized in corporate form?

The use of the quantitative tools of investment analysis, which are common to other analytical problems such as marketability and feasibility studies, appraisal and financial structuring, are a step along the way to the objective of the exercise: settling on a bid price. Hence, the whole frame-work of investment analysis is best understood as a disciplined process of selection.

Most real estate executives would agree that there is no substitute for having seen and worked through the ups and downs of the real estate cycle. The skills and strategies appropriate to a rising real estate market can lead to disastrous results if stubbornly followed as the market enters its contracting phase. Great fortunes have been made in the real estate industry, and great fortunes lost. Reading about these financial dramas is one thing; witnessing them, struggling with them, participating in their resolution is quite another—immensely more valuable—form of learning.

The industry's various accrediting organizations have institutionalized the value associated with acquiring experience. The Appraisal Institute requires substantial specified work experience or a high educational equivalency before granting its MAI designation. The experience threshold for the CRE designation awarded by the Counselors of Real Estate is ten years. These and other organizations recognize that "instant expertise" is an oxymoron.

CONCLUSION

Experience, while a necessary condition for the successful investor, is not sufficient. The lessons of experience must be conceptualized; principles adduced; the patterns of the past translated into a reasonable vision to guide future behavior. Investment analysis, in other words, requires systematic knowledge of the kind formulated in the investment and financial chapters of this book. The need for understanding the data implies that interpretation is an essential element of the analytical process. To know the required hurdle rate, to measure the IRR, to check the accuracy of the computer run, to verify that the initial conditions of the market and the property have been correctly translated into the analytical format: all of these merely demarcate the point at which investment analysis begins. Understanding the implications that all the inputs, taken as a whole, have for the risks and opportunities in the investment vehicle at hand is a *synthetic* task: a task of putting things together rather than taking them apart and examining the pieces.

It is the synthetic effort that requires judgment, and at the level of judgment the finest computers fail. Good judgment requires common sense, that most uncommon of all traits which simultaneously requires the investor to know the consensus of his colleagues and to maintain an independent outlook. Judgment should not be confused with programming "if-then" statements into an investment formula, and then letting the money ride on the result. Investment relies on judgment, and sound investment relies upon prudential judgment. Thus the Delphic counsel, "Know thyself," is well heeded.

ABOUT THE AUTHOR

Hugh F. Kelly, CRE, senior vice president and director of economic research and strategic studies at Landauer Associates, Inc., in New York, is a real estate consultant specializing in market and feasibility studies, appraisal, land use and investment analysis. He is the author of the annual Landauer Real Estate Market Forecast, as well as of numerous other articles and studies, including the annual New York-Metropolitan Market Report for the Urban Land Institute's *Development Review & Outlook,* and is a major contributor to the *Guide to Industrial and Office Real Estate Markets* published by the Society of Industrial and Office Realtors. He holds a BA from Cathedral College and is an adjunct associate professor at the New York University Real Estate Institute.

31

OFFICE INVESTMENT PERFORMANCE MEASUREMENT

by Jeffrey D. Fisher

INTRODUCTION

Many variables affect the performance of office buildings including market rents, vacancy rates, tax influences, the level of risk and the amount of debt financing. This chapter provides the framework for measuring the performance of office building investments. Performance measures such as the equity dividend rate, internal rate of return (before and after tax) and net present value are discussed and illustrated with an office building example. The chapter concludes with a discussion of indices used to measure the performance of office building investments.

PROJECTING CASH FLOWS

Market Rents

The starting point for an analysis of income for an office building is usually a study of market rents for competitive buildings. Rents for the building under evaluation may be established by determining rents being paid for similar properties in the current market. The trend in future rents is more difficult to assess because it depends on many unknown factors including: (1) the outlook for the national economy, (2) the economic base of the area where the property is located, (3) the demand for office space, and (4) the supply of similar competitive office space.

Past trends in market rents are often used to predict future rents. This can be misleading, however, because it assumes that what happened in the recent past is indicative of what will happen in the future. When forecasting future rents, a more complete analysis requires that the analyst relate rents to changes in the demand for office space (e.g., from changes in office employment) and changes in supply due to new construction.

Vacancy

It is difficult to project vacancy for newly constructed properties. While some leases may be signed before a project is completed, it is not likely that full occupancy will be achieved immediately after construction is completed. Projections must be made as to how long it will take for occupancy to reach a normal level. The longer it takes for space to be rented, the less income the investor will receive during the initial years of the project. Because this affects cash flows in the early years of the holding period, it also has a significant impact on value and on the investment performance measures.

Leases

Office space tends to be leased for three to five year terms with the tenant often having the option to lease for one additional three to five year term. National tenants usually require longer term leases. There may be a provision for rent increases each year by either a specified dollar amount or an amount based on an inflation adjustment. Tenants customarily are responsible for paying their share of certain expenses above an agreed level such as property taxes, insurance and maintenance.

To illustrate how an income projection is made, consider the possible purchase of a 100,000 square foot office building by an investor for $8,500,000.[1] Construction of the office building was completed two years ago. The first tenants signed five-year leases at that time. The remaining space was leased at various times during the past two years. Additional assumptions are as follows:

Current Market Rent (per square foot)	$15.00
Gross Rentable Square Feet	100,000
Projected Increase in Market Rent Per Year	4.00%
Management Costs (Percent of Effective Gross Income)	5.00%
Estimated Annual Increase in the Consumer Price Index	4.00%

---

[1] This example and much of the discussion of performance measures in this chapter are based on Chapters 10 and 11 of *Real Estate Finance*, 9th edition (forthcoming) by William B. Brueggeman and Jeffrey D. Fisher, published by Richard D. Irwin, Inc.

TABLE 31-1   Summary Lease Information

Tenant	Square Feet	Current Rent/Sq. Ft.	Current Rental	Remaining Lease Term (years)	CPI Adjustment	Expense Stop
1	30,000	$14.00	$ 420,000	3	50.00%	$4.00
2	25,000	$14.00	350,000	3	50.00%	4.00
3	15,000	$14.00	210,000	3	50.00%	4.00
4	10,000	$14.50	145,000	4	50.00%	4.25
5	10,000	$15.00	150,000	5	50.00%	4.45
6	6,000	$15.00	90,000	5	50.00%	4.45
Total	96,000		$1,365,000			

A summary of the leases that would be honored by the investor if the building is purchased is shown in Table 31-1.[2]

Base Rent

The building has six tenants occupying a total of 96,000 square feet of rentable space. The remaining 4,000 square feet of space is used for heating, air conditioning, stairs, elevators, and so on, and is not rentable. The first three tenants were the first to occupy the building and leased the majority of the space. The market rate at the time they signed the lease (two years ago) was $14.00 per square foot. The leases have a term of five years, so there are three years remaining on each of these leases. A fourth tenant signed a lease last year at $14.50 per square foot. The last two tenants just signed their leases at a rate of $15.00 per square foot, the current rental rate for comparable space.

CPI Adjustment

In an inflationary environment, the real value of fixed rental income will decline each year. Therefore office leases often provide for a rent adjustment based on increases in the consumer price index (CPI). That is, the rental rate is adjusted each year based on any increase in the CPI that occurred that year. Rents may be increased by the same percentage amount that the CPI increases (i.e., if the CPI rises 4%, then the base rent would be increased 4%), or by a lesser amount. Whether inflationary adjustments are included

---

[2] A Lotus 1-2-3™ template was used to make all the cash flow projections (before and after tax) and calculate all the performance measures in this chapter. For information about obtaining a copy of the template, contact the Center for Real Estate Studies, Indiana University School of Business Rm 428, 10th & Fee Lane, Bloomington, IN 47405.

TABLE 31-2   Projected Base Rental Income

	Year					
	1	2	3	4	5	6
Tenant 1	$ 420,000	$ 428,400	$ 436,968	$ 506,189	$ 516,313	$ 526,639
Tenant 2	350,000	357,000	364,140	421,824	430,260	438,866
Tenant 3	210,000	214,200	218,484	253,094	258,156	263,319
Tenant 4	145,000	147,900	150,858	153,875	175,479	178,988
Tenant 5	150,000	153,000	156,060	159,181	162,365	182,498
Tenant 6	90,000	91,800	93,636	95,509	97,419	109,499
Total	$1,365,000	$1,392,300	$1,420,146	$1,589,672	$1,639,992	$1,699,809

in lease terms depends on market conditions and the willingness of tenants to bear the risk of unanticipated inflation. Further, many operating expenses incurred by owners are passed through to tenants. Because tenants will be paying a portion of these expenses (which will increase with inflation), it is not necessary for a building owner to charge rents that fully adjust to the rate of inflation. In the example, it is assumed that rents will increase by 50% of any increase in the CPI. The base rental income can be projected as shown in Table 31-2.

Market rent in the example is $15 per square foot during the first year. This is also the base rent for leases signed that year. Base rent is projected to increase by 2% per year because of the CPI adjustment (50% of 4%). Because it is assumed that market rates will increase at the same rate as the CPI, however, a 4% annual rate of increase is used for projecting market rents that will be in effect when leases are renewed.

Expense Stops

It is common in office leases to include a provision which protects the owner from annual increases in operating expenses. In the example, each lease has an "expense stop" that places an upper limit on the amount of operating expenses the owner must pay. Any operating expenses in excess of the stop must be paid by the tenant. The amount of the stop is usually based on (1) the tenant's pro rata share (percent of total leasable area), (2) categories of expenses that the lessor and lessee agree will be included in the stop, and (3) the actual amount of operating expenses at the time the lease is signed. Some leases also have "expense caps" that limit the amount of expenses that can be passed through to the tenant.[3]

---

[3] A lease may also require the tenant to be responsible for payment of specified operating expenses. That is, the tenant would pay the expenses rather than the owner paying and getting reimbursed from the tenant. The term "net lease" is used when a tenant is responsible for payment of all the operating expenses.

An expense stop assures the owner that net income in subsequent years will be at least equal to the initial net income. Using expense stops is particularly important when leases contain fixed base rents (i.e., no CPI adjustments). If expense stops are not used, operating expenses may rise during the term of the lease and net income will decline. The particular expenses that are passed through to the tenants are negotiable and vary with market conditions. In this example, all expenses except property management expenses will be passed through. Tenants are usually reluctant to have increases in property management expenses passed through because these expenses are the responsibility of the building owner and passing them through to tenants could lead to excessive management fees.

Expense stops in the existing leases are shown in Table 31-1. Based on this information, Table 31-3 shows current expenses for the office building and the estimated annual increase in expenses. The top portion of Table

TABLE 31-3   Summary of Operating Expenses

First Year Expenses and Projected Increases

	Dollars	$/Sq. Ft.	Projected Increases
Property Tax	148,800	1.55	Level 2 Years, 10%, Then Level
Insurance	14,400	0.15	Increase 4.00% Per Year
Utilities	120,000	1.25	Increase 5.00% Per Year
Janitorial	76,800	0.80	Increase 3.00% Per Year
Maintenance	67,200	0.70	Increase 3.00% Per Year
Total	427,200	4.45	

	Year					
	1	2	3	4	5	6
Projection of Expenses						
Property Tax	148,800	148,800	163,680	163,680	163,680	163,680
Insurance	14,400	14,976	15,575	16,198	16,846	17,520
Utilities	120,000	126,000	132,300	138,915	145,861	153,154
Janitorial	76,800	79,104	81,477	83,921	86,439	89,032
Maintenance	67,200	69,216	71,292	73,431	75,634	77,903
Total Operating Expenses	427,200	438,096	464,325	476,146	488,460	501,289
Per Square Foot	4.4500	4.5635	4.8367	4.9599	5.0881	5.2218
Projected Expense Reimbursement						
Tenant 1	13,500	16,905	25,101	0	3,848	7,857
Tenant 2	11,250	14,088	20,918	0	3,207	6,548
Tenant 3	6,750	8,453	12,551	0	1,924	3,929
Tenant 4	2,000	3,135	5,867	7,099	0	1,336
Tenant 5	0	1,135	3,867	5,099	6,381	0
Tenant 6	0	681	2,320	3,059	3,829	0
Total	33,500	44,396	70,625	15,256	19,189	19,670

31-3 shows that total operating expenses subject to expense stops are projected to be $427,200 or $4.45 per rentable square foot during the first year. Projections for the increase in each expense category are shown in the middle portion of the table. Future rates of increase depend on estimates of how each cost is expected to change. In this example, utilities (heat and air conditioning) are expected to increase at a higher rate than the other items shown. Property taxes are assumed to remain level for two years, then to increase with a reassessment of property values scheduled at that time. They are expected to remain level again for at least four years after the reassessment. The information on expense projections and expense stops is used to project expense reimbursements as shown in the bottom portion of Table 31-3.

Net Operating Income

Using the information shown in Tables 31-2 and 31-3, the analyst can project net operating income (NOI) for the office building. Table 31-4 contains a projection of net operating income for the next six years. Recall that management expenses are assumed to be 5% of effective gross income (EGI). EGI is the actual rent expected to be collected after allowing for any vacancy. In the example, vacancy is projected to be 5% of the base rent, beginning in the fourth year when the original leases are renewed. The management expense may be incurred by the owner or paid to a property management company. In either case it is not passed on to the tenant, giving the owner an incentive to control management expenses.

Note that net expenses (before management expenses) are level ($393,700) after gross expenses are netted against the expense reimbursement (before management expenses) for the first three years. This is

TABLE 31-4   Projected Net Operating Income

	Year					
	1	2	3	4	5	6
Base Rent	1,365,000	1,392,300	1,420,146	1,589,672	1,639,992	1,699,809
Vacancy	0	0	0	79,484	82,000	84,990
EGI	1,365,000	1,392,300	1,420,146	1,510,189	1,557,992	1,614,819
Operating Expenses	427,200	438,096	464,325	476,146	488,460	501,289
– Reimbursements	33,500	44,396	70,625	15,256	19,189	19,670
Subtotal	393,700	393,700	393,700	460,890	469,271	481,619
+ Management Expenses	68,250	69,615	71,007	75,509	77,900	80,741
Total Expenses	461,950	463,315	464,707	536,399	547,170	562,360
NOI	903,050	928,985	955,439	973,790	1,010,822	1,052,459

TABLE 31-5   Summary Loan Information

	End of Year				
	1	2	3	4	5
Payment	689,025	689,025	689,025	689,025	689,025
Mortgage Balance	5,851,543	5,742,776	5,622,620	5,489,883	5,343,245
Interest	590,569	580,259	568,869	556,288	542,388
Principal	98,457	108,767	120,156	132,738	146,637

because the expense stops protect owners against any increase in expenses until leases are renewed. The combination of expense stops and CPI adjustments enables the owner to realize an increase in NOI each year.

DEBT FINANCING

Office buildings are typically purchased with a combination of debt and equity capital. To illustrate the impact of debt financing on the cash flow projections and performance measures, assume that a loan can be obtained at a 10% interest rate to be amortized over 20 years with monthly payments. The amount of the loan is 70% of the proposed purchase price. Monthly payments would be $57,418.79, or $689,025 per year. It is traditional in real estate analysis to compute loan payments based on monthly payments, but when financial projections are made, all cash flows are shown on an annual basis in arrears. Table 31-5 shows a summary loan schedule for the property for the first five years. From this point on projections will be made for five years under the assumption that the property will be sold after that time. NOI is projected for an additional year for reasons that will become apparent when estimating the sale price of the property at the end of the five-year holding period. Table 31-6 shows the results of including the financing costs in the calculation of cash flows to the equity investor.

Estimated Sale Price

To calculate measures of investment performance over an investment holding period, the analyst must estimate what the property might sell for. The first step is to choose a holding period over which to analyze the investment. In this example, the holding period chosen is five years. There are two general procedures that investors commonly use to estimate a sale price. The first procedure is to estimate a rate at which property values in that market are expected to increase. This may be related to expected inflation rates, although some areas may do better or worse than the overall economy depending on future employment in office buildings. In this case,

TABLE 31-6   Estimates of Cash Flow From Operations

	Year				
	1	2	3	4	5
Before-Tax Cash Flow					
NOI	903,050	928,985	955,439	973,790	1,010,822
Less: Debt Service	689,025	689,025	689,025	689,025	689,025
Before-Tax Cash Flow	214,025	239,960	266,414	284,765	321,797

an assumption was made that the market rental rate would increase 4% per year. However, the rate at which NOI increases depends on the nature of the expense stops and the degree to which the lease payments are adjusted with the CPI. In the example the increase in NOI over the five-year lease term is about 3% per year. It seems reasonable therefore, that the price for the property would also increase about 3% per year. Using the asking price as a starting point, this would result in a sale price after five years of about $9,850,000.

There are two problems associated with using this approach to estimate the resale price. First, it is based on the assumed purchase price, which the analyst may decide is not what the property is really worth once he completes his analysis. Second, it assumes that the resale price will depend on how the historical value (purchase price) changes over time rather than looking forward to what will happen in the future. The alternative approach to estimating a resale price addresses these issues.

A second way of estimating the resale price is to use a *capitalization rate*. An overall capitalization rate (cap rate for short) is a ratio of net operating income for a given year to the value of the property for the same year. The cap rate used to appraise property is obtained by analyzing sales of comparable office buildings and calculating the ratio of NOI to sale price for each of the properties that sold. This provides an indication of the price that investors are paying for office buildings relative to their first-year NOI.

The analyst has made the assumption that at the time the property will be sold, investors would purchase properties at prices which result in a cap rate of 11%.[4] Because the property will be sold at the end of the fifth year, he uses the NOI in year six, which is the first-year NOI to the new owner. Using NOI of $1,052,459 in year six and a terminal cap rate of 11% results in an estimated resale price of $9,567,809. Note that in this approach

---

[4] As will be emphasized later, the capitalization rate is not considered a rate of return for the entire holding period. It does not explicitly measure expected changes in income and property value over time. It is only a measure of the current yield on the property. The investor's rate of return (IRR) for the entire investment holding period will be higher than 11% in this example because the income and property value are projected to increase over the five-year holding period.

the resale price is not based on either the original purchase price or net operating income that was assumed to occur before the property was sold. Rather, it is based on expected income after the property is sold to the next investor. Furthermore, it is not usually practical to project income for additional years after the end of the initial holding period.

The analyst now has two separate estimates of the resale price. Using a property growth rate of 3% per year, he arrived at an estimate of $9,850,000. Using an 11% terminal cap rate, he arrived at an estimate of about $9,550,000. He might conclude that for purposes of analysis an estimated resale price midway between these two estimates, or about $9,700,000, would be reasonable. Clearly, the analyst must use judgment at this point regarding what is a reasonable estimate of the resale price. He may place more weight on one or the other of the two approaches.

Before-Tax Cash Flow from Sale

When the property is sold, the mortgage balance must be repaid from the sale proceeds. This results in before-tax cash flow from sale. After the fifth year, the mortgage balance is $5,343,245. Subtracting this from the sale price of $9,700,000 results in before-tax cash flow of $4,356,755. This is summarized as follows:

Sale price	$9,700,000
Mortgage balance	-5,343,245
Before-tax cash flow	$4,356,755

PERFORMANCE MEASURES

Should the property be purchased at a price of $8,500,000? To answer this question, the analyst would continue with the pro forma statements from the office building example introduced above.

Measures of Investment Performance Using Ratios

There are several common measures of investment performance that might be referred to as ratio measures. They are simple measures, yet they provide a starting point for the analysis. They are also often used to screen an investment. That is, if one of the ratios indicates a poor investment, the analyst may not take the time to do a more comprehensive analysis.

Capitalization Rate

A preliminary test of the reasonableness of the purchase price for the property is the ratio of first-year NOI to the asking price. Based on the purchase price of $8,500,000, the cap rate is 10.62% ($903,050/$8,500,000), which is just under the 11% capitalization rate used to estimate the resale price. This seems reasonable.

The analyst must be careful when comparing cap rates for a number of reasons. First, the leases for the two properties may have varying expiration dates, renewal options, escalations and other terms. Operating expenses over time may also be different; for example, the building may be older, less functionally efficient, or have a different type of mechanical system. Further, differing locations for the two properties may result in dissimilar future income and expenses and a different potential for price increases. Thus the cap rate is only a starting point in the analysis. It does, however, represent a benchmark or a norm from which the analyst is looking for significant deviations.

Debt Coverage Ratios

To provide financing on the property, the lender must be satisfied that it is a good investment. One consideration is the rate of return the lender will receive over the term of the loan, which depends on such factors as the interest rate charged, points, and so on. But the rate of return is only one consideration. The lender will also evaluate the riskiness of the loan. One widely used indicator of loan risk is the degree to which the NOI from the property is expected to exceed the mortgage payments. The lender would like a sufficient cushion so that if NOI is less than anticipated, for example as a result of unexpected vacancy, the borrower will still be able to make the mortgage payments without using his personal funds.

A common measure of this risk is the *debt coverage ratio* or DCR. The DCR is the ratio of NOI to the mortgage payment. When NOI is projected to change over time, the first year NOI is typically used. For the office building example, NOI in year 1 is projected to be $903,050. The mortgage payment (debt service) is $689,025. This results in a debt coverage ratio of 1.31. Lenders typically want the debt coverage ratio to be at least 1.2. The DCR for each of the five years is as follows:

Year	1	2	3	4	5
DCR	1.31	1.35	1.39	1.41	1.47

The project's debt coverage ratio is 1.31 for the first year, and is projected to increase each year thereafter. Thus it meets the minimum debt coverage ratio typically required by lenders.

Net Present Value (NPV)

The analyst now has the necessary information to calculate different measures of investment performance for the property which consider the

TABLE 31-7   Cash Flow Summary

	End of Year					
	0	1	2	3	4	5
Before-Tax Cash Flow		214,025	239,960	266,414	284,765	4,678,551
Equity	-2,550,000					
Total	-2,550,000	214,025	239,960	266,414	284,765	4,678,551

entire holding period including resale. To simplify calculations, it is common practice to assume that all cash flows will be received at the end of the year (the sum of all monthly cash flows received during the year). He begins with a calculation of the net present value (NPV) before taxes.

A summary of the cash flows for the office building (assuming it is purchased at the asking price) is as follows:

Year	Cash Flow
0 (Equity)	($2,550,000)
1	214,025
2	239,960
3	266,414
4	284,765
5	4,678,551

The cash flow in year five includes both the cash flow from operating the property in year five ($321,797) and the estimated equity sales proceeds ($4,356,755)[5].

The NPV is found by first calculating the present value of all the estimated future cash flows. The initial equity cash outlay to acquire the investment is then subtracted from this present value to obtain the net present value. Thus, NPV measures the extent, if any, to which the present value of cash flows to be received from the investment exceeds the equity invested in the office building. A positive NPV indicates that the value of the investment, in present value terms, exceeds the equity investment. The NPV obviously depends on the discount rate used to calculate the present value of the cash inflows. This discount rate should reflect the minimum rate of return required by the investor to make the investment. It is an *opportunity cost* concept since the return on the investment being analyzed should be at least as good as the return available on comparable investments. By investing in the property being analyzed, the investor must forego the return that could have been earned on alternative investment opportunities.

---

[5] Difference of $1 is due to rounding.

Assuming a discount rate for the office building of 18% and using the cash flows above, the NPV is calculated as follows:

Year	Cash Flow	Present Value of $1	Present Value (18%)
1	214,025 x	0.847457 =	181,377
2	239,960 x	0.718182 =	172,335
3	266,414 x	0.608632 =	162,148
4	284,765 x	0.515787 =	146,878
5	4,678,551 x	0.437109 =	2,045,038
Total present value			2,707,776
Less: Initial equity investment			2,550,000
Net Present Value (NPV)			157,776

The NPV is $157,776, which indicates that the expected rate of return for the investment is greater than the 18% discount rate. The investor could invest $157,776 more equity capital and still earn the required 18% rate of return.

Internal Rate of Return

The IRR is found by finding the discount rate that equates the present value of the future cash inflows with the initial cash outflow. Recall that the initial equity investment is $2,550,000 (the $5,950,000 loan amount less the $8,500,000 purchase price). The cash flows are repeated in Table 31-7.

Using a financial calculator results in a before-tax IRR of 19.64%. This is the before-tax yield that the investor may expect to earn on equity over the investment period.

Is the return adequate? This depends on what the investor can earn on comparable investments, e.g., similar office buildings or even other real estate investments with similar risk characteristics. The investor could compare the investment with the rate of return he would expect to earn had he bought another property at the price paid by another investor. Of course he would have to make his own projections of NOI and resale price. He would also make similar projections and IRR calculations for other properties that are for sale, using their asking price. He should earn a return that is at least as good as the return he could earn on other properties that have similar risk characteristics.

Another test of the reasonableness of the IRR is to compare it with the effective interest cost of any mortgage financing that could be obtained to purchase the property. Normally, one would expect the return on the property to be greater than the effective cost of financing on the property, because the investor accepts more risk than the lender. The lender assumes less risk because he would have first claim on income and proceeds from the sale of the property should there be a default. For example, the IRR for the office building (19.64%) should be more than the 10% mortgage interest rate. Otherwise, the investor would be better off lending on real estate rather than investing in it.

A summary of the calculations for the office building is shown below:

Capitalization rate	10.62%
IRR	19.64%
NPV (18% discount rate)	$157,776

RISK ANALYSIS

When making choices among alternative investments, comparing IRRs or NPVs is usually not possible because of risk differences. Such a comparison may only be made if it is assumed that the risk associated with the different investments being analyzed is the same. Because risk usually is not the same, some techniques for evaluating risk are provided to enable the analyst to make comparisons among alternatives. Following is a brief discussion of sources of risk and how they may differ among investment alternatives.

Types Of Risk

What are the investment characteristics peculiar to real estate that make it riskier than investing in government securities? Similarly, what risk characteristics differentiate real estate investment from alternatives such as common stocks, corporate bonds and municipal bonds? Following is a brief summary of the major investment risk characteristics that investors must consider when they are deciding among alternative investments.

Market Risk

Real estate investors are in the business of renting space in a particular market. They incur the risk of loss due to fluctuations in economic activity that affect the level of income produced by the property. Changes in economic conditions may affect some properties more than others depending on the type of property, its location and existing leases. Many regions of the country and locations within cities experience differences in their rate of growth due to changes in employment, population, and so on. A property with a well-diversified tenant mix is subject to less market risk. Similarly, properties with leases that provide the owner with protection against unexpected changes in expenses (e.g., leases with expense stops) have less market risk.

Financial Risk

The use of debt financing magnifies market risk. Financial risk increases as the amount of debt, the interest cost, or both, on a real estate investment increases. The degree of financial risk also depends on the cost and structure of the debt. For example, there may be less financial risk with a loan that gives the lender a participation in any appreciation in the value of the property in exchange for lower monthly payments.

Liquidity Risk

This risk occurs when there is not continuous market activity with many buyers and sellers and frequent transactions. The more difficult an investment is to liquidate, the greater is the risk that a price concession may have to be given to a buyer should the seller have to dispose of the investment quickly. Real estate has a relatively high degree of liquidity risk.

Inflation Risk

Unexpected inflation can reduce an investor's rate of return if the income from the investment does not increase sufficiently to offset the impact of inflation, thereby reducing the real value of the investment. Real estate has historically done well during periods of inflation. This might be attributed to the use of leases which allow the NOI to adjust with unexpected changes in inflation. During periods of high vacancy rates, however, when there is weak demand for space and new construction is not feasible, the income from real estate does not tend to increase with unexpected inflation.

Management Risk

Most real estate investments require management to maintain the property and keep the space leased to preserve the value of the investment. The rate of return that the investor earns can therefore be highly dependent on the competence of the management. This risk is based on the ability of management to innovate, respond to competitive conditions, and operate the business activity efficiently. Some properties require a higher level of management expertise than others.

Legislative Risk

Real estate is subject to numerous regulations such as tax laws, rent control, zoning and other restrictions imposed by government. Legislative risk occurs because changes in regulations can adversely affect the profitability of the investment. Some state and local governments have more restrictive legislation than others—especially for new development.

Environmental Risk

The value of real estate is often affected by changes in its environment (e.g., contamination by toxic waste) or a sudden awareness that the existing environment is potentially hazardous (e.g., asbestos insulation). Environmental risk can cause a greater loss than other types of risk because the investor can be subject to cleanup costs that far exceed the value of the property.

TAXATION OF OFFICE BUILDING INVESTMENTS

Owners of real estate used in the production of income in a trade or business report income from rents and may deduct expenses incurred in the operation of the property, such as maintenance, repair and utilities. They may also deduct property taxes and interest on loans obtained to acquire property and to operate the business. In addition, they are allowed deductions for depreciation and when properties are sold, certain capital gain and loss provisions also apply.

Taxable income from operating real estate income property differs from before-tax cash flow for two major reasons. First, only the interest portion of a loan payment, not the total payment, is deductible from NOI for tax purposes. Second, the tax code allows owners to deduct an allowance for depreciation from NOI. Thus, taxable income from operating a real estate income property can be stated as follows:

Taxable Income = NOI - Interest - Depreciation Allowance

Depreciation Allowances

Table 31-8 summarizes the methods that have been allowed to compute depreciation allowances under various tax laws in effect in recent years. Congress historically has provided for depreciation allowances in excess of economic depreciation to stimulate investment in real estate in the belief that this would increase the supply of rentable space in the economy. Unfortunately, it may also have contributed to much of the overbuilding in office markets that occurred during the 1980s. As shown in Table 31-8, the 1986 Tax Reform Act (TRA) lengthened the depreciable life of real estate, which reduced the favorable tax treatment real estate had previously enjoyed.

TABLE 31-8   Depreciation Rules for Commercial Real Estate

Years	Depreciable Life	Methods Allowed
1969–1980	Useful life approximately 30–40 years	Accelerated or straight line*
1981–1983	15 years	ACRS based on 175% of straight line depreciation**
1984–1985	18 years	ACRS based on 175% of straight line depreciation**
1986	19 years	ACRS based on 175% of straight line depreciation**
1987–	31.5 years	Straight line

* Investors generally selected accelerated depreciation methods that ranged from 125% to 200% of straight line depreciation, depending on whether the property was residential or nonresidential, and whether it was a new or existing property.

** Because of severe "recapture" rules that affected investors who used accelerated depreciation on commercial real estate, straight line depreciation was used by most investors during this period.

Depreciable Basis

The amount that can be depreciated for a real estate improvement depends on the depreciable basis of the asset. The basis for a real estate investment is generally equal to the cost of the improvements (unless the property was inherited or acquired by gift). Cost is generally defined to include the acquisition price of the improvements plus the cost of placing the property into service. Any capital improvements to the property made during the ownership period are also included in the basis. Only the improvements can be depreciated.

Taxable Income From Disposal Of Depreciable Real Property

The gross sales price is equal to any cash or other property received in payment for the property sold, plus any liabilities against the property assumed by the buyer. Any selling expenses, such as legal fees, recording fees and brokerage fees, may then be deducted. To determine gain or loss, the adjusted basis of the property is subtracted from net sales proceeds. The adjusted basis of a property is its original basis (cost of land and improvements, acquisition and fees), plus the cost of any capital improvements, alterations or additions made during the period of ownership, less accumulated depreciation taken to date. Any excess of the net sales proceeds over the adjusted basis results in a taxable gain, and any deficit results in a taxable loss.

Net gains on the sale of office buildings are treated as long-term capital gains. Net losses from the sale of such property are treated as ordinary losses. Prior to 1986, capital gains received favorable tax treatment. The Tax Reform Act of 1986 eliminated the capital gains exclusion. As a result, capital gains are taxed at the same rate as ordinary income.

AFTER-TAX INVESTMENT ANALYSIS

The analyst must also consider the effect of federal income taxes on performance measures for the office building. In the example, it is assumed that the office building is held by an individual investor.

After-Tax Cash Flow from Operation

After estimating before-tax cash flows from the investment, the analyst must determine the increase or decrease in the investor's taxable income. This must be combined with before-tax cash flows to determine how much cash flow will result on an after-tax basis. To do this the analyst must consider how much taxable income is produced each year from operations and then consider taxes in the year that the property is sold. Table 31-9 shows the calculation of taxable income and after-tax cash flow from operating the property.

Depreciation

Taxable income is also affected by an allowance for depreciation. Under the Tax Reform Act of 1986, nonresidential real property must be depreciated

TABLE 31-9   Taxable Income and After-Tax Cash Flow from Operations

Net Operating Income	903,050	928,985	955,439	973,790	1,010,822
Less: Interest	590,569	580,259	568,869	556,288	542,388
Less: Depreciation	229,365	229,365	229,365	229,365	229,365
Taxable Income (Loss)	83,116	119,361	157,204	188,137	239,069
Tax (at 28%)	23,273	33,421	44,017	52,678	66,939
After-Tax Cash Flow:					
Before-Tax Cash Flow	214,025	239,960	266,414	284,765	321,797
Less Tax	23,273	33,421	44,017	52,678	66,939
After-Tax Cash Flow	190,752	206,538	222,396	232,086	254,857

TABLE 31-10   After-Tax Cash Flow from Sale

Sale Price		$9,700,000
Less: Mortgage Balance		–5,343,245
Before-Tax Cash Flow		$4,356,755
Taxes in Year of Sale:		
Sale Price		$9,700,000
Original Cost Basis	$8,500,000	
Accumulated Depreciation	–1,146,825	
Adjusted Basis		–7,353,175
Capital Gain		$2,346,825
Tax on Gain at 28%		– 657,111
After-Tax Cash Flow From Sale		$3,699,644

over 31.5 years on a straight line basis. Because land cannot be depreciated, the analyst needs to know what portion of the $8,500,000 purchase price represents building improvements as opposed to land. In this example, it is assumed that the land cost is 15% of the purchase price or $1,275,000, leaving improvements of $7,225,000. Dividing the improvement cost by 31.5 results in an annual depreciation deduction of $229,365.[6]

The deduction affects only taxable income, not operating cash flows. In the example, taxable income is $83,116 in year one. Assuming the investor is in a 28% tax bracket, the increase in tax liability will be $23,273 (.28 x $83,116). Subtracting this from before-tax cash flow results in after-tax cash flow of $190,752 in year one.

After-tax cash flow from sale

Table 31-10 illustrates how a sale of the property affects the investor's taxable income. The investor will have depreciated the property for five years. Accordingly, the investor's cost basis in the property will be reduced. In the example, depreciation was $229,365 per year for five years, resulting in accumulated depreciation of $1,146,825. Subtracting the accumulated depreciation from the original cost basis of the property (including the land value) results in an adjusted basis, or book value, of $7,353,175. The difference between the adjusted basis ($7,353,175) and the sale price ($9,700,000) is the capital gain ($2,346,825). Under current tax laws, the entire capital gain is taxable at the ordinary income tax rate. Assuming the investor is still in the 28% tax bracket at the time of sale, taxes resulting from the sale of the property would be $657,111. Subtracting the tax from the before-tax cash flow results in after-tax cash flow of $3,699,644.

---

[6] This approximates the depreciation calculated using the IRS tables assuming the property is purchased in January.

TABLE 31-11   Cash Flow Summary

	End of Year					
	0	1	2	3	4	5
Before-Tax Cash Flow	−2,550,000	214,025	239,960	266,414	284,765	4,678,551
After-Tax Cash Flow	−2,550,000	190,752	206,538	222,396	232,086	3,954,501
Before-Tax IRR	19.64%					
After-Tax IRR	15.17%					

TABLE 31-12   After-Tax Net Present Value (13% discount rate)

Present Value of After-Tax Cash Flow From Operations	+ 765,358
Present Value of After-Tax Cash Flow From Reversion	+ 2,008,018
Original Equity Investment	− 2,550,000
After-Tax Net Present Value	$ 223,376

After-Tax IRR

The information in Tables 31-2 and 31-10 can now be used to calculate the after-tax IRR. The cash flows are summarized in Table 31-11 along with the before-tax cash flows for comparison. As might be expected, the after-tax IRR is lower than the before-tax IRR. However, although the investor's tax rate was 28%, the after-tax IRR is not 28% lower than the before-tax IRR. Rather, it is about 23% lower.[7] Thus the effective tax rate is only 23%.

After-Tax NPV

The NPV can be calculated using after-tax cash flows. Table 31-12 summarizes the calculations. A lower, after-tax discount rate was applied to the after-tax cash flows to obtain the after-tax net present value. With the investor in a 28% tax bracket, his after-tax return on fully taxable investments would be reduced by 28%. If the required before-tax return was 18%, the investor might want to earn 13% after taxes (18% x (1 - .28) = 12.96%). Alternatively, using the 23% effective tax rate calculated earlier, the investor would want to earn 18% x (1 - .23) = 13.86%. The after-tax discount rate depends on the after-tax return that can be earned on alternative investments of comparable risk.

---

[7] { 1 - (15.17/19.64) } = 22.76%}

PERFORMANCE INDICES

Performance measures such as the IRR are designed to measure the performance of a single office building investment. These performance measures are based on projected cash flows over a specified holding period. Investors are also interested in how their office building investments performed historically relative to other office building investments, other real estate investments, and other investment alternatives such as stocks and bonds. To compare the performance of different investments, the analyst needs a measure of the historical rate of return for each of these investment alternatives. The historical rate of return is the IRR that would have been earned by an investor who purchased the investment and sold it after a given period of time. For example, what rate of return would an investor have earned if he invested in an office building one year ago and sold it today? To answer this question one could calculate the IRR by assuming that the building was purchased at its market value one year ago and sold today at its current market value. To facilitate the comparison of different investment alternatives, the IRR is usually calculated on a before-tax basis assuming that the property is purchased without any debt financing. That is, the cash flow received during the investment holding period is the net operating income (NOI).

The IRR (before tax) that would have been earned over the past year (assuming an all-cash purchase) can be calculated as follows:

$$IRR = \frac{NOI + (Sale\ price - Purchase\ price)}{Purchase\ price}$$

In order to construct an index of the historical return (IRR) for a real estate investment, the above calculation can be made for consecutive time periods, e.g., every year for the past ten years. For each annual time period the IRR would be calculated using the market value of the property at the beginning and end of the year and the NOI earned during that particular year. This allows the analyst to know what return an investor would have earned during any particular year if the property was purchased at its market value at the beginning of the year and sold for its market value at the end of the year.

Figure 31-1 shows the quarterly rate of return on office properties reported in the Russell-NCREIF (RN) Index from 1978 to 1991. The RN Index has become the most widely cited index of institutional-grade commercial property returns in the United States. The quarterly RN Index is based on the appraised values of the properties held for institutional investors in the portfolios of the member firms of the National Council of Real Estate Investment Fiduciaries (NCREIF). NCREIF includes 56 of the largest pension fund real estate advisory firms in the country. Begun in the first quarter of 1978 with 234 properties having an appraised market value

FIGURE 31-1

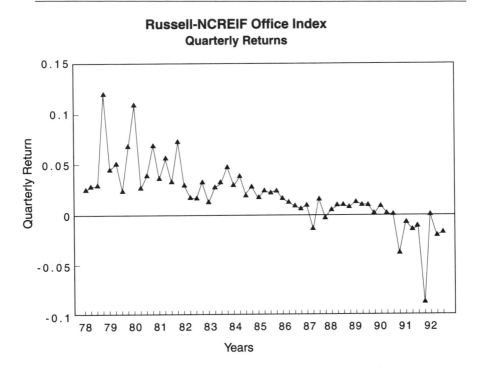

of $587 million, the index has grown rapidly to include more than 1,500 properties appraised at more than $22 billion by the first quarter of 1991.[8] There are about 376 office buildings in the index with a market value of about $7 billion.

Income and Appreciation Return

The annual IRR can be separated into two components: the income return and the appreciation return. This is calculated as follows:

$$\text{Income Return} = \frac{\text{NOI}}{\text{Purchase Price}}$$

$$\text{Appreciation Return} = \frac{(\text{Sale Price}^9 - \text{Purchase Price})}{\text{Purchase Price}}$$

---

[8] The RN-Index is compiled by the Frank Russell Company for NCREIF, and was formerly known as the FRC Index. The formula used to calculate the RN Index is modified to take into consideration capital improvements made to the property during the year.

[9] In the absence of sale, the appreciation return may also be calculated by substituting appraised value for sale price.

FIGURE 31-2

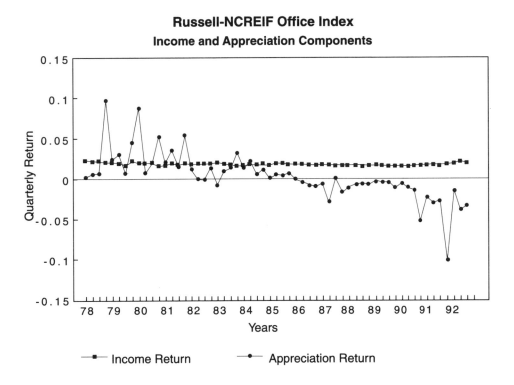

Russell-NCREIF Office Index
Income and Appreciation Components

— Income Return   — Appreciation Return

The income return indicates how much of the IRR comes from the annual cash flow (before debt service) and the appreciation return indicates how much of the IRR comes from any change in the market value of the property over the year. The total return is equal to the sum of the income and appreciation returns. Figure 31-2 shows the breakdown of the RN index into income and appreciation return components. Note that the income return is much more stable. This suggests that capitalization rates for office buildings were fairly constant during this time interval. Although NOI and property values changed over the time period, the ratio of NOI to property value remained fairly constant. Appreciation returns were much more volatile, and have been negative every quarter since the first quarter of 1986, reflecting falling property values.

Limitations of Historical Indices

In order to calculate historical performance measures, the analyst needs to know the market value of the property each year. Because a particular property does not actually sell each year, the market value of the property must be estimated. This can be done by an annual appraisal. Unfortunately, the appraiser must rely on sales of comparable properties that took place at some point in the past. Because of this, the appraised value of a property may not fully capture a sudden change in market conditions. This is particularly true when performance measures are calculated on a quarterly basis.

Because real estate performance measures must be based on appraised values rather than actual transaction prices, care must be taken when comparing the variability of the annual performance of real estate with other assets like stocks and bonds. Because actual transactions can be used to calculate the performance of stocks and bonds, these indices (such as the S&P 500) tend to exhibit more variation in the annual rate of return than published indices of real estate performance such as the Russell-NCREIF index. Figure 31-3 compares the return on office buildings in the RN Index with returns from the S&P 500 index from 1980 to 1991. Note that the S&P 500 returns are much more volatile than the RN Index. This might imply that investment in office buildings was less risky than investment in stocks, but this could be misleading. Some of the lower volatility of the RN Index may be attributed to the use of appraised values to estimate the quarterly change in the market value of the properties in the RN Index. The risk of a portfolio of office building investments is probably comparable to that of the S&P 500.

FIGURE 31-3

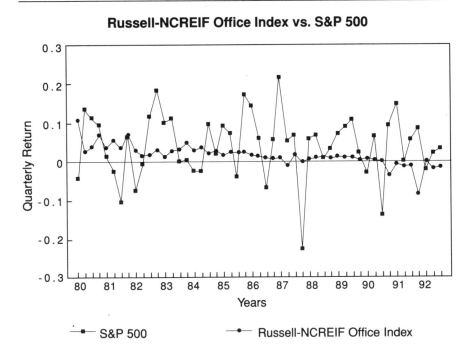

CONCLUSION

This chapter illustrates how an investor can project cash flows for an office building and calculate various measures of investment performance. Investors should not rely on a single measure of investment performance. Rather, several different measures should be used in combination with each other to tell a story about the expected performance of the property. For example, although the internal rate of return (IRR) indicates what the total rate of return is expected to be over the holding period, investors are also concerned with the amount of current cash flow as measured by the capitalization rate. The investor may also want to know how taxes affect the rate of return. Furthermore, rate of return measures should not be evaluated in isolation without considering the relative risk of the property. Although the office building example in this chapter had only six leases and fairly simple lease terms, the same types of performance measures would be calculated for a more complex multi-tenant office building. What is more important is making realistic assumptions and properly interpreting the results. This requires experience and judgment on the part of the real estate advisor.

ABOUT THE AUTHOR

Jeffrey D. Fisher, Ph.D., is director of the Center for Real Estate Studies and associate professor of finance and real estate at the Indiana University School of Business. He served as president of the American Real Estate and Urban Economics Association (AREUEA) in 1990. Fisher currently serves on the board of directors of the National Council of Real Estate Investment Fiduciaries (NCREIF) and is a trustee of The Appraisal Foundation. He has a doctorate in real estate from Ohio State University. Fisher has published numerous books and articles, and has developed and taught seminars and courses for The Appraisal Institute and other real estate organizations.

THE ROLE OF PORTFOLIO MANAGEMENT IN OFFICE INVESTMENTS

by Thomas G. Eastman and
Susan Hudson-Wilson

INTRODUCTION

Ownership of larger office buildings has increasingly come to be dominated by institutional investors. Of these, pension funds have emerged as the most significant. How do these investors become interested in real estate in general and office buildings in particular? How do they determine which properties to buy or finance? The answers to these questions arise from the process of portfolio management.

Portfolio management can be defined as the procedure by which an institutional investor, particularly a pension fund, determines investment goals and turns them into investment decisions. The individuals responsible for portfolio management are distinct from those responsible for property management and asset management. Portfolio managers have an investor-oriented strategic focus—not a regional, property type or urban area focus. They are concerned with the "roll-up" of individual investments—not with the specifics of the individual investments. Portfolio managers set strategy and monitor progress toward the achievement of portfolio objectives. They are foresters, not tree surgeons.

This process is not generally carried out by one individual or even by one organization. In the broadest sense, institutional portfolio management involves the management of a variety of asset classes (e.g., stocks, bonds, real estate, venture capital) and investment vehicles (e.g., commingled funds, joint ventures, direct investments) to achieve the investor's overall investment goals. To understand this process, this chapter will examine:

- How an institutional investor decides to include real estate in its investment portfolio
- What an investor may seek to achieve from real estate investing
- Why office buildings are attractive to investors
- A methodology for the development of investment strategies that are consistent with the investor's objectives and its experience with other asset classes
- Issues in executing the strategy and managing the investment portfolio, including a discussion of the role of office investments in a real estate portfolio

Institutional investors are generally characterized by sophisticated management and a large and diversified pool of investment assets. Because they are relatively new to real estate investing, however, they are only just beginning to understand how to systematically apply the same rigorous analysis and monitoring that they have long applied to other types of investment activity. Similarly, the concept of portfolio management is well established with regard to other asset classes, but is relatively new to real estate investing. In a circular way, portfolio management is both the natural outgrowth of the maturation of real estate as an acceptable asset class for institutional investment and a necessary precursor to the further growth and acceptance of real estate as an investment medium.

It is customary for institutional investors to begin the investment decision-making process with an assessment of their goals for the overall portfolio. These investors look to their liability obligations and seek to design an overall investment strategy that will serve the pace and magnitude of payments they have committed to make. One of their first concerns is whether the return on investment pledged to the investors is high or low, nominal or real. This determination will greatly influence the return requirement, risk tolerance and chosen relationship to the path of inflation of the aggregate portfolio.

Institutional investors set portfolio parameters and then conduct quantitative analyses to determine the proper mix of the various asset classes (stocks, bonds, cash, real estate, venture capital and so on) in the portfolio.[1] This is the first level of portfolio management. When each asset class is considered for inclusion in the mixed asset portfolio, assumptions are made about the assets' expected behavior with respect to the other assets, and their relative performance and risk. Once the aggregate portfolio managers are satisfied with the selected allocation of funds over the various

---

[1] Harry Markowitz, "Portfolio Selection," *Journal of Finance* Vol. 7 (March 1952) pp. 77-91. Harry Markowitz, *Portfolio Selection: Efficient Diversification of Investments* (New York: John Wiley, 1959).

asset classes, the responsibility for fulfilling the allocation is given to those staff responsible for each asset class. Large investors usually have dedicated staff assigned to each asset class, as each requires specialized expertise. The person responsible for the real estate allocation knows what is required in terms of the allocation's risk profile, return expectations and behavior relative to inflation. Then they must determine exactly how they will meet these requirements. That is the task of real estate portfolio management.[2]

Key concepts of real estate portfolio management are still evolving, as are the specific roles and responsibilities of investors, advisors and consultants. At one extreme, the investor might independently develop the strategic vision for the operation of a pool of funds and dictate this vision to an advisor. The strategy might encompass the entire real estate portfolio or only a sub-sector of it. An advisor would then devise tactical approaches to achieve the objectives. In the case of a discretionary relationship, the advisor would have the authority to decide how to implement the portfolio objectives. In a non-discretionary relationship, the advisor would consult with the investor on the hows and whys of implementation.

It is more often the case that while investors have a clear vision of their performance, risk and inflation targets, they understand that there are multiple ways to reach these goals[3] and so are interested in the views of their advisors and consultants. Not all approaches to a problem have equal effectiveness in all market environments. It is important for the investor to select a portfolio management plan that is achievable.

Through the rest of this chapter, task and decisions will be identified, but it is important to keep in mind that who performs these tasks is subject to negotiation among investors, advisors and consultants. What is critical is that relationships based on mutual trust and respect underlie the sharing of portfolio management thinking and mechanics.

The Tasks of Portfolio Management

The tasks performed by those with the title of portfolio manager vary widely among different organizations. Therefore, rather than attempt to describe any single organization's approach to portfolio management, this chapter addresses the tasks that make up the overall activity and, in turn, define the concept. These include:

---

[2] Harris Friedman, "Real Estate Investment and Portfolio Theory," *Journal of Financial and Quantitative Analysis* Vol. 6, Issue 2 (March 1971) pp. 861-874.

[3] Jack Cogel and Michael Oliphant, "One, or More Commingled Real Estate Funds?" *Journal of Portfolio Management* Vol. 17, Issue 4 (Summer 1991) pp. 69-72.

- **Setting goals:** The first step in establishing a real estate portfolio is to determine the role that real estate is to play within the overall investment portfolio. The nominal or real return requirements and risk tolerance of the real estate asset must be defined. Closely related to this is the issue of how much real estate the portfolio should contain if real estate is to be successful in performing its intended role. The ultimate accountability for this decision rests within the investor's organization. Investors are inclined to seek the counsel of trusted advisors and consultants on this important question, yet the leadership is generally exercised by the investor.

- **Portfolio strategy:** Once the goals have been established, an appropriate strategy for investing in real estate can be determined. This chapter will discuss a systematic methodology for designing and monitoring the performance of a real estate portfolio. The underlying principle is that a portfolio of investments is different from simply the sum of its parts. Artful, deliberate planning and careful execution can improve the likelihood that portfolio objectives will be achieved. Accountability for delivering the promised objective generally rests with the advisor; however, the active involvement of the investor is frequently integral to this stage of the process. As in any contractual relationship, leadership qualities emerge and tend to dominate.

- **Portfolio business plan:** The execution of an investment strategy involves translating the overall design of the portfolio into detailed action plans for (1) assembling or improving the composition of the portfolio (new investments); and (2) managing existing assets. Specific plans are developed (typically on an annual cycle) to guide new investment activity and to ensure that the operating plans for each existing asset are consistent with the portfolio's overall objectives. These plans take into consideration renovations and capital improvements, leasing and renewals, and financings or sales. The portfolio manager works closely with the acquisitions and management staffs in the articulation of business plans. The plans must be solidly grounded in the real world. At this point in the process, the advisor generally assumes a lead role, presenting its plans to the investor and keeping the investor informed about the implementation of each plan and its effect on total portfolio performance and the achievement of portfolio goals.

- **Operations:** The final task involved in portfolio management is to ensure that the acquisition, disposition and asset management plans are carried out and that asset objectives are met. As plans are tested by action and results emerge from projections or forecasts, the portfolio manager, usually the advisor, may need to make changes in people, processes and, sometimes, in the plans themselves.

The Decision-Making Hierarchy

Beginning with the strategies that underlie an institution's total investment portfolio, there is a clear hierarchy of decisions (see Figure 32-1). This hierarchy illustrates three general rules:

1. The higher the level of decision, the greater its impact and endurance.
2. All decisions are affected by results dispassionately analyzed.
3. Results affect shorter-term decisions first; their influence then moves up the hierarchy.

One important point should be noted here. A tenant or user of the real estate will have its own hierarchy of decision making coming from the opposite direction. The two hierarchies meet at the box labeled "Actions." This is where asset managers, developers and property managers operate on a daily basis.

There are a variety of places where a particular decision might be made. Using corporate pension funds for illustration, it is common for a fund's staff and investment committee to be advised by consultants who specialize in specific portfolio management activities. These consultants do not have an operational capability; their advisory services are purely passive.

Decision-making authority may rest with different people (or groups) in different pension funds. At one extreme, an investment advisor may be hired to make all decisions regarding real estate portfolio strategy and all the lower order decisions that stem from that strategy. At the other extreme, the advisor's role may be limited to performing asset management services and advising on specific issues, such as the sale or financing of an asset. This advice is communicated to the fund's staff, which in turn makes a recommendation to the fund's investment committee, which then makes the decision (perhaps even with the advice of another real estate or investment consultant).

GOALS AND ASSET ALLOCATION: THE BEGINNING OF STRATEGY

Strategy focuses on the big decisions, those that will do most to determine the outcome of an operation if they are implemented effectively. In the case of investment performance, the most important decision the investor makes is the overall allocation of assets across the myriad of asset classes, at each moment in time as well as over time. This assumes that the investor is operating from a reasonably reliable set of assumptions about the performance of each asset class such as stocks, bonds, venture capital or real estate (a major caveat). Put another way, asset allocation, not individual investment selection, produces most of a portfolio's total return.

Typically, sophisticated mathematical models[4] are used to help make the asset allocation decision. These models rely on data regarding the past

FIGURE 32-1

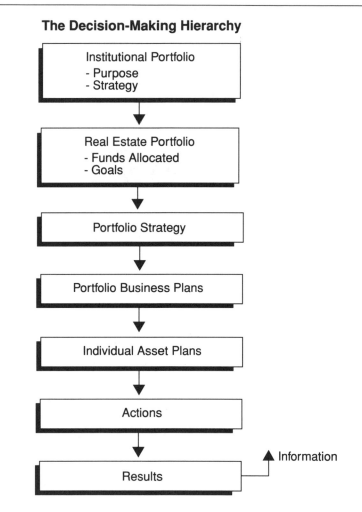

The Decision-Making Hierarchy

behavior of each asset class. If the assumptions used about the performance or behavior of an asset are, in fact, unachievable (or unknown), the
entire asset allocation decision will be severely compromised. It is important for each asset class to be fairly represented in the initial decision-
making framework.

---

[4] Jeffrey D. Fisher, "Portfolio Construction: Real Estate," Chapter 11 in *Managing Investment Portfolios*, edited by Donald Tuttle and John Maginn (Warren, Gorham and Lamont for The Institute of Chartered Financial Analysts, 1983).

James R. Webb and Jack H. Rubens, "How Much in Real Estate? A Surprising Answer" *Journal of Portfolio Management*, Vol. 13, Issue 3 (Spring 1987) pp. 10-14.

There are two significant weaknesses that have led most investors to be less than comfortable with the model they use to determine their allocation to real estate. The first is the historic lack of data from this private market, particularly in any precisely comparable form. While much useful work is being done to overcome this deficit (both in data collection and in its interpretation), data on the real estate industry still runs a poor second to that available on marketable securities.[5]

The second is that all real estate investments are represented as one asset class in the model. This is similar to labeling all investments in corporations as one asset class called, say, "corporate securities." In fact, there are numerous ways to invest in real estate with disparate results. Some types of real estate investing are moderately analogous to types of marketable security investing. (See Figure 32-2.)

Other key factors that influence a pension fund's participation in real estate are its perceived need for liquidity and the level of experience of the fund's staff and the committees to whom they report. As progress is made in each of these areas—information, liquidity and experience—pension investment in real estate will increase both in amount and in the variety of ways pension investments are structured.

What do institutional investors seek to achieve by investing in the real estate asset class? In general, there are three "tasks" that funds have assigned to real estate:

- To produce high risk-adjusted returns
- To bring the benefits of diversification to the aggregate portfolio
- To act as a hedge against inflation

To Produce High Risk-Adjusted Returns

This task presumes that a portfolio of real estate investments can be constructed that will produce high absolute returns with comparatively low attendant risk.[6] There are two ways to achieve this result. One is to

---

[5] The most commonly used source of data is the Russell-NCREIF Property Index, produced jointly by the Frank Russell Company and the National Association of Real Estate Investment Fiduciaries. The majority of the asset returns reflect appraised values rather than transaction-based values, causing the data to be "smoothed" and to lag market movements.

David Geltner, "Bias in Appraisal Based Returns" *AREUEA Journal* Vol. 17, Issue 3 (Fall 1989) pp. 338-352.

George Gau and Ko Wang, "A Further Examination of Appraisal Data and the Potential Bias in Real Estate Return Indexes," *AREUEA Journal* Vol. 18, Issue 1 (Spring 1990) pp. 40-48.

Mike Miles, Rebel Cole and David Guilkey, "A Different Look at Commercial Real Estate Returns," *AREUEA Journal* Vol. 18, Issue 4 (Winter 1990) pp. 403-430.

[6] Stephen E. Roulac, "Can Real Estate Returns Outperform Common Stocks?" *Journal of Portfolio Management* Vol. 2, Issue 2 (Winter 1976) pp. 26-43.

Roger Ibbotson and Laurence B. Siegel, "Real Estate Returns: A Comparison with Other Investments," *AREUEA Journal* Vol. 12, Issue 3 (Fall 1984) pp. 219-242.

FIGURE 32-2

			Relative Risk				→
Lowest							**Highest**
Real Estate Investment	Senior Ground Lease	Mortgage	Hybrid Debt	Free and Clear Equity	Leveraged Equity	Subordinated Ground Lease	Option
Marketable Securities	T-Bills	Bonds	Corporate Convertibles	High Capitalization Stocks	Growth Stocks	Small Company Stocks	Options Futures

identify individual real estate investments each of which has such risk and return characteristics and combine them into a single portfolio. The second way is to assemble a portfolio of investments with differing characteristics that, when combined, will produce this result.

The first idea—that each real estate investment is a producer of relatively higher returns and relatively lower risk—has more credibility than one might at first think. Research has been done that supports the notion that real estate has two investment profiles: one like stocks and one like bonds.[7] Essentially, income from leases (or the fixed-pay portion of the investment's net income stream) behaves like a bond. It exhibits low volatility and cyclical behavior like that of the bond market. The remainder of the real estate asset's return and performance is attributable to the residual value of the property, or the value that might be obtained by signing leases in the future in the context of those future market conditions. This portion of the return cycles similarly to the stock equity market and exhibits much greater volatility than does the bond-like portion.

These two behaviors, operating within the same investment, serve to dampen the volatility of the overall return. Some of the benefits of diversification are thus obtained within a single investment. Real estate practitioners typically call an unleveraged real estate investment an equity, but that is only partially true. It is also a bond. It is, in fact, a hybrid investment.

This explains how individual real estate investments can be asked to provide higher returns and lower volatility than might generally be expected of an asset labelled "equity." It is not because of any anomalous behavior but rather because of the structure of the real estate investment and the math of diversification.

At different times during a market cycle, different property types and different urban areas may be able to "beat the average." A market timing

---

[7] Richard A. Graff and Daniel M. Cashdan, "Some New Ideas in Real Estate Finance," *Journal of Applied Corporate Finance* 1990, No. 3, pp. 77-89.

strategy could be designed that would select "buys" and "sells" to maximize the portfolio's absolute return. Under such a strategy, there might be times when an investor would want to be out of real estate markets entirely.

In addition, it is possible to construct a portfolio of real estate investments that would further dampen the non-systematic risk of real estate.[8] In other words, because there is diversifiable risk in the real estate markets, the thoughtful combination of assets within a portfolio can be a powerful risk manager. This will be discussed at greater length below.

To Diversify the Aggregate Portfolio

Is there a difference between the behavior of real estate and that of other asset classes in the portfolio? If there is a difference, then the combination of these different assets into a portfolio will provide a meaningful reduction of portfolio risk without an attendant loss of return. The answer is yes.[9] In fact, when real estate's bond-like portion is separated from its equity-like portion, the answer becomes resoundingly yes.

The difference in the timing and magnitude of cycles affecting real estate and those affecting other asset classes is the key to achieving the benefits of portfolio diversification. When assets with different behaviors (as manifested by low correlations) are combined in a portfolio, portfolio risk is reduced, while portfolio return remains the weighted sum of the individual assets' returns. This "free lunch" (more benefit/return for less cost/risk) should certainly be exploited whenever practical.

To Hedge Inflation

It has been argued that real estate is better able than other asset classes to pass through to net operating income the effects of both expected and unexpected rates of inflation.[10] The hypothesis is that as inflation rises, and is anticipated to rise, landlords will factor this into the price at which they are willing to rent space. Additionally, in the event of unanticipated inflation, leases roll over frequently enough that the landlord can fairly quickly rewrite a lease to reflect the impact of the higher inflation. This pass-through mechanism is less effective in the office market, where longer

---

[8] Mike Miles, R. Brian Webb and David Guilkey, *"On the Nature of Systematic Risk in Commercial Real Estate,"* University of North Carolina Working Paper (July 1991).

[9] C. F. Sirmans and Jeffrey D. Fisher, *Real Estate in Pension Fund Portfolios: A Review of the Literature and Annotated Bibliography* (Pension Real Estate Association, 1991).

[10] David J. Hartzell, John S. Hekman and Mike Miles, "Real Estate Returns and Inflation," *AREUEA Journal* Vol. 15, Issue 1 (Spring 1987) pp. 617-637.

Michael Giliberto, *"Real Estate in the Portfolio: Then and Now,"* (Salomon Brothers Bond Market Research, July 8, 1991)

Aldrich, Eastman & Waltch, *Why Real Estate?* 1991.

leases may be the norm. Alternatively, long-term leases generally incorporate Consumer Price Index adjustments (or other fixed "bumps" in rental rates) which ensure that the income flow to the landlord will be largely unimpaired by the effects of inflation. If all else fails, the argument continues, capitalization rates will capture any inflation-related return that might not be reflected in rental rates.

This hypothesis held up well until some more basic economics were reasserted. Landlords cannot get nominal rents to rise (let alone real rents) in a severely oversupplied real estate market. Thus, real estate's ability to act as an inflation hedge will ebb and flow with the condition of market fundamentals. While hedging inflation is not always an achievable task for the real estate asset class, on average, over an extended period real estate is significantly more effective as an inflation hedge than stocks or bonds.

In short, the real estate asset class can currently be asked to perform at least two of these tasks reasonably reliably and the third periodically. Still it is not possible for the investor to simply order up all three! An investor must determine the most important priority among its objectives for a real estate portfolio and then set about to design a real estate portfolio that can best achieve that particular objective. (An investor might get lucky and also achieve some portion of the other goals, but shouldn't count on it.)

Different investors will have different needs, depending on their particular circumstances. Some of these circumstances might include:

- Size of the aggregate portfolio
- Need for liquidity
- Investment time horizon
- Tax implications
- Return requirements
- Risk tolerance

For example, an individual investor may have a small investment portfolio and an investment time horizon of ten years, at which time he would need to make college payments. Such an investor probably would not have a high tolerance for risk, would have a moderate return requirement and would require absolute liquidity in ten years. Real estate, held in the traditional fashion, most likely would not serve this investor's needs.

Alternatively, an investor such as a plan sponsor of a large corporate or rapidly growing public pension fund might be characterized by a long liability profile, a low need for liquidity and a moderate risk tolerance. Such an investor probably would be well-suited to the real estate asset class, provided the portfolio were properly structured. Such a plan might place priority on any one of the three tasks described above, depending on the nature of the benefit program. For example, a defined contribution plan might be less concerned with inflation hedging than a defined benefit plan. The former plan specifies what the employer and employee will pay in to the retirement fund, but does not promise a particular payout. The defined benefit plan specifies what benefits will be paid out, but it is up to the employer to figure out how this promise will be met. Clearly the defined benefit plan investor will be more concerned about the real purchasing power of the invested assets and so will need to hedge against the risk of inflation. In addition, each plan has its own sense of risk tolerance and some plans are subject to the diversification principles encouraged by ERISA.

While it is vitally important for the investor to establish a clear sense of its real estate goals, these goals may vary considerably among investors. Once these goals have been articulated and have been "reality checked," the investor will work with its advisors and consultants to design portfolios that can achieve its goals and priorities.

PORTFOLIO STRATEGY

Since strategy focuses on the major decisions that affect the outcome of an activity, the most important thing for a strategist to decide is the hierarchy of factors that will affect the return and the risk of the real estate investment portfolio. Some of these factors include:

- Property type
- Urban economy
- Financial structure
- Specific market location
- Type(s) of tenants

- Quality of design and construction
- Management intensity
- Length of leases
- Local political environment

Clearly, all of these factors will have an influence on the performance and risk of each real estate investment and upon the performance and risk of the portfolio. The question is at what level each factor should be managed. For the purpose of developing and monitoring a real estate portfolio strategy, property type, urban economy and financial structure are important factors. The other factors are best managed at the asset and property management levels.

Two tools have been developed (borrowed in part from the field of finance) to guide the development and monitoring of real estate portfolios: efficient frontiers and capitalization graphs. These tools enable portfolio strategists to design optimal portfolios and to monitor their progress towards achieving their goals. Each is discussed briefly below; those seeking a deeper understanding must refer to the finance literature.[11]

The construction of an optimal portfolio is a goal to be striven for, but never reached. The world is a dynamic place, constantly changing; but responses to change are never instantaneous. In addition, investment goals shift with time and with changes in the fortunes of the other assets in

---

[11] Zvi Bodie, Alex Kane and Alan J. Marcus, *Investments* (Richard D. Irwin, 1989) pp. 183-226.

the aggregate portfolio. The language of portfolio theory appears very precise, but the implementation is always, appropriately, less precise.

The Efficient Frontier

The concept of the efficient frontier can be used to examine the relationship among investments in particular locations and among particular property types. The argument goes as follows: Within any urban area, each of the major property types will behave in a distinct manner. This behavior will be determined by the interaction of supply and demand factors in the market. The demand side of the market is a function of urban economics, i.e., the mix of industries in the urban area, the prospects for these industries, the relative costs of living and doing business, and the amenities of the area. The supply side will be influenced by the demand side, by zoning, by the availability of capital both locally and nationally, and by the cost of land, materials and labor.

A model can be constructed that will inform the analyst about these two sides of the market and the effect of their interaction on returns. An alternative approach to modeling this net effect would be to calculate the actual achieved historic return from a very large data set, were one available. In the very short run, vacancy rates consistently calculated across space, time and property type could be used as a proxy for return (inverted, of course).

The purpose of this data set is to examine the different behaviors of the markets available to investors. Investors will be more or less interested in investing in a particular property type in a particular market if they know how the investment would behave on its own as well as how it can be expected to contribute to, or detract from the performance of the real estate portfolio. In the case of office buildings, the volatility of the investment is high, but the cycle differs from the cycles of retail, industrial and multi-family markets. Thus the office product has an important risk management role in a real estate portfolio.

For example, while the Houston office market began its decline in 1982 and its recovery in 1991, the New York office market remained steady through 1986 and has been in decline ever since. Thus, New York and Houston office markets are complementary in a portfolio context. A risk-sensitive investor would want to combine these investments in a portfolio to dampen overall portfolio risk. Even if each investment independently is quite risky, they will work well together to manage overall portfolio risk. Once the true number of different markets or behaviors is discerned, the concept of the efficient frontier assists the strategist in thinking about constructive combinations of these different behaviors to form a portfolio.

Efficient frontier models operate on a simple principle: the identification of combinations of assets that have different behaviors in order to take advantage of an elementary, yet compelling piece of math. When two assets behave differently (e.g., the return on one rises when the return on the other falls) and are combined in a single portfolio, the return on the portfolio will be the weighted sum of the two assets' returns, but the riskiness of the portfolio will be *less than the weighted sum of the risk of the two assets.* Put another way, for every level of risk the investor is willing to assume, it is possible to obtain an improved rate of return. This is a powerful tool. The efficient frontier model seeks to identify portfolios of assets that are most efficient, i.e., that are able to achieve the most return for the least risk. Return may be thought of as a benefit and risk, a cost. A variety of portfolios underlie the points along the frontier. On the left side are low-return, low-risk portfolios; as one moves up and to the right, the underlying portfolios are characterized by higher return and risk.

For example, point A on the efficient frontier in Figure 32-3 represents a portfolio with a return of 6% and low risk. This combination might be produced by a portfolio consisting of 10% Baltimore office, 10% Miami industrial, 15% Denver multifamily, 20% Denver office, 30% San Francisco retail and 15% San Francisco industrial. Point B on the graph represents a higher risk and return portfolio and so will require a different combination of assets. The points on the efficient frontier represent the most efficient solutions to the portfolio construction problem, i.e., they are the most efficient (least costly in terms of risk) way to achieve a particular rate of return. Points that fall within the frontier are also obtainable and, while inefficient, may represent an improvement over an investor's current position.

FIGURE 32-3

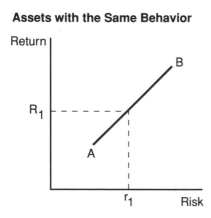

Assets with the Same Behavior

Combinations of "A" and "B" produce portfolios with simple weighted average risk and return characteristics.

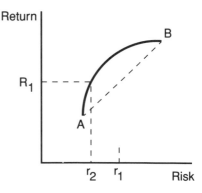

Assets with Different Behavior

Combinations of "A" and "B" produce portfolios with the same returns as before, but with less risk.

The efficient frontier concept can help a portfolio strategist think about the optimal allocation of a portfolio over property types and urban areas. The methodology and discipline are also useful in thinking about an existing portfolio. How is the existing portfolio positioned in terms of risk and return? How can its position be made more efficient and better geared to achieving the portfolio's objectives? How does an incremental investment under consideration fit in? Is it merely a "good deal," or is it also a good portfolio investment? The efficient frontier framework is extremely useful for designing investment strategies and for monitoring progress toward the achievement of investment goals.

Capitalization Graph

The analyst must also consider the financial structure of the portfolio. As with other aspects of portfolio-building, financial structure should be a matter of choice, not chance, and those choices should be made in the context of the aggregate portfolio. It is entirely consistent to have a portfolio that is structured like an unleveraged equity and yet to have each investment within that portfolio be financially structured in some other fashion. Until the investor has examined the financial structure of the portfolio as a whole, however, it is impossible to know the net effect of the investment structuring efforts.

The portfolio capitalization graph (cap graph) seeks to represent the financial structure of a portfolio. It can be used to illustrate the desired portfolio as well as the actual, existing portfolio. (See Figure 32-4 for a construction worksheet.) The first graph depicted in Figure 32-5 illustrates a single, unleveraged equity investment. The even spacing of the quintiles indicates that the investor's capital is uniformly exposed to a loss of property value.

The next cap graph represents a leveraged equity investment in which a $100 million property has been financed with $80 million of debt. In the first case, the investor has $100 million invested and is exposed to a dollar-for-dollar loss if the building declines in value. In the second case, the investor has $20 million invested and stands to lose 100% of that amount if the property value drops by 20%. The third cap graph represents an investment of an $80 million first mortgage loan on a building valued at $100 million. The fourth cap graph in Figure 32-5 illustrates the overall structure of the portfolio. Has the investor chosen this level of risk or has it been acquired unconsciously?

An investor begins the exercise by creating a cap graph that represents the desired portfolio. This should reflect the investor's tolerance for risk and desire for return derived from financial structure. For example, a very conservative investor will wish to use financial structure to shield the real estate portfolio from "first dollar loss." Mortgage debt or structured equity might be used to accomplish this. A more risk-tolerant investor will wish to

FIGURE 32-4

CAP GRAPH WORKSHEET

3 ASSETS

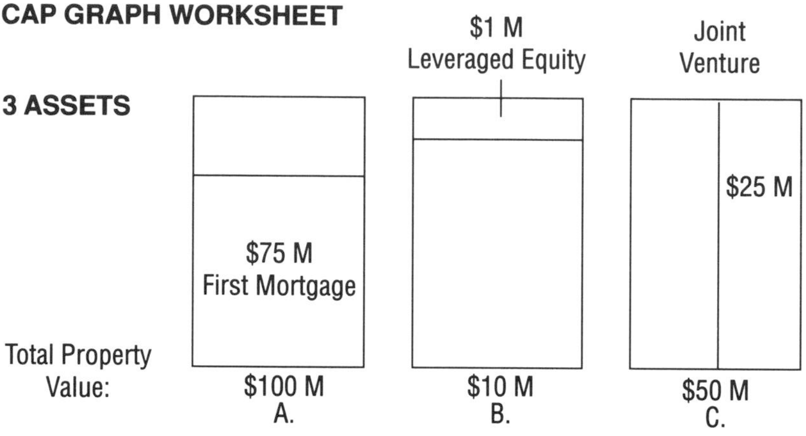

	$1 M Leveraged Equity	Joint Venture
		$25 M
	$75 M First Mortgage	
Total Property Value:	$100 M / A.	$10 M / B.	$50 M / C.

STEPS

1 Assign all invested dollars to quintiles.

A.	B.	C.
$0 M	$1 M	$5 M
$15 M	$0 M	$5 M
$20 M	$0 M	$5 M
$20 M	$0 M	$5 M
$20 M	$0 M	$5 M

2 Sum invested dollars across quintiles.

1+5=6
15+5=20
20+5=25
20+5=25
20+5=25

$101 M

3 Express each quintile as a percent of total invested dollars ($101 M) and re-draw to reflect shares.

— 6 %
20%
25%
25%
25%

$100 %

4 Compare with unleveraged fee.

Sample — 6 %	Unleveraged
20%	20%
25%	20%
25%	20%
25%	20%
25%	20%

FIGURE 32-5

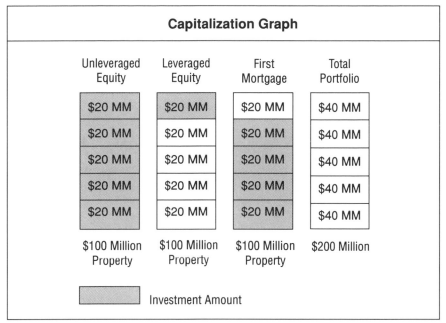

Capitalization Graph

Unleveraged Equity	Leveraged Equity	First Mortgage	Total Portfolio
$20 MM	$20 MM	$20 MM	$40 MM
$20 MM	$20 MM	$20 MM	$40 MM
$20 MM	$20 MM	$20 MM	$40 MM
$20 MM	$20 MM	$20 MM	$40 MM
$20 MM	$20 MM	$20 MM	$40 MM
$100 Million Property	$100 Million Property	$100 Million Property	$200 Million

Investment Amount

leverage at least some investment positions. A risk-neutral investor will want the final portfolio to look like unleveraged equity, even if the individual assets in the portfolio are not all structured as unleveraged equity.

The "desired portfolio" cap graph can then be compared with a cap graph of the existing portfolio. Based on the differences between the two, the portfolio manager can make decisions about how to move the financial structure of the existing portfolio more toward that of the desired portfolio. As with the efficient frontier analysis, the investor/portfolio manager can analyze proposed investments for their suitability based on the financial structure needs of the portfolio.

Decisions about the financial structure of a portfolio also must be continuously reviewed in light of changes in the real estate capital markets environment. The price of debt and the price of equity vary, influenced by many factors. Three of the most significant are investors' inflation expectations, governmental tax policy and perceived strength of user demand for space in relation to supply. (Clearly there are many others, including Federal Reserve policy, strength of the dollar, state of the economy, state of markets abroad and financial soundness of tenants. But the first three dominate.) The following table illustrates the differences between the capital market environment in 1982 and in early 1992:

	1982	1992
Inflation Expectations	High	Moderate to Low
Tax Policy Stimulus	Heavy Real Estate Subsidy	Moderate to Low
Supply/Demand	Strong	Weak

These factors strongly influenced the prices of debt and equity. In 1992, investors desire reliable current income, so they were willing to accept relatively lower rates of current return in exchange for reliability. In 1982, the desire for capital growth (to protect capital in real terms) was paramount. At that time office buildings were a highly desired investment. Leasing risk was acceptable, and short-lease terms were preferred. Ten years later, the opposite was true.

THE PORTFOLIO MANAGER'S OPERATIONAL RESPONSIBILITIES

Once the portfolio manager, in conjunction with the investor, has developed a strategy and evaluated whether the portfolio is structured correctly to implement that strategy, the next issue is implementation and monitoring at the individual property level. There are as many ways to accomplish this as there are institutional investors, staffs and managers. For ease of explanation, assume that there is a single portfolio manager who understands:

- The investor's overall objectives and mission
- The investment strategy
- The investor's reporting and decision-making structure
- What is happening in the real estate and capital markets

Using these points as a frame of reference, the portfolio manager must develop an overall portfolio business plan that is designed to implement the investment strategy. This involves two components: (1) assembling a portfolio of assets, or refining the mix of investments in the existing portfolio; and (2) ensuring that the management of the assets in the portfolio is consistent with the achievement of the portfolio's strategy. To accomplish these tasks, the portfolio manager will work with a variety of in-house or outside specialists, including investors, asset managers, researchers, attorneys and accountants, as well as those with expertise in particular property types or real estate markets. The portfolio manager's job is that of orchestration with an eye toward achieving the goals of the portfolio.

   In constructing a new portfolio or refining the mix of investments in an existing portfolio, the portfolio manager works principally with investment and acquisitions specialists. In focusing their efforts, the manager must make sure that the specialists involved:

- Understand the client's objectives
- Understand the investment strategy
- Have a plan to identify and structure investments that are consistent with both the investment strategy and the realities of the current market

As potential investments are identified, the portfolio manager conducts a preliminary review of the investment proposal to confirm that it meets the client's criteria. If the proposal survives this initial screening, it is subjected to rigorous underwriting not only by the investor but also by the entire array of specialists involved. At this point, the portfolio manager's responsibility is to ensure that the investment is in all respects consistent with the client's objectives and the strategy being pursued. It is also critical to ascertain the views of the asset management team that will be responsible for managing the asset. They must believe that the investment is a good one and that the projected performance can be achieved. Further, they must have a realistic plan for managing the asset after closing, including a plan to add value to the asset, an exit strategy and a target sell date.

In a broader context, the portfolio manager also constantly reviews the entire portfolio to ensure that each investment continues to play its defined role within the portfolio and that the portfolio continues to play its expected role in meeting the client's overall investment needs. In doing so, the manager monitors both asset and portfolio performance closely and compares actual against forecasted results. If performance consistently lags expectations, the portfolio manager must determine whether the problem stems from a flawed investment or asset strategy, poor execution of that strategy, or the uncontrollable factors of market and cycle. Depending on the answer, the manager may decide to make changes in the portfolio mix through additional acquisitions or asset sales, or to review the overall investment strategy. Does the strategy remain a realistic way to achieve the client's investment goals? Any change in strategy must be quickly communicated to all asset managers and investors and reflected in asset operating plans.

Critical Need for Efficient Communication

Communication is one of the most important tasks of the portfolio manager. The goal of downward communication is to make sure that all key participants, especially asset managers, are aware of the overall portfolio strategy and the role their assets play in that strategy. A critical part of this effort is making sure that asset managers support the role their assets have been given and believe the objectives for their assets are realistic and achievable. This will ensure that they are willing to be held accountable for their assets' performance, both as a single investment and as an integral part of the portfolio. In addition, the portfolio manager must always be ready to participate as needed in key investment and operational decisions to ensure that they are consistent with client goals.

Communication extends upward from the portfolio manager to the client. The initial goal is to ensure that the client understands clearly the investment objectives and the strategy agreed on. As the portfolio is assembled, refined and managed, the primary communication concerns results, i.e., how well the portfolio has done in achieving its objectives. If the objectives are not being achieved, why not? What is the plan for the future? While this sounds relatively simple and straightforward, it often is not. Institutional investors and their organizational structures have become more sophisticated, and they are demanding more and better communication from portfolio managers.

Formal Portfolio Reporting

Typically, formal portfolio reports are provided to institutional clients quarterly. It is useful at this regular interval to restate (and re-affirm, if necessary) the portfolio objectives and the strategy for achieving them. This step goes a long way toward focusing discussion and analysis on the truly key issues. As markets go through turmoil, memories fade or become selective. The periodic restatement of goals and strategy reminds everyone involved of the central tasks and tactics. Then progress can be reviewed; issues, problems and proposed solutions can be discussed in light of the goals and strategy.

Each written report contains a balance sheet and income statement for the portfolio. For pension funds, this must be prepared on a market value basis. This means that valuation policies must be determined, as well as accounting policies. Returns are measured, reported and discussed. Attempts are made to measure the extent to which diversification of risk has been achieved and the extent of its impact on return. How close did the portfolio manager come to achieving the efficient frontier and did it make any difference? Is the exposure to "first dollar" loss as planned?

Finally, attempts are now being made to report "value attribution." This is an effort to measure in a rigorous way where, and by whom, value is being added to the portfolio. How did the portfolio manager's selection of the most important factors affecting the risk and return of the investment portfolio (e.g., property type, urban economy, financial structure, market timing) affect performance? What was the role of the efficient frontier in dampening risk? Did property selection add to or detract from portfolio performance?

SUMMARY

Portfolio management is a distinct discipline. It is not property manage-ment, nor asset management, nor simply the sum total of managing multiple assets. It is a strategic, not a tactical, process. Portfolio manage-ment is the art of defining, assembling, refining and monitoring a combina-tion of investments with the objective of producing a specific result. It is a discipline long practiced with regard to other asset classes, but only recently applied to real estate. However, as institutional investors have become more knowledgeable and familiar with real estate, they have begun to demand of their real estate managers the same level of discipline and rigor required from those in charge of other components of their invest-ment portfolios. As the analytic rigor and precision improves, investors will feel more comfortable with the real estate asset class. This comfort will translate into improved allocations and the growth of a wider array of investment vehicles.

Real estate portfolio management remains in the early stages of its evolution. The most appropriate role for each of the participants—investors, advisors and consultants—is yet to be determined. As an industry, real estate still lacks the quantity, quality and consistency of data available in other asset classes. This is a difficult problem, particularly given that real estate is, generally, a private market in which information is often proprietary, closely guarded and a significant source of competitive advantage. Nonetheless, much progress has been made over the past decade in utilizing the data that is available to develop and test theories about the interaction and performance of different types of real estate investments. If real estate is to be viewed by institutional investors as an asset class worthy of the same consideration given to corporate equities and debt instruments, much work remains to be done.

ABOUT THE AUTHORS

Thomas G. Eastman is co-founder and executive director of Aldrich, Eastman & Waltch, where his focus is the management of the firm's client portfolio. Eastman has been investing in real estate on behalf of pension funds since 1972. Before Aldrich, Eastman & Waltch, he was with The Boston Company Real Estate Counsel, Inc. Prior to that, he was director of acquisitions for the closed-end real estate funds sponsored by Coldwell Banker. Eastman holds a BA from Stanford University and an MBA from Harvard. He is a member of The Urban Land Institute (Urban Development/Mixed-Use Council) and a founding member and member of the board of directors of the National Association of Real Estate Investment Managers.

Susan Hudson-Wilson is director, research and development, at Aldrich, Eastman & Waltch, Boston, where she manages the firm's research and the development of new products and new client relationships. She was elected to the board of directors in 1991. Hudson-Wilson is a member of the Association of Investment Management and Research, and the Pension Real Estate Association, and is vice president and treasurer of the NCREIF Research Institute. She has written books on labor economics and quantitative investment analysis, as well as numerous articles. Hudson-Wilson holds a BA in economics from the University of Vermont and is a Chartered Financial Analyst.

SELECTED BIBLIOGRAPHY

PART I

Articles

Brubaker, W. "The Evolution of Chicago's Tall Office Buildings." *Chicago Office* (Building Owners and Managers Association International) (1991).

Iezman, S. L. and N. A. Ihlenfeld. "Real Estate Asset Management." *Real Estate Review* 21(2): 58-63 (1991).

Johnson, W. C. "Office Recycling: One of the 50 Ways to Save the Planet" *Facility Management Journal* (Nov/Dec 1991): 32-34.

Kiechel, W. "Overscheduled and Not Loving It," *Fortune* (April 8, 1991): 105.

MacCormac, R. "The Dignity of Office." *The Architectural Review* (May 1992): 76-82.

Nicholas, J. C. "The Calculation of Proportionate-Share Impact Fees." *Planning Advisory Report* No.408 (American Planning Association) (July 1988): 2.

O'Connor, P. J. "Face It: Recycling is a Job That Must be Done," *The Office: Magazine of Information Systems and Management* 113(6): 35-37 (June 1991).

Oki, J. J. "The Growing Separation Between Real Estate Ownership and Management Expertise." *Real Estate Review* 19(2): 65-74 (Summer 1989).

"OSHA Reaffirms Hazard Warnings for Fibrous Glass." *Textile World* 141(9): 20 (September 1991).

Payne, R. M. "Business Papers: The Time to Recycle Is Now." *The Office: Magazine of Information Systems and Management* 115:30 (April 1992).

Reid, T. and R. A. Maniscalco. "Commercial Management Contracts: A Primer." *Real Estate Review* 21(1): 91-96 (Spring 1991).

Roulac, S. E. "Dimensions of the Restructuring in Real Estate Capital Markets." *The Real Estate Finance Journal* (Spring 1992): 5-12.

Russell, C. "On the Baby-Boom Bandwagon." *American Demographics* 13(5): 12 (May 1991).

Saltz, S. G. and H. J. McCown. "Tenant Representation: A Broker's Duties to Commercial Space Tenants." *Real Estate Review* 19(4): 61-64 (Winter 1990).

White, J. R. "How to Plan and Build a Major Office Building." *Real Estate Review* 10(1): 3-7 (1980).

Books

Atteberry, W. *Modern Real Estate Finance*. Columbus: Grid Publishing, Inc., 1980.

Berger, M. L. *They Built Chicago: Entrepreneurs Who Shaped a Great City*. Chicago: Bonus Books, 1992.

Bluestone, D. *Constructing Chicago*. New Haven: Yale University Press, 1991.

Bruegmann, R. *A Guide to 150 Years of Chicago Architecture*. Chicago: Chicago Review Press, 1985.

Burchel, R. and D. Listokin. *The Fiscal Impact Handbook*. New Brunswick: Center for Urban Policy Research.

Condit, C. W. *American Building*. Chicago: University of Chicago Press, 1968.

Condit, C. W. *The Chicago School of Architecture*. Chicago: University of Chicago Press, 1964.

Costonis, J. J. *Icons and Aliens: Law, Aesthetics, and Environmental Change*. Urbana: University of Illinois, 1989.

Downs, A. *The Structural Revolution in the Commercial Real Estate Industry*. New York: Salomon Brothers, 1992.

Encyclopedia of Architectural Design, Engineering and Construction. Vol. 3. New York: John Wiley and Sons, 1989.

Fletcher, B. *A History of Architecture*. London: Butterworth's, 1987.

Girouard, M. *Cities and People*. New Haven: Yale University Press, 1985.

Goldberger, P. *The Skyscraper*. New York: Alfred A. Knopf, 1982.

Greer, G. E. and M. D. Farrell. *Contemporary Real Estate: Theory and Practice*. Chicago: The Dryden Press, 1983.

Heilbrun, J. *Urban Economics and Public Policy*. 3rd ed. New York: St. Martin's Press, 1987.

Hitchcock, H. R. *Architecture: Nineteenth and Twentieth Centuries*. 3rd ed. Baltimore: Penguin Books, 1971.

King, M. *King's Views of New York, 1911-12*. New York: Moses King, 1912.

Kostof, S. *A History of Architecture*. New York: Oxford University Press, 1985.

Lehman, A. *The New York Skyscraper—A History of Its Development, 1870-1939*. Ph.D. diss., Yale University, 1974.

Lennard, S. C. and H. L. Lennard. *Livable Cities*. New York: Gondolier Press, 1987.

Mayer, H. M. and R. Wade. *Chicago: Growth of a Metropolis*. Chicago: University of Chicago Press, 1969.

Miles, M. E., et al. *Real Estate Development*. Washington: Urban Land Institute, 1991.

Mujica, F. *History of the Skyscraper*. New York: DaCapo Press, 1977.

Norwich, J. J., ed. *Great Architecture of the World*. London: Mitchell Beazley Publishers, Ltd, 1975.

Panati, C. *Panati's Extraordinary Origins of Everyday Things*. New York: Harper & Row, 1987.

Panati, C. *Panati's Browser's Book of Beginnings.* Boston: Houghton Mifflin Co., 1984.

Pevsner, N. *A History of Building Types.* Princeton: Princeton University Press, 1976.

Robinson, R. I. and D. Wrightsman. *Financial Markets: The Accumulation and Allocation of Wealth.* New York: McGraw-Hill Book Company, 1980.

Roth, L. M. *A Concise History of American Architecture.* New York: Harper & Row, 1979.

Russell, B. *Architecture and Design 1970-1980: New Ideas in America.* New York: Harry Abrams, Inc., 1989.

Saliga, P. A., ed. *The Sky's the Limit: A Century of Chicago Skyscrapers.* New York: Rizzoli International Publications, Inc., 1990.

Schultz, E. and W. Simmons. *Offices in the Sky.* Indianapolis: Bobbs-Merrill, 1959.

Seldin, M. and R. Swesnik. *Real Estate Investment Strategy.* New York: John Wiley and Sons, 1979.

Senn, M. A. *Commercial Leases.* 2 vols. New York: John Wiley and Sons, 1990.

Tallmadge, T. E., ed. *The Origin of the Skyscraper.* Chicago: The Alderbrink Press, 1939.

Toll, S. *Zoned America.* New York: Grossman, 1969.

Tolzmann, D. C. *Parties to the Transaction: The Developer.* In *Financing Income-Producing Real Estate,* edited by E. Stevenson. New York: McGraw-Hill Book Company, 1988.

Weber, A.: *The Growth of Cities in the Nineteenth Century* Ithaca: Cornell University Press, 1963.

Whyte, W. H. *City: Rediscovering the Center.* New York: Doubleday, 1988.

PART II

Articles

Aalberts, R. J. and T. M. Clauretie. "Commercial Real Estate and the Americans with Disabilities Act: Implications for Appraisers." *The Appraisal Journal* (July 1992): 347-356.

Dowall, D. E. "Applying Real Estate Financial Analysis to Planning and Development Control." *American Planning Association Journal* 51:84-94 (Winter 1985).

Gold, M. E. "Economic Development Projects: A Perspective" *The Urban Lawyer* 19:199-215 (Spring 1987).

Goodrich, C. "American Development Policy: The Case of Internal Improvements." *The Journal of Economic History* 16(12): 449-460 (December 1956).

Hinda, D. S. and J. B. Corgel. "Understanding the Effect of Transportation on Office Location." *Perspective* No. 1, SIOR (1984).

Keating, A. D. "Public-Private Partnerships in Public Works: A Bibliographic Essay." *Essays in Public Works History* 16(12): 78-108 (December 1989).

Parker, R. A. "Local Tax Subsidies as a Stimulus for Development: Are They Cost Effective? Are They Equitable?" *City Almanac* 16:8-15 (Feb.-April 1982).

Sagalyn, L. "Explaining the Improbable: Local Redevelopment in the Wake of Federal Cutbacks." *Journal of the American Planning Association* 56:429-441 (Autumn 1990).

Sagalyn, L. "Measuring Financial Returns When the City Acts as an Investor: Boston and Faneuil Hall Marketplace." *Real Estate Issues* 24:7-15 (Fall/Winter 1989).

Stark-Hood, M. "The American with Disabilities Act—What Businesses Need to Know Now." *Perspective* No. 32, SIOR (1991).

Wetmore, R. "Bidding for Public Property: Guidelines for Developers." *Urban Land* 50(5):8-13 (May 1991).

Wetmore, R. and C. Klinger. "Land Leases: More Than Rent Schedule." *Urban Land* 59(6):6-9 (June 1990).

Wetmore, R. "Lessor Beware! A Land Lease Is Usually a Partnership." *Urban Land* 47(10):20-23 (October 1988).

Wurtzebach, C. H. "Real Estate Feasibility Analysis and the Emerging Public-Private Partnership in Land Use Decisions." *Real Estate Issues* 6(2): 12-16 (Fall/Winter 1981).

Books

Bateman, M. *Office Development: A Geographical Analysis.* New York: St. Martin's Press, 1985.

Bosselman, F. P. *Downtown Linkages.* Washington: The Urban Land Institute, 1985.

Castells, M. *The City and the Grassroots: A Cross-Cultural Theory of Urban Social Movements.* Berkeley: University of California Press, 1983.

Feagin, J. R. and R. Parker. *Building American Cities: The Urban Real Estate Game.* Englewood Cliffs: Prentice Hall, 1989.

Frieden, B. J. and L. B. Sagalyn. *Downtown, Inc: How America Rebuilds Cities.* Cambridge: MIT Press, 1989.

Getzels, J. and M. Jaffee. *Zoning Bonuses in Central Cities* No. 410. American Planning Association Planning Advisory Service.

Garreau, J. *Edge City.* New York: Doubleday, 1991.

Juergensmeyer, J. C. *Private Supply of Public Services.* Washington: The Urban Land Institute, 1985.

Kayden, J. S. *Incentive Zoning in New York City: A Cost-Benefit Analysis.* Policy Analysis Series No. 201. Lincoln Institute of Land Policy. 1978.

Lassar, T. J. *Carrots and Sticks: New Zoning Downtown.* Washington: Urban Land Institute, 1989.

Lassar, T. J. *City Deal Making.* Washington: Urban Land Institute, 1990.

Mandleker, D. R.; G. Feder; M. P. Collins. *Reviving Cities with Tax Abatement.* New Brunswick: Rutgers University, Center for Urban Policy Research, 1980.

Netzer, D. *Public Finance Context*. In *Private Supply of Public Services*, edited by R. Alterman. New York: New York University Press, 1988.

Porter, D., ed. *Downtown Linkages*. Washington: Urban Land Institute, 1985.

Porter, D.; P. L. Phillips; T. J. Lasser. *Flexible Zoning—How It Works*. Washington: Urban Land Institute, 1988.

Sagalyn, L. B. *Leasing: The Strategic Option*. Working paper, Lincoln Institute for Land Policy and A. Alfred Taubman Center for State and Local Government of Harvard University.

Stout, G. E. and J. E. Vitt. *Public Incentives and Financing Techniques for Co-development*. Urban Land Institute Development Component Series, 1982.

Tarr, J. A. *The Evolution of Infrastructure*. In *Perspective on Urban Infrastructure*, edited by R. Hanson. Washington: National Academy Press, 1984.

Urban Land Institute. *Downtown Development Handbook*. Washington: Urban Land Institute, 1980.

Urban Land Institute. *Joint Development: Making the Real Estate Transit Connection*. Washington: Urban Land Institute, 1979.

Weiss, M. A. *The Rise of the Community Builders, the American Real Estate Industry, and Urban Land Planning*. Irvington, NY: Columbia University Press, 1987.

Witherspoon, R. *Co-Development: City Rebuilding by Business and Government*. Washington: Urban Land Institute, 1982.

PART III

Articles

Anderson, J. E. "A Theoretical Foundation for the Gravity Equation." *American Economic Review* 69:106-111 (1979).

Archer, W. R. "Determinants of Location for General Purpose Office Firms Within Medium Size Cities." *Journal of the American Real Estate and Urban Economics Association* (Fall 1981).

Birch, D. L. "Forecasting Over-built Office Markets." *Perspective* No. 20, SIOR (1988).

Bottum, M. S. "Estimating Economic Obsolescence in Supply-Saturated Office Markets." *The Appraisal Journal* (October 1988): 451-455.

Clark, D. L. and C. G. Dannis. "Forecasting Office Rental Rates: Neoclassical Support for Change." *The Appraisal Journal* (January 1992): 113-128.

Downs, A. "What Have We Learned from the 1980s Experience?" Salomon Brothers, *United States Real Estate Research* (July 1991).

Downs, A. "The Fundamental Shift in Real Estate Finance from a Capital Surplus in the 1980s to a Capital Shortage in the 1990s." Salomon Brothers, *Bond Market Research—Real Estate* (February 1991).

Fanning, S. F. and J. Winslow. "Guidelines for Defining the Scope of Market Analysis in Appraisal Assignments." *The Appraisal Journal* (October 1988): 466-476.

Giliberto, S. M. "Real Estate In the Portfolio: Then and Now." Salomon Brothers (July 1991): 4.

Graham, M. F. and D. S. Bible. "Classifications for Commercial Real Estate." *The Appraisal Journal* (1992): 237-246.

Kelly, H. F. "Industrial and Office Real Estate Survey Reveals Similar Reactions to the Economy Throughout the Country." *Professional Report of Industrial and Office Real Estate*, SIOR (May/June 1991).

Kimball, J. R. and B. S. Bloomberg "Office Space Demand Analysis." *The Appraisal Journal* (October 1987): 567-577.

Legg, W. E. "Analysis of Office Space Markets." *Perspective* No. 7, SIOR (1988).

McFadden, D. "Modelling the Choice of Residential Location." Cowles Foundation Discussion Paper No. 477, Yale University (1987).

Miller, A. "The Migration of Employed Persons to and from Metropolitan Areas of the United States." *Journal of the American Statistical Association* 62:1418-1432 (1967).

Niedercorn, J. H. and B. V. Bechdolt. "An Economic Derivation of the Gravity Law of Spatial Interaction." *Journal of Regional Science* 9:273-282 (1969).

Pickett, N. "Work Force 2000 Executive Summary and Implications for the Commercial Real Estate Industry." *Perspective* No. 31, SIOR (1991).

Pittman, R. H. and G. I. Thrall. "Improving Real Estate Market Research." *Real Estate Issues* 17(1): 1-7 (Spring/Summer 1992).

Pittman, R. H. and M. Seldin. "Real Estate Analyses Using Geographic Data." *Real Estate Issues* 15(1): 32-38 (Spring/Summer 1990).

Powers, R. T. and B. F. Hunter. "Anticipating Office and Industrial Space Demand: How to Effectively Anticipate a Market Area's Turning Points." *Perspective* No. 26, SIOR (1989).

Rages, W. R., et al. "Forecasting Office Space Demands and Office Space Per Worker Estimates." *Perspective* No. 34, SIOR (1992).

Rogers, A. "A Regression Analysis of Interregional Migration in California". *Review of Economics and Statistics* 49: 262-267 (1967).

Weaver, W. C. "Forecasting Office Space Demand with Conjoint Measurement Techniques." *The Appraisal Journal* (July 1984): 389-398.

Williams, D. L. "Suburban Activity Centers and Corporate Decisions." *Perspective* No. 5, SIOR (1985).

Wofford, L. "Significant Trends Affecting Office and Industrial Real Estate: A Twenty-First Century Perspective." *The Appraisal Journal* (January 1987): 94-107.

Books

Clapp, A. and M. Seldin. *Real Estate Analysis Handbook.* New York: Dow-Jones Irwin Press, 1990.

Graaskamp, J. A. *A Guide to Feasibility Analysis.* Chicago: Society of Real Estate Appraisers, 1970.

Graaskamp, J. A. *Fundamentals of Real Estate Development*. Washington: Urban Land Institute, 1981.

Isard, W. *Methods of Regional Analysis: An Introduction to Regional Science*. Cambridge: MIT Press, 1969.

Jarchow, S. P., ed. *Graaskamp on Real Estate*. Washington: Urban Land Institute, 1991.

SIOR and Landauer Real Estate Counselors. *Comparative Statistics of Industrial and Office Real Estate Markets: 1991 Review and 1992 Forecast*.

PART IV

Articles

Adler, R. H. "Revisiting the Smart Building Debate." *Professional Report of Industrial and Office Real Estate*, SIOR (July/August 1991).

Alter, W. A. "Build to Suit: Why Build Empty Buildings When You can Build a Fully Leased Property?" *Perspective* No. 19, SIOR (1987).

Bamberger, D. C. "Developer's Disease can be Hazardous to Your Health." *Real Estate Issues* 17(1): 37-38 (Spring/Summer 1992).

Huffman, F. E. and M. T. Smith. "Suburban Office Development and Work-Residence Relationships." *Real Estate Issues* 14(1): 21-24 (Spring/Summer 1989).

Jahn, H. and D. M. Ludman. "Design Trends: Humanizing the Office Environment." *Real Estate Issues* 4(2): 39-46 (Winter 1979).

King, N. S. "Economic Impact of Current Parking Standards on Office Developments." *Real Estate Issues* 8(2): 49-50 (Fall/Winter 1983).

Merriman, C. L. and M. T. Schmidt. "An Overview: Indoor Air Pollution." *Professional Report of Industrial and Office Real Estate*, SIOR (July/August 1991).

Nahigian, R. J. "Methods of Choosing Amenities for an Office Development." *SIOR Reports* SIOR (May/June 1989).

O'Hara, D. M. and G. E. Lindgren. "Trends Affecting the Planning and Design of Parking Facilities." *Real Estate Issues* 8(2): 47-48 (Fall/Winter 1983).

Rabianski, J. and S. W. Wright. "Non-economic Factors in the Site Selection Process." *Real Estate Issues* 7(2): 25-27 (Fall/Winter 1982).

Taylor, B. D. "Asbestos Update." *Perspective* No. 18, SIOR (1990).

Wail, J. S. "Asbestos and Office Buildings—The Broker's Perspective." *Perspective* No. 23, SIOR (1988).

Books

Beyard, M. D. *Business and Industrial Park Development Handbook*. Washington: Urban Land Institute, 1988.

Reid, E. *Understanding Buildings—A Multi-disciplinary Approach.* Cambridge: The MIT Press, 1984.

PART V

Articles

Bach, W. E. "Subleasing—Some Things to Think About." *Professional Report of Industrial and Office Real Estate,* SIOR (May/June 1992).

Barton, B. "Endurance Will Keep Top Players Alive in 1990s Office Market." *Professional Report of Industrial and Office Real Estate,* SIOR (May/June 1991).

Donnelly, J. C. "Investor Attitudes and the Appraisal of the Major Urban Center Office Building." *The Appraisal Journal* (January 1981).

Ebert, L. P. "Lease vs. Buy: The Corporate Perspective." *Real Estate Issues* 12(1): 15-20 (Spring/Summer 1987).

Eisenberg, J. H. and R. Friedland. "Corporate Headquarters Relocation." *Real Estate Issues* 15(2): 5-7 (Fall/Winter 1990).

Kushner, J. E. "Strategies in Tenant Representation." SIOR (1990).

Lorenc, J. "Image Planning: A Key to Project Success." *Perspective* No. 9, SIOR (1986).

Pearson, T. D. "Location! Location! Location! What is location?" *The Appraisal Journal* (January 1991): 7-20.

Roulac, S. E. "The Syndication Business." *National Real Estate Investor* (August 1983).

Shlaes, J. and M. S. Young. "Evaluating Major Investment Properties." *The Appraisal Journal* (January 1978).

Thorne, O. J. "The Tenant Representation Process." *Perspective* No. 21, SIOR (1988).

Wolken, M. J. "Tenant Representation: Can a Real Estate Broker Serve Two Masters." *Professional Report of Industrial and Office Real Estate,* SIOR (Jan./Feb. 1991).

Books

Alexander, A. A. and R. F. Muhlebach. *Managing and Leasing Commercial Properties.* 2 vols. New York: John Wiley and Sons, 1990.

Institute of Real Estate Management. *Principles of Real Estate Management.* Chicago: Institute of Real Estate Management, 1991.

Messner S. D. *Real Estate Investment and Taxation,* 4th ed. Englewood Cliffs: Prentice Hall, 1991.

Roberts, D. F. *Marketing and Leasing of Office Space.* Chicago: Institute of Real Estate Management, 1986.

White, J. R. *The Real Estate Development Manual.* Warren, Gorham & Lamont, 1990.

PART VI

Articles

Bacow, L. S. "Foreign Investment, Vertical Integration and the Structure of the U. S. Real Estate Industry." *Real Estate Issues* 15(2): 1-8 (Fall/Winter 1990).

Clark, D. "Cash Equivalency Adjustments in Depressed Real Estate Markets." *The Appraisal Journal* (October 1989): 544-550.

Garrigan, R. T. "Wrap-around Mortgage Financing: Enhancing Lender and Investor Wealth" *Real Estate Issues* 4(1): 20-38 (Spring/Summer 1989).

Graaskamp, J. A. "An Approach to Real Estate Finance Education by Analogy to Risk Management Principles." *Real Estate Issues* 2(1): 53-70 (Summer 1977).

Greer, G. and P. T. Kolbe. "Recent Changes in Individual Investors' Attitudes Toward Real Estate." *Real Estate Issues* 16(1): 6-10 (Spring/Summer 1991).

Healy, J. J. and P. R. Healy. "Lenders' Perspectives on Environmental Issues." *Real Estate Issues* 16(2): 1-4 (Fall/Winter 1991).

Hoyt, H. "Financing the Future Commercial and Industrial Requirements in Metropolitan Growth of the United States." *Journal of Finance* 2 (1960).

Koulamas, C. P. and S. R. Stansell. "The Effect of Intertemporal Dependence in Cash Flows on Project Risk." *Real Estate Issues* 16(1): 28-33 (Spring/Summer 1991).

Marcus, M. "Good News for Commercial Real Estate: Safe Harbor's Regulations and Tax-free Transactions." *Perspective* No. 33, SIOR (1992).

Martin, W. B. "Finding and Financing a Turnaround Office Building." *Real Estate Finance* (Summer 1990).

McCoy, B. H. "The New Financial Markets and Securitized Commercial Real Estate Financing." *Real Estate Issues* 13(1): 5-9 (Spring/Summer 1988).

McMahan, J. "Foreign Investment in U. S. Real Estate." *Real Estate Issues* 15(2): 35-37 (Fall/Winter 1990).

Newsome, L. D. "Financing and its Influence on Property Valuation." *Appraisal Review Journal* 2 (1982).

Page, D. E. and C. O. Kroncke. "Finance Subsidiaries: A New Way to Access Capital Markets." *Real Estate Issues* 14(1): 28-31 (Spring/Summer 1989).

Rago, G. and W. J. Kimball. "Appraising Proposed Income-producing Property for Construction Lending." *The Appraisal Journal* (October 1989): 537-543.

Scott, M. A. "Interest Rate Swaps." *Real Estate Issues* 11(2): 37-41 (Fall/Winter 1986).

Sliwoski, L. R. "Understanding the Internal Rate of Return Used in Commercial Real Estate Transactions." *Real Estate Issues* 16(1): 43-45 (Spring/Summer 1991).

South, J. G. "Real Estate Financing." *Appraisal Review Journal* 3 (1984).

Steele, R. A. "Real Estate Investment Yield Linkages." *Real Estate Issues* 17(1): 17-23 (Spring/Summer 1992).

Trippi, R. R. and N. Lare. "Investigation of the Viability of Developer-oriented Real Estate Put Options." *Real Estate Issues* 15(2): 25-34 (Fall/Winter 1990).

Books

Brueggeman, W. B. and J. D. Fisher. *Real Estate Finance*. Homewood: Richard D. Irwin, 1992.

PART VII

Articles

Adelman, M. K. "Effective Facility Management: What It Is and Who Does It." *Real Estate Finance Journal* (Fall 1991).

Barrueta, J. F. and S. M. Wolfson. "Financial Implications of Leasehold Concessions." *Perspective* No. 24, SIOR (1989).

Brooks-Liberator, M. K. "Analyzing Property Management Performance." *Journal of Property Management* (July/Aug. 1990).

Brown, J. R. "A Management Audit for Real Estate Appraisers." *The Appraisal Journal* (July 1983).

Brown, R. K. "Fixed Asset Management and Marketing: Where do We Go From Here?" *Perspective* No. 6, SIOR (1985).

Goodnough, A. "How Institutions Monitor Management Effectiveness." *Journal of Property Management* (July/Aug. 1990).

Ibbotson, R. G. and C. L. Fall. "The United States Market Wealth Portfolio." *The Journal of Portfolio Management* (Fall 1979).

Jensen, B. R. "Building Efficiency: Cost and Value." *The Appraisal Journal* (January 1985): 127-138.

Owers, J. E. and R. C. Rogers. "The Divestiture of Real Estate Assets by Sell-off." *Real Estate Issues* 11(1): 29-35 (Spring/Summer 1986).

Pekala, N. "Short-term Measures, Long-term Markets: A Summary From the 1990 IREM Asset Management Symposium." *Journal of Property Management* (July/Aug. 1990).

Podolsky, R. D. "Asset Management—A Growth-oriented Approach to Property Management." *Professional Report of Industrial and Office Real Estate*, SIOR (Jan./Feb. 1992).

Stafford, E. "Under New Management: The Changing of the Guards." *Journal of Property Management* (May/June 1990).

Books

Building Owners and Managers Association and the Urban Land Institute. *The Changing Office Workplace*. Washington: The Urban Land Institute, 1986.

Institute of Real Estate Management. *Managing the Office Building*. Chicago: Institute of Real Estate Management, 1985.

PART VIII

Articles

Antia, M.; S. D. Kapplin; R. Meyer. "A Certainty-equivalent Approach to the Valuation of Risky Real Estate Investments." *Real Estate Issues* 8(2): 15-20 (Fall/Winter 1983).

Barnes, K. A. "Rental Concessions and Value." *The Appraisal Journal* (Spring 1986): 167-176.

Cogel, J. and M. Oliphant. "One or More Commingled Real Estate Funds?" *Journal of Portfolio Management* 17(4) (1991).

Del Casino, J. J. "European Investment in U. S. Office Markets." *The Appraisal Journal* (January 1986): 21-30.

Del Casino, J. J. "On Assembling Real Estate Portfolios." *Real Estate Issues* 19(2): 47-49 (Fall/Winter 1985).

DeVries, B.; M. E. Miles; S. B. Wolgin. "Prices and Appraisals." *Real Estate Issues* 17(2): 7-11 (Fall/Winter 1992).

Donnelly, J. C. "Investor Attitudes and the Appraisal of the Major Urban Center Office Building." *The Appraisal Journal* (January 1981).

Friedman, H. "Real Estate Investment and Portfolio Theory" *Journal of Financial and Quantitative Analysis* (March 1971): 861-874.

Graff, R. A. and D. M. Cashdan. "Some New Ideas in Real Estate Finance." *Journal of Applied Corporate Finance* 3:77-89 (1990).

Greer, G. and P. T. Kolbe. "Recent Changes in Individual Investors' Attitudes Toward Real Estate." *Real Estate Issues* 16(1): 6-10 (Spring/Summer 1991).

Hartzell, D. J.; J. S. Hekman; M. Miles. "Real Estate Returns and Inflation." *AREUEA Journal* 15(1): 617-637 (1987).

Healy, M. J. "Valuation of a Distressed Office Building." *The Appraisal Journal* (July 1989): 372-377.

Kimball, J. R. and B. S. Bloomberg. "Office Space Demand Analysis." *The Appraisal Journal* (October 1987).

Krumsick, H. L. "It's Coming—The Greatest After-Christmas Sale Ever in Real Estate Investment" *Perspective* No. 29, SIOR (1990).

Ling, D. C. and H. C. Smith. "Linkages Among Capitalization Rates, Discount Rates and Real Estate Cycles." *Real Estate Issues* 17(2): 21-26 (Fall/Winter 1992).

Madura, J. "How to Construct Real Estate Portfolios." *Real Estate Issues* 8(2): 13-14 (Fall/Winter 1983).

Malin, P. "Valuing Property in a World Economy." *The Appraisal Journal* (April 1991): 64-166.

Markowitz, H. "Portfolio Selection." *Journal of Finance* 7(3): 77-91 (March 1952).

McMahan, J. "Measuring Real Estate Returns." *Real Estate Issues* 9(2): 33-44 (Fall/Winter 1984).

O'Connor, J. W. "Real Estate Development: Investment Risks and Rewards." *Real Estate Issues* 11(1): 6-11 (Spring/Summer 1986).

Pagliari, J. L. "Real Estate in 3-D: See It Now!" *Real Estate Issues* 15(2): 16-19 (Fall/Winter 1990).

Patchin, P. J. "The Valuation of Contaminated Properties." *Real Estate Issues* 16(2): 50-54 (Fall/Winter 1991).

Peltzer, K. E. "Computerized Analysis of a Joint-Venture-Investment Office Building." *The Appraisal Journal* (Oct. 1982).

Powers, R. T. "The Worldwide Reappraisal of Real Estate Values." *Real Estate Issues* 17(2): 38-42 (Fall/Winter 1992).

Rosen, K. T. "Toward a Model of the Office Building Sector." *Journal of the American Real Estate and Urban Economics Association* (Fall 1984).

Roulac, S. E. and D. A. King. "Institutional Strategies for Real Estate Investment." *The Appraisal Journal* (April 1978).

Ryan, J. P. "Real Rates of Return—Does Real Estate Make Sense?" *Real Estate Issues* 17(2): 17-20 (Fall/Winter 1992).

Shlaes, J. and M. S. Young. "Evaluating Major Investment Properties." *The Appraisal Journal* (January 1978).

Seldin, M: "Seldin on Change: A Time to Buy, a Time to Sell." *Real Estate Issues* 8(2): 29-31 (Spring/Summer 1983).

Tarantello, R. "The Inflation Dependency of Leveraged Investments." *Real Estate Issues* 10(2): 7-12 (Fall/Winter 1985).

Webb, J. R. and J. H. Rubens. "How Much in Real Estate? A Surprising Answer." *Journal of Portfolio Management* 13(3): 10-14 (Spring 1987).

White, J. R. and D. K. Wiest. "Hybrid Investments: Alternatives." *Real Estate Issues* 10(1): 14-17 (Spring/Summer 1985).

Books

Akerson, C. B. *Capitalization Theory and Techniques: Study Guide*. Chicago: Appraisal Institute, 1988.

Appraisal Institute. *The Appraisal of Real Estate, 10th ed*. Chicago: Appraisal Institute, 1992.

Appraisal Institute. *The Dictionary of Real Estate Appraisal, 2d ed*. Chicago: Appraisal Institute, 1989.

Bodie, Z; A. Kane; A. J. Marcus. *Investments*. Richard D. Irwin, 1989.

Findlay, M. C. and S. D. Messner. *Real Estate Portfolio Analysis*. Lexington: Lexington Books, 1983.

Fisher, J. D. *Portfolio Construction: Real Estate*. In *Managing Investment Portfolios*, edited by D. Tuttle and J. Maginn. Warren Gorham & Lamont for The Institute of Chartered Financial Analysts, 1983.

Himstreet, W. C. *Communicating the Appraisal: The Narrative Report*. Chicago: Appraisal Institute, 1988.

Markowitz, H. *Portfolio Selection: Efficient Diversification of Investments*. New York: John Wiley and Sons, 1959.

Miles, M.; B. R. Webb; D. Guilkey. *On the Nature of Systematic Risk in Commercial Real Estate*. Working paper, University of North Carolina, July 1991.

Sirmans, C. F. and J. D. Fisher. *Real Estate in Pension Fund Portfolios: A Review of the Literature and Annotated Bibliography*. Pension Real Estate Association, 1991.

INDEX